lonely planet

Denmark

Glenda Bendure
Ned Friary

LONELY PLANET PUBLICATIONS
Melbourne • Oakland • London • Paris

SWEDEN

Gothenburg

Halmstad

Hornbæk

Gilleleje

To Oslo
(Norway)

To Oslo
& Larvik
(Norway)

BORNHOLM
This island, located off the southern tip
of Sweden in the Baltic Sea, is a cyclists'
haven with pleasant rural landscapes

BORNHOLM

Christiansø

Svaneke

Nexø

Allinge

Sandvig

Gudhjem

Åkirkeby

Hasle

Rønne

Same Scale as Main Map

To Varberg
(Sweden)

To
Sweden

To
Germany &
Poland

To
Copen-
hagen

Anholt

COPENHAGEN
Scandinavia's grandest city
with splendid museums &
a spirited nightlife

HILLERØD
Site of Frederiksborg Slot,
Denmark's most spectacular
Renaissance castle

To Oslo &
Larvik (Norway)

Kattegat

Østerby
Havn

Byrum

Læsø

Vesterø Havn

REBILD BAKKER
Inviting trails in
Denmark's largest forest

ÅRHUS
University city with a lively
café scene & plenty of
superb sights

Grenaa

Tirstrup

Dråby

Ebeltoft

Nimtofte

Rønde

To Kristiansand
(Norway)

Skagen

Gammel
Skagen

Frederikshavn

Albæk

Sæby

Åsaa

Hals

Auning

Randers

Skagerrak

Hirtshals

Sindal

Tornby

Øster Vrå

Hjørring

Hjallerup

Hadsund

Assens

Mariager

Hobro

Handest

To Bergen &
Egersund (Norway)

Lakken

Brønderslev

Aabybro

Aalborg

Nørresundby

Stavning

Skørping

Mangehøj

Viborg

Bjerringbro

Silkeborg

Blokhus

Nibe

Aars

Bælum

Farsø

Åbenrå

Skive

Karup

Ikast

JUTLAND

Tranum Strand

Fjerritslev

Nykøbing M

Limfjorden

Vinderup

Struer

Holstebro

Herning

To Faroe Islands
& Iceland

Hanstholm

Kliltmøller

Stenbjerg

Agger

Thisted

Hurup

Lemvig

Ulfborg

Lemvig

Ārhus

30km

20miles

15

10

0

0

To Varberg (Sweden)

DENMARK

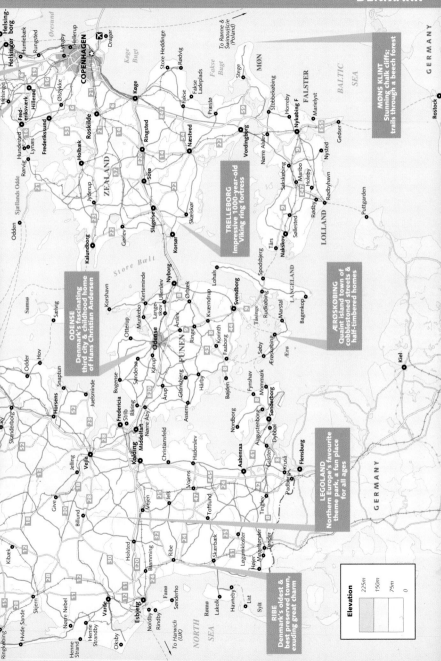

MØNS KLINT
Stunning chalk cliffs; trails through a beech forest

TRELLEBORG
Impressive 1000-year-old Viking ring fortress

ODENSE
Denmark's fascinating third city & childhood home of Hans Christian Andersen

ÆRØSKØBING
Quaint island town of cobblestoned streets & half-timbered homes

LEGOLAND
Northern Europe's favourite theme park, a fun place for all ages

RIBE
Denmark's oldest & best preserved town, exuding great charm

Elevation

225m
150m
75m
0

GERMANY

BALTIC SEA

NORTH SEA

ZENLAND

FUNEN

LOLLAND

FALSTER

MØN

LANGELAND

Store Bælt

Køge Bugt

Fakse Bugt

Øresund

COPENHAGEN

To Rønne & Swinoujście (Poland)

To Harwich (UK)

Rostock

Kiel

Puttgarden

Denmark
3rd edition – February 2002
First published – July 1996

Published by
Lonely Planet Publications Pty Ltd ABN 36 005 607 983
90 Maribyrnong St, Footscray, Victoria 3011, Australia

Lonely Planet offices
Australia Locked Bag 1, Footscray, Victoria 3011
USA 150 Linden St, Oakland, CA 94607
UK 10a Spring Place, London NW5 3BH
France 1 rue du Dahomey, 75011 Paris

Photographs
Many of the images in this guide are available for licensing from
Lonely Planet Images.
w www.lonelyplanetimages.com

Front cover photograph
A square-rigged Hansekogge plies Denmark's Roskilde Fjiord (Marie-
Louise Brimberg, National Geographic)

ISBN 1 74059 075 9

text & maps © Lonely Planet Publications Pty Ltd 2002
photos © photographers as indicated 2002

Printed by The Bookmaker International Ltd
Printed in China

**Although the authors
and Lonely Planet try
to make the informa-
tion as accurate as
possible, we accept
no responsibility for
any loss, injury or
inconvenience sus-
tained by anyone
using this book.**

Contents – Text

2 Contents – Text

NORTH ZEALAND   156

SOUTHERN ZEALAND   178

MØN, FALSTER & LOLLAND   198

BORNHOLM   214

FUNEN   231

Contents – Maps

The Authors

Glenda Bendure & Ned Friary

Glenda grew up in California's Mojave Desert and first travelled overseas as a high school AFS exchange student to India.

Ned grew up near Boston and studied social thought and political economy at the University of Massachusetts in Amherst.

After meeting in Santa Cruz, California, where Glenda was finishing her university studies, they took to the road and spent several years travelling throughout Asia and the Pacific, including stints in Japan where Ned taught English and Glenda edited a monthly magazine. They eventually came back to the USA, settled down on Cape Cod in Massachusetts and began to write for Lonely Planet.

In addition to *Denmark*, Ned and Glenda are the authors of Lonely Planet's guides to *Copenhagen*, *Hawaii*, *Oahu* and *Bermuda* and they have written the Denmark and Norway chapters of Lonely Planet's *Scandinavian & Baltic Europe*.

From the Authors

We'd like to thank Lillian Hess of the Danish Tourist Board in New York, Henrik Thierlein of Wonderful Copenhagen and Merethe Andersen at Use It. Thanks also to Irene Greve of the Copenhagen Jazz Festival, Cathe Jakobsen of Aqua, Susanne Hartz of the Louisiana modern art museum, Kåre Johannessen at Trelleborg, Christian Dorow and Malene Simonsen of Hvidovre Kommune and Svend Ravnkilde of the Dansk Musik Informations Center. A special thanks to Bryan Lantz for his expertise on Danish sports and to Tove and Knud Bøjland in North Zealand for sharing their insights on Danish culture.

This Book

This 3rd edition of *Denmark* was updated by Glenda Bendure and Ned Friary. They also wrote the 1st edition and updated the 2nd edition.

From the Publisher

Denmark 3 was produced in the Melbourne office of Lonely Planet. Yvonne Byron coordinated the editing and was assisted by George Dunford, Shelley Muir and Nina Rousseau. The design and mapping was coordinated by Jody Whiteoak, with assistance by Huw Fowles and Shahara Ahmed. Illustrations were drawn by Martin Harris (MH), Clint Curé (Q-ray & CC) Tamsin Wilson (TW) and Nicky Caven (NC). New illustrations were commissioned by Matt King while Emma Koch put together the language chapter with advice on aa and å by Karin Vidstrup Monk. Mark Germanchis provided invaluable Quark skills during Layout. Thanks also to Barbara Dombrowski and Lonely Planet Images for the great photographs, Kerrie Williams for organising the permissions and Margie Jung for the cover design.

Acknowledgments

Thanks to Rune Baess For the image of Fredrik Lundin playing the sax at the 2001 Copenhagen Jazz Festival on page 61, Karen Schjønning for the Hamlet Sommer logo on page 67, and Carlsberg Breweries for the beer label on page 76.

Thanks

Many thanks to the travellers who used earlier editions of *Denmark* and wrote to us with helpful hints, useful advice and interesting anecdotes. Your names follow:

Philip S Adey, Glenn Ashenden, Andrei Avram, Michael Barr, Daniel Beaumont, Jes Bengtsson, Bo Bjoedstrup, Derek Blice, Guillermo Boughton, DR R Bourne, R Brandwood, Jasper Van Den Brink, Thessa Brongers, Paul Butter, Narelle Castles, Sutapa Choudhury, Ishbel M Curr, Stuart Curran, Warren A & Mary A Dains, Paul Dalton, Nigel Davie, Melinda Drew, HJ Eatwell, Kevin Edwards, Honda Eiki, Anders Ekelund, Stefan Ertmann, Humphrey Evans, Deborah Fink, Sharon Finn, Steve Frandsen, Kieran & Kim Frye, Dave Fuller, Eva Gaarden, Michael Gildersleeve, Jen Gleave, Phyllis Grant, Torben Grue, Ibeth Hansen, Anne Hasselholm, JM Haw-Smalley, Mark Hoewisch, Virginia J Holoday, Stephen Holt, Barry & Deborah Hurwitz, Geoff Hutchison, Stephen Jacob, Peter Johnson, Felicity Kelsale, Imi Kevin, Seamus King, Manfred Lenzen, Sioned Lewis, Gabor Lovei, Henrik Madsen, Silvia Marinovova, Olivier Mauron, Jeppe Mikkelsen, Bruno Moncorge, Geraldine Moran, Giorgia Naccarato, Riccardo Nanni, Thijs Nauta, Douglas M Nelson, Maire Ni Eafa, Urban Ocvirk, Joseph O'Hare, Frank & Pia Olsen, Gustavo Orlando-Zon, Joen Pauli Hansen, Brian Payne, Graham Pointon, Vera Reifenberg, Torben Reitzel, Ray Rodgers, Salvador Sanchez, Dr Julia Saurazas, Gerard Schweng, Johan Segers, Stephen Shapiro, Alan Sirulnikoff, Natasha Skoric, Peter Sluijter, David Smoler, Donna Stark, David Stifel, Stine Suhr, Rebecca & Chuck Theobald, Nick Townsend, Ellie Tzovri, Courtney R Usher, Greta Vanmarcke, Stefan Vanwildemeersch, Tony Walter, Jantine Wijnja, Clare & Nick Wikely, Michael Williams.

Foreword

ABOUT LONELY PLANET GUIDEBOOKS

The story begins with a classic travel adventure: Tony and Maureen Wheeler's 1972 journey across Europe and Asia to Australia. Useful information about the overland trail did not exist at that time, so Tony and Maureen published the first Lonely Planet guidebook to meet a growing need.

From a kitchen table, then from a tiny office in Melbourne (Australia), Lonely Planet has become the largest independent travel publisher in the world, an international company with offices in Melbourne, Oakland (USA), London (UK) and Paris (France).

Today Lonely Planet guidebooks cover the globe. There is an ever-growing list of books and there's information in a variety of forms and media. Some things haven't changed. The main aim is still to help make it possible for adventurous travellers to get out there – to explore and better understand the world.

At Lonely Planet we believe travellers can make a positive contribution to the countries they visit – if they respect their host communities and spend their money wisely. Since 1986 a percentage of the income from each book has been donated to aid projects and human rights campaigns.

Updates Lonely Planet thoroughly updates each guidebook as often as possible. This usually means there are around two years between editions, although for more unusual or more stable destinations the gap can be longer. Check the imprint page (following the colour map at the beginning of the book) for publication dates.

Between editions up-to-date information is available in two free newsletters – the paper *Planet Talk* and email *Comet* (to subscribe, contact any Lonely Planet office) – and on our Web site at www.lonelyplanet.com. The *Upgrades* section of the Web site covers a number of important and volatile destinations and is regularly updated by Lonely Planet authors. *Scoop* covers news and current affairs relevant to travellers. And, lastly, the *Thorn Tree* bulletin board and *Postcards* section of the site carry unverified, but fascinating, reports from travellers.

Correspondence The process of creating new editions begins with the letters, postcards and emails received from travellers. This correspondence often includes suggestions, criticisms and comments about the current editions. Interesting excerpts are immediately passed on via newsletters and the Web site, and everything goes to our authors to be verified when they're researching on the road. We're keen to get more feedback from organisations or individuals who represent communities visited by travellers.

Lonely Planet gathers information for everyone who's curious about the planet – and especially for those who explore it first-hand. Through guidebooks, phrasebooks, activity guides, maps, literature, newsletters, image library, TV series and Web site we act as an information exchange for a worldwide community of travellers.

Research Authors aim to gather sufficient practical information to enable travellers to make informed choices and to make the mechanics of a journey run smoothly. They also research historical and cultural background to help enrich the travel experience and allow travellers to understand and respond appropriately to cultural and environmental issues.

Authors don't stay in every hotel because that would mean spending a couple of months in each medium-sized city and, no, they don't eat at every restaurant because that would mean stretching belts beyond capacity. They do visit hotels and restaurants to check standards and prices, but feedback based on readers' direct experiences can be very helpful.

Many of our authors work undercover, others aren't so secretive. None of them accept freebies in exchange for positive write-ups. And none of our guidebooks contain any advertising.

Production Authors submit their manuscripts and maps to offices in Australia, USA, UK or France. Editors and cartographers – all experienced travellers themselves – then begin the process of assembling the pieces. When the book finally hits the shops, some things are already out of date, we start getting feedback from readers and the process begins again …

WARNING & REQUEST

Things change – prices go up, schedules change, good places go bad and bad places go bankrupt – nothing stays the same. So, if you find things better or worse, recently opened or long since closed, please tell us and help make the next edition even more accurate and useful. We genuinely value all the feedback we receive. A well-travelled team reads and acknowledges every letter, postcard and email and ensures that every morsel of information finds its way to the appropriate authors, editors and cartographers for verification.

Everyone who writes to us will find their name listed in the next edition of the appropriate guidebook. They will also receive the latest issue of *Planet Talk*, our quarterly printed newsletter, or *Comet*, our monthly email newsletter. Subscriptions to both newsletters are free. The very best contributions will be rewarded with a free guidebook.

We may edit, reproduce and incorporate your comments in all Lonely Planet products, such as guidebooks, Web sites and digital products, so let us know if you don't want your comments reproduced or your name acknowledged.

Send all correspondence to the Lonely Planet office closest to you:

Australia: Locked Bag 1, Footscray, Victoria 3011
USA: 150 Linden St, Oakland, CA 94607
UK: 10a Spring Place, London NW5 3BH

Or email us at: talk2us@lonelyplanet.com.au

For news, views and updates see our Web site: www.lonelyplanet.com

HOW TO USE A LONELY PLANET GUIDEBOOK

The best way to use a Lonely Planet guidebook is any way you choose. At Lonely Planet we believe the most memorable travel experiences are often those that are unexpected, and the finest discoveries are those you make yourself. Guidebooks are not intended to be used as if they provide a detailed set of infallible instructions!

Contents All Lonely Planet guidebooks follow roughly the same format. The Facts about the Destination chapters or sections give background information ranging from history to weather. Facts for the Visitor gives practical information on issues like visas and health. Getting There & Away gives a brief starting point for researching travel to and from the destination. Getting Around gives an overview of the transport options when you arrive.

The peculiar demands of each destination determine how subsequent chapters are broken up, but some things remain constant. We always start with background, then proceed to sights, places to stay, places to eat, entertainment, getting there and away, and getting around information – in that order.

Heading Hierarchy Lonely Planet headings are used in a strict hierarchical structure that can be visualised as a set of Russian dolls. Each heading (and its following text) is encompassed by any preceding heading that is higher on the hierarchical ladder.

Entry Points We do not assume guidebooks will be read from beginning to end, but that people will dip into them. The traditional entry points are the list of contents and the index. In addition, however, some books have a complete list of maps and an index map illustrating map coverage.

There may also be a colour map that shows highlights. These highlights are dealt with in greater detail in the Facts for the Visitor chapter, along with planning questions and suggested itineraries. Each chapter covering a geographical region usually begins with a locator map and another list of highlights. Once you find something of interest in a list of highlights, turn to the index.

Maps Maps play a crucial role in Lonely Planet guidebooks and include a huge amount of information. A legend is printed on the back page. We seek to have complete consistency between maps and text, and to have every important place in the text captured on a map. Map key numbers usually start in the top left corner.

Although inclusion in a guidebook usually implies a recommendation we cannot list every good place. Exclusion does not necessarily imply criticism. In fact there are a number of reasons why we might exclude a place – sometimes it is simply inappropriate to encourage an influx of travellers.

Introduction

The world first took notice of Denmark a millennium ago when the Danish Vikings took to the seas and ravaged vast tracts of Europe. Much has changed since then. These days Denmark is the epitome of civilised society, noted for its progressive policies, widespread tolerance and liberal social-welfare system.

The smallest and most southern of the Scandinavian countries, Denmark offers visitors an interesting mix of lively cities and rural countryside. The nation abounds with medieval churches and Renaissance castles as well as tidy 18th-century villages.

Denmark's historic treasures include the preserved bodies of 2000-year-old 'bog people', a scattering of Neolithic dolmens and a number of impressive Viking ruins. Highlights among the latter are a fleet of sleek Viking-era ships that were excavated from the Roskilde Fjord and Scandinavia's best-preserved Viking ring fortresses.

Denmark also boasts quaint towns lined with period half-timbered houses that are so picturesque they could double as the backdrop to a Hans Christian Andersen tale. There's also a lovely coast that's lined with splendid white-sand beaches.

Denmark is a maritime nation, bordered on the west by the North Sea and on the east by the Baltic Sea. Most Danes live within a couple of kilometres of the coast, and no place in Denmark is more than an hour's drive from the sea.

The only part of Denmark that is connected by land to continental Europe is the Jutland peninsula, with the remainder of the country comprised of some 400 islands.

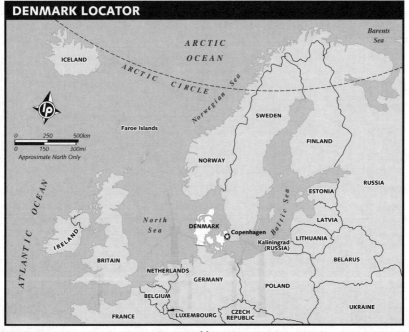

DENMARK LOCATOR

Much of the coast of Denmark is dominated by dunes and heathland, while most of the interior of the country is level farmland accented by the occasional gentle hill.

Of course, not all of Denmark is a pastoral mix of neat farms and snug fishing villages. Copenhagen, Denmark's vibrant capital, is Scandinavia's largest and most cosmopolitan city. In addition to its landmark sites – the *Little Mermaid*, who sits at the waterfront, and Tivoli, the grand old amusement park that enlivens the heart of

the city – Copenhagen also offers visitors renowned museums, a wealth of cultural activities and a spirited music scene that includes northern Europe's top jazz festival. And one of Europe's grandest rock festivals takes place just a 30-minute train ride away in neighbouring Roskilde.

Whether you're relaxing over a glass of beer at an outdoor cafe, cycling your way around the countryside or club-hopping the night away, Denmark offers an endless array of things to see and do.

Facts about Denmark

HISTORY
The Stone Age

There are some indications that present-day Denmark may have been inhabited by humans intermittently during the interglacial period, but the first permanent settlements were probably founded around 12,000 BC. By that time the glacial ice, which once covered all of Denmark, had receded, exposing a low-lying tundra. The tundra's vegetation of lichen and mosses attracted drifting herds of reindeer, which were in turn followed by nomadic hunters.

A Stone Age culture developed that relied primarily on hunting but, as the climate gradually warmed and the tundra gave way to forest, the reindeer migrated farther north. Eventually the hunters were compelled to resettle near the sea and subsisted by fishing and catching sea birds and seals.

As time went on, Stone Age people began to grow more of their own food crops and by 4000 BC agriculture and the keeping of stock animals had become common practice. Woods were cleared by slash-and-burn methods and the grain was sown in the ash that resulted.

Villages developed around the fields and the villagers began to bury their dead in dolmens, a type of grave monument comprising upright stones and topped by a large capstone; you can still find a number of these ancient dolmens in meadows today. There are no indications that social organisation extended beyond that of village life during the Stone Age.

The Bronze Age (1800–500 BC)

Bronze was introduced to Denmark in about 1800 BC, giving rise to a skilled society of artisans who used this pliable metal to make weapons, tools, jewellery and finely crafted works of art. Trade routes to the south were opened up to maintain a supply of bronze; influences from as far away as Crete and Mycenae are found in Danish bronzeworks of the period.

In prehistoric Denmark, objects of great value were often buried in bogs as sacrificial offerings. One superb artefact from that era is the Sun Chariot, crafted in bronze 3500 years ago by followers of a sun cult and found by a farmer in a Zealand field in 1902. It's now on display at Nationalmuseet in Copenhagen, along with Bronze Age *lurs*, curved metal horns that are among the world's oldest surviving musical instruments.

The Iron Age (500 BC–AD 800)

Iron began to replace bronze in about 500 BC. Because iron ore was readily available domestically, long-distance trade trickled off during this period. Iron proved useful for creating ploughs to till fields and as a result large agricultural communities began to develop.

Linguistic and cultural roots of present-day Denmark can be traced back to the late Iron Age and the arrival of the Danes, a tribe that is thought to have migrated south from Sweden in about AD 500.

Threat of the Franks

At the dawn of the 9th century Denmark was still on the outer perimeter of Europe when an expansion-oriented Charlemagne (768–814) extended the power of the Franks northward to present-day northern Germany. Hoping to ward off a Frankish invasion of Denmark, Godfred, king of Jutland, reinforced an impressive earthen rampart that ran the length of his southern border, all the way from the North Sea coast to the town of Hedeby (present-day Schleswig, now part of Germany). However, the rampart, known as the Danevirke, was breached by the advancing Franks who combined their military adventures in Denmark with efforts to establish Christian missions. Both of these measures met widespread resistance from the Vikings.

To some degree the Viking expeditions – at least those that spread southward – were a reaction to the powerful challenge posed by the Frankish Empire, which had changed the political and economic landscape of Western Europe.

Early Viking Era

Although unrecorded raids had probably been occurring for decades, the start of the Viking Age is generally dated from AD 793, when Nordic Vikings brutally raided Lindisfarne Monastery, off the coast of Northumbria in north-eastern England. Survivors of the Lindisfarne attack described the Vikings' sleek square-rigged vessels as 'dragons flying in the air' and the raiders as 'terrifying heathens'.

The early Viking raiders often targeted churches and monasteries, not for their religious significance but because they were rich repositories of gold and jewels. Because the churches also served as centres of learning, many invaluable documents, books and other cultural artefacts went up in flames during the raids. So fearsome were the Vikings that a special prayer was introduced into English church services: 'From the fury of the Northmen, good Lord, deliver us'.

The Vikings were, by and large, adventurous opportunists who took advantage of the turmoil and unstable political conditions that prevailed elsewhere in Europe. In time their campaigns evolved from the mere forays of pirates to organised expeditions that established far-flung colonies overseas.

The Viking groups came from Denmark, Norway and Sweden, and each had its own dominant sphere of influence. The Swedes colonised the Baltic countries, which became the bases for expeditions deep into Russian

The Vikings Slept Here

A fascinating legacy of Denmark's rich Viking history are the four Viking ring fortresses that have been discovered in the Danish countryside. The Trelleborg fortress in Zealand and the Fyrkat fortress near Hobro in Jutland have been excavated and developed as sites of historic significance, with educational displays and reconstructed Viking-style buildings.

The other two fortress sites, which have been identified by archaeologists but not developed as tourist attractions, are the Nonnebakken fortress in Odense on Funen, and the Aggersborg fortress on the northern shore of the Limfjord in Jutland.

These Viking fortresses were constructed in a ring shape with thick earthen walls and gates at the four points of the compass. They were built using the Roman foot (29.33cm) as a unit of measurement and were mathematically precise and strikingly symmetrical. The long wooden stave buildings that once stood inside the walls were all of an equal measure and were clearly used as barracks for soldiers; there were no houses for nobility, as would have been found inside castle walls.

Although the purpose of these Viking camps is not entirely understood, it's now known that all were erected in the early 980s. Researchers, including Poul Nørlund, who excavated Trelleborg in the 1930s, once believed these impressive camps served as staging grounds for the invasion of England by King Sweyn I (Forkbeard). Current research, however, including the more precise dating (to 981) of the timbers used in the Trelleborg fortress, place the construction time far in advance of Forkbeard's raids on England in 993. Furthermore, most of the four base sites were not well located for naval purposes. In the case of Trelleborg, archaeologists now believe that the marsh streams that connect the camp with the sea probably weren't navigable in Viking times.

A popular current theory suggests that these fortified sites may have been used by the monarchy to strengthen its domestic position, rather than being involved in Viking forays overseas. The massive earthen walls and moats of the fortresses certainly lend support to that theory, as they suggest a defensive function rather than an offensive one.

Whatever their exact function, the two excavated fortresses, at Trelleborg and Hobro, are intriguing places to visit, their perfectly symmetrical walls still intact after more than 1000 years.

territory The Norwegian domain included Scotland, Ireland and the Shetland, Orkney and Hebrides island groups. It was a Norwegian explorer, Erik the Red, who colonised Iceland and Greenland; his son, Leif Eriksson, went on to explore the coast of North America.

The main areas visited by the Danes were along the coast of Western Europe and the north-eastern part of England, with the first documented raid by Danish Vikings occurring in 835.

The Danes focused on England in part because it comprised a number of warring kingdoms, and this made it a suitable target for conquest. By 850 the Danish Vikings had established a settlement in Kent and in the years that followed sizable groups of Danish colonists arrived. The new settlers soon came to control the north-western part of England (a region that became known as the Danelaw), although the Anglo-Saxon king Alfred the Great (871–99) successfully repelled their advances to the south and forced the Danes to accept a boundary that recognised his reign over the kingdom of Wessex.

Unification of Denmark

Denmark's lands, like the rest of Scandinavia, have a long history of being ruled by rival regional kings, although by the early 9th century Jutland (and parts of southern Norway) appears to have been more or less united under a single king. In the late 9th century a final move towards Danish unification occurred when warriors led by the Norwegian chieftain Hardegon conquered the Jutland peninsula; Hardegon then began to extend his power base across the rest of Denmark's territory.

The Danish monarchy, the oldest kingdom in Europe, can be traced back to Gorm the Old, Hardegon's son, who established his reign in the early 10th century, ruling from Jelling in central Jutland.

Gorm's son, Harald Bluetooth, took the throne in 950 and, during his 35-year rule, completed the conquest of Denmark. He also spearheaded the conversion of Danes to Christianity, partly in order to appease his

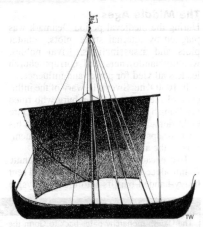

The hulls of Viking ships were clinker built – each hull plank overlapped the one below it.

powerful Frankish neighbours to the south who, a century earlier, had sent the Christian missionary Ansgar to build churches in the Danish towns of Ribe and Hedeby.

End of the Viking Era

Under the reigns of Harald Bluetooth's son Sweyn Forkbeard (985–1014) and grandsons Harald II (1014–18) and Canute the Great (1018–35), England was conquered and a short-lived Anglo-Danish kingdom was formed.

Canute the Great was the first true Danish king to sit on the throne of England, reigning in much the same manner as an English king except that he employed Scandinavian soldiers to maintain his command. The period of Danish rule in England ended when Canute's son Hardecanute died in 1042, after which the balance of power shifted to the English heirs of Alfred the Great. Many of the Danes who had settled in England elected to stay on to live under English rule.

There were a couple of later unsuccessful attempts by the Danes to reclaim England, but the Viking era was clearly on the wane. The defeat of Norwegian Vikings by Harold II of England at the Battle of Stamford Bridge in 1066 marked the end of the Viking Age.

The Middle Ages

During the medieval period Denmark was plagued by internal strife, plots, counter plots and assassinations. Rival nobles, wealthy landowners and corrupt church leaders all vied for power and influence.

In 1060 King Sweyn II, wary of the influence of the bishop of Hamburg who ruled the Danish Church, divided Denmark into eight domestic dioceses and appointed his own bishops, all of whom were trusted members of the aristocracy.

Two decades later Sweyn's son, Canute II, introduced the first personal tax and sent heavy-handed bailiffs into the countryside to collect it. The resistance to the new tax was so widespread that in 1086 Canute was chased from Jutland by a band of rebellious farmers and eventually cornered in an Odense church and stabbed to death.

Following a brief period of stability the monarchy was again thrown into turmoil in 1131 when Knud Lavard, a nephew of the ageing king Niels, was coaxed into the forest and slain in cold blood by his cousin Magnus the Strong. Although Magnus, as Niels' oldest son, was the rightful heir to the throne, he feared that Knud Lavard's popularity as a war hero might put his cousin in a position to declare himself king.

Danish Kings & Queens

The Danish monarchy dates back to Gorm the Old in the 10th century and has continued to the present day; the official name of the country is Kongeriget Danmark (Kingdom of Denmark). The monarchs, and the dates of their reign, are as follows:

Gorm (The Old)	?–950	Valdemar III	1326–30
Harald I (Bluetooth)	950–85	Valdemar IV (Atterdag)	1340–75
Sweyn I (Forkbeard)	985–1014	Oluf III (Håkonsson)	1376–87
Harald II	1014–18	Margrethe I	1387–96
Canute I (The Great)	1018–35	Erik VII (of Pomerania)	1396–1439
Hardecanute	1035–42	Christopher III (of Bavaria)	1440–48
Magnus (The Good)	1042–47	Christian I	1448–81
Sweyn II (Estridsen)	1047–74	John (Hans)	1481–1513
Harald III	1074–80	Christian II	1513–23
Canute II (The Holy)	1080–86	Frederik I	1523–33
Oluf I	1086–95	Christian III	1534–59
Erik I (The Kind)	1095–1103	Frederik II	1559–88
Niels	1104–34	Christian IV	1588–1648
Erik II	1134–37	Frederik III	1648–70
Erik III (The Lame)	1137–46	Christian V	1670–99
Sweyn III & Canute III		Frederik IV	1699–1730
(both claimed the throne)	1146–57	Christian VI	1730–46
Valdemar I (The Great)	1157–82	Frederik V	1746–66
Canute IV		Christian VII	1766–1808
(Son of Valdemar)	1182–1202	Frederik VI	1808–39
Valdemar II (The Victorious)	1202–41	Christian VIII	1839–48
Erik IV (Ploughpenny)	1241–50	Frederik VII	1848–63
Abel	1250–52	Christian IX	1863–1906
Christopher I	1252–59	Frederik VIII	1906–12
Erik V	1259–86	Christian X	1912–47
Erik VI	1286–1319	Frederik IX	1947–72
Christopher II	1320–26	Margrethe II	1972–

The murder of Knud Lavard incited a bitter civil war that resulted in the death of Magnus the Strong, Niels and five of his bishops. Knud's brother Erik Emune, who led the campaign against Magnus the Strong, ascended the throne in 1134 but his tyrannical rule ended abruptly with his assassination at a council meeting just three years later. The civil strife continued unabated throughout a series of brief reigns until Valdemar, the son of Knud Lavard, finally took the throne in 1157.

King Valdemar I united the country, which was weary from civil war, and he enacted Denmark's first written laws, known as the Jyske Lov (Jutland Code). With the cooperation of Bishop Absalon, the militaristic church leader from Roskilde, a series of successful crusades into eastern Germany were launched against the Wends, who had raided the Danish coast with impunity over a long period.

Valdemar's successors enacted other laws that in some respects were quite progressive for their times. In 1282 Erik V signed a coronation charter outlawing imprisonment without just cause and agreed to hold an annual assembly of the *hof*, a national council. In 1360 Valdemar IV, under pressure from the hof, established the first supreme court and instituted a new and more powerful national council, known as the Rigsråd, comprising nobles and bishops.

The Kalmar Union

In 1363 Norway's King Haakon married Margrethe, daughter of the Danish king Valdemar IV. When Valdemar IV died in 1375, Oluf, the five-year-old son of Haakon and Margrethe, was chosen to become king of Denmark. In 1380, after the death of King Haakon, Oluf became the king of Norway as well.

With Oluf too young to take charge, his mother Margrethe assumed de facto control of the Crown. She became the official head of state in 1387 after Oluf died before reaching majority.

In 1388 Swedish nobles, rebelling against their unpopular German-born king, Albert of Mecklenburg, then turned to Margrethe

Flying the Flag

The Danish flag, the Dannebrog, is the oldest national flag in the world. Legend has it that in 1219, during an invasion of Estonia by Valdemar II (the Victorious), an imminent Danish defeat was reversed when a red banner with a white cross fell from the sky. A voice from the mist proclaimed that if the banner was raised, the Danes would win. The Danes followed the instructions, won their battle, and took the banner as their national flag.

Danes continue to take pride in their flag and display it whenever possible. The flag can be seen hanging pennant-style in shopping streets, as a graphic device in magazine ads and flying high on the flagpoles that stand beside virtually every home in the countryside.

for assistance. Sweden and Norway had long maintained royal ties and, indeed, prior to the selection of Albert, King Haakon had sat on the throne of Sweden as well as Norway.

The Swedes hailed Margrethe as their regent and in turn she sent Danish troops to Sweden, capturing Albert and securing victory over his forces.

In 1397 Queen Margrethe established an alliance between Denmark, Norway and Sweden, known as the Kalmar Union. A primary objective of the union was to counter the influence of the powerful German-based Hanseatic League that had come to dominate the region's trade.

In 1410 King Erik of Pomerania, who was Margrethe's grandson, staged an unsuccessful attack on the Hanseatic League, which exhausted the resources of the tri-national government in the process. Erik's penchant for appointing Danes to public offices in Sweden and Norway further soured relations with native aristocrats in those countries and in 1438 the Swedish council withdrew from the union, whereupon the Danish nobility deposed Erik.

Erik's successor, Danish king Christopher III, made amends by pledging to keep the administrations of the three countries separate. The union continued to be a rocky one, however, marred by Swedish rebellions and a few fully fledged wars between Denmark and Sweden. In 1523 the Swedes elected their own king, Gustav Vasa, and the Kalmar Union was permanently dissolved. Norway, however, would remain under Danish rule for another three centuries.

The Lutheran Reformation

A pivotal power struggle involving the monarchy and the Catholic Church was played out during the Danish Reformation.

Frederik I ascended the throne in 1523, promising to fight heresy against Catholicism, but in an attempt to weaken the influence of Danish bishops he switched course and invited Lutheran preachers to Denmark. Their fiery messages against the corrupt power of the Catholic Church, which over the centuries had accumulated an ungodly amount of property and wealth, found a ready ear among the disenchanted.

After Frederik I died in 1533, the Catholic majority in the Rigsråd postponed the election of a new king, afraid that heir-apparent Prince Christian, Frederik's eldest son and a declared Lutheran, would favour the further spread of Lutheranism. They attempted to position Christian's younger brother Hans as a candidate for the throne.

The country, already strained by social unrest, erupted into civil war in 1534. Mercenaries from the Hanseatic city of Lübeck, which hoped to gain control of Baltic trade by allying with Danish merchants against the Danish nobility, invaded southern Jutland and Zealand. By and large the Lübeckers were welcomed as liberators by peasants and members of the middle class.

Alarmed by the revolt against the nobility, the Rigsråd threw its support behind Prince Christian and his father's skilful general, Johan Rantzau. Even the Catholic bishops, who realised the coronation of Christian would signal the end of the Catholic Church in Denmark, felt compelled to add their support rather than face the consequences of a peasant uprising. In 1534 the prince was crowned King Christian III.

The rebellion raged strongest in Jutland, where manor houses were set ablaze and the peasants made advances against the armies of the aristocracy. Rantzau took control and quickly secured Jutland's southern border by cutting Lübeck off from the sea. He then made a sweeping march northward through Jutland, smashing the peasant bands in brutal fighting. Copenhagen, where merchants supported the uprising and welcomed the prospect of becoming a Hanseatic stronghold, was besieged by Rantzau's troops for more than a year. Protected by its ramparts but totally cut off from the outside world, Copenhagen's citizens suffered widespread starvation and epidemics before finally surrendering in 1536, marking the end of the civil war.

With the war's end, Christian III quickly consolidated his power. He took a surprisingly lenient approach to the merchants and Copenhagen burghers who had revolted, and in turn they now pledged their allegiance to the Crown, seeing opportunities for themselves in a stabilised Denmark. On the other hand, the Catholic bishops were arrested and monasteries, churches and other ecclesiastical estates became the property of the Crown.

The Danish Lutheran Church became the only state-sanctioned denomination and was placed under the direct control of the king. For all practical purposes, church officials now became civil servants.

Sharing power only with the nobility, the monarchy emerged from the civil war stronger than ever, buoyed by a treasury that was greatly enriched by the confiscated Church properties.

Wars with Sweden

The first part of Christian IV's long reign (1588–1648) was a period of prosperity and growth. Then in 1625 the king, hoping to neutralise Swedish expansion, entered an ill-advised and protracted struggle known as the Thirty Years' War.

The war resulted in substantial territorial losses for Denmark. In a treaty of 1645, signed after a Swedish invasion of Jutland, the Baltic island of Gotland and two Norwegian provinces were handed over to the Swedes, while a second treaty signed in

1648 relinquished the western half of Pomerania and the bishoprics of Bremen and Verden.

In 1655 the Swedish king invaded Poland and, although the victory was swift, the Swedes found themselves bogged down trying to secure that vast country. Word of the Swedish troubles ignited nationalistic fervour throughout a Denmark that was seething for revenge. In 1657 Christian IV's successor, Frederik III, hoping to take advantage of the Polish situation, once again declared war on the Swedes. For the Danish government, itself ill-prepared for battle, it was a tremendous miscalculation.

Sweden's King Gustave, looking for an honourable way out of Poland, which had already been pillaged to the limit, gladly withdrew and readied for an invasion of Denmark. He led his troops through Germany and into Jutland, plundering his way north.

During the winter of 1657–58 – the most severe winter in Danish history – King Gustave marched his soldiers across the frozen seas of the Lille Bælt between Fredericia and the island of Funen. His uncanny success unnerved the Danes and he proceeded without serious resistance across the similarly frozen Store Bælt to Lolland and then on to Falster.

The Swedish king had barely made it across the frozen waters of the Storstrømmen to Zealand when the thawing ice broke away behind him, precariously separating Gustave and his advance detachment from the main body of his forces. However, the Danes, despite having amassed a substantial army in Zealand to protect Copenhagen, were in such a state of panic that they failed to recognise their sudden military advantage; instead of capturing the Swedish king, they sued for peace and agreed to yet another disastrous treaty.

In February 1658 the Treaty of Roskilde, the most lamented treaty in Denmark's history, was signed. The territorial losses were staggering, with Denmark's borders shrinking by a third. The Danes relinquished the island of Bornholm and lost all Danish territories on the Swedish mainland. Only Bornholm, which eventually staged a bloody revolt against the Swedes, would again fly the Danish flag.

Absolute Monarchy

In 1660 King Frederik III, believing the nobility's wings needed clipping, cunningly convened a gathering of nobles, placed them under siege, and forced them to nullify their powers of council.

With the nobility no longer entitled to a central role in government, Frederik conferred upon himself the right of absolute rule. In 1665 the king enshrined the new system in an absolutist constitution called Kongeloven (The Royal Act), which was to stand as the Danish constitution for almost two centuries. In the spirit of the day, the exact content of the constitution was not made public at the time of its enactment and for nearly 50 years no copies were allowed to be printed. In its essence the document was simple enough: It declared the king to be the highest head on earth, above all human laws and inferior to God alone. Supreme legislative, judicial and military authority was placed solely in the hands of the king.

So concentrated were the royal powers under the new constitution that when Christian V ascended to the throne in 1670 as the first king to be anointed under absolute rule, it was decided that he alone had the authority to crown a king, requiring Christian to place the crown upon his own head during the church service.

The monarchy managed to rebuild the military and put up a reasonable fight in three more wars with Sweden (1675–79, 1699–1700 and 1709–20), but none of these campaigns enabled Denmark to regain its lost territories in southern Sweden.

Throughout the rest of the 18th century Danes and Swedes managed to coexist without serious hostilities. There was even some reconciliation when a Danish princess married the Swedish king Gustav III.

The Age of Reforms

The peace of the 18th century gave Denmark a badly needed economic boost and set the stage for political and social change. In 1784

Palace Follies

One of the most curious political players of the 18th century was not a Danish king but a German doctor named Johan Struensee. In 1768 Struensee was appointed court physician to King Christian VII, who suffered from bouts of insanity. The doctor managed to win favour both with the ailing king, who granted Struensee broad powers of state, and with the 18-year-old queen, Caroline Matilda, who became Struensee's lover.

Emboldened by his assumed powers, the 34-year-old physician dismissed the prime minister and, over the next 16 months, succeeded in proclaiming some 2000 decrees in the name of the monarch. Contemptuous of the aristocracy, Struensee applied the same laws to all citizens regardless of class. The exploitation of peasants for the benefit of landlords was restricted and ill treatment in prisons, orphanages and poorhouses was outlawed. Trade barriers were lifted and money from the king's treasury was transferred to public sources for the support of new social endeavours.

Unfortunately for Struensee, he was ahead of his time – the French Revolution that would stir similar passions was still some 20 years away. Instead of broad support, Struensee elicited widespread resentment that was inflamed by unfounded rumours of his ill treatment of the ailing king. In actuality, however, it seems that the mad king had taken some comfort in being relieved of both his stately and marital duties.

In January 1772 a coup d'etat was instigated at a palace ball and the conspirators, led by the queen mother, forced the king to sign a statement against Struensee, who was being arrested elsewhere in the palace. Unable to prove that Struensee had forcibly taken control of the government or even that he had been corrupt, the court instead condemned him to death for his illicit relations with the young queen, which it ruled to be lese-majesty (an offence against the Crown).

The queen, incidentally, had her marriage dissolved by a special court and was subsequently taken by a British frigate to England to live on the estate of her brother, King George III. Forbidden to take her young daughter (who was deemed to be Christian VII's heir although fathered by Struensee) with her to England, Caroline Matilda died a broken woman at the age of 24.

the crown prince Frederik VI, then just 16, assumed control of the government. More benevolent than his predecessors, Frederik VI brought progressive landowners into government and introduced a sweeping series of reforms. With the French Revolution brewing elsewhere on the continent, the government now took an interest in improving the lot of the Danish peasantry, who in centuries past had received scant attention from the powers that be.

Under the leadership of Frederik VI all feudal obligations were abolished, including those that had required peasants to reside within prescribed geographic boundaries and to provide compulsory labour in the domain of landlords. Large tracts of land were broken up and redistributed to the landless. The reforms also included introduction of compulsory education for all children under the age of 14.

Despite these wide-ranging domestic reforms, Denmark found itself once again embroiled in the mire of new international power struggles with the outbreak of the Napoleonic Wars (1796–1815).

The Napoleonic Wars

At the turn of the 19th century Britain, which dominated the seas, was not all too keen on the growth of Denmark's foreign trade. In 1800, trying to counter potential threats posed by the British, Denmark signed a pact of armed neutrality with Sweden, Prussia and Russia. Britain regarded the act as hostile and in 1801 sent a naval expedition to attack Copenhagen, inflicting heavy damage on the Danish fleet and forcing Denmark to withdraw from the pact.

Denmark managed to avoid further conflicts and actually profited from war trade until 1807, when a new treaty between

France and Russia once again drew the Danes closer to the conflict. The British, weary of Napoleon's growing influence in the Baltic, feared, without solid grounds, that the Danes might be convinced to place their fleet at the disposal of the French.

In September 1807, without attempting diplomacy, the British fleet then unleashed a brutal bombardment on neutral Copenhagen, setting much of the city ablaze and destroying its naval yard. The British then proceeded to confiscate the entire Danish fleet, sailing away with nearly 170 gunboats, frigates, transports and sloops. Ironically, the only ship left standing in Copenhagen harbour was a private yacht that the king of England had given his nephew, Denmark's crown prince Frederik, two decades earlier.

Although the unprovoked attack was unpopular enough back home to have been roundly criticised by the British parliament, Britain nonetheless kept the Danish fleet. The British then offered the Danes an alliance – something that might have been accepted by Denmark a few months earlier but, in the wake of the recent British assault, was now unthinkable. In October 1807 the Danes joined the continental alliance against Britain. In turn, Britain blockaded both Danish and Norwegian waters, causing poverty in Denmark and outright famine in Norway. When Napoleon fell in 1814 the Swedes, by then allied with Britain, successfully demanded that Denmark cede Norway to them.

The Golden Age

Although the 19th century started out dismal and lean, by the 1830s Denmark had awakened to a cultural revolution in the arts, philosophy and literature. The times gave rise to such prominent figures as philosopher Søren Kierkegaard, theologian Nikolaj Frederik Severin Grundtvig and writer Hans Christian Andersen. It was the 'Golden Age' of the arts, with sculptor Bertel Thorvaldsen bestowing his grand neoclassical statues on Copenhagen and Christoffer Wilhelm Eckersberg introducing the Danish School of Art, which paid homage to everyday life.

Spurred on by new ideas and the rising expectations of a growing middle class, the Crown was challenged by an unprecedented interest in democratic principles. Provincial assemblies were formed and, although their jurisdiction was nominal, they provided a vehicle for debate and gave rise to the formation of political parties. While the Crown vacillated about how far it wanted to take the democratisation of power, two growing factions – farmers and liberals – joined forces to form a united liberal party in 1846.

The powers of the absolute monarch were already on the wane when revolution swept across the continent from Paris to Germany in the spring of 1848. The new Danish king, Frederik VII, under pressure from the liberal party, convened a national assembly to abolish the absolute rule of the monarchy and to draw up a democratic constitution.

The constitution, which was enacted on 5 June 1849, established a parliament with two chambers, Folketing and Landsting, whose members were elected by popular vote. Although the king retained a limited voice, legislative powers were now shifted to parliament. An independent judiciary was established and citizens were guaranteed the rights of free speech, religion and assembly. Denmark changed overnight from a virtual dictatorship to one of the most democratic countries in Europe.

Schleswig & Holstein

The duchies of Schleswig and Holstein in southern Jutland, which had long been under Danish rule, became restless during the nationalist fervour of the 1840s. Holstein, which was linguistically and culturally German, had already affiliated itself with the German Federation. Schleswig, on the other hand, was inhabited by people of both Danish and German heritage. When Denmark's new constitution threatened to incorporate Schleswig outright as an integral part of Denmark, the German population in the duchy allied with Holstein, sparking a war against the Danes. The three-year revolt only ended in 1851, when Denmark agreed to accept the status quo rather than further tighten its bonds with Schleswig.

In 1864 the Prussian prime minister, Otto von Bismarck, declared war on a militarily weak Denmark and within a matter of months had captured Schleswig. Denmark's new border in southern Jutland was now drawn at the southern outskirts of Kolding. This further erosion of Denmark's domain opened the question of the very survival of Denmark as a nation.

In the aftermath of the 1864 defeat, a conservative government took power in Denmark and retained power until the end of the century. Although reforms had come to a standstill, the conservatives oversaw a number of welcome economic advances: the railway was extended throughout the country; Danish farmers found a ready grain market in Britain; and Denmark's major industries – shipbuilding, brewing and sugar refining – developed into maturity.

Early 20th Century

In 1901 the conservative landowners, who had long had a stranglehold on government, were ousted by the Venstrereformparti (Left Reform Party). The party carried through a number of broad-minded reforms, including the application of the progressive principles of NFS Grundtvig to the education system and the revision of the constitution to extend the right to vote to women.

Denmark remained neutral during WWI. The northern part of Schleswig was returned to Denmark following a plebiscite that took place in 1920, as required by the accords of the Treaty of Versailles. In the period between the two world wars a social-democratic government emerged, passing some landmark legislation that not only softened the effects of the Great Depression but also laid the foundations for a welfare state.

WWII

Denmark again declared its neutrality at the outbreak of WWII but, with the growing Allied presence in Norway, Germany became intent on acquiring advance coastal bases in northern Jutland.

In the early hours of 9 April 1940, the Germans crossed the frontier in southern Jutland and simultaneously landed troops at half a dozen strategic points throughout Denmark. A military airfield in Copenhagen was attacked and commando troops landed in the city, promptly taking the citadel. The German troops proceeded to Amalienborg Slot, where they met resistance from the royal guards. In the meantime the German envoy delivered an ultimatum, warning that if the Danes resisted, Copenhagen would be bombed.

With German warplanes flying overhead, King Christian X and parliamentary heads hastily met at Amalienborg and decided to yield, under protest, to the Germans. The Danish government did manage to obtain assurances from the Nazis that Denmark would be allowed to retain some degree of internal autonomy.

The Danes, with only a nominal military force, had no capacity to counter the German attack and little alternative but to submit. In all, the lightning blow lasted only a matter of hours, and before nightfall Denmark was an occupied country.

For three years the Danes managed to tread a thin line, basically running their own domestic affairs but doing so under close Nazi supervision, until August 1943 when the Germans took outright control.

The Danish Resistance movement quickly mushroomed. In October 1943, as the Nazis were preparing to round up Jewish Danes, the Resistance, using night-running fishing boats, quickly smuggled 7000 Jews, some 95% of those remaining in Denmark, into neutral Sweden.

Although the island of Bornholm was heavily bombarded by Soviet forces, the rest of Denmark emerged from WWII relatively unscathed.

Modern-Day Issues

Under the leadership of the Social Democrats a comprehensive social-welfare state was established in postwar Denmark and the cradle-to-grave securities that guarantee medical care, education and public assistance were expanded. As the economy grew and the labour market increased, women entered the work force in unprecedented numbers and household incomes reached lofty new heights.

In the 1960s a rebellion by young people, who were disillusioned with the growing materialism, the nuclear arms race and an authoritarian educational system, took hold in the larger cities. Student protests broke out on university campuses and squatters began to occupy vacant buildings.

In Copenhagen the movement came to a head in 1971 when protesters tore down the fence of an abandoned military base at the east side of Christianshavn and turned the site into a commune that they declared to be the 'free state of Christiania'. Thousands of people who were attracted by the idea of transforming a military base into a utopian community flocked to Christiania. The government, so overwhelmed by the scale of the movement, decided to let Christiania stand as a 'social experiment'. After three decades, Christiania continues to serve as a bastion for alternative lifestyles, with a population that has settled to around 800.

One of the most controversial issues of recent times has been Denmark's role in the European Union (EU). Denmark joined the European Community, the predecessor of the EU, in 1973, but Danes have been hesitant to support expansion of the powers of the EU. Indeed when the Maastricht Treaty, which established the terms of a European economic and political union, came up for ratification in 1992, Danish voters rejected it by a margin of 51% to 49%. After being granted exemptions from Maastricht's common defence and monetary provisions, the Danes, in a second referendum held in 1993, voted by a narrow majority to accept the treaty.

In September 2000 the Danes signalled a deeper discontent with European integration when they rejected adoption of the euro, the EU's common currency. Denmark, the first EU country to put that decision in the hands of the people, saw a remarkable 87% voter turnout. Despite a passionate campaign to win support for the euro by the Prime Minister Poul Nyrup Rasmussen and the business community, the euro was rejected by a 6% margin. The opponents to adoption of the euro had been effective in convincing the Danish people they had more to lose than gain, arguing that local control over Danish issues would be ceded to a European bureaucracy dominated by the stronger nations and that Denmark's generous welfare-state securities would also be endangered by the provision.

GEOGRAPHY

Denmark is a small country with a land area of 42,930 sq km, slightly larger than Switzerland.

Iceland, Greenland & the Faroe Islands

When Norway broke its political ties with Denmark in the early 19th century, the former Norwegian colonies of Iceland, Greenland and the Faroe Islands stayed under Danish administration. Iceland, population 279,000, became an independent state within the Danish realm in 1918 and became completely independent in 1944.

The Kingdom of Denmark still includes Greenland and the Faroe Islands. The political situations of the two are not identical, but both are essentially self-governing. The Faroe Islands has had home rule since 1948, Greenland since 1979.

In part because Denmark retains responsibility for their banking, defence and foreign relations, Greenland and the Faroe Islands each have two parliamentary representatives in the Danish Folketing. Unlike Denmark, however, neither Greenland nor the Faroe Islands is part of the EU.

Greenland is the world's largest island (if Australia is regarded as a continent), with a total area of 2,175,600 sq km (of which 341,700 sq km is not under permafrost) and a population of 55,000. The Faroe Islands have a land area of 1399 sq km and a population of about 46,000.

If you want to learn more about these islands, an excellent source of information is Lonely Planet's *Iceland, Greenland & the Faroe Islands*.

The Jutland (Jylland) peninsula, where the 69km-long border with Germany is Denmark's only land connection to the mainland of Europe, encompasses more than half of the land area of the country, stretching 360km from north to south. In addition, Denmark has 406 islands, about 90 of which are inhabited. The capital city, Copenhagen, is on Zealand (Sjælland), the largest island. The next largest islands are Funen (Fyn), the twin islands of Falster and Lolland, and Bornholm to the east.

Denmark is bordered on the west by the North Sea and on the east by the Baltic Sea. To the north, separating Denmark from Norway and Sweden, are the Skagerrak and Kattegat straits. Sweden is just 5km away at its closest point, across a narrow strait called the Øresund.

Most of Denmark is a lowland of fertile farms, rolling hills, beech woods and heather-covered moors. The country hasn't a single mountain; the highest elevation, at Yding Skovhøj in Jutland's Lake District (called Søhøjlandet), is a mere 173m.

There are numerous small rivers, lakes and streams. The largest lake is Arresø on the island of Zealand and the longest river is the 158km Gudenå in Jutland.

The coastline, which includes many inlets and bays, is 7314km in length. No place in Denmark is more than 52km from the sea.

CLIMATE

Denmark lies at a northern latitude stretching from 54° 34' to 57° 45', approximately the same as Moscow, central Scotland and southern Alaska. Considering its northerly location, it has a relatively mild climate, moderated by the effects of the warm Gulf Stream, which sweeps northward along the western coast.

In the coldest winter months of January and February, the average daytime temperature hovers around freezing point – and while that may be cold, it is in fact nearly 10°C above average for this latitude. Winter, however, also has the highest relative humidity (90%) and the cloudiest weather (with more than 80% cloud cover on an average of 17 days each month), both of which can

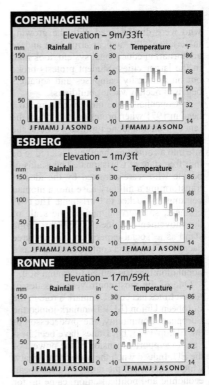

make it feel much colder than the actual mercury reading. By comparison, from May to September the relative humidity drops to a more comfortable level of around 70% and there are about nine predominantly cloudy days a month.

You can expect to see rain and grey skies in Denmark. Measurable rain falls on an average of 11 days in June (the month with the fewest rainy days) and 18 days in November, with the greatest amount of precipitation in the period between July and December – although, when all's said and done, rain is fairly evenly spread over the year. During the most popular months for visitors to Denmark (May, June, July and August) there's an average of 48mm, 55mm, 66mm and 67mm of rain, respectively.

The mean temperature for Denmark is 2.1°C in March, 10.8°C in May, 15.6°C in

July and August, 9.1°C in October and 1.6°C in December.

With its low-lying terrain and proximity to the sea, variations in climate throughout Denmark are minimal. There's a prevalent westerly wind, averaging 13 knots.

You can get a five-day weather forecast in English from the Danish Meteorological Office at its Web site at W www.dmi.dk or by calling ☎ 38 38 36 63.

ECOLOGY & ENVIRONMENT

The Danish environment is one that has been heavily exploited. By the early 19th century, after centuries of deforestation and overgrazing, less than 4% of Denmark's land remained forested, and encroaching heathlands and meadows covered nearly 50% of the total land area. In the late 19th century much of that marginal heathland was turned into agricultural land, heavily reliant on fertilisers and the modification of natural waterways.

In all, about 20% of Danish farmland is at or near sea level, much of it on environmentally sensitive wetlands that have been made arable by draining the water with pumps. The landscape has been so intensely altered that only about 2% of Denmark's naturally winding streams remain intact, the rest having been artificially straightened.

Recent international trade agreements and EU quotas have brought an end to many agricultural subsidies for Danish farmers and the most marginal farmland is no longer economically viable. These conditions, along with a growing environmental awareness, have created a favourable backdrop for the implementation of widespread restoration projects. Under a nature management act passed in 1990, the government has instituted an ambitious program to restore the wetlands, re-establish salt marshes and also realign streams to their original courses. That same act called for the doubling of forest cover over the next 100 years.

On another front, Denmark has vowed not to build nuclear power plants. Instead, it's developed an extensive network of alternative energy sources, most notably wind power, which currently provides nearly 15%

of Denmark's electricity. Rows of sleek wind turbines are an increasingly common sight on the Danish landscape, particularly in breezy coastal areas. In 2001 the world's largest offshore windmill park was built outside Copenhagen harbour, and its 20 giant windmills now generate 3% of the capital's electricity. Despite its reputation for cloudy weather, Denmark has also made some strides in harnessing solar energy and boasts one of Europe's largest solar power stations on the island of Ærø.

Recycling is extensive, with more than 80% of all paper produced from used paper and roughly half of all waste recycled. Over recent decades many air-pollution levels, including those of sulphur dioxide, have dropped by nearly 50%, and since 1993 Danish businesses have been required to pay a tax based on their carbon dioxide emissions.

In 1971 Denmark created a cabinet-level ministry to deal specifically with issues relating to the environment, becoming the first industrialised country to do so. The EU has based its European Environment Agency in Copenhagen and the Danes have taken an active role in promoting international efforts to reduce pollution.

FLORA & FAUNA
Flora

About 12% of Denmark has tree cover but primary forest is rare. Instead, most woods are planted, the bulk of them having been reforested either for conservation and recreation purposes or for timber production. Most of the commercial forests are now planted with fast-growing conifers such as spruce and fir.

Denmark's natural woodlands are largely deciduous with a prevalence of beech and oak trees. Other common trees found in mixed woodlands are hazel, maple, pine, birch, aspen, lime (linden) and horse chestnut. Elm trees are also a common species, but an outbreak of Dutch elm disease that hit Denmark in 1993 has devastated these stately trees in a number of areas. In Copenhagen virtually all of the city's estimated 10,000 elm trees contracted the disease and most have been cut down.

Heath, bogs and dunes cover about 7% of Denmark's land area and are particularly common in western Jutland. In an effort to stem coastal erosion, large tracts of the dunes have been planted with lyme and marram grasses, whose deep root systems help hold the sand in place. Wild pink and white beach roses, of the *Rosa rugosa* variety, are common on sand dunes as well.

In spring, cultivated fields of brilliant yellow rapeseed flowers, a member of the mustard family, are a particularly lovely addition to the farm-belt areas.

In summer, gardens throughout Denmark are planted with the usual colourful mix of temperate-climate flowers. The national flower is the marguerite, a white daisy with a yellow centre that is prolific in sunny open spaces, such as along roadways.

Fauna

The loss of so much natural wilderness habitat to cultivated farmland has spelt the end for numerous animal species in Denmark. Approximately 30% of all mammal species and breeding birds in Denmark are listed as either threatened, vulnerable or rare.

Among the mammals that have actually disappeared are the elk, bear, wolf, wild boar and beaver. Today the most endangered mammal in the country is the freshwater otter, which was plentiful as late as the 1950s and shot by hunters until 1967. By the time protections for the otter were put in place its population had dropped to around 100; it's now making a comeback, with the latest estimates at around 400.

The largest wild species still found is the red deer, which can weigh over 200kg. Denmark is also home to the roe deer, fallow deer, wild hare, fox, squirrel, hedgehog and badger.

Approximately 400 bird species have been observed in Denmark; of these about 160 breed in the country. Some of the more commonly seen birds include the magpie, crow, sparrow, pigeon, coot, goose and duck.

The western coast of Jutland attracts migrating water birds and breeding waders such as the avocet, dunlin, ruff, redshank, lapwing and black-winged godwit. The gull-billed tern, which is a threatened species in Europe, breeds on the uninhabited fjord island of Fjandø, as do some of the country's largest colonies of the sandwich tern, arctic tern and black-headed gull.

The easternmost island, Bornholm, is home to relatively large numbers of rooks and nightingales and is a resting spot for migratory ducks and waders. The nearby Ertholmene Islands provide a bird refuge that hosts breeding eider ducks, razorbills, guillemots and other sea birds.

Birds threatened by extinction, mostly because of the destruction of their habitat, include the wood sandpiper, golden plover and black grouse, all once common birds of the heathland. The national bird is the swan, widespread in urban parks and suburban ponds throughout the country.

There are 68 indigenous species of butterfly, though many are rare; since 1950 nine species have vanished altogether. The national butterfly is the small tortoiseshell, a pretty brownish-orange butterfly with a blue fringe; it's common in all areas of the country from early July and is unusual in that it hibernates as a fully grown insect.

Eleven species of frogs and toads can be found in Denmark, including the common toad, green tree frog and fire-bellied toad; however, because of the loss of wetlands, amphibians have disappeared from approximately 50% of their breeding sites in the past 50 years. Efforts are being made to turn the situation around, most notably on the island of Bornholm where 400 water holes have been restored to create a habitat for the green tree frog, whose breeding area had diminished by 90%.

National Parks

Because Denmark does not have large expanses of wilderness, it's not surprising that it does not have a system of national parks. Its largest contiguous area of woodlands is Rold Skov, a 77-sq-km public forest in central Jutland that contains Denmark's only national park, Rebild Bakker.

Although sizable tracts of wilderness do not exist, numerous state-administered nature conservation areas are spread around the

Thoroughly Modern Monarchy

Denmark's current monarch, Queen Margrethe II, was born on 16 April 1940, the eldest daughter of Frederik IX (1899–1972), who had no sons. As a result of a 1953 referendum that amended the Danish constitution to allow women to succeed to the throne, Margrethe was proclaimed queen on 15 January 1972, the first female monarch of Denmark since the 14th century.

Margrethe II is a popular queen who has been credited with giving a fresh perspective to the monarchy and minimising the privilege that has traditionally separated royalty from commoners.

In addition to performing her ceremonial roles as head of state, the queen is an accomplished artist. She has illustrated a number of books, including Tolkien's *Lord of the Rings*, and has designed Christmas seals for Unicef and stamps for the Danish postal service. The queen has also been active in the theatre, designing costumes for a production of Hans Christian Andersen's *The Shepherdess and the Chimney Sweep* and creating both the settings and costumes for the Royal Theatre's ballet *Et Folkesage* (The Legend). Together with her French-born husband, Prince Henrik, the queen translated Simone de Beauvoir's novel *Tous les hommes sont mortels* (All Men Are Mortal) from its original French into Danish.

Queen Margrethe and Prince Henrik have two sons. Crown prince Frederik was born in 1968 and, like his mother, is a graduate of Århus University, where he studied politics and law. Prince Joachim was born in 1969 and attended a smaller Danish college. Both princes did stints in the armed services after graduation and had work internships overseas, Joachim on a farm in Australia and Frederik at a California winery.

Frederik, who is hands-down Denmark's most eligible bachelor, is a world traveller whose journeys have taken him far and wide. In 2000 the crown prince, along with five companions, completed a 110-day Arctic journey by dogsled across the frozen tundra of northern Greenland. Joachim lives in Møgeltønder with his Hong Kong-born wife and infant son.

country, collectively encompassing about 4% of the nation's land area. These include beaches, coastal forests, heathlands and inland woods and lakes. Many are quite scenic and have been selected for some particular natural quality or historical significance. Most are crossed with hiking and biking trails and, although the majority can be walked in an hour or two, some areas are long and narrow and thus suitable for longer outings.

GOVERNMENT & POLITICS

Denmark is a constitutional monarchy with a single-chamber parliamentary system. The parliament, called Folketing, is responsible for enacting legislation. The prime minister leads the government with assistance from cabinet ministers who head the various government departments. Queen Margrethe II, who has been on the throne since 1972, has a largely ceremonial role but her signature is required on the enactment of new legislation.

The minimum voting age is 18; parliamentary elections are held at least once every four years. There are close to a dozen parties represented in the 179-seat parliament. The two largest parties are Socialdemokratiet (Social Democrats), which received 36% of the vote in the last election in 1998, and Venstre (Liberals – a right-of-centre party), which received 24%. Despite the domination of these two parties, any party that wins 2% of the vote gains representation in the national parliament.

Heated parliamentary debates are not common. Consultation and consensus building across party lines are the norm, with most legislation passed by large majorities. The major parties are quite moderate and most parliamentary members linger near the centre; however, one noteworthy change in the political landscape is the emergence of the far-right Dansk Folkeparti (DPP, Danish People's Party). The DPP was founded in 1995 on a restrictive immigration, anti-EU platform. Largely dismissed by the ruling Social Democrats, the DPP has had little direct influence on the national government but it did capture 13 seats and 7.4% of the vote in the last national election. In a bit of a counterbalance, representation of the other right-leaning party, Fremskridtspartiet (Progress Party), dropped from 11 delegates to just four during that election.

Socialdemokratiet, the largest party, is a moderate socialist party. It's founded on the belief in the right of guaranteed security to all in the form of extensive social-welfare programs that are funded by high taxes. The party first came to power in 1924 and has been in power, either alone or as part of a coalition government, for most of the time since then. Poul Nyrup Rasmussen, who is the leader of Socialdemokratiet, has headed the government under various left-centre coalitions since 1993.

The main domestic issues revolve around reforming taxes in the hope of lowering the nation's 50%-plus income-tax rate, the highest in the EU. The latest tax reform initiatives focus on shifting from direct to indirect taxes by increasing consumption taxes such as those levied on petrol and motor vehicles. In an attempt to capitalise on progressive environmental sentiments, many of the new taxes are being promoted as 'green taxes'.

In addition to having a national government, Denmark is divided administratively into 14 counties and 273 municipalities. Many government services, such as urban transport, health services and primary education, are administered at a local level.

ECONOMY

Denmark has the highest per-capita GNP in the EU and its citizens enjoy a high standard of living. It has a workforce of three million, divided almost evenly between men and women. Relative to other countries in Europe, the Danish economy remains quite strong, despite the fact that the government impounds almost half of its GNP to pay for social services and as transfer payments to the disadvantaged.

Recent changes in employment policy, including more liberal parental leave and enhanced job-training programs, have contributed to a reduction in the unemployment rate to 7%. The generous income-transfer payments, including early retirement pay, pensions and unemployment benefits, have buffered the financial impact on those without work.

Almost all government funding is derived from taxes: More than 50% comes from taxes on personal income and about one-third comes from value-added tax (VAT) and taxes on petrol, alcohol and other dutiable items. A mere 4% is derived from corporate taxes. The government, although having a socialist slant on social-welfare issues, is not involved in the ownership of capital; on the contrary, a number of state-funded services, including such basics as ambulance and firefighting services, are provided by privately owned companies.

Nearly two-thirds of Denmark's land area is under cultivation. Of the country's 60,000 farms, the vast majority are still owned and operated by families. The average farm size is 43 hectares. Although family-operated, farms are highly mechanised and efficient, and 65% of their output is exported abroad. Important crops include wheat, barley, sugar beet and rapeseed, which is used to make canola oil.

Livestock husbandry is also important. Denmark is the world's leading exporter of canned ham and Danish dairy farms supply the milk used to make the country's famous cheeses and butter cookies.

Fishing remains economically important. Denmark boasts the largest fish catches of any EU country. The main fish species that are caught for human consumption are cod, herring, sprat, mackerel and plaice, but about 20% of the catch is industrial fish used to produce fish oil and fish meal.

Danish industry provides roughly 20% of the nation's employment. Important industrial exports include beer, home electronics, furniture, silverware and porcelain. Food processing and the manufacture of machinery are also significant industries. Denmark is self-sufficient in both oil and gas and since 1991 has been an exporter of these fossil fuels.

POPULATION & PEOPLE

Denmark's population is about 5.3 million, with 70% living in urban areas. The four largest cities are Copenhagen (1,785,000), Århus (260,000), Odense (185,000) and Aalborg (154,000).

Denmark is almost entirely inhabited by ethnic Danes, people of the Teutonic ancestry common to all of Scandinavia. Foreign nationals account for approximately 5% of Denmark's population, an increase from just 2% in 1984. Approximately 12% of all foreign nationals come from Nordic countries, 43% from other parts of Europe, 25% from Asia, 12% from Africa and 5% from the Americas.

A relaxation of immigration policies during the economic expansion of the 1960s attracted 'guest workers', many of whom established a permanent niche, and there are now sizable Turkish and Pakistani communities. More recent humanitarian policies, introduced in response to famine and war crises, have resulted in small Somalian and Ethiopian immigrant communities and there is a growing number of refugees from the former Yugoslavia.

EDUCATION

Education is free and nine years of schooling from the age of seven is compulsory. Preschool and kindergarten are optional; about two-thirds of children aged five and six attend.

About half of all Danish students who graduate from secondary school continue on to higher education. Slightly more than half of these graduates enrol in vocational programs that provide training in business, nursing, maritime studies and various other

Great Danes

Thirteen Danes have received the Nobel Prize since 1901, the year in which it was first awarded. They are as follows:

1903 Physiology/Medicine: Niels R Finsen, for his research including the introduction of light-radiation treatment for diseases such as lupus

1908 Peace: Fredrik Bajer, for his work as a peace activist and writer

1917 Literature: Karl A Gjellerup, for poetry inspired by lofty ideals, and Henrik Pontoppidan, for his insightful descriptions of everyday life in Denmark

1920 Physiology/Medicine: Auguste Krogh, for discovering the capillary motor-regulating mechanism

1922 Physics: Niels Bohr, one of the fathers of atomic power, for his investigation into radiation and the structure of atoms

1926 Physiology/Medicine: cancer researcher Johannes AG Fibiger, for his discovery of the Spiroptera carcinoma

1943 Physiology/Medicine: Henrik CP Dam (with Edward Doisy of the USA), for the discovery of Vitamin K

1944 Literature: Johannes V Jensen, for the strength of his poetic imagination

1975 Physics: Aage Bohr and Ben Mottelson (with James Rainwater of the USA), for the discovery of the link between collective motion and particle motion in atomic nuclei and the development of the theory of the structure of the atomic nucleus

1984 Physiology/Medicine: Niels K Jerne (with Georges JF Koehler of Germany and Cesar Milstein of the UK), for theories on the development and control of the immune system and the discovery of the principle of monoclonal antibody production

1997 Chemistry: Jens C Skou (with John Walker of the UK and Paul Boyer of the USA), for discovering aspects of how the body's cells store and use energy

career-specific fields. Most others attend one of the five state-supported universities, of which the most elite is Copenhagen University (founded in 1479); the others are in Århus, Aalborg, Odense and Roskilde. Men and women are evenly represented in higher education, although female students tend to enrol in shorter courses than those chosen by men.

ARTS
Fine Arts
Prior to the 19th century, Danish art tended to revolve around formal portraits of the bourgeoisie, the aristocracy and the royal family. One of the most highly regarded portrait painters was Jens Juel (1745–1802).

Denmark's 'Golden Age' of the arts, from 1800 to 1850, produced luminaries such as

Danish Modern Design

Denmark has distinguished itself as a leader in the field of applied design, with a focus on cool clean lines, graceful shapes and streamlined functionality. These concepts have been applied to everything from coffeepots to the construction of concert halls.

Architecture
In the second half of the 20th century a number of Danish architects have taken a leading role in introducing new designs both at home and abroad. Perhaps the most influential of these is Jørn Utzon who, in the 1950s, took the basic elements of a Californian ranch-house design and modified them into a popular style of suburban Danish house that can be found throughout Denmark today. These homes utilise an open floor plan and an abundance of windows and glass doors that are designed to merge indoor spaces with the outdoors and utilise precious sunlight during long winters. Utzon has also been responsible for designing a number of eminent public buildings in Denmark, such as the performing arts centre Musikhuset Esbjerg in southern Jutland. His most monumental claim to fame, however, lies in Australia, where he designed the Sydney Opera House. Constructed in the 1960s, this striking waterfront building with its multiple shell design is one of the world's most famous and readily recognised landmarks.

Other notable contemporary Danish architects include Johan von Spreckelsen, who designed a European landmark, the huge cube-like La Grande Arche in Paris, in 1984, and Arne Jacobsen, who was an innovator in international modernism, producing Danish interpretations of the Bauhaus style. Some of Jacobsen's best-known works are additions at St Catherine's College in Oxford, England, and the Herrenhaus concert hall in Hanover, Germany, the latter created in collaboration with his partner Otto Weitling. Weitling himself has designed some significant European buildings, including the much-acclaimed Museum of Art in Düsseldorf in 1986.

Furniture
Danish architects place such great emphasis on 'form following function' that they typically design a room only after considering the styles of furniture that are most likely to be used there. Consequently it's not surprising that several Danish architects have crossed over to the field of furniture design, where their work has had an even broader impact.

Modern Danish furniture focuses on the practical refinement of style and the principle that its design should be tailored to the comfort of the user. Kaare Klint, who worked both as an architect and founded the furniture design department at the Royal Academy of Fine Arts in Copenhagen, modified a number of chair designs to add functionality, developing the smooth, unadorned style that was to become the prototype of contemporary Danish furniture design.

In 1949 one of Klint's contemporaries, Hans Wegner, created the Round Chair, whose fluid curving lines made it an instant classic and a model for many furniture designers to follow. So popular

Christoffer Wilhelm Eckersberg (1783–1853), who depicted more universal scenes of everyday Danish life, and Eckersberg's student Christen Købke (1810–48), who was little known in his time but is now regarded as one of the most important painters of the era. The leading Danish sculptor in this period was Bertel Thorvaldsen (1770–1844) who re-created classical sculptures during a long sojourn in Rome, following which he returned to Copenhagen in order to establish his own museum.

The Skagen school was active in the late 18th and early 19th centuries and specialised in romantic seaside subjects with an emphasis on the effects of natural light. Leading Skagen painters included PS Krøyer, Michael Ancher and Anna Ancher.

Danish Modern Design

was the chair at the time that it appeared on the cover of a number of international interior-design magazines, helping to establish the first successful overseas export market for Danish furniture.

A decade later architect Arne Jacobsen created the Ant, a form chair designed to be mass produced, which became the model for the stacking chairs found in schools and cafeterias worldwide. Jacobsen also designed the Egg and the Swan; both are rounded, uncomplicated upholstered chairs with revolving seats perched on pedestal stands.

Danish design prevails in stylish lamps as well. The country's best-known lamp designer is Poul Henningsen, who in his work has emphasised the need for lighting to be soft, for the shade to cast a pleasant shadow and for the light bulb to be blocked from direct view. His PH-5 lamp, which he created in 1958, remains one of the most popular hanging lamps sold in Denmark today.

Silverware & Porcelain

The clean lines of industrial design are also evident in Danish silver, which combines aesthetics with function. Danish silverwork is highly regarded both at home and abroad, the chief design criteria being that the item is attractive yet simple, as well as easy to use. The father of modern Danish silverwork was the sculptor and silversmith Georg Jensen, who artistically incorporated curvilineal designs; his namesake company is still a leader in Denmark silverwork. Two of Jensen's students, Kay Bojesen and Henning Koppel, are also leading names in Danish silverwork.

One of the world's most famous sets of porcelain is the Flora Danica dinner service created by Royal Porcelain Manufactory (now Royal Copenhagen). No two pieces of this 1800-piece set are alike; each is hand-painted with a different native wildflower or other plant, then rimmed with gold. Some of the pieces have trompe l'oeil features, such as cup handles that look like flower stems. Commissioned in 1790 by crown prince Frederik, the original set took 13 years to complete and is still part of the Danish royal collection today; pieces of that original set are on display at Copenhagen's Rosenborg Slot. You can also see examples – or if money is no obstacle, purchase your own reproduction set – at the Royal Copenhagen porcelain shop on Strøget in Copenhagen.

The other leader in Danish porcelain is Bing & Grøndahl, which was founded in 1853 to compete with Royal Copenhagen for the lucrative ceramics market. It too produces a variety of tableware, much of it decorated with finely painted floral designs. Bing & Grøndahl is perhaps most widely known for its annual Christmas plates, which have been issued for more than 100 years. These plates, which are cobalt blue and white with a traditional winter design, are collected by millions of people worldwide.

The trademark gentle curves of Danish design are also evident in industrial and other products ranging from plastic blocks created by Lego to avant-garde sound systems and televisions produced by Bang & Olufsen.

Sage Søren

Denmark's most famous philosopher, Søren Kierkegaard, was born into a prosperous Copenhagen family on 5 May 1813. When Søren was in his early 20s his father died, leaving him with an inheritance that freed him from the need to work. He studied theology and philosophy at Copenhagen University and devoted his entire life to studying and writing.

Kierkegaard was vehemently opposed to the philosophy of Georg Wilhelm Friedrich Hegel, which was prevalent in 19th-century Europe and embraced by the Danish Lutheran Church. In contrast, Kierkegaard's writings challenged the individual to make choices entirely of his or her own among the alternatives that life offered. In his first great work, *Either/Or*, published in 1843, the alternative was between aesthetic pleasures or an ethical life. This work, like many that followed, was in part inspired by Kierkegaard's lifelong pain over breaking off an engagement to a young woman named Regine Olsen. He continued to wrestle with the implications of his broken engagement in subsequent writings, including *Fear and Trembling* (1843), which compares the biblical tale of Abraham's sacrifice of Isaac to Kierkegaard's own sacrifice.

Kierkegaard's greatest attack on Hegelianism, and his most philosophically important work, was *Concluding Unscientific Postscript to the Philosophical Fragments* (1846), which passionately expounded the tenets of existentialism.

Kierkegaard was considered by many members of the establishment to be a fanatic and his friends were few, even in the literary world. His works remained virtually unknown outside Denmark until the 20th century.

The last years of Kierkegaard's life were dominated by an acrimonious battle with the established Church. The toll was so great that it slowly drained his health and he died of exhaustion in a Copenhagen hospital in 1855 at the age of 42. At the time of his death, Kierkegaard felt his works had largely fallen upon deaf ears, but his writings have posthumously become the vanguard for existentialist philosophers worldwide.

The COpenhagen-BRussels-Amsterdam (Cobra) movement, which was formed in 1948 with the aim of exploiting the free artistic expression of the unconscious, had a significant impact on 20th-century Danish art. One of its founders, Danish artist Asger Jorn (1914–73), achieved an international following for his abstract paintings, many of which evoke vivid imagery from Nordic mythology.

Literature

The first half of the 19th century has been characterised as the 'Golden Age' of Danish literature. The foremost writers in that prolific period included Adam Oehlenschläger (1779–1850), a romantic lyric poet who also wrote short stories and plays; Steen Steensen Blicher (1782–1848), a writer of tragic short stories; Hans Christian Andersen (1805–75), whose fairy tales have been translated into more languages than any other book except the Bible; and the noted philosopher Søren Kierkegaard (1813–55), who is considered the father of existentialism.

Around 1870 a trend towards realism emerged, focusing on contemporary issues of the day. A writer of this genre, novelist Henrik Pontoppidan (1857–1943), won the Nobel Prize for Literature in 1917 shortly after publishing the epic *The Realm of the Dead*, which attacked materialism. Another Danish author who won the Nobel Prize for Literature in 1944 was Johannes Vilhelm Jensen (1873–1950), who penned the six-volume novel *The Long Journey* and *The Fall of the King*, a story about Danes during Renaissance times. Better known outside

Denmark is Martin Andersen Nexø (1869–1954), whose novels about the proletariat, the four-volume *Pelle the Conqueror* and *Ditte, Child of Man*, helped draw attention to the conditions of the poor and spurred widespread reform in Denmark.

The most famous Danish writer of the 20th century, Karen Blixen (1885–1962), started her career with *Seven Gothic Tales*, which was published in New York under the pen name Isak Dinesen. She is best known for *Out of Africa*, the memoirs of her farm life in Kenya, which she wrote in 1937. Other works include *Winter's Tales* (1942), *The Angelic Avengers* (1944), *Last Tales* (1957), *Anecdotes of Destiny* (1958) and *Shadows on the Grass* (1960). See the boxed text 'Out of Rungsted' in the Øresund Coast section of the North Zealand chapter for more about her life.

Denmark's foremost contemporary novelist is Peter Høeg, who in 1992 wrote the international bestseller *Miss Smilla's Feeling For Snow* (published in the USA as *Smilla's Sense of Snow*), a suspense mystery that touches upon Danish colonialism and the struggle for Greenlandic cultural identity. Since then, three other Høeg novels have been published in English: *The History of Danish Dreams*, a narrative that sweeps through many generations of a Danish family; *Borderliners*, which deals with social issues surrounding private schooling in Denmark; and *The Woman and the Ape*, the main character of which saves a rare primate from the clutches of scientists. An

Once Upon a Time...

Born on 2 April 1805 in Odense, Hans Christian Andersen was the son of a poor cobbler. At 14 he ran away to Copenhagen 'to become famous' and the following year entered the Royal Danish Theatre as a student of dance and music. In 1822, on the recommendation of the theatre board, he was sent to a preparatory school in Helsingør and in 1828 he passed his university entrance exams.

The following year Andersen self-published his first book, *A Walk From Holmen's Canal to the Eastern Tip of Amager*. In 1831, after being jilted in a love affair with Riborg Voight of Faaborg, he travelled to Germany and wrote the first of a number of stories about his travels abroad.

In 1835 he finally made a name for himself with the successful novel *The Improvisators*. He followed that with his first volume of fairy tales, *Tales, Told for Children*, which included such classics as 'The Tinderbox' and 'The Princess and the Pea'. Over the next few decades he continued writing novels and accounts of his travels, but it was his fairy tales that brought him worldwide fame.

Andersen had a superb talent for humanising animals, plants and inanimate objects without compromising their original character. In his stories the villains are not evil characters such as witches or trolls, but rather human weaknesses such as indifference and vanity, and his tales are imbued with moral realism instead of wishful fantasy. Some of his most famous fairy tales are 'The Little Mermaid', 'The Ugly Duckling', 'The Snow Queen', 'The Constant Tin Soldier', 'The Nightingale' and the satirical 'The Emperor's New Clothes'.

In addition to his fairy tales and poems, Andersen wrote six novels, numerous travel books, many dramatic works and two autobiographies, of which the most highly regarded is *The Fairy Tale of My Life*. In all, he published 156 stories and other works.

Andersen had a penchant for travel and over his lifetime made 29 journeys abroad, several of them lasting many months. On 4 August 1875, at the age of 70, he died of liver cancer at a villa outside Copenhagen. His grave is in the capital's Assistens Kirkegård.

MH

earlier collection of his short stories has also been translated into English under the title *Tales of the Night*. Høeg's works focus on nonconformist characters on the margins of Danish society.

Theatre & Dance

Det Kongelige Teater (The Royal Theatre) in Copenhagen first opened in 1748 as a court theatre, performing the plays of Denmark's most famous playwright, Ludvig Holberg (1684–1754). Today its repertoire encompasses international works, including Shakespearian plays as well as classical and contemporary Danish plays.

In the mid-19th century, Den Kongelige Ballet (The Royal Danish Ballet), which also performs at Det Kongelige Teater, took its present form under the leadership of the French choreographer and ballet master August Bournonville (1805–79). Today Den Kongelige Ballet, which has a troupe of nearly 100 dancers, still performs a number of Bournonville's romantic ballets, such as *La Sylphide* and *Napoli*, along with more contemporary works.

Also based in Det Kongelige Teater is Den Kongelige Opera (The Royal Danish Opera), which has an ensemble of 32 singers and a renowned 60-member opera chorus. It performs about 16 operas each season.

Det Kongelige Kapel (The Royal Danish Orchestra) was founded in 1448, giving it claim to be the oldest orchestra in the world; it accompanies the ballet and opera performances at Det Kongelige Teater.

Cinema

The best-known Danish director of the early part of the 20th century was Carl Theodor Dreyer (1889– 1968), who directed a number of films including the 1928 French masterpiece *La Passion de Jeanne d'Arc*, which was acclaimed for its rich visual textures and innovative use of close-ups. In the midst of WWII, Dreyer boldly filmed *Vredens Dag* (Day of Wrath), which made so many allusions to the tyranny of Nazi occupation that he was forced to flee to Sweden.

It wasn't until the 1980s, that the Danish directors attracted a broader international audience. In 1988 *Babette's Feast*, directed by Gabriel Axel, won the Academy Award for Best Foreign Film. *Babette's Feast* was an adaptation of a story written by Karen Blixen, whose novel *Out of Africa* had been turned into an Oscar-winning Hollywood movie just three years earlier.

In 1989 Danish director Bille August won the Academy Award for Best Foreign Film as well the Cannes Film Festival's Palme d'Or award for *Pelle the Conqueror*, a film adapted from Martin Andersen Nexø's book about the harsh reality of life as an immigrant in 19th-century Denmark. August also directed *Smilla's Sense of Snow* (1997), based on the bestseller by Peter Høeg, starring Julia Ormond and Gabriel Byrne, and *Les Miserables* (1998), adapted from Victor Hugo's classic tale of good and evil, with Liam Neeson and Geoffrey Rush.

The leading director of the new millennium is Lars von Trier, whose better-known films include the melodrama *Breaking the Waves* (1996), featuring Emily Watson, which took the Cannes Film Festival's Grand Prix award, and *Dancer in the Dark* (2000), a musical starring Icelandic pop singer Björk and Catherine Deneuve. *Dancer in the Dark* won the Cannes Film Festival's Palme d'Or in 2000. Von Trier's movies utilise a minimalist approach, which involves using only hand-held cameras, shooting on location with natural light and refraining from the use of special effects and pre-recorded music.

Two Danish actresses that have jumped into the international film scene are Iben Hjejle, who made her Hollywood debut with a leading role in the quirky romantic comedy *High Fidelity* (2000), and Connie Nielsen, who co-starred in the Roman Empire epic *Gladiator* (2000) with Russell Crowe and the thriller *One Hour Photo* (2001) with Robin Williams.

SOCIETY & CONDUCT

Danes pride themselves on being thoroughly modern, and the wearing of folk costumes, the celebration of traditional festivals and the tendency to cling to old-fashioned customs is less prevalent in

Denmark than in most other European countries. There are, of course, traditional aspects of the Danish lifestyle that aren't apparent at first glance.

Perhaps nothing captures the Danish perspective more than the concept of *hygge* which, roughly translated, means cosy and snug. It implies shutting out the turmoil and troubles of the outside world and striving instead for a warm, intimate mood. Hygge affects how Danes approach many aspects of their personal lives, from the design of their homes to their fondness for small cafes and pubs. There's no greater compliment that a Dane can give their host than to thank them for a cosy evening.

Danish family life has changed rather dramatically in the past few decades. These days, about 20% of all couples who live together aren't married and the average age for those who do opt to tie the knot has risen to 35 years. Consequently, family size has dropped to an average of 1.8 children.

Women are often well established in their careers by the time they have their first child, and generous leave schemes make it easy to take a temporary pause from the workplace. The traditional role of homemaker, in which a woman stays home to care for children, has all but disappeared in Denmark. Fewer than 5% of Danish women remain at home full-time after the end of their maternity leave, which typically lasts 24 weeks (but can be extended up to another year with paid parental leave).

From infancy, Danish children spend a significant amount of time away from their home – day-care centres and nursery schools are a normal part of daily life for the vast majority of preschoolers these days.

Perhaps as a result of spending so much time outside the family from an early age, Danes are notably tolerant and have a high degree of social responsibility. They also tend to be more involved in club activities and organisations than most other societies.

Visitors will find Danes to be relaxed, casual and not given to extremes. Danes like to think of themselves as a classless society and there are seldom any hints of chauvinism, sexism or any other ism.

Danes are very open-minded on lifestyle issues. In 1989, Denmark became the first European country to legalise same-sex marriages and to offer gay partners most of the same rights as heterosexual couples. In 1999 a further step in recognising a broader

What's in a Name?

Of the five million-plus Danes on the planet today, two-thirds have a surname ending in 'sen'. The three most common – Jensen, Nielsen and Hansen – account for 23% of all Danish surnames. Next, in order of frequency, are Pedersen, Andersen, Christensen, Larsen and Sørensen.

You may notice a trend here. The most common Danish surnames are derived from the most common given names with 'sen' suffixed on. This is because up until the mid-19th century most peasants and other rural folk did not have a permanent family name but simply added 'sen', meaning 'son', onto their father's first name. Thus if your father was Peder Hansen and your name was Eric, you would be known as Eric Pedersen.

definition of the family was taken when the decade-old Registered Partnership Act was amended to allow married gays to legally adopt the children of their partners.

Dos & Don'ts

Nothing out of the ordinary is expected of visitors, but there are a couple of potential pitfalls to avoid. Danes generally queue by a number system; when you go to the post office, a bakery, the tourist office – just about any place there can be a queue – there's invariably a machine dispensing numbered tickets. Grab one as you enter and wait until your number is called.

Danes love to joke about a lot of things, but can be sensitive to criticism. They have a high degree of respect for the queen and any flippant remark about the royal family is apt to offend most people.

Casual dress is usually perfectly fine. You rarely have to dress up to do anything in Denmark, other than for the fanciest of fine dining. Nonetheless, Danes themselves are often very stylish dressers. If you want to blend in and hit the club scene, black clothing is the key.

RELIGION

More than 90% of Danes officially belong to Folkekirken (Danish People's Church), an Evangelical Lutheran denomination that is the state-supported national church; however, fewer than 5% of Denmark's citizens are regular churchgoers.

Although Folkekirken is connected with the state, Danes enjoy freedom of religion and in most of the larger cities there are also places of worship for Catholics, Anglicans and Jews.

LANGUAGE

The national language is Danish, which belongs to the northern branch of the Germanic language group. Most Danes speak at least basic English, however, and it is easy for English-language speakers to get around without a workable knowledge of Danish. German is also widely spoken.

Use of the letter 'å' was introduced in 1948 to replace 'aa'. However, there are some towns and institutions that opted to continue using the earlier style. So you will sometimes see 'aa' used, eg, Aalborg and Faaborg, in place of the more recent 'å', eg, Århus and Gudenå.

For more information on Danish, including a guide to pronunciation and a list of useful words and phrases, see the language chapter at the back of this book.

For a more comprehensive guide to the language, as well as those of the surrounding countries and Iceland, pick up Lonely Planet's *Scandinavian Europe phrasebook*.

Facts for the Visitor

SUGGESTED ITINERARIES

Depending on the length of your stay and your interests, you might like to see and do the following:

Two Days Buy a Copenhagen Card and explore the capital's splendid museums, palaces, parks and gardens.

One Week Visit Copenhagen and then head for North Zealand's castles and beaches, Roskilde, Trelleborg and perhaps other sights in southern Zealand such as historic Køge, Ringsted and Sorø.

Two Weeks Having covered the areas listed previously, continue to Funen, stopping off at Odense and Ærø, then onwards to Århus, Skagen, Ribe and other places of interest in Jutland.

One Month Extend your range to include Bornholm, southern Funen (including the islands of Tåsinge and Langeland), Møn and Falster.

Two Months Take the opportunity to visit the main places of interest at a more leisurely pace; cycle between sights to experience the gentle charms of the Danish countryside.

HIGHLIGHTS

Be sure to jump in and absorb some of what's quintessentially Danish: pass a sunny afternoon in an outdoor cafe over a plate of herring and a cold Carlsberg, see the country from a cyclist's perspective or spend a night on the town sampling the music scene.

Viking Sites

Denmark is rich with Viking sites, including circular ring fortresses dating back to about AD 980. The best preserved are the Trelleborg fortress in Zealand and the Fyrkat fortress in Jutland; both have reconstructed Viking houses and summer activities.

For maritime history, visit the Viking Ship Museum in Roskilde, Bangsbomuseet in Frederikshavn and Ladbyskibet outside Kerteminde. Also worth a visit is Lindholm Høje outside Aalborg, which contains the largest plot of Viking and Iron Age graves in Scandinavia.

In the summer, several Danish towns hold open-air Viking plays. The performance with the most atmospheric setting is held at the Fyrkat fortress outside Hobro, but there are also plays at Lindholm Høje outside Aalborg and in Frederikssund in North Zealand.

Museums

The most impressive open-air museum is Den Gamle By in Århus, set up as a provincial town, while Den Fynske Landsby folk museum in Odense has the most engaging natural setting.

The best-preserved bog people – intact Iron Age bodies found preserved in peat bogs – are in the Silkeborg Museum in Silkeborg and the Moesgård Museum in Århus. The nation's finest art museums are Ny Carlsberg Glyptotek and Statens Museum for Kunst, both in Copenhagen, and Louisiana in Humlebæk. Copenhagen's Nationalmuseet has a superb collection of Danish historical artefacts, including Viking weaponry and rune stones.

Castles

Egeskov Slot in Funen, surrounded by a moat and formal gardens, has the most striking setting, while Frederiksborg Slot in Hillerød boasts the most elaborately decorated Renaissance interior. In Copenhagen, the king of castles is Rosenborg Slot, which houses the dazzling crown jewels.

Historic Towns

Half-timbered houses, ancient churches and cobblestone streets are thick on the ground in Denmark, but a few places are unique. Ribe, the oldest town in the country, has an exquisite historic centre encircling a 12th-century cathedral.

The tiny fortress island of Christiansø, off Bornholm, retains its ramparts and 17th-century buildings, with almost no trace of modern times. And Ærøskøbing on the island of Ærø has a town centre of 18th-century houses that's arguably the most picturesque in Denmark.

Activities

Denmark, crisscrossed as it is with cycling paths, is a great place for pedal power, and there's barely a nook of it that can't be explored by bicycle. For more information see the special section 'Cycling in Denmark' following the Getting Around chapter.

Windsurfers will find ideal conditions on Jutland's western coast at Hvide Sande, Klitmøller and Rømø. Favourite beaches include Marielyst on Falster, Hornbæk and Tisvildeleje in North Zealand, and Skagen on the northern tip of Jutland. The Lake District is a centre for canoeing and walking, while the Rebild Bakker area is also a splendid place for hiking.

Concerts

Denmark hosts some grand concerts. Each summer Roskilde stages the largest rock festival in northern Europe, while Copenhagen sponsors the region's largest jazz festival and Tønder holds a noteworthy folk festival.

PLANNING
When to Go

Considering its northerly latitude, Denmark has a fairly mild climate year-round. Still, the winter months – cold and with short daylight hours – are certainly the least hospitable. Many tourist destinations are mothballed in the winter and don't come alive until late April, when the weather begins to warm up and the daylight hours start to increase; by October they become sleepers again.

May and June can be delightful months in which to visit: The land is a rich green, accented with fields of yellow rapeseed flowers, the weather is generally warm and comfortable and you'll beat the rush of tourists. Although autumn can also be pleasant, it's not nearly as scenic as the rural landscape has by then largely turned brown.

The peak tourist season of July and August is the time for open-air concerts, lots of street activity and basking on the beach. Other bonuses for travellers during the high season are longer hours at museums and other sightseeing attractions and potential savings on accommodation, as some hotels drop their rates. Of course you won't be the only tourist during summer as many Danes and other Europeans travel during their summer holidays and celebrate midsummer with gusto. The Danish school year is back into full swing by mid-August, so the last half of August can be a particularly attractive time to travel – when there's still summer weather but fewer crowds.

Some sightseeing spots and businesses use the terms 'high season' and 'low season' to define periods when they have different opening hours or prices. These are somewhat elastic terms, depending on the type of business, but generally the high season (when opening hours are longer and some prices are higher) coincides with the school summer holiday, from about mid-June to mid-August. The low season is generally taken to mean any time outside that period.

Before planning a trip, also refer to the Climate section in the Facts about Denmark chapter.

Maps

There are excellent maps of Denmark's larger cities, such as Copenhagen, Århus, Aalborg and Odense, that can be picked up free from tourist offices. Staff at the tourist offices in smaller cities and towns can generally provide simpler maps that are suitable for local sightseeing.

The *Map of Denmark – ferry guide & attractions*, which is a quality foldout, four-colour road map, can be obtained free from Denmark's overseas tourist offices.

If you're renting a car, you can usually obtain a good Denmark road map free from the rental agency when you pick up your car.

Although the aforementioned maps will suit most travellers' needs, if you enjoy exploring back roads, nooks and crannies you may also want to pick up the detailed road map of Denmark published by Kort-og Matrikelstyrelsen in a handy atlas format and labelled *Færdselskort 1:200,000 Danmark*. It's readily found in Danish bookshops and costs 110kr.

What to Bring

Travelling light is always the best policy. It's very easy to find almost anything you need along the way; however, keep in mind that, because of the value-added tax (VAT) and the overall high price of goods, most people won't want to be stocking up excessively in Denmark.

Travelpacks, a combination of backpack and shoulder bag, are very popular for carrying gear. The backpack straps zip away inside the pack when not needed so you have the best of both worlds – a smart-looking soft bag for checking in at hotels, and a suitable backpack for walking. Some packs have sophisticated shoulder-strap adjustment systems so you can use them comfortably even on long hikes. Travelpacks can be reasonably thief-proofed with a small padlock.

The secret of successful packing is using plastic carrier bags inside your travelpack: They keep things organised, and also keep things dry if the bag gets soaked.

Airlines do lose luggage occasionally, but you've got a better chance of it being retrieved if it's tagged with your name and address *inside* as well as outside. Outside tags can always fall off or be removed.

As for clothing, the season you are travelling in will have a major bearing on what you should bring along to wear. However, even during the warmest months, it's a very good idea to carry at least a light jacket, as cool weather can sweep across Denmark at any time.

A minimum packing list could include:

- underwear, socks and swimming gear
- a pair of jeans or trousers
- a pair of shorts or a skirt
- a few T-shirts and shirts
- a warm sweater
- a comfortable pair of shoes
- sandals or thongs (flip-flops) for shared showers
- a coat or jacket
- a raincoat, umbrella, or waterproof jacket
- a medical kit and sewing kit
- a combination padlock
- a Swiss Army knife
- soap and towel
- toothpaste, toothbrush and toiletries
- a small daypack

A tent and sleeping bag are vital for camping. A sleeping sheet with a pillow cover is necessary if you plan to stay in hostels – you'll have to hire or purchase one if you don't bring your own. You can make one of these sleeping sheets yourself out of old sheets or buy one from your hostel association. A bath towel is also necessary if you stay in hostels.

A Swiss Army knife is useful for all sorts of things (any pocket knife is fine, so long as it includes a bottle opener and a strong corkscrew). Note that in Denmark an anti-gang law makes it illegal in most cases to carry a knife with a blade more than 7cm long.

A small daypack will prove convenient for city sightseeing. Other items might include a compass, a torch (flashlight), an alarm clock or a watch with an alarm function, an adapter plug for electrical appliances, a pair of sunglasses and an elastic clothesline.

If you're travelling to Denmark in the summer, when daylight hours are long, you may find an eye mask helpful to fall asleep while it's still light and to avoid being woken by an early dawn.

TOURIST OFFICES

Over 100 tourist offices are found throughout Denmark, and the staff can be amazingly helpful, providing information on virtually anything from what's happening at the concert hall to the location of the nearest coin laundry or bicycle rental shop. Of course they can also help you to book accommodation and provide advice on local sightseeing.

Most offices have multilingual staff who can handle inquiries in English, German and Danish.

Local Tourist Offices

Virtually every good-sized town in Denmark has a tourist office, most often found in the *rådhus* (town hall) or elsewhere on *torvet* (the central square).

Contact information for the local tourist offices is listed under individual towns throughout this book. You can pick up general visitor literature at these offices once you arrive or, upon request, staff at most offices will mail out a package of tourist brochures specific to their area.

If you want to stock up on material before heading off to the countryside, brochures and booklets about all parts of Denmark are available to walk-in visitors at Copenhagen Information opposite Central Station. Although the Copenhagen office is the best-stocked tourist office in Denmark, other major city offices, such as those in Odense and Århus, can also pile visitors high with a good range of brochures pertaining to all parts of Denmark.

The administrative headquarters for the national tourist organisation is: Danish Tourist Board (☎ 33 11 14 15, e dt@dt.dk, w www.dt.dk), Vesterbrogade 6D, 1620 Copenhagen V.

Tourist Offices Abroad

You can receive general information on travel in Denmark, including a road map and a hotel guide, from Danish tourist offices abroad.

Overseas representatives of the Danish Tourist Board include:

Finland
Tanskan Matkailutoimisto (☎ 9-586 0330, e tanska@dt.dk) Salomonsgatan 17 A 6 vån, 00100 Helsinki

France
Conseil du Tourisme de Danemark (☎ 01 53 43 26 26, e paris@dt.dk) 18 boulevard Malesherbes, 75008 Paris

Germany
Dänisches Fremdenverkehrsamt (☎ 40-32 02 10, e daninfo@dt.dk) Glockengiesserwall 2, 20095 Hamburg

Italy
Ente Danese per il Turismo (☎ 2-87 48 03, e info.dk@dt.dk) Via Cappuccio 11, 20123 Milano

Japan
Scandinavian Tourist Board (☎ 03-5212 1121, e scandinavia@stb-japan.com) IzumiKan Gobancho 4F, 12-11 Gobancho, Chiyoda-ku, Tokyo 102-0076

Netherlands
Deens Verkeersburo Benelux (☎ 0900-202 52 80, e denemarken@dt.dk) Postbus 266, 2300 AG Leiden

Norway
Danmarks Turistkontor (☎ 22 00 76 46, e danmark@dt.dk) Tollbugaten 27, Postboks 406 Sentrum, 0103 Oslo

Sweden
Danmarks Turistråd (☎ 08-611 7222, e info@dtab.se) Box 5524, 114 85 Stockholm

UK
Danish Tourist Board (☎ 020-7259 5959, e dtb.london@dt.dk) 55 Sloane St, London SW1X 9SY

USA
Danish Tourist Board (☎ 212-885 9700, e info@goscandinavia.com) PO Box 4649, Grand Central Station, New York, NY 10163

VISAS & DOCUMENTS
Passport

Your most important travel document is your passport, which should remain valid until well after your trip. If it's about to expire, renew it before you go; this may not be easy to do overseas.

Applying for or renewing a passport can take anything from a few days to several months, so don't leave it until the last minute. First check what is required: passport photos, birth certificate, exact payment in cash, whatever.

Australian citizens can apply at post offices, or the passport office in state capitals; Britons can apply at major post offices; Canadians can apply at regional passport offices; New Zealanders can apply at any district office of the Department of Internal Affairs; while US citizens must apply in person (but may usually renew by mail) at a US Passport Agency office or at some courthouses and post offices.

Citizens of a number European countries do not always need a passport for travel within Europe; a national identity card may be sufficient for this group of travellers. Check with a travel agency, airline or embassy before starting your trip.

Once you start travelling, make sure you carry your passport (or national identity card) at all times and guard it carefully. It's a good idea to also carry a photocopy of it in a separate place.

Visas

Visa regulations everywhere are always subject to change, so it's advisable to check the situation before leaving home.

Citizens of the USA, Canada, Australia and New Zealand need a valid passport to enter Denmark, but they don't need a visa for tourist stays of less than three months. In addition, no entry visa is needed by citizens of EU and Scandinavian countries.

Citizens of many South American, Asian African and former Soviet bloc countries do require a visa. The Danish Immigration Service (W www.udlst.dk/sjle5/visumlande .html) publishes a list of countries whose citizens require a visa on its Web site.

Once in Denmark, if you have questions on visa extensions or visas in general, contact the Danish Immigration Service: Udlændingestyrelsen (☎ 35 36 66 00), at Ryesgade 53, Copenhagen.

Travel Insurance

A travel insurance policy to cover theft, loss and medical problems is a good idea. There is a wide variety of policies available, so check the small print.

Some policies specifically exclude 'dangerous activities', which can include scuba diving, motorcycling, and even trekking. A locally acquired motorcycle licence is not valid under some policies.

You may prefer a policy that pays doctors or hospitals directly rather than you having to pay on the spot and claim later. If you have to claim later make sure you keep all documentation. Some policies ask you to call back (reverse charges) to a centre in your home country where an immediate assessment of your problem is made.

Check that the policy covers ambulances or an emergency flight home.

Driving Licence & Permits

Bring your home driving licence: Denmark accepts many foreign driving licences without restriction, including those issued in the USA, Canada, the UK and other EU countries. If you do not hold a European driving licence and plan to drive elsewhere in the region, it's a good idea to obtain an International Driving Permit (IDP) from your local automobile association before you leave – you'll need a passport photo and a valid licence. IDPs are usually inexpensive and valid for one year only.

If you're planning to drive your own car into Denmark, see Paperwork & Preparations in the Car & Motorcycle section of the Getting There & Away chapter.

Hostel Cards

If you have a Hostelling International card be sure to bring it; otherwise, you'll have to buy a guest card once you arrive in Denmark.

Even if you're not planning to stay at hostels on this trip, but happen to have a card, bring it along, as it'll get you discounts at some museums and sightseeing spots.

Student & Youth Cards

The most useful of these is the International Student Identity Card (ISIC), an ID-style card with your photograph, which can provide discounts on some transport and reduced admission to some museums and sights.

There is a worldwide industry in fake student cards, and some places now stipulate a maximum age for student discounts or, more simply, they have substituted a 'youth discount' for a 'student discount'. If you're aged 25 or younger but not a student, you can apply for the International Youth Travel Card (IYTC), formerly called GO25, which gives much the same discounts as an ISIC and is administered by the same organisation.

Both types of card are issued by student unions, hostelling organisations or student travel agencies. They don't automatically entitle you to discounts, but you won't find out until you flash the card.

Other Documents

In many countries, the local camping federations issue a Camping Card International (CCI), which is basically a camping ground ID. These passes incorporate third-party insurance for any damage you may cause. In Denmark your home-country CCI will be accepted if it has the current year's stamp.

If you arrive in Denmark without a CCI, you can buy a Danish camping pass instead; see Camping in the Accommodation section later in this chapter for more details.

Copies

Before you leave home, you should photocopy all important documents (passport data page, credit cards, travel insurance policy, air tickets, driving licence etc). Leave a copy with someone at home and keep another with you, separate from the originals.

It's also a good idea to store details of your vital travel documents in Lonely Planet's free online Travel Vault in case you lose the photocopies or can't be bothered with them. Your password-protected Travel Vault is accessible online anywhere in the world – you can create it at W www.ekno .lonelyplanet.com.

EMBASSIES & CONSULATES
Danish Embassies & Consulates

Danish missions overseas include those listed below.

Australia (☎ 02-6273 2195) 15 Hunter St, Yarralumla, ACT 2600
Canada (☎ 613-562 1811) 47 Clarence St, Suite 450, Ottawa, Ontario K1N 9K1
Finland (☎ 9-684 1050) Centralgatan 1A, 00101 Helsinki
France (☎ 01 44 31 21 21) 77 Avenue Marceau, 75116 Paris
Germany (☎ 5050 2000) Rauchstrasse 1, 10787 Berlin
Iceland (☎ 56 21 230) Hverfisgata 29, 121 Reykjavík
Ireland (☎ 1-475 6404) 121 St Stephen's Green, Dublin 2
Italy (☎ 06-3200 441) Via dei Monti Parioli 50, 00197 Rome
Netherlands (☎ 70-302 5959) Koninginnegracht 30 (Postbus 85654), 2508 CJ Den Haag
New Zealand Contact the embassy in Australia
Norway (☎ 22 54 08 00) Olav Kyrres Gate 7, 0244 Oslo
Sweden (☎ 08-406 7500) Jakobs Torg 1, 11186 Stockholm
UK (☎ 020-7333 0200) 55 Sloane St, London SW1X 9SR
USA (☎ 202-234 4300) 3200 Whitehaven St NW, Washington DC 20008

Embassies & Consulates in Denmark

It's important to realise what your own embassy – the embassy of the country of which you are a citizen – can and can't do to help you if you get into trouble. Generally speaking, it won't be much help in emergencies if the trouble you're in is even remotely your own fault. Remember that you are bound by the laws of the country you are visiting. Your embassy will not be sympathetic if you end up in jail after committing a crime locally, even if such actions are legal in your own country.

In genuine emergencies you might get some assistance, but only if other channels have been exhausted. For example, if you need to get home urgently, a free ticket home is exceedingly unlikely – the embassy would expect you to have insurance. If you have all your money and documents stolen, the embassy might assist with getting a new passport, but a loan for onward travel is out of the question.

Some embassies used to keep letters for travellers or have a small reading room with home newspapers, but these days the mail holding service has usually been stopped and even newspapers tend to be out of date.

The following foreign diplomatic representatives to Denmark are in the greater Copenhagen area:

Australia (☎ 39 29 20 77) Strandboulevarden 122, Copenhagen
Canada (☎ 33 48 32 00) Kristen Bernikows Gade 1, Copenhagen
Finland (☎ 33 13 42 14) Sankt Annæ Plads 24, Copenhagen
France (☎ 33 67 01 00) Kongens Nytorv 4, Copenhagen
Germany (☎ 35 45 99 00), Stockholmsgade 57, Copenhagen
Iceland (☎ 33 15 96 04) Dantes Plads 3, Copenhagen
Ireland (☎ 35 42 32 33) Østbanegade 21, Copenhagen
Italy (☎ 39 62 68 77) Gammel Vartov Vej 7, Hellerup
New Zealand Contact the British embassy
Netherlands (☎ 33 70 72 02) Toldbodgade 33, Copenhagen

Norway (☎ 33 14 01 24) Amaliegade 39, Copenhagen

Poland (☎ 39 46 77 00) Richelius Allé 12, Hellerup

Russia (☎ 35 42 55 85) Kristianiagade 5, Copenhagen

Sweden (☎ 33 36 03 70) Sankt Annæ Plads 15A, Copenhagen

UK (☎ 35 44 52 00), Kastelsvej 40, Copenhagen

USA (☎ 35 55 31 44), Dag Hammarskjölds Allé 24, Copenhagen

CUSTOMS

Coming from outside the EU, you can bring the following into Denmark duty-free: 1L of hard liquor or 2L of fortified or sparkling wine, as well as 2L of table wine, 200 cigarettes and general items of a personal nature.

When you arrive in Denmark, there will be two customs channels. You must use the red channel if you're bringing in more than the usual allowance of duty-free goods or any restricted items (guns, drugs etc). Use the green channel – which is generally a quick exit – if you have nothing to declare.

MONEY
Currency

The Danish krone is most often written DKK in international money markets, Dkr in northern Europe and kr within Denmark. The krone is divided into 100 øre. There are 25 øre, 50 øre, one krone, two kroner, five kroner, 10 kroner and 20 kroner coins. Notes come in denominations of 50, 100, 200, 500 and 1000 kroner.

Exchange Rates

The following currencies convert at these approximate rates:

country	unit		krone
Australia	A$1	=	4.15kr
Canada	C$1	=	5.23kr
euro	€1	=	7.45kr
Japan	¥100	=	6.76kr
New Zealand	NZ$1	=	3.39kr
Norway	1 Nkr	=	0.93kr
Sweden	1 Skr	=	0.78kr
UK	UK£1	=	11.87kr
USA	US$1	=	8.18kr

Exchanging Money

Exchange booths at Copenhagen Airport are open to meet all scheduled incoming flights. If you're on an international ferry to Denmark, you can not only exchange US dollars and local currencies to Danish kroner on board but, if you buy a meal or use one of the shops, regardless of the currency you pay in, many will give you change in Danish kroner upon request.

The US dollar is generally the handiest foreign currency to bring, particularly if you're travelling farther afield than Denmark. However, Danish banks will convert a wide range of currencies including the euro, US dollar, UK pound, Canadian dollar, Swiss franc, Australian dollar, Japanese yen and kroner from Norway and Sweden. Foreign coins are seldom accepted by banks, so offload these before arriving in Denmark.

Exchange Fees All the common travellers cheques are accepted at major banks in Denmark. It's a good idea to bring travellers cheques in higher denominations because bank fees for changing money are a hefty 20kr per cheque, and there's a 40kr minimum. Cash transactions usually incur a 25kr fee however much you change; that doesn't necessarily make cash any more favourable however, because the travellers cheques command about a 1% better exchange rate.

Post offices also exchange foreign currency at comparable rates – the main benefit of this for travellers being that Danish post offices open on Saturday morning.

There are also exchange-only places, but these are limited to Copenhagen and most offer poor exchange rates. An exception is Forex, which has three Copenhagen offices, including one in Central Station, offering good rates and low fees. See Money under Information in the Copenhagen chapter for details.

Travellers Cheques The main benefit of travellers cheques is that they can provide protection from theft. Large companies such as American Express and Thomas Cook generally offer efficient replacement policies.

Keeping a record of the cheque numbers and those you have used is vital when it comes to replacing lost cheques. You should keep this information separate from the cheques themselves.

Eurocheques These guaranteed personal cheques are another way of carrying money or obtaining cash. The most popular of these is the Eurocheque, which requires having a European bank account.

Throughout Europe, when paying for something in a shop or withdrawing cash from a bank or post office, you write out a Eurocheque and show the accompanying guarantee card with your signature and registration number.

The card can double as an ATM card, and should obviously be kept separate from the cheques for safety.

ATMs Most banks in Denmark have automated teller machines (ATMs) that give cash advances on Visa and MasterCard credit cards as well as Cirrus and Plus bank cards. Although ATMs are accessible outside normal banking hours, not all are open 24 hours; particularly outside of Copenhagen, many Danish ATMs shut down for some part of the night, often from around 1am to 6am.

Typically you'll get a good rate when withdrawing money directly from a Danish ATM, but keep in mind that your home bank may charge you a fee (often around US$5) for international transactions. A few banks, especially in Copenhagen, have also installed 24-hour cash-exchange machines that change major foreign currencies, such as the US dollar and the British pound, into Danish kroner.

Credit Cards Credit cards like Visa and MasterCard (also known as Access or Eurocard) are widely accepted in Denmark. Charge cards like American Express and Diners Club are also accepted, but not as often; on the plus side, charge cards have a reputation for quick replacement, often within 24 hours, of reporting the card lost.

If your card is lost or stolen while visiting Denmark, report it to the appropriate agency:

American Express (☎ 80 01 00 21); Diners Club (☎ 36 73 73 73); Visa or Mastercard (☎ 44 89 25 00).

International Transfers The transfer of money from your home bank will be easier if you've authorised someone back home to access your account. Specify the city, the bank and the branch to which you want your money directed or ask your home bank to tell you where there's a suitable one and make sure you get the details right. If you have the choice, find a large bank and ask for the international division.

Costs

By anything other than Scandinavian standards, Denmark is an expensive country. Part of the credit for this lies with the 25% value-added tax (VAT), called *moms* in Danish, which is included in every price from hotel rooms and restaurant meals to car rentals and shop purchases.

Still, your costs will depend on how you travel and it is possible to see Denmark without spending a fortune. If you're travelling on a budget, one way to cut down on expenses is to take advantage of Denmark's extensive network of camping grounds and hostels. The latter are widely used by all age groups and are usually set up more like small hotels than cavernous drop-in centres.

In terms of basic expenses, if you camp or stay in hostels and prepare your own meals you might get by on 250kr a day. If you stay in modest hotels and eat at inexpensive restaurants, you can expect to spend about 500kr a day if you're doubling up, or 700kr if you're travelling alone. Interestingly, top-end hotels, which commonly have good weekend and holiday rates, often cost only about 30% more than the regular rates at budget hotels.

On top of the amounts given above you'll need to budget for local transport, admission fees to museums and other attractions, entertainment and incidentals. Long-distance public transport is reasonably priced and it helps that Denmark is small – the most expensive train ticket between two points in Denmark costs just 300kr.

If you're travelling by car, it's going to be more expensive. Petrol costs around 8.50kr a litre; that's about three times as much as in the USA but 10% less than in the UK. Car ferries are reasonable but the charges can add up, and if you opt to hire a car in Denmark the costs range from expensive to exorbitant. Expect to pay 650kr a day for car hire, although the daily rate drops to around 500kr on longer rentals – in either case this is for the cheapest economy car! One advantage of travelling by car is that you can often find economical accommodation options outside the city centre, so you should save a bit on hotel bills.

Of course there are always ways to circumvent some of the high costs. For instance if you're willing to come into Denmark via Germany you can pick up a rental car there for a fraction of the Danish car-hire fees and then drive north into Denmark.

Tipping & Bargaining

Restaurant bills and taxi fares include service charges in the quoted prices. Further tipping is unnecessary, although rounding up the bill is not uncommon when service has been especially good. Bargaining is not a common practice in Denmark.

Taxes & Refunds

Visitors from countries outside the EU who buy goods in Denmark can get a refund of the 25% VAT, less a handling fee, if they spend at least 300kr at any retail outlet that participates in the 'Tax Free Shopping Global Refund' plan. This includes most shops catering to tourists. The 300kr can be a single item or several items, as long as they're purchased from the same shop.

Be sure to obtain the 'Global Refund cheque' from the store when you make the purchase; it should include the date, both the buyer's and seller's name and address, the number and type of goods, the selling price and the VAT amount.

Contact the Global Refund office at your point of departure from Denmark to get the refund, and allow extra time in case there's a queue at the booth. At Copenhagen airport, you'll find a booth in the international

departure hall; if you depart by ship, inquire at the port as you board.

If you have any questions about these VAT refunds call ☎ 32 52 55 66, or pick up a brochure on the program from any of the participating shops.

POST & COMMUNICATIONS
Post

Most post offices are open either from 9am to 5.30pm or from 10am to 5pm on weekdays, and until noon on Saturday. You can receive mail c/o poste restante at any post office in Denmark, but it's usually held for only two weeks.

It costs 4.50kr to airmail a postcard or letter weighing up to 20g to Scandinavia or Western Europe, 5.50kr to other countries. Heavier letters weighing up to 50g cost 5.25kr within Denmark, 6.75kr to other Scandinavian countries, 9.75kr to Western Europe and 12.25kr to other countries. International mail sent from Copenhagen usually leaves the country within 24 hours.

Telephone

Denmark has an efficient phone system.

If you're going to be making many calls, consider using a debit phonecard (telekort), sold in denominations of 30kr, 50kr and 100kr. These cards can be used for making both local and international calls and are more convenient than pumping coins into a payphone. Cards can be bought at post offices and many kiosks, especially those at train stations.

Payphones can be found in busy public places, such as train stations and shopping centres. It used to be that you'd find an even ratio of coin phones and cardphones side by side, but these days the cardphones are outweighing the coin phones and they may eventually come to replace coin phones altogether.

The good news is that cardphones work out slightly cheaper than coin phones because you pay for the exact amount of time you speak; an LCD screen keeps you posted on how much time is left on the card. It's possible to replace an expiring card with a new card without breaking the call. Cardphones are posted with information in English detailing their use as well as the location of the nearest place that sells phonecards.

Domestic Calls All telephone numbers in Denmark have eight numbers. There are no area codes in the country; all eight numbers must be dialled, even when making calls within the same city.

All domestic calls now have the same rate whether you're calling across town or to some place on the other side of the country. For 2kr you get one minute and 25 seconds of calling time.

For directory assistance dial ☎ 118 but be aware it costs a hefty 5kr per minute.

International Calls to Denmark The country code for Denmark is 45. To call Denmark from another country, dial the international access code for the country you're in followed by 45 and the local eight digit number.

International Calls from Denmark The international access code in Denmark is 00. To make direct international calls from Denmark dial 00 followed by the country code for the country you're calling, the area code, then the local number.

For assistance, including information on rates for international calls, dial toll free ☎ 80 60 40 55. If you want to make a collect (or reverse-charge) call, dial ☎ 80 60 40 50.

You can also dial direct to an operator in your home country with the following services: to the USA and Canada, you can reach AT&T at 80 01 00 10; to Australia, Telstra at 80 01 00 61; to New Zealand, NZ Telecom at 80 01 00 64.

eKno Communication Service
Lonely Planet's eKno global communication service provides low-cost international calls – for local calls you're usually better off with a local phonecard. eKno also offers free messaging services, email, travel information and an online travel vault, where you can securely store all your important documents. You can join online at Ⓦ www .ekno.lonelyplanet.com, where you'll find

the local-access numbers for the 24-hour customer-service centre. Once you have joined, always check the eKno Web site for the latest access numbers for each country and updates on new features.

Fax
Faxes can be sent from larger post offices. The charge for sending within Europe is 35kr for the first page and 20kr for every additional page. If you're sending to a number outside Europe the charge is 50/30kr for the first/additional pages. The cost for receiving faxes is 5kr per page.

Email & Internet Access
Travelling with a portable computer is a great way to stay in touch with life back home, but unless you know what you're doing it's fraught with potential problems. If you plan to carry your notebook or palmtop computer with you, remember that the power supply voltage in the countries you visit may vary from that at home, risking damage to your equipment. The best investment is a universal AC adapter for your appliance, which will enable you to plug it in anywhere without frying the innards. You'll also need a plug adapter for each country you visit – often it's easiest to buy these before you leave home.

Also, your PC-card modem may or may not work once you leave your home country – and you won't know for sure until you try. The safest option is to buy a reputable 'global' modem before you leave home, or buy a local PC-card modem if you're spending an extended time in any one country. Keep in mind that the telephone socket in each country you visit will probably be different from the one at home, so ensure that you have at least a US RJ-11 telephone adapter that works with your modem. You can almost always find an adapter that will convert from RJ-11 to the local variety. For more information on travelling with a portable computer, see Ⓦ www.teleadapt.com or Ⓦ www.warrior.com.

Major Internet service providers such as AOL (Ⓦ www.aol.com) have dial-in nodes throughout Europe; it's best to download a list of the dial-in numbers before you leave home. If you access your Internet email account at home through a smaller ISP, your best option is either to open an account with a global ISP or to rely on public access points to collect your mail.

To use public access points to get your email, you'll need to know your incoming (POP or IMAP) mail server name, your account name and your password. A final option for collecting mail through public access points is to open a free Web-based email account such as HotMail (W www .hotmail.com) or Yahoo! Mail (W mail.yahoo .com). You can then access your mail from anywhere in the world from any Internet-connected machine running a standard Web browser.

A growing number of top-end hotels in Denmark are adding modem hook-ups in guest rooms, so if you intend to use your own computer, you should inquire when making reservations.

Public libraries throughout Denmark have computers with Internet access that are available to everyone. In many situations they are first-come, first-served, but for other computers you may need to book in advance and wait your turn. The good news is that they are free and libraries are adding more computers all the time.

As most families in Denmark have their own computers, and library computers are easily accessible, Internet cafes are not terribly abundant and tend to be short-lived.

DIGITAL RESOURCES

The World Wide Web is a rich resource for travellers. You can research your trip, hunt down bargain air fares, book hotels, check on weather conditions or chat with locals and other travellers about the best places to visit (or avoid!).

There's no better place to start your Web explorations than the Lonely Planet Web site (W www.lonelyplanet.com). Here you'll find succinct summaries on travelling to most places on earth, postcards from other travellers and the Thorn Tree bulletin board, where you can ask questions before you go or dispense advice when you get back. You

can also find travel news and updates to many of our most popular guidebooks, and the subWWWay section links you to the most useful travel resources elsewhere on the Web.

One of the best general Danish Web sites is the Danish foreign ministry site at W www .denmark.org, which has a wealth of information, including updated exchange rates and weather, and links to many other Danish sites, such as the Danish Tourist Board.

BOOKS

Most books are published in different editions by different publishers in different countries. One book might be a hardcover rarity in one country while it's readily available in paperback in another. Fortunately, bookshops and libraries search by title or author, so your local bookshop or library is best placed to advise you on the availability of the following recommendations.

Lonely Planet

If your travels will include other parts of Scandinavia, you'll find these destinations covered in Lonely Planet's *Scandinavian & Baltic Europe* guide. A good companion to help you to communicate with people along the way is Lonely Planet's *Scandinavian Europe phrasebook*. For the most detailed coverage of the Copenhagen area pick up a copy of Lonely Planet's new *Copenhagen* city guide.

History

Numerous books about Viking-era culture and history are available. *The Viking World*, by James Graham-Campbell, is a book with handsome photos that outlines the history of the Vikings by detailing excavated sites and artefacts. *The Viking*, by Bertil Almgren, is an authoritative book tracing Viking history in both the Old and New Worlds.

The hardback *Denmark: A Modern History*, by W Glyn Jones, is one of the more comprehensive and insightful accounts of contemporary Danish society.

Women in Denmark, Yesterday and Today, by Inga Dahlsgård, traces Danish history from a woman's perspective.

Copenhagen, by Michael Frayn, speculates about what may have transpired in Copenhagen during the September 1941 meeting of Danish physicist Niels Bohr and German scientist Werner Heisenberg. These two former colleagues went on to play pivotal roles in the development of atomic weapons, Bohr for the Allies and Heisenberg for the Nazis.

General

Danmark, by John Roth Andersen, is an attractive hardback, four-colour, coffee-table-style pictorial of the country with multilingual commentary.

Discover Denmark – on Denmark and the Danes; Past, Present and Future, by the Danish Cultural Institute, provides a comprehensive overview of Danish society, covering topics such as history, politics, arts, culture and social issues.

Copenhagen Architecture Guide, by Olaf Lind and Annemarie Lund, is a substantial softcover book covering more than 300 noteworthy buildings in Copenhagen, with interesting descriptions and colour photos.

Philosopher Søren Kierkegaard produced volumes of works, including *The Concept of Dread* (1844), which is considered by many to be the first work of depth psychology ever written, and *Concluding Unscientific Postscript to the Philosophical Fragments* (1846), in which Kierkegaard passionately expounded the tenets of the school of thought that would become existentialism. *A Kierkegaard Anthology*, by Robert Bretall, comprises a broad cross section of the philosopher's major works.

There's an avalanche of books by and about Hans Christian Andersen as well as numerous biographies of the author, including the definitive *Hans Christian Andersen* by Elias Bredsdorff.

The Golden Age of Danish Art, by Hans Edvard Norregard-Nielsen, takes a look at the art and artists of the early 19th century; it includes 115 colour illustrations.

Camping Danmark, published annually by Campingrådet (Danish Camping Board), includes detailed information on all approved camping grounds in Denmark.

NEWSPAPERS & MAGAZINES

Denmark has about 50 daily newspapers, of which *Jyllandsposten* and *Politiken* have the largest circulations.

Although none of the dailies is in English, the *Copenhagen Post* is a quality weekly newspaper that publishes an interesting mix of Danish news, events and entertainment information in English.

Foreign English-language magazines and newspapers are readily available at the train-station kiosks in larger towns. Among the more common English-language papers sold in Denmark are the *International Herald Tribune, USA Today,* the *Wall Street Journal,* the *European* and the *Guardian*. In the news magazine category, *Time* and the *Economist* are widely available.

RADIO & TV

Commercial Danish radio offers a blend of Danish-language talk shows, news and contemporary music. You can hear a five-minute news brief in English at 8.40am, 11am, 5.10pm and 10pm Monday to Friday on Radio Danmark International at 1062MHz. The BBC World Service is broadcast on short wave at 6195 and 9410kHz.

Danish TV features a mix of foreign programming and locally produced game shows, news features and light drama. British and US network programs and movies are common evening staples on Danish TV and are usually presented in English with Danish subtitles. Many hotels have live CNN news and BBC World Service as well as other English-language cable and satellite-TV programming.

VIDEO SYSTEMS

If you purchase videos in Denmark, make sure they're compatible with your home system. Denmark uses PAL, which is not compatible with the North American NTSC system.

PHOTOGRAPHY & VIDEO

Both print and slide film is readily available in major cities and towns. A 24-exposure roll of Kodacolor Gold 100 will cost about 40kr to buy and 100kr to develop and print.

Clockwise from top left: Horn-blowing Vikings outside the Rådhus, Copenhagen; National hero Holger Danske in the dungeon of Kronborg Slot, Helsingør; A modern installation at the Kongelige Bibliotek, Copenhagen; Cherubs of the Tivoli, Copenhagen; Carved doorway at Den Gamle By, Århus.

ANDERS BLOMQVIST

NED FRIARY

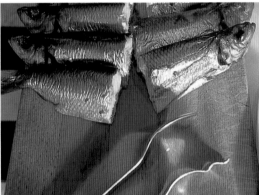

MARTIN MOOS

ANDERS BLOMQVIST

Clockwise from top: Enjoy a sunset cocktail on Roskilde pier; Try the national dish of herring – pickled, salted or smoked; Helsingør is a busy terminal for the ferry from Sweden; Take in the awesome sight of Møns Klint soaring above the incredibly blue sea for 128m.

A 36-exposure roll of Kodak slide film costs about 65kr.

In many larger cities you can find centres that offer a range of photo-processing options. The cost to develop and print a roll of 24-exposure film is about 125kr for one-hour photo processing, 100kr for same-day service and 75kr for three-day service.

For tips on taking advantage of those photo opportunities, read Lonely Planet's *Travel Photography: a Guide to Taking Better Pictures*.

Video

Properly used, a video camera can give a fascinating record of your holiday. As well as videoing the obvious things – sunsets, landmark buildings – remember to record some of the ordinary everyday details of life in the city. Often the most interesting things occur when you're actually intent on filming something else. Remember too that, unlike still photography, video 'flows' – so, for example, you can shoot scenes of the countryside rolling past the train window, to give an overall impression that isn't possible with ordinary photos.

Video cameras these days have amazingly sensitive microphones, and you might be surprised how much sound will be picked up. This can also be a problem if there is a lot of ambient noise – filming by the side of a busy road might seem OK when you do it, but viewing it back home might simply give you a deafening cacophony of traffic noise.

One good rule to follow for beginners is to try to film in long takes, and don't move the camera around too much. Otherwise, your video could well make your viewers seasick! If your camera has a stabiliser, you can use it to obtain good footage while travelling on various means of transport, even on bumpy roads. And remember, you're on holiday – don't let the video take over your life and turn your trip into a Cecil B de Mille production.

Make sure you keep the batteries charged and have the necessary charger, plugs and transformer for Denmark. Larger photo stores sell P-5 videotape; a 90-minute tape costs around 80kr.

Daylight Hours

Throughout the summer, visitors to Denmark can enjoy long lingering hours of daylight. The longest days are in late June, when the sun rises about 4.30am and sets at around 10pm, providing nearly 17½ daylight hours.

month	sunrise	sunset
1 January	8.40 am	3.48 pm
1 February	8.08 am	4.39 pm
1 March	7.06 am	5.40 pm
1 April	6.36 am	7.51 pm
1 May	5.29 am	8.46 pm
1 June	4.36 am	9.40 pm
1 July	4.33 am	9.54 pm
1 August	5.17 am	9.23 pm
1 September	6.16 am	8.02 pm
1 October	7.14 am	6.43 pm
1 November	7.15 am	4.31 pm
1 December	8.23 am	3.37 pm

TIME

Time in Denmark is normally one hour ahead of GMT/UTC, the same as in neighbouring European countries. When it's noon in Denmark, it's 11am in London, 6am in New York and Toronto, 3am in San Francisco, 9pm in Sydney and 11pm in Auckland.

Clocks are moved forward one hour for daylight-saving time from the last Sunday in March to the last Sunday in October. Denmark uses the 24-hour clock system and all timetables and business hours are posted accordingly. *Klokken*, which means o'clock, is abbreviated kl (kl 19.30 is 7.30pm).

Dates are written with the day followed by the month, thus 3/6 means 3 June and 6/3 means 6 March.

ELECTRICITY
Voltages & Cycles

Denmark, like most of Europe, runs on 220V (volts), 50Hz (cycles) AC.

Check the voltage and cycles (usually 50Hz) used in your home country. Most appliances that are set up for 240V (such as those used in the UK) will handle 220V without modifications and vice versa. It's always preferable to adjust your appliance to the exact voltage if you can – a few items, such as some electric razors and radios, will do this automatically. If your appliance doesn't have a built-in transformer, don't plug a 110/125V appliance (the kind used in the USA and Canada) into a Danish outlet without using a separate transformer.

Plugs & Sockets

Denmark uses the 'europlug' with two round pins. Many europlugs and some sockets do not have provision for earth wiring because most local home appliances are double-insulated; when provided, earth usually consists of two contact points along the edge.

If your plugs are of a different design, you'll need an adapter. These are usually available in shops specialising in travel needs; get one before you leave, because most adapters available in Denmark go the other way and are intended for Danes who are travelling to places that don't use the europlug.

WEIGHTS & MEASURES

Denmark uses the metric system. Petrol and beverages are sold by the litre, meats and vegetables are weighed in kilograms, distance is measured in kilometres or metres and speed limits are posted in kilometres per hour (km/h).

Fruit is often sold by the piece *(stykke)*, abbreviated 'stk'. Decimals are indicated by commas and thousands by points.

For those unaccustomed to the metric system, there's a conversion chart on the inside back cover of this book.

LAUNDRY

Møntvaskeri (coin laundries) are relatively easy to find in cities and towns; hostels and camping grounds usually have coin or token-operated machines as well. The cost to wash and dry a load of clothes is generally around 50kr.

TOILETS

Toilets in Denmark are Western-style. Public ones are generally free and easy to find at such places as train stations, town squares and ferry harbours.

HEALTH

Denmark is a healthy place and travellers shouldn't need to take any unusual health precautions.

Visitors whose countries have reciprocal agreements with Denmark are covered by the Danish national health-insurance program. For citizens of EU countries, in most cases you'll need to present EU form E111; inquire at your national health service or travel agency before leaving home. Similar reciprocal arrangements exist between the Nordic countries. However, travel insurance may still be advisable because of the flexibility it offers in where and how you're treated, as well as covering expenses for an emergency flight home.

All visitors, however, regardless of where they are from, receive free hospital treatment in the event of an accident or sudden illness, provided the patient has not come to Denmark for the explicit purpose of obtaining the treatment and is too ill to return home.

Controlled medicine is only available from a pharmacy with a prescription that is issued by a Danish or other Scandinavian doctor. Although most pharmacies have the same opening hours as other shops, in major population centres there's usually at least one *apotek* (pharmacy) open 24 hours; there's an additional charge for using the pharmacy outside normal opening hours. When a pharmacy is closed, it's required to display the address of a nearby outlet that's open.

In medical emergencies, dial ☎ 112; the call can be made without coins from public phones.

Predeparture Planning

Immunisations Jabs are generally not necessary for Denmark or elsewhere in Europe; however, a yellow fever vaccination may be a requirement if you're coming from an affected area.

Health Insurance Make sure that you have adequate health insurance. See Travel

Insurance in the Visas & Documents section earlier in this chapter.

Other Preparations Make sure you're healthy before you start travelling. If you are going on a long trip make sure your teeth are OK. If you wear glasses take a spare pair and your prescription.

If you require a particular medication take an adequate supply, as it may not be available locally. Take part of the packaging showing the generic name of the drug rather than the brand, which will make locating replacements easier. To avoid any problems, it's a good idea to have a legible prescription or letter from your doctor to show that you legally use the medication.

Basic Rules

Tap water is safe to drink throughout the country. Stomach upsets are a possibility anywhere you travel but in Denmark these are likely to be relatively minor.

As a general rule take care with fish and shellfish (for instance, cooked mussels that have not opened properly can be dangerous) and avoid undercooked meat.

Medical Problems & Treatment

Local pharmacies are good places to visit if you have a small medical problem and can explain what it is. Hospital casualty wards will help if it's more serious, and will tell you if it's not. Major hospitals and emergency numbers are mentioned in the text. Staff at tourist offices, pharmacies and hotels can put you in touch with a doctor or dentist.

Environmental Hazards

Jet Lag Jet lag is experienced when a person travels by air across more than three time zones (each time zone usually represents a one-hour time difference). It occurs because many of the functions of the human body (such as temperature, pulse rate and emptying of the bladder and bowels) are regulated by internal 24-hour cycles. When we travel long distances rapidly, our bodies take time to adjust to the 'new time' of our destination, and we may experience fatigue,

Medical Kit Check List

Following is a list of items you should consider including in your medical kit – consult your pharmacist for brands available in your country.

- ☐ **Aspirin or paracetamol (acetaminophen in the USA)** – for pain or fever
- ☐ **Antihistamine** – for allergies, eg, hay fever; to ease the itch from insect bites or stings; and to prevent motion sickness
- ☐ **Cold and flu tablets, throat lozenges and nasal decongestant**
- ☐ **Multivitamins** – consider for long trips, when dietary vitamin intake may be inadequate
- ☐ **Antibiotics** – consider including these if you're travelling well off the beaten track; see your doctor, as they must be prescribed, and carry the prescription with you
- ☐ **Loperamide or diphenoxylate** –'blockers' for diarrhoea
- ☐ **Prochlorperazine or metaclopramide** – for nausea and vomiting
- ☐ **Rehydration mixture** – to prevent dehydration, which may occur, for example, during bouts of diarrhoea; particularly important when travelling with children
- ☐ **Insect repellent, sunscreen, lip balm and eye drops**
- ☐ **Calamine lotion, sting relief spray or aloe vera** – to ease irritation from sunburn and insect bites or stings
- ☐ **Antifungal cream or powder** – for fungal skin infections and thrush
- ☐ **Antiseptic (such as povidone-iodine)** – for cuts and grazes
- ☐ **Bandages, Band-Aids (plasters) and other wound dressings**
- ☐ **Water purification tablets or iodine**
- ☐ **Scissors, tweezers and a thermometer** – note that mercury thermometers are prohibited by airlines

disorientation, insomnia, anxiety, impaired concentration and loss of appetite.

These effects will usually be gone within three days of arrival, but to minimise the impact of jet lag:

- Rest for a couple of days prior to departure.
- Try to select flight schedules that minimise

sleep deprivation; arriving late in the day means you can go to sleep soon after you arrive. For very long flights, try to organise a stopover.
- Avoid excessive eating (which bloats the stomach) and alcohol (which causes dehydration) during the flight. Instead, drink plenty of noncarbonated, nonalcoholic drinks such as fruit juice or water.
- Avoid smoking.
- Make yourself comfortable by wearing loose-fitting clothes and perhaps bringing an eye mask and ear plugs to help you sleep.
- Try to sleep at the appropriate time for the time zone you are travelling to.

Motion Sickness Eating lightly before and during a trip will reduce the chances of motion sickness. If you are prone to motion sickness try to find a place that minimises movement – near the wing on aircraft, close to midships on boats, near the centre on buses. Fresh air usually helps; reading and cigarette smoke don't. Commercial motion-sickness preparations, which can cause drowsiness, have to be taken before the trip commences. Ginger (available in capsule form) and peppermint (including mint-flavoured sweets) are natural preventatives.

Cold If you are cycling or hiking in cool wet weather, be prepared.

Everyday Health

Normal body temperature is up to 37°C or 98.6°F; more than 2°C (4°F) higher indicates a high fever. The normal adult pulse rate is 60 to 100 per minute (children 80 to 100, babies 100 to 140). As a general rule the pulse increases about 20 beats per minute for each 1°C (2°F) rise in fever.

Respiration (breathing) rate is also an indicator of illness. Count the number of breaths per minute: between 12 and 20 is normal for adults and older children (up to 30 for younger children, 40 for babies). People with a high fever or serious respiratory illness breathe more quickly than normal. More than 40 shallow breaths a minute may indicate pneumonia.

It is surprisingly easy to progress from being very cold to dangerously cold due to a combination of wind, wet clothing, fatigue and hunger, even if the air temperature is above freezing. It is best to dress in layers; silk, wool and some of the newer artificial fibres are all good insulating materials. A hat is important, as a lot of heat is lost through the head. A strong, waterproof outer layer is essential, as keeping dry is vital.

Sunburn You can get sunburnt surprisingly quickly, even through cloud. Use a sunscreen, a hat and a barrier cream for your nose and lips. A commercial after-sun preparation or calamine lotion is good for mild sunburn. Protect your eyes with good quality sunglasses, particularly if you will be near water, sand or snow.

Infectious Diseases

Diarrhoea Simple things such as a change of water, food or climate can all cause a mild bout of diarrhoea, but making a few rushed toilet trips with no other symptoms is not indicative of a major problem.

Dehydration is the main danger with any diarrhoea, particularly in children or the elderly, as dehydration can occur quite quickly. Under all circumstances *fluid replacement* (at least equal to the volume being lost) is the most important thing to remember. Weak black tea with a little sugar, soda water or soft drinks allowed to go flat and diluted 50% with clean water are all good. With severe diarrhoea a rehydrating solution is preferable to replace minerals and salts lost.

HIV & AIDS Infection with the human immunodeficiency virus (HIV) may lead to acquired immune deficiency syndrome (AIDS), which is a fatal disease. HIV is a major problem in many countries, including Denmark. Any exposure to blood, blood products or body fluids may put the individual at risk. The disease is often transmitted through sexual contact or via dirty needles – vaccinations, acupuncture, tattooing and body piercing can be potentially as dangerous as intravenous drug use. If you have any questions regarding AIDS while in Denmark, there's an AIDS Hotline (☎ 33 91 11 19) between 9am and 11pm daily.

Sexually Transmitted Diseases Gonorrhoea, herpes and syphilis are among these diseases; sores, blisters or rashes around the genitals, discharges or pain when urinating are common symptoms. In some STDs, such as wart virus or chlamydia, symptoms may be less marked or not observed at all, especially in women. Chlamydia infection can cause infertility in men and women even before any symptoms have been noticed. Syphilis symptoms eventually disappear completely but the disease continues and can cause severe problems in later years. While abstinence from sexual contact is the only 100% effective prevention, using condoms is also effective. The treatment of gonorrhoea and syphilis is with antibiotics. The different sexually transmitted diseases each require specific antibiotics.

Cuts, Bites & Stings
Cuts & Scratches Wash well and treat any cut with an antiseptic such as povidone-iodine. Where possible avoid bandages and Band-Aids, which can keep wounds wet.

Insect Stings Bee and wasp stings are usually painful rather than dangerous. However, in people who are allergic to them severe breathing difficulties may occur and require urgent medical care. Calamine lotion or a sting-relief spray will give relief and ice packs will reduce the pain and swelling.

Ticks You should always check all over your body if you have been walking through a potentially tick-infested area as ticks can cause skin infections and other more serious diseases. If a tick is found attached, press down around the tick's head with tweezers, grab the head and gently pull upwards. Avoid pulling the rear of the body as this may squeeze the tick's gut contents through the attached mouth parts into the skin, increasing the risk of infection and disease. Smearing chemicals on the tick will not make it let go and is not recommended.

Breaking Barriers

Women's roles in Danish society have advanced significantly, though there are still strides to be made. Today more than 80% of all Danish women are in the workplace, nearly twice as many as in 1970. Although Danish law prevents job discrimination between the sexes, opportunities at the highest echelons have nevertheless opened slowly. A third of the members of parliament are now women, but women hold fewer than 10% of the top management positions in the private sector.

Ticks are most commonly found in wooded areas and are most active from late spring to early autumn.

WOMEN TRAVELLERS
Although women travellers are less likely to encounter problems in Denmark than in most other countries, the usual common-sense precautions apply when it comes to potentially dangerous situations such as hitching and walking alone in cities at night.

Center for Information om Kvinde-og Kønsforskning or KVINFO (Danish Centre for Information on Women and Gender; ☎ 33 13 50 88, ⓔ kvinfo@kvinfo.dk), Christians Brygge 3, Copenhagen, is a good place to get involved in feminist issues.

Kvindehuset (☎ 33 14 28 04), Gothersgade 37, Copenhagen, is a help centre and meeting place for women. In Århus, a good place to contact regarding women's issues is Kvindemuseet (☎ 86 13 61 44), at Domkirkeplads 5, which also has a cafe and a women's museum.

Dial ☎ 112 for rape crisis assistance or in other emergencies.

GAY & LESBIAN TRAVELLERS
Danes have a high degree of tolerance for alternative lifestyles of all sorts, and gays are as free as anyone else to express themselves. In 1989, Denmark became the first country in Europe to legalise same-sex marriages and offer gay partners most of the same legal rights as heterosexual couples.

Do You Eric, Take Hans...

In October 1989 the Danish Law of Registered Partnership took effect, allowing people of the same sex to tie the knot. Since then more than 5000 couples have taken advantage of the law and registered their partnerships with city hall.

During the early years of the new law, approximately one-third of the partnerships were lesbian women and two-thirds gay men, although in recent years the numbers have evened out.

If you're interested in learning more about the struggles leading up to the 1989 law, go online to W users.cybercity.dk/~dko12530/, a Web site produced by Axel and Eigil Axgil, the first same-sex couple to be married in Denmark.

Not surprisingly, Denmark is a popular destination for gay and lesbian travellers. Copenhagen in particular has an active, open gay community and lots of nightlife options, but you'll find gay and lesbian venues in other cities as well.

A fun general book if you are looking for something to read before coming to Denmark is *Are You Two...Together? A Gay and Lesbian Travel Guide to Europe*, by Lindsy Van Gelder & Pamela Robin Brandt, which has a particularly enjoyable chapter on Copenhagen.

Landsforeningen for Bøsser og Lesbiske (LBL; ☎ 33 13 19 48, e lbl@lbl.dk), the national organisation for gay men and lesbians, is at Teglgårdsstræde 13 in Copenhagen. It has a library, bookshop, cafe, gay and lesbian support groups, religious services and counselling. There's also a telephone information line (☎ 33 36 00 86) that operates 8pm to 11pm Monday, Thursday and Sunday. LBL also has branches in Århus (☎ 86 13 19 48) and Aalborg (☎ 98 16 45 07).

LBL is also behind the main gay magazine in Denmark, *PAN bladet*, which covers gay-related issues, upcoming events and entertainment; an annual English-language version is published each June. For more information contact PAN Bladet (☎ 33 36 00 82, e lbl-panblad@lbl.dk), Postboks 1023, 1007 Copenhagen K.

The main gay and lesbian festival of the year is the Mermaid Pride parade, a big Mardi Gras-like bash that takes place in Copenhagen on a Saturday in early August. There's also the Copenhagen Gay & Lesbian Film Festival, held each year in October. A good Web site, which includes useful tourist information and listings in English, as well as links to LBL and other gay organisations, is W www.copenhagen-gay-life.dk.

DISABLED TRAVELLERS

If you have a physical disability, get in touch with your national support organisation (preferably the 'travel officer' if there is one). They often have libraries devoted to travel and can put you in touch with travel agents who specialise in tours for disabled travellers.

The UK-based Royal Association for Disability & Rehabilitation (RADAR) publishes a useful guide called *Holidays and Travel Abroad: A Guide for Disabled People*, which gives a good overview of the facilities available in Europe. The book is available by post (UK£6) from RADAR (☎ 020-7250 3222), Unit 12, City Forum, 250 City Rd, London EC1V 8AF.

Most Danish tourist literature, such as the Danish Tourist Board's hotel guide, the camping association listings and the hostel booklet, indicate which establishments have rooms and facilities accessible to people in wheelchairs.

In addition, the Danish Tourist Board, in association with the Committee for Housing, Transportation and Technical Aids, produces a useful English-language publication: *Access in Denmark – a Travel Guide for the Disabled*. The book contains practical information for disabled travellers, including a list of accommodation with suitable access, information on using public transport and the accessibility of museums and sights to people in wheelchairs. The latest edition (60kr) is out of date but it's worth inquiring as an update may be in the works.

Once in Denmark, disabled travellers who have specific questions can contact Dansk Handicap Forbund (☎ 39 29 35 55), Kollektivhuset, Hans Knudsens Plads 1A, 2100 Copenhagen Ø.

SENIOR TRAVELLERS

Many discounts are available to senior citizens for things like public transport and museum admission fees, with proof of age. The minimum qualifying age is generally between 60 and 65. One example is the discount system on the Danish State Railways (DSB), which offers reductions of 25% to 50% to seniors aged 65 and older for travel on most days.

The basic rule is to always inquire about the availability of senior discounts whenever you're visiting a museum or sightseeing attraction or when you're booking transport. Although it's not as common, hotels also occasionally offer promotions that are geared to seniors.

In your home country, there may be a lower age entitling you to special travel packages and discounts (on car hire, for instance) through organisations and travel agencies that cater to senior travellers.

TRAVEL WITH CHILDREN

Denmark is a family-oriented place, with plenty of activities geared for children. Even stuffy history museums often have a hands-on section for the kids; camping grounds commonly have playgrounds; in cities you'll find duck ponds and gardens that invite picnics; and amusement parks abound throughout the country. Staff at local tourist offices are happy to point visitors towards sights and activities of interest to children and they can sometimes provide information on babysitting services.

Successful travel with young children requires planning and effort. Try not to overdo things; even for adults, packing too much into the time available can cause problems. And make sure the activities include the kids as well – balance that day of museum-hopping with a day at Legoland. Include children in the planning of the trip; if they've helped to work out where you will be going, they will be much more interested when they get there. A good book to pick up to help with planning is Lonely Planet's *Travel with Children*, which is loaded with tips and information.

USEFUL ORGANISATIONS

Danish Cultural Institute

The government-sponsored Danish Cultural Institute (Det Danske Kulturinstitut; ☎ 33 13 54 48, fax 33 15 10 91, e dancult@cultur.dk, w dankultur.dk), Kultorvet 2, 1175 Copenhagen K, arranges cultural events and exchanges, sponsors Danish language classes and distributes information on a range of aspects of Danish culture.

The Cultural Institute has branches in the following countries:

Belgium

Deens Cultureel Instituut/Institut Culturel Danois (☎ 02-230 7326, fax 02-230 5565, e d-k-i@innet.be/d-k-i@club.innet.be) rue du Comet/Hoomstraat 22, 1040 Brussels

Estonia

Taani Kultuuriinstituut (☎/fax 6-466 373, e dki@uninet.ee) Vene 14, 0001 Tallinn

Germany

Dänisches Kulturinstitut (☎ 511-6965 005, fax 511-6965 008, e d-k-i@t-online.de) Pelikanstrasse 7, 30177 Hanover

Latvia

Danijas Kulturas Instituts (☎/fax 7-289 994, e d-k-i@mail.bkc.lv) Marijas iela 13, k3, 2sal, 1050 Riga

Lithuania

Danijos Kulturos Institutas (☎ 2-222 607, fax 2-222 412, e d-k-i@post.omnitel.net) Vilniaus 39/6, Room 208, 2001 Vilnius

Poland

Dunski Instytut Kultury (☎ 58-661 5553, fax 58-661 5469, e d-k-i@rubikon.net.pl) ul Kilinskiego 16, 81 393 Gdynia

UK

Danish Cultural Institute (☎ 131-225 7189, fax 131-220 6261, e dci.dancult@dancult.demon.co.uk, w www.dancult.demon.co.uk) 3 Doune Terrace, Edinburgh EH3 6DY

American-Scandinavian Foundation

In the USA, the American-Scandinavian Foundation (☎ 212-751 0714, e mem@amscan.org, W www.amscan.org), 58 Park Ave, New York, NY 10016, arranges cultural exchanges, publishes an English-language magazine and also presents a wide range of cultural programs. It covers not only Denmark but all of Scandinavia. In addition, its members are entitled to discounted air fares between the USA and Scandinavia, which sometimes work out to be good deals. Membership costs $50 per year (seniors and students $25).

DANGERS & ANNOYANCES

Denmark is by and large a very safe country and travelling presents no unusual dangers. Travellers should nevertheless be careful with their belongings, particularly in busy places such as Copenhagen's Central Station.

In cities, you'll need to quickly become accustomed to the busy cycle lanes that run beside roads between the vehicle lanes and the pedestrian pavement, as these cycle lanes (and fast-moving cyclists) are easy to veer into accidentally.

Throughout Denmark, dial ☎ 112 for emergency police, fire or ambulance services.

Theft

As a traveller you're often fairly vulnerable and when you do lose things it can be a real hassle. The most important things to guard are your passport, important papers, tickets and money. It's best to always carry these next to your skin or in a sturdy leather pouch on your belt.

Be careful even in hotels; don't leave valuables lying around in your room. Those planning to stay in hostels should bring a padlock to secure their belongings in the hostel lockers.

Never leave your valuables unattended in parked cars. If you must leave your luggage in a vehicle, be sure that your car has a covered area that keeps bags out of sight and carry the most important items with you in a daypack. Remove all luggage overnight, even if the car is left in a garage.

If you're unlucky enough to have something stolen, immediately report it to the nearest police station. If your credit cards or travellers cheques have been taken, notify your bank or the relevant company immediately.

LEGAL MATTERS

The drinking age in Denmark is 18 years of age. Don't drink and drive, as even a couple of drinks can put you over the legal limit. The authorities are very strict about drink-driving. It's illegal to drive with a blood-alcohol concentration of 0.05% or greater and drivers under the influence of alcohol are liable to receive stiff penalties and a possible prison sentence.

Always treat drugs with a great deal of caution. There is a fair bit of marijuana and hashish available in the region, sometimes quite openly, but note that in Denmark (unlike in the Netherlands) all forms of cannabis are officially illegal.

If you are arrested for any punishable offence in Denmark, you can be held for up to 24 hours before appearing in court. You have a right to know the charges against you and a right to a lawyer, and you are not obliged to answer police questions before speaking to the lawyer. If you don't know of a lawyer, the police will provide one.

You can get free legal advice on your rights from EU Legal Aid (☎ 33 14 41 40) or Emergency Legal Aid (☎ 35 37 68 13), both in Copenhagen.

BUSINESS HOURS

Office hours are generally 9am to 4pm Monday to Friday. Most banks are open 9.30am to 4pm Monday to Friday (to 6pm on Thursday).

Shops are typically open 9.30am to 5.30pm on weekdays (to 2pm on Saturday), although the trend in larger cities is towards longer opening hours.

PUBLIC HOLIDAYS & SPECIAL EVENTS

Summer holidays for school children begin around 20 June and end around 10 August. The schools also take a break for a week in

Jul-tide Celebrations

By far the most eagerly awaited holiday in Denmark is *jul*, or Christmas. Celebrations begin on 1 December with the lighting of candles, the placing of wreaths in windows and the opening of advent calendars. Every day from 1 December to 23 December children unwrap a small gift. A couple of weeks before the holiday a Christmas tree is brought in and decorated with candles, heart-shaped ornaments and strings of miniature Danish flags.

The main celebration for the festive season takes place on 24 December, when Danes have their traditional Christmas dinner. This usually features apple-stuffed roast goose or duck, sweet and sour red cabbage, liver pate, caramelised potatoes and an abundance of sweets, including *brune kager* (gingerbread), *klejner* (fried knotted dough), *pebernødder* (spiced cookies) and *ris à l'amande* (rice pudding with almonds). After the meal, the family joins hands and circles around the tree, singing traditional Christmas songs, followed by the unwrapping of presents.

On 25 December, most Danes have a Christmas lunch featuring a hearty cold table with plenty of leftovers from the day before.

mid-October and over the Christmas and New Year period. Many Danes take their main work holiday during the first three weeks of July.

Banks and most businesses are closed on public holidays, and transport schedules commonly operate on a reduced timetable on those days.

Public holidays observed in Denmark are:

New Year's Day (Nytårsdag)
1 January
Maundy Thursday (Skærtorsdag)
Thursday before Easter
Good Friday (Langfredag)
Friday before Easter
Easter Day (Påskedag)
a Sunday in March or April
Easter Monday (2.påskedag)
day after Easter
Common Prayer Day (Stor Bededag)
fourth Friday after Easter
Ascension Day (Kristi Himmelfartsdag)
sixth Thursday after Easter
Whitsunday (Pinsedag)
seventh Sunday after Easter
Whitmonday (2.pinsedag)
eighth Monday after Easter
Constitution Day (Grundlovsdag)
5 June
Christmas Eve
24 December (from noon)
Christmas Day (Juledag)
25 December
Boxing Day (2.juledag)
26 December

There are lots of small local festivals, agricultural shows, regattas and fairs all around Denmark that can be lots of fun to attend if chanced upon. In addition, most towns of any size have a weekly market in the town square on either Wednesday or Saturday.

For details about some of Denmark's larger annual events see the 'Festive Denmark' special section. Since the dates and venues can change a bit from year to year, check with tourist offices for current schedule information.

ACTIVITIES
Walking

Although Denmark does not have substantial forests, there are numerous small tracts of woodland crisscrossed by a few kilometres of walking trails. Skov og Naturstyrelsen (Forest & Nature Bureau) produces brochures with sketch maps showing trails in nearly 200 such areas. These brochures can be picked up free of charge at public libraries and tourist offices.

There's public access to the coast in Denmark whether the land is publicly or privately owned, and in many areas there are walking tracks along the shoreline. Access is also granted for walkers to virtually all forests; in publicly owned areas you can walk about freely, while in privately owned woodland you must stick to the established trails.

Swimming

Denmark is well endowed with beaches. There are attractive sandy strands all around the country, from the southern shores of Bornholm to Skagen at the northernmost tip of Jutland.

Although topless sunbathing is common on all beaches, nude sunbathing is more restricted and is generally practised only on the more remote sections of beaches. Unless the beach is specifically set aside for nude bathing, follow local custom.

Don't expect tropical conditions. Even in July, water temperatures in the seas around Denmark average just 16°C (61°F) in the north and 17.3°C (63°F) in the south, so most beach-goers are Germans and Scandinavians rather than visitors from warmer climes.

If you find the waters chilly, most larger towns and cities have heated public swimming pools *(svømmehal)* that are open to all for a modest fee. Additionally, there are numerous 'waterworld' parks around the country with pools and water slides that are geared to children.

Windsurfing

Denmark has excellent conditions for windsurfing (often called 'surfing' in Danish), varying from open seas favoured by pros to inland fjords and sheltered coastal areas with calm waters that are ideal for beginners. If you want to hire equipment or take lessons, you can do so at a number of windsurfing shops around Denmark. Most are in Jutland, the west coast of which has some of the country's top wind and wave conditions, but you'll also find a few along the Zealand coast within easy reach of the capital.

Hiring a board and rig typically costs between 300kr and 400kr per day, with the lower prices for beginners gear. You can get a three-hour introductory lesson for about 400kr or a more substantial lesson for about double that price, which includes use of the equipment.

Sailing

With more than 7300km of coastline and hundreds of islands, Denmark offers some

PAUL BERNHARDT

Join the beautiful people windsurfing on the fjords or the open sea.

excellent sailing possibilities. There are lots of calm-water fjords and protected seas such as Smålandsfarvandet (the area nestled between Zealand and Lolland) and the popular island-dotted waters to the south of Funen.

Although most sailors in Danish waters are Scandinavians and Germans with their own boats, it's also possible to hire boats in Denmark, with or without crew. The Maritimt Center Danmark (☎ 62 80 02 16, ⓔ info@maritimt-center.dk), Havnepladsen 2, 5700 Svendborg, can arrange cruises and charters, including some on historic wooden sailing ships. It is also a good source of general information for yachties and can help to arrange maritime school-camp stays and even trips on Viking-style square-rigged vessels.

Eye on the Sky

Denmark offers some fine opportunities for bird-watchers. Perhaps the best locale for spotting waterbirds in all of Denmark is Ringkøbing Fjord, the large brackish lagoon along the West Jutland coast, which teems with both resident and migratory birds. Also uniquely rich in birdlife is the narrow Skagen peninsula at the northernmost tip of Denmark, which is a landing spot for scores of migratory birds on their way to and from northern Scandinavia.

Two excellent places in southern Denmark for spotting waterbirds and shorebirds are Nyord on the north-western tip of Møn and Tryggelev Nor in the south-west of Langeland; both sites have bird-watching towers. Of note right in Copenhagen is Utterslev Mose, a shallow lake that not only provides a year-round habitat for many ducks and swans but also attracts cranes during spring migrations. Also of special interest to urban bird-watchers is Ribe, where the roof atop city hall is crowned by a nesting pair of storks each summer, one of only eight such pairs in all of Denmark.

Fishing

Denmark abounds with streams and lakes, many of which are stocked with pike, perch and trout. In addition, with so much shoreline the saltwater fishing possibilities are nearly endless; the most common saltwater fish are cod, mackerel, plaice and sea trout.

Anglers between the ages of 18 and 67 must buy a fishing licence, which costs 25kr per day or 75kr per week and can be purchased at tourist offices and post offices. There are also a number of privately run 'put and take' fishing holes that allow you to fish for a fee (no licence required).

Golf

In Denmark you are seldom far from a golf course – there are more than 100 scattered around the Danish countryside. By Danish standards, green fees are reasonable: about 275kr on weekdays, 350kr at the weekend. Some of the courses are private clubs, so if you have a membership card from a golf club at home bring it along as it'll sometimes get you temporary membership at Danish golf clubs. You can obtain more information on golf courses from Danish tourist offices.

COURSES

Scandinavia's unique *folkehøjskole*, literally 'folk high school' ('high' denotes an institute of higher learning), provides a liberal education within a communal living environment. Folk high schools got their start in

Denmark, inspired by philosopher Nikolai Grundtvig's concept of 'enlightenment for life'. The curriculum includes such things as drama, peace studies and organic farming.

People aged 17½ and older can enrol; there are no entrance exams and no degrees. Tuition, including room and board, averages €110 a week. For more information, including a catalogue of the nearly 100 schools, contact Højskolernes Sekretariat (☎ 33 13 98 22, e hs@grundtvig.dk, w www .folkehojskoler.dk/old/int), Nytorv 7, 1450 Copenhagen K.

While most folk high schools teach in Danish, the International People's College (☎ 49 21 33 61, w www.ipc.dk), Montebello Allé 1, 3000 Helsingør, has students and teachers from around the world, and most instruction is given in English. Foreigners are welcome to enrol in short-term courses that typically last for two to eight weeks and in summer these include an intensive Danish language and culture program.

Language

Contact the Danish Cultural Institute (see the Useful Organisations section earlier in this chapter) for information on Danish language courses that might be offered in your home country.

In Denmark, there are a number of schools set up to teach Danish to foreigners, but most focus on teaching immigrants or other long-term residents. For others, a good place to try first is HOF, a private

Tracing Your Danish Roots

Many visitors of Danish descent take advantage of their trip to Denmark to trace their roots and seek out the birthplace of their ancestors. If your family hasn't kept in touch with relatives still living in Denmark, establishing your genealogy will generally require some careful investigation.

The best place to begin your research is at home before your trip. People generally hold on to their naturalisation papers; these and other official forms can indicate such vital information as an immigrant's birth date and place of birth. Any old letters from Denmark that have been stowed away may also reveal important clues, including the addresses of relatives. Other possible sources of immigration records are the national archives in your home country.

Once you've determined the birthplace or last Danish address of your ancestors, Det Danske Udvandrerarkiv (Danish Emigration Archives), which maintains the history of Danish emigrants and their offspring, can help you establish your genealogy and make contact with distant relatives. Its address is: Det Danske Udvandrerarkiv (☎ 99 31 42 20, Ⓦ www.emiarch.dk), Postboks 1731, Ved Vor Frue Kirke, 9100 Aalborg.

Among the resources maintained by Det Danske Udvandrerarkiv are copies of the old emigration lists compiled by the police and numerous manuscripts and periodicals relating to emigration. If you contact the organisation in advance of your trip, it can help you to place ads in local newspapers in an effort to make contact with distant relatives. Once in Denmark, you can use the library and research facilities to learn more about your family history.

In addition, Rigsarkivet (National Archives) in Copenhagen keeps various records. The most important for genealogical research are census forms and military draft registers, which date back as far as 1787; note, however, that only people of the peasantry had to register for the draft prior to 1849. The address is: Rigsarkivet (☎ 33 92 33 10, Ⓦ www.sa.dk/ra), Rigsdagsgården 9, 1218 Copenhagen K.

There are also four provincial archives that keep birth, death and marriage certificates and similar records. They are: Landsarkivet for Sjælland (Zealand; ☎ 31 39 35 20), Jagtvej 10, 2200 Copenhagen N; Landsarkivet for Fyn (Funen; ☎ 66 12 58 85), Jernbanegade 36, 5000 Odense; Landsarkivet for Nørrejylland (northern Jutland; ☎ 86 62 17 88), Lille Sankt Hansgade 5, 8800 Viborg; and Landsarkivet for Sønderjylland (southern Jutland; ☎ 74 62 58 58), Haderslevvej 45, 6200 Aabenraa.

school that has a relatively open enrolment; the courses typically meet three times a week, last for two months and the cost is around 800kr.

Following are four of the schools that offer Danish language courses to foreigners:

AOF (☎ 39 16 82 00) Lersø Park Allé 44, 2100 Copenhagen Ø
HOF (☎ 33 11 88 33) Købmagergade 26, 1150 Copenhagen K
   KISS (℅ 35 36 25 25) Nørregade 32, 2200 Copenhagen N
Studieskolen (☎ 33 14 43 22) Antonigade 6, 1106 Copenhagen K

WORK

Denmark has a significant level of unemployment and the job situation is not very promising for non-Danes, doubly so for those who don't speak Danish.

In terms of qualifying to work in Denmark, foreigners are divided into three categories: Scandinavian citizens, citizens of EU countries and other foreigners. Essentially, other Scandinavian citizens have the easiest go of it as they can generally reside and work legally in Denmark without restrictions, and naturally they have fewer language barriers.

Although there can be snarls, EU citizens are entitled to look for work in Denmark and it's fairly straightforward to get a residency permit once a job is established. The main stipulation is that the job provide enough income to adequately cover living expenses.

[Continued on page 69]

The long and lazy days of summer in Denmark are filled with celebration. This is the season for festivals across the country. From Skagen on the tip of Jutland to the island of Rømø and cosmopolitan Copenhagen, you'll find music, kite-flying, theatre, fashion and Viking festivals to choose from. Midsummer eve is celebrated on beaches around the country and the splashy Mermaid Pride parade in the capital is greeted with cheering spectators.

If you visit in the colder months, there will still be fun to join in. A traditional Danish Christmas will be an experience for your taste buds and Tivoli reopens for the holiday period.

Music Festivals

Nearly 200 music festivals are held each year in Denmark. Concerts run the gamut from hard rock music to classical, Nordic ballads to techno, gospel to jazz, and everything in between. The festivals are spread out between May and November, with the vast majority held in July and August.

Denmark's largest rock event is the Roskilde Festival, followed by the Midtfyns Festival in Ringe. Both are large Woodstock-like summer events that last four to five days, include more than 100 performances and attract tens of thousands of rock fans from throughout Europe. Both festivals bring in big-name international musicians; headliners at the Roskilde Festival have included Bob Dylan, Neil Young and UB40, while the Midtfyns Festival has featured the likes of Aerosmith, the Black Crowes and Alanis Morissette.

For jazz fans the major attraction is the 10-day Copenhagen Jazz Festival held in early July. It's a total immersion jazz scene, with nearly 500 concerts, some held in indoor music halls but most held in cafes, pubs and outdoor venues such as parks, squares and pedestrian streets. It's followed the next week by the smaller but still significant Århus Jazz Festival.

The village of Tønder boasts one of northern Europe's largest folk festivals. It's held over four days in late August and features both Danish and international musicians. In addition to traditional folk music there's also bluegrass, Cajun and blues. About half of the performers come from the UK or North America and typically include folk icons such as the USA's Arlo Guthrie or Ireland's Mary Black.

In some festivals all concerts are staged indoors in music halls and clubs, whereas others mix it up, with both indoor and outdoor venues. Admission charges vary according to the festival. At some events you pay for an individual performance, while at others there's a single price for the entire festival.

Most concerts can be booked in advance through BilletNet (☎ 70 15 65 65, W www.billetnet.dk), Denmark's national online ticket system. Dansk Musik Informations Center (☎ 33 11 20 66, W www.mic.dk), Gråbrødretorv 16, 1154 Copenhagen K, has all the lowdown on major music events, and its handy Web site provides links to individual festivals.

Previous Page: Jazz musician Fredrik Lundin performing at Kongens Have, behind Rosenborg Slot, as part of the 2001 Copenhagen Jazz Festiva (Photographer: Rune Bae

More Than Just Festivals

Following are just some of the fun events that take place across Denmark throughout the year. Be sure to check with local tourist offices and see the individual destination sections of this book for more information. The Danish Tourist Board Web site (W www.dt.dk) is a great source for exploring what's on.

January

New Year Concerts Classical music is performed in major cities in early January by the Zealand, Århus, Odense, Aalborg and West Jutland symphony orchestras.

February & March

Despite a paucity of major festivals in winter, there are concerts by local musicians, changing museum exhibitions and full programs by the royal ballet and opera companies.

Night Film Festival (☎ 33 12 00 05, W www.natfilm.dk) Held in Copenhagen in early March, this 10-day festival features more than 100 international films shown in their original languages.

Bakken (☎ 39 63 73 00) An amusement park outside Copenhagen that opens for the season at the end of March; celebrations are kicked off by a parade of some 5000 motorcyclists.

April

Queen Margrethe's Birthday Celebrated on 16 April at Amalienborg in Copenhagen, with the royal guards in full ceremonial dress and the queen waving from the palace balcony at noon.

Tivoli (☎ 33 15 10 01, W www.tivoligardens.com) and **Legoland** (☎ 75 33 13 33, W www.legoland.dk) Tivoli in Copenhagen and Legoland in Billund, Denmark's major amusement parks, open for the season in April.

May

Viking Market (☎ 78 88 11 22, W www.vikinger.dk/english/ribe.html) Held at the Viking Museum in Ribe during the first weekend in May. A Viking marketplace is re-created complete with costumed vendors, craft demonstrations, riding and archery.

Copenhagen Fashion & Design Festival (☎ 33 55 74 80, W www.woco.dk/Aktuelt/Designfestival/DesignFestivalUK_side2.htm) Held in mid-May in Copenhagen, this focuses on Danish design and the latest in fashions.

Copenhagen Marathon (☎ 35 26 69 00, W www.sparta.dk) A 42km race through the streets of Copenhagen, is held on a Sunday in the middle of May and is open to both amateur and professional runners.

Copenhagen Carnival (☎ 35 38 35 04, ⓦ www.karnival.dk) A three-day event in the heart of the capital on Whitsunday weekend. Highlights include an offbeat parade, samba dancing in the streets and various carnival activities. During the day there are special events for children.

Carnival in Aalborg (☎ 98 13 72 11, ⓦ www.karnivaliaalborg.dk) The 'Battle of Carnival Bands' and the parade are features of this four-day celebration that ends with a grand fireworks display. Up to 100,000 visitors share in the excitement.

Swingin' Copenhagen (☎ 33 15 63 53) Held in late May. This jazz event features traditional style jazz played in squares and clubs throughout Copenhagen.

Fyrkatspillet (☎ 98 51 19 27, ⓦ vikinger.dk/english/museum.html) A Viking play presented for two weeks from late May to early June at the Viking-era Fyrkat ring fortress outside Hobro.

June

5-øren (☎ 32 58 15 15, ⓦ www.5-oeren.dk) Held on weekends through-out June. This popular series of outdoor, beachside rock and pop concerts takes place at Copenhagen's Amager Strandpark.

Lace-Making Festival (☎ 74 72 26 65, ⓦ www.kniplings-festival.dk) Held in Tønder during the first weekend in June, this festival celebrates Tønder's history.

Riverboat Jazz Festival (☎ 86 80 16 17, ⓦ www.riverboat.dk) Held in Silkeborg in mid-June. Some 50 bands enliven the city with numerous performances, some taking place on land, others on river boats.

Midsummer Eve Held on 23 June. Known as Sankt Hans eve, the night sky is alight with bonfires on beaches all around Denmark. In Copenhagen events take place at Fælledparken.

Danish Derby Held in late June. Denmark's most important horse race, this is held at Klampenborg near Copenhagen.

Skagen Festival (☎ 98 44 40 04, ⓦ www.skagenfestival.dk) Held over four days at the end of June. This festival in Skagen features folk and world music performed by Danish and international artists.

Round Zealand Boat Race (☎ 49 21 15 67) Held over three days in late June. This substantial yacht race circles the island of Zealand, starting and ending in Helsingør.

Roskilde Festival (☎ 46 36 66 13, ⓦ www.roskilde-festival.dk) Northern Europe's largest music festival rocks Roskilde for four consecutive days each summer on the last weekend in June.

Some 150 rock, techno and world music bands play on seven stages. In 2001, the festival's 31st year, the line-up included Bob Dylan, Robbie Williams, Nick Cave & the Bad Seeds, Neil Young, Coldplay, Beck, Burning Spear and the Danish band Aqua. Over the years the promoters have also been particularly astute at presenting new trends in rock and at booking lesser-known groups (such as UB40 and Talking Heads) who have later gone on to stardom, so you can expect to see some hot bands who haven't yet come into the spotlight.

Right: Thousands take part in the annual Copenhagen marathon. Here runners pass the highest point of the new Øresund bridge, during a special run in June 2000.

Bottom: Check out street posters for music and theatre events – just one way to found out what's happening around town.

ANDERS BLOMQVIST

NED FRIARY

ANDERS BLOMQVIST

ANDERS BLOMQVIST

Top: An Oriental theme in the Nimb Brasserie, Tivoli Gardens.

Left: Danish musicians take the stage at the 10-day Copenhagen Jazz Festival, the biggest event in the city.

The Roskilde Festival is more than just music – it's a huge spirited bash with lots of drinking and partying. The average age of the festival-goers is 24 and about half come from other countries, particularly Germany, Sweden, Finland, the Netherlands, Norway and Belgium. There are stalls selling everything from tattoos to fast food but you may want to bring some food supplies of your own as prices are high.

Over the years, festival organisers have prided themselves in running a safety-conscious event. Nonetheless, tragedy befell the festival in 2000, when nine young men suffocated as they were pressed forward by a crush of fans trying to get closer to a midnight performance by Pearl Jam. Festival organisers have now implemented new safety precautions, including a total ban on crowd surfing, and have limited ticket sales to 70,000, about 10% less than in years past.

The profits from the Roskilde Festival are distributed to charitable causes both at home and abroad. Festival tickets cost around 900kr, including camping near the site, and can be purchased in Denmark through BilletNet (☎ 70 15 65 65) or at Danish post offices. Tickets can also be purchased online at the official concert Web site.

Advance sales typically start in December and the festival does sell out, so the sooner the better...but if you're late, you needn't miss it all, as it's possible to buy a ticket at the gate (350kr) for just the last day of the festival.

Frederikssund Viking Festival (☎ 47 31 06 85, W www.vikingespil.dk) Held in Frederikssund over a two-week period in late June and early July. Costumed 'Vikings' present an open-air drama, followed by a banquet with Viking food and entertainment.

Viking Play at Lindholm Høje (☎ 98 17 33 73, W www.aalborg-tourist .dk) Held north of Aalborg over a two-week period during late June and early July.

July

5-øren Held on weekends throughout July. This popular series of outdoor beachside rock and pop concerts takes place at Copenhagen's Amager Strandpark.

Fourth of July Celebrations (☎ 98 12 60 22, W www.aalborg-tourist.dk/media/ back_again.pdf) Held to commemorate US Independence Day each 4 July in Rebild Bakker. Thousands of Danes and Danish-Americans attend.

Midtfyns Festival (W www.mf.dk) Held in Ringe over five days in early July. It attracts 32,000 fans with international rock, pop, world and jazz musicians in scores of concerts.

Trelleborg Mart (☎ 58 54 95 06, W www.vikinger .dk/english/trelle) Held for a week in early July. This re-created Viking market takes place at the Trelleborg fortress in southern Zealand.

Copenhagen Jazz Festival (☎ 33 93 20 13, W www.jazzfestival.dk) This is the biggest entertainment event of the year in the capital, with 10 days of music beginning on the first Friday in July. The festival features a range of Danish and international jazz, blues and fusion music. It's a cornucopia of nearly 500 indoor and outdoor concerts, with music wafting out of practically every public square, park, pub and cafe from Strøget to Tivoli.

There are always a few big names – in recent years, these have included such renowned artists as Ray Charles, Keith Jarrett and Wynton Marsalis. Many of the outdoor concerts are free; get hold of a festival program and you can plan your own jazz tour. For schedules, prices and ticket information, contact Copenhagen Jazz Festival, Nytorv 3, 1450 Copenhagen K, or check out the Web site.

Århus Jazz Festival (☎ 86 12 13 12) Held the week following the Copenhagen Jazz Festival. Modern and traditional jazz is performed in venues all around Århus.

Maribo Jazz Festival (☎ 40 53 85 84) Held in Maribo for four days in mid-July. Traditional New Orleans jazz and big bands are featured.

Fannikerdage Held in Nordby on Fanø during a weekend in mid-July. This event features islanders wearing traditional costumes and performing folk dances.

Viking Moot (☎ 89 42 11 00, W prehistory.moes.hum.aau.dk/fhm/alme.htm) Held for two days in late July at the Moesgård Museum in Århus, it features a Viking-style market with crafts, food and equestrian events.

August

Esbjerg International Chamber Music Festival (☎ 20 16 23 34, W www.eicmf.dk) Held throughout August. This festival features chamber music concerts in Esbjerg.

Hamlet Summer Plays (☎ 49 28 20 44, W www.hamletsommer.dk) Held the first two weeks in August. Theatre performances of Shakespeare's *Hamlet* take place at Kronborg Slot in Helsingør.

Mermaid Pride Parade (W www.mermaidpride.dk) Held on the first or second Saturday in August. This festive gay pride parade marches with Carnival-like extravagance through the centre of Copenhagen.

Copenhagen Guitar Festival (☎ 33 73 03 73, W www.rundetaarn.dk) This festival takes place during the first two weeks of August at the Rundetårn in Copenhagen's Latin Quarter.

Odense Film Festival (☎ 66 14 88 14, W www.filmfestival.dk) This six-day international film festival is held in Odense in mid-August.

HAMLET
SOMMER
HELSINGØR

Copenhagen International Ballet Festival (☎ 33 32 52 52, Ⓦ www .xproduction.com) Held for 14 days in mid-August in Copenhagen. Features top solo dancers from the Royal Danish Ballet as well as visiting performers from international ballet companies.

Country Music Festival (☎ 86 96 70 11, Ⓦ www.members.tripod .com/sccdk) Held in Silkeborg for three days in mid-August. Features country bands and soloists.

Randers Week (☎ 86 42 44 77) Held in Randers for 10 days in mid-August. Music, dance, theatre, a bicycle race and other sports events are featured.

Copenhagen Fashion Fair (☎ 32 47 21 18, Ⓦ www.ciff.dk) Held over four days in mid-August. This international fashion fair takes place at the Bella Center in the area of Amager. There is another fair in February.

Tønder Festival (☎ 74 72 46 10, Ⓦ www.tf.dk) Held in Tønder for four days in late August, this is one of northern Europe's largest folk festivals, featuring numerous indoor and outdoor performances.

Danish Trotting Derby (☎ 39 96 02 02) Denmark's major trotting event, held in late August at Charlottenlund Travbane near Copenhagen.

Århus Festival Week The 10-day Århus Festuge (☎ 89 40 91 91, Ⓦ www.aarhusfestuge.dk) bills itself as Denmark's largest annual multicultural festival. It begins the last Friday of August and features scores of events at indoor and outdoor venues around Århus. Activities include contemporary and classical music performances, theatre, ballet, modern dance, opera, films and sports. The biggest non-music event is the Marselis Run (Marselisløbet), a 6km (or 12km) run through the Marselisborg woods which attracts close to 20,000 runners of all ages. Tourist Århus (the tourist office) can provide a schedule, or visit the Århus Festuge Web site.

Golden Days in Copenhagen (☎ 35 42 14 32, Ⓦ www.goldendays .dk) Held over two weeks in late August and early September. The city celebrates with art exhibits, poetry readings, theatre, ballet and concerts that focus on Denmark's 'Golden Age' (1800–50).

September

Kite Flying Festival Held over three days in early September on Lakolk beach on Rømø.

Amager Musikfestival Held from mid-September to early October. Features music performances by Danish and international soloists and ensembles at several churches in Amager.

Copenhagen Film Festival (☎ 35 37 25 07) Held during the third week in September. This event in Copenhagen features both Danish and international films.

Odense Folk Festival (☎ 66 16 60 42) Held the last weekend in September. Features regional folk musicians.

October

Cultural Night in Copenhagen (☎ 79 22 24 42) Held on the first night of the autumn school holidays (typically the second Friday in October).

Museums, theatres, galleries and even Rosenborg Slot open their doors between 6pm and midnight.

Copenhagen Gay and Lesbian Film Festival (W www.gayfilm.dk) Held in late October. This week-long event features contemporary gay and lesbian films from around the world.

November

Copenhagen Autumn Jazz (☎ 33 93 20 13, W www.jazzfestival.dk/autumnjazz) Held for four days at the beginning of November. Produced by the Copenhagen Jazz Festival folks, this festival features top jazz musicians performing at clubs around the city.

Copenhagen Irish Festival (☎ 36 45 08 02, W www.irishfestival.dk) Held in Copenhagen for four days in early November. Features traditional Irish folk music.

Musikhøst (Music Harvest) (☎ 66 11 06 63, W www.n-m-o.dk) Held in Odense for five days in mid-November. Classical music and jazz is performed by musicians from Denmark and abroad at Odense Koncerthus and other city venues.

Copenhagen Bluegrass Festival (☎ 36 78 97 09) Held for two days in mid-August. This bluegrass event takes place in the Amager section of Copenhagen.

Tivoli Reopening Copenhagen's Tivoli reopens its gates from mid-November to a few days before Christmas with a holiday market and fair. There's ice-skating on the pond and some Tivoli restaurants offer menus with hot mulled wine and traditional holiday meals.

December

Christmas Fairs Held all around Denmark throughout December. Fairs feature food booths, arts and crafts stalls, and sometimes parades. Particularly atmospheric is the Christmas fair held for two days in early December at Den Gamle By in Århus.

[Continued from page 60]

Citizens of other countries are required to obtain a work permit before entering Denmark. You must first secure a job offer and then apply for a work and residency permit at a Danish embassy or consulate while still in your home country (or the country where you've had legal residency for the last six months). You can enter Denmark only after the permit has been granted. Currently these permits are rarely given to anyone without a specialised skill.

If you do decide to look for work in Denmark, the AF Arbejdsformidling (☎ 33 55 10 20), a public job centre at Kultorvet 17, 1019 Copenhagen K, helps link up the unemployed with employers looking for workers. The newspapers with the best job ads are the Sunday issues of *Politiken* and *Berlingske Tidende*. If you don't mind being a waiter, kitchenhand or cleaning person, restaurants and hotels are two types of businesses that are more likely to offer jobs to foreigners, so you might try inquiring directly.

There are, of course, less formal ways to pick up spare change. Danes are generous to street performers who can put on a good show. Regulations regarding street musicians and other buskers are determined by each municipality and are subject to change, so if you're interested in performing, check first at the local police station. In Copenhagen, for example, individuals or groups of up to three people are currently allowed to perform live acoustic music along Strøget, the city's central pedestrian street, from 4pm to 8pm on weekdays, 10am to 5pm on Saturday and noon to 5pm on Sunday.

ACCOMMODATION

Denmark has a wide range of accommodation options and your budget will be greatly affected by which types you select. Truly cheap hotels are virtually unknown in Denmark, but there are some good alternatives. If you're on a tight budget, you'll save money by camping, staying in hostels or booking rooms in private homes.

If you do opt to stay in hotels there are some schemes, especially in the summer and at weekends, that can bring hotel rates down to a more reasonable level. You may find it works out best to combine different types of accommodation to suit your travelling needs. For example, with a moderate budget, on weekdays you could stay in hostels (most have private rooms available for couples or families) and then end the week in comfortable chain hotels that offer discounted weekend rates. Self-catering flats and cottages may be worth considering if you're with a group and are planning to stay in one place for a while.

Staff at local tourist offices are generally very helpful and can provide lists of accommodation options in their towns. Sometimes they can also call round and do the actual booking for you, for which there may be a nominal fee.

During the high season accommodation can be hard to find and it's advisable to book ahead. Even camping grounds can fill up, especially popular ones in big cities.

Accommodation rates quoted in Denmark, including those listed in this book, include all taxes and service charges.

Camping

Camping is very popular in Denmark and there were, at last count, 512 camping grounds spread around the country. No matter where you're travelling you'll seldom be far from one. In resort areas camping grounds are commonly found right in the thick of it all, whereas in cities and large towns they tend to be more on the outskirts of the municipality. For this reason camping is most popular for people with their own vehicles. If you're on foot the money you save by camping can quickly be outweighed by the money you spend commuting to and from a town centre. Of course you'll also need a tent, sleeping bag, cooking equipment and other bits and pieces – easier to cart around if you have a vehicle.

Although most Danish camping grounds are seasonal, about 100 places stay open year-round. The rest vary quite a bit in their opening season; some, particularly those in seaside resort areas, are open only in the summer months, while others operate from

Danish Camping Terms

Here are some common Danish words and the logo that campers are apt to come across on signs and brochures:

voksne	adult
børn	child
hund	dog
campingvogn	caravan, house trailer
campingbil	motorised caravan
hytte	cabin, hut
udlejning	rental
strøm	electricity charge
handicapvenligt	an area accessible to people in wheelchairs
dag/uge	day/week

spring to autumn. Many of those that have a longer season offer discounted rates outside the summer season.

Although other factors come into play, prices are largely dependent on the camping ground's rating (see Ratings later in this section), and rise by roughly 10% with each additional star. The per-night charge to pitch a tent or park a caravan typically ranges from 45kr to 60kr for each adult and about half that for each child. In the summer, some places also tack on a surcharge of 15kr to 30kr per tent/caravan.

A camping pass is required for stays at all camping grounds. If you don't have a valid Camping Card International, then you can buy a Danish carnet at the first camping ground you visit or from tourist offices. The cost for an annual pass is 75kr, and covers all accompanied children aged under 18.

Camping is regulated in Denmark and is only allowed in established camping grounds or on private land with the owner's permission. Although it may seem tempting, camping in a car or caravan at the beach, in a car park or along the street is prohibited and can result in a fine.

If you're camping with a car or caravan, particularly in the high season, it's wise to make reservations. If you're backpacking or travelling by bicycle, note that even if a camping ground is signposted as fully booked for motorists, it's worth stopping to talk to the warden on duty, as it will often be possible to find a site for a camper who is travelling light.

If you are camping your way around Denmark, a useful book is the annually updated *Camping Danmark*, published by Campingrådet (Danish Camping Board), which lists all approved camping grounds in Denmark and gives details on their facilities, ratings and opening dates. It can be bought in most bookshops and in some tourist offices, and costs 95kr.

Alternately, DK-Camp (☎ 75 71 29 62, W www.dk-camp.dk), which is the largest camping association in Denmark, publishes the annual book *DK Camping Danmark* listing details of its 325 member camping grounds; the publication is available free at larger tourist offices and affiliated camping grounds.

Cabins & Caravans Many Danish camping grounds also rent simple cabins (and/or on-site caravans) that sleep four to six people and costing around 225kr to 500kr per night in the high season, a bit less in the low season. Although cabins often have cooking facilities, bed linen and blankets are rarely provided so it's best to bring your own sleeping bag. Toilet and shower facilities are not in the cabins but are shared with other campers.

Most camping grounds in Denmark gear their facilities to people touring by caravan – in fact, many Danish camping grounds look more like car parks than nature areas. All grounds classified two star or higher are equipped to accommodate caravans, with facilities for emptying toilets, replenishing drinking water and cleaning tanks.

Ratings Camping grounds in Denmark are rated by the Danish Camping Board using a star system. That rating is displayed at the camping ground, as well as in literature that lists camping areas.

One-star camping grounds fulfil minimum standards, providing running water, toilets, at least one shower and at least one electricity outlet for shavers.

Two-star places have a minimum of one shower for every 25 sites, a kitchen with hot tap water and hotplates, as well as a playground for children. To qualify for a two-star rating, the site must also be within 2km of a grocery shop.

Camping grounds with three stars, the most common rating, have more elaborate facilities, including hot water in the wash-basins, a communal lounge, a larger play area for children, nursing rooms for babies, and sinks or washing machines for laundry. They must also be within 1km of a grocery shop.

In recent years the system was expanded to make way for four- and five-star ratings. The higher standards necessary to earn the additional stars are mostly creature comforts, but these higher ratings also require that there be a separate pitch area for tents and an equipped bicycle repair area. So far only a few camping grounds have received the new top ratings but it has provided an incentive for many three-star places to upgrade their facilities, so camping – already of a high standard in Denmark – should become an increasingly comfortable option each year.

When selecting a camping ground keep in mind that, although the stars give a good indication of what to expect, they don't tell the whole story. For example, if a place meets all of the qualifications for a three-star rating but is more than 1km from a grocery shop, it still can't be rated higher than two stars.

Hostels

Denmark has 100 hostels in its national Danhostel association. All are members of the Hostelling International (HI) organisation, which in recent years has changed its name from International Youth Hostel Federation (IYHF) in order to attract a wider clientele and move away from the restricted focus on youth. Some countries have been slow in making the switch to HI, so if your home hostel card says IYHF, HI or YHA, it's all the same thing. Currently in Denmark the word *(vandrerhjem),* meaning youth hostel, is being de-emphasised and Danhostel is taking its place in hostel names.

Most of Denmark's hostels have private rooms in addition to dormitory rooms, which makes them a good-value alternative to hotels. Danish hostels appeal to a wide range of guests in all age categories and are oriented as much towards families and groups as they are to backpackers, students and other budget travellers.

Facilities in hostels vary but most newer hostels have two- and four-bed rooms and are thus well suited for use by couples and small groups. Most hostels list rates for singles and doubles, although during the busier periods some are loathe to rent private rooms to individuals or couples unless you're willing to pay for all of the beds in that room.

Hostels are categorised by a star system, with ratings ranging from one to five stars. One-star hostels meet the basic requirements, whereas two-star hostels also have luggage storage facilities and a small shop; three-star hostels will have a TV lounge. Four- and five-star hostels have more fancy facilities and a minimum of 75% of their rooms have a shower and toilet.

Depending on the hostel category, dorm beds cost from 70kr to 100kr, while private rooms typically range from 150kr to 350kr for singles and 190kr to 400kr for doubles, plus about 50kr for each additional person.

With few exceptions, Danish hostels have single bunk-style beds with comfortable foam mattresses. Blankets and pillows are provided at all hostels but if you don't bring your own sheets you'll have to hire them; they cost around 40kr per stay. Sleeping bags are not allowed. A handy, lightweight pouch-style sleeping sheet with an attached pillow cover can be purchased at many hostels worldwide and will save you a bundle on sheet-rental charges.

Sleeping Green

Ecologically minded Denmark has instituted a system known as Den Grønne Nøgle (The Green Key) to acknowledge environmentally friendly hotels and hostels.

Numerous criteria must be fulfilled for a place to be awarded The Green Key. These include limiting water consumption by using water-saving shower heads, using low-energy light bulbs and ecologically friendly detergents, recycling waste, having smoke-free rooms and serving at least two organic products at breakfast.

Places that qualify for The Green Key display a special logo that looks like a smiling green key standing on end.

Travellers who don't already have an international hostel card can buy one once they arrive in Denmark for 160kr (annual fee) or pay 30kr extra for each night's stay. If you're not sure whether you'll be staying at hostels often enough to make it worth buying an annual card, ask for a sticker each time you pay the 30kr per-night fee; if you accumulate six stickers you'll earn yourself an annual hostel card.

In the summer and other holiday periods many hostels get fully booked, so it's always a good idea to make advance reservations. Outside Copenhagen, you can generally check in between 4pm and 9pm, but in a few places reception closes as early as 6pm. In most hostels the reception office is closed – and the phone not answered – between noon and 4pm.

In the spring and autumn, hostels can get crowded with children on school excursions; many hostels require reservations from individual travellers between 1 September and 15 May. Most Danish hostels close in the winter for a period ranging from a few weeks to several months.

You can pick up the handy 200-page *Danhostel Danmarks Vandrerhjem* guide free from hostels or tourist offices; it provides information on individual hostels, including a breakdown of each hostel's facilities and a simple sketch map showing its location.

All Danish hostels provide an all-you-can-eat breakfast costing 45kr or less and many also provide dinner (65kr maximum). Most hostels also have guest kitchens with pots and pans where you can cook your own food.

The Danish national hostelling association is called Danhostel (☎ 33 31 36 12, fax 33 31 36 26, e ldv@danhostel.dk, W www .danhostel.dk), at Vesterbrogade 39, 1620 Copenhagen V. The individual hostels also have their own Web sites; many of these can be accessed simply by adding the individual hostel name to the end of the association address; hence the Web site for the Ribe hostel is W www.danhostel.dk/ribe.

To join HI before you leave home, ask at your nearest hostel or contact your national hostelling association. Some national offices include:

Australia
Australian Youth Hostel Association (☎ 02-9565 1699, e yha@yha.au), Level 3, 10 Mallett St, Camperdown NSW 2050

Canada
Hostelling International – Canada (☎ 613-237 7884, e info@hostellingintl.ca), 205 Catherine St, Suite 400, Ottawa, Ontario K2P 1C3

England & Wales
Youth Hostels Association (☎ 0870-870 8808, e customerservices@yha.org.uk), Trevelyan House, Dimple Rd, Matlock, Derbyshire DE4 3YH

Ireland
An Óige, Irish Youth Hostel Association (☎ 01-830 4555, e anoige@iol.ie), 61 Mountjoy St, Dublin 7

New Zealand
Youth Hostels Association of New Zealand (☎ 03-379 9970, e info@yha.org.nz), PO Box 436, 193 Cashel St, 3rd Floor, Union House, Christchurch

Northern Ireland

Youth Hostel Association of Northern Ireland (☎ 2890-315 435, e info@hini.org.uk), 22 Donegall Road, Belfast BT12 5JN

Scotland

Scottish Youth Hostels Association (☎ 1786-891 400 e info@syha.org.uk), 7 Glebe Crescent, Stirling FK8 2JA

USA

Hostelling International – American Youth Hostels (☎ 202-783 6161, e hiayhserv@hiayh.org), 733 15th St NW, Suite 840, Washington, DC 20005

Rooms in Private Homes

Staff at many tourist offices can book rooms in private homes in their region for a small fee or can provide a free list of the rooms so travellers can phone for themselves. Rates vary widely but average about 225/300kr for singles/doubles. In most cases, breakfast is available for around 40kr more per person. This is not only a cheaper accommodation option than the hotels, but can also be a good opportunity to meet local families.

In addition, Dansk Bed & Breakfast (☎ 39 61 04 05, w www.bbdk.dk), Postbox 53, 2900 Hellerup, publishes a booklet *Bed & Breakfast in Denmark*, which lists some 500 homes throughout Denmark offering private rooms at similar rates. You can pick up the booklet for 20kr at tourist offices in Denmark.

There's an excellent B&B association in Funen; see the boxed text 'Going Local' in the Funen chapter.

Farm Stays

If you like the countryside, Landsforeningen for Landboturisme (☎ 86 37 39 00, fax 86 37 35 50, w www.bondegaardsferie.dk), Lerbakken 7, Følle, 8410 Rønde, books stays on more than 100 farms throughout Denmark. There's an interesting variety of farmhouses, ranging from modern homes to traditional straw-roofed, timber-framed places. The cost, including breakfast, averages 200kr per person per day (half-price for children under 12 years old). The options also include self-contained flats and small rural houses that can accommodate up to six people and cost around 2000kr to 3500kr per week. Upon request, the organisation will mail you a booklet containing a colour photo and brief description of each place as well as booking details.

Although it's wise to make plans in advance, if you're cycling or driving around Denmark on your own you're also likely to come across farmhouses displaying *værelse* (room) signs.

Manor Houses

For some style, Danske Slotte & Herregaarde (☎ 86 60 38 44, fax 86 60 38 31, e danske .slotte.herregaarde@get2net.dk), Sankt Leonis Stræde 1A, 8800 Viborg, can book rooms in two dozen manor houses and small castles around Denmark. The cost ranges from 600kr to 1300kr for singles and 800kr to 1600kr for doubles, including breakfast. Brochures can be obtained by mail in advance or picked up at larger tourist offices once you arrive in Denmark.

Hotels

Hotels can be found in the centre of all major Danish cities and towns. Prices at the budget end average about 450/600kr for singles/doubles. Although the cheapest places are fairly spartan, Danish hotels are rarely seedy or unsafe. Interestingly, while budget hotels tend to be pricey for what you get, the difference in rates between categories is relatively small. Standard top-end hotels generally cost only about a third more than budget hotels, particularly if you use weekend rates or other hotel schemes.

Kro, a name that implies a country inn but is more commonly the Danish version of a motel, is a type of accommodation typically found along major motorways near the outskirts of town. A kro is generally cheaper than a hotel but the rooms are usually simpler and the walls may well be thin. As a rule, they're not a practical option unless you have your own transport.

Both hotels and kros usually include an all-you-can-eat breakfast, which can vary from a simple meal of bread, cheese and coffee to a generous full-table buffet.

Danish Hotel Terms

Here are some key words you'll come across in hotel brochures:

værelse	room
enkeltværelse	single room
dobbeltværelse	double room
eget bad og toilet	with shower and toilet
bad og toilet på gangen	shower and toilet in the hallway
morgenmad inkl i prisen	breakfast included in the price
senge; køjsenge	beds; bunk beds
med opredning	with extra bed
lejlighed	flat, apartment
adgang til køkken	access to kitchen
vaskemaskine og tørretumbler	washing machine and tumble dryer

Hotel Schemes There are a number of hotel schemes that can pare down room costs in Danish hotels and inns. The two programs outlined below are the most popular ones and are well worth considering if you plan to use hotels as your main accommodation.

Dansk Kroferie This countrywide organisation (☎ 75 64 87 00, fax 75 64 87 20, W www.dansk-kroferie.dk), Vejlevej 16, 8700 Horsens, operates a system of 'Inn Cheques' valid at more than 70 inns that belong to its association. The cheques can be purchased at Danish tourist offices and travel agencies, and cost 645kr for a double room, 725kr for a family of three and 805kr for a family of four. Each cheque covers breakfast and a room with bath. Although most of the association's hotels and inns accept the cheques at face value, some add on a surcharge of 150kr. The association publishes a 60-page booklet providing a brief description of member hotels and noting which add the surcharge.

Best Western Hotels The Best Western group (W www.bestwestern.dk), which runs 34 hotels in Denmark, has a straightforward weekend and holiday discount that doesn't require vouchers or advance payment. Under this plan, a room sleeping up to two adults and two children costs from 795kr per night including breakfast. The rate is effective at weekends year-round and on weekdays during school holiday periods,

including from mid-June to early August. It's best to book as far in advance as possible as the offer is valid on a limited number of rooms, but you can sometimes benefit from the deal on a walk-in basis.

Seaside Cottages & Flats

In many seaside resort areas, cottages and flats account for a significant slice of the accommodation options. They are suited mostly to visitors who are planning to holiday at one specific location, as they are generally booked by the week and require reservations. Rates vary greatly, depending on the type of accommodation and the season, but generally work out to be cheaper than hotels.

One organisation, DanCenter (☎ 70 13 16 16, W www.dancenter.dk), Lyngbyvej 20, 2100 Copenhagen Ø, handles cottage bookings on a nationwide basis and publishes a free catalogue with a colour photo of each place available to rent. Many tourist offices can also help make reservations.

FOOD

Nothing epitomises Danish food more than *smørrebrød* (literally 'buttered bread'), an open sandwich that ranges from very basic fare to elaborate sculpture-like creations. Typically it's a slice of rye bread topped with either roast beef, tiny shrimps, roast pork or fish fillet and finished off with a variety of garnishes. Although smørrebrød is served in most restaurants at lunchtime, it's cheapest in bakeries or specialised smørrebrød takeaway shops found near train stations and office buildings.

Also distinctively Danish is the *koldt bord* (literally 'cold table'), a buffet-style spread of cold foods, including cold cuts, smoked fish, cheeses, vegetables, salads, condiments, breads and crackers, plus usually a few hot dishes such as meatballs and fried fish. The cornerstone of the koldt bord is herring, which comes in pickled, marinated and salted versions. Generally a serving of herring with raw onions is treated as a starter, because it's thought to prime the stomach for the meal. Pickled herring is almost invariably washed down with cold *akvavit* (schnapps), a type of spirit.

Generally the most prominent top-end restaurants feature what's dubbed 'Danish-French' cuisine, a creative fusion combining the flavoursome sauces characteristic of French fare with the addition of fresh Danish vegetables and seafood that are not typical in traditional French recipes.

Among the cheapest places to eat well are those that specialise in Mediterranean buffets and the numerous Italian restaurants that serve the standard pizza-and-pasta fare. Simple Greek eateries selling inexpensive *shawarma*, a filling pitta-bread sandwich of shaved meat, are a favourite alternative to

LEE FOSTER

Anyone for *wienerbrød*?

the ubiquitous American fast-food chains like McDonald's and Burger King. You can also find a cheap, if not particularly healthy, munch at one of the *pølsemandens*, the wheeled carts that sell a variety of hot dogs and sausages.

The sweet pastry known elsewhere in the world as 'Danish' is called *wienerbrød* in Denmark and nearly every second street corner has a bakery with mouthwatering varieties. Less universal in appeal is the salty liquorice *lakrids* that's a favourite among Danes; one popular type is *piratos*, which comes in a flat coin shape.

Dagens ret, which means daily special, is usually the best deal on the menu, while the *børnemenu* is for children.

Although strictly vegetarian restaurants are generally limited to larger cities, vegetarians should be able to get by reasonably comfortably throughout Denmark. Danish cafes commonly serve a variety of salads, and vegetarians can often find something suitable at the smørrebrød counter as well. In addition, there are a growing number of Middle Eastern restaurants with buffets that have separate meat and vegetarian dishes,

Sinfully Sweet

Bakeries abound in Denmark, all selling those sinfully rich breakfast pastries that are so synonymous with Denmark they are known around the world simply as 'Danish'.

Curiously, Danes look elsewhere to give credit. In Denmark, those same mouthwatering treats – flaky, butter-laden pastry with a dollop of jam – are called *wienerbrød,* which translates as 'Vienna bread'.

As legend has it, the naming of the pastry can be traced to a Danish baker who moved to Austria in the 18th century, where he perfected a style of pastry that has since been known to the Danes as *wienerbrød* and to the rest of the world as 'Danish'.

Grinning from Beer to Beer

Danes are great producers and drinkers of beer. Denmark's Carlsberg Breweries, which is an amalgamation of Carlsberg and Tuborg breweries, is the largest exporter of beer in Europe. Not all of the brew makes its way out of Denmark, however: Danes manage to down some seven million hectolitres (roughly two billion bottles) of brew a year, ranking them sixth among the greatest beer drinkers worldwide.

The best-selling beers in Denmark are pilsners, lagers with an alcohol content of 4.6%, but there are scores of other beers to choose from as well. These range from light beers with an alcohol content of 1.7% to hearty stouts that kick in at 8%. You'll find the percentage of alcohol listed on the bottle label. Danish beers are classified with ascending numbers according to the amount of alcohol they contain, with *klasse 1* referring to the common pilsners and *klasse 4* to the strongest stouts.

the latter including sauteed vegetables, salads, rice and couscous. Most Italian restaurants have vegetarian pasta options, and for those who eat cheese, there are scores of pizzerias all around Denmark. Of course all Indian and Pakistani restaurants will have some vegetarian-only dishes.

A comprehensive glossary of Danish food and drink terms can be found in the Language chapter at the back of this book.

Danish Cuisine

Danish cuisine relies heavily on fish, meat and potatoes. The following are some typical Danish dishes:

Flæskesteg – roast pork, usually with crackling, served with potatoes and cabbage
Frikadeller – fried ground-pork meatballs, commonly served with boiled potatoes and red cabbage
Fyldt hvidkålshoved – ground beef wrapped in cabbage leaves
Gravad laks – cured or salted salmon marinated in dill and served with a sweet mustard sauce
Hakkebøf – a ground-beef burger, usually covered with fried onions and served with boiled potatoes, brown sauce and beets
Hvid labskovs – Danish stew made from square cuts of beef boiled with potatoes, bay leaves and pepper

Kogt torsk – poached cod, usually in a mustard sauce and served with boiled potatoes
Mørbradbøf – small pork fillets, commonly in a mushroom sauce
Stegt flæsk – crisp-fried pork slices, generally served with potatoes and a parsley sauce
Stegt rødspætte – fried, breaded plaice, usually served with parsley potatoes
Æggekage – a rich Funen omelette served with dark bread

DRINKS
Nonalcoholic Drinks

All cafes serve coffee *(kaffe)* and tea *(te)*, though caffeine-rich coffee is clearly the more popular. In addition to the common brew, expect to find a good variety of cappuccino, espresso and other specialised coffee drinks.

Mineral water *(mineralvand)* and the standard soft drinks *(sodavand)* such as Coca-Cola are widely available. Tap water is safe to drink throughout Denmark.

Alcoholic Drinks

Denmark's Carlsberg and Tuborg breweries both produce excellent beers. Beer *(øl)* can be ordered as *fadøl* (draught beer), *pilsner* (lager), *lyst øl* (light beer), *lagerøl* (dark lager) or *porter* (stout).

The most popular spirit in Denmark is the Aalborg-produced *akvavit* (aquavit or schnapps). There are several dozen types, the most common of which is spiced with caraway seeds. In Denmark akvavit is not sipped but is swallowed straight down as a shot, usually followed by a chaser of beer. A popular Danish liqueur made from cherries is Peter Heering, which is good sipped straight or served over vanilla ice cream.

Common wine terms used in Denmark include *hvidvin* (white wine), *rødvin* (red wine), *mousserende vin* (sparkling wine) and *husets vin* (house wine). *Gløgg* is a mulled wine that's a favourite speciality during the Christmas season.

Beer, wine and spirits are served in most restaurants and cafes. They can also be purchased at grocery shops during normal shopping hours. Prices are quite reasonable compared with those in other Scandinavian countries. The minimum legal age for consuming alcoholic beverages is 18 years.

ENTERTAINMENT

Denmark's cities have some of the most active nightlife in Europe, with live music wafting through numerous side-street cafes, especially in the university cities of Copenhagen, Århus and Odense. You'll find a wide range of music, including current alternative trends, rock, folk, jazz and blues. Not much begins before 10pm or ends before 3am.

Den Kongelige Ballet (The Royal Danish Ballet) is one of the most highly regarded ballet companies in northern Europe. The larger Danish cities have concert halls with their own symphony orchestras; these halls also double as venues for big-name Danish and international musicians of all genres, including classical music, pop and jazz.

Most towns have cinemas showing first-run English-language films. Foreign films are not dubbed – movies are shown in their original language with Danish subtitles.

Casino gambling can be found in Copenhagen, Odense, Århus and Aalborg.

Following the Ball

Denmark's national football team fares fairly well and is usually rated in the top 20 teams worldwide. Denmark's greatest triumph in recent times was winning the Euro '92 championship, beating Germany 2-0 in the final. In the 1998 World Cup, Denmark made it to the quarterfinals, losing to top-ranked Brazil. If you are keen to watch an international match, games are played at Parken, Denmark's national stadium in Copenhagen.

The national leagues or Serie are headed by the Superliga, the top division containing 12 teams who slug it out through the season (late July to late May, with a break from early December to early March) for the league title. Prominent are teams from Copenhagen such as Brøndby and the more recently formed FC København. The home grounds and contact details of the main Superliga clubs are listed below.

AB (Akademisk Boldklub) Gladsaxe Idrætspark (☎ 44 98 98 42) Skovdiget 1, 2880 Bagsværd

Aalborg Boldspiklub Aalborg Stadion (☎ 98 15 72 22) Hornevej 2, 9220 Aalborg Øst

AGF Århus Stadion (☎ 86 11 27 33) Terp Skovvej 16-18, 8260 Viby J

Brøndby IF Brøndby Stadion (☎ 43 63 08 10) Brøndbyvester Boulevard 8, 2605 Brøndby

FC København Parken (☎ 35 43 31 31) Øster Allé 50, 2110 København

Lyngby FC Lyngby Stadion (☎ 45 88 40 60) Lundtoftevej 61, 2800 Lyngby

Silkeborg IF Silkeborg Stadion (☎ 86 80 44 77)

SPECTATOR SPORTS

The national sport is football (soccer). See the boxed text 'Following the Ball' for details of teams and venues.

Cycling, rowing and sailing are popular in all parts of the country; there are many regional competitions throughout Denmark during the relevant seasons.

Despite the country's small size, over the years Denmark has won Olympic gold medals in cycling and in water sports such as sailing, rowing, kayaking, swimming and platform diving. In 2000 Denmark won two gold medals, one each for yachting and women's team handball.

Denmark is the adopted home of runner Wilson Kipketer, a native of Kenya who took up Danish citizenship in 1990 after completing his studies here. In 1997 he captured the world 800m record and received the IAAF Athlete of the Year award and in the 2000 Olympics in Sydney he won the silver medal in the 800m race.

SHOPPING

Because prices tend to be high, few people come to Denmark for the shopping; however, there are some distinctively Danish products that make fine items to take home. Danish amber, which washes up on Jutland's west coast beaches, makes lovely jewellery and prices are relatively reasonable.

Other popular purchases are silverwork, ceramics and hand-blown glass – all in the sleek style that typifies Danish design. Georg Jensen silverworks, Royal Copenhagen Porcelain and Holmegaard Glass & Crystal are the biggest names in their fields. You'll find their products, and more, along Strøget, Copenhagen's famed shopping street.

In addition to speciality shops, Denmark's larger cities have their share of substantial department stores, such as Magasin du Nord and Salling, that stock virtually everything you can think of, from souvenir picture books to Scandinavian-designed furniture and fluffy goose-down quilts.

Getting There & Away

The information in this chapter details the various ways of getting directly to Denmark – by air, land and sea.

As Copenhagen is one of northern Europe's main gateway cities, you'll find a multitude of international flights to Denmark. In addition there is a range of boat, train and bus services connecting Denmark with the rest of Europe.

AIR
Airports & Airlines
The vast majority of overseas flights into Denmark land at Copenhagen international airport, which is conveniently located on the outskirts of Copenhagen, just a 12-minute train ride south of the city centre.

A few international flights, mostly those coming from other Scandinavian countries or the UK, land at small regional airports in Århus, Aalborg, Esbjerg and Billund.

Scandinavian Airlines (SAS) is the carrier with the most services to Denmark. Other scheduled international carriers flying into Copenhagen include Aer Lingus, Aeroflot, Air France, Alitalia, Austrian Airlines, British Airways, British Midland, Delta Air Lines, EgyptAir, El Al Israel Airlines, Finnair, Go, Iberia, Icelandair, Kenya Airways, KLM Royal Dutch Airlines, LOT Polish Airlines, Lufthansa Airlines, Maersk Air, Olympic Airways, Pakistan International Airlines, Sabena, Swissair, TAP Air Portugal, Thai Airways International, Turkish Airlines and Varig.

Buying Tickets
World aviation has never been so competitive, making air travel better value than ever. But you have to research the options carefully to make sure you get the best deal. The Internet is an increasingly useful source for checking air fares. Generally the more flexibility you have, such as a willingness to travel midweek, and the further in advance you book, the better your odds of finding a good deal.

Full-time students and people under 26 years (under 30 in some countries) often have access to better deals than other travellers. You have to show a document proving your date of birth or a valid International Student Identity Card (ISIC) when purchasing your ticket and boarding the plane.

Generally, there is nothing to be gained by buying a ticket direct from the airline. Discounted tickets are released to selected travel agents and specialist discount agencies, and these are usually the cheapest deals going.

One exception to this rule is the expanding number of 'no-frills' carriers, most of which only sell direct to travellers. Unlike the 'full-service' airlines, no-frills carriers often make one-way tickets available at around half the return fare, meaning that it is relatively easy to put together an open-jaw ticket when you fly to one place but leave from another.

Air Travel Glossary

Alliances Many of the world's leading airlines are now intimately involved with each other, sharing everything from reservations systems and check-in to aircraft and frequent-flyer schemes. Opponents say that alliances restrict competition. Whatever the arguments, there is no doubt that big alliances are the way of the future.

Courier Fares Businesses often need to send urgent documents or freight securely and quickly. Courier companies hire people to accompany the package through customs and, in return, offer a discount ticket which is sometimes a bargain. However, you may have to surrender all your baggage allowance and take only carry-on luggage.

Fares Airlines traditionally offer 1st class (coded F), business class (coded J) and economy class (coded Y) tickets. These days there are so many promotional and discounted fares available that few passengers pay full fare.

Lost Tickets If you lose your airline ticket, an airline will usually treat it like a travellers cheque and, after inquiries, issue you with another one. Legally, however, an airline is entitled to treat it like cash and if you lose it then it's gone forever. Take very good care of your tickets.

Onward Tickets An entry requirement for many countries is that you have a ticket out of the country. If you're unsure of your next move, the easiest solution is to buy the cheapest onward ticket to a neighbouring country or a ticket from a reliable airline which can later be refunded if you do not use it.

Open-Jaw Tickets These are return tickets where you fly out to one place but return from another. If available, this can save you backtracking to your arrival point.

Overbooking Since every flight has some passengers who fail to show up, airlines often book more passengers than they have seats. Usually excess passengers make up for the no-shows, but occasionally somebody gets 'bumped' onto the next available flight. Guess who it is most likely to be? The passengers who check in late. If you do get 'bumped', you are normally offered some form of compensation.

Reconfirmation Some airlines require you to reconfirm your flight at least 72 hours prior to departure. Check your travel documents to see if this is the case

Restrictions Discounted tickets often have various restrictions on them – such as needing to be paid for in advance and incurring a penalty to be altered or cancelled. Others are restrictions on the minimum and maximum period you must be away.

Round-the-World Tickets RTW tickets give you a limited period (usually a year) in which to circumnavigate the globe. You can go anywhere the carrying airlines go, as long as you don't backtrack. The number of stopovers or total number of separate flights is decided before you set off and they usually cost a bit more than a basic return flight.

Ticketless Travel Airlines are gradually waking up to the realisation that paper tickets are unnecessary encumbrances. On simple one-way or return trips, reservations details can be held on computer and the passenger merely shows ID to claim their seat.

Transferred Tickets Airline tickets cannot be transferred from one person to another. Travellers sometimes try to sell the return half of their ticket, but officials can ask you to prove that you are the person named on the ticket. On an international flight, tickets are compared with passports.

The other exception is booking on the Internet. Many airlines, full-service and no-frills, offer some excellent fares to Web surfers. On-line ticket sales work well if you are doing a simple one-way or return trip on specified dates.

However, online super-fast fare generators are no substitute for a travel agent. Good travel agents know all about special deals, have strategies for avoiding layovers and can offer advice on everything from which airline has the best vegetarian food to the best travel insurance to bundle with your ticket.

You may find that the cheapest flights are being advertised by obscure agencies. Most such firms are honest and solvent, but there are some rogue fly-by-night outfits around. Paying by credit card generally offers protection since most card issuers will provide refunds if you can prove you didn't get what you've paid for. Similar protection can be obtained by buying a ticket from a bonded agent, such as one covered by the Air Transport Operators Licence (ATOL) scheme in the UK.

If you feel suspicious about a firm it's best to steer clear, or only pay a small deposit before you actually get your ticket, then ring the airline to confirm that you are actually booked on the flight before you pay the balance. Established organistions such as STA Travel, which has offices worldwide, offer more security and are about as competitive as you can get.

Round-the-World (RTW) tickets are another possibility; for those travelling from a distant country these can be comparable in price to an ordinary, return long-haul ticket. However, some special conditions might be attached to RTW tickets (such as not being able to backtrack on a route). Also beware that there may be cancellation penalties for these and other tickets.

Courier fares, whereby you get cheap passage in return for accompanying an urgent package through customs, offer very low prices. However, there are usually special restrictions attached; in addition, demand for couriers is on the decline in this electronic age.

Travellers with Special Needs

If they're warned early enough, airlines can often make special arrangements for travellers. These arrangements can be anything from receiving wheelchair assistance at airports to being provided with a vegetarian meal on the flight. Children under two years travel for 10% of the standard fare (or free on some airlines) as long as they don't occupy a seat. They don't get a baggage allowance. 'Skycots', baby food and nappies should be provided by the airline if requested in advance, but be sure to let the airline know before the day of your flight. Children aged between two and 12 can usually occupy a seat for half to two-thirds of the full fare, and do get a baggage allowance.

The disability-friendly Allgohere Web site (W www.everybody.co.uk) has an airline directory that provides information on the facilities offered by various airlines.

Departure Tax

Departure taxes, which equal approximately US$20, are included with all the other fees that you pay when you purchase your ticket. There are no separate departure taxes to pay when leaving Denmark.

The UK

Discount air travel is big business in London. Advertisements for numerous travel agencies appear in the travel pages of the weekend broadsheet newspapers, in *Time Out*, the *Evening Standard* and the free magazine *TNT*.

For students or travellers under 26 years of age, a popular travel agency in the UK is STA Travel (☎ 020-7361 6262, W www.statravel.co.uk), with an office at 86 Old Brompton Rd, London SW7, and many branches across the country. Both agencies sell tickets to all travellers but cater especially to young people and students.

There are many scheduled commercial flights between Denmark and the UK, and with all the competition from discount carriers flying can be the cheapest way to travel. Over the past couple of years the lowest fares have typically been available with Go (☎ 0870 607 6543, W www.go-fly.com), which flies daily to Copenhagen from London Stansted, with return fares ranging from UK£39 to UK£129 depending on your day of travel and how far in advance you book. In addition, Ryan Air (☎ 0870-333 1231, W www.ryanair.com) has recently jumped into the fray offering last-minute online fares for travel between London Stansted and Esbjerg for as little as UK£15 each way.

Other airlines flying to Copenhagen include British Airways, which departs from Heathrow; SAS, leaving from Heathrow and Stansted; and Maersk Air, from Gatwick. All three carriers offer numerous daily flights. Unrestricted one-way fares are about UK£250, but these carriers also offer some steeply discounted promotions that can result in a return fare at a fraction of the full one-way price.

Continental Europe

While the cheapest way to travel between Copenhagen and the rest of continental Europe is usually by land, cheap discount flights are often available to travellers aged under 26. As a general guide, discounted youth fares to Copenhagen are typically around f300 from Amsterdam, €105 from Berlin, €140 from Frankfurt and €155 from Paris.

There are many travel agencies throughout Europe where you can purchase discounted tickets. These include: NBBS Reizen (☎ 020-620 5071), 66 Rokin, Amsterdam; Usit Connect Voyages (☎ 01 42 44 14 00), 14 rue de Vaugirard, Paris; STA Travel (☎ 030-311 0950), Goethestrasse 73, Berlin; SSR (☎ 022-818 02 02), 8 rue de la Rive, Geneva; and Passagi (☎ 06-474 0923), Stazione Termini FS, Galleria Di Tesla, Rome.

The USA

The North Atlantic is the world's busiest long-haul air corridor and the flight options can be bewildering. Larger newspapers such as the *New York Times*, the *Chicago Tribune* and the *Los Angeles Times* produce weekly travel sections in which you'll find any number of travel agencies' ads for air fares to Europe.

Discount travel agents in the USA are known as consolidators (although you won't see a sign on the door saying Consolidator). San Francisco is the ticket consolidator capital of America, although some good deals can be found in Los Angeles, New York and other big cities.

Council Travel, America's largest student travel organisation, has around 60 offices in the USA. Call it for the office nearest you (800-226 8624) or visit its Web site (W www.counciltravel.com). STA Travel (☎ 800-777 0112, W www.statravel.com) has offices in Boston, Chicago, Miami, New York, San Francisco, Philadelphia and other major cities. Call the toll-free 800 number for office locations or visit its Web site.

Ticket Planet (W www.ticketplanet.com) is a leading ticket consolidator in the USA and is recommended.

You should be able to fly return to Copenhagen from major east coast cities such as New York, Washington DC or Boston for about US$500 in the low season and US$800 in the high season. Add around US$100 for flights from the midwest and about US$200 from the west coast. You might be able to get better rates if the airlines are battling for passengers with promotional fares or you could end up with a higher fare if all the cheapest fares are booked out on the day you want to leave. Most budget fares between the USA and Copenhagen are valid for either a 30-day or a 60-day stay.

An interesting alternative to a direct flight is offered by Icelandair (☎ 800-223 5500), which allows a free stopover in the capital, Reykjavík. Its prices are usually similar to the direct Copenhagen fares offered by other airlines, though it sometimes undercuts the competition. Icelandair flies from New York, Baltimore-Washington, Boston, Minneapolis and Orlando.

There are other, less orthodox, ways of getting to Europe. For example, Airhitch (☎ 800-326 2009 in New York, ☎ 310-574 0090 in Los Angeles, W www.airhitch.org) specialises in stand-by tickets to Europe for US$180/250 one way from the east coast/west coast, but the destinations are by region (not a specific city or country).

Another possibility is a courier flight, which typically costs US$300 to US$400 return to get to Copenhagen from major cities like New York. Of course, there are a lot of restrictions and you often need to be ready to go on short notice. You can find out more about courier flights from the International Association of Air Travel Couriers (☎ 352-475 1584, W www.courier.org) as well as Now Voyager Travel (☎ 212-431 1616, W www.nowvoyagertravel.com).

Canada

For scheduled commercial flights to Copenhagen, you'll generally have to fly first to New York or Chicago and pick up a connecting flight from there.

However, Air Canada (☎ 800-776 3000) offers a nonstop service a few times a week between Toronto and Copenhagen. Fares vary with the season and because of the limited competition tend to be higher than the lowest fares available from the USA to Copenhagen.

Travel CUTS (☎ 800-667 2887, W www .travelcuts.com) is Canada's national student travel agency and has offices in all the major cities.

Also, scan the budget travel agencies' ads in major newspapers such as the national *Globe & Mail* and the *Vancouver Sun*.

Australia

Round-the-World (RTW) tickets are often real bargains and since Australia is pretty much on the other side of the world from Europe, it can sometimes work out cheaper to keep going right round the world on a RTW ticket than do a U-turn on a return ticket. The cheapest RTW ticket will cost about A$2300.

Cheap flights from Australia to Europe generally go via South-East Asian capitals or the Middle East. When a long stopover between connections is necessary, transit accommodation is sometimes included in the price of the ticket. If it's at your own expense, it may be worth considering a more expensive ticket. A return flight to Copenhagen ranges from A$1600 during the low season to A$2400 in the high season.

Quite a few travel offices specialise in discount air tickets. Some travel agents, particularly smaller ones, advertise cheap air fares in the travel sections of weekend newspapers.

Two well-known agents for cheap fares are STA Travel and Flight Centre. STA Travel (☎ 03-9349 2411, W www.statravel .com.au) has its main office at 224 Faraday St, Carlton, in Melbourne, with offices in all major cities and on many university campuses. Call ☎ 131 776 Australiawide for the location of your nearest branch or visit its Web site. Flight Centre (☎ 131 600 Australiawide, W www.flightcentre.com.au) has a central office at 82 Elizabeth St, Sydney, and there are dozens of offices throughout Australia.

New Zealand

Round-the-World (RTW) and Circle Pacific fares for travel to or from New Zealand are usually the best value, and can often be cheaper than a simple return ticket. Depending on which airline you choose to travel with, you may fly across Asia, with possible stopovers in India, Bangkok or Singapore, or across the USA, with possible stopovers in Honolulu, Australia or one of the Pacific Islands. From New Zealand return fares to Copenhagen start at about NZ$2299 in the low season and go up to NZ$2599 for high-season travel.

Flight Centre (☎ 09-309 6171) has a large central office in Auckland at the National Bank Towers (corner Queen & Darby Sts) and many branches throughout the country. STA Travel (☎ 09-309 0458, W www.statravel .com.au) has its main office at 10 High St, Auckland, and there are other offices in Auckland as well as branches in Wellington, Christchurch, Hamilton, Dunedin and Palmerston North.

Africa

Nairobi and Johannesburg are probably the best places in East and South Africa to buy tickets.

One of the best agencies in Nairobi is Flight Centre (☎ 02-210024), 2nd floor, Lakhamshi House, Biashara St.

Rennies Travel (☎ 011-833 1441), an agent for Thomas Cook, has an office in the Unitas Bldg, 42 Marshall St, Johannesburg, and other offices throughout South Africa.

Asia

Most Asian countries offer fairly competitive air-fare deals with Bangkok, Singapore and Hong Kong the best places to shop around for discount tickets.

Khao San Rd in Bangkok is the budget travellers headquarters. Bangkok has a number of excellent travel agents, but there are also some suspect ones; try to get some advice from other travellers before handing over your cash. STA Travel (☎ 02-236 0262), 33 Surawong Rd, Bangkok, is a good and reliable place to start.

Singapore has hundreds of travel agents, so you can compare prices on flights. You'll find many travel agents at Chinatown Point shopping centre on New Bridge Rd. STA Travel (☎ 65-737 7188), 35a Cuppage Road, Cuppage Terrace, Singapore, offers competitive prices.

Hong Kong has a number of excellent, reliable travel agencies as well as some not-so-reliable ones. A good way to check out a travel agent is to look it up in the phone book: Fly-by-night operators don't usually stay around long enough to get listed. Phoenix Services (☎ 2722 7378) Room B, 6th floor, Milton Mansion, 96 Nathan Rd, Tsimshatsui, is recommended.

In India, reliable travel agents include STIC Travels (☎ 011-332 0239), an agent for STA Travel, which has an office in Delhi on the 1st Floor, West Wing, Chandralok Bldg, 36 Janpath. In Mumbai (Bombay), STIC Travels (☎ 022-218 1431) is at 6 Maker Arcade, Cuffe Parade.

LAND
Bus

If you're coming from elsewhere in Europe travel by bus can be an economical option. Keep in mind that long bus rides can be tedious, so bring along a good book. On the plus side, some of the coaches are relatively luxurious with a toilet, air-con, stewards and a snack bar.

Small bus companies with discount rates come along from time to time but most of them don't remain in business for more than a year or two at the most. Ask around at student and discount travel agencies for the latest information.

Eurolines One of the biggest and most well-established express-bus services is Eurolines, which connects Copenhagen with the rest of Europe. Most of the buses run daily (or near-daily) in summer and between two and five times a week in winter.

Sample one-way Eurolines fares to Copenhagen are €56 from Stockholm, €60 from Oslo, €72 from Amsterdam, €85 from Frankfurt, €92 from Paris and €97 from London. There's a discount of about 10% for those aged 12 to 26 and for those over 60. Children aged four to 11 pay 50% of the adult fare and those three and under pay 20%. Return fares for all age groups are about 15% less than two one-way fares.

There's also a Eurolines pass that covers unlimited travel between nearly 50 European cities, including the Danish cities of Copenhagen and Aalborg. Other cities that the pass covers are as far flung as Dublin, London, Paris, Madrid, Prague, Warsaw and Rome. During the months of June to August a youth pass for travellers aged under 26 costs €200/296/324 for 15/30/60 days and an adult pass costs €240/370/430 for 15/30/60 days. During the rest of the year all passes are about 25% cheaper. Travellers aged over 60 can get a senior pass at the same rates as the youth passes. Eurolines offices in Denmark are:

Copenhagen (☎ 33 88 70 00) Reventlowsgade 8, 1651 Copenhagen V
Aalborg (☎ 70 10 00 10) JF Kennedys Plads 1, 9000 Aalborg

Eurolines representatives elsewhere in Europe include:

Belgium (☎ 02-203 0707) CCN-Gare du Nord, 1000 Brussels
France (☎ 08 36 69 52 52) 28 Avenue du Général de Gaulle, Bagnolet

Germany (☎ 069-79 03 50) Deutsche Touring, Mannheimersbrasse, No 4 Frankfurt am Main
Netherlands (☎ 020-56 08 788) Julianaplein 5, Amsterdam
Norway (☎ 81 54 44 44) Nor-Way Busseks-press, Bussterminalen Galleriet, 0154 Oslo
Sweden (☎ 31 10 02 40) Kyrkogatan 40, 41115 Gothenburg
UK (☎ 08705-143 219) Grosvenor Gardens, London SW1W 0AU

Advance reservations may be necessary on some international buses; either call the bus companies directly or make inquiries at a travel agency.

Busabout This UK-based budget alternative to Eurolines is aimed at the younger traveller, but has no upper age limit. During the summer season it visits 70 European cities, including Copenhagen.

Busabout offers both consecutive day passes, good for successive days of travel, and flexi-passes allowing for a certain number of days of travel within a set period. For example, a flexi-pass good for 10 days of travel during two months costs UK£259/229 for adults/youth, and a standard pass good for 21 consecutive days of travel costs UK£229/209. Youth passes are available to those under 26 years of age.

You are able to buy Busabout tickets directly from the company (☎ 020-7950 1661, W www.busabout.com) or from suppliers such as STA Travel.

Train

Trains are a popular way of getting around; they are good meeting places and in northern Europe they are generally comfortable, frequent and reliable.

If you plan to travel extensively around Europe by train, it might be worth getting hold of the *Thomas Cook European Timetable*, which gives a complete listing of train schedules and indicates where supplements apply or where reservations are necessary; it's available from Thomas Cook outlets worldwide.

In the discussion of rail passes that follows, keep in mind that Denmark is a small country so domestic fares are quite moderate. Squeezing your money's worth out of a rail pass that is used solely in Denmark can be a real challenge (for more details on Denmark's domestic fares, see the Train section in the Getting Around chapter). On the other hand, if you will also be making excursions to neighbouring countries then that will certainly boost the value of a rail pass.

For comparison purposes, standard 2nd class train fares to Copenhagen are 430kr from Oslo, 450kr from Stockholm and €135 from Frankfurt.

Rail Passes A multitude of rail passes are available for travel in Europe and it's important to find a travel agency familiar with the various options.

Two agencies in the USA that specialise in selling rail passes are Budget Europe Travel Service (☎ 800-441 2387), 2557 Meade Court, Ann Arbor, MI 48105, and Europe Through the Back Door (☎ 206-771 8303), 120 Fourth Ave N, PO Box 2009, Edmonds, WA 98020.

Among the agencies selling rail passes in the UK are Wasteels Travel (☎ 020-7834 7066), Victoria train station, London. In continental Europe, rail passes can be purchased at larger train stations and travel agencies.

If you buy a rail pass, read the small print. There are certain rules for validation and the pass cannot be transferred should you decide not to use it.

Keep in mind that rail passes do not cover seat reservation costs and fees for supplements such as sleepers. Also, if you're taking a high-speed train or a business-class train, there is sometimes an extra supplement.

The traveller must fill out in ink the relevant box in the calendar before starting a day's travel. Be sure to get the date right, as tampering with the pass (which includes erasing) or failing to validate it runs the risk of fines and possible forfeiture of the pass. We've had reports of Danish train conductors being extremely scrupulous in their checks, even examining the passes with a magnifying glass.

Eurail Eurailpasses are available to residents of non-European countries, and are intended to be purchased before arriving in Europe.

Eurailpasses are valid for unlimited travel on national railways (and some private lines) in Austria, Belgium, Denmark, Finland, France, Germany, Greece, Hungary, Ireland, Italy, Luxembourg, the Netherlands, Norway, Portugal, Spain, Sweden and Switzerland. Eurailpasses are also valid for free or discounted travel on some of the ferries in and between these countries.

There are two Eurailpasses available to travellers aged under 26. The Eurail Youth Pass is valid for unlimited 2nd-class travel for 15 days (US$388), 21 days (US$499), one month (US$623), two months (US$882) or three months (US$1089). A Eurail Youth Flexipass, which also covers 2nd-class travel, is valid for freely chosen days within a two-month period: 10 days for US$458 or 15 days for US$599.

For those aged over 26, a Eurail Flexipass (available for 1st-class travel only) costs US$654 or US$862 for 10 or 15 freely chosen days within two months. The standard Eurailpass has five versions, all are valid for unlimited travel in 1st class: US$554 for 15 days, US$718 for 21 days, US$890 for one month, US$1260 for two months and US$1558 for three months.

Two or more people travelling together can get a 15% discount by buying a Eurail Saverpass or Eurail Saver Flexipass, which work like the standard Eurailpass and Eurail Flexipass – just keep in mind that you must do all of your travelling together.

Eurailpasses for children are also available; half fare for those aged under 12, free for those under four.

Inter-Rail These train passes are available to residents of European countries.

The Inter-Rail pass is split into zones, with the fare depending upon how many zones you plan to travel within. Zone A comprises Great Britain and Ireland; B is Finland, Norway and Sweden; C is Austria, Denmark, Germany and Switzerland; D is Croatia, the Czech Republic, Hungary, Poland and Slovakia; E is Belgium, France, Luxembourg and the Netherlands; F is Morocco, Portugal and Spain; G is Italy, Greece, Slovenia and Turkey; and H is Bulgaria, Macedonia, Romania and Yugoslavia.

The price, in Danish kroner, for 22 days of travel in any one zone is 1595kr for travellers aged under 26 and 2195kr for adults. Multizone passes are valid for one month: a two-zone pass costs 2095/2895kr for travellers aged under 26/adults, three zones 2295/3295kr and all zones 2695/3795kr.

Terms and conditions vary slightly from country to country, but for travel in the country of origin expect only limited discounts – if you're departing from the UK, for instance, the pass covers the channel crossing but no domestic travel.

Scanrail These rail passes cover travel in Denmark, Norway, Sweden and Finland.

Flexible and consecutive-day passes are available. For travel on any five days within a two-month period, the Scanrail pass costs US$276/204 in 1st/2nd class (US$207/153 for travellers aged under 26). Travel on any 10 days within a two-month period costs US$420/310 for 1st/2nd class (US$315/233 for those aged under 26).

For 21 consecutive days of unlimited travel, the pass will cost US$486/360 for 1st/2nd class (US$365/270 for people aged under 26).

The cost for children aged under 12 is half the adult fare; children aged under four travel free.

If you're 60 years old or over, then you're eligible for a senior pass, which is valid for 1st/2nd class travel over five days in a two-month period for US$246/182, 10 days in a two-month period for US$374/276 and 21 consecutive days for US$432/321.

To get Scanrail passes at these prices, they must be purchased before you arrive in Scandinavia. Scanrail passes can also be purchased in Scandinavia but may cost a bit more, depending on the exchange rate.

The Scanrail pass also includes free or discounted travel on numerous international boats travelling between Denmark and the neighbouring countries.

Other Discounts There are numerous other discount schemes for train travel across Europe, so always ask about off-peak travel, family plans and special promotions. Many routes also have discounted return fares; if you purchase your tickets a couple of days in advance you can sometimes get a return ticket for just a bit more than the one-way fare.

Car & Motorcycle

Denmark's only land border is with Germany. The E45, which is part of the extensive European motorway network, is the main route between Germany and the Jutland peninsula, although there are several smaller border crossings as well. With the new open-border EU regulations that took effect in 2001, the border stations on the Germany-Denmark border have been removed, and drivers now can cross freely between the two countries without stopping.

Until just a few years ago it was necessary to take a car ferry to get to Copenhagen, on the island of Zealand, from anywhere outside Denmark. All that has now changed with the construction of two ambitious bridge-tunnel links.

In 1998, the 18km Storebælts-forbindelsen (the Store Bælt Bridge) was opened, connecting Zealand with the Jutland peninsula and the rest of the European mainland via Germany and the E45 motorway.

In 2000, the 16km Øresundsforbindelsen (the Øresund Fixed Link) was finished, joining Copenhagen with Malmö, Sweden, via the E20 motorway.

Both these recent links are bridge-tunnel combinations with one level carrying motor vehicles and another taking trains. Øresunds-forbindelsen and Storebælts-forbindelsen each charges tolls for cars of 230kr. There are no other toll charges to use the roads or bridges anywhere else in Denmark.

Car ferries haven't disappeared altogether, however, and are still the most efficient way to arrive from some parts of Europe, such as Norway and the UK.

For information on car ferry services to Denmark, see the Sea section later in this chapter. For detailed information on travelling around Denmark by private vehicle, see the Car & Motorcycle section in the Getting Around chapter.

Paperwork & Preparations Your proof of vehicle ownership (such as a Vehicle Registration Document for British-registered cars) should always be carried when you are driving in Europe. Also carry your national driving licence, as well as an International Driving Permit (IDP) if appropriate.

Third-party motor insurance is a minimum requirement in most of Europe. Most UK motor insurance policies automatically provide third-party cover valid in EU countries and some others. Get your insurer to issue a Green Card, which is internationally recognised as proof of insurance, and check that it lists all of the countries you intend to visit. You'll need this in the event of an accident outside the country where the vehicle is insured. Also ask your insurer for a European Accident Statement form, which can simplify things. Never sign statements you can't read or understand – insist on a translation and sign that only if it's acceptable.

It's advisable to have a European breakdown assistance policy, such as the RAC Eurocover Motoring Assistance plan. Ask your motoring organisation for details about free and reciprocal services offered by affiliated organisations in countries you'll be visiting.

Every vehicle that crosses an international border should display a nationality plate of its country of registration. A warning triangle, to be used in the event of a breakdown, is compulsory almost everywhere. Recommended accessories for a driving holiday are a first-aid kit, a spare bulb kit and also a fire extinguisher.

Road Rules Vehicles drive on the right in all the northern European countries. Vehicles brought from the UK or Ireland should have their headlights adjusted to avoid blinding oncoming traffic at night (a simple solution on older headlight lenses is to cover up the triangular section of the lens with tape). Priority is usually given to traffic approaching from the right in countries that drive on the right-hand side. The British RAC publishes an annual *European Motoring Guide*, which gives an excellent summary of regulations in each country, including parking rules. Motoring organisations in other countries produce similar publications.

Take care with speed limits as they vary significantly from country to country. You may be surprised at the apparent disregard of traffic regulations in some places but as a visitor it is always best to err on the side of caution. In many European countries, driving infringements are subject to on-the-spot fines. Always ask for a receipt if you're fined.

For road rules specific to Denmark, see Road Rules in the Car & Motorcycle section of the following Getting Around chapter.

Camper Van Travelling in a camper van can be a surprisingly economical option for the budget traveller, as it can take care of eating, sleeping and travelling in one convenient package. London is a good place to buy your van: look in *TNT* magazine and *Loot* newspaper, or go to the van market on Market Rd, London N7. Expect to spend at least UK£2000 for something reliable.

Note that although discreet free camping, such as in motorway rest areas, is not a problem in many places in Europe, it is illegal in Denmark.

A drawback with camper vans is that they're expensive to buy in spring and hard to sell in autumn. A car and tent might do just as well instead.

Bicycle

A bicycle can make a great travelling companion in cycle-friendly Denmark. If you're flying to Denmark you should be able to take your bicycle along with you on the plane relatively easily. You can dismantle the bicycle and put the pieces in a bike bag or box, but it's easier to simply wheel your bike to the check-in desk, where it should be treated as a piece of baggage. You may have to remove the pedals and turn the handlebars sideways so that it takes up less space in the aircraft's hold. Check all this with the airline well in advance, preferably before you pay for your ticket.

Long Link

Øresundsforbindelsen (the Øresund Fixed Link), which provides the first 'land link' between Denmark and Sweden, ranks as the world's longest combined tunnel and bridge crossing of its kind. A joint construction venture undertaken by the Swedish and Danish governments, it opened in July 2000.

The whole thing stretches nearly 16km across the Øresund from Kastrup, near Copenhagen airport, to Lernacken, near Malmö, Sweden. A 4km-long artificial island, called Peberholm, had to first be built halfway across the sound to provide a point where the 3.5km-long underwater tunnel could be linked with the 8km-long bridge. The system has two decks, with cars moving on the upper deck and trains running on the lower.

Views of the bridge, which has a simple but pleasing design with high pylon towers and clean linear cable patterns, can be seen from many places along the Copenhagen coast all the way north to Klampenborg. The view from Kastrup, near the start of Øresundsforbindelsen, isn't a particularly spectacular one, since the link begins on the Danish side as an underwater tunnel.

It's also possible to send bicycles between Denmark and most other European countries via train as international luggage. The bicycle must be easy to handle; it cannot be locked and anything bulky, such as baskets and panniers, must be removed. The transport time can take as much as three days from other stations in Scandinavia and five days from elsewhere in Europe.

Still, if you have an option, the easiest and cheapest way is to take an international ferry to Denmark. You'll get to travel on the same boat as your bike and the additional fee is usually minimal.

A primary consideration on a cycling tour is to travel light, but you should take a few tools and spare parts, including a puncture repair kit and an extra inner tube. Panniers are essential to balance your possessions on either side of the bike frame. A bike helmet is also a must. Take a good lock and always use it when you leave your bike unattended.

Seasoned cyclists can average 80km a day, but there's no point in overdoing it. The slower you travel, the more local people you are likely to meet.

Once in Denmark, you'll find that many trains and buses are specially equipped to carry bicycles at a nominal fee.

Information on travelling around Denmark by bicycle can be found in the Bicycle section of the Getting Around chapter. There is more detailed information in the special section 'Cycling in Denmark', which follows the Getting Around chapter.

SEA

Ferry travel can be an economical way of getting to Denmark because it often includes overnight accommodation. It's also a pleasant way to travel as the boats are generally of a high standard. The long-distance boats usually have lounges, nightclubs and both cafeterias and formal restaurants.

Many of the boats between Denmark and other Scandinavian countries have floating casinos and small grocery shops on board as well.

The fares in this section are for one-way travel unless otherwise noted. There are often discounts on return tickets, particularly for people travelling by car, and occasionally there are some very good excursion deals – always ask about special promotions. If you're carrying a rail pass or a student card, be sure to flash it when you purchase a ticket, as it may entitle you to a substantial discount. A child's fare is usually half of the adult fare and there are often senior discounts as well.

Keep in mind that the same ferry company can have a whole host of different prices for the same route, depending on the day of the week you travel and on the season. As a general rule, the highest prices occur on summer weekends and the lowest on winter weekdays.

Note that cabin fares are quoted on a per-person (not a per-cabin) basis. Car fares given in this section are for a standard car (generally up to 6m in length and 2m in

height); most fares inch up as the vehicle increases in size, and fares for camper vans are higher still.

Particularly if you are bringing along a vehicle, you should always make reservations well in advance – this is doubly true in summer and at weekends. During busy periods you'll also get the best cabin selection by booking in advance.

Ferry Companies

The following reservation information is for the larger ferry companies operating international routes to and from Denmark.

DFDS Seaways This company (W www .dfdsseaways.com) runs ferries between Copenhagen and Oslo via Helsingborg (Sweden) and from Esbjerg to Harwich (UK). Booking agencies include:

Denmark
Copenhagen: (☎ 33 42 30 00, fax 33 42 30 11) Sankt Annæ Plads 30, 1295 Copenhagen K
Esbjerg: (☎ 79 17 79 17, fax 79 17 79 18) Englandskajen, 6700 Esbjerg
Norway
(☎ 22 41 90 90, fax 22 41 38 38) Utstikker II, Vippetangen, Oslo
Sweden
(☎ 42 26 60 00, fax 42 26 61 77) Sundsterminalen, Atlantgatan, 252 25 Helsingborg
UK
London: (☎ 08705-333 000, fax 020-7616 1450) 28A Queensway, London W2 3RX
Essex: (☎ 1255-240 240, fax 1255-244 370) Scandinavia House, Parkeston Quay, Harwich, Essex CO12 4QG

Color Line This ferry company (W www .colorline.com) operates between Hirtshals and the Norwegian cities of Kristiansand, Oslo and Larvik, and between Frederikshavn and Larvik. The Color Line booking agencies include:

Denmark
(☎ 99 56 19 77, fax 99 56 20 20) Fergeterminalen, 9850 Hirtshals
Norway
Oslo: (☎ 81 00 08 11, fax 22 83 04 30) Postboks 1422 Vika, 0115 Oslo
Kristiansand: (☎ 38 07 88 00, fax 38 07 88

13) Fergeterminalen, Postboks 82, 4665
Kristiansand
Larvik: (☎ 33 12 28 00, fax 33 18 71 67)
Ferjeterminalen, Postboks 2002, 3255 Larvik

Stena Line Stena (W www.stenaline.com)
operates ferries from Frederikshavn to Oslo
in Norway and Gothenburg in Sweden, as
well as from the Danish port of Grenaa to
Varberg in Sweden. Stena's booking agencies include:

Denmark (☎ 96 20 02 00, fax 96 20 02 84)
   Stenaterminalen, 9900 Frederikshavn
Norway (☎ 23 17 90 00; fax 23 17 90 60)
   Utstikker II Vippetangen, Oslo
Sweden (☎ 31 85 80 00; fax 31 85 85 95)
   Danmarksterminalen, 405 19 Gothenburg

Germany
Puttgarden to Rødbyhavn Scandlines (☎
01805-7226 354637 in Germany, ☎ 33 15 15
15 in Denmark, W www.scandlines.de) runs
a busy train, car and passenger ferry service
between these two ports (the quickest way
to Copenhagen) nearly every 30 minutes,
24 hours a day; it takes 45 minutes. If you're
travelling by train, the cost of the ferry will
be included in your ticket. Otherwise the
cost is €25 for a motorcycle with two riders
and €45 for a car with up to nine passengers.

Rostock to Gedser Scandlines also has a
ferry service between Rostock (Germany)
and Gedser (Denmark) several times a day.
The boat takes two hours and costs from
€4.50 to €8 for passengers, from €59 to
€100 for a car with up to nine people.

Sylt to Rømø Rømø-Sylt Linie (☎ 4651-
87 0475 in Sylt, ☎ 73 75 53 03 in Rømø) runs
car ferries between List on the German island
of Sylt and Havneby on the Danish island
of Rømø numerous times each day. The trip
takes one hour and costs €4.50 for a passenger, €23 for a motorcycle and rider and €35
for a car and passengers.

Sassnitz-Mukran to Bornholm Bornholmstrafikken (☎ 038-39 23 52 26 in Sassnitz, ☎ 56 95 18 66 in Bornholm), operates

ferries from Sassnitz-Mukran to Rønne
daily, except Wednesday, in summer and a
few times a week during the rest of the year.
Boats leave Sassnitz at 11.30am, Rønne at
7.30am; the trip takes 3½ hours. The fare
for passengers is €16 between mid-June
and August and it is €8 for the rest of the
year. Depending on the season, it costs from
€64 to €117 to take a car, including up to
five passengers.

Poland
Polferries (☎ 09132-16140 in Poland, ☎ 56
95 10 69 in Denmark, W www.polferries.com
.pl) operates a year-round ferry service between Świnoujście and Copenhagen. The
trip takes 10 hours.

From Świnoujście, the ferries depart at
10.30am on Thursday and Friday and at
10.30pm on Tuesday, Saturday and Sunday.
Ferries from Copenhagen leave at 8am on
Sunday, Monday and Wednesday and
7.30pm on Thursday and Friday. The cost of
the crossing, which Polferries sets in Danish kroner, even if you're travelling from
Poland, are 370kr for a passenger, 520kr for
a car with driver or 920kr for a car with up
to five passengers.

Polferries also runs a ferry between
Poland and Bornholm on Saturday from late
June to August. The trip takes six hours,
with the boat leaving Świnoujście at 10am
and departing from Rønne at 5.30pm. The
one-way fare is 180kr for a passenger,
450kr for a car and driver.

Sweden
Helsingborg to Helsingør The cheapest
ferry route between Denmark and Sweden
is the shuttle between Helsingborg and
Helsingør, which takes 20 minutes and
costs just Skr20. Ferries depart every 20
minutes during the day and once an hour
through the night. The fare for a motorcycle
and driver is Skr115, while a car with up to
nine passengers costs Skr275. There are
various car discounts, and you can often get
a return ticket for around the same price as
a one-way ticket. Both HH-Ferries (☎ 42 19
80 00 in Helsingborg, ☎ 49 26 01 55 in Helsingør) and Scandlines (☎ 42 18 61 00 in

Helsingborg, ☎ 33 15 15 15 in Helsingør)
ply this route.

There's also a frequent passenger-only
hydrofoil service operated by Sundbusserne
(☎ 49 21 35 45) that saves a few minutes on
the travel time but costs about twice as much.

Malmö to Copenhagen Two companies
run passenger-only hydrofoils from Malmö
to Copenhagen.

Pilen (☎ 40 23 44 11 in Malmö, ☎ 33 32
12 60 in Copenhagen) operates hourly between Malmö and Copenhagen, except on
Sunday when it leaves every other hour.
The fare is Skr60 and the crossing takes 45
minutes. Flyvebådene (☎ 33 15 15 15) also
runs a hydrofoil from Copenhagen to
Malmö with hourly service and the same
fare as Pilen.

Gothenburg to Frederikshavn Stena
Line operates car ferries about eight times a
day between Gothenburg and Frederikshavn, charging Skr95 to Skr195 for a passenger, Skr210 to Skr350 for a motorcycle
and driver and Skr595 to Skr995 for a car
with up to five people. Some of the boats
are high-speed catamarans, which take only
two hours, and others are traditional ferries
that take 3¼ hours to make the crossing.

Varberg to Grenaa Stena Line operates
daily service between Varberg and Grenaa.
The crossing takes four hours and costs
Skr95 to Skr195 for a passenger, Skr210 to
Skr350 for a motorcycle and driver and
Skr595 to Skr995 for a car with up to five
people.

Ystad to Rønne There are several daily
ferries run by Bornholmstrafikken (☎ 041-
11 80 65 in Ystad, ☎ 56 95 18 66 in Rønne)
between Rønne and Ystad. The journey
takes 1½ hours. It costs Skr164 to Skr208
for a passenger and Skr560 to Skr900 for a
car with up to five people.

Norway
Oslo to Copenhagen DFDS Seaways
runs daily overnight ferries between Oslo
and Copenhagen, with the cheapest cabin

fare ranging from Nkr595 on winter weekdays to Nkr975 on summer weekends. if you
have a student card, cabin fares are discounted by 25%. The cost to take a car is an
additional Nkr330, a motorcycle Nkr190.
These boats have the cushiest service on the
Denmark-Norway route; opt for the most
economical cabins, as they're of the same
comfortable standard as mid-priced ones.
The departure in either direction is at 5pm,
with arrival at 9am.

Oslo to Frederikshavn Stena Line operates ferries from Oslo to Frederikshavn
daily in summer and every day but Monday
the rest of the year. The ferries leave Oslo
at 7pm, arriving in Frederikshavn at
7.30am. Passenger fares range from Nkr110
to Nkr310 depending upon the day of travel
and season. Cabins, which are mandatory
on overnight sailings, cost an additional fee,
ranging from Nkr100 for a lower-deck four-
person cabin that can be booked as a dorm
to Nkr1300 for a luxury cabin with a sea
view. A motorcycle and driver costs Nkr230
to Nkr830, a car and driver Nkr300 to
Nkr1200.

Larvik to Frederikshavn Color Line operates a daily ferry between Larvik (Norway)
and Frederikshavn (Denmark) year-round.
The schedule varies with the day of the
week and the season, and it can be either a
day ferry (6¼ hours) or an overnight ferry
(9½ hours).

Passenger fares range from Nkr170 on
winter weekdays to Nkr410 on summer
weekends. The additional charge for a car
ranges from Nkr200 to Nkr575. A motorcycle costs from Nkr150 to Nkr300. Cabin
prices begin at an additional Nkr140 in a
four-berth cabin and Nkr240 in a two-berth
cabin during the summer, and slightly less
in winter.

Kristiansand, Oslo & Larvik to Hirtshals
Color Line runs two to five ferries daily
between Hirtshals (Denmark) and Kristiansand (Norway), the busiest ferry connection
between the two countries. The schedule,
which is heaviest in the summer, varies

with the day of the week and the season. The trip takes from 2½ to 4¼ hours, depending on the boat.

There's also a daily ferry between Hirtshals and Oslo. From Oslo the boat operates as an overnight ferry, departing at 7.30pm and arriving at 8am.

Color Line also has a ferry service between Hirtshals and Larvik. The schedule varies with the season but it operates at least once daily from April to September. The trip takes 4½ hours as a day ferry, 10 hours as an overnight ferry.

Color Line fares on all three routes from Hirtshals are exactly the same as on the Larvik-Frederikshavn route listed earlier.

Bergen & Egersund to Hanstholm

Fjord Line (☎ 55 54 88 00 in Norway, ☎ 97 96 14 01 in Denmark) sails year-round from Bergen to Hanstholm at 4.30pm on Monday, Wednesday and Friday, stopping en route in Egersund, Norway, and arriving at Hanstholm the next day at 8am. Sailings from Hanstholm to Bergen are on Sunday, Tuesday and Thursday; times vary. The Bergen-Hanstholm passenger fare ranges from Nkr440 to Nkr800, while a car with up to five passengers costs from Nkr1100 to Nkr2650.

The UK

DFDS Seaways operates car ferries between Harwich in the UK and the Jutland city of Esbjerg.

From May to September, one boat sets sail in each direction every second day; during the rest of the year boats leave Esbjerg on Monday, Wednesday and Friday and Harwich on Tuesday, Thursday and Saturday. Throughout the year the boats depart from Harwich at 4pm, except on Saturday when they sail at 8pm, and from Esbjerg at 6pm. The crossing takes 19 hours.

These are pleasant boats with full amenities. Standard fares, which vary according to the season and the day of week, ranging from UK£52 to UK£92 for a bed in a two-berth cabin. But also ask about promotional fares as cheaper deals are common even in summer.

It costs an additional UK£35 to UK£55 to take a car and UK£14 to UK£19 for a motorcycle. There are discounts on return tickets and for senior travellers and students.

Iceland & the Faroe Islands

The Smyril Line (☎ 298-34 59 00 in Faroe Islands, 33 16 40 04 in Denmark, Ⓦ www .smyril-line.fo) runs weekly ferries, from mid-May to early September, from Tórshavn (Faroe Islands) and Seyðisfjörður (Iceland) to the Danish port of Hanstholm.

The boat departs from Seyðisfjörður at noon Thursday, arriving in Tórshavn at 6am Friday and in Hanstholm at 4pm Saturday.

Summer high-season fares for a couchette are 1480kr from Tórshavn and 2310kr from Seyðisfjörður; these fares are 30% less for travel outside midsummer. There's a 25% discount for students under 26. A car costs 1170kr from Tórshavn, 1940kr from Seyðisfjörður, a motorcycle 460/770kr from Tórshavn/Seyðisfjörður. To travel with a bicycle will cost 80kr.

ORGANISED TOURS

If your time is limited, there are various package tours that include transport to Denmark, hotel accommodation and, in most cases, sightseeing. Standard tours can readily be arranged through your travel agency or through SAS, Icelandair and other airlines.

An array of package tours that include hotels can also be arranged through the large ferry companies, such as Stena Line and DFDS Seaways, the addresses of which are listed under Ferry Companies earlier in this chapter.

The American-Scandinavian Foundation and the Danish Cultural Institute arrange study tours to Denmark. Contact addresses are listed under Useful Organisations in the Facts for the Visitor chapter.

Two commercial travel agents that specialise in tours to Denmark are: Bennett Tours (☎ 212-697 1092), 342 Madison Avenue, Suite 916, New York, NY 10173 USA; and Plantagenet Tours (☎ 1202-521 895), 85 The Grove, Moordown, Bournemouth, BH9 2TY England.

Cruise Ships

In recent years, Copenhagen has grown in popularity as a cruise-ship stopover, usually as part of a larger Scandinavian, Baltic or Western European tour.

Between mid-May and mid-September more than 200 cruise ships call at Copenhagen's Langelinie harbour, just north of the *Little Mermaid*.

There are numerous different itineraries and lines. The Fred Olsen Line, for instance, offers a 13-day cruise from Dover in UK that includes Copenhagen, Oslo, St Petersburg, Tallinn, Stockholm and Kiel, and costs from US$3000.

Travel agencies, particularly those that specialise in cruises, can detail all the possibilities and pile you high with brochures. They can also give you the lowdown on special promotions and discounts, such as those for early booking, which can cut as much as 25% to 40% off the standard fares.

Getting Around

AIR

Domestic air traffic in Denmark is quite limited. The compactness of the country and the ever-increasing efficiency of its rail system have the effect of keeping air routes to a minimum. Still, the two main carriers covering the domestic front, Maersk Air and Scandinavian Airlines (SAS), offer frequent services between Copenhagen and a few of the more distant corners of Denmark.

Maersk Air (☎ 70 10 74 74) links Copenhagen with Billund in Jutland and Rønne on the island of Bornholm. The regular one-way fares from Copenhagen are 800kr to Rønne and 900kr to Billund. There are numerous discount schemes available, for example, a return ticket purchased seven days in advance typically works out a bit cheaper than the one-way fare. Other discounts include a one-way youth fare of 390kr for people aged 21 or under, and various deals for families travelling together.

Scandinavian Airlines (☎ 70 10 30 00) flies from Copenhagen to the two largest Jutland cities, Århus and Aalborg. The one-way fare to either city is 1060kr and return fares can usually be found for around the same price. Ask SAS about any other discounts that could apply such as youth fares, weekend getaway fares and special promotions.

In addition, Cimber Air (☎ 74 42 22 77) flies from Copenhagen to Sønderborg for around 800kr one way or return. There are 50% discounts available for those aged under 26 or over 60.

If your plans include an international flight to and from Copenhagen you can often work in a free domestic flight by getting an open-jaw ticket. This allows you, at either the start of your trip or as part of the return journey, to add a connecting flight between Copenhagen and another Danish city at no extra cost. Buying an open-jaw ticket into Copenhagen and out of Aalborg, for example, would let you rent a car in Copenhagen, self-tour one way, and drop off the car at Aalborg airport on the last day of your stay.

BUS

All of Denmark's major cities and towns have a local bus system and most places are also served by countrywide regional buses. More often than not, the central bus terminal is beside the train station and in many cases regional buses conveniently time their services to dovetail with train schedules.

Stiff competition from trains has left the long-distance bus a very secondary mode of transport in Denmark. There are, however, a handful of cross-country bus routes that can work out about 25% cheaper than train fares.

Daily express buses include a connection between Copenhagen and Århus (200kr, three hours) and another between Copenhagen and Aalborg (220kr, five hours). There's also an express-bus service running a couple of times a day between the Jutland port cities of Frederikshavn and Esbjerg (215kr, five hours).

See the Getting Around sections of the relevant destinations for more details.

TRAIN

Denmark has a good, reliable train system with reasonable fares and frequent services. Most long-distance trains, such as those on the busy Copenhagen-Aalborg route, operate at least hourly throughout the day.

With the exception of a few short private lines, Danske Statsbaner (Danish State Railways), which is invariably referred to as DSB, runs all train services in Denmark. Rail passes such as Scanrail and Eurailpass (see Train in the Getting There & Away chapter) are valid on DSB trains but cannot be used on the private lines.

DSB essentially operates two types of standard long-distance trains; ticket prices are the same on both. The sleek InterCity (IC) trains have ultramodern comforts. The carriage layout resembles a more spacious version of a plane interior, complete with cushioned seats, overhead reading lights and individual music headphone jacks. IC trains also have play areas for children and

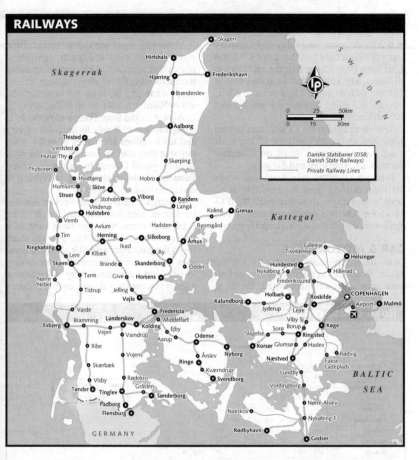

RAILWAYS

Danske Statsbaner (DSB; Danish State Railways)

Private Railway Lines

roomy toilets with nappy-changing facilities. Reservations are generally required for travel on IC trains.

Interregional (IR) trains are older, a bit slower and more basic, but are comfortable in all respects. Reservations are optional on IR trains and in most cases you can find a seat without one, however, if you're travelling a long distance or during rush hour you might prefer to make a reservation to be guaranteed a seat.

In addition to the standard IC trains there are also Business IC trains (designated as InterCityLyn on schedules) on certain routes,

such as Copenhagen to Esbjerg, Århus and Aalborg. These are geared to business travellers, go marginally faster than standard IC trains, are a bit more posh and offer free drinks and snacks. For the pampering you'll pay a 50% surcharge over the standard train fares.

Regardless of distance travelled, the reservation fee is 15kr; on Business IC trains this fee is included in the ticket price. Standard fares work out at about 1kr per kilometre, with the highest fare possible between any two points in Denmark topping out at just 300kr.

Some people are eligible for even lower fares. People aged 65 and over are entitled to a 20% discount on Friday and Saturday and a 50% discount on other days. Children aged from 10 to 15 pay half the adult fare at all times and kids under 10 travel free if they are with an adult. Eight or more adults who are travelling together are entitled to a 30% discount.

Travellers aged from 15 to 25 can buy an *ungdomskort* (youth card) for 150kr; it allows half-price train fares on Tuesday, Wednesday, Thursday and Saturday.

Free pocket-sized schedules that cover the main railway lines are available at all DSB train stations, or you can call ☎ 70 13 14 15 for schedule details and other information on train travel throughout Denmark.

CAR & MOTORCYCLE

Denmark is a pleasant country for touring by car. Roads are in good condition and almost invariably well signposted. Traffic is quite light, even in major cities, except during rush hours.

Motorway signs are colour coded. Blue signs indicate exits and green signs show places that are reached by continuing along the motorway. Petrol stations, with toilets, nappy-changing facilities and minimarkets, are at 50km intervals on all motorways.

Access to and from Danish motorways is straightforward: Roads leading out of city and town centres are named after the main city that they lead to. For instance, the road heading out of Odense to Faaborg is called Faaborgvej, the road leading to Nyborg is called Nyborgvej, and so on.

Denmark's extensive network of domestic ferries carries motor vehicles at quite reasonable rates. Although fares vary, as a rule of thumb, fares for cars average three times the passenger rate. It's always a good idea – and sometimes essential – for drivers to call ahead and make ferry reservations, even if you can only do so a couple of hours

Road Distances (km)

Note: Distances between Jutland & Zealand are via Funen.

	Aalborg	Copenhagen	Esbjerg	Frederikshavn	Grenaa	Helsingør	Kalundborg	Kolding	Næstved	Nyborg	Odense	Ringkøbing	Rødby	Skagen	Thisted	Tønder	Viborg	Århus
Aalborg	---																	
Copenhagen	402	---																
Esbjerg	216	298	---															
Frederikshavn	65	465	278	---														
Grenaa	136	367	216	193	---													
Helsingør	443	47	339	506	408	---												
Kalundborg	345	103	241	408	310	139	---											
Kolding	199	230	72	261	164	271	173	---										
Næstved	342	85	238	405	307	125	71	152	---									
Nyborg	274	228	170	337	239	169	71	102	68	---								
Odense	243	165	139	306	208	206	108	71	105	37	---							
Ringkøbing	174	336	81	236	188	377	279	115	276	208	177	---						
Rødby	410	181	306	473	375	221	176	238	105	136	173	344	---					
Skagen	105	505	319	41	233	546	448	302	445	377	346	277	513	---				
Thisted	90	399	185	138	186	440	342	196	339	271	240	123	407	172	---			
Tønder	284	315	77	347	249	356	258	86	255	187	156	148	323	387	252	---		
Viborg	80	323	136	142	100	354	266	119	263	195	164	94	331	183	87	205	---	
Århus	112	304	153	171	63	345	ferry	101	244	176	145	127	312	212	153	186	66	---

Off the Beaten Track

A special network of scenic routes recommended for people touring by car and motorcycle has been designated and signposted throughout Denmark. Known as the Marguerite Route, it is not a single route that can be taken from end to end but rather a series of routes comprising 3500km of roads in all. Some roads have been chosen for their rural appeal, others have been selected because they pass tourist attractions.

Most of the Marguerite Route is along secondary highways and minor country roads and, consequently, it usually makes an enjoyable alternative to a mundane zip along the main motorways.

The route is marked by a road sign consisting of a white daisy set against a brown backdrop. Virtually all Danish highway maps show the route, either with heavy green dots or solid green outlines. While it's fun to include sections of the Marguerite Route in any self-drive itinerary, at times you'll find alternative country roads parallel to the route to be just as scenic.

The Marguerite Route is not intended for cars pulling trailers, as some of the roads are narrow and cross small bridges. For more details on the route and sights along the way, pick up the small self-touring book *The Marguerite Route,* which is published in English, Danish and German by the Danish Tourist Board. The book can be purchased in larger tourist offices and at Statoil petrol stations.

in advance. Keep in mind that on weekends and holidays it's possible for every ferry on prime crossings to be completely booked. More information on car ferries, including reservation numbers, is given in the destination chapters throughout this book.

Unleaded and super petrol as well as diesel fuel are available. You'll generally find the most competitive prices at petrol stations along motorways. If you don't mind using self-service pumps, the unstaffed OK Benzin stations, which are adjacent to Brugsen grocery shops, charge about 20 øre less per litre than the name-brand stations. OK Benzin pumps are open 24 hours and accept 100kr notes and credit cards.

The Danish Road Directorate (☎ 70 10 10 40) offers a helpful 24-hour telephone service that can provide nationwide information on traffic conditions, roadworks, detours and ferry cancellations; information is available in English. It can also tell you approximately how long your journey should take.

Road Rules

In Denmark vehicles are driven on the right-hand side of the road. Cars and motorcycles must have dipped headlights on at all times and drivers are required to carry a warning triangle, in case of breakdown.

Seat belt use is mandatory. Children aged under three must be secured in a child seat or other approved child restraint appropriate to the child's age, size and weight. Children aged from three to six may use a child seat or booster seat instead of seat belts. Motorcycle riders must wear helmets.

Speed limits are generally 50km/h in towns and built-up areas, 80km/h on major roads and 110km/h on motorways. However, if you're towing a trailer the maximum speed you can travel on major roads and motorways is 70km/h.

Fines for speeding and other traffic offences, which can be collected on the spot, are costly. For each person in the car that isn't wearing a seat belt there's a 500kr fine. Using a hand-held mobile phone while driving is illegal and that too warrants a 500kr fine. Going through a red light carries a 1000kr fine. As for speeding it varies with the offence but, for example, driving 20km over the speed limit in a 50km/h zone can set you back a hefty 2000kr. Breaking a speed limit by more than 70% can trigger fines of up to 8000kr and the immediate confiscation of your driving licence. Although the latter occurrence may be a rare case of madness, Danish drivers do commonly exceed speed limits by a good 10km/h to 20km/h, so don't rely on the flow of traffic as an indication of whether your speed is within legal limits.

The authorities are very strict about driving under the influence of alcohol. It's illegal to drive with a blood-alcohol concentration of 0.05% or greater; driving under the influence will render drivers liable to stiff penalties and a possible prison sentence.

Emergencies

Motorways have emergency telephones at 2km intervals; an arrow on marker posts along the shoulder indicates the direction of the nearest phone. From ordinary payphones, dial ☎ 112 for emergencies.

Parking

To park on the street in the city centres, you usually have to buy a ticket from a kerbside machine, labelled *billetautomat*. This automated ticket machine has an LCD read-out showing the current time and as you insert coins the time advances. Put in enough money to advance the read-out to the time you desire for parking and then push the button to eject the ticket from the machine. Place the ticket, which shows the exact time that your ticket expires, face up inside the car windscreen.

The cost is generally from 5kr to 20kr an hour. Unless otherwise posted, street parking is usually free from 6pm to 8am, after 2pm on Saturday and all day on Sunday.

The billetautomat only charges for hours when a ticket is required, so if you were to park your car at 5pm and leave it overnight in a space where tickets are required from 8am to 6pm, and put in sufficient coins for two hours, the ticket would be valid until 9am the next morning.

In smaller towns, which are delightfully free of coin-hungry billetautomats, street parking is free within the time limits posted. These parking spaces will be marked by a blue sign with the letter 'P'; beneath it will be the time limit for free parking (*1 time* is one hour, *2 timer* is two hours). You will, however, need to use a windscreen parking disk. This is a flat plastic card with a clock face and a movable hour hand which must be set to show the time you parked the car.

Parking disks can be picked up for a small fee from tourist offices and petrol stations.

Parkering forbudt means 'no parking' and is generally accompanied by a round sign with a red diagonal slash. You can, however, stop for up to three minutes to unload bags and passengers. A round sign with a red 'X', or a sign saying *Stopforbud*, means that no stopping at all is allowed.

Rental

Rental cars are expensive in Denmark – you could easily pay as much to hire a car for just one day in Denmark as it would cost to hire one for a week across the border in Germany.

This is one area where it certainly can save you a bundle to do a little research in advance. You'll generally get the best deal on a car rental by booking through an international rental agency before you arrive in Denmark. Be sure to ask about promotional rates, pre-pay schemes and the like, then compare the options. Otherwise if you just show up at the counter at Copenhagen airport you're likely to find the rates for the cheapest cars (including VAT, insurance and unlimited kilometres) beginning at about 650kr per day, or 500kr per day for rentals of two days or more.

One of the better car rental deals that does not require booking before you arrive in Denmark is the weekend rate offered by some companies. This allows you to keep the car from Friday afternoon to Monday morning, including VAT and insurance, for about 1000kr. Be sure to request a plan that includes unlimited kilometres, as some plans begin tacking on an extra fee after 250km.

Avis, Europcar and Hertz are among the largest operators in Denmark with offices in major cities, airports and other ports of entry.

BICYCLE

Cycling is both a practical and an immensely popular way to get around Denmark. There are extensive cycling routes linking towns throughout the country, as well as bike lanes along the streets of most city centres.

Three out of four Danes own bicycles, and half use them on a regular basis. Postal workers are more likely to deliver mail by bicycle than by motor vehicle and it's not uncommon to see executives beating the rush hour by cycling through city traffic.

It's easy to travel with a bike in Denmark, even when you're not riding it, as bicycles can readily be taken on ferries and trains for a modest fee. On DSB trains, reservations should be made at least three hours prior to departure because bikes generally travel in a separate section of the train from the passengers. The DSB pamphlet *Cykler i tog*, available at larger train stations, has details.

If you prefer to leave your bike at home, it's easy to hire bikes throughout Denmark. Prices average around 50/275kr per day/week, although if you want a fancy multispeed bike it'll cost more. You might want to bring your own bike helmet, as helmets are not included with most hired bicycles.

Always be careful locking up your bike, especially if you're travelling with an expensive model, as bike theft is common in Denmark, particularly in larger cities such as Copenhagen and Århus.

For more information on cycling, see the special section 'Cycling in Denmark' following this chapter.

HITCHING

Hitching is never entirely safe in any country in the world and we don't recommend it. Travellers who decide to hitch should clearly understand that they are taking a small but potentially serious risk. People who do choose to hitch will be safer if they travel in pairs and let someone know where they are planning to go.

At any rate, hitching is not a common practice in Denmark and generally not a very rewarding one. Keep in mind that hitching is illegal on motorways. Incidentally, those Danes who do hitch usually only do so when travelling outside their own country.

BOAT

An extensive network of ferries links Denmark's many populated islands. For ferry information see the Getting There & Away sections of relevant destinations throughout this book.

LOCAL TRANSPORT

All cities and towns of any size in Denmark are served by a local bus system. As a general rule, the main terminal for local buses is adjacent to the train station or ferry depot. Copenhagen also has a convenient local train system called the S-train and is constructing a new underground Metro system. For more details on local transport, see the relevant destination sections.

Taxi

Taxis are readily available throughout Denmark in city centres, at train stations and near major shopping centres. If you see a taxi with a lit *fri* sign, you can wave it down, but you can always phone for a taxi as well.

Fares are typically from 20kr to 25kr at flag fall and from 10kr to 13kr per kilometre, with the higher rates prevailing at night and on weekends. There's no need for tipping because a service charge is included in the fare.

New Trains A'Comin'

Copenhagen is constructing a new underground Metro system that was originally scheduled to be fully operational by 2003. However, because of construction snafus only part of the system will open by that date and the final completion will be delayed to at least 2005.

When it does finally open, it will extend 21km, of which half will be underground. In some places it will be side by side with existing S-train stations and in other places there will be new underground stations. Of most interest to travellers will be the line from Copenhagen airport to Kongens Nytorv and Nørreport stations. Most of the rest of the Metro will be serving commuters in the city suburbs.

The system will be fully automated with trains operating as often as every two minutes during the rush hour.

ORGANISED TOURS

Denmark is so small and public transport systems so extensive that organised tours are not all that common.

The main exception is Copenhagen, where day tours explore the metropolitan area and the major sights of North Zealand; see the Organised Tours section of the Copenhagen chapter for details.

A few other Danish tourist offices offer walking tours of their towns and occasionally provide more extensive city tours. For information on sightseeing tours within a specific city, see the relevant destination section.

Cycling in Denmark

Denmark prides itself on being a bicycle-friendly country. With a gentle terrain that tops out at a mere 173m, cycling routes are well suited for recreational cyclists, including families with children. The country is crossed with thousands of kilometres of established cycling routes, some parallelling lightly trafficked roads and others passing through nature preserves and woods.

Denmark is a country of cyclists. Fully half of its citizens ride bicycles on a regular basis; businesspeople unabashedly cycle into their corporate parking spaces; and one of the prime minister's first acts in the international arena was leading cyclists on an anti-nuclear protest to France.

Danish cyclists have rights that in many other countries are reserved for motorists. There are bicycle lanes along major city roads and through

Previous page: See some fun? Just get off your bike and come on in. No problems parking. (Photographer: Ned Friary)

NATIONAL CYCLING ROUTES

central areas; road signs are posted for bicycle traffic; and bicycle racks can be found at grocery shops, museums and many other public places.

For more details of cycling as a mode of transport, see under Bicycle in the Getting Around chapter.

Cycling Maps

There are excellent maps available for every corner of Denmark that show not only cycling routes but also camping grounds, hostels and sights along the way. These maps also indicate which of Denmark's vehicle roads have cycle paths and which vehicle roads prohibit bicycles altogether.

When buying maps, be sure to request an English version; some maps are produced in Danish, English and German versions, while others combine all three languages on the same map. The best all-Denmark map for cyclists is *Cykelferiekort*, a 1:500,000-scale map published by Dansk Cyklist Forbund, the main Danish cycling organisation. It costs 49kr.

Detailed cycling maps cover each of the 14 *amt* (counties) in Denmark. Most are based on maps from Kort-og Matrikelstyrelsen, the company that makes Denmark's highest-quality road maps. The county maps have greater detail than the all-Denmark map, showing such things as grocery stores, cycle repair shops and topography.

The maps are as follows:

- Bornholms Amt (island of Bornholm), 1:50,000, 40kr
- Frederiksborg Amt (North Zealand), 1:100,000, 50kr
- Fyns Amt (Funen county, including Langeland and Ærø), 1:100,000, 75kr
- Københavns Amt (greater Copenhagen area), 1:50,000, 20kr
- Nordjyllands Amt (northernmost part of Jutland), 1:200,000, 55kr
- Ribe Amt (includes Ribe and Esbjerg area), 1:100,000, 50kr
- Ringkjøbing Amt (central part of Jutland's west coast), 1:100,000, 50kr
- Roskilde Amt (Zealand west and south of Copenhagen), 1:100,000, 60kr
- Storstrøms Amt (southernmost part of Zealand, plus Møn, Falster and Lolland), 1:100,000, 60kr
- Sønderjyllands Amt (southernmost part of Jutland), 1:100,000, 50kr
- Vejle Amt (south-east–central Jutland), 1:100,000, 50kr
- Vestsjællands Amt (western Zealand), 1:100,000, 50kr
- Viborg Amt (north-west–central Jutland), 1:100,000, 60kr
- Århus Amt (greater Århus area), 1:100,000, 80kr

Purchasing Maps

All of the maps listed here can be ordered from Dansk Cyklist Forbund (see under Resources). Once in Denmark, the county maps are readily available at larger tourist offices and the whole series of maps can be purchased at bookshops throughout the country.

Resources

The Danish cycling federation, Dansk Cyklist Forbund (☎ 33 32 31 21, fax 33 32 76 83, ⓦ www.dcf.dk), has its headquarters at Rømersgade 7, 1362 Copenhagen K. Cycling maps can be ordered directly from it, with the addition of postage fees; contact the office for details.

CykelGuide, a brochure summarising (in Danish) the national and regional cycle routes of Denmark, is available from the national Road Directorate: Vejdirektoratet (☎ 70 10 10 40), Trafikantservice, Post-boks 1569, Niels Juels Gade 13, 1020 Copenhagen K. This brochure can also be picked up free at tourist offices in Denmark.

There are two free regional cycling publications in English, *Cycling Holidays in West Jutland* and *Funen and the Isles – a bike's eye view*, that suggest routes, things to see and do, and accommodation options along the way. They're available from tourist offices in Denmark.

National Cycling Routes

Over the past decade Denmark has established a mind-boggling network of regional and national cycling routes. For distance cyclists the 10 national cycling routes, which collectively cover more than 3500km, offer a wide range of options that can take you from one end of the country to the other.

1. The West Coast Route (Vestkystruten)

This route runs 550km from Rudbøl on the German border to Skagen at the northernmost tip of Denmark. Along the way it passes Denmark's longest unbroken stretch of sand and sea – though keep in mind the coast is also windswept. You'll keep more of the wind at your back if you take this route heading from south to north. You won't need to trudge across sand, but there are many gravel sections, so it's best suited for a sturdy mountain bike.

2. Copenhagen to Hanstholm

Covering 420km, this route takes you from the bustle of Copenhagen across quiet North Zealand and on by ferry to Ebeltoft, a charming introduction to Jutland. From there it goes to the summer resort of Grenaa and slices west across central Jutland, taking in farmland and fjords before ending at the country's newest port town, Hanstholm. There are some gravel stretches, but the route is mostly on asphalt roads.

3. The Old Military Road (Hærvejen)

Established as Denmark's first national cycling route in 1989, this route actually dates back more than a millennium, having once been travelled by nomadic hunters and Viking armies. It runs 450km from Padborg to Skagen, along Jutland's central ridge, which minimises the need to cross rivers and fjords. With its lengthy history, it's not sur-prising that cyclists pass numerous rune stones, ancient barrows and centuries-old churches along the way.

4. Copenhagen to Søndervig

This 310km route out of the capital heads west via Roskilde with its Viking ships and royal tombs and on to a ferry crossing from Kalund-borg to Århus. From there you'll have a chance to switch gears as the route takes you through the Lake District and Denmark's hilliest country before depositing you at Søndervig where you could trade in your bike for windsurfing gear. It's mostly along municipal roads.

5. The East Coast Route (Østkystruten)

From Sønderborg in southern Jutland to Skagen at the northern tip of Jutland, this route meanders its way along the east coast, winding around so many peninsulas, spits and harbours that it encompasses some 650km – making it the longest of all national cycling routes. As the east coast tends to be more protected than the west, you'll encounter far less wind, not to mention a fine variety of coastal scenery. There are also some fun places to stop along the way, such as Århus, which comes up around the halfway mark.

6. Copenhagen to Esbjerg

Funen has lovely countryside and rolling hills and this route takes in some of them, as well as circling past the fairy-tale sights of Odense. In all, it covers 330km from Copenhagen to Esbjerg, Jutland's second city and Denmark's main port of entry for sea passengers from the UK. This route is particularly attractive in late spring when much of the countryside is ablaze with a brilliant yellow carpet of flowering rapeseed.

7. Gedser to Sjællands Odde

This 230km route follows a more regional track, running from Gedser at the southern tip of Falster to Sjællands Odde at the north-west of Zealand. Falster is a straight and level shot, whereas the journey though Zealand is a bit more varied, passing by the old city of Næstved and some lovely wooded countryside near Sorø. If you would like to lengthen the journey it's possible to take a ferry from Sjællands Odde to Ebeltoft and pick up route No 5 from there.

8. Rudbøl to Møn

After hugging virtually the entire Danish-German border, where most historical sites are dedicated to land struggles and battlefields, this 360km route winds through the agreeable coastal cities of Sønderborg, Faaborg, Svendborg and Rudkøbing. It then crosses Lolland and Falster, with their abundant agricultural fields, before taking in Møn's medieval sites and ending at the white cliffs of Møns Klint, one of Denmark's most stunning coastal vistas.

9. Rødby to Helsingør

This relatively short route covers just 250km from Rødby in sleepy Lolland to Helsingør, the busy port city that's home to Kronborg Slot, the castle made famous in Shakespeare's *Hamlet*. In between there's rural countryside, the seaside village of Præstø, the historic town of Køge, Bakken amusement park and museums at Rungsted and Humlebæk. All in all, a good route for those who want to mix cycling with stops at some of eastern Zealand's sightseeing attractions.

10. Around Bornholm

With hundreds of kilometres of sea between Bornholm and the rest of Denmark, this is strictly a one-island national cycling route – but it doesn't disappoint. Bornholm, with its granite-based geology, offers scenery not found elsewhere in Denmark, as well as unique medieval round churches and picturesque coastal villages. The Bornholm route winds along an enjoyable 115km network of cycling paths utilising former railway lines and forest trails.

Overnighting along the Way

As distances between villages and towns are not great in Denmark, you'll seldom be very far from one of Denmark's 500 camping grounds or one of its 100 hostels. Indeed there are some places, such as the Sorø hostel in southern Zealand, that are located right on a cycling route.

Many camping grounds, particularly those close to cycling routes, have special areas set aside for cyclists and as a general rule they can often make space for cycling campers, even after the camping ground has been closed to motorists. All camping grounds with a four-star or five-star rating have bicycle racks and a covered bicycle repair area where tools can be borrowed; some of the camping grounds with fewer than four stars have these facilities as well.

In addition to conventional camping grounds, some 750 farmers throughout Denmark allow cyclists to pitch a tent on their property. It's primitive camping, but the cost is just 15kr a night. The booklet *Overnatning i det fri*, which is published by Dansk Cyklist Forbund and costs 90kr, lists the location of the farms where camping is allowed.

Rules of the Road

Just as cyclists' rights are taken seriously in Denmark, so too are their responsibilities. Here are some of the traffic regulations that are directly relevant to cyclists.

- All traffic in Denmark, both bicycle and motor vehicle, drives on the right-hand side of the road.
- Cyclists are obliged to obey traffic lights, pedestrian right-of-ways and most other road rules that apply to motor vehicles.
- When making a left turn at crossings, a large left turn is mandatory; that is, you must cycle straight across the intersecting road, staying on the right, before turning left into the right-hand lane of the new road. Do not cross diagonally.
- Use hand signals to indicate turns: your left arm should be outstretched prior to a left turn, and your right arm outstretched before a right turn.
- When entering a roundabout (traffic circle), yield to vehicles already in the roundabout.
- If you're transporting children, the bicycle must have two independent brakes. A maximum of two children under the age of six can be carried on the bicycle or in an attached trailer.

Bicycle Rentals

There are lots of places around Denmark where you can rent three-speed bicycles for around 50kr a day, but they're more suited to local cruising than to cycling across the country.

Finding a good bike to hire for distance touring can be a challenge, but two shops in Copenhagen carry sturdy touring bikes along with regular stock. Københavns Cykler (☎ 33 33 86 13) at Central Station and Østerport Cykler (☎ 33 33 85 13) at the Østerport Station both have 24-speed Trek mountain bikes and high-quality city bikes that can be hired for 900kr a week, 1400kr for two weeks and 2000kr for a month.

Cycling Tours

Denmark's cycling maps make it easy to self-plan your own tour as they show places to stay and all sorts of sightseeing spots, such as castles, museums and historic sights. However, if you're interested in joining a packaged cycling tour, the Dansk Cyklist Forbund (see under Resources) arranges tours, as do the following companies.

BikeDenmark (☎ 48 48 58 00, e bikedenmark@bikedenmark.dk) Oluf Poulsens Allé 1, 3480 Fredensborg

Turistgruppen Vestlyllandferie (☎ 75 28 74 00, e tgv@tvg.dk) Torvet 5, 6830 Nørre Nebel

Sydfyns Turistbureau (☎ 62 21 09 80, e sydfyntb@post7tele.dk) Centrumpladsen 4, 5700 Svendborg

Prices will vary by tour, depending largely on what kind of accommodation is provided. For those willing to camp or stay at hostels, weeklong packages can be under 2000kr; opt for small hotels or inns and the price can surpass 5000kr.

Cycling Races

Each year Denmark hosts more than 150 cycle races. Widely scattered, these events cover virtually every nook and cranny of the country. All but a handful take place between April and September. Most are small regional races that cover just 25km to 100km but there are also some grand cross-country events. The longest cycle touring event in Denmark is the Århus-Copenhagen Race in early June, which covers 359km and attracts 4000 participants. You can find out more about these events, or even enrol online for the next race, at w www.aarhus-koebenhavn.dk.

For a complete list of all races request a copy of the annually updated brochure *Cykel-motion* from Dansk Cyklist Forbund (see the Resources section earlier) or tourist offices.

Copenhagen

pop 1,785,000

Copenhagen (København) is Scandinavia's largest and liveliest city, home to a quarter of all Danes.

Despite its size, Copenhagen is an appealing and still largely low-rise city comprised of block after block of period, six-storey buildings. The church steeples add a nice punctuation to the skyline and only a few modern hotels burst up to mar the scene.

Capital of Denmark since the early 15th century, Copenhagen expanded by gradually radiating out from its centre; consequently most of the city's foremost historical and cultural sites remain concentrated within a relatively small area. A variety of parks, gardens, water fountains, squares and green areas lace the city centre. Along the waterfront you'll discover the scenic row houses that line Nyhavn, the famed statue of the *Little Mermaid* and the canal-cut district of Christianshavn.

For a big city, Copenhagen is surprisingly easy to get around. It's a particularly pleasant place for walking, as many of the sightseeing areas and shopping districts in the city centre are reserved for pedestrians. For those who prefer to move at a faster pace, there are bicycle lanes on Copenhagen's main roads as well as an excellent metropolitan bus and train system.

A cosmopolitan city, Copenhagen boasts a plethora of sightseeing and entertainment possibilities. For music lovers and other revellers there's an active nightlife scene that buzzes into the early hours of the morning, and for sightseers the city has a treasure-trove of old churches, museums and castles to explore.

HISTORY

The city of Copenhagen was founded in 1167 by Bishop Absalon, who constructed a fortress on Slotsholmen Island, fortifying a small and previously unprotected harbourside village. The bishop had been granted the land by King Valdemar I, who wanted to

Highlights

- Have a blast at Tivoli, the famed amusement park in the city centre
- Linger over a cold beer at a pavement cafe on scenic Nyhavn canal
- Visit Copenhagen's world-class museums, most notably Nationalmuseet and Ny Carlsberg Glyptotek
- Board a canal boat for a guided tour of the historic waterfront
- Club-hop your way through the city's spirited nightlife scene
- Peer down on the city from the rooftops of the Rundetårn and Vor Frelsers Kirke
- Enjoy shopping and street entertainment on Strøget, the world's longest pedestrian mall
- Grab one of the free City Bikes and join the Danes pedalling about the city

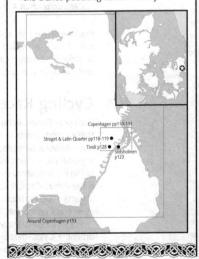

Copenhagen pp110-111

Strøget & Latin Quarter pp118-119 ●
Tivoli p128 ●
Slotsholmen p123

Around Copenhagen p153

put an end to the free movement of marauding Wends who were staging frequent raids along the East Zealand coast.

After the fortification was constructed, the harbourside village grew in importance and took on the name Kømandshavn (Merchant's Port), which was later condensed to København. Absalon's fortress stood until 1369, when it was destroyed in an attack on the town by the powerful Hanseatic states.

In 1376 construction began on a new Slotsholmen fortification, Copenhagen Castle, and in 1416 King Erik of Pomerania took up residence at the site, marking the beginning of Copenhagen's role as the capital of Denmark.

Still, it wasn't until the reign of Christian IV, in the first half of the 17th century, that the city was endowed with much of its splendour. A lofty Renaissance designer, Christian IV began an ambitious construction scheme, building two new castles and many other grand edifices including the Rundetårn observatory and Børsen, Europe's first stock exchange.

By the start of the 18th century Copenhagen's population was 60,000, but in 1711 the bubonic plague reduced it by one-third. Later, two fires, one in 1728 and the other in 1795, wiped out large tracts of the city, including most of its timber buildings. However, the worst scourge in the city's history is generally regarded as the unprovoked British bombardment of Copenhagen in 1807, during the Napoleonic Wars. The attack targeted the heart of the city, inflicting numerous civilian casualties and setting hundreds of homes, churches and public buildings on fire. In the melee that followed, the British captured the Danish fleet and took it as war booty, ostensibly to prevent it from falling into the hands of Napoleon, who had been pressuring a neutral Denmark to close its ports to the English.

Copenhagen flourished in the 19th and 20th centuries, expanding beyond its old city walls and establishing a reputation as a centre for culture and the arts.

ORIENTATION

The main train station, Central Station (also called Hovedbanegården or København H), is flanked to the west by the main hotel zone and to the east by Tivoli amusement park. Opposite the northern corner of Tivoli is Rådhuspladsen, the central city square and the main terminus for city buses.

The world's longest pedestrian mall, Strøget, runs through Copenhagen's city centre between Rådhuspladsen and Kongens Nytorv, the square at the head of the Nyhavn canal. Strøget, which abounds with a variety of shopping, dining and entertainment possibilities, is actually made up of five continuous streets: Frederiksberggade, Nygade, Vimmelskaftet, Amagertorv and Østergade. Pedestrian walkways run north from Strøget into the triangle of streets forming the Latin Quarter.

Maps

The tourist office produces free, detailed, four-colour maps of Copenhagen with street indexes and keys for major attractions. It covers the entire greater Copenhagen area and includes a detailed blow-up of the city centre. You can pick one up from the airport information desk, the tourist office or the front desk of most hotels.

Although there's not much that the free tourist map doesn't show, you can also buy commercial maps at bookshops. These maps are larger and have more complete indexes; one of the best is *Kraks citykort over København*.

INFORMATION
Tourist Offices

Copenhagen Information, which is the city tourist office (☎ 70 22 24 42, fax 70 22 24 52, ℮ touristinfo@woco.dk), Bernstorffsgade 1, is just north of Central Station. Its information desk distributes the useful booklet *Copenhagen This Week*, as well as free maps and brochures covering destinations throughout Denmark; there's also a room- and hotel-booking service on site. Copenhagen Information is open 10am to 4pm Monday to Friday and 10am to 1pm (to 2pm in July and August) on Saturday from May to October; during the rest of the year it's open 10am to 4pm Tuesday to Friday and 10am to 1pm on Saturday.

Use It (☎ 33 73 06 20, fax 33 73 06 49, ℮ useit@ui.dk), at Rådhusstræde 13, is a

COPENHAGEN

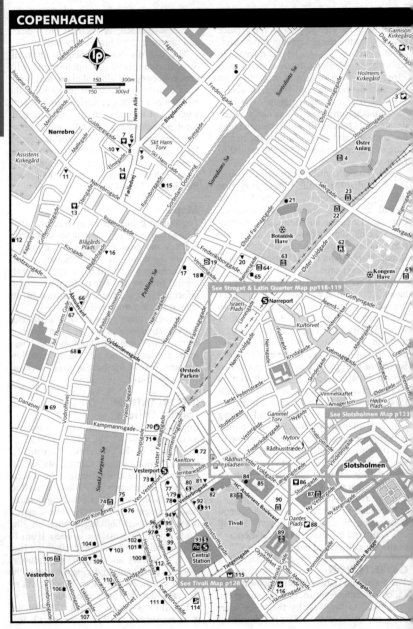

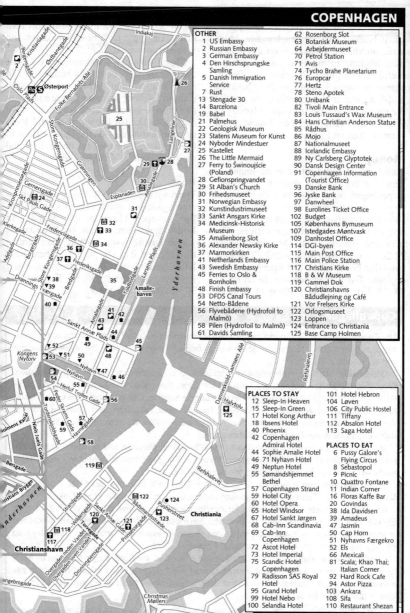

COPENHAGEN

OTHER
1 US Embassy
2 Russian Embassy
3 German Embassy
4 Den Hirschsprungske Samling
5 Danish Immigration Service
7 Rust
13 Stengade 30
14 Barcelona
19 Babel
21 Palmehus
22 Geologisk Museum
23 Statens Museum for Kunst
24 Nyboder Mindestuer
25 Kastellet
26 The Little Mermaid
27 Ferry to Świnoujście (Poland)
28 Gefionspringvandet
29 St Alban's Church
30 Frihedsmuseet
31 Norwegian Embassy
32 Kunstindustrimuseet
33 Sankt Ansgars Kirke
34 Medicinsk-Historisk Museum
35 Amalienborg Slot
36 Alexander Newsky Kirke
37 Marmorkirken
41 Netherlands Embassy
42 Swedish Embassy
45 Ferries to Oslo & Bornholm
48 Finish Embassy
53 DFDS Canal Tours
54 Netto-Bådene
56 Flyvebådene (Hydrofoil to Malmö)
58 Pilen (Hydrofoil to Malmö)
61 Davids Samling

62 Rosenborg Slot
63 Botanisk Museum
64 Arbejdermuseet
70 Petrol Station
71 Avis
74 Tycho Brahe Planetarium
76 Europcar
77 Hertz
78 Steno Apotek
80 Unibank
82 Tivoli Main Entrance
83 Louis Tussaud's Wax Museum
84 Hans Christian Anderson Statue
85 Rådhus
86 Mojo
87 Nationalmuseet
88 Icelandic Embassy
89 Ny Carlsberg Glyptotek
90 Dansk Design Center
91 Copenhagen Information (Tourist Office)
93 Danske Bank
96 Jyske Bank
97 Danwheel
98 Eurolines Ticket Office
102 Budget
105 Københavns Bymuseum
107 Istedgades Møntvask
109 Danhostel Office
114 DGI-byen
115 Main Post Office
116 Main Police Station
117 Christians Kirke
118 B & W Museum
119 Gammel Dok
120 Christianshavns Bådudlejning og Café
121 Vor Frelsers Kirke
122 Orlogsmuseet
123 Loppen
124 Entrance to Christiania
125 Base Camp Holmen

PLACES TO STAY
12 Sleep-In Heaven
15 Sleep-In Green
17 Hotel Kong Arthur
18 Ibsens Hotel
40 Phoenix
42 Copenhagen Admiral Hotel
44 Sophie Amalie Hotel
46 71 Nyhavn Hotel
49 Neptun Hotel
55 Sømandshjemmet Bethel
57 Copenhagen Strand
59 Hotel City
60 Hotel Opera
65 Hotel Windsor
67 Hotel Sankt Jørgen
68 Cab-Inn Scandinavia
69 Cab-Inn Copenhagen
72 Ascot Hotel
73 Hotel Imperial
75 Scandic Hotel Copenhagen
79 Radisson SAS Royal Hotel
95 Grand Hotel
99 Hotel Nebo
100 Selandia Hotel

101 Hotel Hebron
104 Løven
106 City Public Hostel
111 Tiffany
112 Absalon Hotel
113 Saga Hotel

PLACES TO EAT
6 Pussy Galore's Flying Circus
8 Sebastopol
9 Picnic
10 Quattro Fontane
11 Indian Corner
16 Floras Kaffe Bar
20 Govindas
38 Ida Davidsen
39 Amadeus
47 Jasmin
50 Cap Horn
51 Nyhavns Færgekro
52 Els
66 Mexicali
81 Scala; Khao Thai; Italian Corner
92 Hard Rock Cafe
94 Astor Pizza
103 Ankara
108 Sifa
110 Restaurant Shezan

terrific alternative information centre catering to young budget travellers but open to all; it books rooms, stores luggage, holds mail, provides information on everything from hitching to nightlife and produces a useful general guide, *Playtime* – all free of charge. It's open 9am to 7pm daily between mid-June and mid-September; the rest of the year it's open 11am to 4pm Monday to Wednesday, 11am to 6pm on Thursday and 11am to 2pm on Friday.

Money

Banks are plentiful and can be found on nearly every second corner in central Copenhagen. Most are open 9.30am to 4pm on weekdays (to 6pm on Thursday).

You'll usually get better rates by going to one of the Forex exchange offices. The main one, right in Central Station (☎ 33 11 22 20), is open 8am to 9pm daily. There are two other Forex offices in Copenhagen, one opposite Tivoli at Vesterbrogade 2B (☎ 33 93 77 70) that's open 10am to 6pm on weekdays and the other at Nørre Voldgade 90 (☎ 33 32 81 00) in the Nørreport area that's open 9am to 7pm on weekdays and 9am to 3pm on Saturday.

Most banks in Copenhagen have ATMs, many of them accessible 24 hours a day. In addition to regular ATMs, there are specialised 24-hour, cash-exchange machines that change major foreign currencies (bills only) into Danish kroner at several locations, including outside the Danske Bank in Central Station, the Unibank on Axeltorv and the Jyske Bank at Vesterbrogade 9.

Post

The main post office (☎ 33 41 56 00), on Tietgensgade just south-east of Central Station, is open 11am to 6pm Monday to Friday and 10am to 1pm on Saturday. If you're having poste restante mail sent to Copenhagen, it can be picked up there; have letters addressed to: addressee, Poste Restante, Main Post Office, Tietgensgade 37, 1500 Copenhagen V.

Copenhagen Card

The Copenhagen Card is a tourist pass that allows unlimited travel on buses and trains in Copenhagen and throughout North Zealand, as well as free admission to most of the region's museums and attractions.

Copenhagen attractions offering free admission to cardholders include Tivoli, Ny Carlsberg Glyptotek, Nationalmuseet, Statens Museum for Kunst, Rundetårn, Vor Frelsers Kirke, Zoologisk Have, Arken, Zoologisk Museum, Den Hirschsprungske Samling, Orlogsmuseet, Jens Olsen's clock, Kunstindustrimuseet, Musikhistorisk Museum, Frihedsmuseet, Arbejdermuseet, Guinness World of Records Museum, Ripley's Believe It or Not!, Louis Tussaud's Wax Museum and all the Slotsholmen sights except De Kongelige Repræsentationslokaler.

The card also confers free admission to the Viking Ship Museum and cathedral in Roskilde, Frederiksborg Slot in Hillerød, Karen Blixen Museet in Rungsted, Frilandsmuseet in Lyngby, Danmarks Akvarium in Charlottenlund and the museums in Køge.

Discounted admission is available to some other sights, including Rosenborg Slot, Amalienborg Slot, Danish Design Center, Experimentarium and the Louisiana museum in Humlebæk.

An adult card costs 175/295/395kr for one/two/three consecutive days; a child's card costs 85/145/195kr for the same period. Cards can be purchased at Central Station, at tourist offices and in some hotels. Days are calculated on a 24-hour basis; for example, if you begin a one-day card on Saturday at 6pm, it's valid until Sunday at 5:59pm.

If you want to run through a lot of sightseeing in a few days, the Copenhagen Card can be a real bargain. However, for a more leisurely exploration of select places it may work out cheaper to pay individual admission charges and use one of the transport passes (see the Getting Around section later in this chapter for details).

If you're not using the poste restante service, the post office in Central Station will generally prove more convenient. It's open 8am to 9pm on weekdays, 9am to 4pm on Saturday and 10am to 4pm on Sunday.

Telephone & Fax

Payphones can readily be found in public places such as shopping arcades and train stations. You can make international phone calls from any public payphone. Faxes can be sent from hotels and from larger post offices.

Email & Internet Access

The main public library, Hovedbiblioteket (☎ 33 73 60 60), in the Latin Quarter at Krystalgade 15, has computers with Internet access that can be used free of charge for up to 30 minutes, but the queuing time can easily exceed an hour.

If you just want to check your email, a better bet is to drop by Kongelige Bibliotek (☎ 33 47 47 47), Christians Brygge, the national research library on the southern side of Slotsholmen, where more than 100 online computers fill the hallways and visitors can make a quick online run as long as no-one else is waiting to use the computer.

A third freebie is Use It (☎ 33 73 06 20), the youth information centre at Rådhusstræde 13, which offers Internet access but has only three computers available, so online time is generally limited and there can be lengthy queues.

Paid options include Babel (☎ 33 33 93 38), Copenhagen's oldest Internet cafe at Frederiksborggade 33 and the more central Netpoint (☎ 33 42 60 00), in the Radisson SAS Royal Hotel at Hammerichsgade 1. Both places provide Internet access for 30kr an hour.

Digital Resources

Four Web sites that will link you to a wealth of information in English are: W www.woco .dk (run by Wonderful Copenhagen, the tourism office); W www.kbhbase.copenhagen city.dk (by the city of Copenhagen); W www .aok.dk/Copenhagen/Visiting_Copenhagen (in association with the *Copenhagen Post* newspaper); and W www.useit.dk (run by Use It, the youth information centre). Other sites are listed throughout the text under specific attractions and destinations.

Gay & Lesbian Travellers

The Danish national organisation for gays and lesbians, Landsforeningen for Bøsser og Lesbiske (LBL; ☎ 33 13 19 48, e lbl@ lbl.dk), has its headquarters at Teglgårdsstræde 13 in the Latin Quarter. The facility includes a library, bookshop, informal cafe, various gay and lesbian support groups and counselling services.

A network of gay and gay-friendly businesses in the city is Copenhagen Gay Life (W www.copenhagen-gay-life.dk). The Web site includes useful tourist information and listings in English, as well as links to LBL and other gay organisations.

For information on gay and lesbian nightlife, see the Entertainment section later in this chapter.

Travel Agencies

Kilroy Travels (☎ 33 11 00 44) at Skindergade 28, Wasteels (☎ 33 14 46 33) at Skoubogade 6 and STA Travel (☎ 33 14 15 01) at Fiolstræde 18, all specialise in student and budget travel. All three are north of Strøget, just a few minutes' walk from each other.

There are numerous general travel agencies around the city, including Inter-Travel (☎ 33 15 00 77), opposite the Use It office at Frederiksholms Kanal 2.

Bookshops

Substantial bookshops with good selections of English-language titles, travel guides and maps include GAD (☎ 33 15 05 58), on Strøget at Vimmelskaftet 32, Politiken Boghallen (☎ 33 47 25 60) at Rådhuspladsen 37 and Arnold Busck (☎ 33 73 35 00) at Købmagergade 49 in the Latin Quarter.

Nordisk Korthandel (☎ 33 38 26 38), Studiestræde 26, sells guidebooks as well as an extensive range of cycling and hiking trail maps of Denmark and elsewhere in Europe. If you're specifically after travel guidebooks, Kilroy Travels (☎ 33 11 00 44), a travel agent at Skindergade 28, has a comprehensive selection of Lonely Planet titles.

You can buy foreign newspapers and the English-language *Copenhagen Post* at most international hotels and at some of the larger newspaper kiosks, such as those in Central Station and along the pedestrian-only Strøget.

Libraries

Hovedbiblioteket (☎ 33 73 60 60), the central library at Krystalgade 15, holds some international magazines and newspapers in English that visitors are free to browse. It's open 10am to 7pm on weekdays and 10am to 2pm on Saturday.

Kongelige Bibliotek (☎ 33 47 47 47), Christians Brygge, on the southern side of Slotsholmen, is primarily a research library, but it's also open to the public and has a collection of foreign newspapers. It's open 10am to 7pm Monday to Saturday. Both libraries have online computers.

Laundry

Coin laundries (look for the word *møntvask*) are not terribly difficult to find around the Copenhagen. There's one near the hotel district, Istedgades Møntvask (☎ 33 24 46 15) at Istedgade 45.

Watching the Clock

This elaborate clock, designed by Danish astro-mechanic Jens Olsen (1872–1945) and built at a cost of one million kroner, is of special note to chronometer buffs. The clock displays not only the local time but also solar time, sidereal time, sunrises and sunsets, firmament and celestial pole migration, planet revolutions, the Gregorian calendar and even changing holidays such as Easter. Of its many wheels, the fastest turns once every 10 seconds, while the slowest will finish its first revolution after 25,753 years.

The clock was first put into motion in 1955 and its weights are wound weekly. It can be viewed in a side room off the foyer of *rådhus* (city hall) 10am to 4pm on weekdays and 10am to 1pm on Saturday. Admission costs 10kr for adults, 5kr for children.

Medical Services

Frederiksberg Hospital (☎ 38 16 38 16), west of the city centre at Nordre Fasanvej 57, has a 24-hour emergency ward.

Private doctor visits (☎ 33 93 63 00 for referrals) usually cost around 400kr.

There are numerous pharmacies around the city; look for the sign *apotek*. Steno Apotek (☎ 33 14 82 66), at Vesterbrogade 6 opposite Central Station, is open 24 hours.

Emergency

Dial ☎ 112 for police, ambulance or fire services; the call can be made without coins from public phones.

There's a small police office (☎ 33 15 38 01) in Central Station and a major police station (☎ 33 14 14 48) at Politigården, a couple of blocks south-east of the main post office.

WALKING TOUR

Taking a half-day's walk from rådhus (city hall) to the *Little Mermaid* is a good way to get oriented in Copenhagen and to take in many of the city's central sights. As you stroll the narrow streets, be sure to look up now and then to appreciate the gargoyles and other ornamentations that decorate many of the older buildings.

Major sights are marked with an asterisk (*) and described in greater detail under separate headings at the end of this Walking Tour section.

Before heading off, you might want to take a closer look at the red-brick **rådhus**. The building was completed in 1905 and displays elements of 19th-century national Romanticism, medieval Danish design and northern Italian architecture, the latter most notably in the central courtyard. You can see the theatre-like interior for free or take a tour to the top of the 105m tower (☎ 33 66 25 82) at noon Monday to Saturday from October to May, at 10am, noon and 2pm Monday to Friday & noon on Saturday from June to September (20kr).

Rådhuspladsen, the large central square fronting the city hall, is the main terminus for city buses. On the south-western side of the plaza stands a **statue** of Hans Christian Andersen and a **water fountain** with some spouting dragons, while on the eastern side, as you face the Palace Hotel, there's a noteworthy column capped with a bronze **statue of two Vikings** blowing *lurs* (horns).

From Rådhuspladsen, be sure to look over at the Unibank building on the northwestern corner of Vesterbrogade and HC Andersens Blvd. The building is topped with a unique **barometer** that displays a girl on her bicycle when the weather is fair or with an umbrella when rain is predicted. This charming bronze sculpture was created in 1936 by the Danish artist E Utzon-Frank.

From Rådhuspladsen walk down **Strøget** which, after a couple of blocks, cuts between two spirited pedestrian squares, **Gammel Torv** and **Nytorv**. A popular summertime gathering spot in Gammel Torv is the gilded **Caritas Fountain**, erected in 1608 by Christian IV and marking what was once the old city's central market. As in days past, pedlars still sell jewellery, flowers and fruit on the square. At the south-western corner of Nytorv is **Domhuset**, an imposing neoclassical building that once served as the city hall and now houses the city's law courts.

Continuing down Strøget, you'll pass **Helligåndskirken** (the Church of the Holy Ghost), one wing of which dates from medieval times. The interior of the church, most of which was rebuilt after a fire in 1732, is sometimes open to the public on weekday afternoons.

Also along the Amagertorv section of Strøget are some of the city's finest speciality shops, including **Royal Copenhagen Porcelain** and **Georg Jensen**, the latter housing a free display of early 20th-century silverwork. The WØ Larsen pipe shop, diagonally opposite Georg Jensen at Amagertorv 9, boasts another little free speciality exhibition, **Tobaksmuseet** (*Tobacco Museum;* ☎ *33 12 20 50; open 10am-at least 5pm Mon-Sat),* with interesting displays of hand-carved pipes.

The adjacent square, **Højbro Plads**, which contains a water fountain with bronze storks, is a popular venue for street musicians. At the southern end of this elongated square is a **statue** of city founder Bishop Absalon on horseback; behind it, the fitting backdrop is

Slotsholmen, where the bishop erected Copenhagen's first fortress. If you look due east from the northern end of Højbro Plads you'll see the steeple of **Nikolaj Kirke**. The tower of this church dates from the 16th century, although most of the church was rebuilt in 1915. No longer consecrated, the church is now owned by the municipality and is used for contemporary art exhibits.

At the end of Strøget you'll reach **Kongens Nytorv**, a square boasting an equestrian statue of its designer, Christian V, and circled by gracious old buildings. Notable from Christian V's era are *Charlottenborg, a 17th-century Dutch Baroque palace that houses Det Kongelige Kunstakademi (The Royal Academy of Fine Arts), and the 1685 **Thott's Palæ** (Thott's Mansion), which now houses the French embassy. There are also some 100-year-old buildings, including the department store **Magasin du Nord**, with its ornate cupola, and **Det Kongelige Teater** (the Royal Theatre), fronted by statues of the playwrights Adam Oehlenschläger and Ludvig Holberg. The theatre, which is the home of Den Kongelige Ballet (the Royal Danish Ballet) and Den Kongelige Opera (the Royal Danish Opera), has two stages, one on either side of Tordenskjoldsgade. An **archway** with a mosaic depicting Danish poets and artists spans the road connecting the two stages.

To the east of Kongens Nytorv is the picturesque **Nyhavn** canal, which was dug 300 years ago to allow traders to bring their wares into the heart of the city. Long a haunt for sailors and writers (including Hans Christian Andersen, who lived in the house at No 67 for nearly two decades), Nyhavn today is half salty and half gentrified, with a line of trendy pavement cafes and restored gabled townhouses. It makes an invitingly atmospheric place to break for lunch or an afternoon beer. At the head of the canal is a huge frigate **anchor** that commemorates the Danish seamen who died in WWII serving with the Allied merchant marines.

From the northern side of Nyhavn, head north along Toldbodgade, turn right onto Sankt Annæ Plads, then left onto Larsens Plads and continue walking north along the waterfront. You'll pass by a couple of **18th-century warehouses**, converted for modern use, including the Copenhagen Admiral Hotel whose lobby is worth a peek.

When you reach the fountain that graces **Amaliehaven** (Amalie Gardens), turn inland to get to *Amalienborg Slot, home of the royal family since 1794. The palace's four nearly identical rococo mansions, designed by architect Nicolai Eigtved, surround a central cobblestone square and an immense **statue** of Frederik V (1746–66) on horseback sculpted by JFJ Saly. Looking west from the square you'll get a head-on view of the imposing *Marmorkirken (Marble Church), which was designed in conjunction with the Amalienborg complex as part of an ambitious plan by Frederik to extend the city northward by creating a new district geared to the affluent.

From this point you could make a short detour along *Bredgade, where there are a couple of churches and small museums. Otherwise, continue north on Amaliegade to

Churchillparken, where you'll pass *Frihedsmuseet, a museum dedicated to the Danish resistance movement of WWII, then the attractive Gothic **St Alban's Church**, which serves the city's English-speaking Anglican community. The church's location, in the midst of a public park, may seem a bit curious – the site was provided by Christian IX following the marriage of his daughter to the Prince of Wales, who later ascended the British throne as King Edward VII.

Beside the church stands the immense **Gefionspringvandet** (Gefion Fountain), a monument to yet another overseas relationship. According to Scandinavian mythology, when the Swedish king offered the goddess Gefion as much land as she could plough in one night, Gefion turned her four sons into powerful oxen and ploughed the entire area that now comprises the island of Zealand. The bronze statue in the fountain depicts the goddess and her oxen at work.

A 10-minute walk through the park past the fountain and along the waterfront will

The Headless Mermaid

In 1909 the Danish beer baron Carl Jacobsen was so moved after attending a ballet performance of the *Little Mermaid* that he commissioned sculptor Edvard Eriksen to create a statue of the fairy-tale character to grace Copenhagen's harbourfront. The face of the famous statue was modelled after the ballerina Ellen Price, while Eline Eriksen, the sculptor's wife, modelled for the body.

The *Little Mermaid* survived the Great Depression and the WWII occupation unscathed but modern times haven't been so kind to Denmark's leading lady.

In January 1998, in the middle of the night, someone took a saw and decapitated the bronze statue. The next day, international news services spread the gory scene around the world, as divers searched the waters around the statue for clues to no avail. Three days later the severed head mysteriously turned up in a box outside a Copenhagen TV station – and it was speedily reattached.

That wasn't the first time the gentle lady had been the subject of undesired attention. In 1964 the original head was lopped off and in 1983 an arm was sawn off – neither was ever found and both appendages had to be recast and welded back on.

lead you to the statue of the *Little Mermaid* (Den Lille Havfrue), which was designed by Edvard Eriksen in 1913. Inspired by Hans Christian Andersen's fairy tale, the statue depicts a mermaid who fell in love with a prince but had to wait 300 years to become human. This much-photographed bronze figure, perched on a rock at the water's edge, has a certain grace, but don't expect a great monument – the mermaid is indeed little and sports a rather drab, industrial harbour backdrop.

From the *Little Mermaid* continue along the road inland. After just a few minutes you'll reach steps leading down to a wooden bridge that crosses a moat into **Kastellet**, which is a citadel built by Frederik III in the 1660s. The fortress is still surrounded by some of the city's original ramparts. Although the fortress buildings remain in use by the Danish military, the park-like grounds are open to the public from 6am to sunset daily. Walk south through Kastellet and you'll go past its main row of historic buildings before reaching a second bridge that spans the moat and leads back into Churchillparken.

Back at the park entrance, turn right onto Esplanaden to Store Kongensgade; from there you can catch bus No 6 back to Rådhuspladsen or No 1 to Central Station.

Charlottenborg

Fronting Kongens Nytorv is Charlottenborg (☎ 33 13 40 22, Nyhavn 2; adult/child 20kr/free; open 10am-7pm Wed, 10am-5pm Thur-Tues), built in 1683 as a palace for the royal family. Since 1754 Charlottenborg has housed Det Kongelige Kunstakademi. The academy's exhibition hall, on the eastern side of the central courtyard, features changing exhibitions of modern art by Danish and international artists.

Amalienborg Slot

Although most of the royal palace is not open to the public, visitors can enter one wing (☎ 33 12 21 86, Amalienborg Plads; adult/child 40/5kr; open 10am-4pm daily May-Oct, 11am-4pm Tues-Sun Nov-Apr) that features exhibits of the royal apartments

Changing of the Guard

When the queen is in residence at Amalienborg Slot, mainly from December to April, a colourful changing of the guard takes place in the palace square at noon. The ceremony begins with a procession from Rosenborg Slot by the Royal Guard, bedecked in full regalia and marching to the tune of fifes and drums.

The guard contingent leaves the Rosenborg Slot gardens at 11.30am and marches to Amalienborg on a curving route that takes them to Kultorvet in the Latin Quarter, south on Købmagergade and then east along Østergade to Kongens Nytorv. From there the contingent continues to Amalienborg Slot along Bredgade, Sankt Annæ Plads and Amaliegade.

Upon reaching the square, the old guards are ceremoniously relieved of their duties by their fresh replacements, who take up sentry posts in front of the palace. The relieved guards then join the marching band and return to their barracks at Rosenborg Slot, via a route that takes them along Frederiksgade, Store Kongensgade and Gothersgade.

used by three generations of the monarchy from 1863 to 1947.

The rooms, faithfully reconstructed in the styles of the period, are decorated with heavy oak furnishings, gilt-leather tapestries, family photographs and old knick-knacks. They include the study and drawing room of Christian IX (1863–1906) and Queen Louise, whose six children wedded into nearly as many royal families – one eventually ascending the throne in Greece and another marrying Russian tsar Alexander III. Also displayed is the study of Frederik VIII (1906–12), who decorated it in a lavish neo-Renaissance style, and the study of Christian X (1912–47), the grandfather of the present queen Margrethe II.

Marmorkirken

The Marble Church, also called Frederikskirken, is a stately neo-Baroque church on Frederiksgade, a block west of Amalienborg Slot. The church's massive dome, which was

COPENHAGEN

STRØGET & LATIN QUARTER

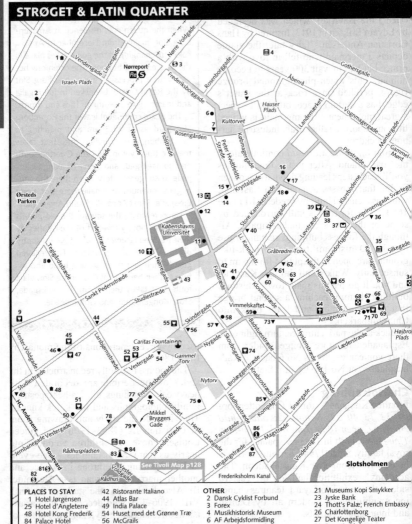

PLACES TO STAY	42 Ristorante Italiano	OTHER	21 Museums Kopi Smykker
1 Hotel Jørgensen	44 Atlas Bar	2 Dansk Cyklist Forbund	23 Jyske Bank
25 Hotel d'Angleterre	49 India Palace	3 Forex	24 Thott's Palæ; French Embassy
48 Hotel Kong Frederik	54 Huset med det Grønne Træ	4 Musikhistorisk Museum	26 Charlottenborg
84 Palace Hotel	56 McGrails	6 AF Arbejdsformidling	27 Det Kongelige Teater
	57 La Glace	8 Landsforeningen for Bøsser og	28 Bang & Olufsen
PLACES TO EAT	60 Restaurant Gråbrødre	Lesbiske (LBL)	29 Guinness World of
5 St Gertruds Kloster	Torv 21	9 Never Mind	Records Museum
7 Klaptræet	61 Jensen's Bøfhus	10 Sankt Petri Kirke	30 Magasin du Nord
15 Ankara	62 Peder Oxe	11 University Library	31 Canadian Embassy
17 Studenterhuset	63 Pasta Basta	12 STA Travel	32 Nikolaj Kirke
19 Den Grønne Kælder	71 Pizza Hut	13 Synagogen	34 Illum
22 Kommandanten	73 Café de Paris	14 Hovedbiblioteket (Public Library)	35 Museum Erotica
33 McDonald's	78 Shawarma Grill House	16 Rundetårn	37 Post Office
36 Café Sommersko	79 Reinh van Hauen	18 Arnold Busck Bookshop	38 Post & Tele Museum;
40 Det Lille Apotek	85 RizRaz	20 Kvindehuset	Café Hovedtelegrafen

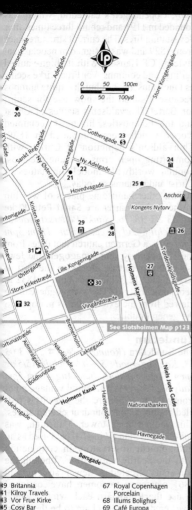

inspired by St Peter's in Rome and measures more than 30m in diameter, is one of Copenhagen's most dominant skyline features.

The original plans for the church were ordered by Frederik V and drawn up by Nicolai Eigtved as part of a grand design that included the Amalienborg mansions. Although church construction began in 1749, it encountered problems as costs overran, due in part to the prohibitively high price of Norwegian marble, and the project was soon shelved.

It wasn't until Denmark's wealthiest 19th-century financier, CF Tietgen, bankrolled the project's revival that it was finally taken to completion. It was consecrated as a church in 1894.

The church's exterior is ringed by statues of Danish theologians and saints. In addition to viewing the interior (*☎ 33 15 01 44; admission free; open 10am-5pm Mon-Fri, noon-5pm Sat & Sun*), with its huge circular nave, you can tour the dome at 1pm and 3pm Saturday and Sunday for 20kr (10kr for children) and catch a broad view of the city from its rim.

Bredgade Sights

There is a cluster of sights between Marmorkirken and Churchillparken.

Heading north, first is **Alexander Newsky Kirke** *(Bredgade 53)*, which was built in Russian Byzantine style in 1883 by Tsar Alexander III. The church is usually open only for services.

Next to the north is **Medicinsk-Historisk Museum** (*☎ 35 32 38 00, Bredgade 62; adult/child 30kr/free*), which is housed in a former surgical academy dating from circa 1786 and deals with the history of medicine, pharmacy and dentistry over the past three centuries. It's open only for guided tours at 11am and 1pm Wednesday to Friday and Sunday in July and August, the 1pm tours are conducted in English.

Sankt Ansgars Kirke (*☎ 33 13 37 62, Bredgade 64; admission free; open 10am-4pm Tues-Fri*) is Copenhagen's Roman Catholic cathedral, and has a colourfully painted apse and a small museum on the history of Danish Catholicism.

COPENHAGEN

Kunstindustrimuseet *(Museum of Decorative Art; ☎ 33 14 94 52, Bredgade 68; adult/child 35kr/free; open 10am-4pm Tues-Fri, noon-4pm Sat & Sun)* is housed in the former Frederiks Hospital (circa 1752). The museum highlights innovations in Danish design and crafts during the 20th century, with displays of furniture, ceramics, silver and textiles.

Frihedsmuseet

This museum *(☎ 33 13 77 14, Churchillparken; adult/child 30kr/free, free Wed; open 10am-4pm Tues-Sat, 10am-5pm Sun May–mid-Sept; 11am-3pm Tues-Sat, 11am-4pm Sun mid-Sept–Apr)* features exhibits on the Danish resistance movement from the time of the German occupation in 1940 to liberation in 1945. There are displays on the Danish underground press, the clandestine radio operations that maintained links with England and the smuggling operations that saved Danish Jews from capture by the occupying Nazis.

LATIN QUARTER

With its cafes and second-hand bookshops, the area north of Strøget that surrounds the old campus of Københavns Universitet (Copenhagen University) is a good place for ambling around. The university, which was founded in 1479, has largely outgrown its original quarters and moved to a new campus on Amager, but parts of the old campus, including the law department, remain here.

In the north of the Latin Quarter is **Kultorvet**, a lively pedestrian plaza and summer gathering place with beer gardens, flower stalls and produce stands. On sunny days you'll usually find impromptu entertainment here, which can range from Andean flute playing to local street theatre.

Climb the stairs of the **university library** *(enter from Fiolstræde; open 10am-7pm Mon-Fri)* to see one quirky remnant of the 1807 British bombardment of Copenhagen: a glass case containing a cannonball in five fragments and the target it hit, a book entitled *Defensor Pacis* (Defender of Peace).

Opposite the university is **Vor Frue Kirke** *(☎ 33 14 41 28, Nørregade 8; admission free; open 8am-5pm Mon-Sat, noon-5pm Sun)*, Copenhagen's cathedral, which was founded in 1191 and rebuilt three times after devastating fires. The current structure dates from 1829 and was designed in neoclassical style by CF Hansen. With its high-vaulted ceilings and columns, Vor Frue Kirke seems as much museum as church – quite apropos because it's also the showcase for sculptor Bertel Thorvaldsen's statues of Christ and the 12 apostles, his most acclaimed works, which were completed in 1839. Thorvaldsen's depiction of Christ, with comforting open arms, became the most popular worldwide model for statues of Christ and remains so today.

Two other handsome places of worship in the Latin Quarter are **Sankt Petri Kirke** *(☎ 33 93 38 76, Sankt Pedersstræde 2; adult/child 20kr/free; open 11am-3pm Tues-Sat)*, a German church that dates from the 15th century, and **Synagogen**, the Jewish synagogue, two blocks to the east at Krystalgade 12, which was built in 1831 in neoclassical style. The synagogue can be viewed from the exterior but is not open to the general public.

Rundetårn

The Rundetårn *(Round Tower; ☎ 33 73 03 73, Købmagergade 52; adult/child 15/5kr; open 10am-8pm daily June-Aug, 10am-5pm daily Sept-May)* is a splendid vantage point from which to admire the old city's redtiled rooftops and abundant church spires. This vaulted brick tower, 35m high, was built by Christian IV in 1642 and used as an astronomical observatory in conjunction with the nearby university. Although the university erected a newer structure in 1861, amateur astronomers have continued to use the Rundetårn each winter, which gives credence to its claim to be the oldest functioning observatory in Europe.

A 209m spiral walkway winds up the tower around a hollow core; about halfway up is a small exhibition hall housing changing displays of art and culture that is worth a visit.

Winter visitors who'd like to view the night sky from the 3m-long telescope that's mounted within the rooftop dome should make inquiries at the ticket booth. The observatory is generally open Tuesday and Wednesday nights from mid-October to mid-March.

ROSENBORG SLOT

This early-17th-century castle (☎ 33 15 32 86, Øster Voldgade 4; adult/child 50/10kr; open 10am-4pm daily May & June, 10am-5pm daily July-Sept, 11am-3pm daily Oct, 11am-2pm Tues-Sun Nov-Apr) with its moat and garden setting, was built by King Christian IV in Dutch Renaissance style to serve as his summer home. A century later King Frederik IV, who felt cramped at Rosenborg, built a roomier palace north of the city in the town of Fredensborg. In the years that followed, Rosenborg was used mainly for official functions and as a place in which to safeguard the monarchy's heirlooms.

In the 1830s the royal family decided to open the castle to visitors as a museum, while still using it as a treasury for royal regalia and jewels. It continues to serve both functions today.

The 24 rooms in the castle's upper levels are chronologically arranged, housing the furnishings and portraits of each monarch from Christian IV to Frederik VII; however, it's the lower level, where the treasury remains, that's the main attraction, with its dazzling collection of crown jewels. These include Christian IV's ornately designed crown, the jewel-studded sword of Christian III and Queen Margrethe II's emeralds and pearls; the latter are displayed here when the queen is not wearing them to official functions.

For information on getting to the castle, see the following Gardens section.

GARDENS

The green stretch of gardens along Øster Voldgade offers a quiet refuge from city traffic. The following gardens are conveniently located opposite each other, so visits to them can be combined in a lengthy stroll.

Kongens Have (King's Gardens), the expansive green space behind Rosenborg Slot, is the city's oldest public park. It has manicured box hedges, lovely rose beds and plenty of shaded areas. Kongens Have is a popular picnic spot and the site of a free marionette theatre that performs on summer afternoons.

If you time your outing well, you can include a visit to **Davids Samling** (☎ 33 73 49 49, Kronprinsessegade 30; admission free; open 1pm-4pm Tue & Thurs-Sun, 10am-4pm Wed), east of Kongens Have, a delightful little museum housing Scandinavia's largest collection of Islamic art.

In the 10-hectare **Botanisk Have** (Botanical Garden; ☎ 35 32 22 40, Gothersgade 128; admission free; open 8.30am-6pm daily Apr-Oct, 8.30am-4pm daily Nov-Mar) you can wander along fragrant paths amid arbours, terraces, rock gardens and ponds. Within the Botanisk Have is the **Palmehus** (Palm House; open 10am-3pm daily), a large walk-through glasshouse containing a lush collection of tropical plants. There's also a cactus house and an orchid greenhouse (open 1pm-3pm Wed, Sat & Sun). One entrance to the Botanisk Have is at the intersection of Gothersgade and Øster Voldgade, while the other is off Øster Farimagsgade.

The modest **Botanisk Museum** (☎ 35 32 22 00; admission free; open noon-4pm daily late June–mid-Aug), in the southern corner of the Botanisk Have, features plants from Denmark and Greenland.

The **Geologisk Museum** (☎ 35 32 23 45, Øster Voldgade 5; adult/child 25/10kr; open 1pm-4pm Tue-Sun), at the eastern corner of the Botanisk Have, is Denmark's foremost geological museum. You'll find the usual exhibits of fossils, minerals, crystals and rocks, including one from the moon. In addition it houses some interesting Danish displays, such as a huge 4.5kg chunk of amber, and some notable finds from Greenland; a highlight is the world's sixth-largest iron meteorite, which weighs in at 20 tonnes.

You can get to the gardens and Rosenborg Slot by taking the S-train to Nørreport station and walking north for two blocks, or via numerous buses including Nos 14, 16, 31, 42 and 43.

Free Browsing

In egalitarian Denmark some of the finest things in life are free – at least one day a week – so you might want to plan your museum browsing accordingly.

Every Wednesday, the Statens Museum of Kunst, Nationalmuseet, Den Hirschsprungske Samling, Post & Tele Museum, Thorvaldsens Museum, Frihedsmuseet, Frilandsmuseet and Ny Carlsberg Glyptotek turn off their cash registers and open their doors gratis to all. Ny Carlsberg Glyptotek is also free on Sunday.

The Københavns Bymuseum is free on Friday.

In addition, there are a few Copenhagen museums that never charge for admission: these include Davids Samling, B & W Museum and Tobaksmuseet.

STATENS MUSEUM FOR KUNST

Denmark's national gallery, Statens Museum for Kunst *(Royal Museum of Fine Arts;* ☎ *33 74 84 94, Sølvgade 48; bus No 10, 14, 40, 42 or 43; adult/child 40kr/free, free Wed; open 10am-8pm Wed, 10am-5pm Tues & Thur-Sun)*, was founded in 1824 to house art collections belonging to the royal family. Originally sited at Christiansborg Slot, the museum opened in its current location in 1896. Statens Museum, which was recently renovated and doubled in size, now lays claim to being the largest art museum in Denmark.

Its collection covers seven centuries of European art, ranging from medieval works with stylised religious themes to free-form modern art. There's an interesting collection of old masters by Dutch and Flemish artists, including Rubens and Frans Hals, as well as more contemporary European paintings by Matisse, Picasso and Munch. The museum also has an extensive collection of drawings, engravings and lithographs representing the works of such prominent artists as Degas and Toulouse-Lautrec.

As might be expected, the museum also contains a good collection of Danish fine art, including works by CW Eckersberg, Jens Juel, Christen Købke and PS Krøyer.

DEN HIRSCHSPRUNGSKE SAMLING

This excellent little museum *(☎ 35 42 03 36, Stockholmsgade 20; bus No 10, 14, 40, 42 or 43; adult/child 35kr/free, free Wed; open 11am-4pm Thur-Mon, 11am-9pm Wed)*, dedicated to Danish art of the 19th and early 20th centuries, is a 10-minute walk from the Statens Museum. Originally the private holdings of tobacco magnate Heinrich Hirschsprung, it contains works by painters of Denmark's Golden Age such as Christen Købke and CW Eckersberg, a notable selection by Skagen painters PS Krøyer and Anna and Michael Ancher, and also works by the Danish symbolists and the Funen painters.

NATIONALMUSEET

If you want to learn more about Danish history and culture, you couldn't do better than spending an afternoon at Nationalmuseet *(the National Museum;* ☎ *33 13 44 11, Ny Vestergade 10; adult/child 40kr/free, free Wed; open 10am-5pm Tue-Sun)*, opposite the western entrance to Slotsholmen.

This quality museum boasts the country's most extensive collection of Danish historical artefacts, dating from the Upper Palaeolithic period to the 1840s and including Stone Age tools, Viking weaponry and impressive Bronze Age, Iron Age and rune-stone collections. Don't miss the exhibit of bronze lurs, some of which date back 3000 years and are still capable of blowing a tune, and the finely crafted 3500-year-old Sun Chariot, unearthed in a Zealand field a century ago.

There are sections related to the Norsemen and Inuit of Greenland, collections of 18th-century Danish furniture, a 'Please Touch' exhibition for sight-impaired visitors and a special children's wing.

The museum also hosts a fine collection of Greek, Roman and medieval coins, and a Classical Antiquities section complete with Egyptian mummies. There's a cafe as well as a gift shop.

SLOTSHOLMEN

Slotsholmen is the seat of Denmark's national government and a veritable repository

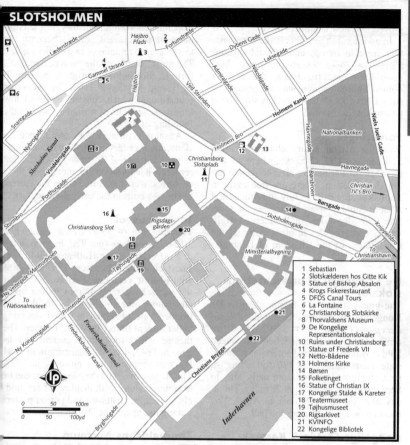

SLOTSHOLMEN

1 Sebastian
2 Slotskælderen hos Gitte Kik
3 Statue of Bishop Absalon
4 Krogs Fiskerestaurant
5 DFDS Canal Tours
6 La Fontaine
7 Christiansborg Slotskirke
8 Thorvaldsens Museum
9 De Kongelige
    Repræsentationslokaler
10 Ruins under Christiansborg
11 Statue of Frederik VII
12 Netto-Bådene
13 Holmens Kirke
14 Børsen
15 Folketinget
16 Statue of Christian IX
17 Kongelige Stalde & Kareter
18 Teatermuseet
19 Tøjhusmuseet
20 Rigsarkivet
21 KVINFO
22 Kongelige Bibliotek

0   50   100m
0   50   100yd

of historical sites. Located on a small island and separated from the city centre by a moat-like canal, Slotsholmen's centrepiece is **Christiansborg Slot**, a large rambling palace that now contains government offices.

Several short bridges link Slotsholmen to the rest of Copenhagen. If you walk into Slotsholmen from Ny Vestergade, you'll cross the western part of the canal and enter Christiansborg's large main courtyard, which was once used as royal riding grounds. The courtyard still maintains a distinctively equestrian character, overseen by a statue of Christian IX (1863–1906) on horseback and

flanked to the north by stables and to the south by carriage buildings.

The stables and buildings surrounding the main courtyard date back to the original Christiansborg palace, which was built in the 1730s by Christian VI to replace the more modest Copenhagen Castle that previously stood there. The grander west wing of Christian VI's palace went up in flames in 1794, was rebuilt in the early 19th century and was once again destroyed by fire in 1884. In 1907 the cornerstone for the third (and current) Christiansborg palace was laid by Frederik VIII and, upon completion, the national parliament and the Supreme Court moved into new chambers there.

In addition to the sights listed here, visitors are also free to enter **Christiansborg Slotskirke** *(open noon-4pm daily July, noon-4pm Sun Aug-June)*, the castle's domed church, which was set ablaze by stray fireworks in 1996 and has since been painstakingly restored.

Folketinget

Visit the parliamentary chamber, called Folketinget *(☎ 33 37 55 00)*, where the 179 members of Parliament meet to debate national legislation. There are free tours in English at 2pm daily in July and August and at 2pm Sunday from September to June. The tour also takes in Wanderer's Hall, which contains the original copy of the Constitution of the Kingdom of Denmark, enacted in 1849.

De Kongelige Repræsentationslokaler

The grandest part of Christiansborg is De Kongelige Repræsentationslokaler *(Royal Reception Chambers; ☎ 33 92 64 92)*, an ornate Renaissance hall where the queen holds royal banquets and entertains heads of state. Tours *(adult/child 40/10kr)* in English start at 11am, 1pm and 3pm daily May to September, 11am and 3pm Tuesday, Thursday and Saturday October to April. You must be on a tour to enter the hall.

Kongelige Stalde & Kareter

Here at Kongelige Stalde & Kareter *(Royal Stables & Coaches; ☎ 33 40 10 10; adult/child 20/10kr; open 2pm-4pm Sat & Sun year-round, also 2pm-4pm Fri May-Aug)*, visitors can view a collection of antique coaches, uniforms and riding paraphernalia, some of which are still used for royal receptions. You can also see the royal family's carriage and saddle horses.

Ruins under Christiansborg

A walk through the crypt-like bowels of Slotsholmen *(☎ 33 92 64 94; adult/child 20/5kr; open 9.30am-4.30pm daily May-Sept, 9.30am-3.30pm Tues, Thur, Sat & Sun*

Oct-Apr) offers a unique perspective on Copenhagen's lengthy history. In the basement of the current palace, beneath the tower, are the remains of two earlier castles. The most notable are the ruins of Absalon's fortress, Slotsholmen's original castle, built by Bishop Absalon in 1167. The excavated foundations, which consist largely of low limestone sections of wall, date back to the founding of the city.

Absalon's fortress was demolished by Hanseatic invaders in 1369. Its foundations, as well as those of Copenhagen Castle that replaced it and stood for more than three centuries, were excavated when the current tower was built in the early 20th century.

Teatermuseet

This museum *(☎ 33 11 51 76; adult/child 20/5kr; open 2pm-4pm Wed, noon-4pm Sat & Sun)* occupies the Hofteater (Old Court Theatre), which dates from 1767 and drips with historic character. Performances over the years have ranged from Italian opera and pantomime to shows by local ballet troupes, one of which included fledgling ballet student Hans Christian Andersen. The theatre, which took on its current appearance in 1842, drew its final curtain in 1881 but was reopened as a museum in 1922. The stage, boxes and dressing rooms can be examined, along with displays of set models, drawings, costumes and period posters tracing the history of Danish theatre.

Thorvaldsens Museum

This museum *(☎ 33 32 15 32, Porthusgade 2; adult/child 20kr/free, free Wed; open 10am-5pm Tues-Sun)* exhibits the works of famed Danish sculptor Bertel Thorvaldsen (1770–1844), who was heavily influenced by Greek and Roman mythology. After four decades in Rome, Thorvaldsen returned to his native Copenhagen and donated his private collection to the Danish public. In return the royal family provided this site for the construction of a museum to house Thorvaldsen's drawings, plaster moulds and statues. The museum also contains antique art from the Mediterranean region that Thorvaldsen collected during his lifetime.

You'll find the entrance to the museum on Vindebrogade.

Tøjhusmuseet

Tøjhusmuseet *(Royal Arsenal Museum; ☎ 33 11 60 37, Tøjhusgade 3; adult/child 20kr/free; open noon-4pm Tues-Sun)* contains an impressive collection of historic cannons, hand weapons and armour. The 163m-long building that houses the arsenal was constructed by King Christian IV in 1600 and boasts the longest vaulted Renaissance hall in Europe.

Kongelige Bibliotek

Kongelige Bibliotek *(Royal Library; ☎ 33 47 47 47, Christians Brygge; admission free; open 10am-7pm Mon-Sat)* is the largest library in Scandinavia. It's an interesting merger of the library's original classical building near parliament and a new ultra-modern extension on the waterfront.

The seven-story extension, dubbed the 'Black Diamond', sports a shiny black granite facade, smoked black windows and a leaning cube-like design. This sleek canal-side addition gives the once solidly historic waterfront a curious futuristic juxtaposition. An enclosed overhead walkway straddles the motorway on Christians Brygge, connecting the Black Diamond with the library's historic wing.

The Royal Library not only serves as a research centre for scholars, but also doubles as a repository for manuscripts and rare books. As Denmark's national library it contains a complete collection of all Danish printed works produced since 1482 and houses some 21 million items in all.

The place is well worth a visit. You'll find a spacious lobby with canal views, a 210-sq-metre ceiling mural by Danish artist Per Kirkeby and various exhibition areas. The lobby contains a bookshop, cafe and restaurant.

Børsen

Another striking Renaissance building is Børsen, the stock exchange, at the eastern corner of Slotsholmen on Børsgade. Constructed in the 1620s, it's of note particularly

---

An Author's Burden

In 1834 Hans Christian Andersen applied for work at the Royal Library in Copenhagen 'to be freed from the heavy burden of having to write in order to live'. Apparently the library administrators weren't too impressed with his resume, as he was turned down. Ironically, Andersen's unsuccessful application is now preserved as part of the library's valued archives, along with many of his original manuscripts. They can be viewed with advance notice.

---

for its ornate spire, formed from the entwined tails of four dragons, and for its richly embellished gables. This still-functioning stock exchange, which first opened during the bustling reign of Christian IV, is the oldest in Europe.

Holmens Kirke

Just across the canal to the north-east of Slotsholmen is Holmens Kirke *(Church of the Royal Danish Navy; ☎ 33 13 61 78, Holmens Kanal; admission free; 9am-2pm Mon-Fri, 9am-noon Sat)*. This historic brick structure, with a nave that was originally built in 1562 to be used as an anchor forge, was converted into a church for the Royal Navy in 1619. Most of the present structure, which is predominantly in Dutch Renaissance style, dates from 1641. The church's burial chapel contains the remains of some important naval figures, including Admiral Niels Juel, who beat back the Swedes in the crucial 1677 Battle of Køge Bay.

It was at Holmens Kirke that Queen Margrethe II took her marriage vows in 1967. The interior of the church has an intricately carved 17th-century oak altarpiece and pulpit.

CHRISTIANSHAVN

Christianshavn is on the eastern flank of Copenhagen. It was established by Christian IV in the early 17th century as a commercial centre and also a military buffer for the expanding city. It's cut with a network of canals, modelled after those in Holland, which leads Christianshavn to occasionally be dubbed 'Little Amsterdam'.

Still surrounded by its old ramparts, Christianshavn today is a hotchpotch of newer apartment complexes and renovated period warehouses that have found second lives as upmarket housing and restored government offices. The neighbourhood attracts an interesting mix of artists, yuppies and dropouts. Christianshavn is also home to a sizable Greenlandic community and was the setting of the public housing complex in the popular novel and movie *Miss Smilla's Feeling for Snow*.

To get to Christianshavn, you can walk over the Knippelsbro from the north-eastern part of Slotsholmen or catch bus No 8 or 2. If you're going to Christiania first, bus No 8 is the best, as it stops near the gate.

Christiania

In 1971 an abandoned 41-hectare military camp on the eastern side of Christianshavn was taken over by squatters who proclaimed it the 'free state' of Christiania (☎ 32 95 65 07), subject to their own laws. The police tried to clear the area but it was the height of the 'hippie revolution' and an increasing number of alternative folk from throughout Denmark continued to pour in, attracted by the concept of communal living and the prospect of reclaiming military land for peaceful purposes.

The momentum became too much for the government to hold back and, bowing to public pressure, the community was allowed to continue as a 'social experiment'. About 1000 people settled into Christiania, turning the old barracks into schools and housing, and starting their own collective businesses, workshops and recycling programs.

As well as hosting progressive happenings, Christiania also became a magnet for runaways and junkies. Although Christiania residents felt that the media played up an image of decadence and criminality – as opposed to portraying Christiania as a self-governing, ecology-oriented and tolerant community – they did, in time, find it necessary to modify their free-law approach. A new policy was established that outlawed

hard drugs in Christiania, and the heroin and cocaine pushers were expelled.

Still, Christiania remains controversial. Some Danes resent the community's rent-free, tax-free situation and more than a few Christianshavn neighbours would like to see sections of Christiania turned into public parks and school grounds.

Although the police don't regularly patrol Christiania, they have staged numerous organised raids on the community and it's not unknown for police training to include a tactical sweep along Pusherstreet.

Visitors are welcome to stroll or cycle in car-free Christiania, though large dogs may intimidate some free spirits. Photography is frowned upon and outright forbidden on Pusherstreet, where marijuana joints and hashish are openly (though not legally) sold and smoked.

Christiania has a small market where pipes and T-shirts are sold, a couple of craft shops and a few places where you can get coffee and something to eat.

The main entrance into Christiania is on Prinsessegade, 200m north-east of its intersection with Bådsmandsstræde. Pusherstreet and most of the shops are within a few minutes' walk of the entrance. You can take a guided tour of Christiania (25kr) at noon or 3pm daily during summer; meet inside the main entrance.

Vor Frelsers Kirke

A few minutes south-west of Christiania is the 17th-century Vor Frelsers Kirke (*Our Saviour's Church;* ☎ 32 57 27 98, *Sankt Annæ Gade 29; admission free; open 11am-4.30pm Mon-Sat & noon-4.30pm Sun Apr-Aug; 11am-3.30pm Mon-Sat & noon-4pm Sun Sept-Mar).* The church, which once benefited from close ties with the Danish monarchy, has a grand interior that includes an elaborately carved pipe organ dating from 1698 and an ornate Baroque altar with marble cherubs and angels.

For a panoramic city view, make the dizzying 400-step ascent (20/10kr adult /child) of the church's 95m spiral tower – the last 150 steps run along the outside rim of the tower, narrowing to the point where they literally disappear at the top. This colourful spire was added to the church in 1752 by Lauritz de Thurah, who took his inspiration from Boromini's tower of St Ivo in Rome.

Orlogsmuseet

The Royal Danish Naval Museum (☎ 32 54 63 63, Overgaden oven Vandet 58; adult/child 30/20kr; open noon-4pm Tues-Sun) occupies a former naval hospital on Christianshavn Kanal. This museum houses more than 300 model ships, many dating from the 16th to the 19th century. Some were built by naval engineers to serve as design prototypes for the construction of new ships; consequently the models take many forms, from cross-sectional ones detailing frame proportions to full-dressed models with working sails.

The museum also displays figureheads, navigational instruments, ship lanterns, and the propeller from the German U-boat that sank the Lusitania.

Other Christianshavn Sights

Christians Kirke (☎ 32 96 83 01, Strandgade 1; admission free; open 8am-6pm daily Mar-Oct, 8am-5pm daily Nov-Feb, except during church services) was designed by the Danish architect Nicolai Eigtved and completed in 1759. This church once served the local German congregation and has an expansive, theatre-like rococo interior.

Nearby is the B & W Museum (☎ 32 54 92 27, Strandage 4; admission free; open 10am-1pm Mon-Fri & 1st Sun of month), which displays the history of Burmeister & Wein, the shipbuilding company that in 1912 pioneered the use of diesel engines in ocean-going ships. In January 1943 Burmeister & Wein became the target of the first Allied air raid on Copenhagen, when British bombers levelled the company's Christianshavn factory to put an end to its production of German U-boat engines.

The architectural museum Gammel Dok (☎ 32 57 19 30, Strandgade 27B; adult/child 30kr/free; open 10am-5pm daily) has changing exhibits of Danish and international architecture, design and industrial art.

TIVOLI

Situated right in the heart of the city, Tivoli (☎ 33 15 10 01, W www.tivoligardens.com, Vesterbrogade 3; adult/child 50/25kr; open 11am-11pm Sun-Tues, 11am-midnight Wed & Thurs, 11am-1am Fri-Sat mid-Apr–Sept) is a tantalising combination of amusement rides, flower gardens, food pavilions, carnival games and open-air stage shows. This genteel entertainment park, which dates from 1843, is delightfully varied. Visitors can ride the roller coaster, take aim at the shooting gallery, enjoy the pantomime of Commedia dell'Arte or simply sit and watch the crowds stroll by.

During the day children flock to Tivoli's Ferris wheel, carousel, bumper cars and other rides. In the evening Tivoli takes on a more romantic aura as the lights come on and the cultural activities unfold, with one stage hosting traditional folk dancing as another prepares a theatrical performance.

Each of Tivoli's numerous entertainment venues has a different character. Perhaps best known is the open-air pantomime theatre, which features mime and ballet, and was built in 1874 by Vilhelm Dahlerup, the Copenhagen architect who also designed the royal theatre. Tivoli also has an indoor cabaret theatre and a large concert hall that features performances by international symphony orchestras and ballet troupes.

Between all the neon and action, Tivoli is a fun place to stroll around, and if you feel like a splurge there are some good restaurants that enjoy stage views and make for a memorable dining experience.

Wednesday and Saturday are the best nights to visit as they include a fireworks display shot off shortly before the clock strikes midnight.

Amusement ride tickets cost 10kr (many rides require two tickets), but there are multi-ticket schemes and passes as well.

The numerous open-air performances are free of charge, but there's usually an admission fee for the indoor performances. For information on the latter, see the Entertainment section in this chapter.

Tivoli also reopens for a few weeks prior to Christmas for various holiday festivities,

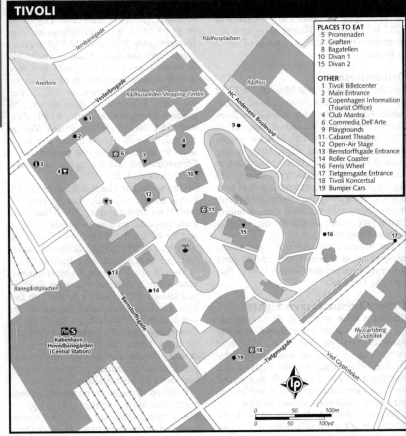

TIVOLI

PLACES TO EAT
5 Promenaden
7 Grøften
8 Bagatellen
10 Divan 1
15 Divan 2

OTHER
1 Tivoli Billetcenter
2 Main Entrance
3 Copenhagen Information (Tourist Office)
4 Club Mantra
6 Commedia Dell'Arte
9 Playgrounds
11 Cabaret Theatre
12 Open-Air Stage
13 Bernstorffsgade Entrance
14 Roller Coaster
16 Ferris Wheel
17 Tietgensgade Entrance
18 Tivoli Koncertsal
19 Bumper Cars

a Christmas market and ice-skating on the lake. Some of Tivoli's restaurants reopen for that period, serving traditional Danish Christmas fare.

NY CARLSBERG GLYPTOTEK

This exceptional museum (☎ *33 41 81 41, Dantes Plads 7; adult/child 30kr/free, free Wed & Sun; open 10am-4pm Tues-Sun*) near Tivoli houses an excellent collection of Greek, Egyptian, Etruscan and Roman sculpture and art. It was built a century ago by beer baron Carl Jacobsen, who was an ardent collector of classical art. The mu-

seum's main building, designed by architect Vilhelm Dahlerup, is centred around a glass-domed conservatory replete with palm trees, creating an atmospheric complement to the collection.

Although Ny Carlsberg Glyptotek was originally – and primarily remains – dedicated to classical art, a later gift of more than 20 works by Paul Gauguin led to the formation of an impressive 19th-century French and Danish art collection. The Danish collection includes paintings by JC Dahl, CW Eckersberg, Christian Købke and Jens Juel.

The French collection is centred around the Gauguin paintings, which now number 50. These are displayed alongside pieces by Cézanne, Van Gogh, Pissarro, Monet and Renoir in a new wing of the museum that opened in 1996. This 'French Wing' also boasts one of only three complete series of Degas bronzes.

A treat for off-season visitors are the chamber concerts given on Sundays from October to March in the museum's concert hall, which is lined by life-size statues of Roman patricians. And you won't have to pay a penny for this high-brow experience since the concerts, like Sunday admission itself, are gratis.

DANSK DESIGN CENTER

The Dansk Design Center (☎ 33 69 33 69, HC Andersens Boulevard 27; adult/child 25/15kr; open 10am-5pm Mon-Fri, 11am-4pm Sat & Sun) opened in 2000 as a place to showcase Danish industrial design alongside international design trends.

The centre has a dual function, providing a meeting place for people in the field of design, as well as display space for exhibitions. The ground floor holds an exhibit of classic Danish chairs, while upstairs are changing exhibits on topics such as the development of fashion trends and the history of the avant-garde audiovisual company Bang & Olufsen.

VESTERBRO

The Vesterbro district has a varied character that's readily observed by walking along its best-known street, Istedgade, which runs west from Central Station. The first few blocks are lined with rows of respectable hotels that soon give way to the city's main red-light area. When Denmark became the first country to legalise pornography in the 1970s, Vesterbro's porn shops and seedy nightclubs became a magnet for tourists and voyeurs. Although it's not necessarily any tamer these days, liberalisation elsewhere has made the area less of a novelty.

About halfway down Istedgade the red-light district recedes and the neighbourhood becomes increasingly multiethnic, with a mix of Pakistani and Turkish businesses. Vesterbro, along with the adjacent district of Nørrebro, is home to much of the city's immigrant community and abounds with good restaurants serving international cuisine.

Københavns Bymuseum

The Copenhagen City Museum (☎ 33 21 07 72, Vesterbrogade 59; bus No 6 or 28; adult/child 20kr/free, free Fri; open 10am-4pm Wed-Mon May-Sept, 1pm-4pm Wed-Mon Oct-Apr) in the Vesterbro district features – not surprisingly – displays about the history and development of Copenhagen, mainly paintings and scale models of the old city. Of particular interest is the small exhibit dedicated to the religious philosopher Søren Kierkegaard, who was born in Copenhagen in 1813 and died in the city in 1855.

NØRREBRO

The Nørrebro quarter of the city developed in the mid-19th century as a working-class neighbourhood. In more recent times it's attracted a large immigrant community and has become a haunt for students, musicians and artists. It consequently boasts lots of interesting Middle Eastern and Asian restaurants and some of Copenhagen's hottest night spots. There numerous second-hand clothing shops in the streets radiating out from Sankt Hans Torv, antique shops along Ravnsborggade and a Saturday morning flea market a few blocks to the west on Nørrebrogade along the wall of the Assistens Kirkegård.

Assistens Kirkegård

This cemetery (☎ 35 37 19 17; bus No 5 or 16; admission free; open 8am-8pm May-Aug, 8am-4pm Nov-Feb, 8am-6pm rest of the year) in the heart of Nørrebro is the final resting place of some of Denmark's most celebrated citizens, including philosopher Søren Kierkegaard, physicist Niels Bohr, authors Hans Christian Andersen and Martin Andersen Nexø, and artists Jens Juel, Christen Købke and CW Eckersberg. It's an interesting place to wander around – as much a park and garden as it is a graveyard.

The cemetery is divided into sectors, which helps in locating specific sites. A good place to start is at the main entrance on Kapelvej, which has an office where you can pick up a brochure mapping famous grave sites.

Zoologisk Museum

This modern zoological museum (☎ 35 32 10 01, Universitetsparken 15; bus No 18, 42, 43 or 184; adult/child 25/10kr; open 11am-5pm Tues-Sun), 1km north of Assistens Kirkegård, displays all sorts of stuffed animals, from North Zealand deer to Greenlandic polar bears. There are also interesting dioramas, recorded animal sounds, a whale skeleton and insect displays.

OTHER ATTRACTIONS
Musikhistorisk Museum

The Music History Museum (☎ 33 11 27 26, Åbenrå 30; adult/child 30/10kr; open 1pm-3.45pm Fri-Wed May-Sept; 1pm-3.45pm Mon, Wed, Sat & Sun Oct-Apr), housed in an 18th-century building just north of Kultorvet in the Latin Quarter, contains a quality collection of musical instruments dating from AD 1000 to 1900.

The exhibits are grouped according to themes, such as folk music of the Middle Ages, Renaissance instruments, 19th-century military music etc; some are accompanied by musical recordings that you can listen to on headphones.

Arbejdermuseet

The Workers' Museum (☎ 33 93 33 88, Rømersgade 22; adult/child 35/20kr; open 10am-4pm daily July-Oct, 10am-4pm Tues-Sun Nov-June) pays homage to the working class with exhibits portraying the lives of Danish labourers during the 1880s, 1930s and 1950s. You can get there by taking the S-train to Nørreport station and walking west on Frederiksborggade or by catching bus No 5, 14 or 16.

Nyboder Mindestuer

This museum (☎ 33 32 10 05, Sankt Paulsgade 20; adult/child 10/5kr; open 11am-2pm Wed & 11am-4pm Sun), which is south-west of Kastellet, stands in the midst of the old residential quarter laid out in 1630 by Christian IV to provide housing for his naval staff. Although the museum is in one of the original buildings, most of the neighbourhood housing – block after block of long ochre-coloured row houses with red-tiled roofs – was built in later years. It presents exhibitions on everyday life in Nyboder from the early 17th to the 20th centuries.

Guinness World of Records Museum

This touristy attraction (☎ 33 32 31 31, Østergade 16; adult/child 69/35kr; open 9.30am-10pm daily June-Aug, 10am-6pm daily Sept-May) on Strøget uses displays, photos and film to depict the world's superlatives – the tallest, fastest, oddest and so on.

Ripley's Believe It or Not!

This cliched museum (☎ 33 91 89 91, Rådhuspladsen 57; adult/child 69/35kr; open 9.30am-10.30pm daily June-Aug, 10am-6pm daily Sept-May) displays the expected collection of unexpected oddities from around the world (such as a six-legged calf) replicated in wax figures and tableaus.

Louis Tussaud's Wax Museum

At this wax museum (☎ 33 11 89 00, HC Andersens Blvd 22; adult/child 68/28kr; open 10am-11pm daily May–mid-Sept, 10am-6pm daily for rest of year), on the northern edge of Tivoli, celebrities such as Elvis and Frankenstein can be found in the company of Danish notables, including the royal family, Søren Kierkegaard and Hans Christian Andersen.

Post & Tele Museum

The Post & Tele Museum (☎ 33 41 09 00, Købmagergade 37; adult/child 30kr/free, free Wed; 10am-5pm Tues & Thurs-Sun, 10am-8pm Wed), 300m north of Strøget, depicts the history of the Danish postal and telecommunications system with displays of historic postal vehicles, uniforms, letter boxes and the like. Not surprisingly, it also boasts a fine stamp collection.

Museum Erotica

A cross between a museum and a peepshow, Museum Erotica (☎ 33 12 03 11, Købmagergade 24; admission 69kr; open 10am-11pm daily May-Sept, 11am-8pm daily Oct-Apr), two blocks north of Strøget, is full of erotic paintings, posters, photographs, statues and sex toys. These items range from hand-coloured daguerreotype photographs from the 1850s to a multiscreen video room playing modern-day porn movies.

Experimentarium

This extensive hands-on technology and natural science centre (☎ 39 27 33 33, Tuborg Havnevej 7, Hellerup; bus No 6 from central Copenhagen; adult/child 85/60kr; open 10am-5pm daily mid-June to early Aug; 9am-5pm Mon &Wed-Fri, 9am-9pm Tues, 11am-5pm Sat & Sun for rest of the year) is housed in a former bottling hall of Tuborg Breweries in Hellerup, north of the city. Containing some 300 exhibits, it's a fun place for kids, featuring such time-honoured standards as the hall of mirrors, as well as computer-enhanced activities that make it possible to compose water music, stand on the moon or ride an inverted bicycle.

Tycho Brahe Planetarium

This planetarium (☎ 33 12 12 24, Gammel Kongevej 10; adult/child 90/71kr; open 10.30am-9pm daily) 750m north-west of Central Station, has a domed space theatre that offers shows of the night sky using state-of-the-art equipment capable of projecting more than 7500 stars, planets and galaxies. The planetarium's 1000-sq-metre screen also shows Omnimax natural science films on subjects ranging from astronauts aboard the space shuttle to divers exploring tropical reefs.

The planetarium was named after the famed Danish astronomer Tycho Brahe (1546–1601), whose creation of precision astronomical instruments allowed him to make more exact observations of planets and stars, and paved the way for the discoveries made by later astronomers.

Zoologisk Have

Copenhagen Zoo (☎ 36 30 20 01, Roskildevej 32; bus No 28 from Rådhuspladsen; adult/child 70/37kr; open 9am-6pm daily June-Aug, 9am-5pm daily Apr-May & Sept-Oct, 9am-4pm daily Nov-Mar), located in the Frederiksberg area, has the standard collection of caged creatures, including lions, elephants, zebras, hippos, gorillas and polar bears. Special sections include the Tropical Zoo, Children's Zoo, Ape Jungle, African Savannah and South American Pampas.

Carlsberg Brewery

The Carlsberg Visitors Center (☎ 33 27 13 14, Gamle Carlsberg Vej 11; bus No 6 from Rådhuspladsen; admission free; 10am-4pm Tues-Sun), adjacent to Carlsberg brewery, has an exhibition area on the history of Danish beer from 1370 BC (yes, they carbon dated a bog girl who was found in a peat bog caressing a jug of well-aged brew!). Dioramas give the lowdown on the brewing process and en route to your final destination you'll pass antique copper vats and the stables that still keep a team of Jutland drayhorses.

The 5m-high elephant gate at the Carlsberg Brewery is made of granite from Bornholm.

The self-guided tour ends, apropos, at a little pub where you get two free beers of your choice – make one of them the Carls Special, a delectably smooth malt that's a local favourite.

SWIMMING
Beaches

If brisk water doesn't deter you, the greater Copenhagen area has several bathing areas. The water is tested regularly and if sewage spills or other serious pollution occurs the beaches affected are closed and signposted.

A popular beach south of Copenhagen is Amager Strandpark (bus No 9, 12 or 13). Playground facilities and shallow water make it ideal for children, while deeper water can be reached by walking out along the jetties. There's another beach, Sydstranden, in Amager along the southern side of Dragør; take bus No 33 or 34.

The most accessible beaches north of central Copenhagen are the Charlottenlund beach and the Bellevue beach at Klampenborg; both can be reached via bus No 6.

Pools

Copenhagen has a handful of swimming pools that visitors can use; the following are the two most central ones.

DGI-byen (☎ 33 29 80 00), Tietgensgade 65, 150m south of Central Station, sports an extravagant new swim centre with several pools, including a grand ellipse-shape affair with 100m lanes, a deep 'mountain pool' with a climbing wall, a hot water pool and a children's pool. Use of the pools costs 40kr for adults, 25kr for children. It's open from 7am to 7pm on Monday, Wednesday and Friday, and from at least 10am to 5pm on other days.

Another option is the municipal pool, Vesterbro Svømmehal (☎ 33 22 05 00) at Angelgade 4, which is open from 10am to 9pm on Monday, from 7am to at least 5pm Tuesday to Friday, from 9am to 2pm on Saturday and Sunday. It costs 24kr for adults and 10kr for children.

BOATING

If you want to explore Christianshavn's historic canals, Christianshavns Bådudlejning og Café (☎ 32 96 53 53) at Overgaden neden Vandet 29 rents out rowing boats on the canal for 60kr an hour. It's open 10am to sunset daily from early May to about the middle of September.

For details of boating in the Lyngby area, see under Lyngby in the Around Copenhagen section at the end of this chapter.

CYCLING

Cycle lanes are found along many city streets and virtually all of Copenhagen can be toured by bicycle, except for pedestrian-only streets such as Strøget. Bicycles are allowed to cross Strøget at Gammel Torv and Kongens Nytorv.

When touring the city, cyclists should be cautious of bus passengers who commonly step off the bus into the cycle lanes, and of pedestrians (particularly tourists) who sometimes absent-mindedly step off the kerb and into the path of oncoming cyclists.

Cycling maps, including a 1:50,000-scale map of the greater Copenhagen area called *Københavns Amt*, are produced by the Danish cycling federation, Dansk Cyklist Forbund, and can be readily purchased at bookshops. For information on bicycle hire, see under Bicycle in the Getting Around section later in this chapter.

Cycle Tour

The most popular self-guided cycling tour in the Copenhagen area is the 12km ride north to Dyrehaven. There's a cycle path the entire way, much of it skirting the Øresund coast.

To begin, take Østerbrogade north from the city. After passing the S-train station Svanemøllen, the road continues as Strandvejen, passing through busy Hellerup, where the intersections have blue-marked crossings to indicate cyclist rights-of-way, and then up through the quiet coastal village of Charlottenlund. Here the cycle lane widens and there's a beach, an old fort and an aquarium that can be interesting diversions (see the Around Copenhagen section at the end of this chapter). Once you reach the Klampenborg station, a bike path leads into Dyrehaven, a woodland crossed by a network of trails, and a perfect place to break out a picnic lunch. Alternatively, if you want to continue farther north, an off-road cycling path runs parallel to the coastal road to Rungsted.

Either way, you have the choice of returning on the same route, taking an alternative route such as the inland road Bernstorffsvej, or putting your bike on the S-train and making it a one-way tour.

ORGANISED TOURS
Bus Tours
Copenhagen is so easy to get around that there's little need to consider a sightseeing bus tour. However, Copenhagen Excursions (☎ 32 54 06 06) does offer various guided tours of the city and surrounding areas. The cheapest tour, in splashy pink-and-yellow double-decker buses with open tops, costs 100kr, lasts one hour and cruises by some of the city's main sights, such as Amalienborg palace, Slotsholmen, the *Little Mermaid* and Nyhavn.

Other tours include a 2½-hour 'grand tour' that takes in a broader swath of city sights and costs 180kr, and a 390kr day-long castle tour of North Zealand that takes in Kronborg Slot in Helsingør, the royal summer palace in Fredensborg and Frederiksborg Slot in Hillerød. Tours leave from Rådhuspladsen, near the Palace Hotel, and tickets can be bought on the bus.

Canal Tours
For a different angle on the city, hop on to one of the boat tours that wind through Copenhagen's canals. Although most of the passengers are usually Danes, multilingual guides give a lively commentary in English as well. All the tours follow a similar loop route, passing by Slotsholmen, Christianshavn and the *Little Mermaid*.

The biggest company, DFDS Canal Tours (☎ 33 42 30 00), operates from April to late October. Boats leave twice an hour from two locations – at the head of Nyhavn and on Gammel Strand, north of Slotsholmen. Tours, which last 50 minutes, run from 10am to 5pm, except in July and August when the Nyhavn departures extend to 7.30pm; the cost is 50kr for adults, 20kr for children.

A better deal is with Netto-Bådene (☎ 32 54 41 02), which charges just 20kr for adults, 10kr for children, and operates from mid-April to mid-October. Its cruises, which last an hour, leave from Holmens Kirke, east of Slotsholmen, as well as from Nyhavn, three times an hour from 10am to 5pm.

Canal boats can also be a fine traffic-free way of getting to some of Copenhagen's famous waterfront sites. DFDS Canal Tours operates a summertime water bus that runs along a route similar to its guided tours but has no commentary. These boats leave Nyhavn every 30 minutes from 10.15am to 4.45pm daily between mid-May and mid-September (to 5.45pm from late June to August), and make 10 stops, including Slotsholmen, Christianshavn and the *Little Mermaid*. A day pass, which costs 40kr for adults and 20kr for children, allows you to get on and off as often as you like. You can also ride from just one stop to another for 30kr.

Walking Tours
From June to late August a 'night watchman' dressed in period clothing and carrying a lantern and spiked mace makes his rounds of the older quarters of the city with sightseers in tow. The one-hour tours, which are conducted in English and Danish, take place on Friday. It's touristy, but colourful and free. Meet at 9pm at Gråbrødre Torv, the small square fronting Peder Oxe restaurant.

Copenhagen Information, the city tourist office at Bernstorffsgade 1, arranges guided walking tours in English from May to September. The tours, which last two hours and leave from the tourist office at 10.30am Monday to Saturday, visit various historic parts of the city. The cost is 50kr.

Royal Copenhagen
Multilingual guided tours (25k) of the Royal Copenhagen porcelain factory (☎ 38 14 92 97, Smallegade 47, Frederiksberg area; bus No 1 or 14 from Rådhuspladsen), are given at 9am, 10am, 11am, 1pm and 2pm Monday to Friday. The factory has been on this site since 1884, though Royal Copenhagen has been making porcelain in Denmark since 1775. The tours last about an hour.

SPECIAL EVENTS

Whatever your interest, you'll be able find an event to suit at some time during the year in Copenhagen. The city plays host to an array of special events ranging from New Year concerts to film festivals and fashion design to the acclaimed Copenhagen Jazz Festival in July.

Other events run the gamut from the Copenhagen Marathon in May to the colourful Mermaid Pride parade in August, Denmark's biggest gay and lesbian event.

For details of festivals and other revelries to consider in planning for your visit to the city, see the 'Festive Denmark' special section.

PLACES TO STAY

Copenhagen is a popular convention city and if you happen to arrive when one is taking place, finding a room could be a challenge. At most other times the following room booking services can land you a room without advance reservations. Still, if you have a particular place in mind it's a good idea to book in advance – rooms in many of the most popular mid-range hotels fill quickly, particularly during the summer season.

Booking Services & Private Rooms

The city tourist office, Copenhagen Information (☎ 70 22 24 42), Bernstorffsgade 1, can help you find accommodation. Rooms in private homes around the city cost from 200kr to 250kr for singles and 300kr to 350kr for doubles. This office also books unfilled hotel rooms, typically at discounted rates that vary from around 100kr off for budget hotels to as much as 50% off for top-end hotels – a situation that can sometimes make a splurge only slightly more costly than going cheap. These discounts, however, are based on supply and demand, and are not always available during busy periods. There's a 50kr fee per booking. The room booking service is open 10am to 8pm Monday to Saturday from May to August (and also 11am to 6pm on Sunday in July and August); during the rest of the year it's open 10am to 4pm on weekdays and 10am to 1pm on Saturday.

The Tourist Information desk in the arrivals area at Copenhagen Airport, just outside customs, also books unfilled Copenhagen hotel rooms at similarly discounted rates for a 50kr booking fee. If you're flying in and looking for a hotel, this is definitely the way to go. It's open longer hours, from 6am to at least midnight daily.

Use It (☎ 33 73 06 20), Rådhusstræde 13, books rooms in private homes, which cost from 150kr to 200kr for singles and 225kr to 300kr for doubles. There's no booking fee for the service. Use It also keeps tabs on which hostel beds are available and is a good source of information on subletting student housing and other long-term accommodation. For opening hours, see Tourist Offices in the Information section earlier in this chapter.

PLACES TO STAY – BUDGET

Camping

Bellahøj Camping (☎ 38 10 11 50, fax 38 10 13 32, Hvidkildevej 66, 2400 Copenhagen NV) Bus No 11 from Rådhuspladsen. Camping per person 57kr. Open June-Aug. This simple one-star camping ground is in a grassy field beside a busy road about 5km west of the city centre in the Bellahøj area. Facilities are minimal, but there are showers and a guest kitchen.

Absalon Camping (☎ 36 41 06 00, fax 36 41 02 93, e absalon@dcu.dk, Korsdalsvej 132, 2610 Rødovre) Camping per person 58kr. Open year-round. This three-star facility is 9km west of the city centre in the Rødovre suburb, near Brøndbyøster station on S-train line B. Facilities onsite include a coin laundry, food kiosk, playground and group kitchen.

Charlottenlund Strandpark (☎ 39 62 36 88, fax 39 61 08 16, e camping-fort@ mail.dk, Strandvejen 144B, 2920 Charlottenlund) Bus No 6. 65kr per person. Open mid-June–mid-Sept. Eight kilometres north of central Copenhagen, this friendly camping ground, on Charlottenlund beach, is set in the tree-lined grounds of an old moat-encircled coastal fortification. Space is limited so advance bookings are recommended. There's a snack kiosk, showers and a coin laundry on site; a bakery and a supermarket are just a few hundred metres away.

Hostels

HI Hostels There are three Copenhagen-area hostels under the auspices of Hostelling International. These hostels often fill early in summer so it's best to make reservations in advance.

Danhostel Copenhagen Bellahøj (☎ 38 28 97 15, fax 38 89 02 10, e bellahoej@ danhostel.dk, Herbergvejen 8, 2700 Brønshøj) Bus No 11 from Central Station. Dorm beds 100kr, doubles 250kr. Open Mar–mid-Jan. The most easily accessible HI-hostel, this place is in the quiet suburban neighbourhood of Bellahøj, 4km north-west of the city centre. Although it has 250 beds, it's quite cosy for its size. Facilities include a laundry room, Internet access, a cafeteria, TV room and table tennis.

Danhostel Copenhagen Amager (☎ 32 52 29 08, fax 32 52 27 08, e copenhagen@ danhostel.dk, Vejlands Allé 200, 2300 Copenhagen S) Dorm beds 95kr, doubles 250kr. Open mid-Jan–Nov. In an isolated part of Amager just off the E20, 5km from the city centre, this place ranks as one of Europe's largest hostels with 528 beds in a series of low-rise wings containing cells of two-bed and five-bed rooms. There's a laundry room, Internet access and a cafeteria. To get there, take the S-train to Sjælør station, then change to bus No 100S, which stops in front of the hostel. On weekdays until 5pm, bus No 46 runs from Central Station directly to the hostel.

Danhostel Lyngby (☎ 45 80 30 74, fax 45 80 30 32, w www.danhostel.dk/lyngby, Rådvad 1, 2800 Lyngby) Dorm beds 95kr, doubles 260kr. Open Apr–late Oct. This hostel, in a small hamlet on the northern side of Dyrehaven, occupies a manor-like house that can accommodate 94 people, mostly in rooms with four to six beds. The area is pretty, with swan-filled ponds; however, it's not a terribly practical place to make a base if your main focus is exploring central Copenhagen. Bus No 187 runs from Lyngby S-train station to the hostel, but it's an infrequent weekday-only bus, so check

the schedule in advance. Otherwise it's a 2km walk between the hostel and the nearest regularly serviced bus stop in Hjortekær.

Other Hostels Even when the HI hostels are full you can almost always find a bed at one of the city-sponsored hostels. Although they tend to be more of a crash-pad scene than the HI hostels, they're also more central and don't require hostel membership.

City Public Hostel (☎ 33 31 20 70, fax 33 55 00 85, e info@city-public-hostel.dk, Absalonsgade 8, Vesterbro, 1658 Copenhagen V) Dorm beds 120kr. Open early May-late Aug. Although there's one large dorm with 68 beds, most rooms contain six to 12 beds. Breakfast is available (20kr), there's a guest kitchen and you'll find affordable restaurants within a few blocks of the hostel. The hostel is less than a kilometre west of Central Station, just a 10-minute walk.

Sleep-In (☎ 35 26 50 59, fax 35 43 50 58, e copenhagen@sleep-in.dk, Blegdamsvej 132A, 2100 Copenhagen Ø) Dorm beds 90kr. Open July-Aug. This place, a few kilometres north of the city centre in the Østerbro district, is Copenhagen's largest summer hostel with some 286 beds occupying a sports hall that's curtained off into 'rooms' with four to six beds; there are no doors, but curtains offer a little privacy. There are free lockers, a guest kitchen and a cafe. You can use your own sleeping bag or rent bed linen (30kr). From the city centre take bus No 1, 6 or 14, get off at Trianglen and walk 300m southwest on Blegdamsvej. A bakery, grocery shop and restaurants are within easy walking distance.

Sleep-In Heaven (☎ 35 35 46 48, e morefun@sleepinheaven.com, Struenseegade 7, 2200 Copenhagen N) Bus No 8. Dorm beds 100kr. Open year-round. This privately run hostel, in the Nørrebro area, has 76 beds in a basement dorm. There's no group kitchen but there are a number of cheap eating places within walking distance. Breakfast is available for 35kr, sheets for 20kr.

Sleep-In Green (☎ 35 37 77 77, fax 35 35 56 40, w www.sleep-in-green.dk, Ravnsborggade 18, 2200 Copenhagen N) Dorm beds

95kr. Open late May-late Sept. This inviting place, with 68 dorm beds, is in the Nørrebro area close to cafes and nightlife. A breakfast of organic fare is available for 30kr. Take bus No 5 or 16, or walk northwest on Frederiksborggade over the canal and then turn right into Ravnsborggade.

Belægningen Avedørelejren (☎ *36 77 90 84, fax 36 77 95 87,* e *info@belaegningen .dk, Avedøre Tværvej 10, 2650 Hvidovre)* Bus No 650S from Central Station. Dorm beds 100kr, singles/doubles 250/350kr, with bath 350/450kr. Open year-round. About 7km south-west of the city centre, this hostel in the renovated barracks of a former military camp has friendly staff, high standards and cosy rooms with just a few beds. Breakfast is available for 40kr, and the hostel offers free Internet access, cheap bicycle rentals and a group kitchen. As an added perk you might spot some of Denmark's hottest screen stars, as the camp's rear buildings have been turned into a Danish 'Hollywood' housing the country's main movie companies.

Also see *Hotel Jørgensen*, which offers dorm beds year-round, in the following hotel section.

PLACES TO STAY – MID-RANGE

Copenhagen's main hotel quarter (and redlight district) is along the western side of Central Station, where rows of six-storey, early 20th-century buildings house one hotel after the other. Despite the porn shops and streetwalkers, the area is neither unpleasant nor notably dangerous, at least not by the standards of large cities elsewhere in Europe. In addition, its central location makes it a convenient spot in which to be based.

Although this Central Station area is jammed with mid-range hotels, Copenhagen has very few hotels that are priced affordably enough to really warrant the term 'budget'. If you're on a tight budget, the cheapest hotel rooms are those with shared bathroom and toilets off the hall.

The hotel rates quoted in this section include service charge, the 25% value-added tax (VAT) and, except where noted, a complimentary buffet-style breakfast.

Around Central Station

Løven (☎ *33 79 67 20, fax 33 15 86 46,* W *www.loeven.dk, Vesterbrogade 30, 1620 Copenhagen V)* Singles 250-350kr, doubles 350-450kr, 3-6–person flats 200kr per person. This place, which has both guest rooms with shared bath and spacious flats with full facilities, is one of the city's best deals. While it's not fancy, there are lots of pleasant touches, such as natural wood floors, and all guests have access to a guest kitchen. Breakfast is available for 40kr, and a bakery and inexpensive restaurants are just outside the front door.

Saga Hotel (☎ *33 24 49 44, fax 33 24 60 33,* e *booking@sagahotel.dk, Colbjørnsensgade 18, 1652 Copenhagen V)* Singles/ doubles 350/480kr, with bath 525/620kr. The Saga has 76 rooms, most of which have been renovated. There's no lift and it's multistorey, so you may have to climb some stairs, but the minimalist approach to lobby amenities keeps the rates low. The rooms are straightforward, but they're tidy, and have a phone and TV.

Absalon Hotel (☎ *33 24 22 11, fax 33 24 34 11,* e *info@absalon-hotel.dk, Helgolandsgade 15, 1653 Copenhagen V)* Singles/ doubles 475/625kr, with bath 850/1075kr; winter rates are about 15% less. This hotel has two wings, an older annexe with rooms that have a shared bathroom, and an upgraded section with modern rooms and full amenities.

Selandia Hotel (☎ *33 31 46 10, fax 33 31 46 09,* e *hotel-selandia@city.dk, Helgolandsgade 12, 1653 Copenhagen V)* Singles/ doubles 525/650kr, with bath 775/950kr; winter rates about 20% less. Although the cheaper rooms have a bathroom off the hall, all 84 rooms have a sink, desk and TV. The rooms are rather average for the money, but the hotel has an excellent breakfast buffet.

Hotel Nebo (☎ *33 21 12 17, fax 33 23 47 74,* e *nebo@email.dk, Istedgade 6, 1650 Copenhagen V)* Singles/doubles 490/680kr with bath 790/890kr; winter rates about 15% less. This hotel is just a stone's throw from Central Station. The 96 rooms are small but perfectly adequate with a sink, TV and phone, and the common areas include large, clean showers and a bright, cheery breakfast room.

Hotel Hebron (☎ 33 31 69 06, fax 33 31 90 67, ✉ tophotel@hebron.dk, Helgolandsgade 4, 1653 Copenhagen V) Singles/doubles 700/900kr, suites 1150/1280kr. Although it's in the middle of the hotel district, this 100-room hotel is smaller and quieter than its neighbours, and offers cosy rooms with the usual amenities as well as roomier suites with sitting areas.

Tiffany (☎ 33 21 80 50, fax 33 21 87 50, ✉ tiffany@hotel-tiffany.dk, Colbjørnsensgade 28, 1652 Copenhagen V) Singles/doubles 795/945kr. This pleasant little all-suite hotel has 24 rooms, each with private bath and all the usual amenities as well as a kitchenette with a refrigerator and microwave oven.

Nyhavn & Around

Sømandshjemmet Bethel (☎ 33 13 03 70, fax 33 15 85 70, Nyhavn 22, 1051 Copenhagen K) Singles/doubles 395/495kr, with bath from 495/595kr. This cosy little place calls itself a seamen's hotel but is open to all. It has a superb location right on Nyhavn canal, a lift to all floors, and two dozen good-sized rooms with an eclectic variety of furnishings. Many also have unbeatable views of Nyhavn – for the best, ask for a corner room.

Sophie Amalie Hotel (☎ 33 13 34 00, fax 33 11 77 07, ✉ anglehot@remmen.dk, Sankt Annæ Plads 21, 1250 Copenhagen K) Singles/doubles 850/1150kr, suites 1450/1550kr for double/triple occupancy; 10% discount for cash or travellers cheque. This popular with business hotel, has 134 modern rooms with the usual amenities. More interesting are the 6th-floor, split-level suites, which have harbour views, a living room with a sofa bed on the lower level and a loft bedroom above. Breakfast costs 95kr.

Hotel City (☎ 33 13 06 66, fax 33 13 06 67, ✉ hotelcity@hotelcity.dk, Peder Skrams Gade 24, 1054 Copenhagen K) Singles/doubles 940/1150kr; winter weekend rate 795kr. This smaller hotel, a Best Western affiliate, has 81 comfortable rooms, each with bath and cable TV.

Copenhagen Strand (☎ 33 48 99 00, fax 33 48 99 01, ✉ copenhagenstrand@arp-hansen .dk, Havnegade 37, 1958 Copenhagen K) Singles/doubles from 995/1195kr. This new mid-range hotel overlooking Copenhagen Harbour has a maritime decor and 174 well-appointed rooms, including some set aside exclusively for nonsmokers. There's an on-site business centre and a lobby bar.

Elsewhere in Copenhagen

Hotel Jørgensen (☎ 33 13 81 86, fax 33 15 51 05, ✉ hotel@post12.tele.dk, Rømersgade 11, 1362 Copenhagen K) Dorm beds 115kr, singles/doubles 425/525kr, with bath 525/650kr. This hotel, conveniently near Nørreport station, is popular with gay travellers but accommodates plenty of straight guests as well. The rooms are simple but have some pleasant touches. The hotel also has 13 dorm rooms with 150 beds. There are lockers for dorm guests.

Hotel Windsor (☎ 33 11 08 30, fax 33 11 63 87, ✉ hotelwindsor@inet.uni-c.dk, Frederiksborggade 30, 1360 Copenhagen K) Singles/doubles from 450/600kr. The Windsor, one block north-east of Hotel Jørgensen, is an exclusively gay hotel in an older building opposite Israels Plads. The two dozen rooms are straightforward but all have TV and most have refrigerators.

Cab-Inn Scandinavia (☎ 35 36 11 11, fax 35 36 11 14, ✉ cab-inn@cab-inn.dk, Vodroffsvej 57, 1900 Frederiksberg C) Singles/doubles 485/595kr. This modern hotel, about 1.5km north-west of Rådhuspladsen, has 201 sleekly compact rooms that resemble cabins in a cruise ship, complete with upper and lower bunks. Although small, the rooms are otherwise comfortable, and have a TV and bath. Breakfast is available for 50kr.

Cab-Inn Copenhagen (☎ 33 21 04 00, fax 33 21 74 09, ✉ cab-inn@cab-inn.dk, Danasvej 32, 1900 Frederiksberg C) Singles/doubles 485/595kr. A few blocks to the south-west of the Cab-Inn Scandinavia, this sister operation has the same type of rooms and the same rates. Both hotels have rooms that are accessible to people in wheelchairs.

Hotel Sankt Jørgen (☎ 35 37 15 11, fax 35 37 11 97, ✉ st.jørgen@teliamail.dk, Julius

Thomsens Gade 22, 1632 Copenhagen V) Singles/doubles 500/600kr. This family-run and pleasantly old-fashioned hotel has 19 spacious doubles and two rather cramped singles. If space is available, single travellers are usually given a double room for the price of a single. Most rooms have three to six beds, so they can easily accommodate families (add 125kr for each person beyond two). All bathrooms are shared.

Ibsens Hotel (☎ 33 13 19 13, fax 33 13 19 16, e hotel@ibsenshotel.dk, Vendersgade 23, 1363 Copenhagen K) Singles/doubles from 895/1100kr. Set in a renovated period building, Ibsens has the character of a 'boutique hotel' with creative decor and no two of its 103 rooms exactly the same. Some rooms have contemporary Scandinavian design, while others are furnished with antiques, but all boast a comfortable bed, TV and private bath.

PLACES TO STAY – TOP END
Around Central Station
Grand Hotel (☎ 33 27 69 00, fax 33 27 69 01, e grandhotel@arp-hansen.dk, Vesterbrogade 9, 1620 Copenhagen V) Singles/doubles from 1125/1460kr. The pleasant 100-year-old Grand, conveniently situated just north of Central Station, has 151 renovated rooms, including some set aside for nonsmokers.

Hotel Imperial (☎ 33 12 80 00, fax 33 93 80 31, e imperial@imperialhotel.dk, Vester Farimagsgade 9, 1606 Copenhagen V) Singles/doubles from 1395/1795kr, summer specials 1095/1395kr. The Imperial, opposite Vesterport S-train station, has a stellar reputation for service among the city's top-end hotels. All of the 163 rooms have modern decor with all the usual amenities plus few special touches including a deep Japanese-style bathtub.

Scandic Hotel Copenhagen (☎ 33 14 35 35, fax 33 32 12 23, Vester Søgade 6, e copenhagen@scandic-hotels.com, 1601 Copenhagen V) Singles/doubles 1200/1700kr. The 465-room Scandic, close to the Tycho Brahe Planetarium, is a well-regarded chain hotel with all the expected facilities, including a health club, secretarial services and a concierge.

Radisson SAS Royal Hotel (☎ 33 42 60 00, fax 33 42 61 00, w www.radissonsas.com, Hammerichsgade 1, 1611 Copenhagen V) Singles/doubles 2140/2340kr. This central 265-room multistorey hotel has modern rooms with full amenities and attracts the well heeled. There's also a centre for business travellers, a nightclub and a fitness centre.

Rådhuspladsen & Around
Ascot Hotel (☎ 33 12 60 00, fax 33 14 60 40, e hotel@ascot-hotel.dk, Studiestræde 61, 1554 Copenhagen V) Singles/doubles from 1190/1490kr. The Ascot occupies a former bathhouse erected 100 years ago by the same architect who designed Copenhagen's rådhus. The lobby boasts some interesting bas-reliefs depicting scenes from the bathhouse days. Most rooms are large and some have a kitchen.

Hotel Kong Frederik (☎ 33 12 59 02, fax 33 93 59 01, e anglehot@remmen.dk, Vester Voldgade 25, 1552 Copenhagen V) Singles/doubles from 970/1570kr. This classic hotel has an historic character with dark woods, antique furnishings and paintings of Danish royalty. The 110 rooms are poshly comfortable. Breakfast costs 105kr.

Palace Hotel (☎ 33 14 40 50, fax 33 14 52 79, e booking@principal.dk, Rådhuspladsen 57, 1550 Copenhagen V) Singles/doubles from 1750/1950kr, discounts up to 50% for last-minute guests. In an interesting period building, the Palace has 162 spacious rooms; the decor is old-fashioned, with upholstered chairs, heavy curtains and brass lamps.

Nyhavn & Around
Copenhagen Admiral Hotel (☎ 33 74 14 16, fax 33 74 14 15, e admiral@admiral-hotel .dk, Toldbodgade 24-28, 1253 Copenhagen K) Singles/doubles 1050/1295kr, suites 1415kr. For nautical atmosphere it's hard to beat this waterfront hotel, in a renovated 18th-century granary replete with brick archways and sturdy beams of Pom-eranian pine. Each of the 366 rooms has a nice blend of period charm and modern conveniences. Breakfast costs 95kr.

71 Nyhavn Hotel (☎ 33 43 62 00, fax 33 43 62 01, e 71nyhavnhotel@arp-hansen.dk,

Nyhavn 71, 1051 Copenhagen K) Singles/ doubles from 1200/1450kr, superior rooms with views 1450/1750kr. Another hotel in a renovated 200-year-old harbourside warehouse, it too has incorporated the building's period features, such as exposed wooden beams. Some of the rooms have fine views of the harbour and Nyhavn canal.

Hotel Opera (☎ *33 47 83 00, fax 33 47 83 01,* e *hotelopera@arp-hansen.dk, Tordenskjoldsgade 15, 1055 Copenhagen K)* Singles/ doubles from 930/1390kr, weekend rates 850/1115kr. The 87-room Opera, just south of Det Kongelige Teater, has an old-world character befitting its theatre-district location. Although it's not as fancy as some other top-end period hotels, the rates are a bit lower and the rooms comfortable.

Neptun Hotel (☎ *33 96 20 00, fax 33 96 20 97,* e *info@neptun-group.dk, Sankt Annæ Plads 18, 1250 Copenhagen K)* Singles/ doubles 1400/1600kr, weekend deals (2 adults & 2 children) 1125kr. This respected 1st-class hotel, a block north of Nyhavn, is affiliated with the Choice Hotels chain.

Phoenix (☎ *33 95 95 00, fax 33 33 98 33,* e *phoenixcopenhagen@arp-hansen.dk, Bredgade 37, 1260 Copenhagen K)* Singles/ doubles 1290/1650kr on weekdays, 950/ 1250kr at weekends. Just a block north of Nyhavn, the Phoenix is one of the city's more popular deluxe hotels. It has 212 plush rooms with heavy carpets, chandeliers, upholstered chairs and the like.

Hotel d'Angleterre (☎ *33 12 00 95, fax 33 12 11 18,* e *anglehot@remmen.dk, Kong ens Nytorv 34, 1050 Copenhagen K)* Singles/ doubles from 2070/2370kr. Visiting celebrities generally opt for this exclusive hotel, which has chandeliers, marble floors and a history dating back to the 17th century. It also has Copenhagen's highest rates but, despite its lengthy history, it no longer enjoys the solidly pre-eminent reputation it once had among Copenhagen's top hotels.

Elsewhere in Copenhagen

Hotel Kong Arthur (☎ *33 11 12 12, fax 33 32 61 30,* e *hotel@kongarthur.dk, Nørre Søgade 11, 1370 Copenhagen K)* Singles/doubles 1095/1320kr. About 1km north of the city

centre, this 107-room hotel is in an attractive 19th-century building that fronts the lake Peblinge Sø.

Radisson SAS Scandinavia Hotel (☎ *33 96 50 00, fax 33 96 55 00,* W *www.radisson sas.com, Amager Blvd 70, 2300 Copenhagen S)* Singles/doubles 1195/1695kr. This 542-room, high-rise hotel south of Christianshavn has services for business travellers, a pool and fitness centre, squash courts and Copenhagen's only casino. Nonsmoking rooms are available.

Hilton Copenhagen Airport (☎ *32 50 15 01, fax 32 52 85 28,* e *res_copenhagen-airport@ hilton.com, Ellehammersvej 20, 2770 Kastrup)* Singles/doubles 1300/1800kr. This new hotel, right at the airport, has 375 rooms with full amenities including top-end touches such as Bang & Olufsen TVs. There's a fitness centre, a swimming pool and conference facilities.

PLACES TO EAT

Copenhagen offers plenty of good dining options for every budget. The selections are varied. You can find old-fashioned Danish pubs with meat-and-potatoes grub; trendy cafes serving a blend of Danish food spiced with Asian influences; and some very fancy restaurants offering authentic international cuisines.

Around Central Station

Central Station has numerous fast-food eateries, including the popular international chains. More interesting is the station's *Gourmet Marked,* a little food court with a half-dozen deli-style eateries, where you can get salads, stir-fries and pizza, all at bargain prices.

Astor Pizza (☎ *33 14 90 14, Vesterbrodgade 7)* Buffet 49/59kr before/after 5pm. Open 11am-11pm daily. Just north of Central Station, this pizzeria offers a reasonable all-you-can-eat deal of pizza and salad.

Ankara (☎ *33 31 92 33, Vesterbrogade 35)* Buffet 39/59kr before/after 4pm. Open noon-midnight daily. This casual 2nd-floor restaurant has a good-value all-you-can-eat buffet of numerous cold and hot traditional Middle Eastern dishes, including calamari, chicken, lamb and salads. Ankara also has a fast-food bar on the street level with inexpensive felafel sandwiches.

Sifa (☎ 33 25 10 10, Vesterbrogade 39) Buffet 49/69kr, 3-course meal 69/88kr, before/after 4pm. Open 11am-midnight daily. Whether you opt for the buffet or the three-course plate, Sifa also offers a wide variety of Middle Eastern dishes to select from. There's belly dancing on the weekends.

Restaurant Shezan (☎ 33 24 78 88, Viktoriagade 22) Veg dishes 50kr, meat dishes 60kr. Open noon-11pm daily. Shezan serves authentic Pakistani food such as *dhal turka* (spiced lentils) or *chana* (chickpea) curry as well as a range of chicken and lamb dishes.

India Palace (☎ 33 12 30 38, HC Andersens Blvd 13) Lunch/dinner buffet 59/115kr. Open 11.30am-11pm daily. If you have a big appetite and fancy Indian food, this restaurant features all-you-can-eat buffets.

Scala, on Vesterbrogade opposite Tivoli, is a multistorey building full of fast-food eateries, though few are notable. The best bets include **Khao Thai** (☎ 33 15 66 99), offering noodle dishes for 55kr, and **Italian Corner** (☎ 33 93 55 93), with various pasta plates for 45kr.

Hard Rock Cafe (☎ 33 12 43 33, Vesterbrogade 3) Lunch specials 49kr, other meals 85-150kr. Open noon-midnight daily. Next to the tourist office, Hard Rock has burgers, barbecued ribs and steaks as well as the expected rock memorabilia decor and a shop selling its logo T-shirts. Happy hour is at 5.30pm with half-price mixed drinks.

Tivoli

Tivoli boasts nearly 30 places to eat. These range from simple stalls offering typical amusement-park fare such as hot dogs and ice cream, to some of the more respected eating establishments in the city. You need to pay Tivoli admission (or have a Copenhagen Card) to eat at these places – and they are only open during the Tivoli season. Kitchens in these restaurants generally stay open until around 11pm; the restaurants close when Tivoli does.

Promenaden (☎ 33 75 07 70) Lunch/dinner mains around 125/175kr. A good, moderately

priced Tivoli restaurant, Promenaden enjoys a view of the open-air stage and serves spareribs and steaks.

Grøften (☎ 33 12 11 25) Smørrebrød 36-90kr, 2-course salmon meal 195kr. The speciality at this popular restaurant is a type of smørrebrød with tiny fjord shrimps spiced with lime and fresh pepper.

Bagatellen (☎ 33 75 07 51) 3-course lunch/dinner deals 150/380kr. One of the trendier choices in Tivoli, Bagatellen blends Mediterranean and Californian influences and offers both indoor dining and outdoor pond-view tables.

Divan 2 (☎ 33 12 51 51) Multicourse meals 375-500kr. Widely considered to be Tivoli's finest restaurant for both food and service, this restaurant serves gourmet French food and has a vintage wine collection. It's been in operation since Tivoli opened in 1843.

Divan 1 (☎ 33 11 42 42) Multicourse meals 375-500kr. The sister restaurant to Divan 2, Divan 1 has a similar history, garden setting and reputation for good food, but with a menu emphasising Danish and international fare.

Strøget & Around

Strøget has an abundance of cheap eateries, including ice-cream, hamburger and hot-dog stands as well as many hole-in-the-wall kebab joints.

Shawarma Grill House (☎ 33 12 63 23, Frederiksberggade 36) Sandwiches 25-40kr. Open 11am-at least midnight daily. A two-minute walk from Rådhuspladsen, this bustling eatery serves an excellent *shawarma* (pitta-bread sandwich of shaved beef and lamb topped with a yogurt dressing), felafel sandwiches and kebabs. It has a sit-down counter on the ground floor and a dining room upstairs.

Reinh van Hauen (☎ 33 12 12 64, Mikkel Bryggers Gade 2) Sandwiches 28kr. Open 7.30am-6pm daily. This excellent bakery uses organic ingredients and has cafe tables where you can sit and eat.

Café de Paris (☎ 33 11 51 75, Vimmelskaftet 39) Buffet 39kr. For a cheap all-you-can-eat meal, try this little pizzeria, which offers a simple pizza and salad buffet.

La Glace (☎ *33 14 46 46, Skoubogade 3*) Desserts around 40kr. Open 8am-5pm Mon-Fri, 9am-5pm Sat, 11am-5pm Sun. This is a classic *konditori* (bakery-cafe) that has been serving tea and fancy cakes to socialites for more than a century.

Pizza Hut (☎ *33 93 99 55, Amagertorv 7*) Buffet 49kr, pizzas from 70kr. Open 11am-11pm daily. Pizza Hut, beside the Tobacco Museum, has a good pizza and salad buffet until 4pm and a wide variety of pizzas made to order.

Huset med det Grønne Træ (☎ *33 12 87 86, Gammel Torv 20*) Sandwiches 40kr, lunch plate 105kr. Open noon-3pm Mon-Sat. This little lunch cafe is at the north-western corner of Gammel Torv and beside the linden tree from which it takes its name. Housed in a period building dating from 1796, it offers quintessential Danish fare, with smørrebrød sandwiches, draught beer and a dozen brands of schnapps.

RizRaz (☎ *33 15 05 75, Kompagnistræde 20*) Daytime/evening buffet 49/59kr, mains 100kr. Open 11.30am-midnight daily. Just south of Strøget, this pleasant cafe offers a delicious Mediterranean-style vegetarian buffet including felafel, pizza, hummus and salads. Many people just go with the buffet but you can also opt to order lamb kebabs or seafood dishes from the menu and the buffet will be included free with the main dish.

Café Hovedtelegrafen (☎ *33 41 09 00, Købmagergade 37*) Light meals around 60kr. Open 11am-5pm Thurs-Tues, 11am-8pm Wed) daily. On the roof of the Post & Tele Museum, this cafe has a splendid view of the city and a good menu as well, featuring items like gazpacho soup, organic feta cheese salads and grilled chicken sandwiches.

Den Grønne Kælder (☎ *33 93 01 40, Pilestræde 48*) Lunch/dinner 50/100kr. Open 11am-10pm Mon-Sat. You'll get healthy meals at this strictly vegetarian restaurant. At lunch, served until 5pm, you can select two salads and a hot dish or quiche for just 50kr. At dinner there's a wider variety of hot dishes to select from.

Slotskælderen hos Gitte Kik (☎ *33 11 15 37, Fortunstræde 4*) Sandwiches 35-75kr. Open 11am-3pm Mon-Fri. A few minutes' walk from Folketinget, this is a compact smørrebrød lunch spot where you can literally rub shoulders with Danish members of parliament.

Krogs Fiskerestaurant (☎ *33 15 89 15, Gammel Strand 38*) 3-course lunch/dinner 278/395kr. Open 11.30am-4pm & 5.30pm-midnight Mon-Sat. North of Slotsholms Kanal, Krogs is a good option for fine dining. It specialises in fresh fish served with organic produce.

Kommandanten (☎ *33 12 09 90, Ny Adelgade 7*) Mains around 250kr; changing 3-course menu 380kr. Open 5.30pm-10pm Mon-Sat. Kommandanten has received numerous accolades, including the Michelin Guides' highest rating among Copenhagen's restaurants. It features French-influenced dishes such as rack of lamb and duck in cabernet sauce.

McGrails (☎ *33 13 20 43, Gammel Torv 6*) This small health-food shop on the north-eastern corner of Gammel Torv sells tofu, snacks, vitamins and organic wines.

Gråbrødre Torv

Greyfriars' Square, between Strøget and the Latin Quarter, has a few popular restaurants grouped around a cobblestone plaza.

Peder Oxe (☎ *33 11 00 77, Gråbrødre Torv 11*) Mains 98-160kr. Open 11.30am-1am daily. For a pleasant dinner treat, try this place, which fronts the square and offers affordable fine dining with a cosy Danish country ambience. The restaurant has tasty fish and organic meat dishes, served with a good salad buffet. It also has a nifty house-wine deal that allows you to pay for only as much of the bottle as you end up drinking. Copenhagen's oldest monastery was built on this site in 1238 and the restaurant's wine cellar retains part of the old stone foundations.

Jensen's Bøfhus (☎ *33 32 78 00, Gråbrødre Torv 15*) Lunch deals 45kr, dinner 90-150kr. Open 11am-11pm daily. Part of a Danish chain of steak restaurants, this place, in another period house fronting Gråbrødre Torv, also has a pleasant atmosphere. Although the food is just average, the lunch specials are a good value.

Pasta Basta (☎ 33 11 21 31, Valkendorfs-gade 22) Buffet 69kr, mains 60-115kr. Open 11.30am-3am Sun-Thur, 11.30am-5am Fri & Sat. The mainstay at this eating place, immediately south of Gråbrødre Torv, is a self-service buffet of various cold pasta and salad dishes. You can also order from the main menu, which includes hot pasta dishes served with the likes of mussels, red snapper or lamb. It's a popular spot with night owls looking for a late meal or drink.

Restaurant Gråbrødre Torv 21 (☎ 33 11 47 07, Gråbrødre Torv 21) Mains around 160kr, 3-course daily special 268kr. Open 6pm-10pm daily. New on the block, this restaurant has excellent Danish food and makes a good choice for a night of fine dining.

Latin Quarter & Around
Studenterhuset (☎ 35 32 38 61, Købmager-gade 52) Light meals 25-40kr. Open noon-midnight Mon-Fri. This low-key student hang-out near the Rundetårn features some good light meals, including vegetarian or meat sandwiches.

Atlas Bar (☎ 33 15 03 52, Larsbjørnstræde 18) Veg/meat mains about 65/110kr. Open 11am-10pm Mon-Sat. This casual basement cafe in the heart of the gay district, has a changing blackboard menu that includes salads, vegetarian fare and chicken. Many of the dishes use organic ingredients.

Klaptræet (☎ 33 13 31 48, Kultorvet 11) Light meals 35-50kr. Open 10am-2pm Mon-Thur, 10am-5pm Fri & Sat, 11am-midnight Sun. This 2nd-floor cafe is a student haunt serving burgers, chilli con carne and salads. Kultorvet itself becomes a popular beer garden in summer, when some of the nearby businesses, including Klaptræet, set up tables in the square and sell beer on tap.

Ankara (☎ 33 15 19 15, Krystalgade 8) Buffet 39/59kr before/after 4pm. Open noon-midnight Mon-Sat, 2pm-midnight Sun. This pleasant Turkish restaurant offers candlelit dining and a tempting buffet of salads, rice and numerous hot and cold dishes.

Det Lille Apotek (☎ 33 12 56 06, Store Kannikestræde 15) Lunch plates around 100kr, 3-course dinner 178kr. Open 11am-midnight Mon-Sat, noon-midnight Sun. An

old favourite for traditional Danish food at moderate prices, this place dates back to 1720 and claims the title of Copenhagen's oldest restaurant. Typical meals include pickled herring, fish fillet and smørrebrød.

Ristorante Italiano (☎ 33 11 12 95, Fiol-stræde 2) Lunch specials 49kr, other dishes 55-165kr. Open 11.30am-11pm daily. Behind Vor Frue Kirke, this place has authentic Italian food and decor. Lunch specials include lasagne or calamari, while the main menu includes everything from pizzas to scampi. In summer the outdoor cafe tables are an agreeable sunny-day option.

Café Sommersko (☎ 33 14 81 89, Kron-prinsensgade 6) Light meals 40-90kr. Open from at least 10am-midnight daily. This cafe draws a high-energy university crowd and serves up 50 different brands of beer. The menu offers the likes of satay with jasmine rice or salmon with pasta. The cafe also serves cakes, desserts and breakfast items.

Govindas (☎ 33 33 74 44, Nørre Farim-agsgade 82) Buffet 55kr. Open noon-8.30pm Mon-Sat. At this pleasant spot, south of the Botanisk Have, Hare Krishna devotees serve up an all-you-can-eat vegetarian Indian meal of savoury hot dishes, basmati rice, soup and salad. There's no religious hard sell, just good wholesome food at honest prices.

St Gertruds Kloster (☎ 33 14 66 30, Hauser Plads 32) Mains from 250kr, 3-course dinner from 350kr. Open 4pm-midnight daily. This elegant restaurant is in a former medieval monastery, sections of which date from the 14th century. The most popular of the four dining rooms is the one that occupies the cellar, which has arched brick walls and is lit by 1500 candles. The restaurant specialises in Danish-French cuisine. Reservations are requested.

Copenhagen's main *produce market* is at Israels Plads, a few minutes' walk west of Nørreport station. Stalls are set up until 5pm Monday to Friday and until 2pm on Saturday, when it doubles as a flea market.

Nørrebrogade
The Nørrebrogade area, with its mix of students and immigrants, has a wide variety of

restaurants serving both Danish and international fare.

Floras Kaffe Bar (☎ 35 39 00 18, *Blågårdsgade 27*) Light meals 40-75kr. Open 10am-at least midnight daily. This relaxed cafe offers a full range of coffees, desserts and reasonably priced soups, sandwiches and salads. There are usually a couple of hot meal specials as well and much of the fare is organic. In summer you can sit outside and soak up the sunshine.

Indian Corner (☎ 35 39 28 02, *Nørrebrogade 59*) Veg dishes around 65kr, meat or fish 90kr. Open 4pm-11pm Wed-Mon. This pleasant little restaurant serves good Indian food at moderate prices.

Sebastopol (☎ 35 36 30 02, *Guldbergsgade 2*) Light meals 50-90kr. Open 9am-1am daily. This stylish cafe, overlooking Sankt Hans Torv, offers baguette sandwiches, Greek salad, vegetarian lasagne, nachos and the like. There's live jazz on Sunday.

Picnic (☎ 35 39 09 53, *Fælledvej 22*) Dishes 50-75kr. Open from at least noon-10pm daily. This small and casual cafe has deli-style dishes including a wide range of salads. Most everything here is organic.

Pussy Galore's Flying Circus (☎ 35 24 53 00, *Sankt Hans Torv*) Mains 60-100kr, breakfast buffet 30kr. Open 8am-2am Mon-Fri, 9am-2am Sat & Sun. Nørrebro's trendiest dig, it has both indoor seating and al fresco tables on the square. The varied menu ranges from salads and burgers to international fare like Goa spiced lamb. On weekday mornings until 10am there's a breakfast buffet of eggs, cereals and bread.

Quattro Fontane (☎ 35 39 39 31, *Guldbergsgade 3*) Mains 55-120kr. Open 4pm-1am daily. This Italian restaurant has good pizza and pasta dishes as well as meat and fish mains.

Mexicali (☎ 35 39 47 04, *Åboulevard 12*) Veg/meat dishes around 80/100kr. Open 5pm-midnight Mon-Sat. Mexicali offers a range of the usual Mexican dishes such as burritos and enchiladas served with rice.

Nyhavn & Around

In the summer season the restaurants that run along the northern side of the scenic Nyhavn canal set tables outside, turning the street into a line of pavement cafes. On sunny days this is a favourite spot for Copenhageners to sit with friends and linger over a cold beer.

Jasmin (☎ 33 13 35 34, *cnr Nyhavn & Toldbodgade*) Combination plates 40kr. Open 11am-11pm daily. This hole-in-the-wall joint shores up Nyhavn's budget end with good Thai food at honest prices. The food is takeaway but you can sit alongside the nearby docks and get a fine canal view.

Nyhavns Færgekro (☎ 33 15 15 88, *Nyhavn 5*) Herring buffet 89kr. Open 11.30am-11.30pm daily. For a thoroughly Danish experience, don't miss the lunchtime buffet at this atmospheric restaurant right on the canal. This all-you-can-eat buffet has 10 different kinds of herring, including baked, marinated and rollmops, with condiments to sprinkle on top, and bread and boiled potatoes to round off the meal. Dinner betrays French influences and is pricier.

Cap Horn (☎ 33 12 85 04, *Nyhavn 21*) Lunch plate 69kr, mains 90-130kr. Open 11.30am-1am daily. This restaurant is also on the canal and specialises in Danish fare, including a smørrebrød lunch plate and herring and steak dishes; it uses predominantly organic ingredients.

Els (☎ 33 14 13 41, *Store Strandstræde 3*) 2-course lunch 200kr, 3-course dinner 388kr. Open noon-3pm & 5.30-10pm Mon-Sat, 5.30pm-10pm Sun. Els offers formal dining and good food in a classic upmarket Danish setting. Although the decor is 19th century, the menu blends French and contemporary Danish influences.

Ida Davidsen (☎ 33 91 36 55, *Store Kongensgade 70*) Smørrebrød 50-150kr. Open 10am-5pm (last order 4pm) Mon-Fri. Considered the top smørrebrød restaurant in Denmark, Ida Davidsen serves an almost limitless variety of open sandwiches and makes for a quintessential Danish lunch experience. It's just a few minutes' walk north of Nyhavn.

Amadeus (☎ 33 32 35 11, *Store Kongensgade 62*) Light meals 60-85kr, 3-course dinner 180kr. Open 11am-11.30pm daily. This gem of a place is a combined cafe and organic bakery with fresh wholesome food. Lunch features creative salads and a variety of tempting sandwiches, ranging from club to smørrebrød. At dinnertime the chef prepares seasonal Danish dishes, offering a three-course menu of the day. There's dining both indoors and in a rear courtyard.

ENTERTAINMENT

Copenhagen is a 24-hour party city. For free entertainment simply stroll along Strøget, especially between Nytorv and Højbro Plads, which in the late afternoon and evening is a bit like an impromptu three-ring circus with musicians, magicians, jugglers and other street performers.

There are scores of backstreet cafes and clubs with live music. As a general rule, entry is free on weeknights, while there's usually a cover charge at weekends or any time someone special is playing. Danes tend to be late-nighters and many places don't really start to get going until 11pm or midnight.

The free publications *Nat & Dag* and *Musik Kalenderen* list entertainment and concert schedules in detail; they're available at the tourist office and various clubs.

See the Public Holidays & Special Events section in the Facts for the Visitor chapter and the 'Festive Denmark' special section for details about festivals, holidays and other major events.

Bars & Cafes

When Danes want to go out for a drink, they head for a cafe. Copenhageners are fond of cosy places and consequently cafes play a leading role in the city's social scene. Cafes are generally places where you can go and stay for hours – they not only serve alcohol, but if you've an inkling for a meal, dessert or coffee, you can order those as well. And some cafes add music to the mix, particularly at weekends.

Absalon's Bar at the western end of Strøget is a small local watering hole best known for its curious basement toilet, which has a couple of stones embedded in the wall that are thought to have once belonged to a 12th-century church constructed by Bishop Absalon.

Australian Bar (☎ 33 15 04 80) at the rear of Vestergade 10, one block north of Strøget, is a casual place with a Down Under decor and a half-dozen pool tables.

Café Europa (☎ 33 12 04 28, *Amagertorv 1*), a continental-style cafe, sets up its tables right on Højbro Plads on sunny days, making it a great place for people-watching.

The Dubliner (☎ 33 32 22 26, *Amagertorv 5*) on the western side of Højbro Plads is a trendy pub with Danish and Irish brews, live Irish folk music and big-screen sports TV.

Trendy ***Krasnapolsky*** (☎ 33 32 88 00, *Vestergade 10*) west of Gammel Torv boasts the longest bar in Copenhagen and attracts a large late-night crowd.

Peder Oxe (☎ 33 11 00 77, *Gråbrødre Torv 11*) has an atmospheric wine cellar that incorporates some of the stone walls from Copenhagen's oldest monastery, built on this site in 1238.

Britannia (☎ 33 14 89 69, *Løvstræde 4*) two blocks south of the Rundetårn is not only a dance club, but also has a bar with darts and eight pool tables.

Base Camp Holmen (☎ 70 23 23 18, *Halvtolv 12*) is a former military-base warehouse that has been converted into a dining and entertainment venue. This huge, cavernous place attracts large crowds on the weekend when there's live music.

A pleasant place to relax on sunny summer days is ***Christianshavns Bådudlejning og Café*** (☎ 32 96 53 53, *Overgaden neden Vandet 29*), a friendly outdoor cafe right on the edge of Christianshavn canal at the boat-rental dock.

Music & Dance Clubs

The Nørrebro area has a number of hot entertainment spots.

Rust (☎ 35 24 52 00, *Guldbergsgade 8*) A bustling place that attracts one of the largest club crowds in Copenhagen, Rust has a couple of dance floors, a wide variety of current music and also hosts occasional international performers.

Stengade 30 (☎ 35 36 09 38, *Stengade 18*) Stengade has a lively alternative scene with everything from new wave and hip-hop to techno and big-name rock.

From top left: Highlights of Copenhagen: A tribute to the city's founder, Bishop Absalon, at Højbro Plads on Slotsholmen; A perfect reflection of the tower of Nikolaj Kirke on Gammel Strand; The classical mythology-inspired *Ganymede with Jupiter's Eagle* on display at Thorvaldsens Museum.

MARTIN MOOS

ANDERS BLOMQVIST

MARTIN MOOS

MARTIN MOOS

MARTIN MOOS

Clockwise from top left: Art in Copenhagen: Hans Christian Andersen in the gardens of Rosenborg Slot; A saxophonist busks near Højbro Plads; An alternative shutter in the Free State of Christiana; Fashion mannequins with attitude in a Kultorvet store; An uninhibited sculpture at Museum Erotica.

Barcelona (☎ 35 35 76 11, Fælledvej 21) Heavily into R&B, hip-hop and soul, Barcelona has a dance floor and a DJ from Thursday to Saturday.

Vega (☎ 33 25 70 11, Enghavevej 40) In the Vesterbro area, this is one of Copenhagen's hottest spots with big-name rock and jazz bands performing on its main stage and underground acts on a smaller stage.

In (☎ 33 11 74 78, Nørregade 1) On the northern side of Strøget's Gammel Torv, this dance club attracts a young crowd with current chart toppers and some world music.

Club Mantra (☎ 33 11 11 13, Bernstorffsgade 3) This disco at Tivoli features reggae and rhythm and blues.

Loppen (☎ 32 57 84 22, Bådsmandsstræde 43) In Christiania, Loppen is a popular spot with live music ranging from funk and soul to punk rock from Wednesday to Saturday.

Copenhagen Jazz House (☎ 33 15 03 66, Niels Hemmingsensgade 10) This is the city's leading jazz spot, featuring top Danish musicians and occasional international performers. The music runs the gamut from bebop to fusion jazz, and there's a large dance floor.

La Fontaine (☎ 33 11 60 98, Kompagnistræde 11) In central Copenhagen, this club is a casual late-night venue for swing and mainstream jazz musicians, including visiting artists who sometimes end up jamming together.

Mojo (☎ 33 11 64 53, Løngangstræde 21) East of Tivoli, this is a hot spot for blues, with live entertainment nightly.

Park Café (☎ 35 42 62 48, Østerbrogade 79) The Østerbro area's main night spot, Park has a couple of large dance floors – the upper level one with live music and the basement floor with a DJ. The music is varied but progressive and the crowd tends to be young and stylish.

Ballet, Opera & Theatre

Det Kongelige Teater (☎ 33 69 69 69, fax 33 69 69 30, Kongens Nytorv) Tickets 50-300kr. Den Kongelige Ballet (The Royal Ballet) and Den Kongelige Opera (The Royal Opera) perform at this theatre. The season runs from mid-August to late May, skipping the main summer months.

An English-language brochure with the season schedule is available from the tourist office, or write to The Royal Theatre, Box Office, PO Box 2185, 1017 Copenhagen K. For bookings and information phone between 1pm and 7pm Monday to Saturday.

There are also a few smaller theatres in Copenhagen that stage performances of popular plays and musicals; programs are published in the daily newspapers and *Copenhagen This Week*.

Of special interest for children are the free marionette shows performed during the months of June, July and August on the eastern side of Kongens Have, the public gardens near Rosenborg Slot. These puppet shows last about half an hour and begin at 2pm and 3pm daily except Monday.

Tivoli The *Tivoli Koncertsal (Concert Hall; ☎ 33 15 10 12, Tietgensgade 30)* is the venue for symphony orchestra, string quartet and other classical music performances by Danish and international musicians. There's a ballet festival each season featuring top international troupes, as well as cabaret performances. They also have modern dance performances by such big names as the Alvin Ailey dance troupe. Tickets are sold at the Tivoli Billetcenter (see the Booking Offices section that follows).

Tivoli also holds numerous free performances for park-goers. One such free show is the Italian-influenced *Commedia Dell'Arte*, a pantomime that plays nightly at the open-air pantomime theatre near the Vesterbrogade entrance.

Booking Offices The Tivoli Billetcenter (☎ 38 88 22 22, fax 38 88 22 23), Vesterbrogade 3, at the main entrance, is a good first stop when looking for tickets of any kind. Not only does it sell Tivoli performance tickets, but it's also the box office for ARTE, which handles tickets for plays in Copenhagen; and an agent for BilletNet, which sells tickets for concerts and music festivals nationwide. Tivoli Billetcenter is open 10am to 8pm daily, but closed Sunday in the low season.

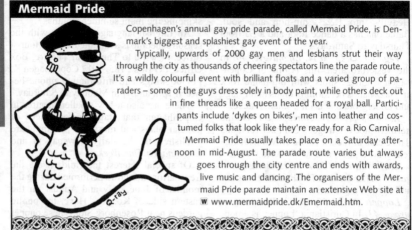

Mermaid Pride

Copenhagen's annual gay pride parade, called Mermaid Pride, is Denmark's biggest and splashiest gay event of the year.

Typically, upwards of 2000 gay men and lesbians strut their way through the city as thousands of cheering spectators line the parade route. It's a wildly colourful event with brilliant floats and a varied group of paraders – some of the guys dress solely in body paint, while others deck out in fine threads like a queen headed for a royal ball. Participants include 'dykes on bikes', men into leather and costumed folks that look like they're ready for a Rio Carnival. Mermaid Pride usually takes place on a Saturday afternoon in mid-August. The parade route varies but always goes through the city centre and ends with awards, live music and dancing. The organisers of the Mermaid Pride parade maintain an extensive Web site at w www.mermaidpride.dk/Emermaid.htm.

Gay & Lesbian Venues

Copenhagen has one of the liveliest gay and lesbian scenes in Europe.

Pan Disco (☎ 33 11 37 84, *Knabrostræde 3*) On the southern side of Strøget, this is the main mixed gay and lesbian dance spot, with three bars and two dance floors. Typically one disco spins the latest sounds and the other focuses on camp pop and romantic music.

Never Mind (☎ 33 11 88 86, *Nørre Voldgade 2*) A trendy dance bar, Never Mind attracts a mixed late-night crowd.

Cosy Bar (☎ 33 12 74 27, *Studiestræde 24*) This is a popular late-night place for men.

Sebastian (☎ 33 32 22 79, *Hyskenstræde 10*) This pleasant bar and cafe attracts a mixed gay and lesbian crowd.

Masken (☎ 33 91 09 37, *Studiestræde 33*) Here you'll find a mellow atmosphere, cheap beer and good sandwiches. It's mainly a hang-out for gay men, but Thursday is Ladies Night.

Copenhagen has about two dozen other gay bars, clubs and cafes, nearly half of them concentrated along Studiestræde in the two blocks between Vester Voldgade and Nørregade. For a complete list pick up a copy of *PAN-bladet*, which is available at gay businesses, including the clubs mentioned here. This monthly newspaper has information on gay organisations, saunas and other places of interest. An English-language version is published each June.

For information on gay-friendly hotels, see Hotel Jørgensen and Hotel Windsor in the earlier Places to Stay section.

Open-Air Concerts

Throughout the summer numerous concerts are held in Copenhagen's parks and squares; most are free, though some charge small fees. The tourist office can provide you with the latest on where the smaller events are taking place. The two leading outdoor venues that have scheduled entertainment throughout the summer are Pavillonen and Femøren.

Pavillonen (☎ 35 26 01 11, *Borgmester Jensens Allé 45*) Bus No 1, 6 or 14 from city centre. This open-air cafe at Fælledparken, a large park in the Østerbro district, stages free concerts on Friday and Saturday nights all summer long. The entertainment can be anything from tango to blues or rock.

Femøren park (☎ 32 59 79 33, *Amager Strandvej*) Bus No 12 or 13. Admission 40-200kr, depending upon the group. This park on the coast of Amager stages beachside open-air concerts on Saturday and Sunday afternoons from June to August. The music is rock or pop, usually by top Danish groups and each summer there are usually a few international names such as Deep Purple or Tower of Power. Get the latest schedule online at **W** www.5-oeren.dk.

Cinema

There are about 20 screens showing first-release movies in the group of cinemas along Vesterbrogade between Rådhuspladsen and Central Station. Tickets for movies range from around 40kr for weekday matinees to 75kr for weekend evenings. As in the rest of Denmark, movies are generally shown in their original language with Danish subtitles.

Casino

Casino Copenhagen (☎ *33 96 59 65, Amager Blvd 70)* Open 2pm-4am daily. If you want to try your hand with the high rollers, this casino at the Radisson SAS Scandinavia Hotel in Amager has slot machines, stud poker and both American and French roulette. Admission is restricted to those aged 18 and over.

SHOPPING

Along Copenhagen's main shopping street, Strøget, you can find numerous speciality shops selling everything from clothing to Danish porcelain and electronics.

Sweater Market (☎ *33 15 27 73, Frederiksberggade 15)* This shop on Strøget sells quality Scandinavian sweaters.

Bang & Olufsen (☎ *33 15 04 22, Østergade 3)* For sleek, top-priced audio equipment, check out Bang & Olufsen products in its shop at the eastern end of Strøget.

China & Silver

Denmark's best-known porcelain and silver are made under the umbrella of Royal Copenhagen Ltd. The two shops mentioned here are side by side on Strøget and have museum-quality displays that are worth a look whether you're a shopper or not.

Royal Copenhagen Porcelain (☎ *33 13 71 81, Amagertorv 6)* Famous for its Flora Danica pattern, Royal Copenhagen Porcelain is in an imposing Renaissance house (circa 1616) near Højbro Plads.

Georg Jensen (☎ *33 13 71 81, Amagertorv 4)* This shop features fine silverwork, including cutlery, candle holders and designer art pieces.

Jewellery

Danish amber can be purchased at reasonable prices from one of the many jewellery shops along Strøget.

Amber Specialist (☎ *33 11 88 03, Frederiksberggade 28)* This Strøget shop has been a stand-by for years and has a good variety of amber pendants, beaded necklaces, earrings and rings.

Museums Kopi Smykker (☎ *33 32 76 72, Grønnegade 6)* This shop, north of Strøget, reproduces Viking designs in bronze, gold and silver, with many of the pieces moulded from authentic Viking-era jewellery.

Department Stores

Magasin du Nord (☎ *33 11 44 33, Kongens Nytorv 13)* Copenhagen's largest department store, it covers an entire block on the south-western side of Kongens Nytorv, and stocks everything from clothing and luggage to books and groceries.

Illums Bolighus (☎ *33 13 71 81, Amagertorv 10)* This store on Strøget stocks stylish Danish-designed furniture, continental quilts, ceramics, silverware and glass, and is also a good place to look for simple gifts like quality wooden toys.

Illum (☎ *33 14 40 02, Østergade 52)* This large department store, also on Strøget, has a 3rd-floor crafts and antique market, which sells items ranging from toys to paintings and furniture.

Airport Shops

Most international airports have the usual duty-free shops and a handful of concessionaires, but Copenhagen airport boasts a fully fledged shopping centre.

There are more than 50 shops in the transfer area of the international terminal selling a wide range of products, including men's and women's clothing, continental quilts, Royal Copenhagen porcelain, Georg Jensen silverware, amber and Viking-design jewellery, photographic and audio equipment,

COPENHAGEN

watches, travel bags, travel books, chocolates and, of course, alcohol.

GETTING THERE & AWAY

Air

Copenhagen airport is Scandinavia's busiest hub, with flights from nearly 150 cities across the world. There are direct flights to Copenhagen from numerous cities in Europe, Asia and North America, as well as a handful of Danish cities. More details about flying to and from Copenhagen can be found in the introductory Getting There & Away and Getting Around chapters.

Copenhagen Airport The modern international airport is in Kastrup, 9km southeast of Copenhagen city centre. It has a large shopping area as well as numerous eateries and bars, most in the transfer area. If you have a flight delay, there's a simple minihotel (☎ 32 31 24 55) with showers, saunas and 'slumber cabins' where you can nap.

You'll find foreign-exchange booths in the arrival hall opposite the tourist information desk as well as on the 2nd floor of the departure hall. The booths are open 6.30am to 10pm daily. The VAT refund bureau is on the 2nd floor of the departure hall.

The post office, in the arrival hall beyond the car-rental desks, is open 10am to 5pm Monday to Friday.

There's a left-luggage room (☎ 32 47 47 32) near the post office where you can store luggage (30kr per piece per day); it's open from 6am to 10pm daily. Self-service lockers (20kr for 24 hours) can be found nearby.

If you're waiting for a flight, note that this is a 'silent' airport and there are no boarding calls, although there are numerous monitor screens throughout the terminal.

Airline Offices Most airline offices are north of Central Station, within a block or two of the intersection of Vester Farimagsgade and Vesterbrogade. Following are the office locations and reservation numbers of major airlines serving Copenhagen:

Aer Lingus (☎ 33 12 60 55) Jernbanegade 4
Air France (☎ 33 12 76 76) Ved Vesterport 6

Alitalia (☎ 33 36 93 69) Vesterbrogade 6D
British Airways (☎ 80 20 80 22) Rådhuspladsen 16
Finnair (☎ 33 36 45 45) Nyropsgade 47
Iberia (☎ 33 12 22 22) Jernbanegade 4
Icelandair (☎ 33 12 33 88) Vester Farimagsgade 1
KLM-Royal Dutch Airlines (☎ 70 10 07 47) Copenhagen Airport
Lufthansa Airlines (☎ 33 37 73 53) Hammerichsgade 1
Scandinavian Airlines (SAS; ☎ 70 10 20 00) Hammerichsgade 1
Swissair (☎ 70 11 30 00) Hammerichsgade 1

Bus

International buses to several European cities are operated by Eurolines (☎ 33 88 70 00), which has a ticket office behind Central Station at Reventlowsgade 8. Most long-distance buses leave from Central Station, though some buses, including those to Sweden, also stop at Copenhagen airport. More information is in the introductory There & Away chapter.

Train

All long-distance trains arrive at and depart from Central Station, which is a huge complex with eateries and numerous services including currency exchange, a post office and a supermarket. There are lockers on the lower level near the Reventlowsgade exit and showers at the underground toilets opposite the police office.

Car & Motorcycle

The main highways into Copenhagen are the E20 from Jutland and Funen and the E47 from Helsingør and Sweden. If you're coming from the north on the E47, exit onto Lyngbyvej (route 19) and continue south to reach the heart of the city.

Hitching

Although hitching is not a very good option and we don't recommend it, if you want to try your luck it's best to start outside the city centre. For rides north, take bus No 1 to Vibenhus Runddel, at the north-western corner of Fælledparken in the Østerbro area. If you're heading towards Funen, take

S-train line A to Ellebjerg station, at the south-western outskirts of the city. Keep in mind that it's illegal to hitch on motorways throughout Denmark.

Use It has a free message board that attempts to link up drivers and riders, though there's usually far more of the latter than the former.

Boat

The Oslo and Bornholm ferries leave from Kvæsthusbroen, north of Nyhavn. Hydrofoils to Malmö leave from Havnegade, south of Nyhavn. Ferries to Świnoujście in Poland leave from Nordre Toldbod, east of Kastellet. Cruise ships use Langelinie harbour, just north of the *Little Mermaid*. More information can be found in the Sea section of the Getting There & Away chapter.

GETTING AROUND
To/From the Airport

If you judge a city by how easy it is to get to from the airport, Copenhagen takes top marks. The rail system has been recently extended to speedily link the airport arrival terminal directly with Copenhagen's Central Station. The trains run every 20 minutes until

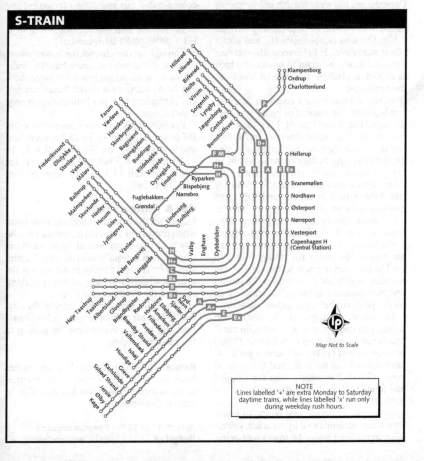

midnight from 4.55am on weekdays, 5.35am on Saturday and 6.35am on Sunday. The trip takes just 12 minutes and costs 19.50kr.

If your baggage is light, you could also take local bus No 250S, which runs frequently between Rådhuspladsen and the airport terminal – but it costs the same as the train and takes about three times longer.

By taxi, it takes about 15 minutes to get between the airport and the city centre, as long as traffic isn't too heavy. The cost is about 150kr.

Bus & Train

Copenhagen has an extensive public transit system consisting of a metro rail network called S-train, with 10 lines passing through Central Station (København H), and a vast bus system called HT (Hovedstadsområdets Trafikselskab), the main terminus of which is at Rådhuspladsen, a couple of blocks to the north-east.

Buses and trains use a common fare system based on the number of zones you pass through. The basic fare of 13kr for up to two zones covers most city runs and allows transfers between buses and trains on a single ticket as long as they're made within an hour. Third and subsequent zones cost 6.50kr more, with a maximum fare of 45.50kr for travel throughout North Zealand. DSB, the national railway, also includes its lines in the common fare system as far north as Helsingør, west to Roskilde and south to Køge.

On buses, you board at the front and pay the fare to the driver (or stamp your clip card in the machine next to the driver). On S-trains, tickets are purchased at the station and then punched in the yellow time clock on the platform before boarding the train.

Instead of buying a single destination ticket, you can buy a *klippekort* (clip card) that is valid for 10 rides in two zones (75kr) or three zones (115kr), or you can get a 24-hour ticket valid for unlimited travel in all zones (75kr). Passengers who are stopped and found to be without a stamped ticket are liable to a fine of 500kr.

Up to two children aged under 10 travel free when accompanied by an adult. Otherwise those aged under 16 travel half-price.

All rides on Copenhagen's regional buses and trains are free for visitors holding a valid Copenhagen Card.

Trains and buses run from about 5am (6am on Sunday) to around 12.30am, though buses continue to run through the night (charging double the usual fare) on a few main routes.

The free Copenhagen city maps that are distributed by the tourist office show bus routes (with numbers) and are very useful for finding your way around the city. If you plan to use buses extensively, you might want to buy HT's hefty timetable book *Busser og tog* (40kr), which comes with a colour-coded bus route map (covering the entire HT route throughout North Zealand), or get just the map for 5kr. Both are sold at HT's booth on Rådhuspladsen.

Throughout this chapter the bus numbers of some of the more frequent buses to individual destinations are listed, but since there can be as many as a dozen buses passing any particular place, our listing is often only a partial one.

For schedules and other information on HT buses call ☎ 36 13 14 15 between 7am and 9.30pm daily; for S-trains call ☎ 33 14 17 01 between 6.30am and 11pm daily; for DSB trains call 70 13 14 15 between 7am and 10pm daily.

Car & Motorcycle

Except for the weekday-morning rush hour, when traffic can bottleneck coming into the city (and vice versa around 5pm), traffic in Copenhagen is usually manageable. Getting around by car is not problematic, except the usual challenge of finding an empty parking space in the most popular places.

To explore sights in the centre of the city, you're best off on foot or using public transport, but a car is convenient for getting to the suburban sights.

Rental The following car hire companies have booths at the airport in the international terminal. Each also has an office in central Copenhagen:

Avis (☎ 33 15 22 99) Kampmannsgade 1
Budget (☎ 33 55 05 00) Helgolandsgade 2

Europcar (☎ 33 55 99 00) Gammel Kongevej 13
Hertz (☎ 33 17 90 21) Ved Vesterport 3

Parking For street parking, you buy a ticket from a kerbside *billetautomat* (automated ticket machine) and place it inside the windscreen. Copenhagen parking is zoned so that the spaces most in demand, such as those in the central commercial area, are the most costly. Your best bet is to search out a blue zone where parking costs just 7kr per hour. If you can't find an empty blue space then opt for a green zone where the fee is 12kr per hour. Avoid red zones where it's a steep 20kr per hour. Parking fees must be paid on weekdays from 8am to 6pm (to 8pm in red zones) and also on Saturday to 2pm in green zones and 8pm in red zones.

If you cannot find street parking, there are car parks at the main department stores, at the Radisson SAS Royal Hotel and on Jerbanegade, east of Axeltorv.

Taxi

Taxis with signs saying *fri* can be flagged down or you can call Københavns Taxa (☎ 35 35 35 35) or Taxa Motor (☎ 38 10 10 10). The cost is 22kr at flag fall, plus about 10kr per kilometre (12kr at night and at weekends). Most taxis accept credit cards. A service charge is included in the fare, so tips are not expected.

Bicycle

Despite the motor traffic Copenhagen, with all its cycle paths, is a great city for getting around by bicycle. One caveat: If you're travelling with a bike, be careful – expensive bikes are hot targets for thieves on the streets of Copenhagen.

If you didn't bring a bike with you, you can readily hire one in Copenhagen. In addition to the rental rates, expect to pay a refundable deposit of around 300kr for a regular bike, 1000kr for a mountain bike or tandem.

One of the most convenient bicycle rental places is Københavns Cykler (☎ 33 33 86 13), at the Reventlowsgade side of Central Station. It's open 8am to 6pm on weekdays and 9am to 1pm on Saturday; in summer, it's also open 10am to 1pm on Sunday. The cost

---

Free Ride

The city of Copenhagen operates a generous scheme, called Bycykler (City Bikes), by which anyone can borrow a bicycle for free. It's motivated in part by an effort to control motor-vehicle traffic in the heart of the city. Sponsors, who paint the bikes with their logos, include private businesses, the local tourism office and the city council. In all there are some 2000 bikes available each summer.

Although the bicycles are not streamlined and are certainly not practical for any long-distance cycling, that's part of the plan – use of the cycles is limited to the city centre. To deter theft and minimise maintenance, the bicycles have a distinctive design that includes solid spokeless wheels with puncture-resistant tyres. The bikes can be found at 125 widely scattered street stands in public places, including S-train stations.

If you're able to find a free bicycle, you deposit a 20kr coin in the stand to release the bike. When you're done using the bicycle you can return it to any stand and get your 20kr coin back.

---

is 50/225kr per day/week for a regular bike, 200/900kr per day/week for a mountain or tandem bike. A sister operation, Østerport Cykler (☎ 33 33 85 13) at Østerport S-train station near track 13, has the same rates and hours as Københavns Cykler, except that it's closed on Sunday year-round.

For a bargain bike, Danwheel (☎ 33 21 22 27), Colbjørnsensgade 3, a couple of blocks north-west of Central Station, hires older bikes for 35/165kr a day/week. It's open 9am to 5.30pm on weekdays, to 2pm on weekends.

Except during weekday rush hours, it's possible to carry bikes on S-trains (buy the 13kr ticket from the red machine). You can load your bicycle in any carriage that has a cycle symbol and you must stay with the bike at all times.

For more information on cycling, see the special section 'Cycling in Denmark', which follows the Getting Around chapter.

Boat

For information on getting around Copenhagen's waterfront by boat, check under Canal Tours in the Organised Tours section earlier in this chapter.

Around Copenhagen

Many places in the greater Copenhagen area make for quick and easy excursions from the city. The following destinations offer a good variety of outings to woodlands, lakes, beaches and historic areas. For other day-trip possibilities a bit farther afield, see the North Zealand chapter.

ARKEN

The Ark (☎ 43 54 02 22, Skovvej 100; S-train to Ishøj station, bus No 128 from there; adult/child 50/20kr; open 10am-5pm Tues &Thurs-Sun, 10am-9pm Wed) is a substantial contemporary art museum on the coast at Ishøj, 17km south of central Copenhagen. Opened in 1996, the stark modernist building rises above the beach and is as much a work of art as the exhibits inside. The Arken collection features the works of leading Danish artists since 1945, with an emphasis on photo-based art, sculpture and installations. Changing exhibits showcase works such as those by the artists from the regional Cobra (COpenhagen-BRussels-Amsterdam) movement and paintings by the Norwegian artist Edvard Munch.

DRAGØR

If Copenhagen begins to feel crowded, consider an afternoon excursion to Dragør, a maritime town on the island of Amager, a few kilometres south of the airport. In the early 1550s Christian II allowed Dutch farmers to settle in Amager to provide his court with flowers and produce, and the town of Dragør still retains a bit of Dutch flavour.

Along the waterfront you'll find smokehouses, fishing boats and the **Dragør Museum** (☎ 32 53 41 06, Havnepladsen; adult/child 20/ 10kr; noon-4pm Tues-Sun May-Sept), a

half-timbered house featuring model ships and period furnishings.

A fun way to spend time is to simply wander the narrow, winding cobblestone streets leading up from the harbour, which are lined with the thatch-roofed, mustard-coloured houses comprising the **old town**. One interesting little ramble is to take Strandgade, a pedestrian alley that begins opposite the museum, and continue up to Badstuevælen, an old square lined with some attractive houses dating from the 1790s (especially house Nos 8 and 12).

If you're in Dragør for lunch, you'll find several places near the waterfront serving sandwiches, fish and chips and other light fare at moderate prices.

You can get to Dragør via bus No 30, 33 or 350S from central Copenhagen.

CHARLOTTENLUND

Charlottenlund is a well-to-do coastal suburb just beyond the northern outskirts of Copenhagen. Despite being so close to the city, it has a decent **sandy beach**, although the smokestacks of Hellerup to the south are part of the backdrop.

Just inland from the beach is the moat-encircled **Charlottenlund Fort**, which now harbours a camping ground as well as an expensive sea-view restaurant. There's not much left of the old fort other than some cannons, but it's still a pleasant place, with wading ducks and lots of birdsong.

Danmarks Akvarium (☎ 39 62 32 83, Kavalergården 1; adult/child 60/30kr; open 10am-6pm daily mid-Feb–mid-Oct, 10am to 4pm daily mid-Oct–mid-Feb) is 500m north of the beach on the inland side of the road. By Scandinavian standards it's a fairly large aquarium and the well-presented collection includes cold-water fish, tropical fish, live corals, nurse sharks, sea turtles, crocodiles and piranhas.

From the aquarium car park a path leads 200m west to **Charlottenlund Slotshave**, an attractive three-storey manor house that's now been converted to offices. Walkways lead around the park-like grounds, making for an enjoyable stroll if you're already in the area.

AROUND COPENHAGEN

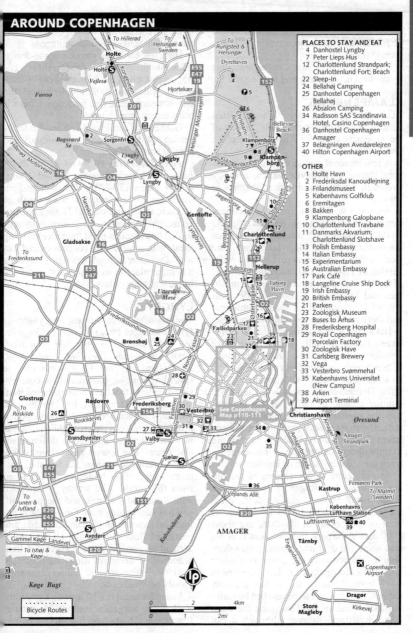

PLACES TO STAY AND EAT
4 Danhostel Lyngby
7 Peter Lieps Hus
12 Charlottenlund Strandpark;
   Charlottenlund Fort; Beach
22 Sleep-In
24 Bellahøj Camping
25 Danhostel Copenhagen
   Bellahøj
26 Absalon Camping
34 Radisson SAS Scandinavia
   Hotel, Casino Copenhagen
36 Danhostel Copenhagen
   Amager
37 Belægningen Avedørelejren
40 Hilton Copenhagen Airport

OTHER
1 Holte Havn
2 Frederiksdal Kanoudlejning
3 Frilandsmuseet
5 Københavns Golfklub
6 Eremitagen
8 Bakken
9 Klampenborg Galopbane
10 Charlottenlund Travbane
11 Danmarks Akvarium;
   Charlottenlund Slotshave
13 Polish Embassy
14 Italian Embassy
15 Experimentarium
16 Australian Embassy
17 Park Café
18 Langeline Cruise Ship Dock
19 Irish Embassy
20 British Embassy
21 Parken
23 Zoologisk Museum
27 Buses to Århus
28 Frederiksberg Hospital
29 Royal Copenhagen
   Porcelain Factory
30 Zoologisk Have
31 Carlsberg Brewery
32 Vega
33 Vesterbro Svømmehal
35 Københavns Universitet
   (New Campus)
38 Arken
39 Airport Terminal

If you're interested in horse races, the major attraction in this suburb will be the **Charlottenlund Travbane**, a trotting (harness racing) track.

Bus No 6 from central Copenhagen runs by the beach, aquarium and trotting track.

KLAMPENBORG

Klampenborg, being only 20 minutes from Central Station on S-train line C, is one of the favourite spots for Copenhageners on family outings.

A few hundred metres east of Klampenborg station is **Bellevue beach**, a sandy stretch that gets packed with sunbathers in summer.

An 800m walk west from Klampenborg station is the 400-year-old **Bakken** (*☎ 39 63 73 00, Dyrehavevej 2; admission free; open noon-midnight late Mar-late Aug)*, the world's oldest amusement park. A blue-collar version of Tivoli, it's a honky-tonk carnival of bumper cars, roller coasters, slot machines and beer halls. Children's rides cost around 15kr, adult rides about double that and there are discounted multi-use passes.

Bakken is at the southern edge of **Dyrehaven** (more formally called Jægersborg Dyrehave), an expansive 1000-hectare area of beech trees and meadows crisscrossed by an alluring network of walking and cycling trails. Dyrehaven was established as a royal hunting ground in 1669 and has evolved into the capital's most popular picnicking area. Dyrehaven also contains the **Københavns Golfklub**, an 18-hole golf course, and **Klampenborg Galopbane**, a horse-racing track immediately south of Bakken.

At the centre of Dyrehaven is the old manor house **Eremitagen**, a good vantage point to spot herds of grazing deer, which are especially abundant in the meadows west of the house. In all, there are about 2000 deer in the park, mostly fallow deer but also some red deer and Japanese sika deer. Among the red deer are a few rare white specimens, descendants of deer imported in 1737 from Germany, where they are now extinct. Eremitagen can be reached by walking 2km north of Bakken along the main route, Kristiansholmsvej, although it can

also be reached from numerous other points in the park as most of the largest trails radiate out like spokes from Eremitagen.

Hackney carriages provide horse-drawn rides into the park from the Dyrehaven entrance just north of Klampenborg S-train station. Rides cost 200kr for 30 minutes; the coaches carry up to five passengers, but it's most romantic with two!

Bakken has numerous fast-food eateries selling hot dogs, burgers, cotton candy and similar carnival fare.

Peter Lieps Hus (*☎ 39 64 07 86, Dyrehaven 8)* Lunch specials around 100kr, dinner mains 130-200kr. Open 11am-8pm Tues-Sun. A few minutes' walk north of Bakken, this quintessential Danish country restaurant occupies an historic thatch-roofed house and is good for a nice relaxing meal, with smørrebrød, venison specialities and other Danish food. On sunny days it's a popular place to sit outside and watch the horse and buggy carts go by.

LYNGBY

The main sight of interest in Lyngby is **Frilandsmuseet** (*☎ 45 85 02 92, Kongevejen 100; adult/child 40kr/free, free Wed; open 10am-5pm Tues-Sun Easter-Sept, 10am-4pm Tues-Sun 1st 3 weeks Oct)*, a sprawling open-air museum of old countryside dwellings that have been gathered from sites around Denmark. Its 110 historic buildings are arranged in 40 groupings that provide a sense of Danish rural life as it was in various regions and across different social strata. The houses range from rather grand affairs to meagre, sod-roofed cottages. Many of the buildings are furnished from the period: The smithy is equipped with irons and a hearth, and the post mill still has functioning sails. Grazing farm animals, selected from old Danish breeds, and costumed field workers add an element of authenticity to the scene. There's a light schedule of demonstrations such as folk dancing, weaving and pottery making, mostly on weekends.

Frilandsmuseet is a 10-minute, signposted walk from Sorgenfri station, 25 minutes from Central Station on S-train line B. You can also take bus No 184 or 194, both of which stop at the entrance.

The Lyngby area also has a number of **lakes**, including Furesø, which is the deepest lake in Denmark. It's possible to hire rowing boats or canoes for 60kr per hour at the lakeside kiosk, **Holte Havn** (☎ 45 42 04 49, 22 Vejlesøvej; open 10am-9pm daily), and row around either Furesø or the smaller Vejlesø, which are connected by a channel.

Holte Havn is near Holte S-train station, two stops north of Sorgenfri.

Frederiksdal Kanoudlejning (☎ 45 85 67 70, Nybrovej 520; open 10am-6pm Tues-Sun), by the locks, hires out canoes and rowing boats for use on the river Mølleåen and the lakes Lyngby Sø, Bagsværd Sø and Furesø, which are interconnected. Boat hire costs 60kr per hour. To get there, get off at Sorgenfri S-train station and take bus No 191.

North Zealand

Considering its proximity to Copenhagen, the northern part of Zealand is surprisingly rural, with small farms, wheat fields and beech woodlands. It also boasts some fine beaches and notable historical sights.

One of the most popular day trips from Copenhagen is a loop tour taking in Frederiksborg Slot in Hillerød and Kronborg Slot in Helsingør, with a stop at Fredensborg Slot in-between. With an early start you might even have time to continue on to one of the north-shore beaches or visit Louisiana, the modern-art museum in Humlebæk, on the way back to the city.

If you're not tight for time, however, North Zealand has a number of destinations that invite a longer stay. You could even hop on a ferry in Helsingør and skip over to Sweden for about the same price as a bottle of beer!

When planning your tour, keep in mind that the Copenhagen Card allows free access to trains, buses and most sightseeing attractions throughout North Zealand; for details see the boxed text under Information in the Copenhagen chapter.

If you're driving between Helsingør and Copenhagen ignore the motorway and take the coastal road, Strandvej (route 152), which is far more scenic.

Information on Charlottenlund, Lyngby and Klampenborg, just north of Copenhagen, is in the Around Copenhagen section at the end of the Copenhagen chapter.

Inland Towns

The inland area of North Zealand, sometimes referred to as the heartland, has two towns of special interest to visitors, Hillerød and Fredensborg.

HILLERØD
postcode 3400 • pop 27,800
Hillerød, 30km north of Copenhagen, is a small town centred around a grand lakeside castle, Frederiksborg Slot.

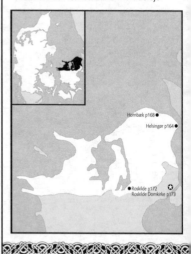

Hornbæk p168
Helsingør p164
Roskilde p172
Roskilde Domkirke p173

An administrative centre and transport hub for North Zealand, Hillerød isn't especially quaint in itself but the castle and the surrounding gardens are splendid. You can enjoy picturesque views of the castle by following the path that skirts the castle lake. If you feel like taking a longer stroll, paths run through Slotshaven, an expansive Baroque-style privet garden immediately north of the castle and lake. The Slotshaven paths connect with trails in the adjacent woodlands of Lille Dyrehave and Indelukket which, taken together, could easily make a pleasant hour's outing.

Orientation

If you arrive at Hillerød by train, follow the signs to the central square, Torvet. The main street through town, Slotsgade, leads directly from Torvet to the gate of Frederiksborg Slot, 500m to the north-west.

Information

The Hillerød Turistbureau (☎ 48 26 28 52, fax 48 24 26 65), Slangerupgade 2, is 50m south of the castle entrance. It's open 10am to 5pm Monday to Friday and 10am to 1pm on Saturday, except between mid-June and August when it's open 10am to 6pm on weekdays and 10am to 3pm on Saturday.

Frederiksborg Slot

This impressive Dutch Renaissance castle ☎ 48 26 04 39, Slotsgade 1; adult/child 45/10kr; open 10am-5pm daily Apr-Oct, 11am-3pm daily Nov-Mar) spreads across three islets on the eastern side of the castle lake, Slotsø. The oldest part of Frederiksborg Slot dates from the reign of Frederik II, after whom the castle is named, but most of the present structure was built in the early 17th century by Frederik II's more extravagant son, Christian IV.

As you enter the main gate you'll pass old stable buildings dating from the 1560s and then cross over a moat to the second islet, where you'll enter an expansive central courtyard with a grandly ornate Neptune fountain. The relatively modest wings that flank the fountain once served as residences for court officers and government officials. A second bridge crosses to the northern-most islet, the site of the main body of the castle, which served as the home of Danish royalty for more than a century.

Frederiksborg Slot was ravaged by a fire in 1859. The royal family, unable to undertake the costly repairs, decided to give up the property. Carlsberg beer baron JC Jacobsen then stepped onto the scene and spearheaded a drive to restore the castle as a national museum, a function it still serves today.

The sprawling castle has a magnificent interior boasting gilded ceilings, wall-sized tapestries, fine paintings, memorabilia and antiques, with exhibits occupying 70 of its rooms. The richly embellished **Riddershalen** (Knights Hall) and **Slotskirken** (Coronation Chapel), where the Danish monarchs were

Brilliant Builder, Faulty Fighter

No Danish monarch has made such a lasting impact on the Danish landscape as Christian IV (1588–1648), who inherited the throne when he was just 10 years old. He ruled for more than 50 years after his coronation in 1596.

When Christian took over power, Denmark had a robust economy and a seemingly boundless treasury. The ambitious king established trading companies and a stock exchange, and built splendid new Renaissance cities, castles and fortresses throughout his kingdom. Many of Denmark's most lavish structures were erected during his reign and you'll find his fancy handiwork when touring Frederiksborg Slot and Kronborg Slot.

Unfortunately, the king's foreign policies weren't nearly as brilliant as his domestic undertakings. In 1625 Christian IV dragged Denmark into the ill-fated Thirty Years' War with Sweden. By the end of the war Denmark was bankrupt and so much territory had been lost to Sweden that there were doubts Denmark would even survive as a nation. The king himself lost an eye to shrapnel when his flagship was attacked in battle. A vivid oil painting of that scene, with the king's eye covered by a bloody handkerchief and his sword raised in defiance, can be seen above Christian IV's crypt in the Roskilde cathedral.

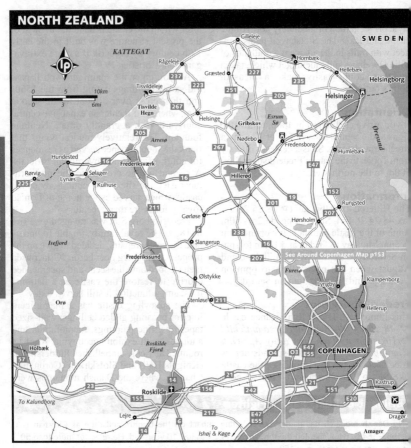

NORTH ZEALAND

crowned from 1671 to 1840, are alone worth the admission fee. The chapel, incidentally, was spared serious fire damage and retains the original interior commissioned by Christian IV, including a lavish hand-carved altar and pulpit created by Mores of Hamburg in 1606 and a priceless **Compenius organ** built in 1610. The organ is played between 1.30pm and 2pm each Thursday.

Outside opening hours, visitors are free to stroll around the grounds and enter the castle courtyard. If you arrive at the castle by car, there's free parking off Frederik-værksgade, west of the castle.

Places to Stay

Hillerød Camping (☎/fax 48 26 48 54, **e** hil camp@post8.tele.dk, Blytækkervej 18) Camp ing per person 56kr. Open Apr–mid-Sept This two-star camping ground is about 20-minute walk directly south of the castl along Slangerupgade.

Hotel Hillerød (☎ 48 24 08 00, fax 48 2 08 74, **e** hotel@hotelhillerod.dk, Milners vej 41) Singles/doubles weekdays 700/900kr weekends 575/625kr. About 2km south o the castle, this hotel has an atrium fille with flowering plants and 62 modern room with bath and kitchenette.

Places to Eat

There are several places to eat a few minutes' walk from the castle on Slotsgade, ranging from the usual fast-food chains to more inviting local options.

Gonzales Cantina (☎ 48 26 19 11, Slotsgade 27D) Lunch specials 29kr, other meals around 50kr. This friendly place serves the best pizza in town and offers good-value lunch specials including lasagne, pizza or beef. At other times you can get the likes of steak or chicken dishes with salad and chips.

Hennessy's (☎ 48 26 04 05, Slotsgade 52) This Irish pub serves up afternoon cake and tea for 30kr on a verandah overlooking the castle.

Getting There & Away

The S-train (A & E lines) runs every 10 minutes between Copenhagen and Hillerød (45.50kr), a 40-minute ride.

Trains from Hillerød run eastward to Fredensborg (13kr, 12 minutes) and Helsingør (36kr, 30 minutes), north to Gilleleje (32.50kr, 31 minutes) and west to Tisvildeleje (32.50kr, 31 minutes); all services operate at least hourly.

Buses also link Hillerød with North Zealand towns but they are much slower than the train and cost just as much.

Getting Around

Bus No 701 departs frequently from the train station and can drop you near the castle gate (13kr).

The little ferry *Frederiksborg* sails across the castle lake about every 30 minutes daily from June to August, landing at three small piers: one just north of Torvet, another near the castle entrance and the third north of the castle on the road to Slotshaven. The fare is 20/5kr for adults/children.

FREDENSBORG

postcode 3480 • pop 8000

Fredensborg is a quiet town with a royal palace, a lakeside location and some pleasant walking tracks. If you're in no hurry, it's a pleasant place to stay for a day or two and unwind the clock.

Information

Fredensborg Turistbureau (☎ 48 48 21 00, fax 48 48 04 65) is just outside the palace at Slotsgade 2. It's open 10am to 4pm Monday to Friday and 11am to 3pm on Saturday, except in July and August when it's open 10am to 6pm on weekdays and 11am to 4pm on Saturday and Sunday.

Fredensborg Slot

Fredensborg Palace (☎ 33 40 31 87, Slotsgade 1), the royal family's residence during most of the summer, was built in 1720 by Frederik IV. It was named Fredensborg, meaning Peace Palace, to commemorate the peace that Denmark had recently achieved with its Scandinavian neighbours. The palace certainly reflects the more tranquil mood of that era and is largely in the style of a country manor house, an abrupt contrast with the moat-encircled fortresses of Kronborg and Frederiksborg that preceded it.

Partly because of its spread-out design, the palace is not as impressive as some other Danish royal palaces in North Zealand. Fredensborg's interior can only be visited during July, when the royal family holidays elsewhere. Guided palace tours (30kr) run every 30 minutes between 1pm and 5pm daily. The grounds are open sunrise to sunset daily year-round.

The main mansion was designed by the leading Danish architect of the day, JC Krieger, and is in Italian Baroque style with marble floors and a large central cupola. It's fronted by an expansive octagonal courtyard framed by two-storey buildings.

The palace is backed by 120 hectares of **wooded parkland**, crisscrossed by trails and open free to the public year-round. Take a stroll through **Normandsdalen**, west of the palace, to a circular amphitheatre with 70 life-sized sandstone statues of Norwegian folk characters – fisherfolk, farmers and so on – in traditional dress. If you continue walking a few minutes west from there you'll reach Esrum Sø, a lake skirted by another trail.

To get to Fredensborg Slot from the train station, turn left onto Stationsvej and then turn right onto Jernbanegade, which merges with Slotsgade near the palace gate; the whole walk is about 1km and takes only 10 minutes.

Other Attractions

Bordering the south-eastern shore of **Esrum Sø**, Denmark's second-largest lake, Fredensborg offers swimming, boating and fishing. Along the shore you can sometimes spot ospreys and cormorants, and the surrounding woods are the habitat of roe deer.

It's a 10-minute walk west from the palace gate along Skipperallé to *Skipperhuset* (☎ 48 48 01 07), a lakeside restaurant where there's a summer ferry service and rowing boats for hire. The main beach is nearby. The ferry can take you to **Gribskov**, a forested area with trails and picnic grounds that borders the western side of Esrum Sø.

Slotsgade, which terminates at the palace gate, has a number of historic buildings, including the **Hotel Store Kro** at No 6. **Villa Bournonville**, the former home of the 19th-century ballet master Auguste Bournonville at Slotsgade 9, is today an art gallery. **Havremagasinet**, Slotsgade 11, once served as horse stables. **Kunstnegården**, an art and crafts gallery a bit farther south at Slotsgade 17, was originally an inn built in 1722.

Places to Stay

Danhostel Fredensborg (☎ 48 48 03 15, fax 48 48 16 56, e danhostel@mail.dk, Østrupvej 3) Dorm beds 95kr, singles/doubles 210/325kr. Open Jan–mid-Dec. This hostel has 88 beds that are mostly in double rooms. It occupies a prime location just 300m south of Fredensborg Slot and 50m west of Hotel Store Kro.

Tourist office staff can book *rooms* in private homes, with doubles costing on average 350kr including breakfast, plus a 25kr booking fee.

Pension Bondehuset (☎ 48 48 01 12, fax 48 48 03 01, e info@bondehuset.dk, Sørupvej 14) Singles/doubles with breakfast 520/840kr. For an upmarket rural getaway, this 18th-century manor house has it all, from comfortable rooms to free rowing boats for guests' use. It's right on the lake on the western side of town.

Hotel Store Kro (☎ 48 40 01 11, fax 48 48 45 61, e reception@storekro.dk, Slotsgade 6) Singles/doubles with breakfast 995/1295kr. This classic inn, just outside the palace gate, was originally built by Frederik IV in 1723 to accommodate palace guests. Not surprisingly, no two rooms are alike but all have traditional decor and full amenities.

Places to Eat

Under Kronen (☎ 48 47 59 02, Jernbanegade 1) Just the place to go for ice cream, sandwiches and coffee, this cafe is conveniently located just outside the palace gate.

Ciao (☎ 48 48 23 24, Christoffer Boecksvej 3) Pizza or pasta at lunch/dinner 39/60kr. A pleasant Italian cafe just off Jernbanegade, Ciao serves good pizza and pasta as well as pricier fish and meat dinners.

Hua Fu (☎ 48 48 23 24, Slotsgade 5) Lunch/dinner 55/120kr. This cosy place has good Chinese food including combination plates that have several items and rice.

Hotel Store Kro (☎ 48 40 01 11, Slotsgade 6) Set dinner 385kr. This is a top-end option offering old-world charm and a three-course Danish dinner with a menu that changes nightly.

You'll pass a good *fruit stand*, a *bakery* and a *grocery shop* on Jernbanegade, about halfway between Fredensborg Slot and the train station.

Getting There & Away

Fredensborg is midway on the train line between Hillerød (13kr, 12 minutes) and Helsingør (30kr, 20 minutes). Trains run about twice hourly from early morning to around midnight.

Øresund Coast

The Øresund Coast, the eastern shore of North Zealand, extends north from Copenhagen to the Helsingør area and is largely a run of small seaside suburbs and yachting harbours. It is the Øresund (Sound) that connects the Baltic Sea to the south with the Kattegat to the north and separates Denmark from Sweden. On clear days you can

Frederiksborg Slot: Built over three islands, the medieval and Renaissance castle, near Hillerød, houses priceless treasures including tapestries, silver, portraits and furniture. The Baroque garden behind the castle re-creates the landscaping style common in the 1720s.

STAEVEN VALLAK

MARTIN LLADÓ

ANDERS BLOMQVIST

ANDERS BLOMQVIST

Clockwise from top: Replicas of a seafaring past at Roskilde's Viking Ship Museum; A small observatory dome in the North Zealand countryside, part of the Niels Bohr Institute; A royal tomb in Roskilde Domkirke; Kronborg Slot, which was the inspiration for *Hamlet*'s castle of Elsinore.

look across the sound and see southern Sweden on the opposite shore.

Partly because of the exclusive homes along the waterfront, the local tourist authorities sometimes rather grandly refer to this area as the Danish Riviera. In reality its main appeal to visitors lies not in its beaches but in two museums, one dedicated to author Karen Blixen, the other to modern art.

RUNGSTED

The coastal town of Rungsted is the site of Rungstedlund, the estate that houses the Karen Blixen museum.

Rungstedlund was originally built about 1500 as an inn. King Karl XII of Sweden stayed there around 1700 and the Danish lyric poet Johannes Ewald, who wrote Denmark's national anthem, was a boarder from 1773 to 1776. The property became a private residence and in 1879 was bought by Karen Blixen's father, Wilhelm Dinesen. Blixen was born at Rungstedlund in 1885 and lived there off and on until her death in 1962.

Karen Blixen Museet

Karen Blixen's former home in Rungsted is now a museum (☎ 45 57 10 57, *Rungsted*

Out of Rungsted

Karen Blixen was born Karen Christenze Dinesen on 17 April 1885 in Rungsted, a well-to-do community north of Copenhagen. She studied art in Copenhagen, Rome and Paris. In 1914, when she was 28 and eager to escape from the confines of her bourgeois family, she married her second cousin Baron Bror von Blixen-Finecke, after having a failed love affair with his twin brother Hans. It was a marriage of convenience – she wanted his title and he needed her money.

The couple moved to Kenya and started a coffee plantation, which Karen was left to manage. The baron, who had several extramarital affairs, eventually infected Karen with syphilis. She came home to Denmark for medical treatment, but subsequently returned to Africa and divorced the baron in 1925.

In 1932, after her coffee plantation had failed and the great love of her life, Englishman Denys Finch-Hatton, had died in a tragic plane crash, Karen Blixen left Africa and returned to the family estate in Rungsted, where she began to write. Danes were slow to take to Blixen's writings, in part because she consistently wrote about the aristocracy in approving terms and used an old-fashioned idiomatic style that some thought arrogant. Her insistence on being called 'Baroness' also took its toll on her popularity in a Denmark bent on minimising class disparity.

Following rejection by publishers in Denmark and England, her first book, *Seven Gothic Tales*, a compilation of short stories set in the 19th century, was published in New York in 1934 (under the pseudonym Isak Dinesen) and was so well received that it was chosen as a Book-of-the-Month selection. It was only after her success in the USA that Danish publishers took a serious interest in her works.

In 1937 Blixen's landmark *Out of Africa*, the memoirs of her life in Kenya, was published in both Danish and English. This was followed by *Winter's Tales* in 1942, *The Angelic Avengers* in 1944, *Last Tales* in 1957, *Anecdotes of Destiny* in 1958 and *Shadows on the Grass* in 1960. Two of her works were later turned into the Oscar-winning films *Out of Africa* and *Babette's Feast*.

A few years before her death in 1962, Blixen arranged for her estate to be turned over to the private Rungstedlund Foundation. For years the foundation had only enough money to maintain the grounds as a bird sanctuary, but the posthumous book sales that were spurred by the success of the films made it possible to turn her former home into a museum in 1991.

Strandvej 111; adult/child 35kr/free; open 10am-5pm daily May-Sept; 1pm-4pm Wed-Fri, 11am-4pm Sat & Sun Oct-Apr). It is furnished in much the way she left it and contains photographs, Masai spears, paintings, shields and other mementoes of her time in Africa, such as the gramophone given to Blixen by her lover Denys Finch-Hatton. On her desk is the old Corona typewriter that Blixen used to write her novels.

One wing of the museum, a converted carriage house and stables, houses a library of Blixen's books in many languages, a cafe and bookshop; there's also an audiovisual presentation on her life. The grounds contain gardens and a wood, part of which has been set aside as a bird sanctuary. Blixen is buried in a little clearing shaded by a sprawling beech tree, the grave marked by a simple stone slab inscribed with just her name.

The museum is opposite the yacht harbour and 1.25km from the train station. To get there, walk north from the train station up Stationsvej, turn right at the lights onto Rungstedvej and then at its intersection with Rungsted Strandvej walk south about 300m and you'll come to the museum.

If you'd like to walk through the museum's bird sanctuary on the way back to the train station, ask at the museum desk for the free *Garden and Bird Sanctuary* brochure, which maps out the route.

Getting There & Away

Trains to Rungsted run every 20 minutes from Copenhagen (45.50kr, 30 minutes) and Helsingør (27.50kr, 25 minutes).

HUMLEBÆK
postcode 3050 • pop 8600

The coastal town of Humlebæk has a couple of harbours and bathing beaches and some wooded areas, but the main focus for visitors to the area is the modern art museum called Louisiana.

Louisiana

Louisiana (☎ 49 19 07 19, *Gammel Strandvej 13; adult/child 60/20kr; open 10am-5pm Thur-Tues, 10am-10pm Wed)*, Denmark's most renowned modern art museum, is on a seaside knoll in a strikingly modernistic complex with sculpture-laden grounds. The sculptures on the lawns, which include works by Henry Moore, Alexander Calder and Max Ernst, create an engaging interplay between art, architecture and landscape. Louisiana is a fascinating place to visit even for those not passionate about modern art.

Items from the museum's permanent collection, mainly paintings and graphic art from the postwar era, are creatively displayed and grouped. There are sections on constructivism, Cobra (COpenhagen-BRussels-Amsterdam)-movement artists, minimalist art, abstract expressionism, pop art and staged photography. Works on display include those by such international luminaries as Pablo Picasso, Francis Bacon and Alberto Giacometti. Some of the more prominent Danish artists represented are Asger Jorn, Robert Jacobsen, Carl-Henning Pedersen and Richard Mortensen.

The museum also has top-notch temporary exhibitions, which over the years have had such diverse themes as the works of Juan Muñoz, Toulouse-Lautrec & Paris and the world of Andy Warhol.

If you're travelling with kids this is one museum that can be real fun. It has an entire children's wing where kids can explore their artistic talents using interactive computers and various hands-on mediums; ask about the free Friday afternoon workshops that attract lots of international youngsters.

The museum has a cafe with a picturesque setting and a shop selling art books, prints and motif mugs.

Louisiana is 1km from Humlebæk train station, a 10-minute signposted walk along Gammel Strandvej.

Places to Eat

There are a number of simple eating options along Gammel Strandvej just outside the Humlebæk train station. On the south side of the station is a ***butcher shop*** with mouthwatering smørrebrød sandwiches, a good ***fruit stand*** and a ***bakery***.

The ***cafe*** at the Louisiana museum has good and reasonably priced sandwiches and cakes.

Getting There & Away

DSB trains leave Copenhagen a few times each hour for Humlebæk, a ride that takes 40 minutes and costs 45.50kr. The train from Helsingør takes 12 minutes and costs 19.50kr.

HELSINGØR

postcode 3000 • pop 34,700

Helsingør (Elsinore), at the narrowest point of the Øresund, is a busy port town, with ferries shuttling to and from Sweden during the day.

Although Swedish shoppers on day trips comprise most of Helsingør's visitors (which accounts for the plethora of liquor shops near the harbour), the town offers enough sightseeing possibilities to make for an enjoyable half-day of touring.

Helsingør has maintained some of its historic quarters, including a block of old homes and warehouses known as Sundtoldkarreen (Sound Dues Square) towards the north-eastern end of Strandgade.

Helsingør's top sight, perched across the harbour on the northern side of town, is the imposing Kronborg Slot, made famous as Elsinore Castle in Shakespeare's *Hamlet*. Kronborg Slot was designated a Unesco World Heritage Site in 2000.

Information

The Helsingør Turistbureau (☎ 49 21 13 33, fax 49 21 15 77), Havnepladsen 3, is opposite the train station. It's open 9am to 4pm on weekdays and 10am to 1pm on Saturday.

Danske Bank (☎ 49 25 52 00), Stengade 55, is open 9.30am to 4pm Monday to Friday (to 6pm on Thursday). The post office (☎ 49 21 05 00), on Jernbanevej 7, is open 9.30am to 5pm on weekdays and 10am to 1pm on Saturday.

The DSB terminus at Helsingør train station and the Scanlines ferry terminal have lockers where you can store your bags while you tour the town.

There's a pharmacy, Stengades Apotek (☎ 49 21 86 00), at Stengade 46.

Walking Tour

This walk through the oldest parts of Helsingør takes a scenic route to Kronborg Slot.

Beginning at the northern side of the tourist office; stroll up Brostræde, a pedestrian alley, and then continue north along Sankt Anna Gade.

You'll soon come to the 15th-century Gothic cathedral **Sankt Olai Kirke** *(admission free)*, which occupies the block between Stengade and Sankt Olai Gade. The cathedral has an ornate altar and baptistry and is open to the public.

One block farther north is **Helsingør Bymuseum** *(☎ 49 21 00 98, Sankt Anna Gade 36; adult/child 10kr/free; open noon-4pm daily)*, built by the monks of the adjacent monastery in 1516 to serve as a sailors' hospital. It did a stint as a poorhouse before being converted to a history museum in 1973. The hotchpotch of exhibits includes about 200 dolls and a model of Helsingør as it was in 1801.

Karmeliterklostret *(Carmelite monastery; ☎ 49 21 17 74, Sankt Anna Gade 38; admission 10kr; open noon-3pm daily)*, the red-brick buildings north of the Bymuseum, is one of Scandinavia's best-preserved medieval monasteries. Christian II's mistress, Dyveke, is thought to have been buried at the monastery when she died in 1517.

From here, follow Sankt Anna Gade north. Turn right on Kronborgvej and at its intersection with Allégade, you'll find a little public **garden** where flowers attract colourful butterflies.

Continue on Kronborgvej. If you'd like to see some fish at close quarters, turn left on Strandpromenaden and go another 250m to **Øresundsakvariet** *(The Sound Aquarium; ☎ 49 21 37 72, Strandpromenaden 5; adult/child 25/15kr; open 10am-5pm daily June-Aug; noon-4pm Mon-Fri, 10am-4pm Sat & Sun Sept-May)*. This little aquarium has exhibits on marine life in the Sound as well as colourful tropical fish.

To get to Kronborg Slot, go back to Kronborgvej and continue walking south-east for another 200m.

Kronborg Slot

Despite the attention this castle *(☎ 49 21 30 78, Kronborgvej; adult/child 30/10kr, including Maritime Museum 45/15kr; open*

HELSINGØR

Walking Tour

Nordhavn

ØRESUND

To Danhostel Helsingør (300m),
Danmarks Tekniske Museum,
Hammermøllen & Hornbæk

Nordhavnsvej

Strandpromenaden

Grønnehavevej

Nordlysvænget

Grønnehave
Station

Allegade

Kronborgvej

Flower
Garden

Møllebakken

Kronborgvej

Kongensgade

Sankt Anna Gade

Allégade

Axeltorv

Sudergade

Sankt Olai Gade

Bjergegade

Brostræde

Strandgade

Havnepladsen

Stengade Hovedvagtsstræde

Havnegade

Søstræde

Bramstræde

Helsingør Station (DSB)

Stengade

Jernbanevej

To Hillerød &
Copenhagen

HHGB Terminal

PLACES TO STAY
1 Helsingør Camping
  Grønnehave
14 Hotel Hamlet

PLACES TO EAT
6 Gæstgivergården
7 Ristorante Italia
8 Kvickly Supermarket
9 Thai Cuisine Restaurant
15 Kammercaféen
17 Rådmand Davids Hus
18 Bakery

OTHER
2 Marienlyst Slot
3 Øresundsakvariet
4 Kronborg Slot; Handels-og
  Søfartsmuseet
5 Karmeliterklostret
10 Helsingør Bymuseum
11 Sankt Olai Kirke
12 Danske Bank
13 Stengades Apotek
16 Helsingør Turistbureau
19 Bus Stop
20 Post Office
21 Scandlines Terminal (Ferry
  to Sweden)
22 HH-Ferries Terminal (Ferry
  to Sweden)
23 Sundbusserne Terminal
  (Hydrofoil to Sweden)

*10.30am-5pm daily May-Sept, 11am-4pm
Tues-Sun Apr & Oct, 11am-3pm Tues-Sun
Nov-Mar)* has received as the setting of
Hamlet, its primary function was not as a
royal residence but rather as a grandiose
tollhouse, wresting taxes from ships passing
through the narrow Øresund. The castle's
history dates from the 1420s, when the
Danish king Erik of Pomerania introduced
the 'sound dues' and built a small fortress,
called Krogen, on a promontory at the narrowest part of the sound.

Financed by the generous revenue from
shipping tolls, the original medieval fortress

was rebuilt and enlarged by Frederik II in
1585 to form the present Kronborg Slot.
Much of Kronborg was ravaged by fire in
1629, but Christian IV rebuilt it, preserving
the castle's earlier Renaissance style. In
1658, during the war with Sweden, the
Swedes occupied Kronborg and removed
practically everything of value, leaving the
interior in a shambles. After that, Danish
royalty rarely visited the castle, although
the sound dues continued to be collected
for another 200 years. In 1785 Kronborg
was converted into barracks; that remained
its chief function until 1922. Since then the

castle has been thoroughly restored and is now open to the public as a museum.

Some of Kronborg's more interesting quarters include the king's and queen's chambers, which have marble fireplaces and detailed ceiling paintings; the small chamber, which boasts royal tapestries; and the great hall, one of the longest Renaissance halls in Scandinavia. The chapel is one of the best-preserved parts of the castle and has some choice wood carvings, while the gloomy dungeons make for more unusual touring.

In the dungeon you'll pass the resting statue of the legendary Viking chief Holger Danske (Ogier the Dane) who is said to watch over Denmark, ever-ready to come to her aid should the hour of need arrive. The low-ceiling dungeon includes areas that once served as soldiers' quarters and store-rooms for salted fish. These days they attract nesting bats!

Also housed in the castle is **Handels-og Søfartsmuseet** *(Danish Maritime Museum; ☎ 49 21 06 85; adult/child 25/10kr, or part of combined ticket to castle; open 10.30am-5pm daily May-Sept, 11am-4pm Tues-Sun Apr & Oct, 11am-3pm Tues-Sun Nov-Mar)*. This comprises a collection of model ships, paintings, nautical instruments and sea charts illustrating the history of Danish shipping and trade. Model ship enthusiasts will find it interesting. The remains of the original Krogen fortress can be seen in the masonry of the museum's showroom Nos 21 and 22.

Although you have to pay to enter the castle's interior, you can cross the moat and walk around the courtyard free of charge, which can be a fun experience in itself.

Outskirts of Town

About 1.5km north-west of the town centre is **Marienlyst Slot** *(☎ 49 28 37 91, Marienlyst Allé 32; adult/child 20kr/free; open noon-5pm daily)*, a three-storey manor house. Built in 1763 in the Louis Seize neo-classical style by French architect NH Jardin, it encompasses parts of an early summer house constructed by Frederik II. The interior exhibits include local paintings and silverwork. The Hornbæk-bound train stops at Marienlyst station, 100m north of the manor house.

If you'd like to examine technological inventions from the late 19th and early 20th centuries, the **Danmarks Tekniske Museum** *(☎ 49 22 26 11, Nordre Strandvej 23; bus No 340; adult/child 25/13kr; open 10am-5pm Tues-Sun)*, opposite the hostel, displays early gramophones, radios, motor vehicles and a 1906 Danish-built aeroplane that's claimed to be the first plane flown in Europe (it stayed airborne for 11 seconds!). It's 200m east of Højstrup train station.

Hammermøllen *(☎ 49 70 88 67, Bøssemagergade 21; adult/child 10/5kr; open 10am-at least 4pm Tues-Sun)*, 5km west of the town centre in the village of Hellebæk, is an old smithy that was founded by Christian IV and used to make muskets for the Kronborg arsenal. The current building, which dates from 1765, has also functioned as a water wheel-operated copper mill and

To Be or Not To Be

At the time Shakespeare penned his tragedy *Hamlet* in 1602, he used Kronborg Slot (calling it Elsinore Castle) as the setting. There is no evidence that Shakespeare ever visited Helsingør but, when the stately Kronborg Slot was completed in 1585, word of it was heralded far and wide and it apparently struck Shakespeare as a fitting setting. Although the play was fiction, Shakespeare did include two actual Danish nobles in his plot – Frederik Rosenkrantz and Knud Gyldenstierne (Guildenstern), both of whom had visited the English court in the 1590s.

The fact that Hamlet, Prince of Denmark, was a fictional character has not deterred legions of sightseers from visiting 'Hamlet's Castle'. Indeed, due to the fame bestowed on it by Shakespeare, Kronborg is the most widely known castle in all of Scandinavia.

Over the years Kronborg Slot has been used many times as the setting for stage performances of *Hamlet*, featuring such prominent actors as Sir Laurence Olivier, Richard Burton and Michael Redgrave.

textile mill. Hammermøllen is 500m south of Hellebæk train station.

Places to Stay

Helsingør Camping Grønnehave (☎ 49 28 12 12, fax 49 28 12 10, ⓔ campingpladsen@ helsingor.dk, Campingvej 1) Bus No 340. Camping per person 50kr. Open year-round. This two-star camping ground is on the beach about 1.5km north-west of the town centre.

Danhostel Helsingør (☎ 49 21 16 40, fax 49 21 13 99, ⓔ helsingor@danhostel.dk, Nordre Strandvej 24) Bus No 340. Dorm beds 95kr, singles/doubles 300/325kr. Open Feb-Nov. This 180-bed hostel is 2km north-west of the town centre in a renovated coastal manor house close to a beach.

Tourist office staff can book **rooms** in private homes for 200/350kr for singles/ doubles, plus a 25kr booking fee.

Hotel Hamlet (☎ 49 21 05 91, fax 49 26 01 30, ⓔ hotelhamlet@internet.dk, Bramstræde 5) Singles/doubles 645/850kr. Best choice for a central hotel is the Hamlet, which has 36 rooms with private bath and TV.

Places to Eat

You'll find the main cluster of eateries around Axeltorv, four blocks north-west of the train station, as well as beer gardens selling Helsingør's own Wiibroe pilsner.

Kammercaféen (☎ 49 28 20 52, Havnepladsen 1) Snacks & meals 30-90kr. In the old customs house behind the tourist office, this cafe specialises in organic fare, including sandwiches, salads and a few hot dishes.

Rådmand Davids Hus (☎ 49 26 10 43, Strandgade 70) This popular cafe is housed in a 300-year-old half-timbered building. The special is the 'shopping lunch' (65kr), a generous plate of traditional Danish foods, typically salmon pate, salad and slices of lamb, cheese and bread.

Gæstgivergården (☎ 49 21 19 78, Kampergade 9) Daily specials 69kr. This pub-like place serves everything from burgers and salads to traditional Danish fare, including some good-value specials.

Ristorante Italia (☎ 49 21 60 22, Kampergade 7) Mains 70-100kr. This pleasant Italian restaurant has all of the usual pasta choices as well as seafood dishes.

Thai Cuisine Restaurant (☎ 49 26 30 01, Torvegade 5) Mains 70-100kr. Here you'll find a full menu of curries, noodle dishes and other Thai specialities.

There's a **bakery** opposite Helsingør train station and another in the **Kvickly** supermarket (Stjernegade 25), a block west of Axeltorv.

Getting There & Away

Train Helsingør train station has two adjacent terminals: the DSB terminal for national trains and the smaller Helsingør-Hornbæk-Gilleleje Banen (HHGB) terminal for the private railway that runs along the north coast. DSB trains to and from Copenhagen (45.50kr, 55 minutes) run about three times hourly from early morning to around midnight. DSB trains to and from Hillerød (39kr, 30 minutes) run at least once hourly until around midnight. The HHGB train from Helsingør to Gilleleje via Hornbæk runs an average of twice hourly (39kr, 40 minutes), with the last train pulling out of Helsingør at 10.54pm.

Car & Motorcycle Helsingør is 64km north of Copenhagen and 24km north-east of Hillerød. There's free parking throughout the city, including at car parks north-east of the tourist office, to the west of the Kvickly supermarket and outside Kronborg Slot.

Boat For information on the frequent ferries to Helsingborg in Sweden (16kr, 20 minutes), see the introductory Getting There & Away chapter. Visitors arriving by train can make a beeline to the Scandlines ferry office by walking through the back exit of the DSB railway terminal.

North Coast

The north coast of Zealand, also known as the Kattegat coast, is a pleasant mix of dunes, heathlands and coastal woodlands. Development is limited to a handful of small fishing towns that date back to the

1500s, their backstreets bordered by half-timbered, thatch-roofed houses with tidy flower gardens. Although the towns have only a few thousand residents in winter, the population swells with throngs of beach-goers in summer.

HORNBÆK
postcode 3100 • pop 3300

Hornbæk has the best beach on the north coast, a vast expanse of soft, white sand that runs the entire length of the town. It's backed by sand dunes with beach grass and thickets of *Rosa rugosa*, a wild pink seaside rose that blooms all summer. Even though it borders the town, the beach is pleasantly undeveloped, with all the commercial facilities on the inland side of the dunes.

Poet Holger Drachmann, who passed away in Hornbæk in 1908, is memorialised by a harbourside monument. These days the salty fisherfolk, about whom Drachmann often wrote, share their harbour with scores of sailing boats and yachts.

Orientation

From the train station it's a five-minute walk directly north along Havnevej to the harbour. Climb the dunes to the left and you're on the beach.

Information

The Hornbæk Turistbureau is inside the library (☎ 49 70 47 47, fax 49 70 41 42), Vester Stejlebakke 2A; to reach it take the walkway at the side of Danske Bank. The tourist office is open the same hours as the library: 2pm to 7pm on Monday, Tuesday and Thursday, 10am to 5pm on Wednesday and Friday, and 10am to 2pm on Saturday.

The post office (☎ 49 25 08 00) is opposite the train station, while Danske Bank (☎ 49 76 01 20) is in the town centre at Nordre Strandvej 350.

There are public toilets and showers at the harbour.

Things to See & Do

The **beach** is without a doubt Hornbæk's main attraction and offers some good swimming conditions and plenty of space for

An Inspiring Rescue

In 1774, Hornbæk fishermen came to the rescue of British captain Thomas Brauwn, whose ship was being battered by a raging storm. These unhesitating Danes, braving treacherous seas, so inspired their countryfolk that a popular play, *Fiskerne*, was written about them by the lyricist poet Johannes Ewald. A song taken from the play became Denmark's national anthem. The rescue was also immortalised by the painter CW Eckersberg, who used it as a theme in a number of his paintings.

sunbathing. If you're interested in **windsurfing**, contact Hornbæk Surfudlejning (☎ 49 70 33 75), Drejervej 19, which rents gear for 250kr a day. To charter a boat to go **fishing**, contact the tourist office or the harbourmaster's office on the southern side of the harbour; prices average 600kr (per boat per day) for up to three passengers. You can rent **bicycles** for 50kr a day at Bjærre Cykler (☎ 49 70 32 82), Nordre Strandvej 338.

If you're up to an enjoyable nature stroll, **Hornbæk Plantage**, a public woodland that extends 3.5km along the coast east from Hornbæk, has numerous interconnecting trails branching out either side of route 237. There are wild roses along the coast and pine trees and flowering Scotch broom inland. One trail hugs the coast from Lochersvej in Hornbæk to the eastern end of the plantage. Other trails go inland, including one path that leads to Hornbæk Camping. There are several areas along Nordre Strandvej (route 237) where you can park a car and start your wanderings. A free forestry map, *Vandreture i Statsskovene, Hornbæk Plantage*, shows all the trails and is available from the tourist office.

Places to Stay

Hornbæk Camping DCU (☎ 49 70 02 23, fax 49 70 23 91, e hornbaek@dcu.dk, Planetvej 4) Camping per person 58kr. Open year-round. This three-star camping ground is on the outskirts of town off Sauntevej, about 1.5km south-east of the centre.

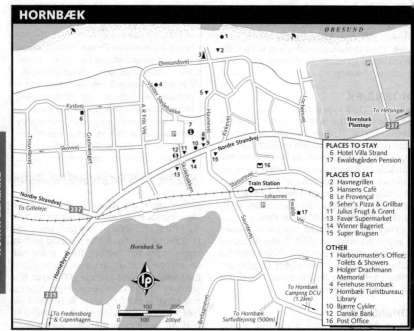

HORNBÆK

ØRESUND

To Helsingør

Hornbæk
Plantage 237

PLACES TO STAY
6 Hotel Villa Strand
17 Ewaldsgården Pension

PLACES TO EAT
2 Havnegrillen
5 Hansens Café
8 Le Provençal
9 Seher's Pizza & Grillbar
11 Julius Frugt & Grønt
13 Favør Supermarket
14 Wiener Bageriet
15 Super Brugsen

OTHER
1 Harbourmaster's Office;
   Toilets & Showers
3 Holger Drachmann
   Memorial
4 Feriehuse Hornbæk
7 Hornbæk Turistbureau;
   Library
10 Bjærre Cykler
12 Danske Bank
16 Post Office

Train Station

Hornbæk Sø

To Hornbæk
Camping DCU
(1.2km)

To Hornbæk
Surfudlejning (500m)

To Gilleleje 237
Nordre Strandvej

To Fredensborg
& Copenhagen 235

0   100   200m
0   100   200yd

Ewaldsgården Pension (☎/fax 49 70 00 82, Johannes Ewalds Vej 5) Singles/doubles with breakfast 385/560kr. This friendly pension, south-east of the train station and about a 10-minute walk from the harbour, occupies an early-18th-century country house. The interior is light and airy with a cosy mix of antiques and cottage-style furnishings. All 12 rooms have a washbasin; showers and toilets are off the hall. There's a guest kitchen for simple preparations such as sandwiches and coffee.

Hotel Villa Strand (☎/fax 49 70 00 88, Kystvej 12) Singles 400-600kr, doubles 700-1100kr. This small hotel on the western side of town has a variety of rooms, with the cheaper ones small and all the pricier ones quite large, but all have private bath and include breakfast, and the place is opposite the beach.

Feriehuse Hornbæk (☎ 49 70 35 20, 49 70 20 94, ✉ morten@feriehuse-hornbaek .dk), at Vestre Stejlebakke 30, is an agency

that handles summer cottage rentals for 2500kr to 4000kr per week.

Places to Eat

Seher's Pizza & Grillbar (☎ 49 70 25 48, Nordre Strandvej 336) Pizza or pasta 40kr. Seher's has straightforward pizza or pasta dishes as well as pitta-bread sandwiches.

Hansens Café (☎ 49 70 04 79, Havnevej 19) Mains 70-90kr. Hansens is in the town's oldest house, a sod-roofed half-timbered building with a pleasant pub-like atmosphere. The menu changes daily but you can expect to find good Danish food at moderate prices.

Le Provençal (☎ 49 76 11 77, Havnevej 1) Mains 100-150kr. This dinner restaurant offers good, upmarket French food, including fresh seafood dishes.

Eating opportunities down at the harbour include a little shop, a fish market and *Havnegrillen*, a fast-food stand selling hot dogs and ice cream. Within 100m of each other on Nordre Strandvej you'll find two supermarkets, a *Favør* and a *Super Brugsen*, as well as the bakery *Wiener Bageriet* and a fruit stand, *Julius Frugt & Grønt*.

Getting There & Away

Trains connect Hornbæk with Helsingør (19.50kr, 25 minutes) and Gilleleje (26kr, 15 minutes) about twice hourly.

GILLELEJE

postcode 3250 • pop 5300

Zealand's northernmost town, Gilleleje has lots of attractive straw-roofed houses as well as the island's largest fishing harbour. Despite its size, the harbour has a certain timeless character, filled as it is with colourful wooden-hulled fishing boats.

Many of the attractions the town has to offer are in one way or another connected with fishing, including smokehouses along the harbour and a little dock-side fish auction that can be viewed by early-risers.

It's a five-minute walk north from the train station to the harbour. Although they are not on a par with those at Hornbæk or Tisvildeleje, there are public beaches on both sides of town.

Information

The Gilleleje tourist office (☎ 48 30 01 74, fax 48 30 34 74) is at Hovedgade 6F in the town centre, 200m east of the train station. It's open 10am to 6pm Monday to Saturday from mid-June to August, and 9am to 4pm on weekdays and 9am to noon on Saturday the rest of the year.

Things to See & Do

The Gilleleje Museum (☎ 48 30 16 31, *Vesterbrogade 56; adult/child 20kr/free, includes entry to eastern lighthouse; open 1pm-4pm Wed-Mon mid-June–mid-Sept*) is on the western side of the town centre. The museum is dedicated to Gilleleje's history, from the Middle Ages to the advent of summer tourism, and includes a 19th-century fisherman's house.

There are coastal trails heading in both directions from the town centre. The trail to the west, which starts near the intersection of Nordre Strandvej and Vesterbrogade, leads

1.75km to a stone **memorial** dedicated to the Danish philosopher Søren Kierkegaard, who used to make visits to this coast.

The trail to the east begins just off Hovedgade and leads 2.5km to the site where two lighthouses with coal-burning beacons were erected in 1772. In 1899 the western lighthouse was modernised with rotating lenses and the eastern one, no longer needed, was abandoned. The eastern lighthouse, **Nakkehoved Østre Fyr** (☎ 48 30 16 31, *Fryvej 20; adult/child 20kr/free, includes entry to the Gilleleje Museum; open 1pm-4pm Wed-Mon mid-June–mid-Sept*) has been restored as a museum. You can get to this lighthouse on the coastal footpath or by turning north off route 237 onto Fyrvejen.

Places to Stay

Tourist office staff can book *rooms* in private homes at around 250/350kr for singles/doubles, plus a 25kr booking fee.

Hotel Strand (☎ 48 30 05 12, fax 48 30 18 59, ⒠ hotelstr@post7.tele.dk, *Vesterbrogade 4*) Singles/doubles with shared toilet 410/610kr, with private facilities 470/720kr. This 25-room hotel is in the centre of town, a short walk west from the harbour. The cheaper rooms are a tad small but have showers (toilets are off the hall); the higher-priced rooms are larger and more modern with full amenities. Rates include breakfast.

Places to Eat

Hos Karen & Marie (☎ 48 30 21 30, *Nordre Havnevej 3*) This excellent little seafood restaurant is in a period building overlooking the harbour. At lunchtime there's a generous sampler plate (139kr) that includes pickled herring, butter-fried plaice, salmon, pork tenderloin and brie.

At the harbour, you'll find *Rogeriet Bornholm*, a simple smokehouse that sells inexpensive smoked fish by the piece, and *Adamsen's Fisk*, with affordable deli items such as fish cakes, rollmops and shrimp salad to take away.

Getting There & Away

Trains run between Hillerød and Gilleleje (32.50kr, 31 minutes) about twice hourly on weekdays, hourly at weekends, and between Helsingør and Gilleleje (39kr, 40 minutes) about twice hourly every day.

TISVILDELEJE
postcode 3220

Tisvildeleje is a pleasant seaside village with an invitingly slow pace and fine nature walks. It's bordered by a stretch of sandy beach that's backed by low dunes; the nearest beach is a short walk from the train station but the most glorious sweep is at the end of Hovedgaden, 1km west of the village centre. That beach has a large car park, a changing room, toilets and an ice-cream kiosk.

Inland from the beach is Tisvilde Hegn, a windswept forest of twisted trees and heather-covered hills that extends south-west from Tisvildeleje for more than 8km. Much of this enchanting forest was planted in the 18th century to stabilise the sand drifts that were threatening to turn the area into desert.

Information

The seasonal tourist office (☎ 48 70 74 51), in the Tisvildeleje train station at Banevej 8, is open 10am to 5pm Monday to Saturday from June to August only.

Walks in Tisvilde Hegn

From the beach parking area at the end of Hovedgaden you can walk, either along the beach or on a dirt path through the woods, about 3km south to **Troldeskoven** (Witch Wood), an area of ancient trees that have been sculpted by the wind into haunting shapes. On the way make a short detour east at Brantebjerg for a nice hill-top view.

Tisvilde Hegn has numerous other trails, including one to **Asserbo Slotsruin**, the moat-encircled ruins of a former manor house and a 12th-century monastery, which are near the southern boundary of the forest. The south-western part of Tisvilde Hegn merges with **Asserbo Plantage**, a wooded area that borders Lake Arresø. Trail maps are available free from the tourist office.

Places to Stay

Danhostel Tisvildeleje (☎ 48 70 98 50, fax 48 70 98 97, ⓔ shc@helene.dk, Bygmarken 30)

Camping per person 25kr, dorm beds 100kr, singles/doubles 330/360kr. Open year-round. This modern 272-bed hostel is 1km east of the town centre and within walking distance of a sandy beach. The hostel is part of the Sankt Helene complex, which runs nature courses and thematic holidays for schoolchildren and other groups. Reservations are essential in summer. Its 12-hectare grounds have walking trails, sports fields and playgrounds and the complex is accessible for wheelchairs. Hostel rooms have four beds, a little sitting area and a bathroom. Campers can pitch a tent in an adjacent field. If you are arriving by train, get off at Godhavns station, one stop before Tisvildeleje station; the hostel is just north of the tracks.

Tisvildeleje Strand Hotel (☎ 48 70 71 19, fax 48 70 71 77, Hovedgaden 75) Singles/doubles 450/500kr, with bath 500/575kr. This 29-room hotel is in the centre of town and within walking distance of the beach. The tariff includes breakfast.

Places to Eat

There's a small cluster of eateries in the town centre on Hovedgaden.

Smitty's Pizzabar (☎ 48 70 21 27, Hovedgaden 78) Opposite the Tisvildeleje Strand Hotel, this eatery caters to the summer crowds, selling ice cream (16kr) and inexpensive pizza.

Tisvildeleje Caféen (☎ 48 70 88 86, Hovedgaden 55) Light meals 40-70kr. This place serves good, moderately priced cafe fare.

There's also a good bakery, **Tisvildeleje Bageri** (☎ 48 70 71 22, Hovedgaden 60), and a little **grocery shop** on the opposite side of the street.

Getting There & Around

Bus No 363 operates between Tisvildeleje and Gilleleje (19.50kr, one hour) every two hours. Trains run between Tisvildeleje and Hillerød (32.50kr, 31 minutes) once an hour; there are a few extra trains in the early morning and the late afternoon.

Bicycles can be hired at the Hydro petrol station (☎ 48 70 80 13), Hovedgaden 53, which is 200m west of the train station, for 50kr per day.

Fjord Towns

North Zealand has two interlinking fjords, the Isefjord and the Roskilde Fjord, that connect with the Kattegat at the town of Hundested. The largest towns in the region, Frederiksværk and Frederikssund, border the Roskilde Fjord and are along the main Tisvildeleje-Roskilde road route.

HUNDESTED
postcode 3390 • pop 8400

The main attraction in Hundested, a small town at the mouth of Isefjord, is the home built by Knud Rasmussen (1879–1933), Denmark's most famous arctic explorer. Near the lighthouse, the home has been turned into a museum, **Knud Rasmussens Hus** (☎ 47 93 71 61, *Knud Rasmussensvej 9; adult/child 10/5kr; open 11am-4pm Tues-Sun mid-Apr–mid-Oct*). It contains original furnishings, but thousands of archaeological artefacts that Rasmussen collected on his expeditions are kept in Nationalmuseet in Copenhagen.

The Lynæs area, a few kilometres south of Hundested, is a **windsurfing** mecca with good wind conditions as well as shallow-water areas suitable for beginners. Nautic Surf og Ski (☎ 47 98 01 00), Lynæs Havnevej 15, has windsurfing gear for hire and also offers lessons.

The train between Hundested and Hillerød (45kr, 45 minutes) runs about twice an hour.

FREDERIKSVÆRK
postcode 3300 • pop 11,600

Frederiksværk, on the northern side of the Roskilde Fjord, is Denmark's oldest industrial town, founded in 1756 by order of King Frederik V, from whom the town takes its name. At that time a canal was dug between the Roskilde Fjord and Arresø Lake to provide water power for mills, a gunpowder factory and a cannon foundry.

The tourist office (☎ 47 72 30 01), in Gjethuset, a former cannon foundry on Torvet that has been converted into a **cultural centre** with changing art exhibits.

Fittingly, Frederiksværk's two museums, both near the canal in the centre of town, are dedicated to the town's industrial history. The **Frederiksværk Bymuseum** (☎ 47 72 06 05, *Torvet 18; adult/child 20kr/free; open noon-4pm Tues-Sun June–mid-Sept*) features artefacts and displays on Frederiksværk's early industries. The open-air **Krudtværksmuseum** (*Gunpowder Factory Museum;* ☎ 47 72 06 05, *Krudtværksalleén 1; adult/child 20kr/free; open noon-4pm Tues-Sun June–mid-Sept*) consists of period buildings equipped with the original machinery and a working water mill.

The town sits on the western shore of Arresø which, at 41 sq km, is Denmark's largest lake. Leisurely **boat excursions** (☎ 47 72 30 01) cruise the lake on summer afternoons (adult/child 60/30kr).

Danhostel Frederiksværk & Frederiksværk Campingplads (☎ 47 77 07 25, *fax 47 72 07 66,* e *strandbo@image.dk, Strandgade 30*) Camping per person 58kr, dorm beds 90kr, singles/doubles 220/360kr. This combined hostel and camping ground is right by the canal in the centre of town.

Frederiksværk is on the railway line between Hundested (20kr, 18 minutes) and Hillerød (29kr, 28 minutes).

FREDERIKSSUND
postcode 3600 • pop 14,500

Frederikssund, at the narrowest part of the Roskilde Fjord, is best known to visitors for the **Viking play** (☎ 47 31 06 85) performed from mid-June to early July by a troupe of 200 local actors. The performance takes place in a large open-air theatre on the fjord, a 10-minute walk south of the train station. Admission costs 100kr, or 140kr if you want to join the feast that follows the play. Phone for information or bookings.

Also in town is the **JF Willumsens Museum** (☎ 47 31 07 73, *Jenriksvej 4; adult/child 30/15kr; open 10am-5pm daily*), which contains paintings, sculpture and drawings by Jens Ferdinand Willumsen (1863–1958), one of Denmark's leading symbolists. The museum also displays some works by other artists, which belonged to Willumsen's private collection.

Frederikssund is at the end of the S-train H line, and is only a 45-minute (45.50kr) ride from Copenhagen.

ROSKILDE

postcode 4000 • pop 52,000

Roskilde, Denmark's first capital, was a thriving trade centre throughout the Middle Ages. It was also the site of Zealand's first Christian church, built by the Viking king Harald Bluetooth in 980.

In 1026 Canute I, in a rage over a chess match, had his brother-in-law Ulf Jarl assassinated in that church. Ulf's widow, Canute's sister Estrid, insisted that the wooden stave church in which her husband was ambushed be torn down, and then donated property for the construction of a new stone church. The foundations of that early stone church are beneath the floor of the present-day Roskilde Domkirke (cathedral). Estrid and her son Svend Estridsen are among the multitude of Danish royals who are now buried in the cathedral.

As the centre of Danish Catholicism, medieval Roskilde was the site of not only a cathedral but also nearly 20 churches and monasteries. After the Reformation swept Denmark in 1536 the monasteries and most of the churches were demolished. Consequently the town, which had been in decline since the capital moved to Copenhagen in the early 15th century, saw its population shrink radically.

Today Roskilde is a likeable, low-profile town. Only 30km west of Copenhagen, it is on Denmark's main east-west train route.

Information

Roskilde Turistbureau (☎ 46 35 27 00, fax 46 35 14 74, e info@destination-roskilde .dk) is at Gullandsstræde 15. It's open 9am to 6pm Monday to Friday and 10am to 2pm on Saturday during July and August. Opening times are 9am to 5pm on weekdays, 10am to 1pm on Saturday for the rest of the year.

There are several banks in the centre, including a Unibank (☎ 46 32 32 33) at Algade 4. The post office (☎ 70 12 40 00) is at Jernbanegade 3, just south-west of the train station.

Heinzes Boghandel (☎ 46 35 43 43), Algade 54, sells books and travel guides.

Walking Tour

Roskilde's most notable sights are within walking distance of each other. **Roskilde Domkirke** is on Stændertorvet, the central square, a 10-minute walk north-west from the train station. From the station, cut diagonally across the old churchyard and go left along Algade.

After visiting the cathedral, you can take a 15-minute walk through the extensive

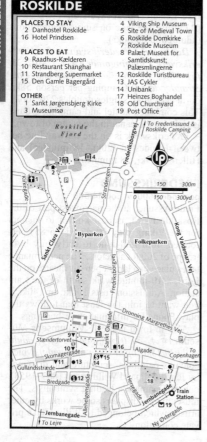

ROSKILDE

PLACES TO STAY	4 Viking Ship Museum
2 Danhostel Roskilde	5 Site of Medieval Town
16 Hotel Prindsen	6 Roskilde Domkirke
	7 Roskilde Museum
PLACES TO EAT	8 Palæt; Museet for
9 Raadhus-Kælderen	Samtidskunst;
10 Restaurant Shanghai	Palæsmlingerne
11 Strandberg Supermarket	12 Roskilde Turistbureau
15 Den Gamle Bagergård	13 JAS Cykler
	14 Unibank
OTHER	17 Heinzes Boghandel
1 Sankt Jørgensbjerg Kirke	18 Old Churchyard
3 Museumsø	19 Post Office

green belt of Byparken on the way down to the Viking Ship Museum. The route begins on the northern side of the cathedral and crosses a field where wildflowers blanket the unexcavated remains of Roskilde's original **medieval town**. The rectangular depression at this site marks the spot where the 12th-century church Sankt Hans Kirke was torn down during the Reformation.

The **Viking Ship Museum** and the adjacent **Museumsø** are fascinating places where you could easily spend a couple of hours touring the various workshops and viewing the archaeological restorations.

From the Viking Ship Museum, a five-minute walk west along the harbour will bring you to the **Sankt Jørgensbjerg quarter**, where the cobbled walkway Kirkegade leads through a neighbourhood of old thatched-roofed houses and into the courtyard of the hill-top **Sankt Jørgensbjerg Kirke**. This church, the nave of which dates from the 11th century, is one of the oldest in Denmark.

Roskilde Domkirke

This imposing cathedral (☎ 46 35 27 00, *Domkirkepladsen; adult/child 15/10kr; open 9am-4.45pm Mon-Fri, 9am-noon Sat, 12.30pm-4.45pm Sun Apr-Sept; 10am-3.45pm Tues-Fri, 11.30am-3.45pm Sat, 12.30pm-3.45pm Sun Oct-Mar*) dominates the city centre. Started in 1170 by Bishop Absalon, Roskilde Dom-kirke has been rebuilt and added to so many times that it represents a millennium of Danish architectural styles.

Roskilde Domkirke boasts tall spires, a splendid interior and the crypts of 37 Danish kings and queens. Some of the crypts are spectacularly embellished and guarded by marble statues of knights and women in mourning, while others are simple unadorned stone coffins. There's something quite awesome about being able to stand next to the bones of so many of Scandinavia's most powerful historical figures.

Of particular interest is the chapel of King Christian IV, off the northern side of the

NORTH ZEALAND

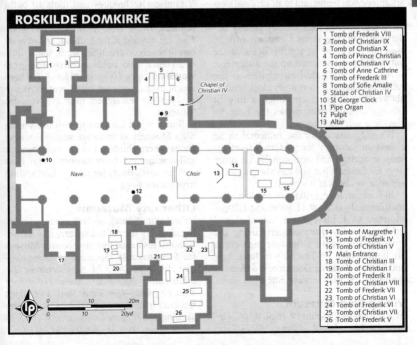

ROSKILDE DOMKIRKE

1. Tomb of Frederik VIII
2. Tomb of Christian IX
3. Tomb of Christian X
4. Tomb of Prince Christian
5. Tomb of Christian IV
6. Tomb of Anne Cathrine
7. Tomb of Frederik III
8. Tomb of Sofie Amalie
9. Statue of Christian IV
10. St George Clock
11. Pipe Organ
12. Pulpit
13. Altar

14. Tomb of Margrethe I
15. Tomb of Frederik IV
16. Tomb of Christian V
17. Main Entrance
18. Tomb of Christian III
19. Tomb of Christian I
20. Tomb of Frederik II
21. Tomb of Christian VIII
22. Tomb of Frederik VII
23. Tomb of Christian VI
24. Tomb of Frederik VI
25. Tomb of Christian VII
26. Tomb of Frederik V

Chapel of Christian IV

Nave

Choir

cathedral. It contains the coffin of Christian flanked by his young son, Prince Christian, and his wife, Anne Cathrine, as well as the brass coffins of his successor, Frederik III, and his wife, Queen Sofie Amalie. The bronze statue of Christian IV beside the entrance is the work of Bertel Thorvaldsen, while the huge wall-sized paintings, encased in trompe l'oeil frames, were created by Wilhelm Marstrand and include a classic scene depicting Christian IV rallying the troops aboard the warship *Trinity* during the 1644 battle of Kolbergerheide.

Some of the cathedral's finest pieces were installed by Christian IV, including the intricately detailed pulpit made of marble, alabaster and sandstone in 1610 by Copenhagen sculptor Hans Brokman.

The enormous gilt 'cupboard-style' altarpiece, made in 1560 in Antwerp, is adorned with 21 plates depicting the life of Christ. The story of how it came to Roskilde is as interesting as the piece. Apparently when the altarpiece was being sent to its original destination Gdansk, its shipper tried to cheat on the sound dues in Helsingør by grossly undervaluing it; the shrewd customs officer, asserting his right to acquire items at the valuation price, snapped up the altarpiece.

An unusually light-hearted item is the cathedral's early-16th-century clock, poised above the entrance, on which a tiny St George on horseback marks the hour by slaying a yelping dragon.

It's not unusual for the cathedral to be closed on Saturday for weddings (particularly in spring) and occasionally on other days for funerals but you can always call in advance to check if it's open.

In summer, tours (30kr) are conducted by multilingual guides at 11.30am and 1.30pm Monday to Friday, 11am Saturday and 1.30pm Sunday. Free concerts using the splendid 16th-century Baroque pipe organ are held at 8pm on Thursday in June, July and August. Roskilde Domkirke is a Unesco-designated World Heritage Site.

Viking Ship Museum

This intriguing museum (☎ 46 30 02 00, *Vindeboder 12; adult/child/family 45/28/98kr;*

open 9am-5pm daily May-Sept, 10am-4pm daily Oct-Apr) displays five reconstructed Viking ships (circa 1000) that were excavated from the bottom of Roskilde Fjord in 1962. The wooden ship fragments have been reassembled on new skeleton frames to recreate the original shapes. As some of the wood was lost over the centuries, none of the ships is complete but all have been reconstructed enough to provide a sense of their original features. The ships include an 18m warship of the type used to raid England and a 16.5m trader that is thought to have carried cargo between Greenland and Denmark.

Appropriately, the museum is on the eastern side of the harbour overlooking Roskilde Fjord, which provides a scenic backdrop for the displays.

The latest addition is **Museumsø** (Museum Island), a new harbourfront facility adjacent to the main museum. On this pier-like island, craftspeople painstakingly use Viking-era techniques and tools to build replicas of Viking ships. Three substantial replicas, *Helge Ask*, *Kraka Fyr* and *Roar Ege*, are moored in the harbour, and numerous other reconstructions are in the works. Museumsø also holds an **archaeological workshop** *(open 10am-3pm Mon-Fri)* where recent excavations are being preserved and analysed by researchers from the National Museum.

Summer is a fun time to visit the Viking Ship Museum as there are seasonal workshops where children can try their hand at sail-making and other maritime crafts, as well as possibilities for taking short sailing trips on the fjord.

Other City Museums

Palæet (the Palace), an 18th-century building, fronting the central square, is a former bishops' residence that now houses **Museet for Samtidskunst** *(Museum of Contemporary Art; ☎ 46 36 88 74, Stændertorvet 3D; adult/child 20kr/free; open 11am-5pm Tues-Fri, noon-4pm Sat & Sun)*, a small art museum with changing exhibits, and **Palæsamlingerne** *(Palace Collections; ☎ 46 35 78 80, Stændertorvet 3E; adult/child 25kr/free;*

Sunken Ships Surface

Towards the end of the Viking era, the narrower necks of Roskilde Fjord were purposely blocked to prevent raids by Norwegian fleets. The five Viking ships that are now displayed at Roskilde's Viking Ship Museum were thought to have been deliberately sunk in one such channel and then piled with rocks to make a reinforced barrier similar to an underwater stone wall. Although people had long suspected that there was a ship beneath the ridge of stones, folklore had led them to believe it was a single ship sunk by Queen Margrethe in the 15th century.

It wasn't until researchers from the National Museum made a series of exploratory dives in the late 1950s that it was discovered that there were several ships at the site and that they dated from the Viking period. Excavations began in 1962 when a cofferdam was built around the ships in the middle of the fjord and pumps were used to drain sea water from the site. Within just four months archaeologists were able to unpile the mound of stones and excavate the ships, whose wooden hulks were now in thousands of pieces. The ship fragments were then reassembled within the purpose-built museum that opened on the harbourfront in 1969.

In the mid-1990s, during the deepening of the harbour and the construction of a new artificial island west of the museum, workers were stunned to discover more ships, seven dating from the Middle Ages and two from the Viking period. The largest is a 36m-long Viking ship thought to have been built in 1030. In response to these new finds, the National Museum established an archaeological workshop right on the site where the recovered ship fragments are cleaned, preserved and documented.

open 11am-4pm daily mid-May–mid-Sept, 2pm-4pm Sat & Sun mid-Sept–mid-May), containing 18th- and 19th-century paintings that once belonged to the wealthy Roskilde merchants.

The well-presented **Roskilde Museum** (☎ 46 36 60 44, Sankt Olsgade 18; adult/child 25kr/free; open 11am-4pm daily) covers Roskilde's history in displays ranging from the Stone Age up to the contemporary 'rock age' of the Roskilde Festival. And naturally there's coverage of Roskilde's glory days as the former capital of Denmark.

Special Events

Roskilde comes alive at the end of June for one of Europe's largest music festivals.

The Roskilde Festival is renowned worldwide and attracts top-name acts as well as a multinational group of followers. For details of this huge event see the 'Festive Denmark' special section.

Places to Stay

Being so close to Copenhagen, Roskilde is usually visited on a day trip but there are a few options if you want to spend a night.

Roskilde Camping (☎ 46 75 79 96, fax 46 75 44 26, e camping@roskildecamping.dk, Baunehøjvej 7, Veddelev) Bus No 603. Camping per person 60kr. Open early Apr–mid-Sept. This three-star camping ground is by a sandy beach right on Roskilde Fjord, 3km north of the Viking Ship Museum.

Danhostel Roskilde (☎ *46 35 21 84, fax 46 32 66 90,* **ⓔ** *danhostel.roskilde@post.tele.dk, Vindeboder 7)* Dorm beds 100kr, 1-3–person rooms 300kr. Open year-round. This new hostel, adjacent to the Viking Ship Museum, has 152 beds in 40 modern rooms, some with water views and each with its own shower and toilet.

Tourist office staff book ***rooms*** in private homes at 150/300kr for singles/doubles, plus a 25kr booking fee; rooms can be booked in town, in the suburbs and on farms.

Hotel Prindsen (☎ *46 35 80 10, fax 46 35 81 10,* **ⓔ** *info@hotelprindsen, Algade 13)* Singles/doubles 970/1125kr, summer family special (2 adults, 2 children) 945kr. First opened in 1695, this city-centre place is Denmark's oldest continuously operating hotel. Its guest list reads like a who's who of great Danes, from King Frederik VII to Hans Christian Andersen. As befits an old hotel, the rooms are different sizes and have varied decor, but all have modern amenities and include breakfast. The hotel is a member of the Best Western chain, not.

Places to Eat

On Skomagergade, the pedestrian street that runs west from Stændertorvet, there are numerous places to eat.

Strandberg Café (☎ *46 35 14 49, Skomagergade 11)* Light meals around 30kr. This cafeteria-style place on the upper floor of the Strandberg grocery store has a varied menu that includes breakfast items, sandwiches and inexpensive chicken lunches.

Restaurant Shanghai (☎ *46 35 01 82, Skomagergade 4)* Mains 60-80kr. This family-run restaurant is the place to go for reasonably priced Chinese fare.

Raadhus-Kælderen (☎ *46 36 01 00, Stændertorvet)* Lunch specials 68kr, dinner mains around 200kr. For a treat, try this atmospheric restaurant in the cellar of the old town hall (circa 1430). Lunchtime specials include such dishes as fish fillet with shrimp and asparagus. Dinner features a changing menu of creative, French-inspired meat and seafood dishes.

Den Gamle Bagergård (☎ *46 35 01 12, Algade 6)* Sandwiches 24kr. This is a good bakery with a range of pastries and take-away sandwiches.

On Wednesday and Saturday mornings there's a ***market*** on Stændertorvet selling fresh produce as well as local handicrafts and flowers.

Getting There & Away

Trains from Copenhagen to Roskilde are frequent (45.50kr, 25 minutes). Trains also run between Roskilde and Køge (39kr, 25 minutes) and Næstved (45kr, 42 minutes).

If you're coming from Copenhagen by car, route 21 leads to Roskilde. Upon approaching the city, exit onto route 156, which leads into the centre. There are car parks south of Strandberg Supermarket and down by the Viking Ship Museum.

Getting Around

Bicycles can be rented from JAS Cykler (☎ 46 35 04 20), Gullandsstræde 3, for 50kr a day.

LEJRE

postcode 4320

The countryside on the outskirts of Lejre, a village 8km south-west of Roskilde, has two sightseeing attractions that could be combined for an afternoon outing.

Lejre Forsøgscenter

This 'archaeological experimental centre' (☎ *46 48 08 78, Slangeallen 2; adult/child 60/30kr; open 10am-5pm daily May–mid-Sept)* contains a reconstructed Iron Age village where Danish families can volunteer to spend their summer holidays as 'prehistoric families', using technology and dressed in clothing from that period. The reconstructed houses they live in and the tools they use are modelled on finds from archaeological excavations around Denmark.

The centre is a popular destination for school outings and also has craft demonstrations and a small cottage-farm area where the lives of 19th-century Danish farmers are re-enacted. In summer, when the place is most active, children can paddle dugout canoes and partake in other hands-on activities such as grinding flour.

Ledreborg Slot

This grand manor house (☎ 46 48 00 38, *Ledreborg Allé; adult/child 50/25kr; open 11am-5pm daily mid-June–Aug, 11am-5pm Sun May–mid-June & Sept)*, set on a knoll overlooking 80 hectares of lawns and woods, was built by Count Johan Ludvig Holstein in 1739 and has been home to the Holstein-Ledreborg family ever since. The interior has barely changed since the house was originally decorated and consequently it's considered one of the finest period manor houses in Denmark.

Visitors are required to put on booties to prevent damage to the marble and parquet floors. The house is chock-full of antique furniture, gilded mirrors, chandeliers, oil paintings and wall tapestries. One of the most superb rooms is the banquet room, designed by architect Nicolai Eigtved, the creator of Copenhagen's Amalienborg Slot. Also in the house is a chapel, constructed by JC Krieger in 1745, which served as the parish church until 1899.

Getting There & Away

From Roskilde it's just a short train ride to Lejre station, where bus No 233 continues to both Ledreborg Slot and Lejre Forsøgs-center (11kr).

By car, from Roskilde take Ringstedvej (route 14), turn right on route 155 and then almost immediately turn left onto Ledreborg Allé. Follow the signs to Ledreborg, 6km away, where a long drive lined by old elm trees leads to the entrance. Lejre Forsøgscenter is 2km farther west along the same road.

NORTH ZEALAND

Southern Zealand

Steeped in history, southern Zealand has played an important role in the shaping of Denmark since the Viking era. In medieval times it was a stomping ground for significant historical characters such as Bishop Absalon and the royal Valdemar family. In the 17th century the area was the stage for some of the most important battles of the lengthy wars between Denmark and Sweden. The most pivotal defeat in Danish history was played out here in 1658 when the Swedish king Gustave marched across southern Zealand en route to Copenhagen, where he forced a treaty that nearly cost Denmark its sovereignty.

Today the region is a mix of peaceful towns, rural villages and patchwork farmland. Highlights of include: two notably engaging towns, Køge and Sorø; one of Denmark's most impressive Viking sites, the 1000-year-old ring fortress at Trelleborg; and some interesting medieval churches.

If you're travelling across the region between Køge and Korsør using your own transport, the rural route 150 makes an excellent alternative to zipping along on the E20 motorway. Not only is it a slower, greener route, but it will take you right into the most interesting towns and villages.

KØGE
postcode 4600 • pop 33,200

Køge has a rich history stretching back to 1288, when it was granted its municipal charter by King Erik VI. With its large natural harbour, Køge quickly developed into a thriving fishing and trade centre.

In 1677 one of the most important naval engagements of the Danish-Swedish wars was fought in the waters off Køge. Known as the Battle of Køge Bay, it made a legend of Danish admiral Niels Juel, who resoundingly defeated the attacking Swedish navy and thwarted the attempted invasion.

Today the harbour still plays an important role in Køge's economy, having developed into a modern commercial facility. Although

Highlights

- Wander around Sorø, a charming town with a rich cultural background
- Explore the Viking past at the fascinating ring fortress at Trelleborg
- Stroll through the well-preserved historic quarter of the ancient town of Køge
- Poke around the rural hamlet of Vallø, with its castle and woodland
- Enjoy centuries-old frescoes at Sankt Bendts Kirke, Ringsted's medieval church

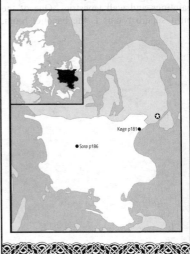

Køge p181

Sorø p186

parts of the city have been industrialised, Køge has done a superb job of retaining the period character of its central historic quarter. The narrow streets that radiate from Torvet, the town square, are lined with old buildings, some having survived a sweeping fire in 1633, and many others built in the construction boom spawned by that blaze.

Information

The Køge Turistbureau (☎ 56 65 58 00, fax 56 65 59 84, e post@kogeturistbureau.dk),

SOUTHERN ZEALAND

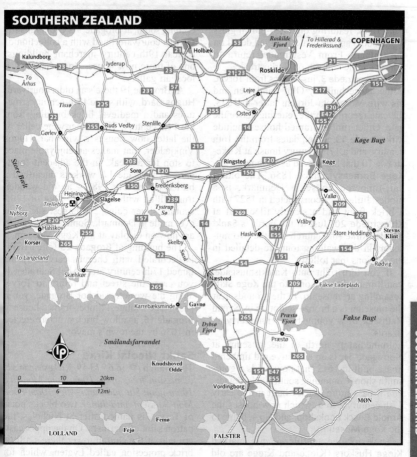

Vestergade 1, distributes a 90-page booklet, with English translations, describing the town's sights; this booklet is free. The office is open 9am to 5pm on weekdays year-round. Saturday opening hours are 9am to 2pm from June to August, 10am to 1pm the rest of the year.

The Unibank (☎ 56 63 33 33), Torvet 14, is open 9.30am to 4pm on weekdays (to 6pm Thursday).

The post office (☎ 70 12 40 00), which is at Jernstøbervænget 2, is open 10am to 5pm on weekdays and 10am to 12.30pm on Saturday.

Walking Tour

Most of Køge's finest historical sites are within easy walking distance of each other. A pleasant little stroll around these sites can be made in about an hour, although if you take your time, stopping at Sankt Nicolai Kirke and the two museums along the way, you could easily turn it into a half-day outing.

Begin the walk from Torvet by making a short detour west along the first block of **Vestergade**. There are two half-timbered houses on this street: house **No 7**, which dates from the 16th century, and **No 16** (the Richters Gaard restaurant), a remarkably

SOUTHERN ZEALAND

well-preserved merchant's house dating from 1644, featuring old hand-blown glass in the doors and intricately carved detail on the timbers. From Vestergade, return to Torvet and head north on Kirkestræde.

At **Kirkestræde 3**, just metres from Torvet, is the house built by Oluf Sandersen and his wife Margareta Jørgensdatter in 1638, the date recorded in the lettering above the gate. Other timber-framed houses include **Kirkestræde 13**, which dates from the 16th century, and a 17th-century house at Kirkestræde 10 that has served as a kindergarten, **Køge Børneasyl**, since 1856. The oldest half-timbered house in Denmark, is a modest little place constructed in 1527 with a brick front and a steeply tiled roof at **Kirkestræde 20**. Just to the north is **Sankt Nicolai Kirke** (the church and the two museums in this walking tour are detailed in the sections that follow).

If you turn right onto Katekismusgade, you'll immediately come to the **Køge Skitsesamling** art museum. In the grounds near the museum is a bronze sculpture by Svend Rathsack of a young boy with scurrying lizards.

Immediately north of the museum, at Nørregade 31, is an attractive red timbered house built in 1612 that now holds a **goldsmith shop**. Continuing south on Nørregade, you'll pass more houses built in the early 17th century: No 5, which now houses the **Arnold Busck bookshop**, and No 4, home to the **Køge Museum**.

Look for the marble plaque marked **Kiøge Huskors** (Kiøge and Kjøge are old spellings of Køge) on the green corner building at Torvet 2, which honours the victims of a witch-hunt in the 17th century. Two residents of an earlier house on this site were among those burned at the stake.

Along the eastern side of Torvet is the yellow neoclassical **Køge Rådhus**, which boasts of being the oldest functioning town hall in Denmark. At the rear of this complex is a building erected in 1600 to serve as an inn for King Christian IV on journeys between his royal palaces in Copenhagen and Nykøbing.

At Brogade 1, by the south-eastern corner of Torvet, is **Køge Apotek**, a pharmacy

that has occupied this site since 1660. Proceeding south, at Brogade 7 is **Oluf I Jensens Gård**, a courtyard lined with a collection of typical 19th-century merchant buildings; one of these now houses **Køge Galleriet**, a local art gallery.

At Brogade 19 there's an older courtyard, **Hugos Gård**, with some 17th-century structures and a medieval brick building from the 14th century. The former wine cellar of the latter now houses a wine bar, Hugos Vinkjælder, that makes an enjoyable place to stop for a break. In the adjacent courtyard, at Brogade 17, workers unearthed a buried treasure in 1987 – an old wooden trunk filled with more than 30kg of 17th-century silver coins, the largest such find ever made in Denmark. Some of these coins are now on display at the Køge Museum.

The building at **Brogade 23** (circa 1638) is decorated with cherubs carved by the famed 17th-century artist Abel Schrøder. If you cross the street and return to Torvet along the western side of Brogade, you'll pass Køge's longest timber-framed house at **Brogade 16**, a yellow-brick structure erected in 1636 by the town's mayor.

Sankt Nicolai Kirke

This church (*☎ 56 65 13 59, Kirkestræde 31; admission free; open 10am-4pm Mon-Fri, 10am-noon Sat mid-June–Aug; 10am-noon Mon-Sat Sept–mid-June*), two blocks north of Torvet, is named after St Nicholas, the patron saint of mariners. On the upper eastern end of the church tower there's a little brick projection called Lygten, which for centuries was used to hang a burning lantern as a guide for sailors returning to the harbour. It was from the top of the church tower that Christian IV kept watch on his naval fleet as it successfully defended the town from Swedish invaders during the Battle of Køge Bay.

The church dates from 1324 but was largely rebuilt in the 15th century. Most of the ornately carved works that adorn the interior were added later, including the altar and pulpit, which date from the 17th century. In summer you can climb the tower between 10.30am and 1.30pm.

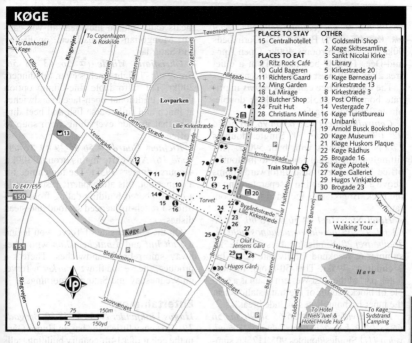

KØGE

PLACES TO STAY	OTHER
15 Centralhotellet	1 Goldsmith Shop
	2 Køge Skitsesamling
PLACES TO EAT	3 Sankt Nicolai Kirke
9 Ritz Rock Café	4 Library
10 Guld Bageren	5 Kirkestræde 20
11 Richters Gaard	6 Køge Børneasyl
12 Ming Garden	7 Kirkestræde 13
18 La Mirage	8 Kirkestræde 3
23 Butcher Shop	13 Post Office
24 Fruit Hut	14 Vestergade 7
28 Christians Minde	16 Køge Turistbureau
	17 Unibank
	19 Arnold Busck Bookshop
	20 Køge Museum
	21 Køge Huskors Plaque
	22 Køge Rådhus
	25 Brogade 16
	26 Køge Apotek
	27 Køge Galleriet
	29 Hugos Vinkjælder
	30 Brogade 23

Walking Tour

Køge Museum

Køge Museum (☎ 56 63 42 42, Nørregade 4; adult/child 20/10kr including entry to Køge Skitsesamling; open 11am-5pm daily June-Aug; 1pm-5pm Sun-Fri, 11am-3pm Sat Sept-May) occupies a lovely building dating from 1619 that was once a wealthy merchant's home. Its rooms now feature exhibits illustrating the cultural history of the Køge area. As well as the expected period furnishings and artefacts, there's an interesting hotchpotch of displays ranging from a Mesolithic-era grave to hundreds of recently discovered silver coins, including those unearthed in the courtyard at Brogade 17, part of a huge stash thought to have been hidden during the Swedish wars of the late 17th century.

The museum also has a desk used by Danish philosopher NFS Grundtvig, who lived on the outskirts of Køge, and a window-pane onto which Hans Christian Andersen, during an apparently stressed-out stay at a nearby inn, scratched the words 'Oh God, Oh God in Kjøge'.

Køge Skitsesamling

The Køge Art and Sketch Collection (☎ 56 63 34 14, Nørregade 29; adult/child 20/10kr, including entry to the Køge Museum; open 11am-5pm Tues-Sun) is a unique art museum that specialises in outlining the creative process from an artist's earliest concept to the finished work. The displays include original drawings, clay models and mock-ups by 20th-century Danish artists.

Places to Stay

Køge Sydstrand Camping (☎ 56 65 07 69, fax 56 66 07 68, e koege.sydstrand.camping@ fritid.tele.dk, Søndre Badevej) Camping per person 50kr. Open Apr–mid-Sept. This two-star facility, south of the harbour, is the closest camping ground to town. On a beach with an industrial backdrop, it's about a 20-minute walk from the train station.

Danhostel Køge (☎ 56 65 14 74, fax 56 66 08 69, e koegedanhostel@koegekom .dk, Vamdrupvej 1) Bus No 210. Dorm beds 90kr, 1-4–person rooms 400kr. Open Apr–mid-Dec. This 80-bed hostel is in a quiet area 2km north-west of the town centre.

The tourist office can book *rooms* in private homes for 375kr to 450kr a double, plus a 25kr booking fee.

Centralhotellet (☎ 56 65 06 96, fax 56 66 02 07, Vestergade 3) Singles/doubles 270/490kr, doubles with bath 590kr. This fittingly named hotel adjacent to the tourist office has a dozen straightforward rooms above a small bar and in a separate wing at the back. Breakfast is included in the room rate.

Hotel Niels Juel (☎ 56 63 18 00, fax 56 63 04 92, e hotelnielsjuel@post.tele.dk, Toldbodvej 20) Singles/doubles 905/1125kr, summer & weekend family rate (2 adults, 2 children) 795kr. This 50-room, modern hotel, part of the Best Western chain is a couple of blocks south of the train station near the inner harbour. Rates include breakfast.

Hotel Hvide Hus (☎ 56 65 36 90, fax 56 66 33 14, e koge@hotelhvidehus.dk, Strandvejen 111) Singles/doubles 905/1125kr, summer & weekend family rate 795kr. This Best Western hotel is near the beach at the less-developed end of town to the south, with 126 modern rooms. Prices include breakfast.

Places to Eat

Guld Bageren (☎ 56 65 10 75, Torvet 30) Light meals 20-35kr. An unbeatable budget choice is this combination bakery and self-service cafe, which offers mouth-watering fruit tarts, delicious brie sandwiches and oversized cups of coffee. Enjoy it all in the upstairs dining area overlooking the square.

La Mirage (☎ 56 65 88 08, Nørregade 9) Pizzas 40kr, lunch specials 30kr. In addition to pizza, this casual place has inexpensive burgers and chicken.

Ritz Rock Café (☎ 56 65 33 77, Torvet 22) Mains 100kr, lunch specials 50kr. This Tex-Mex place features nachos, salads, fajitas and generous steaks.

Ming Garden (☎ 56 65 12 23, Vestergade 20) Meals or barbecues 120kr. This Chinese

restaurant offers a variety of three-item meals daily and an indulgent all-you-can-eat, Mongolian-style barbecue on Friday and Saturday.

Christians Minde (☎ 56 63 68 56, Brodgade 7) Light lunches 60kr, full dinners 200kr. This affordable fine-dining option features traditional open-faced sandwiches at lunch and full-course fish and beef dinners that include everything from soup to coffee.

Richters Gaard (☎ 56 66 29 49, Vestergade 16) A la carte mains around 200kr, 4-course dinners 395kr. The top choice for a dinner out, this atmospheric restaurant in a half-timbered building dating from 1644 offers French-influenced seafood and steak dishes.

On the eastern side of Torvet you'll find a *fruit hut* and a *butcher shop* with takeaway smørrebrød sandwiches. There's a produce, cheese and flower *market* at Torvet on Wednesday and Saturday mornings.

Entertainment

Hugos Vinkjælder (☎ 56 65 58 50, Brogade 19) This cosy little wine bar, in Hugos Gård in the cellar of a 14th-century building, sells half a bottle of wine for just 60kr and also serves inexpensive beer. In summer, live jazz bands play in the courtyard at noon on Saturday.

Getting There & Away

Train Køge is at the end of the E and A+ lines, the southernmost station on greater Copenhagen's S-train network. Trains from Copenhagen (42kr, 38 minutes) run three to six times an hour. Køge is also on the rail line between Roskilde (37kr, 25 minutes) and Næstved (45kr, 34 minutes).

Car & Motorcycle Køge is 42km southwest of Copenhagen and 25km south-east of Roskilde. If you're coming by road take the E47/E55 from Copenhagen or route 6 from Roskilde and then pick up route 151 south into the centre of Køge. There's free parking on Torvet with a one-hour limit during business hours as well as less-restricted parking off Havnen, north of the harbour.

VALLØ
postcode 4600

Vallø is a charming little hamlet with cobblestone streets, a dozen mustard-yellow houses and an attractive moat-encircled Renaissance castle, Vallø Slot. Situated in the countryside about 7km south of Køge, Vallø makes an enjoyable little excursion for those looking to get off the beaten path. If old-world character and mildly eccentric surroundings appeal, it could also be a fun place to spend the evening.

Vallø Slot

The red-brick Vallø Slot dates from 1586 and retains most of its original style, even though much of it was rebuilt following a fire in 1893.

The castle has a rather unusual history. On her birthday in 1737 Queen Sophie Magdalene, who owned the estate, established a foundation that turned Vallø Slot into a home for 'spinsters of noble birth'. Until a few decades ago unmarried daughters of Danish royalty who hadn't the means to live in their own castles or manor houses were allowed to take up residence at Vallø, supported by the foundation and government social programs.

In the 1970s, bowing to the changing sentiments that had previously spared this anachronistic niche of the Zealand countryside, the foundation amended its charter to gradually make the estate more accessible to the general public. For now, the castle remains home solely to a handful of ageing blue-blooded women who had taken up residence prior to 1976.

Vallø Slot is surrounded by 2800 hectares of woods and ponds and 1300 hectares of fields and arable land reaching down to the coast. Although the main castle buildings are not open to the public, visitors are free to walk in the gardens and the adjacent woods.

Hestestalden (*☎ 56 63 42 42; admission 10kr, free with a same-day Køge Museum ticket; open 11am-4pm daily mid-May–Aug)*, the stables at Vallø Slot, feature an exhibition on the history of the castle.

Places to Stay & Eat

Vallø Slotskro (☎ 56 26 70 20, fax 56 26 70 71, e hotel@valloeslotskro.dk, Slotsgade 1)

Singles/doubles 485/675kr, with bath from 735/825kr. This 200-year-old inn, just outside the castle gate, has 11 quite pleasantly decorated rooms that combine antique furnishings with modern conveniences such as minibars and TV. Prices include breakfast and the inn's dining room serves Danish country fare featuring three-course meals from 100kr.

Getting There & Away

Take the train to Vallø station, two stops south of Køge, and from there it's an easy 1.25km stroll east down a tree-lined country road to the castle.

If you're travelling by road take route 209 south from Køge, turn right onto Billesborgvej and then left (south) onto Valløvej, which leads to Slotsgade.

There's a signposted cycle route from Køge that leads into Valløvej.

RINGSTED
postcode 4100 • pop 18,100

Situated at a crossroads in central Zealand, Ringsted was an important market town during the Middle Ages and also served as the site of the *landsting*, a regional governing assembly. The town grew up around Sankt Bendts Kirke, which was built during the reign of Valdemar I (1157–82). This historic church, which still marks the town centre, is Ringsted's most interesting sight.

Immediately east of the church is Torvet, the central square, which features a statue of Valdemar I, sculpted by Johannes Bjerg in the 1930s, as well as three sitting stones that were used centuries ago by the landsting members.

Ringsted's town centre is 10 minutes' walk north from the train station.

Information

The Ringsted Turistbureau (*☎ 57 62 66 00, fax 57 62 66 09*) is at Sankt Bendtsgade 6, just north of Sankt Bendts Kirke. It's open 9am to 5pm from Monday to Friday and 10am to 2pm on Saturday from mid-June to September; 10am to 5pm on weekdays and 10am to 1pm on Saturday during the rest of the year.

The Dagmar Cross

Queen Dagmar, the first wife of Valdemar II, was born a princess in Bohemia. Although she lived in Denmark for only a few years before her premature death in 1212, she was much loved by the Danes and is revered in several ballads as a kind, good-hearted woman.

In 1683, as Queen Dagmar's tomb was being removed from Sankt Bendts Kirke in Ringsted, a small gold cross with finely detailed enamel work was found at the site. Now known as the Dagmar Cross, it is thought to date from AD 1000. One side shows Christ with arms outstretched on the cross and the other side depicts him with the Virgin Mary, John the Baptist, St John and St Basil.

This perfectly preserved cross of Byzantine design is now in Nationalmuseet in Copenhagen. It has been widely replicated as a pendant by Ringsted jewellery shops and is popularly worn as a necklace by brides who marry in Sankt Bendts Kirke.

Sankt Bendts Kirke

This imposing church (☎ 57 61 14 01, Sankt Bendtsgade 1; admission free; open 10am-noon & 1pm-5pm daily May–mid-Sept, 1pm-3pm daily mid-Sept–Apr) was erected in 1170 by Valdemar I, partly to serve as a burial sanctuary for his father, Knud Lavard, who had been canonised a saint by the Pope. It was also a calculated move to shore up the rule of the Valdemar dynasty and intertwine the influences of the Crown and the Catholic Church.

Although Sankt Bendts Kirke was substantially restored in the 1900s, it retains much of its original medieval style and still incorporates travertine blocks from an 11th-century abbey church that had earlier occupied the same site.

The nave is adorned with magnificent frescoes, including a series depicting Erik IV (known as Erik Ploughpenny, for the despised tax he levied on ploughs), which were painted in about 1300 in a failed campaign to get the assassinated king canonised. These frescoes show Queen Agnes seated on a throne; on her left is a scene of

Ploughpenny's murderers stabbing the king with a spear, while the right-hand scene depicts the king's corpse being retrieved from the sea by fishermen.

Sankt Bendts Kirke was a burial place for the royal family for 150 years. In the aisle floor beneath the nave are flat stones marking the tombs of (in order from the font) Valdemar III and his queen, Eleonora; Valdemar II, flanked by his queens Dagmar and Bengærd; Knud VI; Valdemar I, flanked by his queen, Sofia, and his son Christopher; and Knud Lavard. Also buried in the church are Erik VI (Menved) and Queen Ingeborg, whose remains lie in an ornate tomb in the chancel, and King Birger of Sweden and his queen Margarete, who occupy the former tomb of Erik Ploughpenny.

Some of the tombs, including the empty one that once held Queen Dagmar, have been disturbed over the centuries to make room for later burials. A few of the grave relics removed from these tombs can be found in the church's museum chapel, along with a copy of the Dagmar Cross (see the boxed text).

The church has interesting carved works, including pews from 1591 (note the dragons on the seats near the altar), an elaborate altarpiece from 1699 and a pulpit from 1609. The church's oldest item is the 12th-century baptismal font which, despite its historical significance, once served a stint as a flower bowl in a local garden.

Note that the church is closed whenever there are weddings, a particularly common occurrence on Saturdays in spring.

Ringsted Museum

This small museum of local cultural history (☎ 57 62 69 00, Køgevej 41; adult/child 25/10kr; open 11am-4pm Tues-Sun), which includes a restored 1814 Dutch windmill, is on the eastern side of town, within walking distance of Torvet and the train station.

Places to Stay

Tourist office staff can book *rooms* in private homes for 180kr to 250kr per person; there's a 25kr booking fee.

Danhostel Ringsted (☎ 57 61 15 26, fax 57 61 34 26, W www.danhostel.dk/ringsted, Sankt Bendtsgade 18) Dorm beds 95kr, singles/doubles 240/290kr. Open mid-Jan–mid-Dec. This modern 78-bed hostel has an ideal location opposite the Sankt Bendts Kirke.

Scandic Hotel Ringsted (☎ 57 61 93 00, fax 57 67 02 07, e ringsted@scandic-hotels .se, Nørretorv 57) Singles/doubles 895/1095kr, summer & weekend family specials 725kr. On the northern side of the town centre, this hotel, a member of the Scandic chain, has 75 modern rooms with 1st-class amenities; breakfast is included.

Places to Eat

Restaurant Kina (☎ 57 61 23 18, Sankt Bendtsgade 10) Chinese dishes 50-70kr. This eatery, 20m east of the tourist office, offers a variety of Chinese selections served with rice, as well as cheap hot dogs and chicken dishes.

Raadhuskroen (☎ 57 61 68 97, Sankt Bendtsgade 8) Steaks 130kr. This pub-style restaurant next to the tourist office specialises in steaks of all sorts.

Italy & Italy (☎ 57 61 53 53, Torvet 1C) Multicourse lunch/dinner 89/198kr. Facing the south-eastern side of the church, this place serves good Italian food ranging from pizzas and pasta to a mouth-watering cognac salmon.

Getting There & Away

Ringsted is on route 150 and just off the E20 motorway, 27km west of Køge and 16km east of Sorø. Roskilde is 30km to the north via route 14.

There are numerous trains throughout the day to Ringsted from Roskilde (29kr, 18 minutes) and Næstved (29kr, 20 minutes).

SORØ

postcode 4180 • pop 6800

Bordered by lakes and woodlands, Sorø is a delightful little town steeped in history. Bishop Absalon established a Cistercian monastery here in 1161, six years before he founded Copenhagen. The bishop and four Danish monarchs lie buried in Sorø Kirke, the church that Absalon erected in the monastery grounds.

After the Reformation, when Catholicism was banned and Church properties were turned over to the Crown, Frederik II set aside the monastery grounds to be used as a school. His successor, Christian IV, developed it into the Sorø Academy of Knights, an elite school dedicated to the education of the sons of the nobility.

The great Danish playwright Ludvig Holberg (1684–1754), a summer resident of Sorø and a patron of the academy, helped to revive the school during faltering times by bequeathing it his substantial estate.

During Denmark's 'Golden Age' of national romanticism (1800–50), Sorø became a haunt for some of the country's most prominent cultural figures, including Bertel Thorvaldsen, NFS Grundtvig and Adam Oehlenschläger.

Sorø is a pleasant destination with an interesting air of culture and history. The streets of the town centre are thick with old timber-framed houses, and the academy grounds and surrounding lakeside park are open to the public.

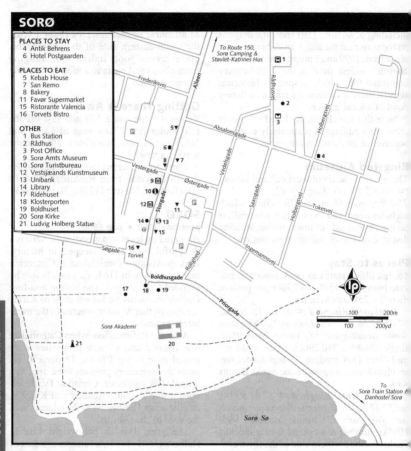

SORØ

PLACES TO STAY
4 Antik Behrens
6 Hotel Postgaarden

PLACES TO EAT
5 Kebab House
7 San Remo
8 Bakery
11 Favør Supermarket
15 Ristorante Valencia
16 Torvets Bistro

OTHER
1 Bus Station
2 Rådhus
3 Post Office
9 Sorø Amts Museum
10 Sorø Turistbureau
12 Vestsjæands Kunstmuseum
13 Unibank
14 Library
17 Ridehuset
18 Klosterporten
19 Boldhuset
20 Sorø Kirke
21 Ludvig Holberg Statue

To Route 150,
Sorø Camping &
Støvlet-Katrines Hus

Frederiksvej

Alleen

Rådhusvej

Absalonsgade

Holbergsvej

Vestergade

Østergade

Vedelsgade

Saxogade

Storgade

Tokesvej

Ingemannsvej

Søgade

Rolighed

Boldhusgade

Priorgade

Torvet

Sorø Akademi

To
Sorø Train Station &
Danhostel Sorø

Sorø Sø

0   100   200m
0   100   200yd

Information

Sorø Turistbureau (☎ 57 82 10 12, fax 57 82 10 13, **e** soroe@turisme.dk) is in the town centre at Storgade 15. It's open 9.30am to 5pm Monday to Friday and 9.30am to 3pm on Saturday (to noon on Saturday from September to May). In addition to the usual services, staff here can arrange bicycle rentals.

There are several banks in town including a Unibank (☎ 57 83 05 00) at Storgade 22.

The post office (☎ 58 56 78 00), Rådhusvej 6, is just south of the rådhus. The library (☎ 57 87 01 01), at Storgade 7, has Internet access.

Sorø Akademi

Although it's no longer reserved for the sons of the nobility, the Sorø Akademi remains a prominent Danish school. The extensive grounds are owned by a private foundation, though the school itself is still funded by the state.

The southern end of Sorø's main street, Storgade, leads directly to the academy via **Klosterporten**, the medieval gate that once served to cloister the monks from the outside world.

Although both Klosterporten and Sorø Kirke date back to the Middle Ages, other monastery buildings that once occupied the academy grounds were long ago demolished and replaced with Renaissance structures thought to be more conducive to learning.

Ridehuset, immediately west of Klosterporten, was built by Christian IV to stable the horses and dogs used to train students in the art of hunting.

Boldhuset, just east of Klosterporten, also dates from the reign of Christian IV and now houses the library, which contains an outstanding collection of first editions of Ludvig Holberg's works.

A **statue** of Ludvig Holberg by the sculptor Vilhelm Bissen can be found in the garden area in the western part of the grounds. Walking **trails** lead west from the statue down to the lake, Sorø Sø.

Sorø Kirke

The 12th-century Sorø church *(☎ 57 82 10 12; admission free; open 10am-4pm Mon-Sat, noon-4pm Sun Apr–mid-Sept; reduced hours in low season)*, in the centre of the academy grounds, is one of Denmark's oldest brick structures and the country's largest monastery church. It was built to serve as a sepulchral church for Bishop Absalon and his prestigious family, the Hvides, whose landholdings included the Sorø region. The fact that five monarchs opted to be buried next to Absalon bears witness to the bishop's prominence; many historians consider Absalon, who wielded both sceptre and sword, to be the most significant Danish statesman of medieval times.

The church stands largely as Absalon erected it, in the Romanesque style typical of Cistercian monasteries. Its huge central nave is flanked by two aisles. At the end of the left aisle is the marble sarcophagus of Ludvig Holberg.

Absalon lies directly behind the main altar; keeping him company are the sarcophagi of kings Valdemar IV, Christopher II and Oluf II. Queen Margrethe I, the architect of the 1397 Kalmar Union that brought Norway and Sweden under Danish rule, was originally buried here as well, but her remains were later transferred to Roskilde Domkirke.

In 1827 Absalon's grave was opened. The gold and sapphire ring he was wearing and the silver chalice that was cupped between his hands were removed; they're now in a little display area to the right of the altar, along with some interpretive descriptions in English.

The church's grand interior includes medieval frescoes, a 6m-high crucifix by Odense sculptor Claus Berg and a beautifully detailed altar and pulpit, both carved in the 1650s in Baroque style.

The 16th-century organ, rebuilt by Christian IV's master organist Johan Lorenz, is the centrepiece of a classical concert series on Wednesday evening from late June to early September; advance tickets (90kr) are available from the tourist office.

Sorø Amts Museum

This regional cultural museum *(☎ 53 63 40 63, Storgade 17; adult/child 20kr/free; open 1pm-4pm Tues-Sun)* is housed in a handsome half-timbered building dating from 1625.

Bishops & Bricks

Shortly after the end of the Viking era, two things happened that had a significant and lasting impact on church architecture in Denmark. First, King Sweyn II (1047–74) found himself deep in a power struggle with the Archbishop of Bremen, the leader of the Danish Church. To weaken the influence of the archbishop, the king divided Denmark into eight separate dioceses, which set the stage for a flurry of new church and cathedral building.

Then, in the 12th century, the art of brickmaking was introduced to Denmark from Italy. Before then, most churches were constructed from wood or calcareous tufa and rough stone. The use of bricks allowed construction on a much larger scale and within a few decades grand churches were being built all around Denmark. Some of the buildings from that era still stand today, including stalwart churches in Sorø and Ringsted, and the cathedrals in Roskilde and Århus.

SOUTHERN ZEALAND

It contains rooms with period furnishings, ranging from a peasant's simple quarters to the stylish living room of an aristocrat. There's also a grocery shop from 1880 and a room furnished with the personal belongings of the 19th-century poet BS Ingemann, who taught at Sorø Akademi.

Vestsjællands Kunstmuseum

Another worthwhile stop is the Art Museum of West Zealand (☎ 57 83 22 29, Storgade 9; admission free; open 10am-4pm Tues-Sun mid-May–mid-Aug, 1pm-4pm Tues-Sun mid-Aug–mid-May), which is housed in a period building. Its varied collection of regional art runs the gamut from medieval wood carvings and stodgy portraits by CW Eckersberg to wildly expressionist modern art.

Other Attractions

Inside the courtyard at Storgade 7 is a fine timber-framed **Renaissance building**, constructed by King Christian IV, that now holds a wing of the town library.

From Torvet, an intersting option is to walk west down **Søgade**, an inviting street of leaning half-timbered, mustard-yellow houses with red tiled roofs. You can follow this street 400m down to the lake and its garden-like setting, where there are trails in both directions.

Places to Stay

Sorø Camping (☎ 57 83 02 02, fax 57 82 11 02, ℮ soroe.camping@adr.dk, Udbyhøjvej 10) Bus No 234. Camping per person 59kr. Open Mar-Oct. This three-star camping ground borders the lake Pedersborg Sø to the north-west of town, about 150m north of Slagelsevej. The camping ground is about a 20-minute walk from the town along a lakeside trail.

Tourist office staff can book *rooms* in private homes for 175/350kr for singles/doubles; there's a 25kr booking fee.

Antik Behrens (☎/fax 57 83 53 52, Absalonsgade 19) Singles/doubles with breakfast 225/350kr. A 10-minute walk east of the town centre, this private home has four comfortable rooms. The owners are former antique dealers and the breakfast room is so laden with period paintings and furniture that it resembles a museum.

Hotel Postgaarden (☎ 57 83 22 22, fax 57 83 22 91, Storgade 25) Singles/doubles with breakfast 495/695kr. This inn-style hotel with a 300-year history is in the town centre and has 23 rooms with private bath and TV.

Danhostel Sorø (☎ 57 84 92 00, fax 57 84 92 01, ℮ info@kkfg.dk, Skælskørvej 34) Bus No 83 from Sorø. Dorm rooms 100kr, singles/doubles 275/320kr, with bath 300/400kr. Open Apr-Oct. This appealing lakeside place, also known as Kongskilde Friluftsgård, 7km south-west of town on route 157, is a combined hostel and country inn. In the midst of a nature reserve, it's a popular respite for both hikers and cyclists – two national cycle routes, Nos 6 and 7, cross right at the inn, and nature trails lead from the front door. Reasonably priced breakfast and dinner are available, but advance notice is needed for dinner.

Places to Eat

Torvets Bistro (☎ 57 83 21 92, Torvet) This fast-food eatery sells burgers, sandwiches and ice cream, and you can sit right on the square and watch the world go by.

San Remo (☎ 57 82 00 83, Storgade 38) Pizzas 50kr. You can get good, reasonably priced pizza and pasta at this place.

Wufu Chinese & Thai (☎ 57 83 53 88, Storgade 25) Dinner buffet 98kr. This restaurant at Hotel Postgaarden has a nightly buffet of Chinese and Thai dishes.

Ristorante Valencia (☎ 57 83 16 13, Storgade 6) Mains 70-120kr. This upmarket Italian restaurant has a good variety of meat and fish dishes, including some French and Spanish options.

Støvlet-Katrines Hus (☎ 57 83 50 80, Slagelsevej 63) 3-course meals 285kr. This atmospheric restaurant on the western edge of town was originally built as a home for Christian VII's mistress. Today it serves splendid French-influenced Danish dishes such as smoked duck with apricot compote or poached turbot with ginger-lemongrass sauce. There's a daily selection of wines (35kr a glass) to match each course. It's an unbeatable spot for a night out.

There are a few places to get cheap meals along Storgade near the Hotel Postgaarden, including a **kebab eatery** and a **bakery**. You can pick up groceries at the **Favor** supermarket (☎ 57 83 06 26, Storgade 28).

Getting There & Away
Sorø is 15km east of Slagelse and 16km west of Ringsted via route 150 or the E20.

Trains run about hourly to Sorø from Slagelse (20kr, 10 minutes) and Ringsted (20kr, 8 minutes). Sorø train station is in Frederiksberg, 2km south of the town centre; bus Nos 806 and 807 run between the two at least hourly. There's also a frequent bus service (No 234) between Sorø and Slagelse (28kr, 24 minutes). The bus station is on Rådhusvej between Absalonsgade and Fægangen.

SLAGELSE
postcode 4200 • pop 31,400
Slagelse is best known to visitors as the starting point for outings to the nearby Viking fortress of Trelleborg (see the Trelleborg section that follows). Although Slagelse itself doesn't have any particular allure, there are a couple of local sights you could take in if time permits and it's an agreeable enough place to stay if you need to break for the night.

The town centre is dominated by Sankt Mikkels Kirke, a Gothic church built of brick in the early 14th century. To the east of the church is Nytorv, the main commercial square.

Information
The Slagelse Turistbureau (☎ 58 52 22 06, fax 58 52 86 87), Løvegade 7, is a 10-minute walk south of the train station and 300m west of Nytorv. It's open 9am to 5pm Monday to Friday and 9am to 3pm on Saturday from mid-June to August; opening hours are 10am to 5pm on weekdays and 10am to 1pm on Saturday for the rest of the year.

Slagelse Museum
This local museum (☎ 53 52 83 27, Bredegade 11; adult/child 20kr/free; open 1pm-5pm Tues-Sun mid-June–Sept, 1pm-5pm Sat & Sun Oct–mid-June) is a short walk southwest from Nytorv. It displays the craft and industrial history of Slagelse, featuring the old tools and workshops of a grocer, barber, butcher, blacksmith and other tradespeople.

Ruins of Antvorskov
The brick ruins of Antvorskov, a monastery founded by Valdemar I in 1164, are about 2km south of the town centre. Antvorskov's most significant role in history is its connection with Hans Tausen, the renegade monk who took his monastic training here. Hans was vexed by the excessive privilege he found at Antvorskov, which was one of the wealthiest monasteries in Denmark and open only to those of noble birth. After touring Germany, where he heard Martin Luther preach, Hans returned to Antvorskov, and in 1525 delivered a fiery speech that helped spark the Danish Reformation.

After the Reformation, Antvorskov was confiscated by the Crown and became a favourite hunting manor of King Frederik II, who died here in 1588. Eventually it was sold off and the buildings, including the old monastery church, were demolished.

About half of the former monastery grounds are now buried under the E20 motorway, but remnants of the brick foundations can still be seen and interpretive plaques help explain the ruins. Although historically significant, the ruins are not overwhelmingly interesting in themselves and are pretty much out of the way if you don't have your own transport. You can get there by taking Slotsalléen from the town centre to its end, then turning right and proceeding about 200m to the car park opposite Munkebakken.

Places to Stay
Slagelse Campingplads (☎ 58 52 25 28, fax 58 52 25 40, Bjergbygade 78) Bus No 303. Camping per person 52kr. Open Apr-Sept. This small one-star camping ground is 2km south of the train station.

Danhostel Slagelse (☎ 58 52 25 28, fax 58 52 25 40, W www.danhostel.dk/slagelse, Bjergbygade 78) Bus No 303. Dorm beds 100kr, singles/doubles 250/350kr. Open mid-Jan–mid-Dec. This hostel is run by the same management as the adjacent Slagelse Campingplads.

Tourist office staff can book **rooms** in private homes for around 150/250kr for singles/doubles, plus a 20kr booking fee.

Hotel Frederik den II (☎ 58 53 03 22, fax 58 53 46 22, e hotel@fr2.dk, Idagårdsvej 3) Singles/doubles with breakfast 905/1125kr. This modern Best Western hotel, near the intersection of route 22 and the E20, at the south side of town, has comfortable rooms.

Places to Eat

There are several places to eat on Nytorv, the central square, from bakeries and fast-food joints to sit-down restaurants.

Siang Jiang (☎ 58 52 04 45, Nytorv 3) Specials 38kr. This restaurant on the square has tasty Chinese food and six good-value specials every day.

Nat Toget (☎ 58 53 10 66, Gammel Torv 8) Dishes from 75kr. This pleasant pub-style place, 100m south of Nytorv, specialises in Mexican fare.

Getting There & Around

Slagelse is at the intersection of routes 150 and 22 and by the E20 motorway. It's 37km south-east of Kalundborg and 19km north-east of Korsør.

Slagelse is on the main east-west railway line between Copenhagen and Jutland and has frequent train services. From Slagelse, it's 33 minutes (52kr) to Roskilde, 12 minutes (20kr) to Korsør and 10 minutes (20kr) to Sorø.

Getting Around

Bicycle hire can be arranged at HJ Cykler (☎ 58 52 28 57), Løvegade 46 near the tourist office, for 50kr per day.

TRELLEBORG

Trelleborg (☎ 58 54 95 06, Trelleborg Allé 4; adult/child 35/20kr; open 10am-5pm daily Easter-Oct, 1pm-3pm Nov-Easter), in the countryside 7km west of Slagelse, is the best preserved of the four Viking ring fortresses in Denmark.

Despite the passing of a millennium since its construction, this circular earthen mound fortress is amazingly intact. Naturally the wooden structures that once stood within the fortress have long since decayed but several Viking-era buildings have been reconstructed using materials and methods authentic to the period.

The most impressive is the longhouse, built in Viking stave style, using rough oak timbers erected above mud floors. The inside has benches of the type used by warriors for sleeping and a central hearth with a simple opening in the roof for venting smoke.

Other reconstructions are clustered together to give the sense of a Viking village, complete with costumed interpreters doing chores of the period such as sharpening axes, chopping wood and baking bread. In the summer season the interpreters also conduct activities for children, such as archery demonstrations and pottery workshops.

In addition, the site has a small museum with exhibits of pottery, bronze jewellery, spearheads, human skeletons and other items excavated from the fortress grounds. It also shows a 20-minute video on Trelleborg's history.

Still, the highlight at Trelleborg is simply strolling the grounds. You can walk up onto the grassy circular rampart and readily grasp the geometric design of the fortress. From atop the rampart, Trelleborg appears strikingly symmetrical and precise; cement blocks have been placed to show the outlines of the elliptical house foundations. Grazing sheep wandering in from the surrounding farmland imbue the scene with a timeless aura.

Places to Eat

Hos Hulda og Hjalmar (☎ 58 54 95 06, Trelleborg Allé 4) Snacks 35kr, mains 100kr. Right at the entrance to Trelleborg, this is a fun place to eat, with burlap-covered tables on a sand floor and waiters dressed in Viking clothes. You can get anything from hot dogs and burgers to organic salads and steak dinners. Be sure to try the local speciality, a beer-like Viking-era drink called mjød (mead).

Getting There & Away

Bus No 312 goes from Slagelse to Trelleborg (12kr, 12 minutes), but in summer it only

Trelleborg's Precise Design

Trelleborg's military origins are visible in its precise mathematical layout and use of the Roman foot (29.33cm) as a unit of measure.

The Trelleborg compound consists of two wards that encompass about 7 hectares in all. The inner ward is embraced by a circular earthen rampart 6m high and 17m thick at its base. Four gates, one at each point of the compass, cut through the rampart. The ward is crossed by two streets, one east-west, the other north-south, which has the effect of dividing it into four symmetrical quadrants. In Viking times, each quadrant contained four long elliptical buildings surrounding a courtyard. Each of the 16 buildings was exactly 100 Roman feet long and contained a central hall and two smaller rooms.

Following the arc along the exterior of the inner rampart was an 18m-wide ditch; two bridges spanned the ditch, crossing over to the outer ward. This outer ward contained a cemetery holding about 150 graves and 15 houses, each of which was 90 Roman feet long and lined up radially with its gable pointing towards the inner rampart. A second earthen ward separated the outer ward from the surrounding countryside.

runs to Trelleborg at 10am, noon and 2pm on weekdays, at 12.40pm on Saturday and not at all on Sunday. During the rest of the year, when it doubles as a school bus, the schedule is more frequent. Or just take a taxi to the site, which costs around 100kr.

To get to Trelleborg from Slagelse using your own transport, take Strandvejen to its end at the village of Hejninge and then follow the signs to Trelleborg, 1km farther on.

A good alternative to relying on the bus is to cycle your way across the rural countryside between Slagelse and Trelleborg (see the Slagelse Getting Around section for bike-hire details).

KORSØR

postcode 4220 • pop 14,800

Situated at the narrowest point of the Store Bælt (Great Belt), the channel that separates Zealand from Funen, Korsør takes much of its character from its strategic location. The town boomed in the 1850s with the construction of the Zealand railway and until recently all vehicles – trains and cars alike – had to board ferries in Korsør to continue across the channel to Funen. In 1998 all that changed with the opening of the 18km-long Storebæltsforbindelsen (the Great Belt Fixed Link), which now connects Zealand and Funen, providing a 'land link' between the two islands.

With the new link and Korsør's new train station both situated 3km north of the town

centre, Korsør is now largely bypassed by travellers. There are a couple of local sights in town that could be visited, but if time is tight Nyborg, on the other side of the channel, holds far more allure.

Information

The Korsør Turistbureau (☎ 58 35 02 11, fax 58 35 02 66), Nygade 7, is open 9am to 5pm Monday to Friday and 10am to 2pm on Saturday.

Things to See

Fæstning (Fortress) tower, near the town centre on the southern side of the harbour, is one of Denmark's few remaining medieval towers. About 24m high and 9m wide, the tower was built using monkstone, a type of oversized brick. It's part of **Korsør By-og Overfartsmuseum** *(Korsør Town & Ferry Service Museum; ☎ 58 37 47 55, Søbatteriet 3; adult/child 15/5kr; open 11am-4pm Tues-Sun)*, which features ship models as well as displays on the history of the ferries and icebreakers that have crossed the Store Bælt over the past two centuries.

Kongegården *(☎ 58 37 78 90, Algade 25; admission free; open 10am-4pm Thur-Tues, 10am-8pm Wed)*, in the town centre, is a small art museum that has one floor dedicated to the works of Harald Isenstein, a Jewish sculptor who fled Nazi Germany in the 1930s. There are also temporary exhibitions of regional

Shrinking Denmark

The largest engineering scheme ever undertaken in Denmark was Storebælts-forbindelsen (the Great Belt Fixed Link), an 18km bridge and tunnel project across the narrowest point of the Store Bælt, the body of water that separates Zealand from Funen.

Opened in 1998, it has two bridges, the Østbro (East Bridge) and the Vestbro (West Bridge), linking at the little island of Sprogø near the centre of the Store Bælt.

The Østbro, which has a total length of 6790m, has a free span above the fairway of 1624m, which makes it the world's second-longest suspension bridge. The Østbro's two towers, which reach a height of 254m, are the highest structures ever erected in Scandinavia.

The Østbro carries cars, while trains travel through an undersea tunnel that runs beneath the bridge. On the 6.6km-long Vestbro, both cars and trains cross above the water, with a four-lane motorway and a double-track railway.

By eliminating the fleet of ferries that used to leisurely shuttle both cars and trains across the Store Bælt, the project effectively made little Denmark an even smaller country, reducing travel time across the channel from one hour to just 10 minutes.

work. Kongegården is in a neighbourhood of interesting 18th-century buildings.

Places to Stay

Halskov Camping (☎ 58 37 50 80, fax 58 37 50 30, e halskovcamping@vip.cybercity.dk, Revvej 175) Camping per person 56kr. Open year-round. This two-star camping ground is on the beach just south of the E20.

Danhostel Korsør (☎ 58 37 10 22, fax 58 35 68 70, e korsoer@svanegaarden.dk, Tovesvej 30F) Dorm beds 100kr, singles/doubles 300/350kr. Open Jan–mid-Dec. This modern 80-bed hostel is on the eastern outskirts of town, midway between the train station and the city centre.

Jens Baggesen Hotel (☎ 58 35 10 00, fax 58 35 10 01, e jbagge@post10.tele.dk,

Batterivej 3) Singles/doubles with bath 630/870kr, summer specials 500/700kr, including breakfast. This 40-room hotel is in a converted period warehouse, south of the fortress.

Places to Eat

In the town centre, near the intersection of Nygade and the pedestrian walkway Algade, you'll find several **bakeries**, **cafes** and **restaurants**.

Toscana (☎ 58 37 59 99, Algade 58) Lunch specials 38kr, 3-course dinners 120kr. This popular Italian restaurant has a varied menu and outdoor dining on warm days.

Getting There & Around

As Korsør is on the main railway line between Zealand and Funen, there are frequent train services to Copenhagen (92kr, one hour) and Odense (100kr, 28 minutes). Local buses connect Korsør's town centre and train station.

On the northern outskirts of Korsør the E20 crosses the Store Bælt channel to Nyborg on Funen; the car toll for the 18km bridge is 230kr.

KALUNDBORG

postcode 4400 • pop 15,500

For those heading directly to Århus from Zealand, Kalundborg makes a convenient jumping-off point. The railway line ends at the central harbour, so you can walk off the train and right onto the boat.

If you have time to spare before catching a ferry, consider a stroll over to Vor Frue Kirke, an intriguing medieval church and Kalundborg's main site of interest.

Things to See

Vor Frue Kirke (Aldegade; admission free; open 9am-5pm Mon-Sat, noon-5pm Sun) was erected in the late 12th century and, with its five towers, is one of the most unique medieval churches in Denmark. Built as a castle church by Esbern Snare, Bishop Absalon's brother, it has a Byzantine-like design based upon the Greek cross. The cross shape takes the form of a square central tower connected by cross appendages to four equidistant octagonal towers. The church was originally part of an extensive fortress but in 1658 the townspeople tore down the fortress walls to minimise the risk of an attack by Swedish forces. The church is just west of Torvet and a short walk north-west from the harbour. The site of Snare's castle is in **Ruinparken**, a few minutes farther west, but there's little left to decipher among the ruins.

If you make a loop around Vor Frue Kirke via Præstegade and Adelgade you'll pass through the oldest part of town, where there are cobbled streets and 16th-century homes, one of which houses the **Kalundborg-og Omegns Museum** (☎ 59 51 21 41, Adelgade 23; adult/child 20kr/free; open 11am-4pm Tues-Sun May-Aug, 11am-4pm Sat & Sun Sept-Apr), the local-history museum.

Places to Stay & Eat
Danhostel Kalundborg (☎ 59 56 13 66, fax 59 56 46 26, e kalundborg@danhostel.dk, Stadion Allé 5) Dorm beds 100kr, 1-6–person rooms 360kr. Open year-round. This modern 118-bed hostel is just north-west of Ruinparken, within walking distance of the train station and the boats to Århus.

There are several restaurants in the town centre.

Restaurant Bispegården (☎ 59 51 25 35, Adelgade 6) Mains 100kr. This old-fashioned restaurant near Vor Frue Kirke has a good reputation for its fish dishes.

Getting There & Away
Train Services between Copenhagen and Kalundborg operate at least hourly, take 1¾ hours and cost 92kr.

Car & Motorcycle Kalundborg is at the terminus of routes 22 and 23, some 51km north of Korsør and 69km west of Roskilde.

Boat Mols-Linien (☎ 70 10 14 18) runs ferries between Århus and Kalundborg six times a day on weekdays, three times a day on weekends. The trip takes 2¾ hours. The fare is 130/65kr for adults/children, 225kr for a car with up to five people, and 170kr for a motorcycle and up to two people.

NÆSTVED
postcode 4700 • pop 45,000
Located at the mouth of the Suså River, the town of Næstved has been an important trading centre since medieval times. Industry grew following the introduction of the railway in the 19th century and with the later dredging of a new commercial harbour.

Today Næstved is the largest town in southern Zealand. The town centre has a few interesting historical buildings, including two medieval Gothic churches, all within easy walking distance of each other.

Orientation
The bus and train station are close together on Farimagsvej, opposite its intersection with Jernbanegade. To get to Axeltorv, the central square, take Jernbanegade west to Sankt Mortens Kirke and then continue west on Torvestræde; it's a walk of about five minutes in all. All of the town's sights are within a few minutes' walk of Axeltorv.

Information
Næstved Turistbureau (☎ 55 72 11 22, fax 55 72 16 67) is a few blocks south of Axeltorv at Det Gule Pakhus, Havnegade 1. It's open 9am to at least 5pm Monday to Friday and 9am to noon on Saturday from mid-June to August; opening hours are 9am to 4pm weekdays and to noon on Saturday the rest of the year.

There are banks in the town centre including a Unibank (☎ 55 72 05 27) on Axeltorv. The post office (☎ 55 78 75 00) is on the south side of the train station on Farimagsvej.

Sankt Peders Kirke
This large Gothic brick church (☎ 55 72 31 90; admission free; open 10am-noon & 2pm-4pm Tues-Fri May–mid-Sept, 10am-noon Tues-Fri mid-Sept–Apr), just south of Axeltorv, dominates Sankt Peders Kirkeplads. The church features notable 14th-century frescoes, including one depicting King Valdemar IV and Queen Helvig kneeling before God. The Latin inscription to the left of the king translates as 'In 1375, the day before the feast of St Crispin, King Valdemar died, do not forget it'.

Sankt Mortens Kirke

Also built with brick, this smaller church (☎ 55 76 00 82, Kattebjerg 2; admission free; open 9am-11am & 1pm-5pm Mon-Fri mid-June–mid-Sept, 9am-11am Mon-Fri mid-Sept–mid-June), midway between the train station and Axeltorv, has a strikingly similar design to Sankt Peders Kirke. The interior has period frescoes and a 6m-high altar created by the master Næstved carver Abel Schrøder in 1667. The pulpit, which dates from the early 17th century, is thought to have been carved by Schrøder's father.

Næstved Museum

The Næstved Museum (☎ 55 77 08 11; adult/child for both sections 20kr/free; open 10am-4pm Tues-Sun) has two sections. Fittingly, the local-history section is in Næstved's oldest building, the 14th-century Helligåndshuset (House of the Holy Ghost; Ringstedgade 4), just north of Axeltorv. It contains 13th- and 14th-century church carvings and exhibits of farm, trade and peasant life from Næstved's past. The Boderne section (Sankt Peders Kirkeplads) displays Næstved silverwork, Holmegaard glass and locally made pottery.

Other Central Attractions

Kompagnihuset (Kompagnistræde), just south-east of Sankt Peders Kirke, is said to be the only medieval guildhall remaining in Denmark. This timber-framed building was constructed in 1493 and has been restored It's architecture can be appreciated from the outside, however, the interior is not open to the public.

Apostelhuset (Riddergade 5), a half-timbered medieval building just south of Sankt Mortens Kirke, takes its name from the 13 wooden exterior braces that separate the windows, each carved with the figure of Christ or one of the 12 apostles. Dating from about 1510, they are some of the oldest and best preserved timber-frame carvings in Denmark.

Also with roots in the medieval period is the old town hall, Rådhuskirken, the brick and half-timbered building at the northern side of Sankt Peders Kirke.

The town's most novel curiosity is Denmark's smallest equestrian statue, a tiny bronze atop a tall brick pedestal depicting Næstved's founder, Peder Bodilsen. It's located at Hjultorv, a small square just north of Axeltorv.

Holmegaards Glasværker

If you have your own transport you might want to drive to Fensmark, about 8km northeast of Næstved, to visit the Holmegaard Glassworks (☎ 55 54 50 00, Glasværksve, 1; admission free; open 10am-4pm Mon-Fri, 11am-4pm Sat & Sun). Founded in 1825 this is Denmark's principal producer of quality glass. Visitors can view the process of glass being blown by hand; there's also a shop and a little museum.

Canoeing

The Suså River, which runs through the western part of town, has calm waters tha make for good canoeing. You can rent canoes for 70kr for the first hour, 50kr each additional hour, from Suså Kanoudlejning (☎ 57 64 61 44) at Slusehuset at the southern end of Rådmanshave, a large park north of the town centre.

Places to Stay

Danhostel Næstved & Næstved Camping (☎ 55 72 20 91, fax 55 72 56 45, e nstvh@ post4.tele.dk, Frejasvej 8) Camping per person 35kr, dorm beds 80kr, singles/doubles 150/200kr. Open mid-Mar–mid-Nov (hostel), June-Aug (camping ground). This combined hostel and small one-star camping ground is 1km from the town centre. To reach this place, head south when you leave the train station and then continue eas along Præstøvej.

The tourist office maintains a list of private rooms available for rent in the greater Næstved area.

Hotel Vinhuset (☎ 55 72 08 07, fax 55 72 03 35, e vinhuset@post4.tele.dk, Sank Peders Kirkeplads 4) Singles/doubles with breakfast 640/795kr. This 18th-century hotel has pleasant rooms with modern amenitie, and a prime location on the square opposite Sankt Peders Kirke.

Places to Eat

DSB Café (☎ 55 72 89 90, Banegårdspladsen) Light meals around 50kr. If you're waiting for a train, this eatery at the station offers affordable fare.

China House (☎ 55 73 18 88, Jernbanegade 15) Mains 80-100kr. This place, a few minutes' walk west of the train station, serves a full range of Chinese dishes.

The central square, Axeltorv, has a few simple eateries where you can get a sandwich and beer. For something more upmarket, try one of the two romantic *restaurants* at Hotel Vinhuset.

Getting There & Away

Næstved is 25km south of Ringsted and 28km north of Vordingborg, at the crossroads of routes 14, 22, 54 and 265.

Trains run about hourly from Copenhagen (76kr, one hour), Roskilde (45kr, 42 minutes) and Ringsted (29kr, 20 minutes). There are also regular services to Vordingborg (29kr, 20 minutes) and to Køge (45kr, 34 minutes).

PRÆSTØ

postcode 4720 • pop 3500

This seaside village on the southern coast of the Præstø Fjord largely retains the look of a sleepy 19th-century provincial town. It has a small centre with older homes and handsome buildings that can make for a pleasant hour or so of wandering; however, the main activity is at the yacht harbour, which spreads across the northern side of the town centre. Although foreign tourists are few, Præstø attracts plenty of Danish visitors, particularly sailors with their own boats.

Præstø's bus station is in the village centre. The main commercial street, Algade, is on the southern side of the bus station, while the waterfront is to the north.

Information

Præstø Turistinformation (☎ 55 99 11 90, fax 55 99 15 51), Jernbanevej 22, is open 9am to at least 4pm from Monday to Friday year-round and also 9am to 2pm on Saturday from mid-June to August.

Things to See & Do

On the eastern side of the town centre is **Præstø Kirke** *(Klosternakken; admission free; open irregular hours)*, whose north nave dates from the 13th century. Before the Reformation it was an abbey church for monks of the order of St Anthony. Each of its two naves has an altar; most notable is the detailed altarpiece in the south nave, which was created by Abel Schrøder in 1657. The religious philosopher NFS Grundtvig was the parish rector here from 1821 to 1822.

A kilometre north-west of town is **Nysø**, a private manor house built in the 1670s. Baroness Christine Stampe, who owned Nysø in the mid-19th century, opened it as a retreat for Danish artists, including sculptor Bertel Thorvaldsen who set up a studio here. The manor isn't open to the public but a building in the grounds contains **Thorvaldsen-samlingen** *(☎ 53 79 55 99, Nysøvej 1; adult/child 15/10kr; open 11am-5pm Sat & Sun May, June & Aug, 11am-5pm Tues-Sun July)*, a collection of Thorvaldsen's works.

The waters around Præstø are mostly shallow – a challenge for sailors but quite suitable for waders. There's a public **beach** good for children on the north-eastern side of town.

Places to Stay

Præstø Camping (☎ 55 99 11 48, Spangen 2). Camping per person 50kr. Open Apr-Sept. This simple one-star facility is 300m south of the town centre.

Hotel Frederiksminde (☎ 55 99 10 42, fax 55 99 17 65, ℮ frederiksminde@post.tele.dk, Klosternakken 8) Singles/doubles with breakfast 550/675kr. This hotel, built in 1868, is set on a seaside knoll. The two dozen rooms are all different, some quite spacious, some with ocean views, others with balconies.

Places to Eat

There are half a dozen places to eat along Aldegade.

Restaurant Kaktus (☎ 55 99 12 46, Adelgade 45) Pizzas or pasta 50kr, Mexican dishes 90kr. This pleasant restaurant has a mix of Mexican and Italian fare.

Skipperkroen (☎ 55 99 22 00, Havnevej 1)
Light lunches about 75kr, 2-course dinners
215kr. Down at the harbour in the attractive
old customs house, this is a sure winner
for some really good fish dishes and an
engaging atmosphere.

Getting There & Away
Route 265 passes Præstø on its way between
Næstved (25km) and Møn (26km). Bus No
79 connects Præstø with Næstved (32kr, 40
minutes) hourly, and bus No 256 connects
Præstø with Møn (32kr, 40 minutes) every
two or three hours. There are no train services to Præstø.

VORDINGBORG
postcode 4760 • pop 8700
Strategically located on the strait between
Zealand and Falster, Vordingborg played an
important role in Denmark's medieval history. It was the royal residence of Valdemar
I, whose ascension to the throne in 1157
marked the end of a contentious period of
rebellion and served to reunite the Danish
kingdom, and it continued to be a favoured
residence of other kings of the Valdemar
dynasty. With its large natural harbour,
Vordingborg also served as the staging area
for late-12th-century military campaigns
led by Bishop Absalon against the Wends of
eastern Germany.

During the 15th century Vordingborg slip-
ped from prominence, in part because the
Kalmar Union had so greatly expanded
Danish rule elsewhere in Scandinavia that
the royal family now took little interest in it.

Vordingborg is today a quiet town built
around the ruins of the old castle and
fortress. It's also the jumping-off point for
trips to Møn if you are travelling by public
transport.

Information
The Vordingborg Turistkontor (☎ 55 34 11
11, fax 55 34 03 08), Algade 96, just east of
Gåsetårnet, is open 9am to 5pm Monday to
Friday and 9am to 2pm Saturday from June
to August. Opening hours are 9.30am to
5pm on weekdays and 9.30am to 1pm on
Saturday from September to May.

There are several banks on Algade, including a Unibank (☎ 55 34 33 33) at Algade
78. The post office (☎ 55 37 00 67) is just
north of the train station at Årsleffsgade 1.

Things to See & Do
The 14th-century **Gåsetårnet** *(Goose Tower;*
☎ 55 37 25 51, Slotsruinen 1; adult/child
20/10kr, including Sydsjællands Museum;
open 10am-5pm daily June-Aug, 10am-4pm
Tues-Sun Sept-May), once part of a huge
royal castle and fortress, is Scandinavia's
best-preserved medieval tower and the only
intact structure remaining from the Valdemar era. The name stems from 1368, when
Valdemar IV placed a golden goose on top
of the tower to express his scorn for the
German Hanseatic League's declaration of
war (Valdemar referred to the league as
'cackling geese'). The rest of the fortress,
including seven other towers, has been demolished over the centuries but the 36m-
high Gåsetårnet was spared because of its
function as a navigational landmark. The
tower's 101 steps can be climbed for a good
view of the surrounding area.

The fortress grounds, which have been
turned into a pleasant park with walking
paths, also contain various brick and stone
foundation ruins and an attractive little
botanical garden *(admission free)*.

In addition, the grounds of Gåsetårnet
hold the **Sydsjællands Museum** *(☎ 55 37*
25 54; adult/child 20/10kr, including Gåse-
tårnet; open 10am-5pm daily June-Aug,
10am-4pm Tues-Sun Sept-May). Southern
Zealand's regional history museum, it has
a Stone Age collection as well as sections
on the Middle Ages and the Renaissance,

Law of the Land

The Jutland Code, which codified traditional
law and was thus one of the most important
doctrines of the Middle Ages, was sanctioned
by Valdemar II in Vordingborg in 1241. Today
virtually every schoolchild in Denmark can
recite the code's preamble 'Mæth logh skal
land byggiæs' (With law shall a land be built).

including trade and craft exhibits, church decorations and textiles.

To get there from the train station, walk north to the nearby post office and then turn south-east onto Algade, which leads directly to the fortress grounds.

Along the way, on the western side of Algade, is **Vor Frue Kirke** *(Kirketorvet; admission free; open 10am-noon Mon-Sat)*, which has a nave dating from the mid-15th century, frescoes and a Baroque altarpiece carved by Abel Schrøder in 1642.

Walking Track If you have your own transport and are up to a walk, **Knudshoved Odde**, the narrow 18km-long peninsula west of Vordingborg, offers some hiking opportunities in an area known for its 'Bronze Age landscape'. The peninsula also has a small herd of American buffalo brought in by the Rosenfeldt family who own Knudshoved Odde. There's a car park (10kr) about halfway down the peninsula, where the trail begins.

Places to Stay

Danhostel Vordingborg (☎ 55 36 08 00, fax 55 36 08 01, **e** *vandrerhjem@videnscentret .dk, Præstegårdsvej 18)* Dorm beds 100kr, singles/doubles 220/280kr. Open year-round. This 112-bed hostel is in the countryside about 2km north of town.

Hotel Kong Valdemar (☎ 55 34 30 95, fax 55 34 04 95, Algade 101) Singles/doubles 645/825kr. This hotel, in the town centre opposite Gåsetårnet, has 60 rooms with bath, TV and minibar.

Places to Eat

There are numerous cafes, bakeries and restaurants on Algade, the town's principal commercial street.

Xanthos Pizzaria (☎ 55 37 69 76, Algade 16) Pizzas at lunch/dinner 29/48kr. Here you'll find a good variety of tasty pizzas at reasonable prices.

La Mexicana (☎ 55 37 32 32, Algade 22) Mains from 69kr. This Mexican restaurant offers a free salad bar with meals.

Restaurant Påfuglen (☎ 55 37 01 90, Algade 88) Lunches 50-68kr, dinners 80-165kr. This is a good choice for traditional Danish food in a pleasant setting.

Getting There & Away

Vordingborg is 28km south of Næstved via route 22, and 13km from Møn via route 59.

By train, Vordingborg is 80 minutes from Copenhagen (92kr) and 20 minutes from Næstved (29kr). If you're en route to Møn, you'll need to switch from the train to the bus at Vordingborg train station; see the Møn Getting There & Away section of the Møn, Falster & Lolland chapter for more details.

SOUTHERN ZEALAND

Møn, Falster & Lolland

The three main islands south of Zealand – Møn, Falster and Lolland – are all connected with Zealand by bridges. Møn is known for its unique chalk sea cliffs and Falster has fine white-sand beaches. Lolland, the largest of the three islands, has a handful of scattered sights that are only practical to explore if you have your own transport. All three islands are predominantly rural and, except for Møn's rolling hills, the terrain is largely flat.

Møn

pop 11,000

Although its main allure is the spectacular white cliffs of Møns Klint on the east coast, Møn is a thoroughly appealing island. The scenery is rustic and the pace slow. There are some good beaches, prehistoric passage graves and medieval churches with outstanding frescoes.

Møn's interior is largely given over to fields of rapeseed, grain and sugar beet, although agriculture has been in decline since the island's only sugar refinery closed in the early 1990s. Møn's rich clay soil has led to the rise of numerous pottery shops, and 'keramik' signs are commonplace along its country roads.

Travellers using public transport should note that the island lacks a train system and the bus service is sketchy. Still, for those with time to explore, Møn offers a generous dose of what Danes call 'lovely nature'.

GETTING THERE & AWAY

Route 59 connects southern Zealand with the island of Møn.

As there's no train service to Møn, visitors need to take the Copenhagen-Nykøbing F train to Vordingborg in southern Zealand and switch to a bus. The trains from Copenhagen to Vordingborg (92kr, 80 minutes) leave about hourly from early morning until around midnight.

Highlights

- Hike along the gleaming white chalk cliffs at Møns Klint
- Tour Møn's medieval churches, admiring their splendid frescoes
- Join the holiday-makers at Marielyst, Falster's premier summer beach resort
- Visit Maribo, a peaceful town with lakeside walking trails (Lolland)
- Drive through Knuthenborg Safari Park with its free-roaming animals (Lolland)

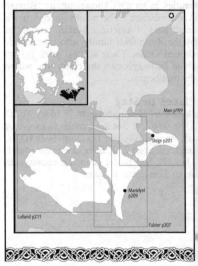

Bus No 62 from Vordingborg to Stege (32kr, 45 minutes), on Møn, connects with train arrivals, leaving Vordingborg about once an hour; as with the train, there's a somewhat fuller service during weekday rush hours and a lighter service at weekends. Bus No 50 runs between Stege and Nykøbing F, (42kr, 55 minutes), on Falster, about once every two hours. For more information on buses contact Storstrøms Trafikselskab (☎ 54 88 04 00).

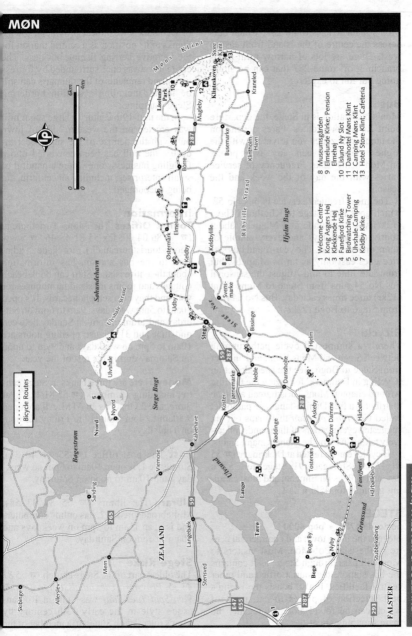

MØN

Bicycle Routes

1 Welcome Centre
2 Kong Asgers Høj
3 Klekkende Høj
4 Fanefjord Kirke
5 Birdwatching Tower
6 Ulvshale Camping
7 Keldby Kirke
8 Museumsgården
9 Elmelunde Kirke; Pension Elmehøj
10 Lislund Ny Slot
11 Danhostel Møns Klint
12 Camping Møns Klint
13 Hotel Store Klint; Cafeteria

GETTING AROUND

Møn's main road is route 287, which cuts across the centre of the island from east to west. There are lots of narrow rural roads branching off route 287 that can be slow-going but fun to explore.

Bus

Møn's bus station is in Stege, the departure point for all bus routes. Fares depend on the number of zones you travel in, with the highest fare between any two points on Møn being 22kr. Frequency of service varies with the day of the week and the season.

The most frequent service is bus No 52, which goes from Stege to Klintholm Havn (12kr) via Elmelunde and Magleby about hourly on weekdays and every couple of hours on weekends. The year-round bus service goes east only as far as Magleby, but from late June to mid-August the seasonal bus No 54 runs from Stege to Møns Klint (12kr) three times each day. Bus No 64 runs from Stege to Bogø (22kr).

Bicycle

There's a signposted cycle path running between Stege and Møns Klint, and another from Stege to Bogø. See the special section 'Cycling in Denmark' following the Getting Around chapter. Møns Turistbureau at Stege distributes a free Danish-language pamphlet called *Cykelture på Møn* that maps out six suggested cycling tours of the island, collectively taking in all of the island's major sights.

Bicycles can be rented at Dækringen (☎ 55 81 42 49), Storegade 91, Stege, for 35kr a day, and at Pension Elmehøj and most camping grounds for 45kr a day.

STEGE

postcode 4780 • pop 4000

Stege is the main town and commercial centre of the island of Møn. Most visitors to Møn will pass through Stege, as it contains the bus station, the tourist office and other central facilities. It also boasts the island's best selection of places to eat, most of which can be found along Storegade, the main shopping street.

During the Middle Ages, Stege was one of Denmark's wealthiest provincial towns, thanks to its position as a central market for the lucrative herring fishing business. The entire town was once surrounded by fortress walls, and remnants of the ramparts can still be found, including a section bordering Stege Camping.

In the mid-19th century a large sugar mill was erected on the western side of town but, with the demise of the sugar beet industry, the mill has been converted into a fledgling business zone where a handful of small enterprises, including an eel farm, are being encouraged.

Information

Tourist Offices The Møns Turistbureau (☎ 55 86 04 00, fax 55 81 48 46, **W** www .moen-touristbureau.dk), Storegade 2, adjacent to the bus station, has information about the entire island. Staff can book beach cottages and rooms in island farmhouses for you, and they also sell phonecards. It's open 10am to 5pm weekdays, 9am to 6pm on Saturday and 11am to 1pm on Sunday between mid-June and 31 August; opening hours are 10am to 5pm on weekdays and 9am to noon on Saturday during the rest of the year.

Money There are three banks in Stege centre, including a Unibank (☎ 55 81 11 11) at Storegade 23 that has an ATM. All are open 9.30am to 4pm Monday to Friday (to 6pm on Thursday).

Post The post office (☎ 55 81 40 31), Storegade 1, is open 10am to 5pm on weekdays and 10am to noon on Saturday.

Library The library (☎ 55 81 43 54), Møllebrøndstræde 12, has online computers and is open 11am to 5pm on weekdays and 10am to 1pm on Saturday.

Stege Kirke

The oldest part of the Stege church *(☎ 55 81 43 35, Provstestræde; admission free; open 9am-5pm Tues-Sun)* was built in Romanesque style in the early 13th century by Møn's ruler, Jakob Sunesen, a member of the

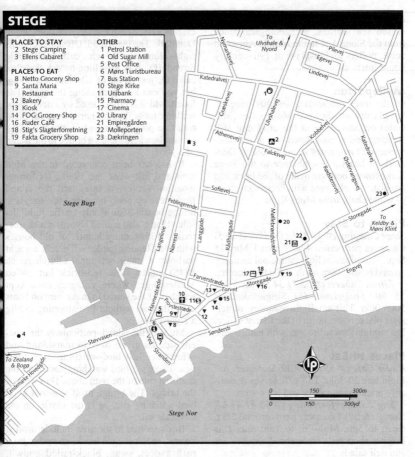

STEGE

PLACES TO STAY
2 Stege Camping
3 Ellens Cabaret

PLACES TO EAT
8 Netto Grocery Shop
9 Santa Maria
   Restaurant
12 Bakery
13 Kiosk
14 FOG Grocery Shop
16 Ruder Café
18 Stig's Slagterforretning
19 Fakta Grocery Shop

OTHER
1 Petrol Station
4 Old Sugar Mill
5 Post Office
6 Møns Turistbureau
7 Bus Station
10 Stege Kirke
11 Unibank
15 Pharmacy
17 Cinema
20 Library
21 Empiregården
22 Molleporten
23 Dækringen

Stege Bugt

Stege Nor

To Zealand & Bogø

To Ulvshale & Nyord

To Keldby & Møns Klint

0   150   300m
0   150   300yd

---

powerful Hvide family that controlled much of southern Zealand. In the late 15th century this 60m-long church was expanded to its present dimensions; the main nave is flanked by two smaller naves, each of which boasts high vaulted ceilings and pointed arch windows.

Noteworthy are the primitive-style ceiling frescoes, some with whimsical jester-like characters, including one depicting a hunter with a pack of dogs chasing a fox and hare. The frescoes, which were whitewashed over centuries ago, were exposed and restored in 1892. The church also has a splendidly carved pulpit dating from 1630, featuring reliefs of biblical scenes. Each relief is separated by a narrow vertical panel depicting virtues such as hope and truth, and below each of those is a grotesque little caricature mask to serve as a reminder of the horrors that await the less virtuous.

Empiregården
The Møn Museum has two sections, one in Stege and the other that's near Keldbylille village. The Stege section, called Empiregården (☎ 55 81 40 67, Storegade 75; adult/child 20kr/free; open 10am-4pm Tues-Sun)

covers local cultural history. There are fossilised sea urchins, archaeological finds from the Stone Age to the Middle Ages, old coins, pottery and displays of 19th-century house interiors.

Mølleporten

Of the three medieval gates that once allowed entry into the town, Mølleporten (Mill Gate) on Storegade is the only one still standing and is considered one of the best-preserved town gates in the whole of Denmark. It bears a resemblance to the Stege Kirke tower; both are made of red brick and are distinctively lined with horizontal strips of white chalk from Møns Klint.

Places to Stay

Stege Camping (*☎ 55 81 84 04, Falcksvej 5*) Camping per person 42kr. Open 1 May-15 Sept. This pleasant little municipal camping ground is just 500m north of the town centre.

Ellens Cabaret (*☎ 55 81 54 54, fax 55 81 58 90, Langelinie 48*) Singles/doubles 500/600kr. This small, three-storey, motel-style place, 600m north of the tourist office, has straightforward rooms with bathrooms.

Places to Eat

Ruder Café (*☎ 55 81 17 00, Storegade 68*) Light fare 20-35kr. This cafe serves reasonably priced sandwiches and ice cream.

Stig's Slagterforretning (*☎ 55 81 42 67, Storegade 59*) Takeaway items around 20kr. Open to 5pm Mon-Fri, to 1pm Sat. This butcher shop sells smørrebrød sandwiches and deli salads.

Santa Maria Restaurant (*☎ 55 81 18 55, Storegade 7*) Pizzas 40kr, pastas from 50kr, meat & fish dishes 100kr. Open noon-10pm daily. This friendly family-run restaurant offers good food and a varied menu that includes Italian, Spanish and Iranian dishes.

There's a good **bakery** (*Storegade 36*) and three **grocery shops** along Storegade. On Torvet you'll find a **kiosk** selling inexpensive hot dogs and burgers.

ULVSHALE & NYORD

The north-eastern side of the Ulvshale peninsula, 6km north of Stege, boasts one of Møn's best beaches and a primeval forest that's one of the few virgin woods left in Denmark. The main road, Ulvshalevej, runs right along the beach, called Ulvshale Strand. If you're travelling by car, there's a car park just south of Ulvshale Camping, but you can also park along the road. The forest, which is crisscrossed by a network of walking trails, begins north-west of Ulvshale Camping and extends to the end of the peninsula, where there's a bridge to the island of Nyord.

Nyord has been connected to the Møn mainland just since the 1980s. Its former isolation served to safeguard the island from development; now its little one-lane bridge boasts Møn's only traffic light! Its sole village, also named Nyord, is a characteristic 19th-century hamlet of old houses with well-tended gardens. There's a yacht harbour, a small octagonal church (circa 1846) and a little red-brick hut called Møllestangen where villagers once kept watch over the sound to make sure no boats came through without first stopping to hire a Nyord pilot.

Much of the island, particularly the eastern side, is given over to marshland and offers excellent **bird-watching** opportunities. There's a bird-watching tower on the northern side of the road about 1km west of the bridge. The bridge itself is also a good bird-watching site, as is the marsh on the Ulvshale side.

Birds spotted in the area include osprey, kestrel, rough-legged hawk, snow bunting, ruff, avocet, swan, black-tailed godwit, arctic tern, curlew and various ducks.

Places to Stay & Eat

Ulvshale Camping (*☎ 55 81 53 25, fax 55 81 55 23, [e] info@ulvscamp.dk, Ulvshalevej 236*) Camping per person 52kr. Open Apr-Oct. This two-star municipal camping ground is right by the beach and on the main road through Ulvshale. The complex includes a shop selling fresh bakery items and limited groceries, and bicycles are available for hire.

Fætter Fiks (*☎ 55 81 85 03, Ulvshalevej 151*) Fast food 15-60kr. Opposite Ulvshale strand, this popular place offers reasonable burgers, ice cream and chicken and chips.

Lolles Gård (☎ *55 81 86 81, Nyord*) Eels 35kr, light dishes around 70kr. This pleasant lunch spot in the village centre specialises in fried eels but also serves omelettes and other light meals.

KELDBY

The Keldby area, about 5km east of Stege, is noted mainly for its roadside church, but there's also a small farm museum 3km south of route 287.

Keldby Kirke

Keldby's brick church (*Route 287; admission free; open 7am-5pm daily Apr-Sept, 8am-4pm daily Oct-Mar*), the nave of which dates back to the early 13th century, has a splendid collection of fresco paintings splashed across its walls, arches and ceiling. The frescoes were painted over a period of two centuries, with the oldest (1275) decorating the chancel walls and depicting scenes from the book of Genesis. Scores of other expressionistic scenes, ranging from the vivid sacrifice of Cain and Abel to a large mural of doomsday, make this one of the most intriguing collection of church frescoes in Denmark. The church pulpit was carved in 1586. You'll find an interesting tombstone at the northern side of the chancel that dates back to 1347 and shows three nobles in period dress.

Museumsgården

This low-key museum (☎ *55 81 30 80, Skullebjergvej 15; adult/child 25kr/free; open 10am-4pm Tues-Sun May-Oct*), in a four-winged farmhouse south of Keldbylille, depicts life on a small Møn farm in the 19th century. Essentially it's an old farmstead that remained in the same family for generations and was turned over to the Møns Museum after its bachelor owner, Hans Hansen, died in 1964. The drive to it takes you, appropriately, through fields of sugar beet and wheat.

ELMELUNDE

Elmelunde is a small, rural hamlet with an appealing guesthouse and an ancient church,

Church Frescoes

Møn's churches are enlivened with some of the best-preserved frescoes in Denmark. A vivid form of peasant art, the paintings are so splendid that the churches can be likened to medieval art galleries. The frescoes, which served as a means of describing the Bible to illiterate peasants, run the gamut from light-hearted scenes from the Garden of Eden to depictions of grotesque demons and the fires of hell.

Frescoes are created by painting with watercolours on newly plastered, still-wet walls or ceilings, which allows the colours to penetrate deep into the plaster before it dries. The frescoes in Stege Kirke were painted solely in black and ochre-red, whereas those in the other Møn churches employ a fuller range of colour.

Møn's frescoes were whitewashed over in the 17th century by Lutheran ministers who thought they too closely represented Catholic themes of the pre-Reformation days. Ironically, the whitewashing didn't destroy the paintings, but rather served to preserve this medieval art from soiling and fading, in part due to a protective layer of dust that separated the frescoes from the whitewash. The whitewash wasn't removed from most of the churches until the 20th century, at which time the frescoes were restored by artists under the auspices of Denmark's national museum.

When you visit Møn's churches you may notice a similar style in many of the frescoes. This is because most of those dating from the 15th century were painted by the same artist, whose exact identity is a mystery but who has come to be known over the centuries as Elmelundemesteren (the Elmelunde master). This artist used distinctive warm earth tones: russet, mustard, sienna, brick red, chestnut brown, soft grey and pale aqua.

both on the main road between Stege and Møns Klint. Bus No 52 stops right in front of the church.

Elmelunde Kirke

Elmelunde Kirke (Kirkebakken 41; admission free; open 7am-5pm daily Apr-Sept, 8am-4pm daily Oct-Mar) is one of Denmark's oldest stone churches; the section around the choir dates back to 1080. The nave was lengthened during the Romanesque period and the lower section of the tower was added around 1300. The church features wonderful frescoes whose subjects range from Adam and Eve's expulsion from the Garden of Eden at the rear of the church to heavenly scenes above the altar. The altar, from 1646, is intricately carved and painted, while the pulpit, its weight carried by a figure of the apostle Peter, dates back to 1649. The three-pointed vaults over the nave were added in 1460 and painted by the 'Elmelunde master' (see the boxed text 'Church Frescoes').

Places to Stay & Eat

Pension Elmehøj (☎ 55 81 35 35, fax 55 81 32 67, e pension-moen@vip.cybercity.dk, Kirkebakken 39, 4780 Stege) Singles/doubles with breakfast 265/430kr. This pension, right next door to Elmelunde Kirke, makes a convenient base as it's equidistant from Stege, Klintholm Havn and Møns Klint. Møn-born Brit and her Australian husband, Jonathan Olifent, have taken a former home for the elderly and turned it into a good-value guesthouse. There are 23 pleasant rooms, all of which have shared toilets and showers. Guests have access to a shared kitchen and a TV lounge. Pension Elmehøj is accessible to people in wheelchairs and has a lift.

In the high season, the pension operates an informal basement **cafe** with cakes, sandwiches and other reasonably priced light eats.

Kaj Kok (☎ 55 81 35 85, Klintevej 151) Dishes 60-90kr. Located on the main road, this is the closest restaurant to the pension, which is 2km east. Kaj Kok serves steaks, schnitzels and chicken.

MØNS KLINT & KLINTESKOVEN

The chalk cliffs at Møns Klint were created 5000 years ago when the calcareous deposits from aeons-worth of seashells were lifted from the ocean floor. The gleaming white cliffs rise sharply 128m above an azure sea presenting one of the most striking landscapes in Denmark. The cliffs are a repository for fossilised Cretaceous-period shells, many of them from creatures long extinct.

Møns Klint is a popular destination for Danish tourists. The main visitor area, Store Klint, has a cafeteria, a small hotel, souvenir shops, a car park (25kr) and picnic grounds. Still, none of this detracts from the natural beauty of the cliffs themselves.

You can walk down the cliffs to the beach and directly back up again in about 30 minutes; alternatively, you can head along the shoreline in either direction and then loop back up through a thick forest of wind-gnarled beech trees for a harder walk lasting about 1½ hours. Either way, start on the steps directly below the cafeteria – it's a quick route to the most scenic stretch of the cliffs.

You needn't limit your hiking to the coast. Klinteskoven (Klinte Forest), the woodland that extends 3km inland from the cliffs, is crisscrossed by an extensive network of footpaths and horse trails. Although most people start their hikes from the cliffs there's a trail from Camping Møns Klint as well. One interesting track leads 1km west from Store Klint to Timmesø Bjerg, a hilltop that is the site of castle ruins dating back to around AD 1100. Other trails lead to lakes, marshes, ancient barrows and old-growth forests where deer run free.

Places to Stay & Eat

Camping Møns Klint (☎ 55 81 20 25, fax 55 81 27 97, e camping@klintholm.dk, Klintevej 544, 4791 Borre) Camping per person 59kr. Open Apr-Oct. This three-star camping ground borders Klinteskoven. It has a 25m swimming pool, a guest kitchen, a coin laundry, bicycles for hire and a shop selling bread, beer and other basics.

Danhostel Møns Klint (☎ 55 81 20 30, fax 55 81 28 18, w www.danhostel.dk/moen, Langebjergvej 1, 4791 Borre) Dorm beds 95kr.

Møns Klint's Unusual Flora

The unique ecosystem at Møns Klint is the result of its unusual soil. The beech trees along this coast keep their fresh spring-green hue throughout the summer thanks to the soil's high chalk content, which inhibits their intake of iron and magnesium, the elements that cause leaves to darken.

The calcareous soil also provides ideal conditions for orchids. Klinteskoven, the wood that backs the cliffs, is the habitat of 20 species of orchid, the greatest variety anywhere in Denmark. The flowering season is from May to August. The grassy hills in the Mandemarke area in the southern part of the woods are particularly abundant with wild orchids.

Two of the more beautiful flowers are the pyramidal orchid (Anacamptis pyramidalis), which has a mounded, multiblossomed pink head, and the dark red helleborine (Epipactis atrorubens), which has an oval leaf and a tall stem with numerous crimson flowers. Look but don't touch, as many of the orchids are rare and all are protected.

singles/doubles 200/260kr. Open May-15 Sept. This hostel is in a former hotel 3km north-west of Møns Klint, opposite Camping Møns Klint. It has a pleasant location, right on a lake, with lots of shady trees and scurrying hares. The 29 rooms contain 105 beds in all. From late June to mid-August you can take the Møns Klint bus No 54 from Stege, but during the rest of the year the nearest stop is in Magleby, 2.75km west of the hostel, where bus No 52 drops you off.

Hotel Store Klint (☎ 55 81 90 08, fax 55 81 90 09, Stengårdsvej 6, 4791 Borre) Singles/doubles with shared bathroom 400/550kr. This 18-room hotel offers the only accommodation right at Møns Klint. Three storeys high, the hotel is perched above the cliffs a stone's throw from the cafeteria, where you check in. Rates include breakfast

Liselund Ny Slot (☎ 55 81 20 81, fax 55 81 21 91, Langebjergvej 6, 4791 Borre) Singles/doubles with breakfast 765/1100kr. For those who would like to stay in a small

manor-house hotel, this place occupies an upmarket 19th-century home in the midst of an expansive estate that's been turned into a park of lawns, duck ponds and gardens. There are 15 rooms with bath. There's also an expensive fine-dining *restaurant*. Liselund is near the coast, 2km north of the hostel.

Møns Klint cafeteria (☎ 55 81 91 83, Store Klint) Sandwiches 35kr, chicken & fish dishes 60kr. Open 10.30am-6pm daily. This place offers typical cafeteria fare such as chicken or fish with chips. There's a little *kiosk* below the cafeteria where you can buy ice cream.

KLINTHOLM HAVN

Klintholm Havn is a pleasant little harbourside village with a long sandy beach. Half touristy, half local, it has one harbour filled with working fishing boats and an adjacent harbour given over to yachts, many belonging to German tourists.

This one-road village has a grocery shop, a handful of eateries, a large harbourside resort and a little seaside inn.

Beyond that, it's mostly beach, which extends in both directions from the two harbours. The section that runs east is particularly appealing and pristine, with light grey sand backed by low dunes; it can be a fun place to stroll and also has the best surf. The safest swimming is found along the western section. There are public toilets and showers near the end of the road by the western part of the beach.

Places to Stay

Klintholm Søbad (☎ 55 81 91 23, Thyravej 19, 4791 Borre) Cottages 375-675kr, double rooms 375-575kr. This small inn has cottages with kitchens and TV, that can each accommodate a small family, and a handful of double rooms with shared bathroom in the main building.

Danland Feriehotel Østersøen (☎ 55 81 90 55, fax 55 81 90 56, Klintholm Havn, 4791 Borre) Apartments from 2150kr for 3 nights. This is a large apartment resort spread across an artificial peninsula separating the two harbours. It's modern and has a pool, sauna, restaurant, coin laundry and

MØN, FALSTER & LOLLAND

other conveniences. Each of the units has two bedrooms, bath, kitchen and TV.

Places to Eat
Half a dozen restaurants line the waterfront road, ranging from a beachside hot-dog and burger joint to seafood restaurants.

Klintholm Søbad (☎ *55 81 91 23, Thyravej 19)* Lunch specials around 50kr, dinner fish meals 100kr. For a typically Danish experience, try this place, which has a dining room with a sea view and fresh fish dishes.

Hyttefadet (☎ *55 81 92 36, Klintholm Havn)* Mains 85kr. Open noon-10pm daily. This lively, if touristy, eatery is opposite the fishing harbour.

Klintholm Røgeri (☎ *55 81 92 90, Margrethevej 14)* Fish 12-20kr a piece. Open 10am-6pm daily. For Klintholm's best value, take the coastal road 250m east of the fishing harbour to this casual place where you can buy smoked and fried fish by the piece, enjoy a beer and sit down to feast at picnic tables.

WESTERN MØN
The western end of Møn is largely farmland crisscrossed by narrow country roads. This part of the island has a few worthwhile historic sights but you'll need your own transport to visit them, as the public bus system primarily serves route 287.

Passage Graves
Møn's two best-known Stone Age passage graves, Kong Asgers Høj and Klekkende Høj, are not far from each other on the western side of the island. Both are about 2km from the village of Røddinge and are signposted.

Kong Asgers Høj *(Kong Asgers Vej)* is in a farmer's field north-west of Røddinge; you can see the mound clearly from the road. This is Denmark's largest passage grave, with a burial chamber 10m long and more than 2m wide. Bring a torch (flashlight) and watch your head!

Klekkende Høj, south-east of Røddinge, is the only double passage grave mound on Møn. It has two entrances side by side, each leading to a 7m-long chamber.

Fanefjord Kirke
Fanefjord Kirke *(Fanefjordvej; admissio free; open 8am-4pm Mon-Sat)*, overlookin the Fanefjord, was built in around 1250 i the early Gothic style. The current churc still incorporates parts of the original struc ture but there have been several addition over the centuries. The church is adorne with superb frescoes; the oldest, which dat back to 1350 and can be seen at the roo arch, depict St Christopher carrying Chris across a ford. Most of the other frescoe date from around 1450 and were created b the Elmelunde master, whose mark (whic resembles a stick man with rabbit ears) ca be seen on an altar-facing rib in the north eastern vault.

BOGØ
The island of Bogø, west of Møn, is con nected to Møn by a causeway and to Zealan and Falster via the impressive Farø bridges

Bogø chocolate, well known throughou Denmark, hails from the island, which als has a Dutch windmill built in 1852 and Gothic church. A car ferry, dating back t the days when Bogø had no causeways c bridges, still shuttles in summer betwee the southern side of the island and Stubbe købing in Falster. Bicycles are not allowe on the Farø bridges so cyclists will need t take the ferry (65kr), which operates onc an hour.

Near the ramp to the Farø bridges is **welcome centre** housing a cafeteria, toilets money exchange and the **Bogø chocolat production centre** *(☎ 55 89 33 02; admis sion 35kr)*. There's also a tourist offic where you can load up with brochures fror 10am to 5pm daily (to 6pm in summer).

Falster

pop 43,000
The island of Falster is almost completel given over to agriculture and its roads liter ally slice across farmers' fields. Althoug the scenery of the interior can become a bi repetitive, Falster's south-eastern coast is summer haven, lined with lovely white-san

beaches that are a magnet for German and Danish holiday-makers.

If you're poking around Falster, the rural hamlets and small towns contain a few sights, including a restored **windmill** in Gedesby and **frescoes** by the Elmelunde master at the church in Nørre Alslev.

NYKØBING F

postcode 4800 • pop 25,000

Nykøbing F is Falster's only large town. The F, incidentally, stands for Falster and is used to differentiate the town from Denmark's two other Nykøbings, one in Zealand and one in Jutland.

The grand medieval castle of Nykøbing F was torn down in the 18th century (you can see a model of it in the local-history museum) and with few exceptions the town has a predominantly modern facade. Still, if you need to stay overnight there are some reasonable places to stay and enough sights to occupy a day.

Torvet, the town centre, is a 10-minute walk west of the train station.

Information

Nykøbing F Turistinformation (☎ 54 85 13 03, fax 54 85 10 05) is just south of Torvet at Østergågade 7. It's open 10am to 5pm Monday to Thursday, 10am to 7pm on Friday and 10am to 1pm on Saturday.

The post office (☎ 54 84 81 00), Banegårdspladsen 4, is on the northern side of the train station.

Things to See & Do

Climb the old **water tower** (Hollandsgård 1; admission 20kr; open 10am-4pm Mon-Fri, 10am-1pm Sat May-Oct) off Østergågade, just south of Nykøbing F Turistinformation, for a bird's-eye view of the town.

Museet Falsters Minder (☎ 54 85 26 71, Langgade 2; admission 20kr; open 11am-5pm Tues-Fri, 11am-3pm Sat, 2pm-4pm Sun May–mid-Sept; afternoons mid-Sept–Apr), the local-history museum, is housed in one of Nykøbing F's oldest houses, a half-timbered building dating back to around 1700. The house itself is referred to as Czarens Hus for the Russian tsar Peter the

Great who stayed here in 1716. It's on the corner of Langgade and Færgestræde, on the western side of Torvet.

There's a children's **zoo** (☎ 54 85 20 26, Østre Allé 97; admission free; open 9am-8pm daily June-Aug, 9am-4pm Sept-May), 1km east of the train station, featuring flamingos, goats, deer, monkeys and llamas.

The area's most popular attraction is **Middelaldercentret** (Medieval Centre; ☎ 54 86 19 34, Ved Hamborgskoven 2, Sundby; adult/ child 75/35kr; open 10am-4pm daily May-Sept), which re-creates a 14th-century medieval village with costumed interpreters demonstrating crafts, games, falconry and

FALSTER

the like. There's a large wooden catapult, a distillery, a smithy and a number of buildings constructed as they would have been in the Middle Ages. A good time to visit is during one of the jousting tournaments, which occur at 2.30pm daily from mid-June to mid-August. It's on the outskirts of town, across the bridge on Lolland. Take bus No 2 from Nykøbing F train station.

Places to Stay

Nykøbing F Camping (☎/fax 54 85 45 45, Østre Allé 112) Camping per person 56kr. Open Apr–Sept. This two-star camping area is near the hostel.

Danhostel Nykøbing F (☎ 54 85 66 99, fax 54 82 32 42, [e] *nyk.f@danhostel.dk, Østre Allé 110)* Dorm beds 100kr, singles/ doubles 230/290kr. Open mid-Jan–mid-Dec. This 94-bed facility, Falster's only hostel, is 1km east of the train station and opposite the zoo. Take bus No 42 (12kr) from the Nykøbing F station.

The tourist office keeps a list of *rooms* available in private homes; prices start at 150kr per person.

Hotel Falster (☎ 54 85 93 93, fax 54 82 21 99, [e] *info@hotel-falster.dk, Skovalléen 2)* Singles/doubles 610/775kr. This hotel, part of the Dansk Kroferie association, has comfortable, modern rooms and friendly management.

Places to Eat

Torvet, the central square, has a handful of reasonably priced places to eat.

Bjørnebageren (☎ 54 85 58 77, Torvet 2) Light eats & desserts 15-40kr. This cafe is a nice spot for a sandwich or to treat yourself to cake and coffee.

Nykøbing F train station has a **kiosk** selling fresh fruit and a **snack bar** offering drinks, ice cream and sandwiches. There's a *McDonald's* opposite the station.

Getting There & Away

Nykøbing F is 128km south-west of Copenhagen and 24km north of Gedser. The north-south E55 highway goes directly through Nykøbing F, while route 9 connects Nykøbing F with Lolland via the Frederik IX bridge.

Trains leave Copenhagen hourly for Nykøbing F (108kr, two hours).

The bus stop is to the south of the train station. Bus Nos 40, 41 and 42 run to Marielyst (22kr, 25 minutes) frequently particularly on weekdays.

MARIELYST
postcode 4873

The most glorious stretch of beach in Falster is at Marielyst, which, with 6000 summer cottages, ranks as one of Denmark's prime holiday areas. It has all of the expected beach-resort facilities including numerous places to eat and drink and a variety of places to stay. Although Marielyst draws lots of visitors in the summer, the beach extends for many kilometres and there's easy access to its entire length so that it never feels crowded.

Information

Marielyst Turistbureau (☎ 54 13 62 98, fax 54 13 62 99), Marielyst Strandpark 3, is next to the bowling alley on the north-western outskirts of town. It's open 9am to 5pm Monday to Saturday from mid-June to August, and 9am to 4pm on weekdays and 10am to 2pm on Saturday the rest of the year.

The Unibank (☎ 54 13 60 85) at Marielyst Strandvej 54 is open 10am to 3pm Monday to Friday from June to September, and 10am to 12.30pm Tuesday to Friday in the low season.

Marielyst Møntvask (☎ 54 13 15 30), a coin laundry at Marielyst Strandvej 23, is open 7am to 10pm daily.

Places to Stay

Smedegårdens Camping (☎ 54 13 66 17, fax 54 13 66 16, [e] *camping@marielyst.dk, Bøtøvej 5)* Camping per person 58kr. Open June-Aug. This simple one-star camping ground has cooking facilities and is a mere two-minute stroll from the beach.

The tourist office maintains a list of *rooms* in private homes for 250/350kr for singles/doubles. Staff there can also help you to book small *apartments* costing about 2000kr per week and *summer houses* ranging from 3000kr to 15,000kr per week. There

lockwise from left: Gåsetårnet in Vordingborg is topped with a golden goose – Valdemar IV's insult ɔ the Hanseatic League; The remains of Trelleborg fortress reveal the precise design of Viking settle-ɔents; Half-timbered houses at Haderslev; Summer activities at Trelleborg re-create Viking lifestyles.

Clockwise from top left: An old-style windmill at Frilandsmuseum at Maribo on Lolland; The modern Møn bridge contrasts with the island tradition; Quench your thirst in a cosy Lolland inn; Simple Lutheran frescoes in a Møn church were painted to describe the Bible to illiterate peasants.

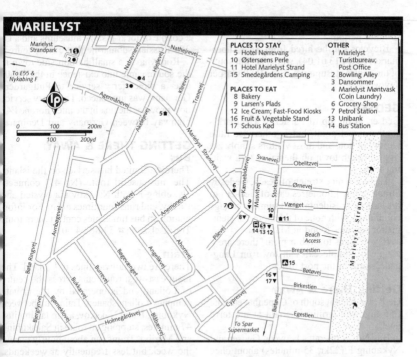

MARIELYST

PLACES TO STAY	OTHER
5 Hotel Nørrevang	1 Marielyst
10 Østersøens Perle	Turistbureau;
11 Hotel Marielyst Strand	Post Office
15 Smedegårdens Camping	2 Bowling Alley
	3 Dansommer
PLACES TO EAT	4 Marielyst Møntvask
8 Bakery	(Coin Laundry)
9 Larsen's Plads	6 Grocery Shop
12 Ice Cream; Fast-Food Kiosks	7 Petrol Station
16 Fruit & Vegetable Stand	13 Unibank
17 Schous Kød	14 Bus Station

are no booking fees. You can also book cottages from Dansommer (☎ 54 13 66 22, fax 54 13 16 22) at Marielyst Strandvej 26D.

Hotel Marielyst Strand (☎ 54 13 68 88, Marielyst Strandvej 61) Singles/doubles 475/625kr. This small hotel, a short stroll from the beach, has just undergone a complete renovation.

Hotel Nørrevang (☎ 54 13 62 62, fax 54 13 62 72, Marielyst Strandvej 32) Singles/doubles from 745/945kr; discounts often available. Marielyst's most upmarket hotel, this has 26 standard rooms with bath, phone and TV, as well as 57 bungalows and apartments that also have kitchens and can accommodate from two to six people. The hotel also books and manages *Østersøens Perle (Marielyst Strandvej 59)*, which has a handful of double rooms for 550kr.

Places to Eat
Marielyst is thick with cafes and fast-food joints.

Schous Kød (☎ 54 13 64 69, Bøtøvej 12) Fish & chips 30kr, chicken & chips 40kr. This place, 200m south down Bøtøvej from the corner with Marielyst Strandvej, offers a good alternative to junk food. There's a little *fruit and vegetable stand* next door.

Larsen's Plads (☎ 54 13 21 70, Marielyst Strandvej 53) Veg mains from 70kr, steaks from 100kr. This pleasant restaurant abounds with true Danish character and offers hearty beef and potato dishes as well as vegetarian offerings.

On the corner of Bøtøvej and Marielyst Strandvej you'll find an *ice-cream shop* and three *kiosks* selling pizzas, burgers, hot dogs and beer. There's a good *bakery* just west of the bus station.

Getting There & Around
From Nykøbing F train station it's a 25-minute bus ride to Marielyst (22kr). Buses are frequent, particularly on weekdays; you can catch bus No 40, 41 or 42. Bus No 45

runs to Gedser (12kr, 20 minutes) during the summer period.

Bicycles can be hired from Spar supermarket (☎ 54 13 61 04), which is 2km south of the centre at Lupinvej 1, for 35/200kr per day/week.

GEDSER

Gedser, at the tip of Falster, is Denmark's southernmost point, but is otherwise little worthy of note and most visitors simply zip right through town on their way to a waiting ferry.

There is a nice stretch of beach, Gedesby Strand, a few kilometres east of Gedser but it's largely a residential and summer cottage community with none of the more transient-visitor services found in Marielyst.

If you want to grab a meal, there are a couple of simple cafes in town on Langgade, north of the post office.

Getting There & Away

Gedser is 152km south of Copenhagen. The E55 highway terminates right at the ferry dock.

Bus No 39 operates between Gedser and Nykøbing F (22kr, 35 minutes) about once an hour throughout the day. In the summer bus No 45 runs between Gedser and Marielyst (12kr, 20 minutes).

There are daily car ferries from Gedser to Rostock in Germany; for details see the Getting There & Away chapter.

Lolland

pop 72,000
Lolland has some of Denmark's best farming land, much of it planted with sugar beet. Being a farm belt it's not an particularly interesting area to tour but it does have a few scattered sights, including a safari park and a notable car museum.

Maribo, in a little lake district in the central part of Lolland, is the most appealing of the island's towns. Sakskøbing, about 9km north-east of Maribo, has a water tower painted with a cheery smiling face, and Nakskov, at the western end of Lolland, has

a few half-timbered waterfront warehouses, a couple of local-history museums and a U-359 Russian submarine that can be toured.

Rødbyhavn, a small harbourside town in the south, came into existence in the 1960s after a direct ferry service to Puttgarden, Germany, was introduced. That ferry service now provides the link in the inter-Europe E47 highway between Germany and Denmark.

GETTING THERE & AWAY
Bus

There's a limited bus service on the island. The most useful route (No 47) connects Nykøbing F with Nakskov via Nysted and Rødby, and runs four times a day. For information on bus timetables contact Storstrøms Trafikselskab (☎ 54 88 04 00).

Train

There are two railway lines in Lolland. The main east-west route cuts across the centre of Lolland and is operated by the private company Lollandsbanen. Trains run between Nykøbing F and Nakskov, a trip lasting just 47 minutes, stopping en route in Sakskøbing and Maribo. Trains run about hourly during the week but less frequently at weekends. The fare between Nykøbing F and Nakskov is 48kr; the fare to Maribo from either Nykøbing F or Nakskov is 30kr.

The other railway line, between Rødby and Nykøbing F (37kr, 23 minutes), is run by DSB. Trains leave Rødbyhavn several times a day in conjunction with the ferry service from Puttgarden, Germany; most of the trains continue on from Nykøbing F to Copenhagen.

Car & Motorcycle

Route 9 cuts across central Lolland from Nykøbing F in the east to Tårs in the west (61km). There are no services at Tårs; it's simply a car-ferry terminal.

Boat

Scandlines (☎ 33 15 15 15) runs a car ferry between Tårs and Spodsbjerg (in Langeland) about once every 30 minutes during the height of the day and hourly in the early morning and late evening. It costs 230kr for a car carrying up to nine people, and 120kr for a motorcycle with up to two riders.

For information about the ferry between Rødbyhavn and Puttgarden, Germany, see the Getting There & Away chapter.

AALHOLM SLOT & AUTOMOBIL MUSEUM

Aalholm Slot, one of northern Europe's oldest inhabited castles, dates back to the 12th century. The Danish king Christopher II was imprisoned in his own dungeon here in 1332 by his half-brother, Count Johan the Mild. The castle is now privately owned and is not open to the public, but part of the estate houses the Aalholm Automobil Museum (☎ 54 87 19 11, Aalholm Parkvej 17, Nysted; adult/child 65/30kr; open 10am-5pm daily June-Aug), which contains nearly 200 antique cars and is one of Europe's largest collections.

Rare models include an 1899 Daimler, a 1900 Decauville, 1902 Renault, 1903 Ford Model A, 1905 Cadillac, 1911 Rolls Royce and a 1931 Bugatti.

The castle and museum are at the west side of the small town of Nysted, which is connected to Nykøbing F via route 297 and to Sakskøbing via route 283.

MARIBO
postcode 4930 • pop 5500

If you decide to stop for a night in Lolland, the town of Maribo, the geographical and commercial centre of the island, is an agreeable place. It has a choice setting, nestled around the northern arm of a large inland lake, Søndersø. A historic cathedral sits on the eastern shore and Bangshave, a wood thick with beech trees, sits on the western shore.

The town centre, Torvet, is marked by Maribo's neoclassical 19th-century rådhus (town hall), fronted by a water fountain and backed by a few 18th-century timber-framed houses. Beyond that the main attraction is the lake and woods; there are trails along

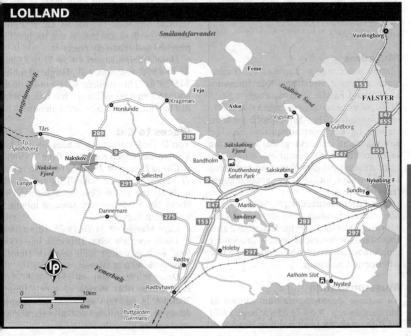

LOLLAND

Smålandsfarvandet

Vordingborg

Femø

Fejø

Kragenæs

Askø

FALSTER

Horslunde

Vigsnæs

Guldborg Sund

Guldborg

Langelandsbælt

Tårs

To Spodsbjerg

Nakskov

Nakskov Fjord

Langø

Søllested

Sakskøbing Fjord

Bandholm

Knuthenborg Safari Park

Sakskøbing

Nykøbing F

Sundby

Dannemare

Maribo

Søndersø

Holeby

Rødby

Aalholm Slot

Nysted

Rødbyhavn

Femerbælt

To Puttgarden (Germany)

0 5 10km
0 3 6mi

MØN, FALSTER & LOLLAND

both sides of the lake beginning only minutes from the town centre.

The train/bus station is north of Torvet, about a five-minute walk via Jernbanegade.

Information

Maribo Turistbureau (☎ 54 78 04 96), Rådhuset, Torvet, is open 9am to 5pm Monday to Friday and 10am to 1pm on Saturday.

There are a number of banks in the town centre including a Sparekassen bank (☎ 54 78 15 44) on Østergade 2, opposite the rådhus. The post office (☎ 54 84 81 00) is at the western side of the train station.

Maribo Domkirke

Maribo's lakeside cathedral was erected in the 15th century and named, like the town itself, after the Virgin Mary. Maribo Domkirke was once part of a larger complex including the convent in which Leonora Christine, the daughter of Christian IV, spent the last years of her life after her release from imprisonment in Copenhagen Castle in 1685. You can see her crypt in the cathedral. Maribo Domkirke is 200m southwest of Torvet.

Museums

Maribo is home to a couple of small museums. Adjacent **Storstrøms Kunstmuseum** and **Lolland-Falster Stiftsmuseum** (☎ 54 78 11 01, Jernbanepladsen; admission 20kr; open noon-4pm Tues-Sun), beside the train station, have a joint admission fee. The Kunstmuseum features regional art from the 18th to the 20th centuries, while the Stiftsmuseum exhibits church art and some social displays, including one about migrant farm labourers.

The **Frilandsmuseum** (☎ 54 78 11 01, Meinckesvej 5; admission 20kr; open 10am-5pm daily May-Sept), in the Bangshave area about 1km south-west of town, is an open-air museum with a wooden windmill and a few other period buildings.

Museumsbanen

An antique steam-engine train known as Museumsbanen (☎ 54 78 85 45; adult/child 40/20kr) makes a jaunt north to Bandholm

on Tuesday, Thursday and Sunday from July to mid-August. The train leaves Maribo station at 10.20am and the return trip takes 90 minutes.

Places to Stay

Maribo Sø Camping (☎ 54 78 00 71, fax 54 78 47 71, e camping@maribo-camping.dk, Bangshavevej 25) Camping per person 58kr. Open Apr-Oct. This three-star camping ground right on Søndersø is about a 20-minute walk south-west from the town centre. It has a kitchen, laundry and TV lounge and is accessible to people in wheelchairs.

Danhostel Maribo (☎ 54 78 33 14, fax 54 78 32 65, w www.danhostel.dk/maribo, Søndre Boulevard 82B) Dorm beds 85kr, 1-3–person rooms 255kr. Open year-round. About 2km south-east of Torvet, this modern hostel near Søndersø has 96 beds. There's a lakeside trail to the town centre.

Ebsens Hotel (☎ 54 78 10 44, fax 54 78 60 44, Vestergade 32) Singles/doubles 385/485kr. This small local hotel is just a few minutes' walk south-west from the train station. Although the rooms are straightforward, with shared bathrooms, the hotel is pleasant and relatively cheap.

Hotel Maribo Søpark (☎ 54 78 10 11, fax 54 78 05 22, Vestergade 27) Singles/doubles 745/795kr. This modern 63-room lakeside hotel, 500m west of Torvet, has rooms with full amenities and lake-view balconies.

Places to Eat

You'll find numerous places to eat on Vestergade, which runs west from Torvet.

China House (☎ 53 88 13 66, Vestergade 4) Mains with rice 70kr. This restaurant with all the usual Chinese standards, is above the Fakta grocery store, a minute's walk from Torvet.

Café Maribo (☎ 54 78 39 76, Vestergade 6) Daily specials 50kr. This cafe has good food such as quiche with salad or Danish roast pork with potatoes.

Omer's Pizza Bar (☎ 54 78 41 90, Vestergade 13A) Pizzas at lunch/dinner 30/50kr. In addition to pizza, this simple eatery sells pasta dishes and tasty shawarma sandwiches.

Restaurant Bangs Have (☎ 54 78 19 11, *Bangshavevej 23*) Mains around 100kr. Popular for its lakeside setting, this restaurant is in an old manor house east of Maribo Sø Camping; it has a great view of Maribo Domkirke across the water.

KNUTHENBORG SAFARI PARK

Knuthenborg Safari Park (☎ 54 78 80 88, *Bandholm; adult/child 88/46kr; open 9am-5pm daily May–Sept*), 7km north of Maribo via route 289, is a large drive-through safari park with free-roaming zebras, antelopes, llamas, giraffes, rhinoceroses, camels and other exotic creatures. The park, which occupies the lawns of what was once Denmark's largest privately held estate, is enclosed by a 7km-long wall. In addition to the animals, there are 500 varieties of trees and flowering bushes, an aviary, an enclosed tiger section and some simple amusement rides for young children.

Bornholm

pop 45,000

Bornholm is a delightful, slow-paced island that makes for a pleasant getaway. Lying 200km east of Copenhagen, Bornholm is closer to Germany and Sweden than it is to the rest of Denmark and consequently sees more foreign tourists than Danes.

Topographically, it's a varied island. The centre of Bornholm is a mixture of wheat fields and forests, the coast is dotted with small fishing villages and there's a scattering of half-timbered houses across the island. The northern part of Bornholm has sea cliffs and a rocky shoreline, while the southern coast has long stretches of powdery white sand.

The island is easy to explore, with both a good island-wide bus system and an impressive network of bicycle paths.

In addition to its fortified rundkirke (round churches) and medieval fortress, Bornholm is renowned for its smokehouses. Be sure to try Bornholm's smoked herring, called *bornholmer*, and the spiced herring from the nearby island of Christiansø, considered the best in Denmark.

HISTORY

Bornholm's rich history, which goes back at least 5000 years, has been traced through Bronze Age burial mounds, rock engravings and monoliths. During the Iron Age Bornholm served as a trading centre for the Baltic region. Archaeological finds, including numerous Roman coins, indicate that trade between Bornholm and the rest of Europe was widespread.

In the Middle Ages Bornholm was administered by the Archbishop of Lund (now part of southern Sweden, Lund was then Danish territory), who ruled from Hammershus, an expansive fortress on the island's northern coast.

During the wars between Sweden and Denmark in the mid-17th century, Bornholm fell into Swedish hands, along with Danish territories at the southern end of the Swedish mainland. In 1658, when it looked likely

Highlights

- Visit one of Bornholm's unique 12th-century rundkirke, its unique fortified round churches
- Cycle some of the island's splendid bicycle trails
- Soak up history at the ruins of the 13th-century fortress Hammershus Slot
- Explore Dueodde's fine white-sand dunes and beach
- Saunter around the picturesque harbourside villages of Gudhjem and Svaneke
- Take a day visit to Christiansø, an offshore island with a well-preserved, 17th-century character

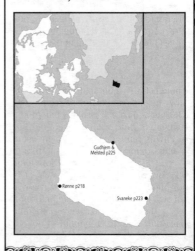

Gudhjem & Melsted p225

Rønne p218

Svaneke p223

that the island might become a permanent part of Sweden, the Swedish commandant on Bornholm was murdered in an uprising. The rebels, led by Bornholm native Jens Kofoed, went on to expel the Swedish garrison from Bornholm and in 1660 returned the island to Danish rule. As a consequence,

Bornholm managed to prevail as Denmark's easternmost province in a period when the country's borders were being substantially eroded by Swedish conquest.

Peace in the 18th century brought prosperity to the island and to its merchants, who built timber-framed mansions along waterfront villages such as Svaneke and Rønne. Many of those harbourside homes still stand today.

Bornholm, like the rest of Denmark, was occupied by the Nazis during WWII. When Germany surrendered to the Allies on 4 May 1945, the German commander on Bornholm refused to step down and the Soviets bombed Rønne and Nexø, causing heavy damage. On 9 May the island was turned over to the Soviets, who occupied it until the spring of the following year.

GETTING THERE & AWAY

Bornholm can be reached by air, boat or a combination that couples the boat with a bus or train.

Air

Maersk Air (☎ 70 10 74 74) operates several flights a day between Copenhagen city and Rønne. The one-way fare for this route is 825kr, but return fares as low as 625kr are available if you book at least seven days in advance.

The island's airport, Bornholms Lufthavn, is 5km south-east of Rønne, on the road to Dueodde. Bus No 7 stops on the main road in front of the airport.

Train & Boat

The Danish national railway system DSB (☎ 70 13 14 15) operates a combined train/boat service to Bornholm. You catch a train between Copenhagen's Central Station and Ystad in Sweden, then connect with a ferry to Rønne. The service runs at least four times daily, including departures from Copenhagen at 6.50am and 10.30am; it takes just three hours to reach Rønne and the fare is 239/120kr for adults/children.

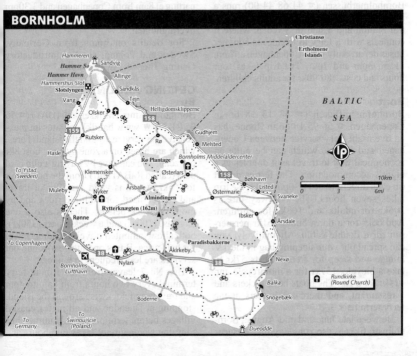

BORNHOLM

Delayed Liberation

At the end of WWII, when Germany surrendered to the Allies, Bornholm was occupied by a German garrison of about 20,000 soldiers. At that time the German naval commander in charge of Bornholm, Captain von Kamptz was fearful of Soviet reprisals and insisted on surrendering his troops only to the British. On 7 May 1945, when Soviet surveillance planes flew over the island, von Kamptz fired off a round from his anti-aircraft guns. Later that day the Soviets returned with a squadron of bombers, which released their loads onto the harbourfront towns of Nexø and Rønne. No warning was given to the islanders, who were still in the midst of celebrating the war's end, and 10 people died in the attack.

The Soviets gave the Germans until 10am the next morning to surrender but von Kamptz held his ground, insisting once again on turning the island over to the British. He did, however, order a civilian evacuation of the two towns. The next morning, at 9.45am, the Soviets attacked Nexø and Rønne again, this time using incendiary bombs that levelled one-third of the houses. On 9 May the Germans finally capitulated and within a matter of days the Nazi soldiers had been repatriated from the island.

After the Germans left, the Soviets built up their forces and continued to occupy the island instead of turning Bornholm over to the Danish government. For a while it looked as if Stalin was going to wrap Bornholm within his Iron Curtain – but in March 1946 he abruptly announced plans to withdraw and within a month all the Soviet troops had left the island.

Bus & Boat

Bornholmerbussen (☎ 44 68 44 00) runs a bus (No 866) between Copenhagen's Central Station and Ystad in Sweden, where it connects with a ferry to Rønne. In summer buses depart daily from Copenhagen at 7am, 11am, 3pm and 7pm. The trip takes four hours and costs 180/90kr for adults/children.

Boat

Bornholmstrafikken (☎ 33 13 18 66 in Copenhagen, ☎ 56 95 18 66 in Rønne) has an overnight ferry service between Copenhagen and Rønne, which can be quite an economical way to travel as it doubles as a night's accommodation. The ferries depart (in each direction) at 11.30pm daily; the trip takes seven hours. The one-way fare is 206kr for adults and 103kr for children. Add 66kr for a dorm bunk, 161kr per person for a double cabin. Alternatively, you can spread out your sleeping bag in the TV lounge and sleep for free. It costs 57kr to take a bicycle, 157kr for a motorcycle and 424kr for a car. The boats have lockers and a restaurant, and there are lockers at the ferry terminals.

Between late June and mid-August, Bornholmstrafikken also runs daytime services every day except Tuesday and Thursday, departing at 8am from Copenhagen and 3.30pm from Rønne. These cost the same as the overnight boat.

For details on boats from Germany, Sweden and Poland, see the introductory Getting There & Away chapter.

GETTING AROUND
Bus

Bornholms Amts Trafikselskab (BAT) (☎ 56 95 21 21, ⓦ www.bat.dk) operates an inexpensive bus service around the island. Fares, which are based on a zone system, cost 8kr per zone. You can save by buying a clip card pass (called RaBATkort) from the bus driver for 65kr, which is valid for 80kr of travel and can be used for multiple rides and by more than one person. There's also a one day pass (100kr) and a weekly pass (350kr); both allow unlimited travel. Children travel for half-price. Buses operate year-round but services are less frequent in winter.

Bus No 7 leaves from the Rønne ferry terminal every two hours from 8am to 4pm and travels anticlockwise around the island, stopping at Dueodde and all major coastal villages before terminating at Hammershus Slot; the whole circuit takes two hours and

40 minutes. Other buses make direct runs from Rønne to Nexø, Svaneke, Gudhjem and Sandvig.

Standard fares on the main routes are: 24kr from Rønne to Åkirkeby (bus No 5 or 6); 32kr from Rønne to Sandvig (bus No 1) or Gudhjem (bus No 3); and 40kr from Rønne to Svaneke (bus No 4), Nexø (bus No 6) or Dueodde (bus No 7).

In July and August BAT runs special sightseeing buses for passholders: The Bondegårdsbussen services visit farms on Wednesday; Kunsthåndværkerbussen stops at craft studios on Tuesday and Friday; Veteranbussen, an antique bus, visits 20th-century historical sights on Wednesday; Middelalderbussen visits medieval sights including the Bornholms Middelaldercenter and the Hammershus Slot ruins on Thursday; and Havebussen visits gardens on Thursday. The tours leave Rønne at 10am and last between five and six hours. You can use either the daily or weekly pass mentioned above; refreshments and admission fees (if applicable) are extra.

For details of buses and schedules contact the main bus office (☎ 56 95 21 21) or visit BAT's Web site.

Car & Motorcycle

Hiring a car is expensive on Bornholm. Even with advance reservations, expect to pay about 650kr per day for short-term rentals, although the rates can drop a bit if you keep the car for a longer period.

Europcar and Avis have offices within walking distance of the Rønne ferry terminal. The Avis office (☎ 56 95 22 08) is at Rønne Autoudlejning ApS, Snellemark 19. Europcar (☎ 56 95 43 00), Nordre Kystvej 1, is at the Q8 petrol station. Both companies also serve the airport.

Europcar hires motor scooters from 210kr per day.

Bicycle

Cycling is a great way to get around Bornholm, which is crisscrossed by more than 200km of bike trails. Some of the trails are built over former train routes, some slice through forests and others run alongside main roads. Together they connect Bornholm's largest towns, cross a wide variety of landscapes and lead to most of the island's sightseeing attractions.

You can start right in Rønne, where bike routes fan out to Allinge, Gudhjem, Nexø, Dueodde and the Almindingen forest.

If you don't feel like pedalling the entire way, you can take your bike on public buses for an additional 20kr.

The tourist office in Rønne sells the handy 60-page English-language *Bicycle Routes on Bornholm* (40kr), which maps out routes and describes sights along the way.

Rental Three-speed bicycles can be hired for about 50/200kr per day/week; mountain bikes 70/350kr. Two of the larger Rønne rental shops are Cykel-Centret (☎ 56 95 06 04) at Søndergade 7 and Bornholms Cykeludlejning (☎ 56 95 13 59), next to the tourist office at Nordre Kystvej 5. Elsewhere on the island most hostels and camping grounds hire out bicycles.

RØNNE
postcode 3700 • pop 15,000
Rønne, Bornholm's administrative centre and largest town, has one-third of the island's total population.

Spread around a large natural harbour, Rønne has been the island's commercial centre since the Middle Ages. Over the years the town has expanded and taken on a more suburban look, but there are still some well-preserved quarters that provide pleasant strolling, most notably the old neighbourhood west of Store Torv with its handsome period buildings and cobblestone streets.

Rønne is seen more as a watering hole and shopping locale for Swedes on day trips, rather than a sightseeing destination, but it can be an agreeable place to begin or end a longer tour of the island.

Information
Bornholms Velkomstcenter (☎ 56 95 95 00, fax 56 95 95 68, e turist@bornholminfo .dk), Nordre Kystvej 3, is a few minutes' walk from the harbour and has information on the whole island. It's open 10am to 6pm

BORNHOLM

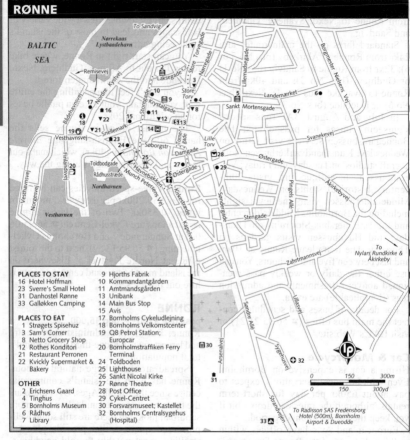

RØNNE

To Sandvig
Nørrekaas
Lystbaadehavn
BALTIC SEA
Remisevej
Rådhusvej
Nordre Kystvej
Vesthavnsvej
Finlandsvej
Vesthavnsvej
Norgesvej
Vesthavnsvej
Vesthavnen
Toldbodgade
Rådhusstræde
Nordhavnen
Munch Petersens Vej
Havnebakken
Søborgstr.
Snellemark
Store Torvegade
Nørregade
Laksegade
Krystalgade
Store Torv
Sankt Mortensgade
Lillemadegade
Borgmester Nielsens Vej
Landemærket
Svanekevej
Tornegade
Damgade
Østergade
Kirkebakken
Kirkebrede
Kapelvej
Sandergade
Pingels Allé
Østergade
Lille Torv
Stengade
Zahrtmannsvej
Sandre Allé
Ullasvej
Sygehusvej
Arsenalvej
Strandvejen
To Nylars Rundkirke & Åkirkeby
To Radisson SAS Fredensborg Hotel (500m), Bornholm Airport & Dueodde
LP
0   150   300m
0   150   300yd

PLACES TO STAY	
16	Hotel Hoffman
23	Sverre's Small Hotel
31	Danhostel Rønne
33	Galløkken Camping

PLACES TO EAT	
1	Strøgets Spisehuz
3	Sam's Corner
8	Netto Grocery Shop
12	Rothes Konditori
21	Restaurant Perronen
22	Kvickly Supermarket & Bakery

OTHER	
2	Erichsens Gaard
4	Tinghus
5	Bornholms Museum
6	Rådhus
7	Library
9	Hjorths Fabrik
10	Kommandantgården
11	Amtmandsgården
13	Unibank
14	Main Bus Stop
15	Avis
17	Bornholms Cykeludlejning
18	Bornholms Velkomstcenter
19	Q8 Petrol Station; Europcar
20	Bornholmstraffiken Ferry Terminal
24	Toldboden
25	Lighthouse
26	Sankt Nicolai Kirke
27	Rønne Theatre
28	Post Office
29	Cykel-Centret
30	Forsvarsmuseet; Kastellet
32	Bornholms Centralsygehus (Hospital)

daily between June and August, and 10am to 5pm on weekdays and noon to 3pm on Saturday during the rest of the year.

There's a Unibank (☎ 56 95 14 20) at Store Torv 18. The post office (☎ 56 94 38 00) is at Lille Torv 18.

The library (☎ 56 95 07 04), Pingels Allé 1, is on the western side of town. The hospital, Bornholms Centralsygehus (☎ 56 95 11 65), Sygehusvej 9, is at the southern end of town.

Walking Tour

A good place to begin a walking tour of Rønne's older quarters is **Store Torv**, which

once served as the military parade ground. Now the central commercial square, it's the site of a **public market** on Wednesday and Saturday mornings year-round. On the eastern side of the square, at Store Torv 1, is **Tinghus**, a neoclassical building dating from 1834 that once housed Rønne's city hall, courthouse and jail.

Continue up Store Torvegade and turn left on Laksegade, a picturesque cobblestone street with a number of attractive houses built in the early 19th century. **Erichsens Gaard** (☎ 56 95 87 35, Laksegade 7; adult/ child 25/10kr; open 10am-5pm Tues-Sat *mid-May–mid-Oct)*, a merchant's house dating back to 1806, has been turned into a museum complete with period furnishings.

At the end of Laksegade turn left onto Storegade; at No 42 you'll find **Kommandantgården**, an imposing building erected in 1846 as a residence for the Bornholm military commander.

If you enjoy arts and crafts, take a short detour to **Hjorths Fabrik** (☎ *56 95 01 60, Krystalgade 5; adult/child 25/10kr; open 10am-5pm Tues-Sat)*, which is a working ceramics museum.

Return to Storegade and proceed south to **Amtmandsgården**, a half-timbered 18th-century structure at Storegade 36 that is now the Bornholm prefect's residence. Jens Kofoed, who liberated Bornholm from the Swedes in 1658, was born in a house that once stood on this site.

When you reach Rådhusstræde, turn right and you'll soon come to **Toldboden**, at Toldbodgade 1; this was constructed as a storehouse in 1684 and is one of the town's oldest timber-framed buildings. On the wall by the harbour-facing gable you can spot figurines of two menacing Dalmatians flanking a cloaked figure that is said to represent Satan.

Continue back down Rådhusstræde to Havnebakken, where you'll pass a quaint octagonal **lighthouse** (built in 1880) before reaching the attractive **Sankt Nicolai Kirke**, built in 1915. South of the church is **Bombehusene**, a neighbourhood that encompasses Kapelvej and Kirkestræde; this is one of the areas that was levelled by Soviet bombers in May 1945.

If you continue east from the church on Østergade, at the corner with Teaterstræde you'll pass the restored **Rønne Theatre**, which was built in 1823 and is one of the oldest functioning theatres in Denmark. Continue north onto Nellikegade and turn right at Tornegade to get back to Store Torv.

Bornholms Museum

This museum (☎ *56 95 07 35, Sankt Mortensgade 29; adult/child 30/5kr; open 10am-5pm Tues-Sat May-Sept, shorter low-season hours)* has a local-history collection

that includes a hotch-potch of nature displays, antique toys, excavated Roman coins, pottery, paintings and an exhibition of *Bornholmerur*, a type of grandfather clock that's made on the island.

Forsvarsmuseet

The Defence Museum (☎ *56 95 65 83, Kastellet; adult/child 25/5kr; open 10am-4pm Tues-Sat May-Oct)* is in the 17th-century citadel called Kastellet, south of the town centre. It has the usual collection of armaments and military uniforms as well as displays on the bombing of Rønne and Nexø by the Soviets at the end of WWII and the subsequent Soviet occupation of the island.

Nylars Rundkirke

The attractive Nylars Rundkirke (☎ *56 97 20 13, Kirkevej 17; admission free; open 9am-5pm Mon-Sat)*, built in 1150, is the most well-preserved and easily accessible round church in the Rønne area. Its central pillar is painted with 13th-century frescoes, the oldest in Bornholm, depicting scenes from the Creation myth, including Adam and Eve's expulsion from the Garden of Eden. The cylindrical nave has three storeys, the top one of which has a watchman's gallery that served as a defence lookout in medieval times.

Inside the church, the front door is flanked by two of Bornholm's 40 rune stones, carved memorial stones that date back to the Viking era.

Nylars Rundkirke is about 8km from Rønne, on the road to Åkirkeby. It's only a 15-minute ride from Rønne on bus No 6; alight at the bus stop near the Dagli Brugsen shop and turn north on Kirkevej for the 350m walk to the church. The cycle path between Rønne and Åkirkeby also passes the church.

Places to Stay

Galløkken Camping (☎ *56 95 23 20, fax 56 95 37 66,* e *info@gallokken.dk, Strandvejen 4)* 58kr per person. Open mid-May–Aug. This camping ground, a little over 1km south of the town centre, is in a pleasant setting on the bike trail along the southern coast.

Bornholm's Round Churches

Unique among Bornholm's sights are its four 12th-century rundkirke (round churches), constructed with 2m-thick whitewashed walls and black conical roofs. The churches were built at a time when pirating Wends from eastern Germany were ravaging coastal areas throughout the Baltic Sea. They were designed not only as places of worship but also as refuges against enemy attacks – their upper storeys doubling as shooting galleries. Each church was built about 2km inland, and all four are sited high enough on knolls to offer a lookout to the sea. Fittingly, these bold churches have a stern, ponderous appearance, more typical of a fortress than of a place of worship.

Another unique architectural feature of each church is the detached belfry, made of stone and tarred timber. All four churches are still used for Sunday services.

Danhostel Rønne (☎ 56 95 13 40, fax 56 95 01 32, ℮ rvh@post4.tele.dk, Arsenalvej 12) Dorm beds 100kr, singles/doubles 220/340kr. Open Mar-Oct. This 140-bed hostel, just north of Galløkken Camping, is a 30-minute walk, or a 50kr taxi ride, from the harbour.

The tourist office can book *rooms* in private homes in Rønne for singles/doubles 195/280kr; there's no booking fee.

Sverre's Small Hotel (☎ 56 95 03 03, fax 56 95 03 92, ℮ sverreshoteldk@mail.tele.dk, Snellemark 2) Singles/doubles with shared bathroom 290/460kr in summer, 260/390kr at other times; 130kr more for private bathroom. This central budget hotel, run by a friendly jazz musician, has 24 rooms that vary in size, but are all clean and adequate. Breakfast is included in the room rates.

Hotel Hoffmann (☎ 56 95 03 86, fax 56 95 25 15, ℮ info@hotelhoffmann.dk, Nordre Kystvej 32) Singles/doubles with breakfast 695/795kr. This mid-range hotel has 85 modern rooms with bath and TV, some with sea views, and a convenient location just a few minutes north of the tourist office.

Radisson SAS Fredensborg Hotel (☎ 56 95 44 44, fax 56 95 03 14, ℮ info@hotel-fredensborg.dk, Strandvejen 116) Singles/doubles 900/1150kr. The Fredensborg, the area's most upmarket hotel, is perched on a quiet knoll in a wooded coastal section at the southern end of Rønne. It has 72 well-appointed rooms and there's a sauna, pool and tennis court.

Places to Eat

Rothes Konditori (☎ 56 95 04 39, Snellemark 41) Snacks 8-25kr. Opposite the main bus stop, this place has good pastries, sandwiches and minipizzas, with takeaway and sit-down service.

Store Torv has a number of *fast-food outlets* selling hamburgers, hot dogs and pizzas, as well as a *grocery shop*.

Sam's Corner (☎ 56 95 15 23, Store Torv 2) Pizza & cafe fare 40-70kr. This unpretentious eatery on the square has sandwiches, pizza and simple meals.

Strøgets Spisehuz (☎ 56 95 81 69, Store Torvegade 39) Mains 80-120kr. This quintessentially Danish restaurant has hearty meat-and-potato dishes, including a good selection of steaks.

Restaurant Perronen (☎ 56 95 84 40, Munch Petersons Vej 3) Mains around 100kr. This stylish restaurant south-east of the tourist office has an international menu that includes Mexican fare.

For a quick breakfast, the ferry terminal has an upstairs *cafeteria* serving pastries and coffee at reasonable prices.

Kvickly (☎ 56 95 17 77, Nordre Kystvej 28), the supermarket opposite the tourist office, has a good, inexpensive *bakery* that opens at 6.30am daily, although the supermarket itself doesn't open until 9am.

ÅKIRKEBY

Åkirkeby is an inland town with a mix of old half-timbered houses and newer homes with slightly less character.

The tourist office, car park and a couple of simple eateries are at the eastern side of the church on Jernbanegade. The town square, post office and bank are 150m east of the tourist office.

The town takes its name from its main sight, the 12th-century Romanesque stone church **Aa Kirke** (☎ *56 97 41 03, Nybyvej 2; admission 6kr; open 10am-4pm Mon-Sat in spring & autumn, 9.30am-5pm in summer)*, which is built on a knoll overlooking the surrounding farmland. The largest church on Bornholm, its crossroads location made it a convenient place of assembly for people from all over the island. Although it has been altered and renovated in recent centuries, the interior still houses a number of historic treasures, including a 13th-century baptismal font of carved sandstone depicting scenes of Christ and featuring runic script. The ornate pulpit and altar date from around 1600 and are notable for their fine detail. For a 360° view of the town, climb the 22m-high bell tower, but watch your head on the low ceilings en route!

About 2km south of Åkirkeby centre, on the road to Dueodde, is the **Bornholms Automobilmuseum** (☎ *56 97 45 95, Grammegaards-vej 1; adult/child 30/10kr; open 10am-5pm Mon-Sat May-Oct)*, a small museum featuring 1920s vintage cars and motorcycles.

INTERIOR WOODLANDS

Bornholm is the most forested county in Denmark, with one-fifth of the island covered with woodland. Beech, fir, spruce, hemlock and oak are dominant. There are three main areas, each laid out with walking trails (you can pick up free maps at tourist offices). A single bicycle trail connects them all.

Almindingen, the largest forest (2412 hectares), is in the centre of the island and can be reached by heading north from Åkirkeby. It's the site of Bornholm's highest point, the 162m hill **Rytterknægten**, which has a lookout tower called Kongemindet from where you can view the surrounding countryside.

Paradisbakkerne (Paradise Hills), 2km north-west of Nexø, contains wild deer and a trail that passes an ancient monolithic gravestone. **Rø Plantage**, about 5km south-west of Gudhjem, has a terrain of heathered hills and woodlands.

DUEODDE
postcode 3730

Dueodde, the southernmost point in Bornholm, is a vast stretch of beach backed by pine trees and expansive dunes. Its soft white sand is so fine-grained that it was once used in hourglasses and ink blotters.

There's no real village at Dueodde – the bus stops at the end of the road where there's a hotel, a restaurant, a couple of food kiosks and a footpath to the beach.

Dueodde is a true beach-bum hang-out. The only 'sight' is a **lighthouse** on the western side of the dunes; you can climb the 197 stairs for a view of endless sand and sea.

The beach at Dueodde is a good place for children: the water is generally calm and is shallow up to about 100m out, after which it becomes deep enough for adults to swim.

Places to Stay

Møllers Dueodde Camping (☎ *56 48 81 49, fax 56 48 81 69, ℮ moeller@dueodde-camp .dk, Duegårdsvej 2)* Camping per person 54kr. Open mid-May–mid-Sept. This three-star camping ground is in a wooded area that's a 10-minute walk north-east of the bus stop. There's a small shop on site.

Dueodde Vandrerhjem & Camping (☎ *56 48 81 19, fax 56 48 81 12, ℮ info@ dueodde.dk, Skrokkegårdsvejen 17)* Camping per person 48kr; 1-4–person rooms 440kr mid-June–Aug, 300kr other times. Open Apr-Oct. This place, which borders the beach and is a 10-minute walk east of the bus stop, is a two-star camping ground that also has some simple rooms for rent.

Dueodde Badehotel (☎ *56 48 86 49, fax 56 48 89 59, ℮ mail@dueodde-badehotel .dk, Sirenevej 2)* Units 3360-6400kr per week, depending on season. Right next to the bus stop, this modern apartment-style place rents units by the week. The convenient one-bedroom units have a sofa bed in the living room and can sleep up to five people. There's a coin laundry, tennis court and sauna.

Places to Eat

Restaurant Granpavillonen (☎ *56 48 81 75, Fyrvej 5)* Pizza 70kr, mains around 120kr.

Also at the end of the road, this place has pizza as well as Danish and German dishes.

Dueodde Vandrerhjem & Camping (☎ 56 48 81 19, Skrokkegårdsvejen 17) Fast food 20-40kr. This place has a cafeteria that sells hamburgers and other simple fare and a minimarket selling ice cream, fresh bread and a few basic supplies.

There are a few **kiosks** selling ice cream, hot dogs and snacks at the end of the road opposite the bus stop.

SNOGEBÆK

A quaint seaside village of older homes, Snogebæk makes a nice little detour if you are travelling by car or bike between Nexø and Dueodde. Down by the water, on Hovedgade, you'll find a shop selling quality hand-blown glass at reasonable prices. Immediately next to it is a good smokehouse where you can get smoked fish, deli items and cold beer. The end of the road beyond the glassworks is a good site for spotting migratory ducks and other waterbirds. If you want to explore more, there's a coastal footpath leading north along the beach.

NEXØ

postcode 3730 • pop 3800
Nexø (also spelt Neksø), Bornholm's second-largest town. It has a large modern harbour where fishing vessels unload their catch. The harbour, and much of the town, was reconstructed after being destroyed by Soviet bombing in WWII. Despite taking a back seat to more touristy towns such as Gudhjem and Svaneke, Nexø has its fair share of picturesque buildings.

Information

The Nexø-Dueodde Turistbureau (☎ 56 49 32 00, fax 56 49 43 10) at Åsen 4 is in the centre of town, two blocks inland of the harbour. It has information on both Nexø and Dueodde.

There are a couple of banks on Torvet, the central square, just south of the tourist office.

Things to See & Do

Nexø Museum (☎ 56 49 25 56, Havnen 2; adult/child 15/5kr; open 10am-4pm Mon-Fri

& 10am-2pm Sat mid-May–mid-Oct) is in a picturesque building constructed in 1796 from Nexø sandstone (once a major export of the town). Opposite the waterfront, it features exhibits on Nexø's history with an emphasis on fishing and shipping. Particularly notable are the reconstructions of fishers' houses.

The childhood home of author Martin Andersen Nexø is a **museum** (☎ 56 49 45 52, cnr Andersen Nexøvej & Ferskeøstræde; adult/child 15/5kr; open 10am-4pm Mon-Fri & 10am-2pm Sat mid-May–mid-Oct), in the southern part of the town. Those interested in Nexø's life will find photos of the author, along with some of his letters and other memorabilia.

There's a butterfly farm, **Bornholms Sommerfuglepark & Tropeland** (☎ 56 49 25 75, Gamle Rønnevej 14; adult/child 50/40kr; open 10am-6pm daily Jun-Aug, 10am-5pm May, Sept & Oct), on the western side of town. You can walk among these colourful creatures, which are at all stages of their development, from foraging caterpillars to fluttering butterflies.

Although Nexø's central waterfront is industrial, 2km south of town there's a popular seaside area called **Balka** with a gently curving, white-sand beach.

Places to Stay

Few people stay in Nexø proper because the beaches on the outskirts are much more appealing.

Hotel Balka Strand (☎ 56 49 49 49, fax 56 49 49 48, e info@hotelbalkastrand.dk, Boulevarden 9) Rates per person 300-500kr depending on season, apartments 3000-5750kr per week. This hotel, 200m from Balka's sandy beach, has double rooms as well as cheery apartments, all with modern decor. There's a sauna, pool, tennis court, bar and restaurant. The per person rates include breakfast.

Hotel Balka Søbad (☎ 56 49 22 25, fax 56 49 22 33, e hotel-balkasoebad.dk, Vester Strandvej 25) Rates per person 370-530kr depending on season. Also in the Balka area, this hotel by the beach has 106 commodious rooms in modern two-storey buildings.

Rooms have at least two twin beds, a sofa bed and a balcony; some have a second bedroom. There's a pool, tennis court, bar and restaurant. Breakfast is included in the price.

Places to Eat

Jørgens Cafe (☎ 56 49 49 45, Torvet 5) Sandwiches 25-40kr. This cosy little cafe in the centre of town specialises in smørrebrød sandwiches.

Both of the beachside hotels have moderately expensive *dinner restaurants*.

Kvickly (☎ 56 49 21 37, Købmagerade 12) If you want to pack a lunch for the beach,

head to this supermarket near the bus stop in the town centre, which has a good bakery and a deli section.

SVANEKE
postcode 3740

Svaneke is an appealing town of red-tiled 19th-century buildings that has won international recognition for maintaining its historic character. In 1975 its efforts were rewarded with the prestigious Council of Europe's gold medal for town preservation. The harbourfront is lined with mustard-yellow half-timbered former merchants'

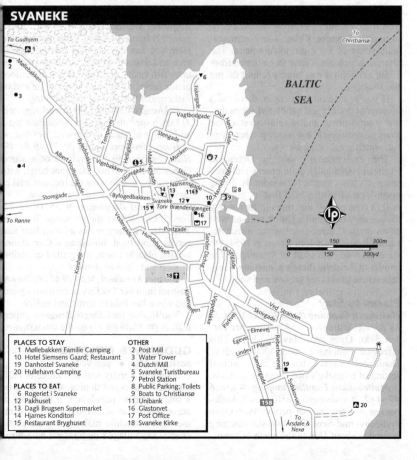

SVANEKE

To Gudhjem
To Christiansø

BALTIC SEA

To Rønne

To Årsdale & Nexø

PLACES TO STAY
1 Møllebakken Familie Camping
10 Hotel Siemsens Gaard; Restaurant
19 Danhostel Svaneke
20 Hullehavn Camping

PLACES TO EAT
6 Rogeriet i Svaneke
12 Pakhuset
13 Dagli Brugsen Supermarket
14 Hjarnes Konditori
15 Restaurant Bryghuset

OTHER
2 Post Mill
3 Water Tower
4 Dutch Mill
5 Svaneke Turistbureau
7 Petrol Station
8 Public Parking; Toilets
9 Boats to Christiansø
11 Unibank
16 Glastorvet
17 Post Office
18 Svaneke Kirke

houses, some of which have been turned into restaurants and hotels.

Information

Svaneke Turistbureau (☎ 56 49 63 50, fax 56 49 70 10), in the rådhus, Storegade 24, is open 9.30am to 4.30pm Monday to Friday and 9am to noon on Saturday June to August. It's open 10am to 4pm Monday to Wednesday and 11am to 5pm Thursday and Friday for the rest of the year.

There's a Unibank (☎ 56 49 64 20) at Nansensgade 5 and the post office (☎ 56 94 38 00) is at Postgade 2.

Things to See & Do

You'll find some interesting period buildings near **Svaneke Kirke**, a few minutes' walk south of Torv, the town square. The church, which has a rune stone, dates from 1350, although it was largely rebuilt during the 1880s.

If you're interested in **crafts**, there are a number of pottery and handicraft shops dotted around town, and at Glastorvet in the town centre there's a workshop where you can watch glass being blown.

The easternmost town in Denmark, Svaneke is generally quite breezy and consequently has a number of **windmills**. To the north-west of town you'll find an old post mill (a type of mill that turns in its entirety to face the wind) and a Dutch mill, as well as an unusual three-sided water tower designed by architect Jørn Utzon in 1951. On the main road 3km south of Svaneke, in the hamlet of Årsdale, there's a working windmill where grains are ground and sold.

Places to Stay

Hullehavn Camping (☎ 56 49 63 63, fax 56 49 63 90, Sydskovvej 9) Camping per person 52kr. Open mid-May–mid-Sept. This three-star camping ground, 400m south of Danhostel Svaneke, has the more natural setting of Svaneke's two camping grounds.

Møllebakken Familie Camping (☎/fax 56 49 64 62, e molcamp@post10.tele.dk, Møllebakken 8) Camping per person 48kr. Open mid-May–mid-Sept. This two-star camping ground is about 1km to the north of town.

Danhostel Svaneke (☎ 56 49 62 42, fax 56 49 73 83, e danhostel-svaneke@bornholm .net, Reberbanevej 9) Dorm beds 100kr, singles/doubles 300/360kr. Open Apr-Oct. A kilometre south of the centre on the bus route, this is a chalet-like place with 152 beds

Hotel Siemsens Gaard (☎ 56 49 61 49, fax 56 49 61 03, e hotel@siemsens.dk, Havnebryggen 9) Singles/doubles with breakfast 495/790kr. This 51-room hotel has a fine location opposite the harbour, pleasant rooms and a bit of old-world character. All rooms have a bath and refrigerator, and some have water-view balconies.

Places to Eat

Rogeriet i Svaneke (☎ 56 49 63 24, Fiskergade 12) Items 10-25kr. A fun place to eat. Here you can buy smoked herring, mackerel and salmon by the piece, as well as tasty fish cakes, and chow down at outdoor picnic tables. It's by the water at the end of Fiskergade, north of the town centre.

Pakhuset (☎ 56 49 65 85, Brænderigænget 3) Lunch specials 50kr. This restaurant has a wide range of reasonably priced beef dishes.

Hotel Siemsens Gaard (☎ 56 49 61 49, Havnebryggen 9) Smørrebrød or seafood dishes 50-100kr. This restaurant hotel, with patio dining overlooking the harbour, makes an ideal lunch choice on a sunny day.

Restaurant Bryghuset (☎ 56 49 73 21, Torv 5) Lunch 50kr, dinner mains 70-120kr. This friendly place brews its own beer and serves good food, including a Christiansø herring plate at lunch, and grilled spareribs, salmon and chicken dinners.

Hjarnes Konditori (☎ 56 49 61 56, Torv 8) Pastries from 6kr. On Torvet, the town square, this place has bakery items and coffee.

You'll also find *Dagli Brugsen* supermarket *(☎ 56 49 60 41)* on the town square.

GUDHJEM & MELSTED

postcode 3760 • pop 900

Gudhjem is a pretty seaside village of half-timbered houses and sloping streets. Despite a small resident population, it manages to accommodate an substantial influx of summer visitors while maintaining its rustic charm. The village's picturesque harbour is

NED FRIARY

NED FRIARY

NED FRIARY

NED FRIARY

Clockwise from top left: A post mill in Svaneke – the mill can turn on its foundation to take advantage of changing winds; Dried fish for sale on Bornholm; A customer visits the Nexø fish market; Even the barn doors of Christiansø reflect a rural focus.

Clockwise from top left: Wherever you wander in Odense, you'll find allusions to the master of fairy tales; HC Andersens Hus is a now a museum; A cottage window at Den Fynske Landsby, Odense; Steensgaard Manor near Faaborg is just one example of Denmark's past rural affluence.

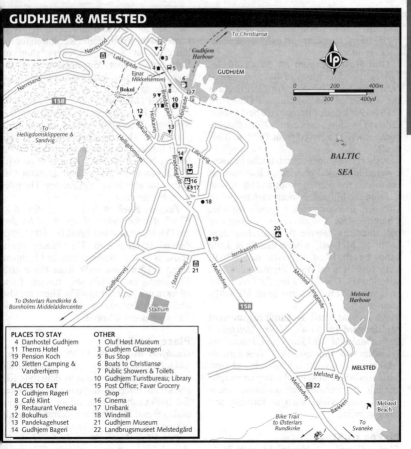

GUDHJEM & MELSTED

PLACES TO STAY
4 Danhostel Gudhjem
11 Therns Hotel
19 Pension Koch
20 Sletten Camping &
   Vandrerhjem

PLACES TO EAT
2 Gudhjem Røgeri
8 Café Klint
9 Restaurant Venezia
12 Bokulhus
13 Pandekagehuset
14 Gudhjem Bageri

OTHER
1 Oluf Høst Museum
3 Gudhjem Glasrøgeri
5 Bus Stop
6 Boats to Christiansø
7 Public Showers & Toilets
10 Gudhjem Turistbureau; Library
15 Post Office; Favør Grocery
   Shop
16 Cinema
17 Unibank
18 Windmill
21 Gudhjem Museum
22 Landbrugsmuseet Melstedgård

so well-preserved that it served as one of the
period settings for the filming of Martin
Andersen Nexø's *Pelle the Conqueror*.

Gudhjem would make a good base for
exploring the rest of Bornholm; it has cycle
paths, walking trails, convenient bus connections, reasonably priced places to stay
and a boat service to Christiansø. It is also
an enjoyable place to just wander about and
soak up the harbourside atmosphere.

Information

Gudhjem Turistbureau (☎ 56 48 52 10, fax
56 48 52 74), Åbogade 7, is at the library, just

a block inland from the harbour. There's a
Unibank (☎ 56 48 51 51) at Brøddegade 6.
The post office (☎ 56 94 38 00) is inside the
Favør grocery shop. There are toilets and
showers at the harbour.

Things to See & Do

At the dockside **Gudhjem Glasrøgeri** (☎ 56
48 54 68, Ejnar Mikkelsensvej 13A; open
daily in summer), you can watch top-quality
Bornholm glass being hand blown.

Gudhjem Museum (☎ 56 48 54 62, Stationsvej 1; adult/child 20/5kr; open 10am-5pm
Mon-Sat, 2pm-5pm Sun mid-May–mid-Sept),

in the handsome former train station in the southern part of town, features displays of local history, temporary art exhibits and outdoor sculptures.

Oluf Høst Museum (☎ *56 48 50 38, Løkkegade 35; adult/child 40/15kr; open at least 1pm-5pm Tues-Sun Apr-Oct)* features the workshops and paintings of Oluf Høst (1884–1966), one of Bornholm's best-known artists. The museum occupies Norresân, the home where Oluf lived from 1929 until his death.

A short five-minute climb up the heather-covered hill **Bokul** provides a fine view of the town's red-tiled rooftops and out to sea.

From the hill at the south-eastern end of Gudhjem harbour you'll be rewarded with a **harbour view**. You can continue along this path that runs above the shoreline 2km south to Melsted, where there's a little **sandy beach**. It's a delightful nature trail, with lots of swallows, nightingales and wildflowers. Gudhjem's beaches are rocky so if you want to see some sand, Melsted's your best bet.

Also in Melsted is **Landbrugsmuseet Melstedgård** (☎ *56 48 55 98, Melstedvej 25; adult/child 30/15kr; open 10am-5pm Tues-Sun mid-May–mid-Oct)*. This agricultural history museum is housed in old farm buildings where costumed interpreters tend animals and demonstrate traditional techniques in activities such as farming and wool spinning.

Places to Stay

Sletten Camping & Vandrerhjem (☎ *56 48 50 71, fax 56 48 52 56,* e *sletten@post10 .tele.dk, Melsted Langgade 45)* Camping per person 48kr, double rooms 295kr. Open mid-May–mid-Sept. This two-star facility is the nearest camping ground to town and is a 15-minute walk south of Gudhjem harbour. In addition to camping, this place also has a hostel-like building with comfortable double rooms and shared bathrooms.

Danhostel Gudhjem (☎ *56 48 50 35, fax 56 48 56 35,* e *dgh@mail.tele.dk, Ejnar Mikkelsensvej 14)* Dorm beds 100kr, singles/doubles in private homes 295/350kr. Open year-round. This hostel is in an attractive

tile-roofed building opposite the harbour-side bus stop. It also offers rooms in private homes in the town centre. Reception for the hostel is at a small grocery shop on Løkkegade, about 75m north-west of the hostel. Mountain bikes can be hired for 70kr per day.

Therns Hotel (☎ *56 48 50 99, fax 56 48 56 35,* e *post@therns.dk, Brøddegade 31)* Singles/doubles 350/550kr, with bath from 550/650kr. This reasonably priced central hotel (under the same management as the hostel) has 30 pleasant rooms, most with TV, a small refrigerator and an extra sofa bed; some also have kitchenettes. The rates include breakfast.

Pension Koch (☎ *56 95 72 95, fax 56 95 67 95,* e *info@pensionkoch.dk, Melstedvej 15)* Double rooms with breakfast 600-750kr depending on season. This cheery guest house is in the southern part of Gudhjem, about a 10-minute walk from the centre. The rooms are comfortably furnished and all have private bath and TV. There are also apartments that can be rented by the week. Smoking is not allowed.

Places to Eat

Gudhjem Røgeri (☎ *56 48 57 08, Ejna Mikkelsensvej)* Buffet 75kr. This pleasant waterfront smokehouse sells deli-style fish and salads, offers an all-you-can-eat smoked fish buffet and has both indoor and outdoor dining areas. There's live folk music nightly in summer.

Pandekagehuset (☎ *56 48 55 17, Brøddegade 15)* Light meals 30-60kr. This casual cafe specialises in pancakes and also has good omelettes.

Restaurant Venezia (☎ *56 48 53 53, Brøddegade 33)* Pizza & pasta 60-85kr. This popular Italian restaurant has a pleasant atmosphere and good food.

Café Klint (☎ *56 48 54 59, Ejna Mikkelsensvej 20)* Light meals 40-65kr. On a sunny day the patio is the spot for a leisurely cappuccino or beer, with a view of the harbour.

Bokulhus (☎ *56 48 52 97, Bokulvej 4)* Lunch specials 75kr, two-course dinner 150-190kr. This old-fashioned restaurant highly regarded for its fish dishes, is Gudhjem's top fine-dining choice.

Gudhjem Bageri (☎ *56 48 56 03, Brøddegade 16*) Bakery goods 6-20kr. This bakery has a rooftop patio where you can have pastries and coffee.

There's a **Favør** grocery shop around the corner to the south-east.

ØSTERLARS RUNDKIRKE

The largest and most impressive of the island's round churches is Østerlars Rundkirke (☎ *56 49 82 64, Vietsvej 25; adult/child 5kr/free; open 9am-5pm Mon-Sat)*, which dates from 1150 and is set in the midst of wheat fields and half-timbered farmhouses. This fortress-like church has seven weighty buttresses and an upper-level shooting gallery. It's thought that the roof was originally constructed with a flat top to serve as a battle platform, complete with a brick parapet but, because of the excessive weight this exerted on the church walls, the roof was eventually replaced with its present conical one.

The interior is largely whitewashed, although a swath of medieval frescoes has been uncovered and restored. There's a rune stone dating back to 1070 at the church entrance and a sundial above it.

A cycle path to the church leads inland 4km south from Gudhjem; the church can also be reached on bus No 9.

BORNHOLMS MIDDELALDER-CENTER

The new 10.5-hectare Bornholms Middelaldercenter *(Bornholm's Medieval Centre;* ☎ *56 49 83 19, Stangevej 1; adult/child 45kr/free, 60/25kr in July; open 9am-5pm daily May-Sept)* re-creates a medieval village. People in period dress operate a smithy, tend fields, grind wheat in a water mill and perform other chores of yesteryear throughout the summer months. However, the best time to visit is in July when the activity schedule is beefed up, adding falconry presentations, archery demonstrations as well as hands-on craft activities for children.

The medieval centre is 500m north of Østerlars Rundkirke and can be reached by bus No 9.

HELLIGDOMSKLIPPERNE

Perhaps because Denmark hasn't much in the way of hills or lofty rocks, those that it

MH

The distinctive Østerlars Rundkirke served as a defence and supply warehouse as well as a church.

does have are almost revered. Such is the case with Helligdomsklipperne (Sanctuary Cliffs), where moderately high **coastal cliffs** of sharp granite rock formations attract sightseers. About 5km north of Gudhjem on the eastern side of the main coastal road, the Helligdomsklipperne area also has **nature trails** and an art museum.

Bornholms Kunstmuseum (☎ 56 48 43 86, Helligdommen; adult/child 40kr/free; open 10am-5pm Tues-Sun May-Oct; 1pm-5pm Tues, Thur & Sat Nov-Apr), a 100-year-old museum housed in a stylish modern building, exhibits paintings by artists from the Bornholm School, including Olaf Rude, Oluf Høst and Edvard Weie, who painted during the first half of the 20th century. The museum also has works by other Danish artists, most notably paintings of Bornholm, by Skagen artist Michael Ancher. There's a cafe on site. Buses stop in front of the museum (bus No 2 from Rønne or Sandvig, bus No 7 between Gudhjem and Sandvig).

SANDVIG & ALLINGE
postcode 3770
Sandvig is a quiet little seaside hamlet with attractive older homes, many with rose bushes and tidy flower gardens. Sandvig itself is fronted by a sandy beach and borders a network of interesting walking trails (see the Hammeren section later in this chapter).

Allinge, the larger and more developed half of the Allinge-Sandvig municipality, is 2km south-east of Sandvig. Although not as quaint as Sandvig, Allinge has the lion's share of commercial facilities, including banks, grocery shops and the area's tourist office, Nordbornholms Turistbureau (☎ 56 48 00 01, fax 56 48 00 20), Kirkegade 4.

Seven kilometres south-east of Sandvig, in the small village of **Olsker**, is the most slender of the island's four round churches. If you take the inland bus to Rønne, you can stop off en route to visit the church or catch a passing glimpse of it as you ride by.

Places to Stay & Eat
Sandvig Familie Camping (☎ 56 48 04 47, fax 56 48 04 57, Sandlinien 5) 50kr per person. Open Apr-Oct. This three-star camping

ground on the northern side of Sandvig is backed by heathered hills and has an ideal location just minutes from the beach, nature trails and bus stop.

Danhostel Sandvig (☎ 56 48 03 62, fax 56 48 18 62, **e** danhostel.sandvig@get2net .dk, Hammershusvej 94) Dorm beds 100kr, singles/doubles 200/350kr. Open June-Sept. The hostel has a pleasant, rural location between Sandvig and Hammershus Slot, just 10 minutes' walk from the ruins and 100m from a bus stop. Breakfast is available but other meals are not served.

Hotel Pepita (☎ 56 48 04 51, fax 56 48 18 51, **e** pepita@post5-tele.dk, Langebjervej 1) Singles/doubles with bath 370/620kr. This convenient place in the centre of Sandvig has 36 reasonably priced rooms with amenities that include refrigerators and satellite TV. Breakfast is included in the rate.

Ella's Konditori (☎ 56 48 03 29, Strandgade 42) Light meals 50-80kr. Ella's relaxed eatery has a pretty garden setting and a menu that includes fish and chips, grilled chicken and salads.

There's a **snack bar** by the beach and a number of **restaurants** within easy walking distance of the camping ground.

HAMMERSHUS SLOT
The impressive 13th-century castle ruins of Hammershus Slot, dramatically perched on top of a sea cliff, are the largest in Scandinavia. It is thought that construction was begun around 1250 by the Archbishop of Lund, who wanted a fortress to protect his diocese against the Crown, which at that time was engaged in a power struggle with the Church. In the centuries that followed, the castle was enlarged, with the upper levels of the square tower added on during the mid-16th century.

Eventually, improvements in naval artillery left the fortress walls vulnerable to attack and in 1645 the castle temporarily fell to Swedish troops after a brief bombardment. Hammershus not only served as a military garrison but also as a prison; from 1660 to 1661 King Christian IV's daughter, Leonora Christine, was imprisoned here on treason charges.

In 1743 the Danish military abandoned Hammershus and many of the stones were carried away to be used as building materials elsewhere. Still, there's much to see and you shouldn't miss a stroll through these extensive fortress ruins. The grounds are always open and admission is free.

Looking north from the coastal sections of the ruins you can see Hammer Havn, a little harbour that was originally built to carry quarried rock to Germany but now shelters yachts, and beyond it Hammeren, a rocky jut of land that's set aside as a nature reserve.

Getting There & Away
There's an hourly bus (No 7) from Sandvig to Hammershus Slot, but the most enjoyable way to get there is via footpaths through the hills of Hammeren – a wonderful hour's hike. The well-trodden trail begins by the Sandvig Familie Camping ground and the route is signposted.

If you're coming from Rønne, bus No 1 makes the trip to Hammershus Slot about once an hour.

HAMMEREN
Hammeren, the hammerhead-shaped crag of granite at the northern tip of Bornholm, is crisscrossed by **walking trails** leading through hillsides thick with purple heather. Some of the trails are inland, while others run along the coast.

In addition to just wandering about, you can follow trails between Sandvig and Hammershus Slot. The shortest route to Hammershus travels along the inland side of Hammeren and passes **Hammer Sø**, Bornholm's largest lake, and **Opalsøen**, a deep pond in an old rock quarry. A longer and more windswept route goes along the rocky outer rim of Hammeren, passes a **lighthouse** at Bornholm's northernmost point and continues south along the coast to a harbour, **Hammer Havn**.

From Hammershus Slot there are trails heading south through another heathered landscape in a nature area called **Slotslyngen**, and east through public woodlands to **Moseløkke granite quarry**. Moseløkke is also

the site of a small **museum** (☎ 56 48 04 68, Moseløkkevej 4; adult/child 20kr/free; open 10am-noon & 1pm-4pm Mon-Fri April-Oct) where you can see traditional rock-cutting techniques being demonstrated.

The whole area is a delight for people who enjoy nature walks. For a detailed map of the trails and terrain, pick up the free *Hammeren og Hammershus, Slotslyng* forestry brochure at any one of the island's tourist offices.

CHRISTIANSØ
postcode 3740 • pop 100
Tiny Christiansø is a charmingly preserved 17th-century fortress island one hour's sail north-east of Bornholm. The largest of a cluster of small granite islands known collectively as Ertholmene, Christiansø has an intriguing history.

A seasonal fishing hamlet since the Middle Ages, Christiansø fell briefly into Swedish hands in 1658, after which Christian V decided to turn the island into an invincible naval fortress. Bastions and barracks were built; a church, a school and a hospital followed. Christiansø became the Danish Navy's forward position in the Baltic, serving to monitor Swedish trade routes and in less congenial times as a base for attacks on Sweden.

In 1808, keen on capturing Christiansø for its strategic significance, the British Navy bombarded the island but withdrew after it was unable to make a landing. The island also played an infamous role in Danish history when a jail was built in 1825 for political prisoners, the most famous of whom was Dr Dampe, an insurgent who railed against the despotism of Frederik VI.

By the 1850s Christiansø was no longer needed as a base for defence from Sweden and the navy withdrew. Soldiers who wanted to stay on as fishermen were allowed to live as free tenants in the old cottages. Their offspring, and a few latter-day fisherfolk and artists, currently comprise Christiansø's residents.

The entire island is an unspoiled reserve – there are no cats or dogs, no cars and no modern buildings allowed. Instead there's a sense of history conveyed by the old, stone-block fortifications and attractive yellow-washed houses.

Christiansø is connected to its smaller sister island, **Frederiksø**, by a footbridge.

Græsholm, the island to the north-west of Christiansø, is a wildlife refuge and an important breeding ground for guillemots, razorbills and other sea birds.

All of the Ertholmene Islands, including Christiansø and Frederiksø, serve as spring breeding grounds for up to 2000 eider ducks. The ducks nest near coastal paths and visitors should take care not to scare the mothers away from their nests because predator gulls will quickly swoop and attack the unattended eggs. Conservation laws also forbid the removal of any plants from this unique ecosystem.

Things to See & Do

A leisurely walk of around an hour is all that's needed to explore both Christiansø and Frederiksø – ideal for a day trip.

The two main sights are the two stone circular defence towers. **Lille Tårn** (Little Tower) on Frederiksø dates from 1685 and is the site of the **local-history museum** (☎ 56 46 20 71; adult/child 10/5kr; open 11.30am-4pm daily May-Sept). The ground floor features fishing supplies, hand tools and iron works; upstairs there are cannons, period furnishings, models and a display of local flora and fauna.

Christiansø's **Store Tårn** (Great Tower), built in 1684, is an impressive structure measuring a full 25m in diameter. The tower's 100-year-old **lighthouse** offers a splendid 360° view of the island; for 4kr you can climb to the top.

The main activity on Christiansø is the walk along the fortified stone walls and cannon-lined batteries that surround the perimeter of the island. There are skerries

(rocky islets) with nesting sea birds and a secluded **swimming cove** on Christiansø's eastern side.

Places to Stay & Eat

Duchess Battery (☎ 30 34 96 05) Camping per person 45kr. Camping is allowed in summer in a small field called the Duchess Battery, at the northern end of Christiansø, but because of limited space it can be difficult to book.

Christiansø Gæstgiveriet (☎ 56 46 20 15, fax 56 46 20 86) Doubles with breakfast 460kr. Open May-Oct. Built in 1730 as the naval commander's residence, this is the island's only inn. It has half a dozen rooms with shared bathrooms.

The inn has a moderately priced **restaurant** and there's a small **food store** and **snack shop** nearby.

Getting There & Away

Christiansøfarten (☎ 56 48 51 76, **W** www .christiansoefarten.dk) operates passenger ferries to Christiansø from Allinge and Gudhjem in the high season, while the mail/passenger boat from Svaneke makes the trip year-round.

A boat leaves Gudhjem at 10.15am daily from May to late September and departs from Christiansø for the return trip at 2.15pm. Between mid-June and August there's also a boat that leaves Gudhjem at 12.15pm daily.

A boat leaves Allinge at 12.45pm from Monday to Saturday between May and mid-September, departing from Christiansø at 4.30pm.

From Svaneke, a boat leaves at 10am (9.30am in winter) on weekdays, returning from Christiansø at 2.30pm (at 1.15pm during winter).

All boats charge 150kr return for a day trip and 250kr for an open return. Children aged from four to 14 pay half price.

Funen

Funen (Fyn) is the name of Denmark's second largest island as well as the county (Fyn Amt) that includes Funen island and about 90 neighbouring islands. While most of these nearby islands are small and privately owned, the largest three – Ærø, Langeland and Tåsinge – have appealing seaside towns and are fine destinations in themselves. All of Funen county has a bucolic character, with picturesque rural scenery and thatched farmhouses.

The main railway line from Copenhagen runs straight through Odense, Funen's main city, and west to Jutland, but it would be a shame to zip through without stopping to explore more of Funen. As well as Odense, places of special merit include Egeskov Slot, the historic maritime town of Faaborg and the unspoiled island of Ærø.

Odense

pop 185,000

Odense, which translates as 'Odin's shrine', was named after the powerful Nordic god of war, poetry and wisdom. The city's history dates back to pre-Viking times, with the first known reference to Odense appearing in a letter written by the German emperor Otto III in 988.

By the middle of the 18th century Odense was the largest provincial town in Denmark, with 5000 inhabitants. But it was the only major Danish town without a harbour and thus failed to benefit directly from the maritime trade that prospered in coastal towns such as Faaborg.

In 1800, in the largest construction project of that era, a canal was dug to connect Odense to the Odense Fjord, 5km to the north. With the new sea link Odense became an industrial city with products ranging from refined sugar to textiles.

Odense is now Denmark's third largest city, the capital of Funen county and a transportation hub for the region.

Highlights

- Admire Ærøskøbing's leaning half-timbered houses
- Wander around the cobblestone streets of Faaborg, an enjoyable coastal town
- Tour Egeskov Slot, a splendid moat-encircled Renaissance castle
- Explore the city of Odense with its interesting Gothic cathedral and intriguing museums
- Cycle through Funen's undulating countryside with its picturesque farms and villages
- Hop on a boat to one of the small islands off Funen's southern coast

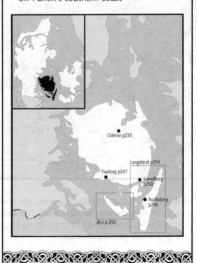

The city makes much ado about being the birthplace of Hans Christian Andersen, but Andersen himself got out of Odense as fast as he could, after a fairly unhappy childhood.

Whatever Andersen's experiences may have been, Odense today is an affable university city with lots of pedestrian streets

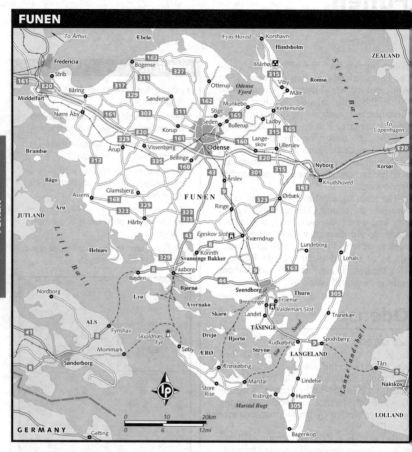

and cycle paths, an interesting cathedral and a number of museums worth a visit. It's also relatively light on the wallet, with two hostels and some good-value hotels.

Orientation

The train station is in a large modern complex called the Odense Banegård Center, which contains restaurants, shops, the public library and travel-related facilities. The tourist office, at rådhus, is a 10-minute walk south from the train station. The cathedral, Sankt Knuds Kirke, is on Klosterbakken, a two-minute walk from the tourist office,

and most other sights are also within walking distance of each other in the city centre.

Information

Tourist Offices The Odense Turistbureau (☎ 66 12 75 20, fax 66 12 75 86, ⓦ www .odenseturist.dk), Rådhuset, 5000 Odense C, is open 9am to 7pm Monday to Saturday and 10am to 5pm on Sunday from mid-June to August. It's open 9.30am to 4.30pm Monday to Friday and 10am to 1pm on Saturday from September to mid-June. The office is well stocked with regional brochures and handles everything from currency exchange outside banking hours to sales of hostel cards and the Odense Eventyrpas (see the boxed text 'Adventuring on the Cheap' for details).

Money There's a Sydbank (☎ 65 40 92 80) at Kongensgade 74 and a Unibank (☎ 66 12 73 25) at Vestergade 64.

Post & Communications The main post office (☎ 65 42 02 00), north of the train station at Dannebrogsgade 2, is open 9am to 6pm Monday to Friday and 9am to 1pm on Saturday. There's also a branch in the centre at Gråbrødrestræde 1, open until at least 5pm on weekdays and until 1pm on Saturday.

Net Café (☎ 65 91 02 78), Vindegade 43, offers inexpensive Internet access from noon to midnight daily.

Travel Agencies Kilroy Travels (☎ 66 17 77 80), Pantheonsgade 7, specialises in youth and discount travel.

Bookshops The GAD Bookshop (☎ 66 13 17 42) at Vestergade 37 and the Arnold Busck Bookshop (☎ 66 12 14 91) at Vestergade 82 both have good selections of books in English. Antikvariatet (☎ 66 13 35 76), Kongensgade 13, is a good place to pick up second-hand paperback novels at reasonable prices.

Libraries The library (☎ 66 14 88 14), in Odense Banegård Center, subscribes to a few English-language foreign newspapers. Library hours vary with the season; it's open 10am to at least 4pm Monday to Saturday from May to September. You can buy foreign newspapers at the kiosk on the 3rd floor of the same building.

Medical Services There's a 24-hour chemist, Ørnen Apoteket (☎ 66 12 29 70), at Vestergade 80.

Meet the Danes Staff at the tourist office can arrange for foreign travellers to meet with a Danish family at home for tea and conversation. Because they try to match people of similar ages and interests, you should request the 'Meet the Danes' program at least a day in advance. There's no fee.

Walking Tour

The following route takes in many of the city's historic sights and museums. Although the walk itself takes only about an hour, if you stop at all the sights along the way it could easily take you the better part of a day to complete the tour. (The major sights listed in this walk are described in more detail later in this section.)

Start at **rådhus**, the city hall, which is predominantly of 1950s vintage, though the west wing dates from the late 19th century. Hour-long tours of city hall (10kr) are conducted at 2pm Monday to Thursday in summer.

From rådhus head east on Vestergade, which becomes Overgade, and then turn right onto **Nedergade**, a cobblestone street with leaning half-timbered houses and antique shops.

At the end of Nedergade, a left turn onto Frue Kirkestræde will bring you to **Vor Frue Kirke** *(Admission free; open 10am-noon Mon-Fri)*, erected in the 13th century. It has a rather plain, whitewashed interior, though there's an ornate Baroque pulpit that dates from the mid-17th century.

From Vor Frue Kirke turn left back onto Overgade; you'll soon reach **Møntergården**,

FUNEN

Adventuring on the Cheap

The Odense Eventyrpas (Adventure Pass) gives free admission to most of the city sights, including the Hans Christian Andersen museums, Brandts Klædefabrik, Carl Nielsen Museet, Den Fynske Landsby, Fyns Kunstmuseum, Fyrtøjet, Møntergården and the Odense Zoo, and a 25% reduction on the Odense Åfart riverboat. The pass also includes unlimited use of buses and trains within the city limits.

If you're up to a lot of sightseeing, the pass is a real bargain at 85kr (40kr for children) for one day or 125kr (60kr for children) for two days. It can be purchased at the tourist office, the train station, the hostels and some hotels.

the city museum, and then turn right into Claus Bergs Gade, where you'll pass the city's only casino. Immediately to the north is the **Odense Koncerthus** (Concert Hall) and a museum dedicated to composer Carl Nielsen.

Just past the casino, turn left onto Ramsherred (which quickly changes into Hans Jensens Stræde) to reach the children's cultural centre, **Fyrtøjet**, and **HC Andersens Hus**, the principal museum dedicated to Hans Christian Andersen. The museum is in a pleasant neighbourhood of narrow cobbled streets and old tile-roofed houses. If you desire some green space there's a little **park and duck pond** south of the museum.

Continue down Hans Jensens Stræde, cross Thomas B Thriges Gade and follow Gravene to Slotsgade; **Fyns Kunstmuseum**, Odense's notable fine arts museum, is on the corner of Slotsgade and Jernbanegade. Turn left and proceed down Jernbanegade to Vestergade. Along the way you'll pass the site of **Gråbrødre Kloster**, a medieval Franciscan monastery that has been converted into a home for the elderly.

When you reach Vestergade, turn east back to rådhus and then go south to **Sankt Knuds Kirke**, Odense's intriguing cathedral. Opposite the cathedral, turn down Sankt Knuds Kirkestræde and then go south on Munkemøllestræde, where you'll pass **HC Andersens Barndomshjem**, the writer's childhood home.

Loop back around on Klosterbakken and take the path into the **HC Andersen Haven**, a riverside park with a prominent statue of the author. You can walk north through the park to get back to your starting point at rådhus.

Sankt Knuds Kirke

Odense's 12th-century Gothic cathedral (☎ *66 12 03 92, Flakhaven; Admission free; open 9am–5pm Mon-Sat, noon–3pm Sun Apr–Oct, 10am–4pm Mon-Sat, noon–3pm Sun Nov–Mar*) is one of the city's most interesting sights. It boasts an ornate gilded altar dating from 1521 that's considered the finest work of master woodcrafter Claus Berg. An intricately detailed triptych, the altar stands 5m high and has nearly 300

The Unsaintly Saint

Canute (Knud) II reigned over Denmark from 1080 to his untimely death six years later. A ruthless tyrant, Canute led Viking raids abroad and instituted numerous taxes at home, often using brutal methods to collect them.

In 1086 Canute, trying to evade a crowd of angry farmers who had pursued him from Jutland, fled into Sankt Albans Kirke in Odense in an attempt to take sanctuary. There, while kneeling before the altar, he was killed by the mob.

Although less than saintly, in 1101 Canute II was canonised as Canute the Holy by the pope in a move to secure both the Crown and Church in Denmark. Despite being Denmark's first saint, Canute the Holy has never been widely popular and his name is still invoked as a term of abuse among farmers in Jutland.

---

carved figures, most depicting the life and death of Christ, although the bottom row also works in King Hans on the left and Queen Christine on the right. It was Christine, a friend of Berg's, who commissioned the work. Berg also created the large limestone sepulchral monument bearing the king's and queen's portraits in bas-relief.

The cathedral's most intriguing attraction lies in the basement beneath the altar, where you'll find a glass case containing the 900-year-old skeleton of King Canute (Knud) II and another displaying the skeleton of his younger brother, Benedikt. An inconspicuous set of stairs leads from the right-hand side of the altar down to these basement treasures.

A few metres to the left of the coffins, steps lead down to the remains of Sankt Albans Kirke, which stood on this site before Sankt Knuds Kirke was built. It was at the altar of Sankt Albans Kirke that Canute II and Benedikt were killed during a tax revolt.

HC Andersens Hus

This museum (☎ *66 14 88 14, Hans Jensens Stræde 39; adult/child 35/15kr; open 9am–7pm daily mid-June–Aug, 10am–4pm Tues-Sun Sept–mid-June*), on a cobbled pedestrian

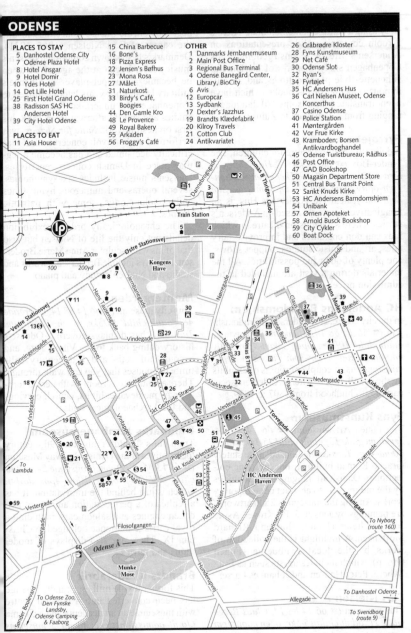

ODENSE

PLACES TO STAY
- 5 Danhostel Odense City
- 7 Odense Plaza Hotel
- 8 Hotel Ansgar
- 9 Hotel Domir
- 10 Ydes Hotel
- 14 Det Lille Hotel
- 25 First Hotel Grand Odense
- 38 Radisson SAS HC Andersen Hotel
- 39 City Hotel Odense

PLACES TO EAT
- 11 Asia House
- 15 China Barbecue
- 16 Bone's
- 18 Pizza Express
- 22 Jensen's Bøfhus
- 23 Mona Rosa
- 27 Målet
- 31 Naturkost
- 33 Birdy's Café, Boogies
- 44 Den Gamle Kro
- 48 Le Provence
- 49 Royal Bakery
- 55 Arkaden
- 56 Froggy's Café

OTHER
- 1 Danmarks Jernbanemuseum
- 2 Main Post Office
- 3 Regional Bus Terminal
- 4 Odense Banegård Center, Library, BioCity
- 6 Avis
- 12 Europcar
- 13 Sydbank
- 17 Dexter's Jazzhus
- 19 Brandts Klædefabrik
- 20 Kilroy Travels
- 21 Cotton Club
- 24 Antikvariatet
- 26 Gråbrødre Kloster
- 28 Fyns Kunstmuseum
- 29 Net Café
- 30 Odense Slot
- 32 Ryan's
- 34 Fyrtøjet
- 35 HC Andersens Hus
- 36 Carl Nielsen Museet, Odense Koncerthus
- 37 Casino Odense
- 40 Police Station
- 41 Møntergården
- 42 Vor Frue Kirke
- 43 Kramboden; Borsen Antikvardboghandel
- 45 Odense Turistbureau; Rådhus
- 46 Post Office
- 47 GAD Bookshop
- 50 Magasin Department Store
- 51 Central Bus Transit Point
- 52 Sankt Knuds Kirke
- 53 HC Andersens Barndomshjem
- 54 Unibank
- 57 Ørnen Apoteket
- 58 Arnold Busck Bookshop
- 59 City Cykler
- 60 Boat Dock

FUNEN

FUNEN

street, tells Hans Christian Andersen's life story using a barrage of memorabilia. There's a room containing slide presentations on Andersen's life, a reconstruction of his Copenhagen study, displays of his fanciful silhouette-style paper cuttings and a voluminous selection of his books, which have been translated into some 80 languages ranging from Azerbaijani to Zulu.

Fyrtøjet

A delightful cultural centre for children, The Tinder Box (☎ 66 14 44 11, Hans Jensens Stræde 21; admission 35kr; open 9.30am-7pm daily June-Aug, 10am-4pm Tues-Sun Sept-May), near HC Andersens Hus, is an imaginative playworld based on Andersen's stories. There's a hands-on theatre in which kids can don costumes and improvise fairy tales; art and music studios; puppet shows; and plenty of other fun possibilities. All the materials during a visit are included in the admission price.

HC Andersens Barndomshjem

In the city centre, HC Andersens Barndomshjem (☎ 66 14 88 14, Munkemøllestræde 3; adult/child 10/5kr; open 10am-4pm daily mid-June–Aug, 11am-3pm Tues-Sun Sept–mid-June) has a couple of rooms of exhibits in the small home where Andersen spent part of his childhood from 1807 to 1819.

Fyns Kunstmuseum

The Funen Art Museum (☎ 66 14 88 14, Jernbanegade 13; adult/child 25/10kr; open 10am-4pm Tues-Sun), housed in a stately Graeco-Roman building, boasts a fine collection of Danish art, ranging from paintings by the old masters to abstract contemporary works. Among the museum's 2500 artworks are paintings by Jens Juel, PS Krøyer, Asger Jorn, Vilhelm Hammershøi and Richard Mortensen. A highlight is the collection of works by the local Fynboerne (Funen Group), which includes artists such as Fritz Syberg, Peter Hansen and Johannes Larsen.

Carl Nielsen Museet

This museum (☎ 66 14 88 14, Claus Bergs Gade 11; adult/child 15/5kr; open noon-4pm Tues-Sun June-Aug, noon-4pm Thurs-Sun Sept-May), in the Odense Koncerthus, details the career of Carl Nielsen (1865–1931), Denmark's best-known composer. Nielsen's music career began at the age of 14 when he became a trumpet player in Odense's military band. Four years later he moved to Copenhagen to undertake formal music studies and shortly afterwards, in 1888, his first orchestral work, Suite for Strings, was performed at the Tivoli concert hall. It was critically acclaimed and has become a regular piece in Danish concert repertories. Nielsen's music includes six symphonies, several operas and numerous hymn tunes and popular songs, some with patriotic themes.

The chronologically ordered exhibition details not only the life of Nielsen but also that of his wife, sculptor Anne Marie Brodersen. Displays include Brodersen's works and studio and Nielsen's study and piano.

Møntergården

This city museum (☎ 66 14 88 14, Overgade 48; adult/child 15/5kr; open 10am-4pm Tues-Sun) has displays covering Odense's history dating back to the Viking Age, and a couple of 16th- and 17th-century half-timbered houses that you can walk through. There are numerous rooms with period furnishings, medieval exhibits, church carvings and local archaeological finds.

Danmarks Jernbanemuseum

Train buffs shouldn't miss the 19th-century locomotives at the Danish Railway Museum (☎ 66 13 66 30, Dannebrogsgade 24; adult/child 30/10kr; open 10am-4pm daily), which is just behind the train station. It has a replica of a period station and about two dozen engines and saloon cars, including a royal carriage that once belonged to Christian IX. There are also displays of model trains and ferries.

Brandts Klædefabrik

This former textile mill on Brandts Passage has been converted into a cultural centre with museums, an art academy and a cinema (Joint admission ticket to all 3 museums

50kr; open 10am-5pm daily July & Aug, 10am-5pm Tues-Sun).

The **Danmarks Grafiske Museum/Dansk Pressemuseum** *(Danish Graphic Museum/ Danish Press Museum; ☎ 66 12 10 20; admission 25kr)* traces the development of printing in Denmark over the last three centuries. One section covers old-fashioned lithography, engraving, bookbinding and paper-making, and the other concentrates on newspaper production. Former workers, now retired, re-enact the techniques they used in their working days (such as setting cold type), which have been made obsolete by computerised presses.

Museet for Fotokunst *(Museum of Photographic Art; ☎ 66 13 78 16; admission 25kr)*, dedicated to the art of photography, has both a permanent collection and changing exhibitions by national and international photographers.

Kunsthallen *(☎ 66 13 78 97; admission 30kr)*, a modern art gallery, has four large halls with changing exhibitions focusing on new trends in the visual arts. Displays include paintings, sculpture and installations as well as exhibits on Scandinavian design. There's also a videotheque with a library of art videos that can be viewed by visitors.

Odense Slot

Kongens Have, the park directly opposite the train station, is the site of Odense Slot, a two-storey castle with red-tiled roofs and a cobbled courtyard. Modest as castles go, it was erected in 1720 by Frederik IV to serve as a royal residence during his visits to Odense. The king died here in 1730, a victim of tuberculosis. Odense Slot was later converted into a governor's residence and now serves as administrative offices for the municipal and county governments. It's not open to visitors but you can stroll through the grounds.

Den Fynske Landsby

This delightful open-air museum *(The Funen Village; ☎ 66 14 88 14, Sejerskovvej 20; take bus No 42; adult/child 35/15kr; open 9.30am-7pm daily mid-June–mid-Aug, 10am-5pm Tues-Sun mid-Aug–Oct &*
Apr–mid-June, 11am-3pm Sun Nov-Mar) contains furnished period buildings laid out as they might have been in a small country village of the mid-19th century, complete with barnyard animals, a duck pond, apple trees and flower gardens. There are about two dozen thatched houses and farm buildings in all, including a windmill, a water mill and a smithy, which have been moved here from rural areas in Funen.

Den Fynske Landsby is in a green zone 4km south of the city centre. In summer you can take the boat operated by Odense Åfart (see Boat under Getting Around later in this section) and get off at Erik Bøghs Sti, from where it's a refreshing 15-minute woodland walk south-east along the river to Den Fynske Landsby.

Odense Zoo

Denmark's second largest zoo *(☎ 66 11 13 60, Sondre Boulevard 306; take bus No 31; adult/child 75/40kr; open daily year-round: 9am-7pm July, 9am-6pm May, June & Aug, 9am-at least 4pm Sept-Apr)* borders the river Odense Å, 2km south of the city centre. Some of the animals on display include tigers, lions, giraffes, zebras, chimpanzees and colourful African birds and there's a new 'oceanium' with penguins and manatees.

Odense Åfart (see Boat under Getting Around later in this section) stops at the zoo, or you could walk the entire way along the wooded riverside path that begins at Munke Mose.

Places to Stay

Camping *Odense Camping (☎ 66 11 47 02, fax 65 91 73 43, e odense@dcu.dk, Odensevej 102, 5260 Odense S)* Bus No 21 or 22. Camping per person 58kr. Open year-round. This pleasant three-star camping ground is in a wooded area not far from Den Fynske Landsby, 3.5km south of the city centre. It has cooking and laundry facilities and cabins for hire.

Hostels & Rooms *Danhostel Odense*
(☎ 66 13 04 25, fax 65 91 28 63, W www .odense-danhostel.dk, Kragsbjergvej 121, 5230 Odense M) Bus No 61 or 62. Dorm

beds 94kr, doubles 310kr. Open 15 Feb-30 Nov. This hostel is in an exclusive suburb 2km south-east of the city centre. The hostel buildings, formerly a manor house, surround a cobbled courtyard and are half-timbered; the interior has been renovated and the rooms are modern. The 168 beds are mostly in four-bed rooms.

Danhostel Odense City (☎ 63 11 04 25, fax 63 11 35 20, Østre Stationsvej 31, W www .cityhostel.dk, 5000 Odense C) Dorm beds 100kr, doubles 320kr. Open year-round. You can't be more central than at this new hostel, which is right at the train station in a renovated 19th-century hotel. It has 143 beds in 39 rooms, each room with its own bathroom.

The tourist office can book *rooms* in private homes for 175/300kr for singles/ doubles, plus a 25kr booking fee.

Hotels *Det Lille Hotel* (☎/fax 66 12 28 21, Dronningensgade 5, 5000 Odense C) Singles/ doubles with shared bathroom 250/380kr. This guesthouse-like place with 14 straightforward rooms is a 10-minute walk west of the train station. The room rates also include breakfast.

Hotel Domir (☎ 66 12 14 27, fax 66 12 14 13, Hans Tausensgade 19, e reception@ ydes.dk, 5000 Odense C) Singles/doubles 390/480kr, including breakfast. This 35-room hotel has reasonable prices and is in a convenient spot just minutes from the train station. The rooms are cheery with phone, desk, TV and bath.

Ydes Hotel (☎ 66 12 11 31, fax 66 12 17 82, Hans Tausensgade 11, e reception@ ydes.dk, 5000 Odense C) Singles/doubles 330/450kr, including breakfast. Domir's nearby sister-operation, the Ydes Hotel has 26 compact but spotlessly clean and modern rooms with TV, desk and bath.

Hotel Ansgar (☎ 66 11 96 93, fax 66 11 96 75, Østre Stationsvej 32, e ansgar@ email.dk, 5000 Odense C) Singles/doubles 565/795kr, summer & weekends 525/650kr, including breakfast. This central hotel has pleasantly renovated rooms with TV, minibar and bath. Overall the rooms are on a par with some of the city's top-end hotels but it

also offers some reasonable weekend and summer rates.

City Hotel Odense (☎ 66 12 12 58, fax 66 12 93 64, e reception@city-hotel-odense .dk, Hans Mules Gade 5, 5000 Odense C) Singles/doubles 795/895kr. Convenient to a number of the city's museums, this modern hotel has 43 inviting rooms with full amenities, free parking, a good breakfast and friendly service.

Odense Plaza Hotel (☎ 66 11 77 45, fax 66 14 41 45, e info@odenseplaza.dk, Østre Stationsvej 24, 5000 Odense C) Singles/ doubles 1025/1250kr; weekend & summer rate (2 adults, 2 children) 795kr, including breakfast. This period hotel south-west of the train station is a member of the Best Western chain. It has 68 well-appointed rooms and a pleasant sunroom where a better-than-average breakfast is served.

First Hotel Grand Odense (☎ 66 11 71 71, fax 66 14 11 71, Jernbanegade 18, e odense@firsthotels.dk, 5100 Odense C) Singles/doubles from 895/1095kr. The city's other historic hotel, the central First Hotel Grand has a variety of rooms, most of them large and all with full amenities including minibars.

Radisson SAS HC Andersen Hotel (☎ 66 14 78 00, fax 66 14 78 90, Claus Bergs Gade 7, W www.radisson.com/odensedk, 5000 Odense C) Singles/doubles 1050/1195kr. The rooms at this contemporary four-storey hotel have the expected amenities and there's a casino on site.

Places to Eat

Budget Bakeries and cheap fast-food outlets are easy to find all around the city. The *Royal Bakery* (☎ 66 12 06 17, Vestergade 26) has good pastries and during the summer monthsit sets up a pavement stand selling organic ice cream.

On Wednesday and Saturday mornings there's a large *produce market* along Claus Bergs Gade, the pedestrian street that runs south from the Odense Koncerthus.

At the train station you'll find a *bakery* with both eat-in and takeaway items, some *fast-food eateries* and a small *grocery store* that's open until midnight. There are more cheap eateries and fast-food chains on the pedestrian street Kongensgade.

Pizza Express (☎ 65 91 09 03, *Vindegade 73)* Pizza 39kr, sandwiches 25kr. Open 3pm-11pm Tues-Thur, 3pm-2am Fri & Sat. Pizza Express has numerous varieties of thin-crust takeaway pizza as well as pitta-bread sandwiches.

Café Biografen (☎ 66 13 16 16, *Brandts Passage 43)* Dishes 30-65kr. Open 11am-at least midnight daily; kitchen closes 9pm. This French-influenced cafe is a popular student haunt offering inexpensive pastries, coffees, light meals and beer.

Naturkost (☎ 66 13 70 13, *Gravene 8)* Open 9am-5.30pm Mon-Fri, 9am-1pm Sat. This is a well-stocked health-food shop. There are also conventional *grocery stores* along the pedestrian section of Vestergade.

Mid-Range There are moderately priced restaurants and cafes along both Vestergade and Kongensgade, many of which chalk up daily specials. One cluster can be found at the *Arkaden* complex, at the southern end of Kongensgade on Vestergade, which contains Greek, Italian, Brazilian and a few other ethnic restaurants offering lunchtime specials for around 50kr and full dinners for about 100kr.

Froggy's Café (☎ 65 90 74 47, *Vestergade 68)* Light meals 40-60kr. Open 11am-2am daily. A good people-watching spot overlooking the main pedestrian street, Froggy's has reasonably priced burgers, pastas, omelettes and salads.

Jensen's Bøfhus (☎ 66 14 59 59, *Kongensgade 10)* Dinner mains around 90kr, lunch specials 40kr. Open 11am-11pm daily. Part of a nationwide chain, it offers grilled chicken and steaks at dinner, and cheap lunch specials. There's a second Jensen's Bøfhus at the train station.

Målet (☎ 66 17 82 41, *Jernbanegade 17)* Schnitzel 79kr. Open 11am-10pm daily for food, 11pm for drinks. This sports pub and restaurant features 10 different kinds of schnitzel.

Birdy's Café (☎ 66 14 00 39, *Nørregade 23)* Dishes around 75kr. Open 4pm-after midnight Mon-Sat. You can get international fare such as Mexican fajitas or Indian curry at this popular student spot.

China Barbecue (☎ 66 13 66 16, *Kongensgade 66)* Lunch/dinner buffet 49/88kr. Open lunch noon-3pm Mon-Sat, dinner 5.30pm-at least 10pm nightly. Here you can get a good-value Chinese buffet with six different dishes at lunch and 10 at dinner.

Mona Rosa (☎ 65 91 49 13, *Vintapper-stræde 4)* Lunch dishes 60kr, dinner 100kr. Open noon-10pm daily. This popular place on a quiet side street has a pleasant atmosphere and serves Mexican fare, steaks and salads.

Top End *Bone's* (☎ 66 11 18 16, *Vindegade 53)* Sparerib meal 120kr. Open 4.30-10.30pm Sun-Fri, noon-10.30pm Sat. This popular place specialises in spareribs – servings are generous and include a serving from the salad bar. On Monday to Thursday if you dine before 7pm you can get a 25% 'early birdy' discount.

Asia House (☎ 66 12 19 24, *Østre Stationsvej 40)* A la carte mains 100kr, buffet 139kr. Open from 5pm nightly. Head here for delicious, authentic Thai food. Best time is Friday or Saturday night, when there's a grand buffet spread.

Le Provence (☎ 66 12 12 96, *Pogestræde 31)* 3-course meal from 168kr. Open 5.30pm-midnight Mon-Sat. This pleasant French restaurant on a quiet back street in the city centre offers cosy candlelit dinners.

Den Gamle Kro (☎ 66 12 14 33, *Overgade 23)* Lunch/dinner around 125/250kr. Open 10am-10.30pm Mon-Sat, 10am-9.30pm Sun. This restaurant, which is located in a historic building dating from 1683, offers traditional Danish fare. There are a few dining rooms, the most atmospheric in the brick-vaulted cellar.

Entertainment
Ryan's (☎ 65 91 53 00, *Fisketorvet 12)* University students hang out at this friendly Irish pub near rådhus. It has Guinness and Kilkenny on tap, and in the evening there's often live Irish folk music.

Boogies (☎ 66 14 00 39, *Nørregade 23)* In the same building as Birdy's Café, Boogies is a dance spot popular with students.

FUNEN

FUNEN

Dexter's Jazzhus (☎ 66 13 68 88, Vindegade 65) This is a good place to hear jazz; there's live music from Thursday to Saturday.

Cotton Club (☎ 66 19 38 55, Pantheonsgade 5) The Cotton Club, which also has weekend jazz, tends to attract an older crowd.

Casino Odense (☎ 66 14 91 50, Claus Bergs Gade 7) At this casino in the Radisson SAS HC Andersen Hotel you can try your luck at blackjack, roulette and slot machines.

Odense Koncerthus (☎ 66 12 44 80, Claus Bergs Gade 9) Symphony orchestra and other classical music performances are held here, with a program that commonly includes works by native son Carl Nielsen.

BioCity (☎ 70 13 12 11, Odense Banegård Center) If you're up for a movie this new cinema features the largest screen in Denmark and it's eminently convenient – right at the train station!

Café Biografen (☎ 66 13 16 16, Brandts Passage 43) This cafe, at Brandts Klædefabrik, also screens first-run movies, but often has art-house flicks as well.

Brandts Klædefabrik (☎ 66 13 78 97, Brandts Passage) This venue is an open-air amphitheatre that holds free summertime rock, jazz and blues concerts, particularly on Saturday.

The *outdoor cafes* on Vintapperstræde are good spots for a quiet evening drink.

Lambda (☎ 66 17 76 92, Vindegade 100) This gay and lesbian organisation hosts occasional events.

Shopping

You can find a wide variety of clothing and speciality shops in the city centre along Kongensgade and Vestergade.

Magasin (☎ 66 11 92 11, Vestergade 20) The city's largest department store, Magasin stocks just about everything from food delicacies to cosmetics and clothing.

Kramboden (☎ 66 11 45 22, Nedergade 24) The place to head for antiques, Kramboden offers the buyer an interesting hotchpotch of items including porcelain, toys, glass and pewter.

Borsen Antikvarboghandel (☎ 66 11 37 76, Nedergade 26) Next door to Kramboden, this shop specialises in antique books.

Getting There & Away

Odense is 34km west of Nyborg, 44km north-west of Svendborg, 37km north-east of Faaborg and 50km east of the bridge to Jutland.

Bus Regional buses leave from the bus station at Dannebrogsgade 6, at the rear of the train station. There are bus services from Odense to all major towns on Funen (see individual destinations for bus information).

Train Odense is on the main railway line between Copenhagen (188kr, 1½ hours) and Århus (164kr, 1¾ hours) via Nyborg (37kr, 20 minutes); the service is frequent throughout the day. The only other train route in Funen is the hourly run between Odense and Svendborg (52kr, one hour).

Car & Motorcycle Odense is to the north of the E20; you can exit the E20 and go into the city via route 9, 43 or 168. Odense is connected to Nyborg by route 160 and the E20, to Kerteminde by route 165, to Jutland by the E20, to Faaborg by route 43 and to Svendborg by route 9.

Cars can be rented from Avis (☎ 66 14 39 99), Østre Stationsvej 37; Europcar (☎ 66 14 15 44), Kongensgade 69; and Hertz (☎ 66 14 90 96), in the Odense Banegård Center.

Getting Around

Bus The main transit point for city buses is in front of Sankt Knuds Kirke. The fare is 11kr.

Car & Motorcycle Outside rush hour, driving in Odense is not difficult, but many of the central sights are on pedestrian streets and it's best to park your car and explore on foot.

Near the city centre, there's metered parking along the streets, but spaces fill quickly. A better bet is the large multistorey car park on the northern side of Filosofgangen or the smaller car parks around Brandts Klædefabrik and at the northern side of Carl Nielsen Museet.

Taxi Taxis are readily available at the train station, or you can order one by phoning Odense Taxa (☎ 66 15 44 15).

Bicycle Hire bikes at City Cykler (☎ 66 13 97 83), Vesterbro 27, from 50kr per day.

Boat From May to August, Odense Åfart (☎ 65 95 79 96) runs a little covered boat down the Odense Å to Erik Bøghs Sti, a landing in the woods at Fruens Bøge. The boat departs from Munke Mose, to the south-west of the city centre, at 10am, 11am, 1pm, 2pm, 3pm and 5pm (and also at noon and 4pm between June and mid-August). Take it as a 70-minute return excursion or break your journey at the zoo or the woods. The cost is 30/45kr one-way/return, 18/27kr for children.

Around Funen Island

The island of Funen, nicknamed 'Denmark's garden island', is largely rural and green, with rolling woodlands, pastures, wheat fields and lots of old farmhouses. The terrain is gentler in the north, where it eventually levels out to marshland, and more hilly in the south. In May the landscape is ablaze with solid patches of yellow rapeseed flowers.

NYBORG
postcode 5800 • pop 15,800

Nyborg is the easternmost town on Funen and the western terminus of the Store Bælt bridge. While most people pass right through the town without pause, seeing little more than its industrial harbourfront, Nyborg can make an enjoyable stop for those with time to spare.

The most appealing part of town is around Torvet, the main square, where there is an attractive brick rådhus, the remains of a medieval castle and some classic half-timbered houses. All are just few hundred metres apart and only a 10-minute walk west of the train station.

There are white-sand beaches on the east of town, about 1.5km from the centre.

Information

The Nyborg Turistbureau (☎ 65 31 02 80, fax 65 31 03 80), Torvet 9, is open 9am to 5pm Monday to Friday and 9am to 2pm on Saturday mid-June to August; 9am to 4pm Monday to Friday and 9.30am to 12.30pm on Saturday from September to mid-June.

Nyborg Slot

Nyborg Slot (☎ 65 31 02 07, Slotsgade 11; adult/child 30/15kr; open 10am-4pm daily June & Aug, 10am-5pm July, 10am-3pm daily Mar-May & Sept-Oct) was one of half a dozen fortresses erected in strategic locations during the late 12th century to secure Denmark's coast. In 1282 Erik V, under pressure from nobles who wanted to limit royal power, signed an important charter here that established an annual parliament known as the Danehof. The castle was used as a royal residence for centuries and was the birthplace of King Christian II.

The fortress once had an enclosing defence wall and four corner towers but only part of the original structure remains. Two of the towers fell victim to earlier modifications and in 1870 most of the ramparts were torn down to make room for the town's expansion.

Still, what does remain is fun to explore. The **Danehof room**, where the Danehof met, has walls painted with an intriguing 16th-century, three-dimensional cube design that seems strikingly contemporary. You'll find old royal paintings, suits of armour, antique guns and swords. You can climb a spiral staircase to the loft and walk along the running boards past the machicolations through which boiling tar was once poured onto attacking Swedes.

Mads Lerches Gård

This engaging half-timbered merchant's house (☎ 65 31 02 07, Slotsgade 11; adult/ child 30/15kr; open 10am-4pm daily July & Aug, 10am-3pm Tues-Sun May, June & Sept), built in 1601 and just south of Nyborg Slot, has displays of local cultural history. Some of its 30 rooms have period furnishings, others the usual assortment of old toys, model ships and antique tools.

Vor Frue Kirke

This church (Gammel Torv 1; admission free; open 9am-6pm daily June-Aug, 9am-4pm

FUNEN

Going Local

Funen has a countywide B&B association that encompasses 100 homes. Some are modern places right in the city, others are centuries-old farmhouses in quiet countryside settings. Staying in one of these B&Bs is a great way to experience a slice of Denmark up close, to sit down at the breakfast table and rub shoulders with local families.

The association publishes an annually updated catalogue with a photo of each B&B along with a brief description that includes the number of guestrooms, the price, and information on facilities available, such as a kitchen, TV or play area for children. The descriptions also note which foreign languages each host speaks – the majority speak English and German, but some also speak French. Pictograms let you know which places have farm animals and which are close to good angling spots, hiking trails or beaches. The catalogue includes a map of Funen county with the location of each B&B.

Prices, which include breakfast, bed linen and a towel, range from 165kr to 225kr per person based on double occupancy. The per-person charge runs a little higher for singles and a bit lower if there are more than two people to a room.

Advance reservations are advised, especially in the high season, and because many of the hosts work outside their homes it's wise to call at least an evening ahead to make arrangements at any time of the year. You can pick up the catalogue free at any tourist office in Funen.

Sept-May), Nyborg's central place of worship, dates from 1388 but has been altered many times over the years, most extensively in 1870. Its beautifully detailed Baroque pulpit was carved in 1653 by Anders Mortensen of Odense. From left to right the pulpit sections depict the birth of John the Baptist, Christ's baptism, the Transfiguration, the Resurrection and the Ascension. There's also a wooden baptismal font dating from 1585. Entry is via the small southern door on Korsbrødregade.

Places to Stay

Nyborg Strandcamping (☎ 65 31 02 56, fax 65 31 07 56, e mail@strandcamping.dk, Hjejlevej 99) Camping per person 54kr. Open Apr-Sept. This three-star camping ground, on a white-sand beach about 2km east of the town centre, has a view of the Store Bælt bridge.

Hotel Villa Gulle (☎ 65 30 11 88, fax 65 30 11 33, e post@villagulle.dk, Østervoldgade 44) Singles/doubles 325/475kr, with bath 425/625kr. This hotel, which has 26 straightforward rooms, is the cheapest in town.

Hotel Hesselet (☎ 65 31 30 29, fax 65 31 29 58, e hotel@hesselet.dk, Christianslundsvej 119) Singles/doubles 1090/1590kr. The Hesselet, in a quiet spot 2km north-east

of town, is one of Funen's most exclusive hotels. Its 46 rooms have modern amenities and, in most cases, ocean views. There's an indoor swimming pool, a billiards room and a lounge with a fireplace.

Hotel Nyborg Strand (☎ 65 31 31 31, fax 65 31 37 01, e nyborgstrand@nyborgstrand .dk, Østerøvej 2) Singles/doubles 905/1125kr, weekend & summer family rates 795kr. This large Best Western hotel, with 240 rooms, is north of Hotel Hesselet.

Places to Eat

There are several places to eat in the streets south of Torvet.

Gertz Conditori (☎ 65 31 00 96, Kongegade 16) Light meals 25kr. On sunny days sit outside and enjoy pastries and sandwiches at one of the pavement tables.

Fiskehallen (☎ 65 31 16 60, Korsgade 11) Fish & chips 25kr. This fish shop offers fresh takeaway seafood.

Pappas Pizzaria (☎ 65 31 69 69, Korsgade 10) Pizza 40kr. This is a good choice for reasonably priced pizza.

Restaurant Østervemb (☎ 65 30 10 70, Mellemgade 18) Lunch about 120kr, 3-course dinner 268kr. For a treat try this atmospheric restaurant, which specialises in fresh seafood and home-style Danish food.

Getting There & Away
Nyborg is on the E20, 34km east of Odense. Trains run an average of twice an hour between Nyborg and Odense (37kr, 20 minutes).

KERTEMINDE
postcode 5300 • pop 5500
Kerteminde is a seaside town with a pleasantly slow pace and a couple of minor sights. While it still has a few fishing boats, the town's waterfront has largely been given over to leisure craft, with yachties comprising the lion's share of Kerteminde's visitors.

Kerteminde is fronted by a harbour and a long marina, but there are sandy beaches on both sides of the town: Nordstranden extends from the northern end of the marina, Sydstranden begins on the southern side of the harbour. A statue of Amanda the fishergirl, a town symbol of sorts, stands on the southern side of the Langebro, the bridge that crosses the Kerteminde Fjord and connects the northern and southern parts of Kerteminde.

Information
Kerteminde Turistbureau (☎ 65 32 11 21, fax 65 32 18 17) is in the town centre at Strandgade 1B. It's open 9am to 5pm Monday to Saturday between mid-June and August, and 9am to 4pm on weekdays and 9.30am to 12.30pm on Saturday from September to mid-June.

There are a few banks in the town centre, including a Danske Bank (☎ 63 32 07 00) at Langegade 31. The post office (☎ 63 21 68 68) is at Strand-vejen 4, immediately south of the bus station.

Museums
The local-history museum **Farvergården** (☎ 65 32 37 27, Langegade 8; adult/child 15kr/free; open 10am-4pm Tues-Sun Mar-Oct), in the town centre, is in a handsome, half-timbered farm building erected in 1630. Many of the rooms remain as they would have been in centuries past, with period furnishings, pottery and paintings.

Johannes Larsen Museet (☎ 65 32 11 71, Møllebakken 14; adult/child 40kr/free; open 10am-5pm daily June-Aug, 10am-4pm Tues-Sun Sept-May), on the northern side of town, is in the artist's former home and retains its original furniture and decor. Larsen (1867–1961), one of the Fynboerne painters, is known for his paintings of wildlife and provincial Danish scenes. Also here is **Svanemøllen**, a windmill dating from 1853, and a modern 15-room exhibition centre with paintings by several dozen artists. This museum has parking spaces for disabled people only; other travellers with cars should use the car park at the corner of Hindsholmvej and Marinavejen.

Romsø
For a quiet outing, consider a visit to the island of Romsø, a 30-minute boat ride from Kerteminde. The only residents are the boatman's family, about 200 deer and numerous rabbits and birds. You can walk a 3km coastal trail around the 109 hectare island or just soak up the solitude. Bring a picnic lunch because there are no facilities.

The Romsø-Båden boat service (☎ 65 32 13 77) takes passengers to the island on Wednesday and Saturday, departing from Kerteminde at 9am and from Romsø at 3pm. Reservations are required. The return trip costs 85kr for adults and 45kr for children.

Places to Stay
Kerteminde Camping (☎ 65 32 19 71, fax 65 32 18 71, e kerteminde camp@dk-camp .dk, Hindsholmvej 80) Camping per person 55kr. Open Apr-Sept. This three-star camping ground is opposite the beach and just 1.5km north of the town centre.

Danhostel Kerteminde (☎ 65 32 39 29, fax 65 32 39 24, e info@dkhostel.dk, Skovvej 46) Dorm beds 100kr, private room for 1-3 people 300kr. Open Jan–mid-Dec. This hostel is at the edge of a pleasant wooded area just a five-minute walk from a sandy beach and 15 minutes south of the town centre. The 30 rooms each have a maximum of four beds, a shower and a toilet.

The tourist office can provide a list of ***rooms*** in private homes for singles/doubles costing around 200/300kr.

Tornøes Hotel (☎ 65 32 16 05, fax 65 32 48 40, e tornoes@tornoeshotel.dk, Strandgade 2) Singles/doubles 450/550kr, with bath

FUNEN

595/795kr. This 27-room hotel has an ideal location, on the harbour right in the centre of town.

Places to Eat

There are a few places right in the centre where you can grab something inexpensive to eat.

Burger Caféen (☎ 65 32 18 78, Lange-gade 19) Light meals 20-40kr. This central fast-food eatery has ice cream, burgers and a variety of sandwiches.

Restaurant Sejlklub (☎ 65 32 24 53, Marinavej 2) Dishes 50-100kr. For afford-able waterfront dining, this place at the yacht marina on the northern side of town offers beef and seafood dishes, and both in-door and patio seating. It's also a nice spot to have a cold beer on a sunny afternoon.

Rudolf Mathis (☎ 65 32 32 33, Dosserin-gen 13) 3-course lunch/dinner 265/395kr. This waterside restaurant on the southern side of Kerteminde harbour specialises in fresh fish and is widely regarded as one of Funen's best restaurants.

Getting There & Around

Kerteminde is on route 165, 19km north-west of Nyborg and 21km north-east of Odense.

There are hourly bus services connecting Kerteminde with Odense (Nos 885 and 890) and Nyborg (Nos 890 and 891). Both of these routes take about 35 minutes and cost 27kr.

Amanda Cykler (☎ 65 32 21 32), Hans Schacksvej 5, hires bicycles for 50kr per day.

LADBYSKIBET

The remains of a 22m-long Viking ship have been preserved in Ladby, at the site where it was originally excavated in 1935. The ship, which once formed the tomb of a Viking chieftain, was buried in the 10th century and covered with an earthen mound. Although it was not uncommon for the high-ranking Vikings to be buried in their wooden ships, along with those supplies considered to be of use in the afterlife, Ladbyskibet (the Ladby ship) is the only Viking Age ship burial site uncovered in Denmark to date.

Unlike the spectacularly preserved Viking ships dug from clay burial sites in Norway and now on display in Oslo, all of the wooden planks from the Ladby ship, which was buried in turf, decayed long ago. What is preserved is the imprint of the hull moulded into the earth, along with iron nails, an anchor and the partial remains of the dogs and horses that were buried with their master.

An exhibition hall (☎ 65 32 16 67, Vikingevej 123; adult/child 25kr/free; open 10am-5pm daily June-August, 10am-4pm Tues-Sun Sept-Oct & Mar-May, 11am-3pm Wed-Sun Nov-Feb), which resembles a bur-ial mound from the exterior, has been erected around the excavation. There's also a sepa-rate visitor centre near the car park with a 1:10-scale model of the ship and back-ground information about the site.

Getting There & Away

In the little village of Ladby, 4km south-west of Kerteminde via Odensevej, turn north onto Vikingevej, a one-lane road that ends after 1.2km at the Ladbyskibet car park. From there it's a five-minute walk along a dirt path to the mound.

Local bus No 482 makes the six-minute trip from Kerteminde to the village of Ladby (12kr) eight times a day from Mon-day to Friday only. Check the schedule with the driver, as the last return bus is typically around 4pm. Also, you'll have to walk the Vikingevej section.

HINDSHOLM

The Hindsholm peninsula, stretching north from Kerteminde, is a rural area of small villages boasting 16th-century churches and old half-timbered farmhouses. The most fetching village is **Viby**, which has a pic-turesque windmill and an early Gothic church with frescoes. Viby is at the south-ern end of the peninsula, only a 15-minute drive from Kerteminde.

Farther north, in Mårhøj, is Funen's largest single-chamber **passage grave**, which dates from 200 BC; it consists of a 10m-long chamber that visitors can enter, but it's only about 1m high so bring a torch and be prepared to crawl. The mound is easy to spot, in a farmer's field about five minutes' walk from the road.

At the northernmost tip is **Fyns Hoved**, an island-like extension of the Hindsholm peninsula that's connected by a narrow causeway. You can walk to the edge of its 25m-high cliffs (high by Danish standards), from where there's a view of the northern Funen coast and, on a clear day, Jutland and Zealand as well.

Getting There & Away

Route 315 runs the length of the peninsula from south to north; villages and sightseeing spots along the way are signposted off the road.

There are a couple of buses from Kerteminde to Hindsholm. Bus No 481 connects Kerteminde with Viby, while Nos 484 and 483 run up the peninsula to Korshavn, ending about 1km shy of Fyns Hoved. Both routes are covered about half a dozen times a day on weekdays only and cost 12kr.

However, the best way to visit laid-back Hindsholm is by bicycle. There's a regional loop cycle route from Kerteminde to Fyns Hoved that makes a good day-long bike tour. You can get more information on cycling from the Kerteminde tourist office.

EGESKOV SLOT

Egeskov Slot (☎ *62 27 10 16*, W *www .egeskov.com, Egeskov Gade 18; adult/child: grounds, labyrinth & museum 60/30kr, castle additional 55/27.50kr; grounds open 10am-5pm May & Sept, 10am-6pm June & August, 10am-8pm July; castle open 10am-5pm May-June & Aug-Sept, 10am-7pm July)* is a gem of a Renaissance castle complete with a moat and drawbridge. Egeskov, literally 'oak forest', was built in 1554 in the middle of a pond on a foundation of thousands of upright oak trunks.

While it's most impressive from the outside, you can also tour the castle interior. It has antique furnishings, grand period paintings and an abundance of hunting trophies that include elephant tusks and the skins and heads of tigers, cheetahs and other rare creatures. Apparently the former owner, Count Gregers Ahlefeldt-Laurvig-Bille, was one of the more active hunters of African big game of his day.

The expansive 15-hectare park that surrounds the castle was designed in the 18th

Egeskov Slot was built with defence in mind, complete with moat, drawbridge and scalding holes.

FUNEN

century and includes century-old privet hedges, topiary work, free-roaming peacocks and manicured English gardens.

However, not everything is formal – you can laugh your way through the a-maze-ing bamboo grass labyrinth, designed by the contemporary Danish poet-artist Piet Hein. A sign at the entrance of this 3m-high maze admonishes visitors 'Don't be afraid. We inspect the maze thoroughly each autumn' – in actuality, most people make it through in about 15 minutes.

Also in the castle grounds is an antique vehicle museum that displays hundreds of period cars and motorcycles as well as some early aeroplane models. For children, there's a playground and a small petting zoo.

Getting There & Away

Egeskov Slot is 2km west of Kværndrup on route 8. From Odense take the Svendborg-bound train to Kværndrup station (45kr) and continue on foot or by taxi.

Alternatively, you could take bus No 801 from Odense to Kværndrup Bibliotek and there catch bus No 920, which stops in front of Egeskov Slot (it's a 700m walk to the entrance) on its way between Faaborg and Nyborg; be sure to ask for a through ticket (32kr) from the bus driver in Odense.

FAABORG

postcode 5600 • pop 7300

In the 17th century Faaborg was a bustling harbour town with one of Denmark's largest merchant fleets. A sleepier place today, the town retains many vestiges of that earlier era, and its picturesque cobbled streets lined with leaning half-timbered houses make for delightful walking. Three streets particularly notable for their attractive period buildings and hollyhock-trimmed doorways are Holkegade, Adelgade and Tårngade.

Faaborg also has two interesting museums, one dedicated to town history and the other concentrating on regional art. All in all, it's an appealing place to break a journey.

Information

Faaborg Turistbureau (☎ 62 61 07 07, fax 62 61 33 37), adjacent to the bus station at Banegårdspladsen 2A, has general brochures and sells cycling maps and telephone cards. It's open 9am to 5pm Monday to Saturday between May and September; 10am to 5pm Monday to Saturday during the rest of the year.

There are a few banks in the town centre, including a Sparekassen (☎ 63 61 18 00) at Torvet 6 and a Jyske Bank (☎ 63 61 10 20) at Østergade 36.

The post office (☎ 63 21 68 68) is at Banegårdspladsen 4, just east of the bus station. It's open 10am to 5pm Monday to Friday and 10am to noon on Saturday.

Den Gamle Gaard

This well-presented museum (☎ 62 61 33 38, Holkegade 1; adult/child 25kr/free; open 10.30am-4.30pm 15 May-15 Sept), just west of Torvet, is in a timber-framed merchant's house that dates back to about 1725 and retains much of its original character. The 22 rooms are arranged to show how a wealthy merchant lived at the start of the 19th century; part of the house holds the family quarters and other sections contain workshops and storerooms. The museum is full of intriguing antiques, ranging from furniture, porcelain and toys to maritime objects and a hearse carriage. One room contains personal items that belonged to Riborg Voigt, a merchant's daughter with whom Hans Christian Andersen had a brief relationship and a lifelong infatuation. The mementoes include one of Andersen's business cards and a lock of his hair.

Faaborg Museum

In an attractive neoclassical building, Faaborg Museum (☎ 62 61 06 45, Grønnegade 75; adult/child 35kr/free; open 10am-5pm June-Aug, 10am-4pm Apr-May & Sept-Oct, 11am-3pm Nov-Mar) contains Denmark's best collection of Funen art, featuring works by Peter Hansen, Johannes Larsen, Poul Christensen and Fritz Syberg. Also on display is sculptor Kai Nielsen's original sandstone Ymerbrønd, the bronze copy of which stands on Torvet. Based on a Nordic creation myth, this controversial statue, depicting a man, a child and a cow entwined,

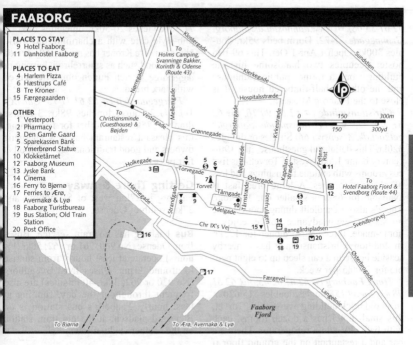

FAABORG

PLACES TO STAY
9 Hotel Faaborg
11 Danhostel Faaborg

PLACES TO EAT
4 Harlem Pizza
6 Hæstrups Café
8 Tre Kroner
15 Færgegaarden

OTHER
1 Vesterport
2 Pharmacy
3 Den Gamle Gaard
5 Sparekassen Bank
7 Ymerbrønd Statue
10 Klokketårnet
12 Faaborg Museum
13 Jyske Bank
14 Cinema
16 Ferry to Bjørnø
17 Ferries to Ærø,
Avernakø & Lyø
18 Faaborg Turistbureau
19 Bus Station; Old Train
Station
20 Post Office

To Holms Camping,
Svanninge Bakker,
Korinth & Odense
(Route 43)

To
Christiansminde
(Guesthouse) &
Bøjden

To
Hotel Faaborg Fjord &
Svendborg (Route 44)

To Bjørnø

To Ærø, Avernakø & Lyø

Faaborg
Fjord

FUNEN

created a minor uproar when it was unveiled in 1913.

Other Things to See & Do

Vesterport (West Gate), the brick town gate that was erected in the 15th century to allow entry into the city, still spans Vestergade, 500m north-west of Torvet. One of only a handful of such gates remaining in Denmark, it owes its existence primarily to Faaborg's economic decline in the 19th century, a time when many town gates elsewhere were torn down to make room for wider roads and municipal expansion.

Klokketårnet (*cnr Tårngade & Tårn-stræde; admission 10kr; open 11am-4pm Mon-Fri mid-June–Aug*), a belfry that was once part of a medieval church, now serves as the town's clock tower; in summer you can climb it.

Between mid-June and late August a cos-tumed **night watchman** winds his way through the old town, welcoming visitors

to follow in his footsteps. He begins his rounds at Klokketårnet at 9pm from Thurs-day to Sunday.

The antique train **Syd Fyenske Veteran-jernbane** (*☎ 63 63 36 96; adult/child 40/20kr; departs 10am, 1pm & 3pm Sun late June-early Aug*) makes three leisurely runs from the old Faaborg train station north to Korinth. The return trip lasts 80 minutes.

Svanninge Bakker, the countryside north of Faaborg, has some pretty rolling hills, amusingly dubbed the Funen Alps by local tourism authorities. Here you'll find cycling and walking trails and a golf course.

Places to Stay

There are half a dozen camping grounds within a 10km radius of Faaborg. Most cen-tral is **Holms Camping** (*☎ 62 61 03 99, fax 62 61 33 63, e post@holms-camp.dk, Odensevej 54*) Camping per person 45kr. Open 1 May-15 Sept. This two-star camping ground is on route 43, just 1km north of the town centre.

Danhostel Faaborg *(☎ 62 61 12 03, fax 62 61 35 08,* **W** *www.danhostel.dk/faaborg, Grønnegade 71-72)* Dorm beds 95kr, doubles 300kr. Open 1 Apr-1 Oct. This 69-bed hostel occupies two handsome historic buildings, one a former public bathhouse and the other a half-timbered house. It is close to the Faaborg Museum.

Christiansminde *(☎ 62 61 90 18, fax 62 61 90 72,* **e** *christiansminde-faaborg@ get2net.dk, Assensvej 66)* Singles or doubles 320kr. This delightful guesthouse, in a 19th-century home 1.5km west of Torvet, has five cosy rooms with antique furnishings and lots of pleasant touches. A large breakfast is available for 65kr, a smaller one for 40kr. There's also a candlelit dining room where guests can, with advance notice, enjoy a home-made, three-course dinner for 125kr. In addition, Christiansminde has a nearby seaside house that can sleep up to eight people for 7500kr per week.

Hotel Faaborg *(☎ 62 61 02 45, fax 62 61 08 45, Torvet 15)* Singles/doubles 515/620kr. In an old brick building overlooking Torvet, this small hotel has a dozen rooms, each with bath, TV and a refrigerator. There's a bar and a restaurant on the ground floor if you need some sustenance.

Hotel Faaborg Fjord *(☎ 62 61 10 10, fax 62 61 10 17,* **e** *faaborgfjord@get2net.dk, Svendborgvej 175)* Singles/doubles 895/1095kr. A member of the Quality Hotel chain, this large hotel on the eastern outskirts of town has standard tourist amenities, including 131 modern rooms and a restaurant, pool and sauna.

Places to Eat
There is a variety of places to eat in Faaborg, many of them within a few minutes' walk of Torvet.

Hæstrups Café *(☎ 63 61 00 20, Torvet 2)* Salads, burgers and sandwiches around 50kr. This is a popular central spot for light meals and drinks.

Harlem Pizza *(☎ 62 61 41 62, Torvegade 10)* Pizzas and pastas 30-50kr. This pizzeria has good pizza with a range of toppings, as well as reasonably priced pitta-bread sandwiches, lasagne and spaghetti.

Tre Kroner *(☎ 62 61 01 50, Strandgade 1)* Sandwiches 20-50kr, omelettes 60kr. A pub-style cafe with a charming old-world character, Tre Kroner has moderately priced Danish food such as smørrebrød, herring or *æggekage,* a rich Funen omelette served with dark bread.

Færgegaarden *(☎ 62 61 11 15, Chr IX's Vej 31)* 2-course lunches 98kr, 3-course dinners 175kr. A good bet for fine dining, this pleasant restaurant has new energetic owners and good traditional Danish food at fair prices.

Getting There & Away
Faaborg is 27km west of Svendborg and 37km south of Odense.

Bus Faaborg has no train service. Buses from Odense (No 960, 961 or 962; 50kr, 1¼ hours) operate at least hourly from sunrise to around 11pm. Buses from Svendborg (No 930 or 962; 32kr, 40 minutes) are also frequent throughout the day, running at least hourly. Faaborg's bus station is on Banegårdspladsen, at the old train station on the southern side of town.

Car & Motorcycle Getting to Faaborg by car is straightforward: if you are coming from the north, simply follow route 43, which is called Odensevej as it enters the town. From Svendborg, route 44 leads directly west into Faaborg, entering the town as Svendborgvej.

Boat Ferries run to and from Faaborg daily to the island of Ærø; see Getting There & Away in the Ærø section later in this chapter.

There are also ferries from Faaborg to the nearby offshore islands of Bjørnø, Lyø and Avernakø; see the following section for details.

Getting Around
Bicycles can be hired at the tourist office for 50kr a day.

BJØRNØ, LYØ & AVERNAKØ
If you are looking for a quiet getaway while you're in the Faaborg area, consider a day

trip to one of the three small offshore islands, Bjørnø, Lyø and Avernakø. All three islands are rural, unspoilt and connected by a daily ferry service to Faaborg. If you're interested in staying overnight, staff at the Faaborg tourist office can arrange stays with local families.

The nearest and smallest island, Bjørnø, 3km south of Faaborg, is just 3km long and 1km wide. It has one small village with about 40 inhabitants. You can walk around the island but there are no real sights.

Lyø, about 10km south-west of Faaborg, is the most heavily populated of the islands – with all of 150 residents. Roughly 4km long and 2km wide, it has a small village perched in the middle of the island, with half-timbered houses, a school and a church with an unusual circular churchyard. It also has a few scattered sights, including a bell stone on the western side of the island, and enough narrow roads to make for an interesting day's cycling.

Avernakø, 6km south of Faaborg, is shaped a bit like a pair of spectacles, with two oval-shaped sides, both about 4km long, connected by a thin rim of land. There's a small village, Avernak, on the north-western side of the island and scattered farmsteads throughout. In all, about 120 people live on Avernakø.

Getting There & Away

The M/S *Lillebjørn* (☎ 20 29 80 50), a little 20-passenger boat, makes six crossings between Faaborg and Bjørnø on weekdays, fewer on weekends. It takes about 20 minutes. The return trip costs 40kr (children 20kr). Bicycles cost an additional 12kr return.

The M/F *Faaborg II* (☎ 62 61 23 07) carries 150 passengers and 12 cars and operates between Faaborg, Avernakø and Lyø at least six times daily. From Faaborg it takes between 30 and 70 minutes to get to your destination, depending on which island the boat pulls into first. It costs 70kr return (children 45kr), plus 20kr for a bicycle, 60kr for a motorcycle.

Because the roads are narrow, visitors are not encouraged to bring cars to Avernakø or Lyø; there's no car ferry to Bjørnø.

SVENDBORG
postcode 5700 • pop 39,000

During the 19th century Svendborg was a busy harbour town with nearly two dozen shipyards producing almost half of all of the wooden-hulled ships built in Denmark. AP Møller, one of the world's largest shipping companies, was founded in Svendborg in that period of peak activity. With its excellent port facilities, Svendborg also became the site of foundries, tanneries, tobacco-processing plants and mills.

Today Svendborg, the largest municipality in southern Funen, remains an industrial city with commercial port facilities. It also has a couple of shipyards that still build wooden ships and provide repair services to the scores of yachts that ply the waters off southern Funen.

Svendborg offers some nicely restored buildings and a comfortable hostel right in the city centre, so it can be a pleasant enough place to spend the night; however, some of the less-developed islands around Svendborg – such as Tåsinge, Langeland and Ærø – hold more allure.

Information

Sydfyns Turistbureau (☎ 62 21 09 80, fax 62 22 05 53), Centrumpladsen, in the city centre, has information on all of southern Funen. It's open 9.30am to 6pm on weekdays and 9.30am to 3pm on Saturday from mid-June to August; the hours are 9.30am to 5pm on weekdays and 9.30am to 12.30pm on Saturday during the rest of the year.

There are several banks in the city centre, including a Unibank (☎ 62 21 52 21) at Centrumpladsen 8, south of the tourist office, and Danske Bank (☎ 63 21 43 30) a few minutes' walk from the train station at Møllergade 2.

The post office (☎ 63 21 68 68), Klosterplads 11, is to the south of the train station.

Things to See & Do

Near Torvet you'll find a couple of attractive period buildings. The handsome brick church, **Vor Frue Kirke** *(Torvet 1; admission free; open 8am-4pm high season, 8am-noon low season)*, was originally built in the 13th

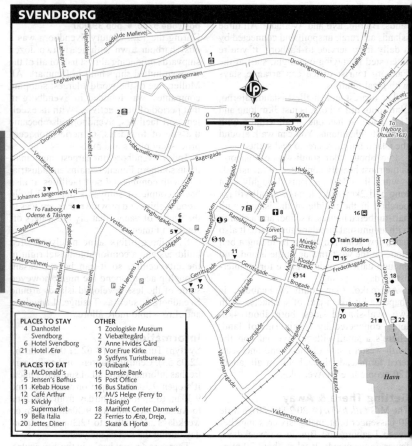

SVENDBORG

PLACES TO STAY
4 Danhostel Svendborg
6 Hotel Svendborg
21 Hotel Ærø

PLACES TO EAT
3 McDonald's
5 Jensen's Bøfhus
11 Kebab House
12 Café Arthur
13 Kvickly Supermarket
19 Bella Italia
20 Jettes Diner

OTHER
1 Zoologiske Museum
2 Viebæltegård
7 Anne Hvides Gård
8 Vor Frue Kirke
9 Sydfyns Turistbureau
10 Unibank
14 Danske Bank
15 Post Office
16 Bus Station
17 M/S Helge (Ferry to Tåsinge)
18 Maritimt Center Danmark
22 Ferries to Ærø, Drejø, Skarø & Hjortø

century in Romanesque style, although subsequent alterations have given it a Gothic appearance. The church has a late-16th-century pulpit and altar.

Just west of Vor Frue Kirke is the city's oldest secular building, **Anne Hvides Gård** (☎ 62 21 02 61, Fruestræde 3; admission 15kr), a large and lovely timber-framed house that dates from 1560. It's now a local-history museum displaying antiques, including locally made pottery, silverware and glass.

Viebæltegård (☎ 62 21 02 61, Grubbemøllevej 13, admission 20kr) was formerly a poorhouse. It exhibits its old workshops and displays some archaeological finds.

The **Zoologiske Museum** (☎ 62 21 06 50, Dronningemaen 30; admission 30kr) displays the usual stuffed birds and mammals, as well as the skeleton of a baleen whale that beached on Tåsinge. All three museums are open 10am to 5pm in high season, with slightly shorter hours in low season.

Maritimt Center Danmark (☎ 62 80 02 16, e info@maritimt-center.dk) at Havnepladsen arranges **cruises** and charters. You can even experience shipboard life on a historic wooden sailing ship.

Places to Stay

The nearest camping grounds are on Tåsinge, on the southern side of the Svendborg sound; for details see the Tåsinge Places to Stay section.

Danhostel Svendborg (☎ 62 21 66 99, fax 62 20 29 39, e danhostel.svendborg@ get2net.dk, Vestergade 45) Dorm beds 100kr, private rooms (1-3 people) 330kr. Open year-round except Christmas & New Year holidays. This highly rated hostel is in a pleasantly renovated 19th-century iron foundry in the city centre. It has 34 double rooms, 28 three-bed rooms and 22 four-bed rooms, each with a shower and toilet. The hostel has laundry facilities and also rents bicycles.

Hotel Ærø (☎ 62 21 07 60, fax 62 21 06 78, e post@hotel-aeroe.dk, Brogade 1) Singles/doubles 250/400kr. This hotel, opposite the Ærø ferry terminal, has 12 clean, basic rooms. Communal toilets and showers are off the hall.

Hotel Svendborg (☎ 62 21 17 00, fax 62 21 90 12, e booking@hotel-svendborg.dk, Centrumpladsen 1) Singles/doubles with bath 750/920kr. This modern hotel in the city centre is popular with business travellers.

Places to Eat

The lion's share of places to eat in Svendborg are conveniently along Brogade and Gerritsgade, which connect the ferry terminal with the city centre.

Kebab House (☎ 62 22 99 00, Gerritsgade 28) Burgers, kebabs and pitta-bread sandwiches 15-30kr. This hole-in-the-wall eatery offers a variety of quick inexpensive eats.

Café Arthur (☎ 62 21 11 01, Gerritsgade 35) Various pastas from 35kr. This pleasant little cafe has good prices and is in a central location.

Jensen's Bøfhus (☎ 62 80 08 84, Tinghusgade 1) Lunch specials 45kr, dinners around 100kr. In the complex opposite the Hotel Svendborg, this steak and chicken restaurant has a good salad bar and some cheap lunch deals.

Jettes Diner (☎ 62 22 16 97, Kullinggade 1) Creative burgers 45kr, veg specials 56kr, fish 85kr. Don't let the name mislead you,

this cosy cafe, 200m south of the train station, is the trendiest place in town with a varied menu that combines Danish and Mexican influences.

Hotel Ærø (☎ 62 21 07 60, Brogade 1) Daily special 72kr; dinner mains 100-150kr. This popular restaurant, opposite the ferry terminal, has an agreeable dining room with hearty daily specials, such as Danish beef and potatoes.

Bella Italia (☎ 62 22 24 55, Brogade 2) Pizza & spaghetti 54-85kr. Just north of Hotel Ærø, this Italian restaurant has good pizza and pasta dishes.

McDonald's (☎ 62 21 87 87, Johannes Jørgensens Vej) The plus here is that it's cheap and close to the hostel.

Kvickly (Vestergade 20) This central supermarket also has a bakery and a simple cafeteria-style eatery.

Getting There & Away

For most travellers, Svendborg is the transit point between Odense and the southern Funen islands. It is 44km south-east of Odense on route 9, 33km south-west of Nyborg on route 163 and 27km east of Faaborg on route 44.

Bus & Train There are frequent bus services between Svendborg and Faaborg (No 930; 32kr, 40 minutes), Rudkøbing (27kr, 25 minutes) and other Funen towns. Trains leave Odense for Svendborg about once an hour (52kr, one hour). The bus and train stations are a few streets north of the ferry terminal.

Boat Ferries to Ærøskøbing depart from Svendborg several times a day. For more information see the Ærø Getting There & Away section later in this chapter.

For information on the M/S *Helge*, which sails between Svendborg and Tåsinge, see Getting There & Away in the following Tåsinge section.

DREJØ, SKARØ & HJORTØ

Many of Svendborg's visitors are yachties who sail the protected waters along the southern Funen coast. Three popular local sailing spots are the small offshore islands of Drejø, Skarø and Hjortø, all 10km to 15km south-west of Svendborg.

Camping is allowed at designated sites on all three islands; Drejø has a restaurant and grocery shop, while Skarø has a small food shop and a snack bar.

Drejø, which has about 75 inhabitants, is the largest island, covering 412 hectares and extending about 5km in length. Its small central town, Drejø By, was devastated during a Midsummer Eve bonfire in 1942 when an ember landed on the vicarage's thatched roof – within minutes, 17 closely clustered half-timbered farmhouses had burned to the ground. Despite the fire, Drejø still has some attractive old houses and a community church that dates from 1535. The island is largely given over to moors and meadows (home to the endangered fire-bellied toad) and has a large protected harbour with good mooring facilities.

Skarø (population 20) is shaped a bit like a rabbit's head, covers 189 hectares and reaches an altitude of just 9m at its highest point. Part of the island's salt meadows is set aside as a bird sanctuary, and it is home to about 50 species of breeding birds each summer. Skarø has mooring space for about 50 boats.

Hjortø (population 15) is the smallest of the three islands, measuring just 2km at its widest point. It's free from cars and motorcycles, attracts lots of sea birds and shore birds, and has some protected beaches. You can walk around the island in just a couple of hours. About 25 boats can moor in the Hjortø harbour.

Getting There & Away

If you don't have your own boat, it's possible to visit these islands on a day trip via small ferries that leave from Svendborg's harbour. The Hjortø ferry (☎ 62 54 15 18) generally sails twice daily, while the ferry to Drejø and Skarø (☎ 62 21 02 62) runs three to five times a day. The sailing time is 30 to 75 minutes, depending on the island and the route. The return trip costs 60kr for adults, 40kr for children, plus 20kr for a bicycle. Detailed timetables are available at the Svendborg tourist office.

TÅSINGE
postcode 5700 • pop 2300

Tåsinge, the fourth largest island in Funen county, is connected by bridge to both Svendborg and Langeland. Most of the island is typically rural, a mix of woods and open fields.

The island's main road, route 9, cuts straight across Tåsinge, but it's well worth making a detour through the north-eastern quarter of the island, where you'll find Tåsinge's main sights: the old sea captains' village of Troense and the 17th-century castle Valdemars Slot.

Troense is a well-to-do seaside village with lots of quaint thatched houses and a small yachting harbour. The main activity for visitors is just strolling around and admiring the old homes; two particularly interesting streets are Grønnegade and Badstuen. There's also a small maritime museum, **Søfartssamlingerne i Troense** (☎ 62 22 52 32, Strandgade 1; admission 25kr; open 10am-5pm daily May-Sept), housed in the old village schoolhouse (dating from about 1790), which sports a rooftop belfry. The museum holds paintings, photos, model ships, figureheads and items from China brought back by local merchant ships in the 19th century.

From Troense the tree-lined Slotsalléen leads south-east to **Valdemars Slot** (Valdemar's Castle), constructed by Christian IV in 1639 for his son Valdemar. In 1677 the castle was transferred to the naval commander Niels Juel as part of the payment for his victory in the decisive Battle of Køge Bay; Juel's heirs still own the property today.

The main building, a brick manor house, is open to the public as a museum (☎ 62 22 61 06, admission 55kr; open 10am-5pm daily May-Sept, Sat-Sun Apr & Oct). About two dozen of its rooms can be toured; they contain period furniture, wall tapestries, royal portraits and a few of Juel's personal belongings.

The road leading from Troense passes right through the castle's two decorative gatehouses, which are open 24 hours. There is no admission charge to the castle grounds or to the sandy beach that's just outside the castle's southern gate.

About 1km south-west of the castle, look for a grand oak tree along the northern side of the road. **Ambrosius Egen** (Ambrosius' Oak), which is marked by a plaque, is named after Ambrosius Stub, a romantic poet who worked at Valdemars Slot about 1700 and who composed many of his verses while relaxing beneath the shade of this tree. The oak tree is thought to be at least 400 years old and has a girth of nearly 7m.

The small village of **Bregninge**, on route 9, is home to the Bregninge Kirke, a church that dates from medieval times. One of the church's three votive ships was built in 1727 as a replica of the battleship sailed by Niels Juel in the Battle of Køge Bay, but the main attraction is the panoramic view from the **church tower** (admission 5kr; open 8am-10pm daily), which at 72m is the highest point on the island. Across the road is a local-history museum, **Tåsinge Skipperkjem og Folkemindesamling** (☎ 62 22 71 44, Kirkebakken 1; admission 30kr; open 10am-5pm Tues-Sun June-Aug).

Landet, 3km south of Bregninge, also has a medieval church, most notable for the churchyard graves of the famous lovers Elvira Madigan and Sixten Sparre who died in a suicide pact in 1889.

Places to Stay

Vindebyøre Camping (☎ 62 22 54 25, fax 62 22 54 26, e mail@vindebyoere.dk, Vindebyørvej 52) Camping per person 54kr. Open early Apr–mid-Sept. This seaside three-star facility is the closest camping ground to Svendborg. It has a coin laundry, a TV lounge and a guest kitchen. The local ferry, M/S *Helge*, docks out front and bicycles can be hired.

Tåsinge Camping (☎ 62 54 13 27, Sundbrovej 130) Camping per person 45kr. Open May–mid-Sept. A bit cheaper, this one-star camping ground is on route 9 on the southeastern side of the island of Tåsinge. It's a small friendly place with basic facilities and a snack bar.

Det Lille Hotel (☎ 62 22 53 41, fax 62 22 52 41, e eriksen@detlillehotel.dk, Badstuen 15) Singles/doubles 395/510kr, including breakfast. This half-timbered guesthouse in

the village of Troense has eight rooms with shared bathroom.

Hotel Troense (☎ 62 22 54 12, fax 62 22 78 12, e mail@hoteltroense.dk, Strandgade 5) Singles/doubles 550/785kr, including breakfast. Perched above the harbour in the village centre, the hotel has 27 rooms with bath, TV and phone. It's part of the Dansk Kroferie association and accepts 'Inn Cheques' (see Hotel Schemes in the Accommodation section of the Facts for the Visitor chapter).

Slotspension Valdemars Slot (☎ 62 22 59 00, fax 62 22 72 67, e slot@valdemarsslot .dk, Slotsalléen 100) Singles 450-950kr, doubles 750-1200kr. If you've ever wanted to live like royalty, here's your chance. One wing of Valdemars Slot now has eight plush guestrooms with four-poster beds, courtyard views and full amenities. Rates include breakfast at Restaurant Valdemars Slot.

Places to Eat

Troense village centre has a *bakery* and a *minimarket*.

Hotel Troense (☎ 62 22 54 12, Strandgade 5) 3-course lunch 138kr, dinner mains 150kr. This hotel restaurant serves typical Danish fare.

Restaurant Valdemars Slot (☎ 62 22 59 00, Slotsalléen 100) 3-course lunch/dinner 175/320kr. For an atmospheric treat you can't beat this upmarket restaurant in the basement of Valdemars Slot. The food is Danish with French accents; the changing menu typically includes venison and fresh fish and the wine list is extensive.

Getting There & Away

Route 9 connects Tåsinge with Svendborg on Funen and with Rudkøbing on Langeland; there are cycle paths running the entire way.

The Svendborg city bus service operates between the city and Tåsinge, but the most enjoyable public transport option is the vintage ferry M/S *Helge* (☎ 62 21 09 80), which operates mid-May to early September. The boat leaves Svendborg harbour at 9am, 11am, 1.30pm, 3.30pm and 5.30pm from June to mid-August. Ten minutes later it docks at Vindebyøre on the northern tip of Tåsinge and then crosses back across the sound to Christiansminde, a beach area to the east of Svendborg. The boat continues on to Troense and then to Valdemars Slot. Return departures from Valdemars Slot are at 9.55am, 11.55am, 2.25pm, 4.25pm and 6.25pm. In May and late summer, the *Helge* operates the three middle sailings only. Fares range from 12kr to 36kr one way (children half price), depending on the distance. Bicycles are allowed on for an extra 15kr provided space is available.

Langeland

Langeland is a long, narrow island with good beaches, cycling paths and a wealth of birdlife. It has an unhurried provincial character with small farming villages and a countryside dotted with windmills, both modern and vintage. There are ceramics shops and galleries selling local handicrafts scattered all around the island.

Langeland's only large town, Rudkøbing, has a handful of historic sights, but the island's most frequented visitor attraction is the medieval castle at Tranekær.

GETTING THERE & AWAY
Route 9, via the Langeland bridge, connects Langeland with Tåsinge and Svendborg.

Buses make the 20km run from Svendborg to Rudkøbing (27kr, 25 minutes) at least hourly.

There's a ferry service from Rudkøbing to Marstal on Ærø (see Getting There & Away in the Ærø section) and from Spodsbjerg to Tårs on Lolland (see the Lolland Getting There & Away section).

GETTING AROUND
Route 305 runs from Lohals to Bagenkop, nearly the full length of the island.

Bus
All buses that run the length of Langeland are all marked No 910, so you'll need to check the destination sign on the bus to see in which direction it's headed. Buses travel

from Rudkøbing north to Lohals and south to Bagenkop at least once an hour (about half as often on weekends), connecting all of Langeland's major villages en route. The maximum one-way fare from Rudkøbing to anywhere else on Langeland is 32kr, while the Lohals-Bagenkop fare is 56kr.

Within Rudkøbing there are special green buses that make a loop around the city outskirts, going as far east as the Spodsbjerg harbour, about a dozen times a day from Monday to Friday. There are no charges to use these buses. The whole loop takes about an hour; hop on for an interesting little tour

LANGELAND

All buses leave from the Rudkøbing bus station on Ringvejen.

Bicycle

There are asphalt cycle paths running north from the Rudkøbing area to Lohals, east to Spodsbjerg and south to Bagenkop. The tourist office in Rudkøbing has a bicycle map of Langeland available for 15kr. In Rudkøbing you can hire bicycles at Profa (☎ 62 51 11 08) at Ørstedsgade 5; elsewhere on the island they can be hired at the camping grounds.

RUDKØBING

postcode 5900 • pop 5000

Rudkøbing is Langeland's commercial centre and the island's only sizable town. It's also the departure point for ferries to Ærø, which leave from the ferry harbour right in the town centre. North of the ferry harbour is a fishing harbour and a 260-berth marina that attracts Germans in summer and Danes year-round.

Information

You can pick up information on the entire island from Team Langeland (☎ 62 51 35 05, fax 62 51 43 35), Torvet 5. It's open 9am to 5pm Monday to Saturday from mid-June to August; the hours are 9.30am to 4.30pm on weekdays and 9.30am to 12.30pm on Saturday during the rest of the year.

There's a Unibank (☎ 62 51 11 04) on Østergade 39, open 10am to 4pm Monday to Friday (to 5.30pm on Thursday).

The post office (☎ 63 21 68 68), Brogade 9, is open 10am to 5pm Monday to Friday and 10am to noon on Saturday.

Things to See & Do

Rudkøbing can appear rather nondescript from the ferry harbour, but it definitely warrants a closer look. Just east of Havnegade, the main harbour road, is a series of one-lane carriage roads that date from medieval times and are lined with old houses. Three of the most interesting streets – Ramsherred, Smedegade and Vinkældergade – can be combined in a pleasant 15-minute stroll between Havnegade and Brogade.

The town also has a few sights along its main street, which begins inland of the harbour as Brogade and changes to Østergade after Torvet. On Brogade, just east of Ramsherred, is a **statue of HC Ørsted**, the Danish physicist who advanced the development of electromagnetic theory. Across the street is the old Rudkøbing Apotek, the site where Ørsted was born. It now houses the small museum **Det Gamle Apotek** (☎ 62 51 13 47, Brogade 15; adult/child 15kr/free; open 11am-4pm Mon-Fri mid-June–Aug). This place contains replicas of the interiors of two pharmacy shops, one from the 18th century and the other from the 19th century.

Fiskeri-og Søfartsudstilling (☎ 62 51 13 47, Østergade 25; admission free; open 10am-4pm Mon-Fri, 10am-1pm Sat), a nautical museum, features fishing gear, dinghies and model ships.

Langelands Museum (☎ 62 51 13 47, Jens Winthers Vej 12; adult/child 20kr/free; open 10am-4pm Mon-Thur, 10am-1pm Fri), about 500m farther east, is the region's history museum. Its displays are primarily archaeological finds from Langeland and Ærø, but it also has a collection of glass, silver and furniture from the 18th century.

On Torvet you'll find the 19th-century **rådhus** backed by the town church **Rudkøbing Kirke**, which dates from the early 12th century, although most of the current building is from the post-Reformation era.

Places to Stay

Danhostel Rudkøbing & Camping (☎/fax 62 51 18 30, W www.danhostel.dk/rudkobing, Engdraget 11) Camping per person 45kr, dorm beds 100kr, doubles 290kr. Open 15 Mar-31 Oct. Langeland's only hostel is just a 10-minute walk from Torvet in the town centre. Tents can be pitched in the field at the side of the hostel.

The tourist office can provide a list of private homes with *rooms* for rent. Some are in villages, others on farms; a few are in Rudkøbing, the rest spread around the island. Doubles cost around 350kr.

Det Gamle Hotel Rudkøbing (☎ 62 51 36 18, e solem@worldonline.dk, Havnegade 2) Singles/doubles 380/595kr, with breakfast.

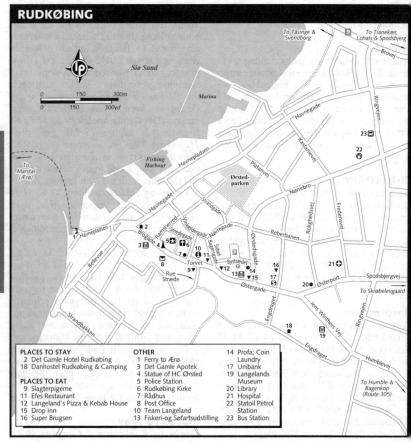

RUDKØBING

Siø Sund

To Tåsinge &
Svendborg

To Tranekær,
Lohals & Spodsbjerg

Brovej

Marina

0   150   300m
0   150   300yd

Havnegade

23

22

Fishing
Harbour

Havnepladsen

Platanvej

Ørsted-
parken

Ringvejen

Kastanjevej

To
Marstal
(Ærø)

Havnepladsen

Bellevue

Brogade

Ramsherred

Smedegade

Vinfeldergade

Nørregade

Strandgade

Sidsel
Bagers
gade

Ørstedsgade

Bystrædet

Østergade

Engdraget

Reberbanen

Rollighedsvej

Fredensvej

Nørrebro

Spodsbjergvej

Østerport

To Skrøbelevgaard

Strandbakken

Jens Winthers Vej

Ringvejen

Engdraget

Humlevej

To Humble &
Bagenkop
(Route 305)

Rue
Stræde

Torvet

PLACES TO STAY	OTHER	14 Profa; Coin
2 Det Gamle Hotel Rudkøbing	1 Ferry to Ærø	Laundry
18 Danhostel Rudkøbing & Camping	3 Det Gamle Apotek	17 Unibank
	4 Statue of HC Ørsted	19 Langelands
PLACES TO EAT	5 Police Station	Museum
9 Slagterpigerne	6 Rudkøbing Kirke	20 Library
11 Efes Restaurant	7 Rådhus	21 Hospital
12 Langeland's Pizza & Kebab House	8 Post Office	22 Statoil Petrol
15 Drop Inn	10 Team Langeland	Station
16 Super Brugsen	13 Fiskeri-og Søfartsudstilling	23 Bus Station

This pleasant little hotel, in a period building opposite the waterfront, has newly renovated rooms, some with sea views.

Skrøbelevgaard (☎ 62 51 45 31, fax 62 51 45 32, e jensen@skroebelevgaard.dk, Skrøbelev Hedevej 4) Singles 300-450kr, doubles 400-750kr, including breakfast. This cosy inn 4km east of Rudkøbing in the village of Ny Skrøbelev is a fine option if you enjoy historic settings and the quiet of the countryside. Occupying a 17th-century manor house, Skrøbelevgaard has 10 cosy rooms. The free city bus stops near the inn's gate on weekdays.

Places to Eat

Super Brugsen (☎ 62 51 13 54, Ahlefeldtsgade 5) In the town centre, this grocery store has a good bakery and a cafe serving simple, cheap fare.

Drop Inn (☎ 62 51 42 20, Ostergade 29) Sandwiches, salads and chicken dishes 25-50kr. This cheery cafe has a nice variety of healthy light meals.

Slagterpigerne (☎ 62 51 10 72, Torvet 6) Sandwiches 20kr. This butcher shop prepares creative smørrebrød for takeaway.

Langeland's Pizza & Kebab House (☎ 62 51 50 04, Østergade 11) Pizza slice 20kr,

Clockwise from top left: A traditional windmill on the island of Ærø; Viking parade; Kai Nielsen's *Ymerbrønd* at Faaborg is a controversial depiction of an ancient creation myth; Special delivery; Doorway of a traditional Danish half-timbered house, a style that is common in Ærøskøbing.

The double walls of Egeskov Slot, in the heart of Funen, conceal secret staircases in case of siege.

other items 35-50kr. This is a good choice for inexpensive pizza, pitta-bread sandwiches and pastas.

Efes Restaurant (☎ 62 51 46 00, *Østergade 5)* Pasta, meat or fish mains 50-90kr. This is a popular place to linger over a good, reasonably priced meal.

NORTHERN LANGELAND
Northern Langeland has a run of small villages separated by farmland. You'll see the occasional sign advertising organic produce for sale and a few roadside windmills, but the main sights are at Tranekær, a quiet village surrounding a lovely medieval castle.

You could continue travelling north from Tranekær to Lohals, a fair-sized village near the northern tip of Langeland. It and the neighbouring seaside area of Hov have a couple of camping grounds and hotels, but Lohals lacks the charm of Tranekær and its beaches are not as good as those in the south.

Tranekær
postcode 5953
Tranekær has a quaint character and quite a number of timber-framed houses, but its dominant sight is the salmon-coloured **Tranekær Slot** which, reflected in its swan pond, looks like something torn from the pages of a fairy tale.

The castle dates from around 1200 and was at one time the centrepiece of a royal estate that included more than half of Langeland. Although it's been altered several times, most recently in 1862, Tranekær Slot has been in the same family since 1659. Its current owner, Count Preben Ahlefeldt-Laurvig, still maintains it as a residence, so the castle interior cannot be toured, but much of the grounds have been converted into a sculpture park called **Tickon** that's open to the public.

The park, the main path of which circles the castle pond, contains the environmental works of a dozen international artists who have used straw, stones and sticks to give their art a distinctively Nordic appearance. In addition, 70 different types of exotic trees, ranging from Norway spruce to California sequoia, are numbered and identified in a

corresponding park brochure. It costs 20kr (children free) to walk around the castle grounds and view the sculptures; after hours, drop your coins into the box.

In the old water mill opposite the castle is **Tranekær Slotsmuseum** (☎ 62 51 13 47, *Slotsgade 95; adult/child 20kr/free; open 10am-5pm Mon-Fri, 1pm-5pm Sun mid-May–30 Sept),* which displays exhibits on the history of the castle and Tranekær village.

One kilometre north of the castle is **Tranekær Slotsmølle,** an attractive Dutch windmill dating from 1846. It's been restored as a museum and, wind permitting, still grinds flour. It has the same admission fees and opening hours as the Tranekær Slotsmuseum.

Places to Stay & Eat *Tranekær Gæstgivergaard* (☎ 62 59 12 04, e *info@ tranekaerkro.dk, Slotsgade 74)* Singles/ doubles with bath 500/650kr, including breakfast. This half-timbered village inn 200m south of the castle dates from 1802 and retains its period ambience.

Tranekær Gæstgivergaard's *restaurant* offers traditional Danish country dinners for around 150kr.

Café Herskabsstalden (☎ 62 59 14 26, *Slotsgade 92)* Most items 20-65kr. This large cafe fronting the castle offers chicken dishes, fish and chips, hot dogs and burgers.

SOUTHERN LANGELAND
Southern Langeland has the island's best beaches, several passage graves and a couple of bird sanctuaries.

Heading south from Rudkøbing you will pass a number of small villages. Three kilometres south-east of Lindelse is **Skovsgaard,** which is an estate managed by the conservation group Danmarks Naturfredningsforening; it contains an old manor house and a large organic farm complete with a windmill and thatched farm buildings. Visitors are welcome, there's an organic food cafe and the stable has been converted into a carriage museum (☎ 62 51 13 47, *Kaagårdsvej 12; adult/child 35kr/free; open 10am-5pm Mon-Fri, 1pm-5pm Sun mid-May–Oct)* with 25 horse-drawn vehicles, ranging from a wedding carriage to farm wagons.

A few kilometres away, just south of Kædeby, is **Kong Humbles Grav**, the largest long dolmen on Langeland. Dating from approximately 3000 BC, the barrow is edged with 77 stones, extends 55m in length and has a single burial chamber. Its size has given rise to local folklore that a king was buried here, although historians give little credence to the tale. The dolmen is on private property in a field of grain and rapeseed, but visitors are free to walk to the site along a path that begins near the whitewashed church in Humble. To get to the dolmen walk north-east from the car park, which is just past the church, and bear left at the first intersection; follow that trail past the farmhouses. The walk takes about 20 minutes each way.

If the crops aren't too tall you'll also be able to see the site from route 305 about 150m south of Kædeby; the mounded dolmen is about 800m east of the road.

The village of **Humble**, the little commercial centre of southern Langeland, has a bank, a pizzeria and a petrol station. Humble is also the turn-off for Ristinge.

Ristinge, a little seaside village with thatched houses, is bordered by a long stretch of sandy beach backed by dunes and wild roses. Despite being the island's favourite bathing area Ristinge is pleasantly low-key, its main visitor facility being the camping ground.

At the southern end of the island is **Bagenkop**, an attractive little fishing village. Just beyond Bagenkop at the southernmost tip of the island is **Dovnsklint**, an area of 16m-high cliffs and pebble beaches that's popular with bird-watchers during the autumn southern migration. About 500m north of the cliffs is **Gulstav Mose**, a marshy bird sanctuary that provides a habitat for hawks, herons, ducks, reed buntings and small songbirds. East of the sanctuary are the adjacent woodlands **Gulstav Skov**. All three sites are connected by footpaths. Another area of interest to bird-watchers is **Tryggelev Nor**, a coastal nature reserve with a sighting tower, midway between Bagenkop and Ristinge.

Places to Stay & Eat

Ristinge Camping & Feriecenter (☎ 62 57 13 29, fax 62 57 13 47, e info@ristinge.dk Ristingevej 104, 5932 Humble) Camping per person 54kr. Open mid-Apr–early Sept This three-star camping ground is within walking distance of the beach in Ristinge. I has a grocery shop and a snack bar.

Humble Hotel (☎ 62 57 11 34, fax 62 57 11 24, Ristingevej 2, 5932 Humble) Singles doubles with bath 595/710kr. The neares hotel to Ristinge, this little hotel, which ha six rooms, is in Humble village centre Breakfast is included in the room rate.

The larger villages, such as Humble and Bagenkop, have *bakeries*, *grocery shops* and at least a couple of places where you ca stop for a meal.

Ærø

Well off the beaten track, Ærø is an idyllic island with small villages, rolling hills and patchwork farms. It's a popular place to tour by bicycle – the country roads are enhanced by thatched houses and old wind mills, and the island offers some ancien passage graves and dolmens for visitors to explore.

Ærø is a favourite destination of yachties and each of the three main towns – Ærø skøbing, Marstal and Søby – has a modern marina. Sailing is so popular that, with a total of 800 berths, there are about fou times as many yacht moorings as there are hotel rooms. Each of the three towns also has a commercial ferry harbour.

GETTING THERE & AWAY

Det Ærøske Færgetrafikselskab (☎ 62 52 40 00) operates year-round car ferries to Søby from Faaborg, to Ærøskøbing from Svendborg, and to Marstal from Rud købing. All run an average of five times a day, take about an hour and cost 70kr for adults, 35kr for children, 20kr for a bicycle 40kr for a motorcycle and 155kr for a car These prices are one way; if you buy a return ticket there's a 15% discount. If you have a car it's a good idea to make advance

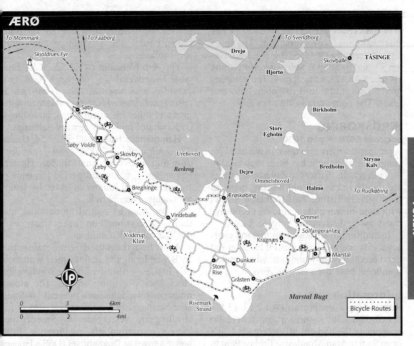

ÆRØ

reservations, particularly at weekends and in summer high season when ferries can be booked out several days in advance.

There is also a ferry (☎ 62 58 17 17) between Søby and Mommark (on the island of Als in Jutland), which runs three to five times daily from April to September, but much less frequently during the rest of the year. The trip takes one hour and costs 65kr for adults, 30kr for children, 15kr for a bicycle and 275kr for a car with two people.

GETTING AROUND
Bus
Fyns Amt (☎ 63 11 22 33) operates a bus service (No 990) from Marstal to Søby via Ærøskøbing. It runs hourly from 5.30am to 7.30pm on weekdays. Weekend buses are about half as frequent, with the first bus leaving Marstal at 8.30am. It takes about an hour to get from one end of the island to the other. Fares range from 12kr to 27kr, depending on the distance, but there's also a

pass for unlimited one-day travel that costs 50/25kr for adults/children.

Car
Cars can be rented at the harbourside Q8 petrol station (☎ 62 53 18 55) in Marstal.

Bicycle
Cycle Routes Cycling is a great way to enjoy Ærø, with three well-signposted cycle routes to follow. Cycle route 91 begins at Marstal and continues along the southern side of the island up to Søby, while cycle route 90 runs along the northern side of the island from Søby to Ærøskøbing and continues as route 92 from Ærøskøbing to Marstal. If you were to cover the entire route as a circular tour of the island you would cycle about 60km – a hardy outing considering the island's hilly terrain.

Ærø's tourist offices sell an inexpensive English-language cycling map of the island, listing sights along the routes.

Rental You can hire bicycles in Ærøskøbing at Pilebækkens Cykelservice (☎ 62 52 11 10), Pilebækken 11; in Marstal at Thygesen Cykelforretning (☎ 62 53 14 77), Mølleve-jen 77; and in Søby at Søby Cykelforretning (☎ 62 58 18 42), Langebro 4. The camping ground and hostel in Ærøskøbing also rent bikes. The going rate is 40kr per day.

ÆRØSKØBING
postcode 5970 • pop 1050

A prosperous merchant town in the late 17th century, Ærøskøbing has been preserved in its entirety. Its narrow cobblestone streets are tightly lined with old houses, many of them gently listing half-timbered affairs with hand-blown glass windows, decorative doorways and streetside hollyhocks.

In addition to its engaging historic char-acter, Ærøskøbing has a central location and good accommodation options, which makes it an ideal base for a stay on Ærø.

Information

Ærøskøbing Turistbureau (☎ 62 52 13 00, fax 62 52 14 36, e turistar@post1.tele.dk) is opposite the harbour at Vestergade 1. It's open 9am to 5pm Monday to Friday, 9am to 2pm on Saturday and 10am to noon on Sun-day between June and August; 9am to 4pm Monday to Friday and 9am to noon on Saturday during the rest of the year.

There's an Amtssparekassen bank (☎ 62 52 10 81) on Torvet and a Danske Bank (☎ 63 52 25 40) at Vestergade 56.

The post office (☎ 63 21 68 68), on the northern side of town at Statene 6, is open noon to 4.30pm Monday to Friday and 10am to noon on Saturday.

Things to See & Do

In keeping with the town's character, sights are low-key. The main attraction is **Flaskes-kibssamlingen** (☎ 62 52 29 51, Smedegade 22; adult/child 25/17kr; open 10am-5pm daily May-Sept; 1pm-3pm Tues-Thur & 10am-1pm Sun Oct-Apr), in the former poor-house. This museum is dedicated to the lifetime work of Peter Jacobsen, a local sailor nicknamed Bottle Peter for the 1700 ships-in-a-bottle he created before his death in 1960 at the age of 86. In addition to the model ships, many of which are in hand-blown bottles, the museum contains other local folk art.

The **Ærø Museum** (☎ 62 52 29 50, Bro-gade 3; adult/child 15/10kr; open 10am-4pm Tues-Sun mid-June–late Aug, 10am-1pm in spring and autumn) features antique furnish-ings and other historical items, including a collection of mid-19th-century paintings.

Hammerichs Hus (☎ 62 52 27 54, Gyden 22; adult/child 15/10kr; open 11am-3pm Tues-Sun June-Aug), a half-timbered house, has antiques, china and period furnishings from Funen and Jutland collected by sculp-tor Gunnar Hammerich.

If you want to visit all three museums, there's a combination ticket that costs 40/20kr for adults/children.

Apart from the museums, the main activ-ity is wandering the quaint streets with their tidy houses – it's all a bit like winding the clock back a century or two. The **oldest house** in town dates back to about 1645 and is at Søndergade 36. Other fine streets for strolling are Vestergade and Smedegade; there's a particularly picturesque little house known as **Dukkehuset** (Doll's House) at Smedegade 37.

Places to Stay

Ærøskøbing Campingplads (☎ 62 52 18 54, fax 62 52 14 36, e turistar@post1.tele.dk, Sygehusvej 40) Camping per person 50kr. Open May-Sept. This three-star camping ground is near a shallow beach just 1km from the town centre.

Danhostel Ærøskøbing (☎ 62 52 10 44, fax 62 52 16 44, e stormaeroe@mail.tele.dk, Smedevejen 15) Dorm beds 100kr, doubles 240kr. Open Apr-Sept. This 87-bed hostel is 750m from the town centre on the road to Marstal.

The Ærøskøbing tourist office maintains a list of islanders who rent out **rooms** in pri-vate homes around Ærø; singles/doubles cost 210/340kr. Staff can also book houses, cottages and flats by the week, starting at around 3200kr.

Hotel Ærøhus (☎ 62 52 10 03, fax 62 52 21 23, e mail@aeroehus.dk, Vestergade 38)

Singles/doubles 280/480kr, with bath 550/780kr, including breakfast. This timber-framed, 30-room hotel has an old-fashioned character right down to its creaky hallways and fine china at the breakfast table. The hotel is part of the Dansk Kroferie association and accepts 'Inn Cheques' (see Hotel Schemes under Accommodation in the Facts for the Visitor chapter).

Pension Vestergade 44 (☎ 62 52 22 98, *Vestergade 44*) Singles/doubles 350/500kr with shared bathroom, including breakfast. This friendly six-room pension in the centre of town occupies a picturesque house that dates from 1784.

Graasten Farm (☎ 62 52 24 25, fax 62 52 13 49, ⓔ aeroe-graasten@forum.dk, *Øster-marksvej 20*) Singles/doubles 275/400kr, including breakfast. For a homy country experience consider this working dairy farm run by a Danish-English couple, on the main road midway between Ærøskøbing and Marstal. It has three guest bedrooms and lots of common space including a kitchenette.

Places to Eat

Ærøskøbing Bageri (☎ 62 52 10 31, *Vestergade 62*) Sandwiches 20kr. This is the place for takeaway sandwiches and yummy pastries.

Ærøskøbing Røgeri (☎ 62 52 40 07, *Havnen 15*) Simple meals 20-50kr. This place, adjacent to the harbour, serves inexpensive smoked fish and shrimp dishes.

Café Lille Claus (☎ 62 52 40 02, *Havne-pladsen*) Light meals 35-90kr. This cafe opposite the tourist office has sandwiches, salads and fish dishes.

Hotel Ærøhus (☎ 62 52 10 03, *Vestergade 38*) 2-course special 100kr. This hotel has a pleasant dining room with a full menu of Danish fish and meat dishes. For good value choose one of the daily two-course specials.

MARSTAL
postcode 5960 • pop 2500

Marstal, at the eastern end of the island, is Ærø's most modern-looking town although it too has a nautical character, with a maritime museum, a shipyard and a marina. There's a reasonably good beach, half sandy and half rocky, on the southern side of town, about a 15-minute walk from the centre.

Although Marstal is quiet today, until the 19th century it was one of the region's busiest harbours, with more than 300 merchant ships pulling into port annually. The sea was such an integral part of people's lives that even the gravestones at the seamen's church on Kirkestræde are engraved with maritime epitaphs, the most frequently quoted being 'Here lies Christen Hansen at anchor with his wife; he will not weigh until summoned by God'.

Information

Marstal Turistbureau (☎ 62 52 13 00, fax 62 52 14 36), Havnegade 5, is five minutes' walk south from the harbour. It's open 9am to 5pm Monday to Friday and 10am to 3pm on Saturday between mid-June and 31 August; and also 10am to 3pm on Sunday in July. Low-season hours are 9am to 4pm Monday to Friday and 10am to 1pm on Saturday.

There's a Danske Bank (☎ 63 52 60 00) at Prinsensgade 8, one block inland from the tourist office. The post office (☎ 63 21 68 68), at Havnegade 1, is open 10am to 5pm Monday to Friday and 10am to noon on Saturday.

> ### Soaking up the Sun
>
> Ærø, with its many windmills, has a centuries-old tradition of harvesting renewable energy. It therefore seems fitting that Europe's largest solar power station, Solfangeranlæg, opened on the island in 1996. The facility, on the western outskirts of Marstal, encompasses an 8064-sq-metre field of solar collectors that are capable of providing year-round heating for 270 homes.
>
> The solar collectors have special glass faces designed to absorb heat from the sun, which is then transferred through a network of pipes to a heat exchange and generator installation, from where it enters the island's power grid. In all, the solar facility provides an annual output of power that previously required 350,000L of oil to produce.

Marstal Søfartsmuseum

The Marstal Søfartsmuseum (☎ 62 53 23 31, Prinsensgade 1; adult/child 30/25kr; open 9am-5pm daily Jun & Aug, 9am-8pm daily July, 10am-4pm Tues-Fri & 11am-3pm Sat Sept-May) has a collection of maritime paraphernalia including paintings and models of some of the schooners and brigs that filled the town harbour during its heyday.

Places to Stay

Marstal Camping (☎ 62 53 36 00, fax 62 53 36 40, e marstal.camping@mail.tele.dk, Egehovedvej 1) Camping per person 55kr. Open Apr-Sept. This camping ground is behind the marina, 1km south of the harbour.

Danhostel Marstal (☎ 62 53 10 64, fax 62 53 10 57, e mav@adr.dk, Færgestræde 29) Dorm beds 100kr, doubles 250kr. Open May-Aug. This 82-bed hostel is central, only 500m south of the ferry harbour and within walking distance of restaurants and the beach.

Hotel Marstal (☎ 62 53 13 52, Dronningestræde 1A) Singles/doubles 325/425kr, including breakfast. Just a few minutes walk south-west of the harbour, this hotel has a handful of simple rooms above a restaurant, all with shared bathroom.

Places to Eat

At the ferry harbour there's a small *food shop* and a *grill restaurant* serving inexpensive burgers, pizzas and other simple eats.

Hotel Marstal (☎ 62 53 13 52, Dronningestræde 1A) 2-course daily special 98kr. For something a little more substantial try this hotel restaurant.

Super Brugsen (☎ 62 53 17 80, cnr Kirkestræde & Skovgyden) This grocery shop, about 300m west of the ferry harbour, has good deli, produce and wine sections.

STORE RISE

The village of Store Rise, in the middle of the island, has an attractive medieval **church**, though much of the current structure is from the 17th century. The churchyard is surrounded by a medieval circular wall and contains graves separated from each other by hedges. The church interior includes an ornately carved altar from the late Gothic period.

In the field just behind the church is **Tingstedet**, a 54m-long Neolithic passage grave thought to be at least 5000 years old. The cup-like markings in the largest stone near the church indicate that the grave may have belonged to a fertility cult. It takes only a few minutes to get there along a footpath that is marked from the church.

A couple of kilometres south of the village is **Risemark Strand**, the best of Ærø's few sandy beaches.

SØBY

postcode 5985 • pop 900

Søby has a shipyard which is the island's biggest employer, a sizable fishing fleet and a popular marina. It's a pleasant enough place with some thatched houses, but the town doesn't pack the same charm as Ærøskøbing and most of its visitors are yachties.

The tourist office (☎ 62 58 13 00) operates a branch at Søby harbour from 9.30am to 3.30pm Monday to Friday and 2pm Saturday from June to August.

Things to See & Do

Five kilometres beyond Søby, at Ærø's northern tip, is **Skjoldnæs Fyr**, a 19th-century, granite-block lighthouse with a narrow stairway; you can climb the lighthouse for a fine view of the sea. A few minutes' walk beyond the lighthouse is a pebble beach.

Along the main cross-island road, roughly 3km south of Søby, you'll see **Søby Volde**, the mounded-over earthen ramparts that were once part of a 12th-century fortress.

Places to Stay & Eat

Søby Camping (☎/fax 62 58 14 70, e soby cam@image.dk, Vitsø 10) Camping per person 44kr. Open Mar-Oct. This is a small two-star facility about 1km west of town.

Søby Kro (☎ 62 58 10 06, fax 62 58 27 10, Østerbro 2) Singles/doubles with shared bathroom 210/360kr, breakfast included. This small inn, in the centre of town three blocks south of the harbour, also has good fresh-fish dinners for 98kr.

There are a couple of *fast-food kiosks* near the harbour and a *bakery* 200m south of the harbour at Nørrebro 2.

Southern Jutland

The Jutland (Jylland) peninsula, the only part of Denmark connected to the European mainland, was originally settled by the Jutes, a Germanic tribe whose forays included an invasion of England in the 5th century.

Jutland's southern boundary has long been a fluid one. It was last redrawn in 1920 when Germany returned part of the Schleswig region to Denmark following a postwar plebiscite on self-determination.

Southern Jutland has a number of well-preserved historic towns, the most notable of which is Ribe. However, many southerly towns tend to be modern and nondescript, in part due to the destruction unleashed during the border wars with Germany.

As is the case throughout Jutland, the bulk of the land is given over to fields and pastures, with only sporadic patches of woodland. The east coast of southern Jutland is cut by deep fjords whereas the west coast is bordered by marshland and moors.

ESBJERG
postcode 6700 • pop 83,000
Esbjerg, the youngest city in Denmark, owes its rise to the territorial losses that beleaguered Denmark in the 19th century. Following the loss of the Schleswig and Holstein regions to Germany in 1864, farmers in Jutland suddenly needed a new export harbour for shipping grain to England. To serve that purpose the coastal town of Esbjerg was founded in 1868 on a site that had previously been farmers' fields.

Esbjerg's port opened in 1874 and within only a few decades the town's population had grown to nearly 20,000. It's now Denmark's fifth-largest city, the centre of the country's North Sea oil activities and its largest fishing harbour.

Although Esbjerg has its fair share of late-19th-century buildings, it lacks the intriguing atmosphere of the medieval quarters of other cities and isn't on the itinerary of most travellers, unless they're travelling to or from the UK.

Highlights

- Step back in time in Ribe, Denmark's oldest and best-preserved town
- Take an excursion to quaint Møgeltønder village and its lavish church
- Join the action on the island of Rømø, a haven for windsurfers
- Revel at Denmark's largest folk music festival, held in Tønder each August
- Tour Sønderborg with its seaside castle and 1864 battlefield sites

Esbjerg p266
Ribe p270
Rømø p276
Haderslev p282

Orientation
Torvet, the city square where Skolegade and Torvegade intersect, is bordered by cafes, banks, the post office and the tourist office. The train and bus stations are about 300m east of Torvet, while the ferry terminal is 1km to the south.

Information
Tourist Offices For information about the city, the Esbjerg Turistkontor (☎ 75 12 55 99,

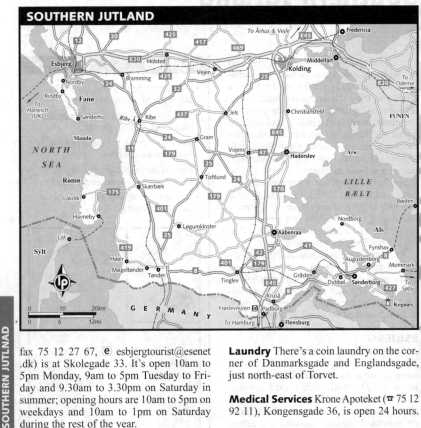

SOUTHERN JUTLAND

fax 75 12 27 67, e esbjergtourist@esenet
.dk) is at Skolegade 33. It's open 10am to
5pm Monday, 9am to 5pm Tuesday to Friday and 9.30am to 3.30pm on Saturday in
summer; opening hours are 10am to 5pm on
weekdays and 10am to 1pm on Saturday
during the rest of the year.

Money There are many banks in the centre, including a Danske Bank (☎ 79 15 72
00) at Torvet 18 and a Unibank (☎ 79 12 60
00) around the corner on Kongensgade 48.

Post The post office (☎ 79 12 12 12),
Torvet 20, is open 9.30am to 5pm Monday
to Friday (to 5.30pm on Thursday) and
10am to 1pm on Saturday.

Library The library (☎ 75 12 13 77), Nørregade 19, has Internet access and foreign
newspapers and magazines. It's open 10am
to 7pm Monday to Thursday, 10am to 5pm
on Friday and 10am to 2pm on Saturday.

Laundry There's a coin laundry on the corner of Danmarksgade and Englandsgade,
just north-east of Torvet.

Medical Services Krone Apoteket (☎ 75 12
92 11), Kongensgade 36, is open 24 hours.

Things to See
There are a few local museums to explore,
or you could pick up a free walking-tour
map at the tourist office and stroll along a
route that traces Esbjerg's architectural development, unassuming as it is.

In the centre of Torvet stands a **statue** of
Christian IX, who held the throne in 1899
when Esbjerg obtained its municipal charter.

Esbjerg Vandtårn (*Esbjerg Water Tower;*
☎ *75 12 78 11, Havnegade 22; adult/child*
15/5kr; open 10am-4pm daily June–mid-
Sept, 10am-4pm Sat & Sun mid-Sept–May),
two blocks south of Torvet, was erected in
1897 by town architect CH Clausen, who incorporated medieval features in an attempt

to give Esbjerg a more historic look. Climb the tower for a view of the city and harbour.

Esbjerg Museum (☎ 75 12 78 11, Torvegade 45; adult/child 30kr/free; open 10am-4pm daily June-Aug, 10am-4pm Tues-Sun Sept-May), three blocks north of Torvet, is known mostly for its amber collection of both ancient and modern pieces, but also has some minor historical exhibits.

Esbjerg Kunstmuseum (Esbjerg Art Museum; ☎ 75 13 02 11, Havnegade 20; adult/child 30kr/free; open 10am-4pm daily), near Esbjerg Vandtårn, features Danish paintings by several 20th-century artists of the Cobra (COpenhagen-BRussels-Amsterdam) movement, including Richard Mortensen, Robert Jacobsen and Per Kirkeby.

Fiskeri-og Søfartsmuseet (Museum of Fishing & Shipping; ☎ 76 12 20 00, Tarphagevej; adult/child 60/30kr; open 10am-6pm daily July & Aug, 10am-5pm Sept-June), 4km north-west of the city centre, is a 25-tank aquarium featuring North Sea fish, an outdoor seal pool (feeding times at 11am and 2.30pm) and various fisheries exhibits. Take bus No 1 or 8 from the train station.

On the waterfront opposite the aquarium is Esbjerg's newest landmark, **Mennesket ved Havet** (Man Meets the Sea), comprising four stark white, 9m-high, stylised human figures created by Danish sculptor Svend Wiig Hansen to commemorate the city's centennial. Strike a pose on their toes for a photo.

There's also an old wooden **lightship** (☎ 21 62 11 04; adult/child 20/10kr; open 10am-4pm daily June-Aug) that's moored down at the fishing harbour.

Places to Stay

Camping & Hostels There are a few options in these categories around town.

Ådalens Camping (☎ 75 15 88 22, fax 75 15 97 93, e info@adal.dk, Gudenå-vej 20) Bus No 1. Camping per person 55kr. Open year-round. This three-star facility is 5km north of the city centre on route 447.

Danhostel Esbjerg (☎ 75 12 42 58, fax 75 13 68 33, e esbjerg@danhostel.dk, Gammel Vardevej 80) Bus No 1 or 4. Dorm beds 100kr,

singles/doubles 250/300kr. Open Feb-Nov. This 130-bed hostel is in a former folk high school 3km north of the city centre. There are bicycles for hire and sports facilities.

Private Rooms Staff at the tourist office can book *rooms* in private homes, both in the city and in the surrounding countryside. The cost averages 150kr per person, plus 35kr for breakfast if required.

Hotels The *Hotel Bell-Inn* (☎ 75 12 01 22, fax 75 13 16 40, Skolegade 45) Singles/doubles with shared bathroom 350/475kr. This 30-room place is not terribly appealing but it does have the city's cheapest hotel rooms.

Cab-Inn Esbjerg (☎ 75 18 16 00, fax 75 18 16 24, e cab-inn@cab-inn.dk, Skolegade 14) Singles/doubles 485/595kr. A member of the Copenhagen chain of the same name, this is the best-value hotel in town. It occupies an attractive century-old building that has been thoroughly renovated. The 82 modern, comfortable rooms all have bath, TV and phone.

Hotel Ansgar (☎ 75 12 82 44, fax 75 13 95 40, w www.hotelansgar.dk, Skolegade 36) Singles/doubles with breakfast 535/780kr. This old place has straightforward rooms with bath, TV, phone and minibar.

Hotel Britannia (☎ 75 13 01 11, fax 75 45 20 85, e manager@hotelbritannia.dk, Torvet 22) Singles/doubles 840/900kr, summer family rate 795kr. This modern Best Western hotel has a central location, 79 rooms with modern amenities, a bar and a restaurant. The room rates include breakfast.

Places to Eat

In addition to the following restaurants, there are numerous grocery stores in the centre of the town.

Kongensgade A variety of eating options can be found east of Torvet on Kongensgade, the main pedestrian shopping street.

Baker Street (☎ 75 13 41 07, Kongensgade 25) Pastries around 10kr, sandwiches 22kr. This bakery cafe has big mouthwatering sandwiches on wonderfully crispy bread.

Town Pizza Bar (☎ *75 13 00 52, Kongensgade 9B*) Pizza slices 20kr. This tiny pizzeria is a local favourite and serves giant slices of tasty pizza that are a meal in themselves for most people.

Sunset Boulevard (☎ *75 18 03 88, Kongensgade 38*) Salads & submarine sandwiches 25-40kr. This is a popular place to grab a quick eat; for even cheaper fast food there's an adjacent ***McDonald's***.

Jensen's Bøfhus (☎ *75 18 18 70, Kongensgade 9*) Lunch/dinner mains 45/90kr. This place has courtyard dining and good-value lunch deals on grilled chicken and steaks.

Torvet You will find plenty of eating places around the city square.

Dronning Louise (☎ *75 13 13 44, Torvet 19*) Sandwiches, salads & light eats 40-65kr. This restaurant, on the eastern side of Torvet, sets out pavement tables on the square on warm summer days. Specialities include good quiche served with smoked salmon salad.

Papa's Cantina (☎ *75 13 08 00, Torvet 17*) Buffet before/after 4pm 89/129kr. This basement restaurant features buffets with spareribs, a salad bar, tacos and various other Mexican dishes.

Elsewhere in Esbjerg The ***Kunstpavillonen*** (☎ *75 12 64 95, Havnegade 20*) Lunch buffets 78-98kr, 3-course dinners 198kr. This new restaurant adjacent to the art museum has reasonably priced fine dining. The buffets feature a variety of herring dishes, while the full-course meals include a seafood soup, fresh salmon and other fish specialities.

Sand's (☎ *75 12 02 07, Skolegade 60*) Lunch specials around 80kr, 2-course dinners 178kr. This is a traditional restaurant specialising in Danish cuisine including smørrebrød and various fish and beef dishes.

Entertainment
You'll Never Walk Alone (☎ *75 45 40 60, Kongensgade 10*) This English-style pub,

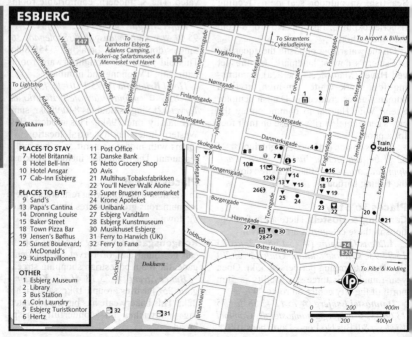

ESBJERG

PLACES TO STAY
7 Hotel Britannia
8 Hotel Bell-Inn
10 Hotel Ansgar
17 Cab-Inn Esbjerg

PLACES TO EAT
9 Sand's
13 Papa's Cantina
14 Dronning Louise
15 Baker Street
18 Town Pizza Bar
19 Jensen's Bøfhus
25 Sunset Boulevard;
   McDonald's
29 Kunstpavillonen

OTHER
1 Esbjerg Museum
2 Library
3 Bus Station
4 Coin Laundry
5 Esbjerg Turistkontor
6 Hertz
11 Post Office
12 Danske Bank
16 Netto Grocery Shop
20 Avis
21 Multhus Tobaksfabrikken
22 You'll Never Walk Alone
23 Super Brugsen Supermarket
24 Krone Apoteket
26 Unibank
27 Esbjerg Vandtårn
28 Esbjerg Kunstmuseum
30 Musikhuset Esbjerg
31 Ferry to Harwich (UK)
32 Ferry to Fanø

complete with darts and English brews on tap, has live TV broadcasts of British football and sometimes has live music as well.

Papa's Cantina (☎ 75 13 08 00, Torvet 17) This Mexican restaurant turns into a disco at midnight on Friday and Saturday.

Musikhuset Esbjerg (☎ 76 10 90 10, Havnegade 18) This performing arts centre, designed by famed Danish architect Jørn Utzon, is the city's main venue for classical music concerts.

Multihus Tobaksfabrikken (☎ 75 18 02 22, Gasværksgade 2) Rock and jazz concerts are held at this venue.

Getting There & Away
Air Ryan Air provides inexpensive air service daily between London and Esbjerg. See the Getting There & Away chapter for details.

Bus An express bus (☎ 70 10 00 30) runs between Esbjerg and Frederikshavn (215kr, five hours) at least twice daily.

Train Trains run hourly between Copenhagen and Esbjerg (260kr, 3¼ hours) during the day.

There's also a train service that runs north to Struer (140kr, 2¼ hours) and south to Ribe (37kr, 35 minutes) and Tønder (76kr, 1½ hours), and another to Kolding (68kr, 55 minutes).

Car & Motorcycle Esbjerg is 77km northwest of Tønder, 59km south-west of Billund and 92km west of the Funen-Jutland bridge.

If you're driving into Esbjerg, the E20, the main expressway from the east, leads directly into the heart of the city and down to the ferry harbour. If you're coming from the south, route 24 merges with the E20 on the outskirts of the city. From the north, route 12 makes a beeline for the city, ending at the harbour.

There's a Hertz car-rental office (☎ 75 12 60 88) by Hotel Britannia and an Avis office (☎ 75 13 44 77) at Exnersgade 19. Both companies also have booths at the airport, but you'll need to make advance reservations for airport pick-up.

Boat For details of ferry services to the UK see the Getting There & Away chapter. For information on boats leaving for Fanø, see the Getting There & Away section under Fanø, following.

Getting Around
To/From the Airport The airport is 10km east of the city centre. Public bus No 9 runs about once an hour between the airport and the train station.

Bus Most city buses can be boarded at the train station. The cost is 14kr per ride, or you can buy a 80kr card valid for 10 rides.

Car & Motorcycle There's free central parking with a two-hour limit west of Hotel Britannia (enter from Danmarksgade), and free parking with no time limit at the car park on Nørregade east of the library.

Bicycle Bikes can be hired from Skræntens Cykeludlejning (☎ 75 45 75 05), at Skrænten and Kirkegade north of the city centre, for 60kr a day. The tourist office has free English-language brochures detailing suggested cycling tours.

FANØ
postcode 6720 • pop 3200

Fanø, just 15 minutes by ferry from Esbjerg, is a long, flat island with a landscape dominated by heathland, dunes and broad sandy beaches. The two main villages, at opposite ends of the island, are Nordby and Sønderho, both of which have narrow streets and attractive period houses.

The best beaches are on the exposed north-western side of the island in the area around Fanø Bad and Rindby Strand. To the north of Fanø Bad is Soren Jemsens Sand, a 3km-long sand spit that can be explored on foot, while the packed-sand beach extending to the south is open to both cars and pedestrians. Windsurfers take to the beach south of Rindby Strand.

Information
Fanø Turistbureau (☎ 75 16 26 00, fax 75 16 29 03), Færgevej 1, is at the ferry harbour

A Cunning Deal

Until 1741 the island of Fanø was Crown property but when Christian VI, in the midst of grand construction projects across Denmark, found the royal coffers running dry he decided to sell it. He put the island up for auction, much to the chagrin of the Fanø natives, who were convinced that wealthy Ribe merchants would purchase it and impose hefty taxes.

According to one oft-told tale, on the eve of the auction Fanø's attractive young women lured the would-be bidders to a night of drink and merriment and, while they were distracted, wound the men's watches back an hour. When the auction took place the next morning at 8am, only a contingent of Fanø islanders and a single lord from Tønder appeared. The Tønder lord was forcibly squeezed behind a door by a crowd of Fanø men and the Fanø islanders put in the sole bid.

This bit of local lore aside, history does record that the Fanø islanders were able to piece together enough money to buy their island from the Crown. Along with the land, the deed also bestowed the right to own and build ships and in the next 150 years nearly 1000 sailing vessels were constructed on Fanø.

in Nordby. Opening hours are 8.30am to 6pm Monday to Saturday and 9am to 5pm on Sunday from mid-June to August. The hours are 8.30am to 5.30pm weekdays, 9am to 1pm on Saturday and 11am to 1pm on Sunday from September to mid-June.

There's a Danske Bank (☎ 76 66 07 20) at Hovedgaden 74 in Nordby. The post office (☎ 75 16 20 18), at Hovedgaden 15 in Nordby, is open 1pm to 5pm Monday to Friday and 10am to noon on Saturday.

Things to See & Do

Fanø has quite a number of sights. Most of them are seasonal; the hours fluctuate a bit, but all are open in the afternoon during the summer months.

In Nordby, just 200m west of the tourist office, is **Fanø Skibsfarts-og Dragtsamling** (☎ 75 16 22 72, Hovedgaden 28; admission 15kr), a museum of model ships, maritime displays and local costumes. **Fanø Museum** (☎ 75 16 61 37, Skolevej 2; admission 15kr), 300m to the east, is another local-history museum, this one concentrating on period furnishings.

The following attractions are in Sønderho's centre, within easy walking distance of each other. **Fanø Kunstmuseum** (☎ 75 16 40 44, Nordland 5; admission 25kr) is a small museum featuring paintings of Fanø. **Hannes Hus** (☎ 75 16 41 71, Øster Land 7; admission 12kr) is a 17th-century sea captain's home complete with decor from the period. The 18th-century **Sønderho Kirke** (☎ 75 16 40 32, Sønderho Strandvej 1) is known for its 14 votive ships.

In the centre of the island, midway between Nordby and Sønderho, is a wooded area of 1162 hectares called **Fanø Klitplantage** and crisscrossed by walking trails; it provides a habitat for deer, rabbits and birds.

Places to Stay

There are nine camping grounds on Fanø, most of which have cabins for rent in addition to the usual tent and caravan sites.

Tempo Camping (☎ 75 16 22 51, fax 75 16 12 51, Strandvejen 34, Nordby) Camping per person 51kr. Open mid-May–mid-Sept. This facility is about 1km north of Nordby.

Feldberg Strand Camping (☎ 75 16 24 90, fax 75 16 33 33, Rindby Strand) Camping per person 56kr. Open mid-Apr–mid-Oct. If you like being close to the beach, this camping ground is within walking distance of Rindby Strand.

Fanø Krogaard (☎ 75 16 20 52, fax 75 16 23 00, e mail@fanokrogaard.dk, Langelinie 11, Nordby) Singles/doubles 495/595kr, with bath 545/695kr. This 11-room inn, in Nordby near the waterfront, has pleasant rooms and reasonable rates, which include breakfast.

Sønderho Kro (☎ 75 16 40 09, fax 75 16 43 85, e sonderhokro@mail.dk, Kropladsen 11, Sønderho) Singles/doubles with breakfast from 750/940kr. An intimate, up-market choice, this small inn dates back to 1722. It's a member of the Relais & Châteaux chain.

For information on booking *summer holiday flats*, which cost 3000kr to 5000kr a week and can typically sleep four to six people, contact the tourist office.

Places to Eat
Mage's Pizza (☎ 75 16 11 22, Valdemarsvej 4) Pizzas 50kr. This eatery in the centre of Nordby has good pizzas.

Nordby Kro (☎ 75 16 35 89, Strandvejen 2) Mains around 150kr. This pleasant dinner restaurant, on the southern side of Nordby, has a good reputation for its fish dishes.

Sønderho Kro (☎ 75 16 40 09, Kropladen 11) Mains 200-240kr. This upmarket restaurant in Sønderho has traditional Danish decor and creative dishes that merge French and Danish influences.

There are *bakeries* and *cafes* in Nordby, Fanø Bad and Sønderho.

Getting There & Away
Scandlines (☎ 33 15 15 15) shuttles a car ferry between Nordby and Esbjerg from early morning until after midnight, departing two to three times an hour in the middle of the day. The return fare is 27kr for adults, 13kr for children, 27kr for a bicycle, 75kr for a motorcycle with rider and 290kr for a car with up to six people.

Getting Around
There's a local bus service from the ferry dock that runs about once an hour in summer, connecting Nordby with Fanø Bad (12kr), Rindby Strand (12kr) and Sønderho (16kr).

Bicycles can be hired in Nordby from Havnekiosken (☎ 75 16 21 20), a kiosk next to the tourist office, and from Fanø Cykler (☎ 75 16 25 13) at Hovedgaden 96.

RIBE
postcode 6760 • pop 8,000
Ribe, the oldest town in Denmark, is chock-full of historic sites. Recent excavations, which unearthed a number of silver coins, indicate that a market town existed on the northern side of the Ribe Å River as far back as 700. In 850 Saint Ansgar built the first church in Ribe and the town began to grow. During the Viking era Ribe, linked to the sea by its river, flourished as a centre of trade between the Frankish Empire and the Scandinavian states to the north.

In the 12th century the Valdemar dynasty fortified the town, building a castle and establishing Ribe as one of the king's Jutland residences.

During the late medieval period, as power shifted to eastern Denmark, the importance of Ribe declined. In 1580 a sweeping fire destroyed a third of the town's buildings and, in the century that followed, the incessant wars with Sweden strangled trade and further impoverished the town. Meanwhile the Ribe Å silted up and the town's population began to drop off. With the founding of the port city of Esbjerg in 1868, Ribe was completely bypassed as a trade centre.

Ironically, in terms of town preservation, Ribe's economic misfortunes have served to spare its historic buildings from modernisation. As a result the town centre, which surrounds an imposing medieval cathedral, retains a unique centuries-old character. With its crooked cobbled streets and half-timbered 16th-century houses, Ribe is a bit like a living history museum. Indeed, the entire old town is a preservation zone, with more than 100 buildings registered by the National Trust.

Orientation
Ribe is a tightly clustered place, easy to explore. Everything, including the hostel and the train station, is within a 10-minute walk of Torvet, the central square.

Information
The Ribe Turistbureau (☎ 75 42 15 00, fax 75 42 40 78, ⓔ infotur@ribekom.dk), Torvet 3, is conveniently located on Torvet and is open 9.30am to 5.30pm Monday to Friday and 10am to 5pm on Saturday in July and August. It's open 9am to 5pm Monday to Friday (to 4.30pm between November and March) and 10am to 1pm on Saturday during the rest of the year.

Danske Bank (☎ 76 88 68 20) at Overdammen 4, just east of Torvet, has an outdoor ATM. The post office (☎ 79 12 12 12), Sct

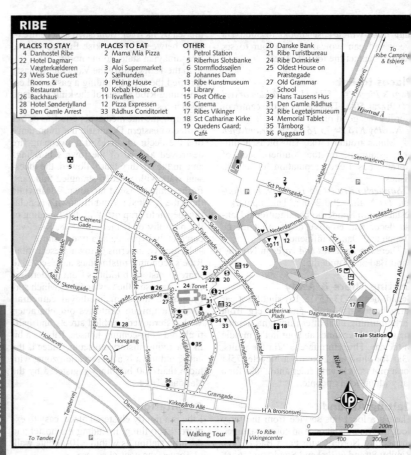

RIBE

PLACES TO STAY
4 Danhostel Ribe
22 Hotel Dagmar;
    Vægterkælderen
23 Weis Stue Guest
    Rooms &
    Restaurant
26 Backhaus
28 Hotel Sønderjylland
30 Den Gamle Arrest

PLACES TO EAT
2 Mama Mia Pizza
   Bar
3 Aloi Supermarket
7 Sælhunden
9 Peking House
10 Kebab House Grill
11 Isvaflen
12 Pizza Expressen
33 Rådhus Conditoriet

OTHER
1 Petrol Station
5 Riberhus Slotsbanke
6 Stormflodssøjlen
8 Johannes Dam
13 Ribe Kunstmuseum
14 Library
15 Post Office
16 Cinema
17 Ribes Vikinger
18 Sct Catharinæ Kirke
19 Quedens Gaard;
    Café

20 Danske Bank
21 Ribe Turistbureau
24 Ribe Domkirke
25 Oldest House on
    Præstegade
27 Old Grammar
    School
29 Hans Tausens Hus
31 Den Gamle Rådhus
32 Ribe Legetøjsmuseum
34 Memorial Tablet
35 Tårnborg
36 Puggaard

Nicolajgade 12, is open 10am to 5pm week-days and 10am to noon on Saturday.

The library (☎ 75 12 17 00), Giørtzvej 1, has Internet access and is open 10am to 6pm on weekdays and 10am to 1pm on Saturday.

Walking Tour

You can visit central Ribe's historic sights on a leisurely looped walk that takes a couple of hours.

The walk begins at Torvet and follows Overdammen east to Fiskergade, where you turn left. On Fiskergade you'll notice many alleys leading east to the riverfront. Take a

look at the 'bumper' stones on the house corners; the alleys are so narrow that the original residents installed these stones to protect their houses from being scraped by the wheels of horse-drawn carriages.

At the intersection of Fiskergade and Skibbroen you'll find **Stormflodssøjlen**, a wooden flood column commemorating the numerous floods that have swept over Ribe. Note the ring at the top of the column indicating the water's depth (6m above normal!) during the record flood of 1634, which claimed hundreds of lives. Although these days low-lying Ribe is afforded somewhat more protection by a system of dikes, residents are still subject to periodic evacuation.

At Stormlodssøjlen, look south-east along the waterfront to find the **Johanne Dan**, a replica of an 1867 sailing ship designed with a flat bottom that allowed it to navigate the shallow waters of the Ribe Å; it's occasionally open in summer for boarding.

Continue north-west along Skibbroen, which skirts the old medieval quay, now lined with small motorboats.

From Skibbroen then turn south onto Korsbrødregade and head south-east along Præstegade. About halfway down on the right, you'll pass this street's **oldest house**, constructed in 1580, as noted on the plaque above the door; it was once the residence of the cathedral curate. Continue back to **Ribe Domkirke**, skirting around the cathedral's western side and onto Skolegade.

On the corner of Skolegade and Grydergade is an **old grammar school** that first opened in the early 16th century. On the opposite side of Skolegade is the two-storey **Hans Tausens Hus**, which dates from the early 17th century and is one of Denmark's oldest bishops' residences. A **statue** of Hans Tausen, who helped spark the Danish Reformation, stands opposite in the churchyard.

From Skolegade continue south on Puggårdsgade, a cobbled street lined with older homes. The timber-framed **brick house** on the corner of Sønderportsgade and Puggårdsgade has an interesting 2nd storey that overhangs the road. A couple of buildings down on the left is **Tårnborg**, a 16th-century manor house that now serves as a local government office. On the same side of the street, but a little farther south, is a half-timbered house dating back to 1550.

When you reach Gravsgade go right for about 50m and on the northern side of the street you'll find the brick **Puggaard**, a canon's residence constructed in about 1500. From there turn around and walk east on Gravsgade, then turn north onto Bispegade.

On the corner of Bispegade and Sønderportsgade you'll find a **memorial tablet** dedicated to Maren Spliid, burned at the stake on 9 November 1641, one of the last victims of Denmark's witch-hunt persecutions.

From that corner continue north past **Den Gamle Rådhus** (the Old Town Hall) and back to your starting point on Torvet.

Ribe Domkirke

Standing as a fine testament to Ribe's prominent past is the town's dominant landmark, Ribe Cathedral (☎ 75 42 06 19, Torvet; adult/child 12/5kr; open 10am-5.30pm Mon-Sat, noon-5.30pm Sun, July-Aug; 10am-5pm Mon-Sat, noon-5pm Sun, May, June & Sept; reduced hours in winter). The diocese of Ribe was founded in 948 but its original cathedral was just a modest wooden building. In 1150 Ribe's Bishop Elias, with considerable financial backing of the royal family, began work on a more stately stone structure.

The new cathedral was constructed primarily from tufa, a soft porous rock quarried near Cologne and shipped north along the Rhine. It took a century for the work to reach completion. The later additions included several Gothic features, but the core of the cathedral remains decidedly Romanesque, a fine example of medieval Rhineland influences in architecture.

One notable feature is the original 'Cat's Head' door at the south portal of the transept, which boasts detailed relief work including a triangular pediment portraying Valdemar II and Queen Dagmar positioned at the feet of Jesus and Mary. At noon and 3pm the cathedral bell plays the notes to a

Sepulchral Monuments

In the Renaissance period, arranging for burial inside Ribe Domkirke became trendy among those wealthy enough to afford the floor space. Most of these graves are marked by simple carved stones in the aisles, but there are also more ostentatious memorials and chapels containing the remains of bishops and other distinguished citizens of the day. The highest-ranked bones within the confines of the cathedral are those of King Christopher I, who was buried in 1259 directly beneath the great dome in the middle of the sanctuary.

folk song about Dagmar's death during childbirth.

The interior decor is a hotchpotch of later influences. Among the highlights are an organ with a facade designed by renowned 17th-century sculptor Jens Olufsen and an ornate altar created in 1597 by Odense sculptor Jens Asmussen. You can find frescoes dating from the 16th century along the northern side of the cathedral, while in the apse are modern-day frescoes, stained-glass windows and seven mosaics created in the 1980s by artist Carl-Henning Pedersen.

For a towering view of the countryside, climb 27m up the cathedral tower, which dates back to 1333. A survey of the surrounding marshland makes it easy to understand why the tower once doubled as a lookout station for floods.

Sct Catharinæ Kirke

St Catharine's Church (*☎ 75 42 05 34, Sct Catharinæ Plads; admission free; open 10am-noon & 2pm-5pm daily*) was founded by Spanish Black Friars in 1228. The original church, which built on reclaimed marshland, eventually collapsed. The present structure dates back to the 15th century. Of the 13 churches built in Ribe during the pre-Reformation period, Sct Catharinæ Kirke and Ribe Domkirke are the only survivors.

In 1536 the Reformation forced the friars to abandon Sct Catharinæ Kirke and, in the years that followed, the compound served as, among other things, an asylum for the mentally ill and a wartime field hospital. The abbey is currently used as housing for the elderly.

In the 1920s Sct Catharinæ Kirke was restored at tremendous cost (due to its still-faulty foundations) and was reconsecrated in 1934. The interior boasts a delicately carved pulpit dating back to 1591 and an ornate altarpiece created in 1650. Entry to the adjacent garden courtyard costs 3kr.

Den Gamle Rådhus

This building (*☎ 76 88 11 22, Von Støckens Plads; adult/child 15/5kr; open 1pm-3pm daily June-Aug, 1pm-3pm Mon-Fri May & Sept*), opposite the south-eastern corner of

---

Stork Watch

A look at the top of Den Gamle Rådhus in Ribe will reward you with the rare sight of a large, round nest built of sticks and reaching a couple of metres in diameter. Each year around 1 April a pair of storks returns to this nest. Ribe residents enthusiastically follow the comings and goings of these great birds and even have a little ceremony on the first Thursday after the birds return.

Ribe Domkirke, dates back to 1496, making it the oldest town hall in Denmark. In addition to being the site of council meetings it also houses a small collection of historical artefacts, including medieval weapons and the executioner's axe.

Before entering the rådhus, take a look at the highest point of its gable, which doubles as a nesting site for a pair of storks.

Quedens Gaard

This history museum (*☎ 76 88 11 22, Over-dammen 10; adult/child 20/5kr; open 10am-5pm daily June-Aug, 11am-3pm Tues-Sun Sept-May, 11am-1pm in midwinter*) is in a half-timbered former merchant's house, the oldest wing of which was built in 1583. Part of the house retains merchants' furnishings from the early 17th century; other rooms exhibit furniture and crafts from earlier periods plus trade and industry displays from more recent times.

Ribes Vikinger

Opposite the train station is the Vikings of Ribe (*☎ 77 88 11 22, Odin Plads 1; adult/child 50/20kr; open 10am-6pm daily July-Aug, 10am-4pm daily Sept-Oct & Apr-June, 10am-4pm Tues-Sun Nov-Mar*) This substantial and well-presented museum features informative displays on Ribe's Viking and medieval history.

One exhibition hall reproduces a marketplace in AD 800, complete with a cargo-laden Viking ship, while another hall has a late-medieval scene set in the town centre. There are also many interesting archaeological

GLENDA BENDURE

NED FRIARY

NED FRIARY

Clockwise from top left: Aalborg's prosperous past meant businessmen could build stately homes like that of early mayor, Jørgen Olufsen; Since those heady times, towns like Ribe have become sleepy villages with preserved medieval streets; Legoland's version of Old Amsterdam.

Thatched roof, the Lake District, Central Jutland.

Cleaning the daily catch, Skagen.

Below the thatched roof, the Lake District.

Preserving a maritime history on the *Danmark*.

A fishing boat on Ebeltoft harbour.

finds including pottery shards, glass and amber beads and an anchor from a Viking ship. Facilities include a museum shop and a cafe serving light meals.

Ribe Vikingecenter

The Ribe Vikingecenter (☎ 75 41 16 11, Lustrupvej 4; adult/child 50/20kr; open 11am-4.30pm daily July-Aug; 11am-4pm Tues-Sun May, June & Sept), 3km south of the town centre, is affiliated with the Ribes Vikinger museum. The Vikingecenter tries to re-create a slice of life in Viking-era Ribe using various reconstructions, including a 34m Fyrkat-style longhouse. The staff, who dress in period clothing, cook over open fires, demonstrate Viking-era crafts, such as pottery and leatherwork, and offer falconry demonstrations.

Ribe Kunstmuseum

Housed in a 19th-century villa, Ribe Kunstmuseum (☎ 75 42 03 62, Sct Nicolajgade 10; adult/child 30kr/free; open 11am-5pm daily mid-June–Aug, 1pm-4pm Tues-Sun Sept–mid-June) is one of the oldest art museums in Denmark and has consequently acquired a good collection, particularly of works by the 19th-century Danish 'Golden Age' painters. Exhibits include works by Juel, Abildgaard, Eckersberg, Købke and Michael Ancher.

Other Attractions

A costumed **night watchman** makes his rounds from Torvet at 8pm and 10pm between June and August and you can follow him as he sings his way through the old streets. The tour starts in front of the Weis Stue restaurant and proceeds south from Torvet. It's an unabashedly touristy scene that's both fun and free. In May and during the first half of September the watchman makes the rounds once each night at 10pm.

Ribe Legetøjsmuseum (☎ 75 41 14 40, Von Støckens Plads 2; adult/child 30/15kr; open 10am-5pm daily June-Aug, 1pm-5pm daily Sept-Oct & Apr-May, 1pm-4pm Nov-Mar), just south-east of Ribe Domkirke, features a collection of 19th- and 20th-century antique toys, including porcelain dolls.

Riberhus Slotsbanke, 1km north-west of the town centre, is the moated site of a former 12th-century royal castle; it served as a fort until the 17th century and was then dismantled for its stones. In the south-western corner of the grounds is a statue of Queen Dagmar.

Places to Stay

Camping & Hostels The following are good options for budget accommodation.

Ribe Camping (☎ 75 41 07 77, fax 75 41 00 01, e ribe@dk-camp.dk, Farupvej 2) Camping per person 56kr. Open year-round. This three-star camping ground in a field about 2km north of Ribe centre is the nearest to town.

Danhostel Ribe (☎ 75 42 06 20, fax 75 42 42 88, e ribe@danhostel.dk, Sct Pedersgade 16) Dorm beds 100kr, singles/doubles 250/295kr. Open Feb-Nov. This modern 140-bed hostel has helpful management and

NC

Tour Ribe with one who watches over the city.

comfortable rooms. The location is ideal – on a quiet marsh but within walking distance of the main sights. All rooms have a bath and some are accessible to people in wheelchairs. Common facilities include a kitchen, sitting areas and a TV lounge. This is a popular hostel, so reservations are recommended.

Private Rooms The tourist office distributes an annually updated brochure listing some 20 private homes that rent *rooms*. Some are in the town centre, others are in Ribe's outskirts. Rates are 200/350kr for singles/doubles in Ribe, 150/250kr for places a few kilometres outside town.

Hotels & Inns The *Hotel Sønderjylland* (☎ 75 42 04 66, fax 75 42 21 92, Sønderportsgade 22) Singles/doubles with breakfast 350/550kr. This hotel, 300m west of Torvet, has straightforward rooms above a small pub.

There are also two restaurants in town that rent similar 2nd-storey rooms: *Weis Stue* (☎ 75 42 07 00, Torvet) with singles/doubles for 250/450kr, and *Backhaus* (☎ 75 42 11 01, Grydergade 12) at 250/500kr. Both places include breakfast.

Den Gamle Arrest (☎ 75 42 37 00, fax 75 42 37 22, e dga2505@post4.tele.dk, Torvet 11) Singles/doubles from 400/540kr, with bath 550/690kr. This is Ribe's most unusual place to stay. It was the town jail from 1893 until 1989 and has now been turned into an 11-room hotel. There's a certain austere quaintness in entering your room through the old steel doors but, as might be expected, converted jail cells make rather cramped quarters. Prices include breakfast.

Hotel Dagmar (☎ 75 42 00 33, fax 75 42 36 52, e dagmar@hoteldagmar.dk, Torvet 1) Singles/doubles with breakfast from 775/975kr. This red-brick hotel in the centre of Ribe dates back to 1581, giving some credence to its claim of being the oldest hotel in Denmark. Restored to retain its period character, it has 50 rooms with bath, TV, phone and minibar.

Places to Eat
Rådhus Conditoriet (☎ 73 42 01 50, Hundegade 2) Pastries & sandwiches 8-25kr. Just a couple of minutes' walk south-east from Torvet, this is a nice spot for a dessert o light lunch.

Pizza Expressen (☎ 75 41 14 10, Nederdammen 28) Pizza slices 20kr. This place has long hours and serves large slices o good pizza.

Isvaflen (☎ 75 41 06 88, Nederdammen 18) You'll find all-natural Underground ice cream (two-scoop cones 15kr) here.

Kebab House Grill (☎ 75 42 50 15, Nederdammen 18) Hot dogs 18kr, kebab sand wiches 33kr. This fast-food eatery is adjacent to the ice-cream shop.

Peking House (☎ 75 41 16 00, Nederdammen 21) Lunch/dinner buffets 30/109kr Open 11am-10pm. This little restaurant of fers Chinese buffets that are a good deal especially for lunch, which is served unti about 4.30pm.

Mama Mia Pizza Bar (☎ 75 41 17 67, Sc Pedersgade 4) Lunch/dinner pizzas 30/50kr Open 11am-10.30pm. Just outside the hos tel and opposite the Aloi supermarket, this convenient pizzeria has bargain pizza price: from 11am to 3pm.

Quedens Gaard Café (☎ 76 88 11 22 Overdammen 10) Soup or sandwiches 40kr Beside Quedens Gaard museum, this cafe i. a pleasant place for light meals.

Sælhunden (☎ 75 42 09 46, Skibbroen 13 Lunch specials 54-84kr, dinner mains 100 160kr. Kitchen open noon-9pm. Top choice for a leisurely meal is this atmospheric restaurant, which has the best seafood i town and offers generous servings as well The smoked ham and asparagus sala makes a delicious lunch, while the frie plaice with shrimp and mussels is the din ner favourite here.

Weis Stue (☎ 75 42 07 00, Torvet) Dan ish beef plate 85kr, dinner specials 130kr For a old-fashioned dining experience, hea to this leaning half-timbered tavern wit wooden plank tables, dating back to 1704 which serves Danish and German food.

Vægterkælderen (☎ 75 42 00 33, Torvet 1 Mains 100-140kr. Kitchen open noon-10pm This basement restaurant at the histori Hotel Dagmar shares the kitchen with the Dagmar's expensive main dining room, bu has less fastidious service and a more basic menu. The best deal in the basement is the 500g spareribs plate (109kr) that can easily feed two.

Getting There & Away

Ribe is 30km south of Esbjerg via route 24 and 47km north of Tønder via route 11.

Trains from Ribe run hourly on weekdays and slightly less frequently at weekends to Esbjerg (37kr, 35 minutes) and to Tønder (52kr, 50 minutes).

Getting Around

There's parking with a two-hour limit on the southern side of Ribe Domkirke, a parking area with a three-hour limit at Ribes Vikinger and parking with no time limit at the end of Sct Pedersgade near the hostel.

Bicycles can be hired from Danhostel Ribe for 57kr a day.

RØMØ
postcode 6792 • pop 850

Rømø, the largest Danish island in the North Sea, extends 17km from north to south and about 6km across. Lying off the coast midway between Ribe and Tønder, just 5km north of the German island of Sylt, it's connected to the Jutland mainland by a 10km causeway that passes over scenic marshland with grazing sheep and wading water birds. The causeway has a cycle lane.

For more than a hundred years Rømø has been a popular summer resort for German tourists, although in the low season it is a windswept sleeper.

The western side of the island, exposed to the North Sea, is lined with expansive sandy beaches that attract scores of windsurfers. The busiest beach area is at Lakolk, on the central west coast.

Lakolk 'village' is essentially a large strip-mall shopping centre and a camping ground on the inland side of the dunes. Although Lakolk is separated from the beach by just 100m, the beach itself is more than 1km wide, so it's a pretty hefty walk over the sand flats to the water's edge, particularly at low tide. Some people drive out, but be careful not to park your car in an incoming tide zone.

Despite a few unsightly caravan parking areas, most of Rømø is a rural scene with thatched houses, open spaces and the scent of the sea heavy in the air. The main settlements are on the east coast in the 7km stretch from the causeway bridge south to the harbourside village of Havneby.

Rømø is rich in birdlife and its west coast provides a habitat for about 1500 seals, which haul themselves onto sandbanks to sunbathe during the day. The north-western corner of the island is a restricted military zone.

Information

The Rømø Turistbureau (☎ 74 75 51 30, fax 74 75 50 31, e romo@romo.dk), at Havnebyvej 30, Tvismark, is 1km south of the causeway. It's open 9am to 7pm Monday to Saturday and 10am to 6pm Sunday from April to October; 9am to 5pm daily the rest of the year.

Tønder Bank (☎ 74 75 56 77) is at Havnebyvej 102 in Kongsmark, and there's an after-hours ATM.

The post office (☎ 74 75 52 69), Havnebyvej 60 in Kongsmark, is open 11am to 4pm Monday to Friday.

Things to See

Kommandørgården (☎ 74 75 52 76, Juvrevej 60, Toftum; adult/child 15kr/free; open 10am-6pm Tues-Sun May-Sept, 10am-3pm Tues-Sun Oct), 1.5km north of the causeway, is a handsome sea captain's house (circa 1748), that retains much of its original decor, including 4000 Dutch wall tiles. It displays local history which, in Rømø, is strongly tied to the sea. In the 18th century a disproportionately high number of Rømø men served as kommandører (sea captains) on German and Dutch whaling ships that hunted in the waters off Greenland.

Another remnant of the whaling era, a **whale jawbone fence**, can be found 1km farther north on the eastern side of the main road in the village of Juvre.

The island's 18th-century church, **Rømø Kirke**, is on the main road in Kirkeby, about midway between Havneby and the causeway. It's noted for its unique Greenlandic gravestones erected by sea captains and

SOUTHERN JUTLAND

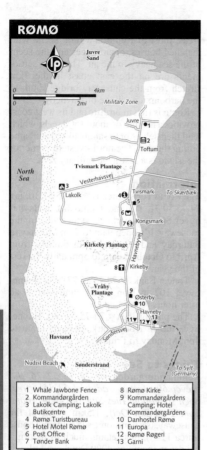

ROMØ

1 Whale Jawbone Fence	8 Rømø Kirke
2 Kommandørgården	9 Kommandørgårdens
3 Lakolk Camping; Lakolk	Camping; Hotel
Butikcentre	Kommandørgårdens
4 Rømø Turistbureau	10 Danhostel Rømø
5 Hotel Motel Rømø	11 Europa
6 Post Office	12 Rømø Røgeri
7 Tønder Bank	13 Garni

decorated with reliefs of their boats and families; these stones can be seen lining the northern wall of the churchyard.

Walking
The inland section of this flat island has trails through both heathered moors and wooded areas, offering quiet hiking spots. There are three forest zones, each with a couple of kilometres of trails: Tvismark Plantage, along Vesterhavsvej, the main east-west road; Kirkeby Plantage, to the west of Kirkeby; and Vråby Plantage, a less diverse area dominated by pines, about 1km farther south.

Water Sports
Water activities are based largely along the west coast, with the main **windsurfing** zone south of Lakolk. Almost all windsurfers arrive with their own equipment so hired gear is not usually available, but try inquiring at the tourist office or at Lakolk Camping.

There's a **nudist beach** in the Sønderstrand area, at the south-western tip of the island; to reach it, take Søndersvej to its western end, from where it's a 2km hike across the sand flats to the ocean.

Places to Stay
Both of Rømø's camping grounds are three-star rated with full facilities and have food shops and restaurants nearby.

Lakolk Camping (☎ 74 75 52 28, fax 74 75 53 52, Lakolk) Camping per person 59kr. Open early Apr–mid-Oct. This camping ground is on the west-coast beach at Lakolk.

Kommandørgårdens Camping (☎ 74 75 51 22, fax 74 75 59 22, Havnebyvej, Østerby) Camping per person 60kr. Open year-round. This camping ground is adjacent to the hotel of the same name and is managed by the same people.

Danhostel Rømø (☎ 74 75 51 88, fax 74 75 51 87, e romo@danhostel.dk, Lyngvejen 7, Østerby) Dorm beds 100kr, doubles from 250kr. Open 15 Mar-Oct. This 91-bed hostel on the south-eastern side of the island near Havneby is in a traditional thatched roof building.

Hotel Motel Rømø (☎ 74 75 51 14, Gamle Færegevej 1, Kongsmark) Singles/doubles with bath & breakfast 325/395kr. About 1km south of the tourist office, this is a simple motel-style place with good-value rooms.

Hotel Kommandørgårdens (☎ 74 75 51 22, fax 74 75 59 22, e info@kommandoer gaarden.dk, Havnebyvej 201, Østerby) Singles or doubles with bath in summer 795kr, singles/doubles at other times from 425/595kr; huts & apartments per week 1525-4950kr, depending on size and season. This 80-unit hotel has a large pool, tennis courts and a minimarket. Breakfast is included in the tariffs for singles and doubles.

The vast majority of accommodation on Rømø is found in some 1300 *summer houses* scattered around the island. Prices vary, with rates for a simple six-person cabin-like place ranging from 1500kr to 3000kr per week, depending on the season. A ritzier chalet costs roughly twice that. The tourist office can provide a catalogue with photos and prices of the houses and handle the bookings.

Places to Eat

Rømø Røgeri (☎ 74 75 54 52, Havnevej 1, Havneby) Seafood items 15-60kr. Not far from the harbour, this place sells delicious smoked herring and cooked shrimp by weight and has a small cafe with reasonably priced fish dishes.

Europa (☎ 74 75 59 73, Vestergade 3, Havneby) Dishes 50-100kr. This restaurant serves pizzas, other Italian food and Greek dishes at moderate prices.

Kommandørgårdens Restaurant (☎ 74 75 51 22, Havnebyvej 201, Østerby) Meat & fish mains around 100kr. At Hotel Kommandørgårdens, this sit-down restaurant features grilled salmon and steak dishes.

There's a *grocery shop* and *bakery* in Østerby, within walking distance of the hostel.

There's a *supermarket*, *bakery* and various *eateries* at the Lakolk Butikcentre, which fronts Lakolk Camping; these include hot-dog stands, a cafe, a pizzeria and a cafeteria.

Getting There & Away

Rømø is on route 175, about 14km west of Skærbæk.

Bus No 29 runs from Skærbæk to Havneby (12kr, 35 minutes) about once an hour on weekdays, less often at weekends. From Skærbæk there are trains about once an hour to Ribe (37kr, 19 minutes), Tønder (45kr, 28 minutes) and Esbjerg (84kr, one hour).

Rømø-Sylt Linie (☎ 73 75 53 03) operates car ferries between Havneby and the German island of Sylt (46kr, one hour) several times each day.

Getting Around

From late May to early September bus No 29/591 makes a 20-minute trip from Havneby up the east-coast road and over to Lakolk. There are about 10 runs on weekdays, and about half that weekends. It costs 12kr to go anywhere on the island.

The best choice, if you don't have your own transport, is to rent a bicycle, as Rømø is flat and small enough to explore. You can hire bikes from Garni (☎ 74 75 54 80) at Nørre Frankel 15 in Havneby for 35/175kr per day/week and at Hotel Kommandørgårdens (☎ 74 75 51 22) in Østerby for 45/270kr.

TØNDER

postcode 6270 • pop 8200

Tønder, is just 4km north of the German border. It is a historic town that retains a few curving cobblestone streets lined with half-timbered houses.

Tønder's town charter was issued in 1243. Although it's surrounded by marshland today, it was once a busy market town with access to the sea. Because it's low-lying, Tønder has always been subject to serious flooding and in medieval times it was nearly swept away altogether. In the 16th century a network of dikes was erected to protect the town from flooding but the dikes also contributed to the transformation of the tidal flats and the seas eventually receded, leaving the town landlocked.

By the 18th century Tønder was again prospering; it had become the centre of a high-quality lace-making industry which, at its peak, employed some 12,000 workers in the greater Tønder area. Many of the town's finest houses were erected by wealthy lace merchants.

These days the high point in town is the last weekend of August when the Tønder Festival (☎ 74 72 46 10, W www.tf.dk), one of Denmark's largest folk festivals, attracts a multitude of international and Danish musicians for more than 40 concerts.

Information

The Tønder Turistbureau (☎ 74 72 12 20, fax 74 72 09 00) is in the centre of town at Torvet 1. It's open 9.30am to 5.30pm on weekdays and 9.30am to 3pm on Saturday between mid-June and August; opening hours are 9am to 4pm on weekdays and 9am to noon on Saturday for the rest of the year.

SOUTHERN JUTLAND

There are a couple of banks near Torvet, the central square. The post office (☎ 73 22 40 00) is at Vestergade 83, a few minutes' walk north of the train station.

Things to See

Some of the town's most picturesque streets lined with period houses are off Søndergade, just a couple of minutes' walk south of Torvet. The best-preserved is the cobbled Uldgade.

Tønder Museum (☎ 74 72 26 57, Kongevej 51; adult/child 30kr/free; open 10am-5pm daily June-Aug, 10am-5pm Tues-Sun Sept-May) exhibits objects relating to regional history, including a collection of delicate Tønder lace, period furniture and Dutch wall tiles. In an adjacent wing, **Sønderjyllands Kunstmuseum** features Danish surrealist and modern art, mostly by lesser-known artists. A single ticket covers entry to both sections. The site is a 10-minute walk east of the train station.

Kristkirken (Torvet; admission free; open 10am-4pm Mon-Sat), the large church on the north-eastern side of the square, dates back to the late 16th century. The 47.5m-high tower, part of an earlier church that once stood on this site, doubled as a navigational marker in the days when Tønder was connected to the sea. The church interior boasts some impressive carvings and paintings, including a font from 1350, an ornate pulpit from 1586 and a series of memorial tablets from around 1600.

Det Gamle Apotek (Østergade 1), on Torvet, is noted mainly for its elaborate 1671 Baroque doorway flanked by two lions. Also worth a look is the old-fashioned interior, which was converted from a pharmacy to a gift shop just a decade ago.

Places to Stay

Tønder Campingplads (☎/fax 74 72 18 49, Holmevej 2) Camping per person 50kr. Open Apr-late Sept. East of the town centre and adjacent to the hostel, this three-star facility is part of Tønder Fritidscenter (sports centre), which includes tennis courts, a swimming pool and squash courts.

Danhostel Tønder (☎ 74 72 35 00, fax 74 72 27 97, ✉ danhostel@tonder-net.dk, Sønderport 4) Dorm beds 100kr, doubles 325kr. Open Feb-late Dec. This hostel, jus a few minutes' walk east of the town centre has comfortable rooms, each with four bed and a bathroom.

The tourist office can provide a list o *rooms* in private homes in the Tønder area which cost 200/300kr for singles/doubles.

Hostrups Hotel (☎ 74 72 21 29, fax 74 7: 07 26, Søndergade 30) Singles 490-610kr doubles 610-725kr. This old hotel, a fev minutes' walk south-east of Torvet, has 2: rooms, most with bath, desk and TV.

Hotel Tønderhus (☎ 74 72 22 22, fax 7 72 05 92, Ⓦ www.hoteltonderhus.dk, Jom frustien 1) Singles/doubles from 775/900kr Opposite Tønder Museum, this hotel is in a modern brick building with 50 standard motel-style rooms with bath, TV and phone

Places to Eat

Choices are limited and many people jus drive south to Germany where food i cheaper. Otherwise your best bet for restau rants is to look around Torvet.

Torve Bistroen (☎ 74 72 41 55, Torvet Fast-food standards 35-50kr. This popula cafe serves fish and chips, vegetarian ome lettes, sandwiches and burgers.

Torvets Restaurant (☎ 74 72 43 73 Torvet) Mains around 100kr. In the same building as Torve Bistroen, this is the town's upmarket spot with a varied menu o meat and fish dishes.

Konfekturen (☎ 74 72 65 22, Østergade 2A) This little place, 20m east of Torvet sells organic ice cream, cappuccino and espresso, for 15kr to 25kr.

Spisehuset Asian (☎ 74 72 38 36, Øster gade 37) Chinese mains around 42kr. Thi is the place for cheap Chinese dishes and some inexpensive grilled items.

Pizzeria Italiano (☎ 74 72 53 05, Øster gade 40) Pizzas & pastas at lunch/dinne from 49/65kr. A short walk east of Torvet this pizzeria has good pizza and past dishes. Immediately west of the pizzeria i a *bakery*.

There's a *market* selling fruit, vegetable and cheese at Torvet on Tuesday and Frida mornings.

Getting There & Away

Tønder is on route 11, 4km north of the border with Germany and 77km south of Esbjerg.

The train station is on the western side of town, 1km from Torvet via Vestergade. Trains run hourly on weekdays and slightly less frequently at weekends from Ribe (52kr, 50 minutes) and Esbjerg (76kr, 1½ hours).

MØGELTØNDER

If you're in the Tønder area, don't leave without first visiting the fetching village of Møgeltønder, 4km to the west.

The centre of the village is the cobbled main street Slotsgade, lined with period brick houses sporting thatched roofs and colourful wooden doors. At the western end of Slotsgade is **Schackenborg**, a small castle that was presented by the Crown to Field Marshal Hans Schack in 1661 following his victory over the Swedes in the battle of Nyborg. Members of the Schack family occupied the castle until 1978, when it was returned to the royal family.

Since their marriage in 1995, Queen Margrethe's youngest son, Prince Joachim, and his wife, Princess Alexandra, have made Schackenborg their primary residence. Although the castle building is off limits to the public, the moat-surrounded grounds on the opposite side of the street have been turned into a small public park that's open to all.

At the eastern end of Slotsgade is **Møgeltønder Kirke** *(Slotsgade 1; admission free; open 8am-5pm daily May-Sept, 9am-4pm Oct-Apr)*, which has one of the most lavish church interiors in Denmark. The Romanesque nave dates back to 1180 and the baptismal font is from 1200, but the church has had numerous additions – the Gothic choir vaults were built during the 13th century, the tower dates from about 1500 and the chapel on the northern side was added in 1763.

The interior is rich in frescoes, gallery paintings and ceiling drawings. Here too is one of the oldest church pipe organs in Denmark, dating back to 1679. The elaborately detailed gilt altar dates back to the 16th century. Note the 'countess bower', a balcony with private seating for the Schack family,

who owned the church from 1661 until 1970.

Places to Stay & Eat

Schackenborg Slotskro *(☎ 74 73 83 83, fax 74 73 83 11, Slotsgade 42, 6270 Tønder)* Singles/doubles from 845/990kr. This place in the village centre has 11 comfortable if pricey rooms. It has a pavement *cafe* with lunchtime omelettes and other light meals for around 75kr, and an upmarket Danish *restaurant* with three-course meals for 275kr.

Getting There & Away

Møgeltønder is 4km west of Tønder on route 419.

Bus No 66 connects Tønder with Møgeltønder (11kr, 10 minutes) about once every hour on weekdays, and less frequently on the weekend.

HØJER

If you're heading directly to the island of Rømø from Møgeltønder you'll pass right through Højer, a rural market town that once served as a port for shipping southern Jutland cattle. Constructed only a few metres above sea level, Højer is bordered by marshland and is protected by an extensive network of sluice gates and dikes, some of which date back to the 16th century.

Although it's not a must-see town, Højer does have some distinctive red-brick houses with thatched roofs and claims the only **thatched town hall** in Denmark. The main site of interest, in the centre of town next to the tourist office, is a nicely restored **Dutch windmill** *(☎ 74 78 29 11; Møllegade 13; admission 20kr; 10am-4pm Mon-Fri Apr-Oct)* that was built in 1857 and houses a little local-history museum.

If you're interested in **bird-watching**, the coastal marshland west of Højer is a rich habitat for wading birds, sea birds and shore birds.

Getting There & Away

Højer is on route 419, about 7km west of Møgeltønder. Bus No 66 connects Højer with Møgeltønder (22kr) and Tønder (22kr) about hourly.

SOUTHERN JUTLAND

KOLDING
postcode 6000 • pop 57,000

Kolding, unassuming as it is, ranks as Jutland's fifth-largest city. Despite its industrial edge, Kolding has a pleasant centre with a lakeside castle and a few other historic buildings. In addition there's a worthwhile art museum on the city outskirts.

Information

The Kolding Turistbureau (☎ 76 33 21 00, fax 76 33 21 20), Akseltorv 8, is open 9.30am to 7pm Monday to Friday, and to 4.30pm on Saturday from July to mid-August; it's open 9.30am to 5.30pm weekdays, and until 2pm on Saturday during the rest of the year.

There's a branch of Danske Bank (☎ 76 34 35 00) on the southern side of Akseltorv and a post office (☎ 79 43 50 00) at the train station.

Central Attractions

Akseltorv, the central square, is the site of **Borchs Gård**, a decorative Renaissance building which dates from 1595. Pedestrian streets radiate out from Akseltorv. Helligkorsgade, a few minutes' walk south of Akseltorv at the end of Østergade, is a pleasant street for a stroll; you'll find Kolding's **oldest house** at No 18, a lovely timber-framed affair built in 1589. Just west of Akseltorv, on the other side of the rådhus, is **Sankt Nicolai Kirke** *(Nicolai Plads; admission free)*, a medieval church that was largely rebuilt in the 19th century. It's not grandly interesting but the interior does have a late-16th-century altar and pulpit.

Koldinghus

The town's main landmark is Koldinghus *(☎ 76 33 81 00, Adelgade 1; adult/child 50/25kr; open 10am-5pm daily)*, a castle fortress immediately north of Akseltorv. The first fortress on this site was built in 1268 by Erik V to guard the border between Denmark and the Duchy of Schleswig. The oldest parts of the current castle, the north and west wings, date from around 1440. The distinctive tower was added in around 1600 by Christian IV, who spent much of his childhood at Koldinghus.

In 1808 Spanish troops stationed at Koldinghus during the Napoleonic Wars tried to fight off the chilly Danish weather by building a roaring fire in one of the castle's hearths; the fire got out of hand, engulfing a defective chimney, and the castle went up in flames. Koldinghus was left in ruins until 1890, when the north wing was restored to house a museum. The work continued piecemeal over nearly a century. The exterior now has an 18th-century Baroque appearance while the castle interior retains some original Gothic and Renaissance influences innovatively fused with modern Scandinavian architecture.

Koldinghus has displays of church sculpture, paintings, period furnishings and some historical exhibits, including one about the Schleswig wars.

Kunstmuseet Trapholt

The Trapholt Museum of Modern Art *(☎ 7 30 05 30, Æblehaven 23; adult/child 50kr/free; open 10am-5pm daily)* is on the eastern outskirts of the city on the northern side of the Kolding Fjord. Opened in 1988 this is one of Denmark's largest museums dedicated to 20th-century art. The fine arts collection includes works by Anna Archer, Richard Mortensen, Franciska Clausen and Per Kirkeby. The applied arts section shows the influence of Danish design on ceramics, textiles and furniture. There are also quality changing exhibits. Take bus No 4 from the train station.

Places to Stay

Vonsild Camping *(☎ 75 52 13 88, fax 75 52 45 29, Vonsildvej 19)* Camping per person 60kr. Open year-round. This three-star camping ground is on the southern outskirts of Kolding.

Danhostel Kolding *(☎ 75 50 91 40, fax 75 50 91 51,* e *kolding@danhostel.dk, Ørnsborgvej 10)* Dorm beds 90kr, doubles 270kr. Open Feb-Nov. This 90-bed hostel is 1km north-west of the city centre.

Saxildhus *(☎ 75 52 12 00, fax 75 53 53 10,* e *saxildhus@mail.tele.dk, Banegårdspladsen)* Singles/doubles with breakfast from 695/845kr. This classic period hotel opposite the train station has modernised rooms, most of which are comfortable and have bath, TV and minibar.

Places to Eat
The main cluster of eateries are near Akseltorv, the central square. Take Jernbanegade west from the station and it's just a 10-minute walk to Akseltorv.

Jensens Bøfhus (☎ 75 53 50 55, Jernbanegade 11) Lunch/dinner mains 45/90kr. This steakhouse, between the station and Akseltorv, has affordable steaks and grilled chicken.

Café Piano (☎ 75 52 26 57, Akseltorv 3) Salads & light meals 35-60kr. This friendly cafe is right on the square.

China Garden (☎ 75 53 32 18, Østergade 19) Dishes 60-90kr. This place, 100m south of Akseltorv, has good Chinese food at moderate prices.

Getting There & Away
Train There are regular train services from Kolding south to Padborg on the German border (84kr, 70 minutes) and north all the way to Frederikshavn (230kr, four hours). There's a second line to Esbjerg (68kr, 55 minutes). Trains run roughly hourly, except for services to Padborg (every two hours).

Car & Motorcycle Kolding is 92km east of Esbjerg and 82km north of the German border. The E20 (which continues east to Funen) and the E45 connect Kolding with other major towns in Jutland. If you're travelling leisurely by road north to south, route 170 is a pleasant alternative to the E45.

HADERSLEV
postcode 6100 • pop 30,000
Haderslev is a likeable town at the head of the Haderslev Fjord. Established as a market town in the 13th century, its centre has been well restored. You'll find some of the town's finest period buildings on **Torvet**, a cobbled square bordered by half-timbered buildings and filled with sculptures by Erik Heide.

In addition to the fjord, the town also borders a lake, Haderslev Dam, which offers some good canoeing opportunities.

Information
The Haderslev Turistbureau (☎ 74 52 55 50, fax 74 53 46 67), Honnøkajen 1, is on the town outskirts, 1km east of the centre. It's open 9.30am to 4.30pm on weekdays and 9.30am to 2.30pm on Saturday.

There are several banks along Nørregade, including a Jyske Bank (☎ 73 53 12 00) at No 22 and a Danske Bank (☎ 73 22 46 46) at No 23.

The post office (☎ 73 22 40 00) is at Gravene 8, to the north of the town centre.

Haderslev Domkirke
Haderslev's cathedral *(Apotekergade; admission free; open 10am-5pm daily May-Sept, 10am-3pm Oct-Apr)*, on a knoll above Torvet, is the most imposing building in town. Parts of the building, including the transept and nave, date back to the mid-13th century, while other additions were made in the centuries that followed. It's said that in 1525 it was the site of the first Lutheran teachings in Denmark.

Haderslev Domkirke has an impressive interior. Particularly notable is the altar, which has a crucifix dating back to about 1300 and alabaster figures of the 12 apostles created around 1400. There's also a grand Sieseby organ and a baptismal font dating from 1485.

Haderslev Museum
This museum *(☎ 74 52 75 66, Dalgade 7; adult/child 15kr/free; 10am-4pm Tues-Sun June-Aug, 1pm-4pm Tues-Sun Sept-May)*, 1km north-east of Torvet, features exhibits on southern Jutland's archaeological history as well as a small open-air museum with a windmill and a few other period buildings.

Ehlers-samlingen
This museum *(☎ 74 53 08 58, Slotsgade 20; admission 20kr; open 10am-5pm Tues-Fri, 2pm-5pm Sat & Sun; closed Wed & Fri in low season)* specialises in displays of Danish pottery from the Middle Ages to 1900, when the regional distinctions in Danish pottery styles began to erode. The museum is housed in an attractive timber-framed building dating back to 1577.

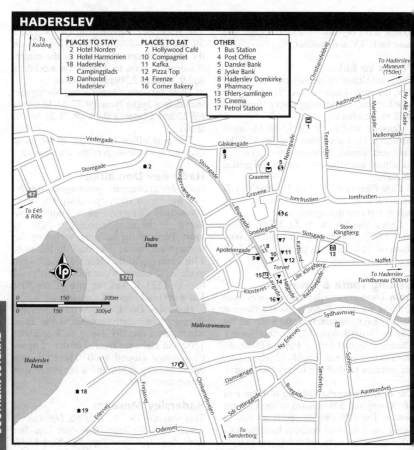

HADERSLEV

PLACES TO STAY
2 Hotel Norden
3 Hotel Harmonien
18 Haderslev Campingplads
19 Danhostel Haderslev

PLACES TO EAT
7 Hollywood Café
10 Compagniet
11 Kafka
12 Pizza Top
14 Firenze
16 Corner Bakery

OTHER
1 Bus Station
4 Post Office
5 Danske Bank
6 Jyske Bank
8 Haderslev Domkirke
9 Pharmacy
13 Ehlers-samlingen
15 Cinema
17 Petrol Station

SOUTHERN JUTLNAD

Places to Stay

Danhostel Haderslev & Haderslev Campingplads *(☎ 74 52 13 47, fax 74 52 13 64, e bh-had@post12.tele.dk, Erlevvej 34)* Camping per person 60kr, dorm beds 100kr, doubles 250kr. Hostel open Feb-Nov, camping ground open June–mid-Oct. This site, 1km south-west of the town centre, on the southern shore of the Haderslev Dam, has both a camping ground and an 80-bed hostel. There's a playground and canoes for hire.

Hotel Harmonien *(☎ 74 52 37 20, fax 74 52 44 51, e hotel.harmonien@mail.tele.dk, Gåskærgade 19)* Singles/doubles 695/795kr.

Amenities at this 28-room hotel include private bath, TV and phone.

Hotel Norden *(☎ 74 52 40 30, fax 74 52 40 25, e sales@hotel-norden.dk, Storegade 55)* Singles/doubles 885/1085kr. A rather upmarket option, this 68-room hotel, about 500m north-west of Torvet, has an indoor swimming pool and rooms with modern amenities including minibars. There's a restaurant, a bar and conference facilities.

Places to Eat

There are numerous places to grab a bite on or near the central square, Torvet.

Pizza Top (☎ 74 53 47 00, Torvet 8) Pizzas 30-45kr. This simple pizzeria on the eastern side of Torvet has a pizza of the day for 30kr as well as a range of sandwiches and hot dogs.

Firenze (☎ 74 53 05 05, Torvet 13) Pizzas & pastas 75kr, meat & fish dishes 150kr. This Italian restaurant on the southern side of Torvet is a more upmarket option than Pizza Top.

Kafka (☎ 74 53 00 08, Nørregade 6) Mains 50-60kr. This stylish cafe serves good coffee and a variety of dishes including pastas and Danish lunches of fish and smørrebrød.

Hollywood Café (☎ 74 53 55 57, Nørregade 12) Lunch 39kr, dinner 70kr. This agreeable place has inexpensive omelettes and salads at lunch, and lasagne and similar dishes at dinner.

Compagniet (☎ 74 53 54 44, Torvet 7) Lunch 50kr, 2-course dinner 200kr. This upmarket cafe right on Torvet has good Caesar salads and sandwiches at lunch, and steaks and fresh fish at dinner.

Corner Bakery (☎ 74 52 30 15, Lavgade 10) Baguette sandwiches 22kr. This bakery a block south of Torvet serves good pastries and filling sandwiches.

Getting There & Away
Bus & Train Bus Nos 33 and 35 frequently run between Haderslev and Vojens (22kr, 20 minutes), the nearest train station. Trains to Vojens run about hourly from Fredericia (45kr, 45 minutes) and a bit less often from Sønderborg (45kr, one hour).

Bus No 34 runs hourly between Haderslev and Kolding (24kr), taking 45 minutes.

Car & Motorcycle Haderslev is 31km south of Kolding via route 170 or the E45 and 51km east of Ribe via routes 24 and 47. There's a large free car park at the southern side of Sydhavnsvej with no time limit.

PADBORG
postcode 6330 • pop 4700
Padborg, near the German border, is the site of **Frøslevlejren** (Frøslev Camp), an internment camp opened near the end of WWII to detain members of the growing Danish Resistance. Built just 5km from Germany to avoid having to deport Danes from Danish soil, Frøslevlejren held 12,000 prisoners during its nine months of operation.

The camp buildings now house a collection of displays and museums. The most prominent is **Frøslevlejrens Museum** *(☎ 74 67 65 57, Lejrvejen 83; admission 25kr; open 10am-5pm daily late June-early Aug, 9am-4pm Tues-Fri & 10am-5pm Sat & Sun in low season; closed Dec & Jan)*, which depicts the Danish Resistance movement and daily prison life at Frøslev. Other buildings house free exhibits by Amnesty International and branches of the Danish defence forces. On a lighter note there's also an exhibit on local wildlife.

Frøslevlejren is on the north-western outskirts of Padborg, 1km west of the E45 (take exit 76).

ALS
pop 3200
The 33km-long island of Als is separated from the Jutland mainland by the narrow Als Sund. Its only large town, Sønderborg, sits at the south-western corner of Als; the rest of the island is a quiet provincial region of small farming villages. The best beaches are in the south, where there are seaside camping grounds.

Sønderborg
postcode 6400 • pop 26,700
Sønderborg, an agreeable seaside town on the island of Als, traces its origins back to medieval times when Valdemar I (the Great) erected a castle fortress along the waterfront. The town grew up around the castle and, with its fine natural harbour, prospered as a fishing and trading centre.

Sønderborg played a notable role in Denmark's history as the site of the final battle in the German invasion of 1864. The Danish loss at the pivotal Battle of Dybbøl, fought on the western outskirts of town, marked the beginning of a German occupation in the region that continued until the end of WWI. One legacy of that 1864 battle is Sønderborg's predominantly modern appearance:

The heavy artillery bombardment that took place during the fighting left much of the town in rubble.

Today Sønderborg has a distinctively peaceful appearance and caters in equal measure to German and Danish tourists.

Orientation Sønderborg spreads along both sides of the Als Sund (Als Sound), which is spanned by two bridges. The town centre and Sønderborg Slot are to the east, on the island of Als, while the Dybbøl area and the train station are on the western side, which is part of mainland Jutland. There's a small sandy beach right in town by the southern side of the castle.

Information The Sønderborg Turistbureau (☎ 74 42 35 55, fax 74 42 57 47), Rådhustorvet 7, is on the main town square. It's open 9.30am to 6pm Monday to Friday and 8.30am to 1pm on Saturday between mid-June and mid-August; the hours are 9.30am to 5pm weekdays and 9.30am to 1pm on Saturday during the rest of the year.

There's a post office (☎ 73 43 62 00) as well as a couple of banks along the pedestrian street Perlegade, immediately north of Rådhustorvet.

Things to See The town's dominant sight is the waterfront **Sønderborg Slot**, a castle dating back to the 12th century, when it was constructed as a circular fortress to defend against marauding Wends. The deposed king, Christian II, was held captive here from 1532 to 1549 – not in the dungeon but in comfortable royal chambers. Sønderborg Slot has been rebuilt over the years, with its current Baroque design dating back to 1718. Of special interest is the chapel, built in 1568 by the dowager queen Dorothea, widow of Christian III, because it is Denmark's first Lutheran chapel and one of Europe's oldest preserved royal chapels.

The castle now houses **Museet på Sønderborg Slot** (☎ 74 42 25 39, Slotsbakken; adult/child 25/10kr; open 10am-5pm daily May-Sept, reduced hours in low season), featuring exhibits on the wars of 1848 and 1864, the maritime history of Sønderborg,

medieval church art and the German occupation of Denmark.

Dybbøl, on the western side of the Als Sund, was the site of the most important battle in the Danish-German war of 1864. The **Historiecenter Dybbøl Banke** (☎ 74 48 90 00, Dybbøl Banke 16; adult/child 40/15kr; open 10am-5pm daily mid-Apr–Sept) museum has a multimedia display commemorating the bloody battle that marked the fall of southern Jutland to the Germans. The reconstructed windmill **Dybbøl Mølle** (☎ 74 48 90 00, Dybbøl Banke 15; adult/child 25/10kr; open 10am-5pm daily mid-Apr–Sept), on the opposite side of the street, was damaged in the battle of 1864 and is now a national historic site.

Places to Stay Sønderborg has a reasonable range of accommodation to cater for its tourist trade.

Sønderborg Camping (☎/fax 74 42 41 89, Ringgade 7) Camping per person 54kr. Open Apr–mid-Sept. This three-star camping ground is set in a wooded area near the yacht harbour, 1km south-east of the town centre.

Danhostel Sønderborg (☎ 74 42 31 12, fax 74 42 56 31, e sonderborg@danhostel.dk, Kærvej 70) Dorm beds 100kr, doubles 300kr. Open Feb-Nov. This modern hostel 1km north of the centre, is almost motellike with comfortable guest rooms, a lounge with a fireplace, a sauna and sports fields. Most of the 44 rooms have just four beds, and all have baths and double entry doors to ensure quiet.

Hotel Arnkilhus (☎ 74 42 23 36, fax 74 42 23 39, Arnkilgade 13) Singles/doubles with breakfast from 375/550kr. This hotel, about 500m north of the centre, is Sønderborg's cheapest, with 13 straightforward rooms.

Quality Hotel Sønderborg (☎ 74 42 00 00, fax 74 42 76 00, e info.soenderborg@quality.choicehotels.dk, Ellegårdvej 27) Singles/doubles 895/1095kr, in summer 595/795kr. This modern hotel, on the northern outskirts of town, has an indoor pool, comfortable rooms and good summer deals.

Places to Eat You'll find plenty of eating places on or near Rådhustorvet.

Byens Smørrebrød *(☎ 74 43 28 30, Råd-hustorvet 3)* Dishes around 35kr. This place offers fast food such as chicken with chips, mostly for takeaway, but on warm days there are a couple of pavement tables where you can sit and eat.

Maybe Not Bob *(☎ 74 42 52 28, Rådhus-torvet 5)* Sandwiches 25-30kr. This has some outdoor seating on the square, and draws a young crowd with Kilkenny beer on tap and reasonably priced sandwiches.

Café Druen *(☎ 74 43 43 90, St Rådhus-gade 1)* Sandwiches & veg dishes 30-65kr. You'll find creative sandwiches and other simple dishes at this pleasant cafe 100m south of the tourist office.

On most days a ***greengrocer*** selling organic fruits and vegetables sets up a van in front of the tourist office.

Getting There & Away Sønderborg is 30km north-east of the German border crossing at Kruså, via route 8.

The airport is 6km north of town. The commuter airline Cimber Air offers daily direct flights to Copenhagen. For more information, see the Getting Around chapter.

Sønderborg is connected by numerous trains a day to Kolding (108kr, 1¼ hours) and the rest of Jutland. It's also possible to go from Sønderborg to Padborg (52kr), changing trains in Tinglev; with a good connection it takes about an hour.

Getting Around If you want to cycle between sights, bicycles can be hired from Stavgaard Eft (☎ 74 42 33 75) on Kastanie Allé 2, a block north-east of Rådhustorvet.

Around Als

Tourist sights on the rest of Als are limited; many of the villages have small churches of varying antiquity that can be visited, and there's a dolmen and a Viking burial site on the eastern coast at Blommeskobbel.

Augustenborg, 8km north-east of Sønderborg along route 8, is one of Als' more easily accessible and interesting villages. It has a compact centre, of which the main street begins at the gate of **Augustenborg Slot**, an 18th-century Baroque palace that now serves as a psychiatric hospital. The grounds are open to all, as is the small exhibition in the gatehouse and the courtly palace chapel (if the chapel door is locked, ask to borrow the key from the hospital caretaker). The Augustenborg Turistbureau (☎ 74 47 17 20) is at Storegade 28, just 300m west of the palace in a picturesque house, which dates back to about 1769.

For those with their own transport the area around **Kegnæs**, the island at the southern tip of Als, is an enjoyable destination for a short outing, with gently pastoral countryside and sandy beaches. Fifteen kilometres south-east of Sønderborg via route 427, Kegnæs is connected to the rest of Als by a short causeway. On Kegnæs, 1km west of the causeway, is a hill-top **lighthouse** *(admission 5kr)* that can be climbed for a coastal view. If you want to try your luck at angling, the fishing is said to be good at the western end of Kegnæs; otherwise the only place on the island that you're likely to find any company is at the beach.

Places to Stay & Eat Outside of Sønderborg, accommodation and dining options are naturally more limited.

Drejby Camping *(☎ 74 40 43 05, fax 74 40 49 73, Kegnæsvej 85)* Camping per person 56kr. Open Mar-Oct. In Skøvby, to the north-east of the causeway to Kegnæs, there's a long sandy beach and the four-star Drejby Camping, Als' most popular seaside camping ground, which has 500 sites, a grill-style eatery and a minimarket.

Getting There & Away On weekdays bus No 13 leaves from the Sønderborg bus station about twice hourly for Augustenborg (22kr, 12 minutes).

As bus services in the more rural parts of Als are sketchy, a pleasant alternative for those without their own transport is to hire a bike in Sønderborg. The Sønderborg tourist office sells a map (30kr) with suggested cycling tours.

Central Jutland

Central Jutland covers a broad swath of Denmark extending from Fredericia in the south to the Limfjord in the north. The western side is an expansive plain of windswept moors, bordered by a coastline of beach flats and sand dunes. Although this western region was predominantly wild heathland until the 19th century, much of it has now been turned into pasture and sugar beet fields. The more protected eastern side of central Jutland has fertile soil, small farms, a coastline indented with shallow fjords, and the largest cities and towns.

East Central Jutland

This section of the Jutland region has two significant – but quite dissimilar – tourist destinations. Children who have grown up playing with Lego blocks will undoubtedly want to make a beeline for Legoland, Jutland's most visited attraction, while adults travelling without kids may be more interested in Jelling, one of Denmark's most important historic sites.

FREDERICIA
postcode 7000 • pop 36,700

Fredericia is an industrial city that's notable to visitors mainly for its old fortified ramparts. The town dates from 1650, when Frederik III began construction of the fortress to guard the narrow sound between Jutland and Funen. Over the centuries the Fredericia fortress played a significant role in the frequent wars between Denmark and its neighbours.

In the winter of 1657–58 Swedish troops, on their way to Copenhagen, overran the fortress and killed the entire garrison before marching on across the frozen waters of the Lille Bælt. The most celebrated battle that was fought here took place two centuries later when, in 1849, the successful defence

Highlights

- Enjoy Århus' trendy cafe life and Viking-era sights
- Wander around Den Gamle By, the largest open-air museum in Denmark (Århus)
- Get active in the Lake District with its hiking, canoeing and cycling possibilities
- Come eye to eye with the remains of the 'bog people' at museums in Silkeborg and Århus
- Relive your childhood at Legoland amusement park, Denmark's most-visited family destination
- Examine historic rune stones at Jelling Kirke
- Follow quiet trails through the heather-covered hills of Rebild Bakker
- Marvel at the 1000-year-old Fyrkat Viking ring fortress near Hobro

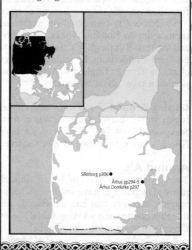

Silkeborg p306 •
Århus pp294-5 •
Århus Domkirke p297

of Fredericia from German assault halted the northward advance of the Schleswig-Holstein troops.

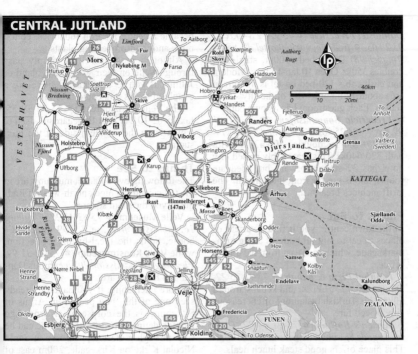

CENTRAL JUTLAND

Orientation

The train and bus stations are together to the west of the town centre. To get to the tourist office, walk north from the stations, turn right onto Vesterbrogade and follow it to the ramparts, then enter the old town gate at Danmarks Port through the rampart wall to Danmarksgade. The walk takes approximately 10 minutes.

Information

Fredericia Turistbureau (☎ 75 92 13 77, fax 75 93 03 77, ⓔ *turisme@fredericiakom.dk*) Danmarksgade 2A, is open 9am to 6pm on weekdays and 9am to 3pm on Saturday from June to August; it's open 9.30am to 5pm on weekdays and 10am to 1pm on Saturday during the rest of the year.

There are several banks on Gothersgade, just a few minutes' walk south-east of the tourist office.

The post office (☎ 80 20 70 30) is on the northern side of the train station.

Things to See & Do

The old earthen **ramparts** of the Fredericia fortress remain largely intact, and form a mounded park-like green belt around the oldest section of the city. The ramparts themselves extend about 2km and are topped with scattered war memorials, cannons and a footpath. You can get the best overview of it all from the top of the rampart wall at the western end of Danmarksgade, where there's a water tower that can be climbed in summer. A free English-language brochure detailing the history of different parts of the wall is available at the nearby tourist office.

The other main sight is the **Fredericia Museum** (☎ 72 10 69 80, Jernbanegade 10; adult/child 20kr/free; open 11am-4pm daily in summer, noon-4pm Tues-Sun rest of the year), which displays local military and civilian history exhibits in an attractive collection of historic buildings, just a few minutes walk south of the train station.

CENTRAL JUTLAND

Places to Stay

Danhostel Fredericia (☎ *75 92 12 87, fax 75 93 29 05,* e *fredericia@danhostel.dk, Vestre Ringvej 98)* Dorm beds 100kr, singles or doubles 350kr. Open 10 Jan-15 Dec. Modern and cushy, this 120-bed hostel is in a green area about 1km north-west of the city's train station. Each guestroom has its own bath.

Fredericia Sømandshjem (☎ *75 92 01 99, fax 75 93 25 90,* e *fsh@fsh.dk, Gothersgade 40)* Singles/doubles 300/420kr, with bath 520/640kr. This reasonably priced city hotel has 32 straightforward but adequate rooms, and is not far from the harbour. The tariff includes breakfast.

Places to Eat

In the town centre, you'll find a variety of places to eat to suit all budgets along Danmarksgade, which runs east from the tourist office.

Istanbul Pizza & Kebab (☎ *75 93 25 22, Danmarksgade 5)* Pizza and kebabs around 50kr. This Turkish restaurant offers reasonably priced fare.

Jensen's Bøfhus (☎ *75 91 44 32, Danmarksgade 8)* Lunch/dinner mains 45/100kr. This place offers good steak lunch deals.

Bøf & Vino (☎ *75 93 08 08, Danmarksgade 36)* Mains 50-100kr. This friendly Italian restaurant serves everything from pizza and pasta to beef dishes.

The train station has a *minimarket* and a cheap *snack bar* where you can get burgers and sandwiches.

Getting There & Away

Fredericia has good train connections, being on the north-south line between Padborg and Frederikshavn and also on the Copenhagen to Århus route. Train fares are 68kr to Odense (25 minutes), 100kr to Padborg (75 minutes) or Århus (1 hour) and 230kr to Copenhagen (2 hours).

Fredericia is north of the E20, 80km from Nyborg and 92km from Esbjerg.

VEJLE

postcode 7100 • pop 48,100

Vejle, at the head of the Vejle Fjord, is a bustling industrial city. In the 19th century,

after the railway was extended to here, Vejle became a centre for iron foundries, cotton mills and food-processing plants.

Although most travellers simply pass through Vejle on their way to Legoland or Jelling, if you're less hurried there are a couple of sights you could take in.

The Vejle Turistbureau (☎ 75 82 19 55, fax 75 82 10 11) is at Banegårdspladsen 6, which is on the southern side of the train station.

Things to See

The following two adjacent museums are in the town centre, a block north-west of Rådhustorvet, the main square.

Vejle Museum (☎ *75 82 43 22, Flegborg 18; admission free)*, in a 1799 merchant's house, holds the local-history collection, while **Vejle Kunstmuseum** (☎ *75 72 31 99, Flegborg 16; admission 20kr)* exhibits Danish and European art.

More interesting, if you haven't already seen one of the 'bog people' in Århus or Silkeborg, is the corpse of an **Iron Age woman** dating back to 450 BC. She can be seen through a glass-topped case at Sankt Nicolai Kirke on Kirkegade, 200m east of Rådhustorvet.

Places to Stay & Eat

Danhostel Vejle (☎ *75 82 51 88, fax 75 83 17 83,* e *info@vejle-danhostel.dk, Gammel Landevej 80)* Dorm beds 90kr. This hostel is 5km south-east of the city, near the E45.

Staff at the tourist office can book *rooms* in private homes and there are a few moderately priced *hotels* in the centre.

You'll find the usual array of *bakeries*, *cafes* and *restaurants* in the central streets around Rådhustorvet.

Getting There & Away

Vejle is off the E45, 73km south-west of Århus and 30km north of Kolding.

Vejle has frequent train departures because it's on both the main Jutland line and the branch line to Jelling and Herning. From Vejle it's 45 minutes (76kr) to Århus, 36 minutes (52kr) to Kolding and an hour (68kr) to Herning.

JELLING

postcode 7300

Jelling is a small town with a rich history. Although its sleepy rural character provides few hints to its past, Jelling once served as the royal seat of King Gorm the Old, the first in a millennium-long chain of Danish monarchs that continues unbroken to this day. The site of Gorm's ancient castle remains a mystery but other vestiges of his reign can still be found at Jelling Kirke.

Information

The Jelling Turistbureau (☎ 75 87 13 01) is 100m west of Jelling Kirke at Gormsgade 4. This seasonal office is open 10am to 4pm (until 6pm in July) daily from June to August.

Jelling Kirke

Jelling Church *(cnr Gormsgade & Vejlevej, admission free; open 8am-5pm Mon-Fri, 8am-2pm Sat; grounds open outside these hours)*, erected in about 1100, is one of Denmark's most significant historical sites. Inside this small whitewashed church you'll find some vividly restored 12th-century **frescoes** that are among the oldest in Denmark. The main attractions, however, are the two well-preserved **rune stones** just outside the church door.

The smaller stone was erected in the early 10th century by Gorm the Old in honour of his wife. The larger one, raised by Gorm's son Harald Bluetooth, is adorned with the oldest representation of Christ found in Scandinavia and reads:

Harald king bade this be ordained for Gorm his father and Thyra his mother, the Harald who won for himself all Denmark and Norway and made the Danes Christians.

Harald Bluetooth did, in fact, succeed in routing the Swedes from Denmark and begin the peaceful conversion of the Danish people to Christianity, and away from the pagan religion celebrated by his father. The larger stone, commonly dubbed 'Denmark's baptismal certificate', not only represents the advent of Christianity but also bids a royal farewell to the ancient gods of prehistoric Denmark. One side of the stone, which depicts a snake coiled around a mythological creature, is thought to symbolise this change of faith.

Two huge **burial mounds** flank Jelling Kirke. The barrow to the north was long believed to contain the bones of Gorm and his queen Thyra, but when it was excavated in 1820 no human remains were found. In 1861 Frederik VII oversaw the excavation of the southern mound but, again, only a few objects were found with no mortal remains among them.

In the 1970s a team of archaeologists excavated beneath Jelling Kirke itself and hit pay dirt. They found the remains of three earlier wooden churches; the oldest is thought to have been erected by Harald Bluetooth. A burial chamber was also unearthed at this time and human bones and gold jewellery were discovered. The jewellery was consistent with pieces that had been found earlier in the northern burial mound.

Archaeologists now believe that the skeletal remains found beneath the church are those of Gorm, who had originally been buried in the northern mound but was later re-interred by his son. Presumably Harald Bluetooth, out of respect, moved his parents' remains from pagan soil to a Christian place of honour within the church. The bones of Queen Thyra have yet to be found.

The Jelling burial mounds, church and rune stones are a designated Unesco World Heritage Site.

The large rune stone at Jelling Kirke dedicated to Harald Bluetooth.

Jelling Kirke is in the centre of town, just a two-minute walk due north from the train station along Stationsvej.

Kongernes Jelling

This new exhibition centre (☎ 75 87 23 50, Gormsgade 23; adult/child 30/15kr; open 10am-5pm Tues-Sun 15 Apr-15 Oct, 1pm-4pm Tues-Sun 16 Oct-14 Apr), which is directly opposite the church, traces the history of the Jelling church and burial grounds using changing exhibits to explore related themes.

Places to Stay & Eat

Jelling Camping (☎ 75 87 16 53, fax 75 87 20 82, e jelling@dk-camp.dk, Mølvangvej 55) Camping per person 52kr. Open mid-Apr–mid-Sept. This three-star facility is right in town, 1km west of Jelling Kirke, and has a swimming pool.

Jelling Kro (☎ 75 87 10 06, fax 75 87 10 08, Gormsgade 16) Singles/doubles with shared bathroom for 395/595kr, which includes breakast. This place has six rooms and is just 200m north of the Jelling Kirke. You can also get a daily two-course meal here for 138kr.

Harald Blåtand (☎ 75 87 10 03, Gormsgade 11) Meals 65-90kr. Also nearby the church, this restaurant offers reasonably priced meat and potato specials.

Getting There & Away

Jelling is 10km north-west of Vejle on route 442. From Vejle (20kr, 15 minutes) trains run at least hourly on weekdays, slightly less frequently at weekends.

LEGOLAND

postcode 7190

Legoland, 1km north of the small town of Billund, is Denmark's most visited tourist attraction outside Copenhagen. A 10-hectare theme park built from plastic Lego blocks, Legoland has hosted some 30 million visitors, more than half of them from outside Denmark, since opening in 1968.

Legoland has its own bank, post office, tourist office, hotel and restaurants, and even its own airport.

Information

The Billund Turistbureau (☎ 76 50 00 55, fax 75 35 31 79), Legoland Parken, is inside Legoland, but also has an entrance facing the outside of the park. It's open 10am to 6pm daily during the Legoland season (to 8pm in July and August).

The Danske Bank, inside the tourist office, is open 10am to 4pm daily (to 7.30pm during summer).

Things to See & Do

The park's main attraction (☎ 75 33 13 33, W www.legoland.dk, Aastvej; adult/child 150kr/140kr, under 3 free; open 10am-8pm daily Apr–mid-July & mid-Aug–early Sept; 10am-9pm daily mid-July–mid-Aug; 10am-6pm Mon-Fri, 10am-8pm Sat & Sun early Sept-end Oct) is a Lilliputian world of 45 million plastic blocks arranged into miniature cities, plus scenes with Lego pirates and safari animals. Most replicas are on a scale of 1:20 and include the medieval town of Ribe, Amalienborg Slot in Copenhagen and a handful of recognisable international cities and sights such as Amsterdam, Los Angeles and the Acropolis.

At times the park employs as many as 30 'builders', who spend their days snapping together the creations. The tallest piece, a model of the American Indian chief Sitting Bull, reaches 14m in height and contains 1.4 million Lego blocks. The most elaborate piece is the 3.5-million-block Copenhagen Harbour exhibit, which features electronically controlled ships, trains and cranes.

Legoland also features numerous amusement rides. Most of the rides are along the lines of merry-go-rounds, miniature trains and mechanical boats geared to children but there are a few, like the water slide, that can be fun for adults as well. All are included in the admission price except for the children's traffic school (25kr), a driving course with little electric cars.

There's also an antique doll collection, a children's theatre and Mindstorms Center, where visitors can build programmable robots. The various theme-park sections include Legoredo, a small Wild West town with a few costumed gunslingers and Indians in

Plastic Fantastic

Lego got its start more than 60 years ago when a local carpenter, Ole Kirk Christiansen, tried his hand at making wooden toys to earn money during a Depression-era construction slump. In 1934, after a couple of years of making pull-toys and piggy banks, Ole selected the business name Lego, a contraction of the Danish words *leg godt*, meaning 'play well', and expanded his line to four dozen toy designs.

In the late 1940s Lego became the first company in Denmark to acquire a plastics injection-moulding machine and began making interlocking plastic blocks called 'binding bricks', the forerunner of today's Lego blocks. In 1960, when Lego's wooden-toy warehouse went up in flames, the company decided to concentrate solely on plastic toys. By that time Lego blocks had become the most popular children's toys in Europe.

Lego continued to expand. In 1969 it created the Duplo series for younger children, with bricks twice as long and twice as wide as basic Lego blocks. Later, it introduced little vehicles, wooden families and complex theme sets of trains, pirate ships and the like. Although there are now advanced kits incorporating motors and fancy gadgets, the basic appeal of Lego continues to be the simple interlocking blocks that can be snapped together in endless creative combinations.

Lego is still a family-run business, today headed by Ole Kirk's grandson, but it's grown into one of Denmark's best-known companies and Europe's largest toy manufacturer. Lego now has 50 branches on six continents. It's estimated that in the past 50 years some 300 million children worldwide have at one time or another played with Lego toys.

feather headdresses; Pirateland, with ships and swordplay; Castleland, featuring a train ride through a castle; and Duplo Land, with gentle rides for very young children.

Note that the activities and rides usually shut down two hours before Legoland closes and there's no admission charge after the rides stop. In this evening period when it is open gratis to the public you can still view the Lego block sights – so for those just curious to see what the park is all about it's an ideal time to swing by for a free stroll.

Places to Stay

In the high season places to stay near Legoland are often fully booked, so advance reservations are advised. Nonetheless, even then tourist office staff can usually find you a hotel, or a room in a private home (175kr per person), though you may have to go 10km to 20km outside town. There's no booking fee for the service.

Billund FDM Camping (☎ *75 33 15 21, fax 75 35 37 36,* **e** *c-billund@fdm.dk, Ellehammer Allé 2*) Camping per person 59kr, 2-6–person cabins 250-500kr. Open year-round. This three-star facility is 400m east of the Legoland gate. It is one of Denmark's largest camping grounds, with 550 sites, a food store, lounges and playground.

Danhostel Billund (☎ *75 33 27 77, fax 75 33 28 77,* **e** *billund@danhostel.dk, Ellehammer Allé 2*) Dorm beds 100kr, 4-bed family rooms 400kr. Open year-round. This modern five-star facility, with 228 beds, is adjacent to Billund FDM Camping.

Billund Kro (☎ *75 33 26 33, fax 75 35 31 91,* e *billund-kro@billund-kro.dk, Buen 6)* Singles/doubles 645/710kr. This place is 1km south-west of Legoland, near route 28. Part of the Dansk Kroferie association, it has 30 rooms, each with bath, phone and TV. For the double rate buy an 'Inn Cheque' at the tourist office.

Hotel Legoland (☎ *75 33 12 44, fax 75 35 38 10,* e *hotel@legoland.dk, Aastvej 10)* Singles/doubles with breakfast from 1030/1355kr. This hotel is opposite Legoland itself, but is connected by an overhead walkway. It is the largest hotel in the area. The rooms are comfortable with bath, TV, phone and minibar.

Hotel Svanen (☎ *75 33 28 33, fax 75 35 35 15, Nordmarksvej 8)* Singles/doubles with breakfast 785/825kr. A cheaper option, this motel-style place is 600m south-east of Legoland, in the same neighbourhood as the hostel. It has 24 modern rooms with bath, phone and TV.

Places to Eat
Legoland has about a dozen food stands serving the expected amusement park fare. The names given to these simple eateries – Hotdogs, Burger House, Coffee & Pastry, Pizza Slice, Pancakes and Soft Ice – simply reveal the menus. You can snack at any of them for around 40kr.

Hotel Legoland Restaurant (☎ *75 33 12 44, Aastvej 10)* Lunch/dinner buffet 158/196kr. This is the Legoland choice for a more substantial meal, with grand buffet spreads after a hard day in the park.

Café Bistro (☎ *75 33 27 77, Ellehammer Allé 2)* Breakfast/dinner 40/65kr. This hostel cafe serves a buffet-style breakfast and changing two course dinners.

Getting There & Away
Billund is on route 28, 59km north-east of Esbjerg and 28km west of Vejle.

Air Billund's airport sits right outside Legoland's gate, serving not only Legoland but, but because of its central Jutland location, has grown into Denmark's second busiest airport.

Maersk Air (☎ 70 10 74 74) has the heaviest schedule here, operating numerous daily flights to Billund from Copenhagen (730kr return); it also provides daily international services to Billund from many European cities including Amsterdam, Frankfurt and London.

Bus There's no train service so if you're travelling by train the most common route is to get off at Vejle and catch a bus from there. Bus No 244/44 (35kr, 30 minutes) runs hourly from Vejle to Legoland. In addition, public bus No 244 runs about once an hour from Esbjerg to Legoland (70kr, 1½ hours).

You could also hop onto one of the airport buses, timed to meet scheduled flights, between Billund airport and Århus (130kr, 1½ hours) or Fredericia (65kr, one hour).

Car Four international car rental agencies have booths at the Billund airport: Avis (☎ 75 33 29 99), Budget (☎ 75 35 39 00), Europcar (☎ 75 33 15 33) and Hertz (☎ 75 33 82 50).

Århus

pop 260,000
Århus, Denmark's second largest city, is the commercial and cultural centre of Jutland. It's a lively university city with one of Denmark's best music and entertainment scenes, offering everything from symphony performances and theatre to a thriving night-owl cafe life.

Århus boasts a well-preserved historic quarter and plenty to see and do, ranging from good museums and intriguing old churches in the city centre to woodland trails and beaches along the city outskirts. Some of the highlights are: Den Gamle By, a quality open-air museum; Århus Domkirke, Denmark's largest church; and the Moesgård Museum, which has notable Bronze and Iron Age collections, and an enjoyable trail through a landscape rich in prehistoric sights.

History
In the middle of Jutland's eastern coast, Århus has been an important trading centre

and seaport since Viking times; it was originally named Aros, meaning 'at the river mouth'. Archaeological excavations indicate that Århus was founded around 900, when a semicircular rampart was constructed at the waterfront. The rampart, only a few city blocks in diameter, encompassed the area where the current cathedral, theatre and casino now stand. Remnants of the original city can be seen in the excavated basement of the Unibank west of Århus Domkirke.

In medieval times Århus' central location often left it in the thick of conflict with neighbouring states; King Sweyn II of Denmark and King Magnus of Norway engaged in a major battle off Århus in 1043 and just a few years later, in 1050, Århus was ravaged by the Norwegian warrior-king Harald Hardrada. In the decades that followed, its prosperity was kept in check by raids from other rival Vikings and attacks by fearsome Wend pirates.

Over the following centuries stability was slowly achieved and Århus grew as a centre of trade, art and religion. Its large, protected harbour became increasingly important. Århus flourished as a transport hub for central Jutland in the 18th century and to this day virtually all regional roads and railway lines lead to the city.

A lengthy dispute between Århus and the national government led the city to found its own university in 1928, but by the time the new campus was ready to open its doors in 1933 the national government had come around to recognise and support the university. Today students at Århus University, along with those at Århus' engineering college, dental school, business college, music academy and school of architecture, account for nearly 40,000 of the city's residents.

Orientation

Århus is fairly compact and easy to get around. The train station (Århus Hovedbanegård) marks the south side of the city centre. The pedestrian shopping streets of Søndergade and Sankt Clements Torv lead to Århus Domkirke in the heart of the old city. The small streets north-west of the cathedral are filled with cafes and restaurants.

Information

Tourist Offices Tourist Århus (☎ 89 40 67 00, fax 86 12 95 90, e turist-aarhus@aar-turist.dk), Rådhuset, 8000 Århus C, is in the rådhus on Park Allé. It's open 9.30am to 6pm Monday to Friday, 9.30am to 5pm on Saturday and 9.30am to 1pm on Sunday from mid-June to early September. Opening hours are 9.30am to 4.30pm Monday to Friday (to 5pm from May to mid-June) and 10am to 1pm on Saturday during the rest of the year.

Money There's a Sydbank (☎ 86 12 40 88) at the front of the train station, many more banks along Søndergade and a Unibank (☎ 89 42 11 00) near Århus Domkirke at Sankt Clements Torv 6.

Post & Communications The main post office (☎ 89 35 80 00), beside the train station, is open 9.30am to 6pm Monday to Friday and 10am to 1pm on Saturday.

Århus has a couple of Internet cafes: Net-City (☎ 86 76 11 99), on the 2nd floor of the rear building at Frederiksgade 45, and Net House (☎ 87 30 00 96), Nørre Allé 66A. Both are open noon to midnight daily.

Gay & Lesbian Travellers Better known as LBL, Landsforeningen for Bøsser og Lesbiske (☎ 86 13 19 48), the national organisation for gays and lesbians, has its Århus branch at Jægergårdsgade 42.

Travel Agencies Kilroy Travels (☎ 86 20 11 44), Fredensgade 40, specialises in youth and discount travel.

Bookshops GAD bookshop (☎ 86 13 10 66), Søndergade 20, and Svend A Larsen (☎ 86 12 56 11), Sønder Allé 4, have English-language books, including travel guides. The English Book Store (☎ 86 19 54 55), Frederiks Allé 53, specialises in both new and second-hand English-language books.

Library & Newspapers You can read the international news at the main public library (☎ 86 12 48 44), a large modern facility off Vester Allé. International newspapers are sold at the kiosk in the train station.

ÅRHUS

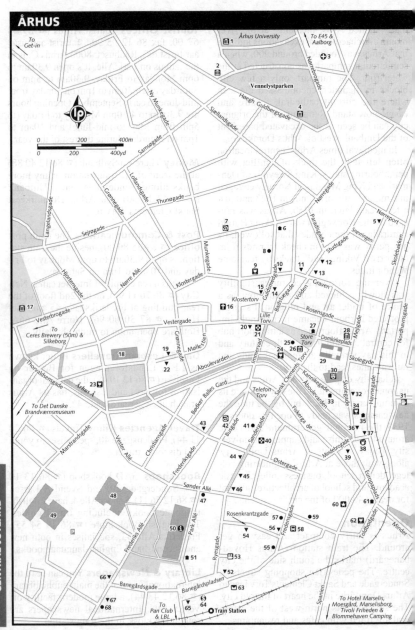

To Get-in

Århus University

To E45 & Aalborg

1

2

3

Vennelystparken

Høegh Guldbergsgade

4

Nørrebrogade

Sjællandsgade

Ny Munkegade

Samsøgade

Lollandsgade

Grønnegade

Thunøgade

Langelandsgade

Sejrøgade

Nørreport

5

Snevringen

Studsgade

Paradisgade

Nørregade

Skolebakken

Nørre Allé

Hjortensgade

Vesterbrogade

17

7

6

8

9

10

11

12

13

Munkegade

Klostergade

Guldsmedgade

14

15

Klostertorv

16

Badstuegade

Volden

Graven

Rosensgade

To Ceres Brewery (50m) & Silkeborg

Vestergade

Lille Torv

20

21

Store Torv

Domkirkeplads

28

27

Nordhavnsgade

Mejlgade

Thorvaldsensgade

18

19

22

Grønnegade

Møllesti

Åboulevarden

Immervad

24

25

26

29

Skolegyde

30

31

Havnegade

Sankt Clemens Torv

Kannikegade

33

32

34

35

36

37

Århus Å

23

To Det Danske Brandværnsmuseum

Booker Bailes Gard

Telefon Torv

Åboulevarden

Fiskerge de

Mindebrogade

38

39

Marstrandsgade

Vester Allé

Christiansgade

Frederiksgade

43

42

41

40

Bülowsgade

Sandenvej

Østergade

44

45

46

Europaplads

Toldbodgade

Sønder Allé

47

48

49

50

Rosenkrantzgade

57

56

54

55

58

59

60

61

62

Fredensgade

Park Allé

Ryesgade

51

53

52

66

67

68

Banegårdsgade

Frederiks Allé

Banegårdspladsen

63

64

65

To Pan Club & LBL

Train Station

Spanien

Minder

To Hotel Marselis, Moesgård, Marselisborg, Tivoli Friheden & Blommehaven Camping

0   200   400m
0   200   400yd

CENTRAL JUTLAND

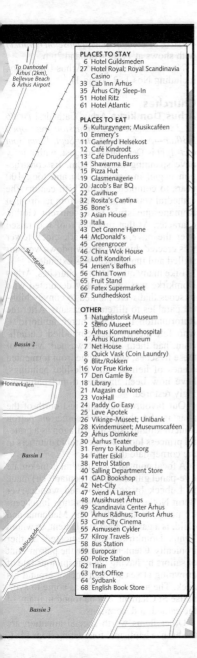

PLACES TO STAY
6 Hotel Guldsmeden
27 Hotel Royal; Royal Scandinavia
    Casino
33 Cab Inn Århus
35 Århus City Sleep-In
51 Hotel Ritz
61 Hotel Atlantic

PLACES TO EAT
5 Kulturgyngen; Musikcaféen
10 Emmery's
11 Ganefryd Helsekost
12 Café Kindrodt
13 Café Drudenfuss
14 Shawarma Bar
15 Pizza Hut
19 Glasmenagerie
20 Jacob's Bar BQ
22 Gavlhuse
32 Rosita's Cantina
36 Bone's
37 Asian House
39 Italia
43 Det Grønne Hjørne
44 McDonald's
45 Greengrocer
46 China Wok House
52 Loft Konditori
54 Jensen's Bøfhus
56 China Town
65 Fruit Stand
66 Føtex Supermarket
67 Sundhedskost

OTHER
1 Naturhistorisk Museum
2 Steno Museet
3 Århus Kommunehospital
4 Århus Kunstmuseum
7 Net House
8 Quick Vask (Coin Laundry)
9 Blitz/Rokken
16 Vor Frue Kirke
17 Den Gamle By
18 Library
21 Magasin du Nord
23 VoxHall
24 Paddy Go Easy
25 Løve Apotek
26 Vikinge-Museet; Unibank
28 Kvindemuseet; Museumscaféen
29 Århus Domkirke
30 Aarhus Teater
31 Ferry to Kalundborg
34 Fatter Eskil
38 Petrol Station
40 Salling Department Store
41 GAD Bookshop
42 Net-City
47 Svend A Larsen
48 Musikhuset Århus
49 Scandinavia Center Århus
50 Århus Rådhus; Tourist Århus
53 Cine City Cinema
55 Asmussen Cykler
57 Kilroy Travels
58 Bus Station
59 Europcar
60 Police Station
62 Train
63 Post Office
64 Sydbank
68 English Book Store

Laundry Quick Vask (☎ 86 13 16 25), a coin laundry at Guldsmedgade 27, is open 7.30am to 9.30pm.

Medical Services Løve Apotek (☎ 86 12 00 22), opposite Hotel Royal at Store Torv 5, is open 24 hours.

Emergency Dial ☎ 112 for police or ambulance. Århus Kommunehospital (☎ 89 49 29 31), Nørrebrogade 44, has a 24-hour emergency ward. Krisecenter for Voldsramtekvinder (☎ 86 15 35 22) helps women in crisis and can provide a safe haven overnight if necessary.

Central Museums

Den Gamle By The Old Town (☎ 86 12 31 88, Viborgvej 2; bus No 3, 14 or 25; adult/child 60/15kr; open 9am-6pm daily June-Aug; 10am-5pm Apr, May, Sep & Oct; 10am-4pm Feb-Mar & Nov-Dec; 11am-3pm Jan) is a picturesque open-air museum comprising 75 restored buildings brought here from all over Denmark and reconstructed as a provincial town, complete with a functioning bakery, silversmith, bookbinder and so on. Most of the buildings are half-timbered 17th- and 18th-century houses but there's also a water mill, a windmill and a few buildings from the late-19th century.

Den Gamle By is about 1.5km west of the city centre. Outside opening hours, you can walk through the old cobbled streets for free – this is a delightful time to visit because the crowds are gone and the light is ideal for photography, but you won't be able to enter individual buildings.

Vikinge-Museet Pop into the basement of the Unibank (☎ 89 42 11 00, Sankt Clements Torv 6; admission free; open 10am-4pm Mon-Fri, 10am-6pm Thur) for a look at artefacts from a Viking village excavated at this site in 1964 during the bank's construction. The excavated artefacts, dating from 900 to 1400, indicate that this neighbourhood was one of the earliest settlements in Århus. The display includes photos of the excavation, a skeleton, a reconstructed house, 1000-year-old carpentry tools and pottery.

CENTRAL JUTLAND

Århus Pass

Århus has a nifty city pass that allows unlimited transport on municipal buses as well as admission to most city sights, including Den Gamle By, Århus Kunstmuseum, Moesgård Museum, the two university museums, Det Danske Brandværnsmuseum, Kvindemuseet and Tivoli Friheden.

The cost of a two-day pass is 110kr for adults and 55kr for children aged 15 and under. A seven-day pass costs 155/75kr for adults/children. The pass can be purchased from hotels, camping grounds and Tourist Århus.

Kvindemuseet The Women's Museum *(☎ 86 13 61 44, Domkirkeplads 5; adult/child 25kr/free; open 10am-5pm daily June-Aug, 10am-4pm Tues-Sun Sept-May)* features changing exhibits on the culture and history of women. With its cafe and occasional activities Kvindemuseet is also a good place for women travellers meet Danish women involved in the feminist movement.

Århus Kunstmuseum This museum *(☎ 86 13 52 55, Vennelystparken; bus No 1, 2, 3 or 6; adult/child 40kr/free; open 10am-5pm Tues-Sun, 10am-8pm Wed)*, south of the university, contains a comprehensive collection of 19th- and 20th-century Danish art. There is also a foreign collection, predominantly of German and American art, and periodic special exhibitions.

University Museums There are two museums in Universitetsparken, the grounds of Århus University. **Naturhistorisk Museum** *(☎ 86 12 97 77; adult/child 35/10kr; open 10am-5pm daily July & Aug, 10am-4pm Sept-June)* features a large collection of domestic and foreign stuffed birds and animals, many set in dioramas. There are also exhibits on subjects covering Danish ecology, evolution and minerals.

Steno Museet *(☎ 89 42 39 75; adult/child 40/15kr; open 10am-4pm Tues-Sun)*, a history of science museum, features exhibits on medicinal herbs, anatomy and medicine. The museum also has a planetarium *(adult/child 40/20kr, or combined with museum 60/30kr)* with shows at 11am, 1pm and 2pm.

Numerous buses go to Århus University, including Nos 1, 2, 3 and 11.

Churches
Århus Domkirke Århus Cathedral *(☎ 86 12 38 45, Bispetorv; admission free; open 9.30am-4pm Mon-Sat May-Sept, 10am-3pm Oct-Apr)* is Denmark's longest, with a lofty nave spanning nearly 100m. Its construction began in around 1200 and took 100 years to complete. In the 15th century the cathedral was transformed from its original Romanesque style to its current Gothic character. At that time the roof was raised over the nave, the landmark clock tower was erected, high Gothic windows were installed and the chancel was extended.

Like many other Danish churches, Århus Domkirke was once richly decorated with frescoes that were painted to convey biblical parables to illiterate peasants. After the Reformation in 1536 Church authorities, who felt the frescoes embodied Catholicism, had them all whitewashed. Many of these frescoes, which range from tormented scenes of hell to fairy-tale-like paintings, have now been uncovered and painstakingly restored.

Our favourite painting, just north of the altar, is of a chipper St George, the patron saint of knights, slaying a dragon as a grateful princess looks on; the Arabic numbers in the corner date it to 1497.

A focal point of the cathedral is the ornate five-panel gilt altarpiece (pentaptych) made in Lubeck by the renowned woodcarver Bernt Notke in the 15th century. In its centre panel, to the left of the Madonna and child, is a gaunt-faced St Clement, to whom Århus Domkirke was dedicated. Rather ironically, Clement became the patron saint of sailors by having the inauspicious fate of drowning at sea with an anchor around his neck. The anchor, which has come to symbolise St Clement, can be found in many of the cathedral decorations.

Other items worth special attention are the bronze baptismal font dating from 1481,

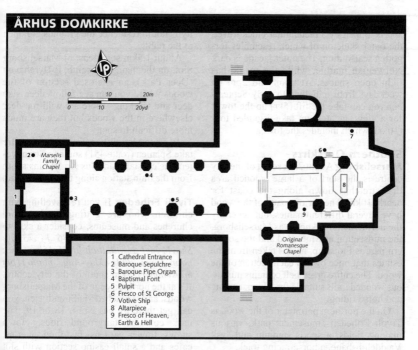

ÅRHUS DOMKIRKE

0   10   20m
0   10   20yd

2 ● Marselis Family Chapel

1

3 ●

4 ●

5 ●

7

6 ●

8

9

Original Romanesque Chapel

1	Cathedral Entrance
2	Baroque Sepulchre
3	Baroque Pipe Organ
4	Baptismal Font
5	Pulpit
6	Fresco of St George
7	Votive Ship
8	Altarpiece
9	Fresco of Heaven, Earth & Hell

the finely carved Renaissance pulpit created in 1588, the magnificent Baroque pipe organ made in 1730, the large 18th-century votive ship and the Baroque sepulchre in the Marselis family chapel.

As with all churches, no visits are allowed during funerals, wedding and other services.

Vor Frue Kirke This church (☎ 86 12 12 43, Frue Kirkeplads; admission free; open 10am-2pm Mon-Fri, 10am-noon Sat), set back from Vestergade, is like a Russian mat-ryoshka doll, opening to reveal multiple layers beneath the surface. It was here that the original Århus cathedral was erected shortly after 1060 when Sweyn II, bent on weakening the power of the archbishop who led the Danish church, divided Denmark into eight separate dioceses, one of which was Århus. The cathedral was constructed from rough stone and travertine, and stood until about 1240 when it was replaced by the current Vor Frue Kirke.

Built of red brick, the church has a largely whitewashed interior although the chancel features a few exposed frescoes depicting the coats of arms of wealthy families from the 14th century. There's also a detailed trip-tych altar carved by Claus Berg in 1530. However, the main treasure is in the church basement – the vaulted crypt of the original cathedral, the oldest surviving church in-terior in Denmark. Entered via the stairs beneath the chancel, the crypt was uncov-ered by chance in 1956 during a restoration of Vor Frue Kirke by the national museum.

Vor Frue Kirke has yet another chapel, this one boasting early-16th-century frescoes, which can be entered through the garden courtyard; it's behind the first door on the left.

Århus Rådhus

Århus city hall (☎ 89 40 20 00, Rådhus-pladsen) was designed by architect Arne Jacobsen, a pioneer of Danish modernism, and completed in 1942. This controversial building has a ponderous, functional design and is topped by a rectangular clock tower, the outer skeleton of which resembles forgotten scaffolding. The outer facade is dark Norwegian marble, while the inside has light open spaces. At noon and 2pm on weekdays from mid-June to early September you can take the lift (5kr) up the tower for a view; or at 11am take a guided tour (10kr), which includes the tower.

Southern Outskirts

Marselisborg About 2km south of the city centre is the start of a large wooded area that stretches down along the coast for nearly 10km. The various parts of the wood have several different names, but generally the northern end is known as Marselisborg, the midsection as Moesgård and the southern part as Fløjstrup, names taken from the estates that once owned each section of the wood. The entire green belt contains numerous wooded trails suitable for hiking, cycling and horse riding.

On the northern perimeter of the wood is Tivoli Friheden amusement park, various playing fields, a sports stadium and Jysk Væddeløbsbane, a horse-racing track.

Farther south, near the intersection of Carl Nielsens Vej and Kongevejen, is **Marselisborg Slot**, a big white manor house built in 1902 and occasionally used in summer by the royal family. When the queen is in residence there's a changing of the guard at noon. The palace can't be toured but you can catch a glimpse of it, along with the palace guards, from the road; when the royal family is not in residence the grounds are open to the public.

About 1.5km south-east of Marselisborg Slot, on the main road south, is **Dyrehaven** (Deer Park), an enclosed section of the woods where you can see fallow deer, sika deer and wild pig. There are wild roe deer elsewhere in the woods but they are much more difficult to spot.

To get to Marselisborg from the city centre take Spanien (route 451) south to Strandvejen, the coastal road. Bus No 19 runs south from the train station along the coastal road.

Tivoli Friheden If you're travelling with children who are getting tired of old churches and museums, consider a skip to this amusement park (☎ 86 14 73 00, *Skovbrynet 1; adult/child 35/15kr; open noon-10pm daily May-Aug, noon-11pm midsummer)*, 2km south of the city centre. It's at the northern edge of the Marselisborg woods, and is reached via Strandvejen; you can get there by bus No 4, 18 or 19. The park contains fairground rides, clown shows, flower gardens, fast-food eateries, cafes and a small casino section with slot machines for wayward adults.

Moesgård Eight kilometres south of the city centre, the Moesgård area makes for an absorbing half-day outing. The main focal point is the **Moesgård Museum** (☎ 89 42 11 00, *Moesgård Allé 20; adult/child 35kr/free; open 10am-5pm daily Apr-Oct,*

Grauballe Man

Grauballe-manden (Grauballe Man), now displayed at Moesgård Museum, was discovered in April 1952 in a peat bog near the village of Graubelle, 35km west of Århus. Grauballe Man died in around 80 BC, a slash across his throat indicating he may have been the victim of a murder or execution. One theory is that he was the object of a ritualistic sacrifice, perhaps killed as an offering to one of the pagan gods thought to be responsible for warding off plagues and assuring abundant harvests.

Grauballe Man was about 30 years old when he died. Tannic acids and iron deposits in the bog preserved his body and literally tanned his hide, giving his skin a brown, leather-like appearance.

Two millennia after Graubelle Man's last supper, scientists were able to discover a great deal about his eating habits by examining his stomach, which contained remnants of a porridge of barley and rye as well as 66 different types of seeds.

10am-4pm Tues-Sun Nov-Mar), which features quality displays from the Stone Age to the Viking Age including flint axes, tools and pottery and a roomful of **rune stones**.

The museum's most unique exhibit, displayed in a glass case, is the 2000-year-old **Graubelle Man**, who was found preserved in a nearby bog in 1952 (see the boxed text). The dehydrated, leathery body is amazingly intact, right down to his red hair and his fingernails.

An enjoyable **trail** dubbed the 'prehistoric trackway' leads from behind the museum through fields of wildflowers, grazing sheep and beech woods down to **Moesgård Strand**, Århus' best sandy beach. The trail, marked by red-dotted stones, passes reconstructed historic sights including a dolmen, burial cists and an Iron-Age house. Before you start off pick up a brochure at the museum. You can walk one way and catch a bus from the beach back to the city centre or follow the trail both ways as a 5km round trip.

If you're at Moesgård Strand in the last weekend in July, a Viking Moot re-enactment takes place along the waterfront – an ideal opportunity to combine a day at the beach with some historical enrichment.

Bus No 6 from Århus train station terminates at the museum year-round, while bus No 19 terminates at Moesgård Strand during the summer season; both buses run about twice an hour.

Det Danske Brandværnsmuseum
The Danish Fire Brigade Museum *(☎ 86 25 41 44, Tomsagervej 25; bus No 12 or 18; adult/child 45/15kr; open 10am-5pm daily Apr-Oct, 10am-4pm Tues-Sat Nov & Feb-Mar, closed Dec & Jan)* is one of the largest museums of its kind in Europe, housing nearly 100 antique fire-fighting vehicles, both horse-drawn and engine-driven. The museum is 5km west of the city centre, just off Viby Ringvej.

Hiking & Cycling
Århus Kommune distributes the handy detailed brochure *Nature Around Århus-South*, which maps out suggested hiking and cycling tours of the green space south of the city.

This brochure (10kr), which includes short but interesting titbits about the local flora, fauna and history, can be picked up at the tourist office. Be sure to ask for the English-language version.

Specifically for cyclists is the *Cyclist Turistkort*, a detailed map produced by Århus Amt (Århus County). The county has 1200km of cycling routes over a mix of surfaced secondary roads, forest paths and abandoned railway tracks. The cycling map, available in English, details various county-wide touring routes, including those in the immediate Århus area, the Lake District and the Grenaa/Ebeltoft region. It also gives information on things to see and do en route with some useful tips and the addresses of cycle repair shops. The map costs 80kr and can be purchased at tourist offices and bookshops.

Swimming
There are sandy beaches on the outskirts of Århus. The most popular one to the north is Bellevue, about 4km from the city centre (bus No 6 or 16), while the favourite to the south is Moesgård Strand, 8km from the centre on bus No 19.

Windsurfing
Windsurfers will find suitable spots in Århus Bay to the north of the city centre near Risskov and to the south at Marselisborg. For more on windsurfing, including information on classes, call Surfline (☎ 86 17 67 65).

Other Sports
Tourist Århus has a Tourist Sport program (☎ 89 40 67 00); staff can help to arrange various sporting activities including sailing, tennis, golf, ice-skating and windsurfing.

Organised Tours
Ceres Brewery Tours of the brewery, on Vesterbrogade opposite Den Gamle By, are given at 2pm Wednesday year-round. There is an additional tour at 2pm Tuesday from mid-June to July. Passes (25kr) are distributed at the tourist office; pick them up as soon as you arrive in Århus as the tours commonly book out days in advance.

Sightseeing Tour For a good overview of the city consider taking the guided, 2½-hour public-bus tour that leaves from the tourist office at 10am daily between mid-June and early September. Conducted by knowledgeable multilingual guides, it gives a drive-by glimpse of the main city sights and a more detailed tour of Århus Domkirke. At 45kr this is a great deal because it includes entry into Den Gamle By and also leaves you with a 24-hour bus pass. Not surprisingly the tour often fills to capacity, but you can book in advance at the tourist office (☎ 89 40 67 00).

Special Events
The Århus Festival is a multicultural event held every August. If you're the physical kind, join in the marathon. If your style is more to relax and enjoy a musical performance, then there is lots to choose from. For more details of the festival see the 'Festive Denmark' special section.

Århus also has a couple of noteworthy events in July: the Viking Moot, with some re-created Viking-era activities, and the Århus Jazz Festival, the city's big annual jazz happening, featuring big-name acts.

Places to Stay
Camping Just 6km south of the city centre is *Blommehaven Camping* (☎ 86 27 02 07, fax 86 27 45 22, e info@blommehaven.dk, Ørneredevej 35, 8270 Århus) Camping per person 55kr. Open early Apr-mid Sept. This three-star camping ground has a nice beachside setting in the Marselisborg woods. It has full facilities and a minimart. From Århus train station you can take bus No 19 (which stops in front of Blommehaven Camping) or No 6 (which stops 400m away).

Private Rooms & Hostels The staff at the tourist office can book *rooms* in private homes; singles/doubles cost 175/275kr, plus a 25kr booking fee.

Danhostel Århus (☎ 86 16 72 98, fax 86 10 55 60, e danhostel.aarhus@get2net.dk, Marienlundsvej 10, 8240 Risskov) Dorm beds 90kr, 3-person rooms 270kr. Open 25 Jan-20 Dec. This 145-bed hostel is in a renovated 1850s dance hall in the midst of the Risskov woods, 4km north of the city centre. Take bus No 1, 6 or 9; from the bus stop it's a 300m walk east along Marienlundsvej.

Århus City Sleep-In (☎ 86 19 20 55, fax 86 19 18 11, e sleep-in@citysleep-in-dk, Havnegade 20, 8000 Århus C) Dorm beds 95kr, doubles 270/300kr no bath/bath. Although the place can get a bit noisy, it's an affordable alternative to a hotel and has a good central location. Now run by the city youth and culture centre, the building was originally a seamen's hotel, so the sleeping quarters are hotel rooms rather than large dorms. If you don't have a sleeping sheet you'll need to rent linen for an additional 15kr. There's a guest kitchen, a TV room, a pool table and laundry facilities. Breakfast is available for 50kr. Reception is open 24 hours and reservations are accepted.

Guesthouse & Hotels Hotels in Århus tend to be pricey but there are a few good-value options.

Get-in (☎ 86 10 86 14, fax 86 10 86 24, Jens Baggesensvej 43) Bus No 7 from the train station. Singles/doubles 250/300kr, with bath 300/350kr. This 62-room guesthouse near Århus University is midway between a hostel and a hotel in both style and price. The rooms are simple but clean and adequate. Common space includes a TV room and guest kitchen. Breakfast is available for 35kr.

Hotel Guldsmeden (☎ 86 13 45 50, fax 86 13 76 76, e hotel-guldsmeden@mail.tele.dk, Guldsmedgade 40, 8000 Århus C) Singles/doubles 495/695kr, with bath 675/795kr. This cosy place, on the northern side of the city centre, has just 20 rooms and the atmosphere of an upmarket bed and breakfast. The owner is an architect who has creatively added modern Scandinavian aspects to an older building. Pleasant touches include a hearty organic breakfast.

Cab Inn Århus (☎ 70 21 62 00, fax 70 21 62 24, e cab-inn@cab-inn.dk, Kannikegade 14, 8000 Århus C) Singles/doubles 485/595kr. This new 192-room economy hotel is a particularly good value. All rooms have private bath, TV and free coffee, and the location is great for sightseeing and club-hopping. One thing that separates it

CENTRAL JUTLAND

from most other hotels, however, is that breakfast is not included in the rates. Some rooms are designed to accommodate people in wheelchairs.

Hotel Ritz (☎ *86 13 44 44, fax 86 13 45 87,* e *info@bestwestern.dk, Banegårdsplads 12, 8100 Århus C)* Singles/doubles 635/965kr. A member of the Best Western chain, this older 68-room hotel is central, just a two-minute walk from the train station. Rooms can be a bit small but they're comfortable with the usual amenities.

Hotel Atlantic (☎ *86 13 11 11, fax 86 13 23 43, Europaplads 12, 8000 Århus C)* Singles/doubles 945/1195kr, summer & weekend rate 695/795kr. This modern hotel, between the bus station and the harbour, has 102 pleasant rooms with TV and minibar. There's free guest parking.

Hotel Royal (☎ *86 12 00 11, fax 86 76 04 04,* W *www.hotelroyal.dk, Store Torv 4, 8100 Århus C)* Singles 1395-1895kr, doubles 1545-2195kr. This historic hotel, on the same square as Århus Domkirke, is the city's top hotel with its casino and deluxe rooms catering for high rollers. All rooms have full amenities with minibars, video-TV and the like.

Hotel Marselis (☎ *86 14 44 11, fax 86 11 70 46,* e *info@marselis.dk, Strandvejen 25, 8000 Århus C)* Singles/doubles 1065/1265kr Sun-Thur, weekend family rate (Fri & Sat) 900kr (2 adults, 2 children). This 101-room hotel is in a well-to-do suburb 3km south of the city centre. It fronts the beach and is backed by forest. The rooms have modern amenities and ocean-view balconies and there's a pool, bar and restaurant.

Places to Eat
Train Station Area There are a number of eating options within easy walking distance of the train station.

China Town (☎ *86 19 62 64, Fredensgade 46)* Lunch 50kr, dinner 75-95kr. Open noon-11pm daily. This Chinese restaurant opposite the bus station has 10 daily lunch specials. For dinner there's a multicourse meal or you can order from the a la carte menu.

Jensen's Bøfhus (☎ *86 12 44 88, Rosenkrantzgade 23)* Lunch 39kr, dinner 100kr.

Open 11.30am-11pm daily. This steakhouse offers the chain's usual steak or chicken lunch deals.

Sundhedskost (☎ *86 12 77 76, Frederiks Allé 49)* Open 10am-6pm Mon-Fri. As the city's largest natural-food store it has a good selection, from cereal and teas to fresh organic produce.

Loft Konditori (☎ *86 13 33 34, Banegårdsplads)* Open from 7am Mon-Sat. Across the street from the train station, this is a good bakery with a small dining room that opens for breakfast.

Føtex (☎ *86 12 04 00, Frederiks Allé 22)* Open 9am-8pm Mon-Fri, 8am-5pm Sat. This chain supermarket, diagonally opposite Sundhedskost, has a bakery and a deli that can provide elements for a cheap takeaway meal.

The station itself houses a small **supermarket**, open until midnight, as well as the usual DSB chain eateries serving up cafeteria fare, hot dogs, burgers and beer. There's a *fruit stand* at the front.

Central Area You'll find plenty of places to stop for a bite along the pedestrian street Søndergade.

China Wok House (☎ *86 12 69 23, Sønder Allé 9)* Takeaway 20kr, lunch/dinner buffet 49/98kr. Open 11am-10.30pm daily. This casual Chinese restaurant has good, cheap three-item takeaway deals. Or walk through to the dining room and enjoy a generous all-you-can-eat buffet meal.

Det Grønne Hjørne (☎ *86 13 52 47, Frederiksgade 60)* Lunch/dinner buffet 59/89kr, mains 100-120kr. Open 11.30am-11pm Mon-Sat, 5pm-10pm Sun. This cosy cafe specialises in Turkish buffets with a good variety of hot and cold items, creative salads and fresh fruit. It also offers chicken and lamb dishes to order.

Italia (☎ *86 19 80 22, Åboulevarden 9)* Pizza & pasta from 50kr, meat & fish mains from 100kr. Open noon-11pm Mon-Sat, from 5pm Sun. This Italian restaurant boasts a wood-fired pizza oven for an authentic flavour.

Rosita's Cantina (☎ *86 13 27 72, Skolegade 21)* Mexican-style meal 100kr. Open

5pm-10.30pm daily. This long-established restaurant offers a full menu of Mexican dinners served with rice and beans. There's live music on weekends.

Bone's (☎ *86 13 27 55, Skolegade 33)* Mains 120kr. Open 5pm-10.30pm Sun-Fri, 1pm-10.30pm Sat. This popular restaurant has good spareribs and steaks, accompanied by a helping from the fresh salad bar.

Salling (☎ *86 12 18 00, Søndergade 27)* Open 9.30am-6pm Mon-Wed, 9.30am-8pm Thurs & Fri, 9am-5pm Sat. This department store has a supermarket and deli in its basement, a bakery on the ground floor and an upstairs 'bistro' with good croissants, tempting smørrebrød sandwiches and a salad bar.

In the first block of Søndergade there's a **greengrocer** and a **McDonald's**.

Northside Cafes & Restaurants The narrow streets of the old quarter north of Århus Domkirke are thick with cafes and offer a fun choice of dining options.

Café Drudenfuss (☎ *86 12 82 72, cnr Graven & Studsgade)* Dishes 20-50kr. One of the more popular meeting places, this cafe has inexpensive sandwiches, empanadas and drinks.

Café Kindrødt (☎ *86 18 56 88, Studsgade 8)* Salads & pasta from 50kr. Open 10am-1am Mon-Sat, 11am-midnight Sun. This cafe offers affordable candlelit dining.

Shawarma Bar (☎ *86 19 49 25, Guildsmedgade 8)* Light meals from 25kr. Open 11.30am-at least 8pm daily. This popular hole-in-the-wall Middle Eastern sandwich shop commonly has a queue out the door – but it's worth the wait for felafel or the shawarma pita-bread sandwiches.

Museumscaféen (☎ *86 13 61 44, Domkirkeplads 5)* Salads & sandwiches 25-50kr. Open 10am-5pm daily in summer, 10am-4pm Tues-Sun in winter. This cosy cafe at Kvindemuseet (The Women's Museum) makes an inviting place for women to meet. The menu also includes wine, coffee and cakes – all at reasonable prices.

Kulturgyngen (☎ *86 19 22 55, Mejlgade 53)* Lunch 35kr, dinner 55kr. Food service 10am-9pm Mon-Sat. This youth and culture centre serves hearty portions of good food, offering a different vegetarian meal as well as a fish or meat meal each night. There are also cakes and coffee. After the kitchen has closed it stays open for drinks and conversation until at least midnight and commonly until 2am.

Pizza Hut (☎ *86 13 20 55, Klostertorv)* Lunch buffet 49kr. Open 11.30am-11pm daily. Here you'll get the chain's standard pizzas, pasta and salads.

Jacob's Bar BQ (☎ *86 12 20 42, Vestergade 3)* Steaks from 100kr, other mains from 80kr. Open 11am-1.30am daily. In a historic merchant's house, this bustling place is known for its grilled steaks, and also has fish, lamb and kebab dishes.

Emmery's (☎ *86 13 04 00, Guildsmedgade 24)* Snacks 30kr, mains 100kr. Open 7.30am-midnight Mon-Sat, 8am-5pm Sun. A more upmarket option, this trendy cafe serves organic bakery items, cakes, sandwiches, salads and light meals.

Ganefryd Helsekost (☎ *86 12 54 15, Klostergade 2)* Open to 5pm Mon-Fri. This pleasant little natural-food store in the midst of the cafe district sells produce, organic nuts and the like.

Entertainment

Being a university city, there's always a lot happening in Århus. For listings of current events, music and other entertainment pick up *Musik Kalenderen* or the tourist office's *What's On in Århus*, both of which are free.

Music Clubs Much of the vibrant music scene is centred around backstreet cafes that offer a variety of choice.

VoxHall (☎ *87 30 97 97, Vester Allé 15)* The city's newest music venue features a wide range of quality music, from rock and metal to world music and jazz.

Train (☎ *86 13 47 22, Toldbodgade 6)* One of the hottest spots in town, Train features good rock, pop and jazz bands from Denmark and the UK, and also has a disco.

Musikcaféen and **Gyngen** (☎ *86 76 03 44, Mejlgade 53)* These are part of Kulturgyngen, a youth and culture centre that occupies a renovated factory on the northern side of the city centre. Both places offer an interesting alternative scene with a wide range of music including rock, techno and world music.

Plasma (☎ *87 30 39 39, Klostergade 34)* This dance spot bustles at weekends to both live rock music and disco.

Fatter Eskil (☎ *86 19 44 11, Skolegade 25)* This cafe has jazz or blues music most nights.

Paddy Go Easy (☎ *86 13 83 33, Åboulevarden 60)* Not surprisingly, this authentic Irish pub has live Irish music at weekends and is also a spot to watch football games on a wide-screen TV.

Concert Hall In the city centre is Århus' modern concert venue **Musikhuset Århus** (☎ *89 40 40 40, Thomas Jensens Allé)*. This complex contains two concert halls, the larger of which seats 1600, and is the arena for numerous events including dance performances, operas and musicals. Offerings range from performances by the city symphony orchestra to concerts by international pop and jazz stars. The foyer, which houses the ticket office and a cafe, occasionally has free musical performances, so if you're strolling by it's worth a look. A monthly program schedule is available from the ticket office which is open 11am-9pm.

Theatre South of Århus Domkirke, **Århus Teater** (☎ *89 33 26 22, Bispetorv)* is a splendid century-old building richly embellished with gargoyles and various other decorative elements, including a scene from a Ludvig Holberg play painted across the front gable. Jutland's largest theatre, it has five stages, a permanent theatre troupe and an affiliated drama school. The theatre season is from early September to mid-June.

Gay & Lesbian Venues The **Pan Club** (☎ *86 13 43 80, Jægergårdsgade 42)* is a cafe and weekend disco just a short walk south-west of the train station. It is the city's main gay and lesbian hang-out.

Cinema The nine-screen **Cine City** (☎ *86 13 70 90, Sankt Knuds Torv 15)* is a centrally located cinema and generally features first-run English-language movies.

Casino If you have extra cash burning a hole in your pocket, head for the casino at the Hotel Royal.

Royal Scandinavia Casino (☎ *86 19 21 22, Store Torv 4)* Open 2pm-4am daily. To keep you entertained, you can choose between slot machines, other electronic games, American roulette, French roulette and blackjack. Entrance requires proper dress but men can borrow a jacket at the door. Admission is 50kr after 7pm.

Shopping

Department Stores & Speciality Shops

One of the city's largest department stores is **Magasin du Nord** (☎ *86 12 33 00, Immervad 2)* This place takes up an entire block between Vestergade and Åboulevarden. It stocks just about anything you can imagine, or need, from gourmet foods to designer clothing, Danish silverware and tax-free gift items.

Salling (☎ *86 12 18 00, Søndergade 27)* Another enormous department store, Salling has 30 departments and stocks the same kind of merchandise as Magasin du Nord.

Søndergade, a busy pedestrian shopping street, has numerous speciality stores, many selling fashionable clothing. Other shops and boutiques, specialising in both Danish design and imported clothing, are thick along Badstuegade and Volden, streets that run north from Lille Torv.

If you're interested in antiques, there are a few shops north of Århus Domkirke on Graven that stock everything from old furniture, silver and china to rare books.

Crafts Telefon Torv, a small pedestrian square off the northern end of Søndergade, has a few open-air stalls selling jewellery and other simple handicrafts.

Quality Danish handicrafts can be found in shops along Møllestien, a cobbled street east of the library.

Glasmenageriet (☎ *86 13 81 81, Møllestien 50)* This gallery sells the works of leading Danish glass-blowers.

Gavlhuset (☎ *86 13 06 32, Møllestien 53)* This shop sells its own traditional Danish pottery and raku-style earthenware.

Getting There & Away

Air Århus airport, in Tirstrup 44km north-east of the city (50kr, 45 minutes by airport bus), is primarily a domestic airport. Scandinavian Airlines (SAS) has numerous daily flights to and from Copenhagen, and Ryan Air has a twice-daily flight from London.

Bus All long-distance buses stop at Århus bus station, 500m north-east of the train station. The bus station has lockers, a small grocery shop and an inexpensive cafe.

Express buses (☎ 70 21 08 88) run a few times daily between Copenhagen's Valby station and Århus (200kr, 2¾ hours).

Train Trains to Copenhagen (260kr, 3¼ hours), via Odense, leave Århus about hourly from early morning to midnight. There's also an hourly train service north to Frederikshavn (172kr, 2½ hours) and south to Vejle (76kr, 45 minutes) and Fredericia (100kr, 1¼ hours). For details on trains to Grenaa and the Lake District, see those sections.

Car & Motorcycle The main highways to Århus are the E45 from the north and south and route 15 from the west. The E45 curves around the western edge of the city as a ring road. There are several turn-offs from the ring road into the city, including Åhavevej from the south and Randersvej from the north.

Boat Mols-Linien (☎ 70 10 14 18) runs car ferries between Århus and Kalundborg six times a day on weekdays, three times a day on weekends. The trip takes 2¾ hours and costs 225kr for a car with up to five people, 170kr for a motorcycle and up to two people.

The company also operates a ferry service from Århus to Odden a few times daily with the same price structure; the trip takes 65 minutes.

Getting Around

Bus Århus has an extensive public bus system with frequent services throughout the city. Most city buses stop in front of the train station or around the corner from it on Park Allé. Tickets are bought from a machine in the back of the bus for 13kr and are valid for unlimited rides within the time period stamped on the ticket (about two hours); you can change buses during that time as often as you like. You can also buy a 24-hour pass valid for bus travel in Århus municipality alone (45kr) or one that is valid throughout Århus County, which includes Grenaa and the Lake District (90kr). There are also 75kr *klippekort* (clip card) tickets valid for nine rides. Klippekort tickets and passes can be bought at newsstands and the tourist office. For information on bus routes and departure times call ☎ 89 46 56 00.

Car & Motorcycle A car is quite convenient for getting to sights such as Moesgård on the city outskirts, though the city centre is best explored on foot.

Århus has numerous *billetautomats* (parking meters) along its streets. Parking costs around 10kr an hour from 8am to 6pm Monday to Thursday, 8am to 8pm on Friday and 8am to 2pm on Saturday. Outside those hours parking is usually free of charge.

There are several car parks around town, including large ones in front of and beneath the conference centre, Scandinavia Center Århus.

Cars can be rented in town from Avis (☎ 86 16 10 99) Jens Baggesensvej 88A or Europcar (☎ 89 33 11 11) Sønder Allé 35.

Taxi Taxis are readily available at the train station. You can also order a taxi by phoning ☎ 89 48 48 48 or ☎ 86 16 47 00.

Bicycle You can rent bicycles at Asmussen Cykler (☎ 86 19 57 00) at Fredensgade 54 near the bus station; the cost is 50kr for the first day, 35kr for each additional day. The shop also sells quality bikes and accessories.

The Lake District

The Lake District (Søhøjlandet), the closest thing Denmark has to hill country, is a popular active-holiday spot for Danes, offering good opportunities for canoeing, cycling and hiking. The scenery is pretty, but placid and pastoral rather than stunning. The district contains Gudenå, Denmark's longest river; Mossø, Jutland's largest lake; and Yding Skovhøj, Denmark's highest point – none of which are terribly long, large or high!

SILKEBORG
postcode 8600 • pop 37,200

Silkeborg is the Lake District's largest and youngest town. It was founded in 1846 when Michael Drewsen – whose statue graces Torvet – built a paper mill on the eastern side of the river. The mill and other industries still form the backbone of the economy. Because of its modern facade, the town may seem a bit bland but it has a pretty setting, bordered by both a river (Remstrup Å) and a lake (Silkeborg Langsø). If you're strolling through the town at night, walk down by the rådhus, where a colourfully lit fountain spurts up from the lake.

Information

Tourist Offices The Silkeborg Turistbureau (☎ 86 82 19 11, fax 86 81 09 83, ⓔ info@ tourist.silkeborg.dk), Åhavevej 2A, is north-east of the Silkeborg Museum. It's open 9am to 5pm Monday to Friday, 9am to 3pm on Saturday and 9.30am to 12.30pm on Sunday between mid-June and 31 August. The opening hours are 9am to 4pm on weekdays and to noon on Saturday during the rest of the year.

Money There are a number of banks on Vestergade, a block west of Torvet, including a Unibank at Vestergade 13 (☎ 86 82 53 33) and a Jyske Bank (☎ 89 22 22 22) at Vestergade 16.

Post & Communications The post office (☎ 76 26 86 00) is at Drewsensvej 1, just east of the train station. The library (☎ 86 82 02 33), Hostrupsgade 41, has a central location and many computers with Internet access.

Other Facilities There's a pharmacy (☎ 86 82 15 00) at Vestergade 9 and a coin laundry (☎ 86 80 57 51) a couple of blocks from Torvet at Hostrupsgade 21.

Silkeborg Museum

This quality regional museum of cultural history (☎ 86 82 14 99, Hovedgårdensvej 7, ⓦ www.silkeborgmuseum.dk/english; adult/child 30/10kr; open 10am-5pm daily May-Oct, noon-4pm Wed, Sat & Sun in winter) is housed in the 18th-century Hovedgården manor house, east of the town centre, the oldest building in town. Its Bronze and Iron Age collections include pottery, flint daggers and jewellery, most of which has been found in nearby peat bogs. Other exhbitions feature trade workshops from the end of the 19th century, including those of a cooper, a dentist and a shoemaker, and also a good glass collection.

The museum's main attraction, however, is **Tollund Man**, an Iron Age man who met an untimely end in his late 30s in 200 BC. His blackened, leather-like body, complete with a rope still around his neck, was discovered in a nearby bog in 1950. He was apparently hanged as a sacrifice to the gods. When discovered, Tollund Man was wearing only a sheepskin cap and a simple leather belt. The face is so amazingly well preserved that you can count the wrinkles on his forehead.

Silkeborg Kunstmuseum

The Silkeborg Museum of Art (☎ 86 82 53 88, Gudenåvej 7; adult/child 30kr/free; open 10am-5pm Tues-Sun Apr-Oct; noon-4pm Tues-Fri, 10am-5pm Sat & Sun Nov-Mar), 1km south of the town centre, features the works of native son Asger Jorn and other modern artists. Built around Jorn's private collection, it contains hundreds of his own paintings, sculptures and etchings, as well as works by other artists. The emphasis is on 20th-century art: early expressionism, spontaneous abstract art of the 1930s and 1940s, and also the Cobra (COpenhagen-BRussels-Amsterdam) movement that came next. Among the artists whose works are on display are Jean Dubuffet, Richard Mortensen, Carl-Henning Pedersen and Per Kirkeby.

Aqua

This complex (☎ 89 21 21 89, Vejsøvej 55; adult/child 65/35kr; open 10am-6pm daily

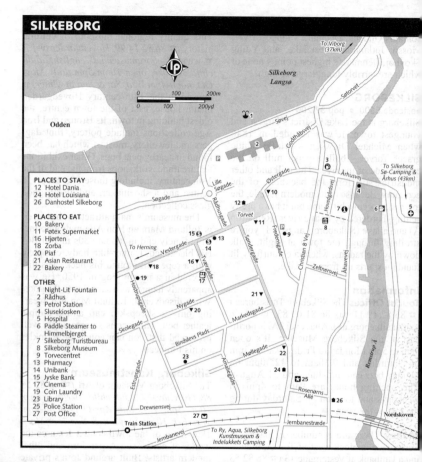

SILKEBORG

PLACES TO STAY
12 Hotel Dania
24 Hotel Louisiana
26 Danhostel Silkeborg

PLACES TO EAT
10 Bakery
11 Føtex Supermarket
16 Hjørten
18 Zorba
20 Piaf
21 Asian Restaurant
22 Bakery

OTHER
1 Night-Lit Fountain
2 Rådhus
3 Petrol Station
4 Slusekiosken
5 Hospital
6 Paddle Steamer to Himmelbjerget
7 Silkeborg Turistbureau
8 Silkeborg Museum
9 Torvecentret
13 Pharmacy
14 Unibank
15 Jyske Bank
17 Cinema
19 Coin Laundry
23 Library
25 Police Station
27 Post Office

CENTRAL JUTLAND

June-Aug; 10am-4pm Mon-Fri, 10am-5pm Sat & Sun Sept-May) is about 2km south of the town centre, displaying fish, otters, waterfowl and other fauna found in a freshwater environment. It's a great place to spend a rainy day – all the displays are presented in a way that'll capture the interest of adults and kids alike.

Hiking & Canoeing

To get to **Nordskoven**, a beech forest with hiking and cycling trails, simply walk over the old railway bridge at the eastern end of Jernbanestræde.

You can hire **canoes** for about 60/300kr per hour/day at a few places around town, including the camping grounds and Slusekiosken (☎ 86 80 08 93) on the river. as well as just touring for the day, it is possible to paddle through the Lake District and spend nights at lakeside camping areas. The canoe hire shops can help you plan an itinerary to suit your schedule.

Places to Stay

Indelukkets Camping (☎ 86 82 22 01, fax 86 80 50 27, e indelukket@get2net.dk, Vejlsøvej) Camping per person 59kr. Open early Apr–mid-Oct. This three-star camping ground, 1km south of the Silkeborg Kunst-museum, is near the river and surrounded by quiet woods.

Silkeborg Sø-Camping (☎ 86 82 28 24, fax 86 80 44 57, e mail@seacamp.dk, Århusvej 51) Camping per person 59kr. Open early Apr–mid-Sept. Also three star, this camping ground is beside a lake 1.5km east of the town centre.

Danhostel Silkeborg (☎ 86 82 36 42, fax 86 81 27 77, e silkeborg@danhostel.dk, Åhavevej 55) Dorm beds 80-100kr. Open Mar-Nov. This 93-bed hostel has friendly management and a scenic riverbank loca-tion about 600m east of the train station.

The tourist office can give you a list of about 30 private homes that let *rooms*; costs range from 150kr to 200kr for singles, 250kr to 400kr for doubles.

Hotel Dania (☎ 86 82 01 11, fax 86 80 20 04, e info@hoteldania.dk, Torvet 5) Singles/doubles with breakfast 955/1145kr. This old-fashioned hotel has front rooms over-looking Torvet and quieter rear rooms that overlook the lake. Most rooms are large with a bath and TV.

Hotel Louisiana (☎ 86 82 18 99, fax 86 80 32 69, e info@louisianahotel.dk, Chris-tian 8 Vej) Singles/doubles 905/1125kr, weekend rate 795kr per room. A Best West-ern affiliate, this modern, central hotel has 27 rooms with the expected comforts, including cable TV and minibar. The prices include breakfast.

Places to Eat

Asian Restaurant (☎ 86 81 32 99, Sønder-gade 18) Lunch specials 39kr, dinner mains 90kr. This place serves Thai and Vietnam-ese dishes with a full menu of salads, soups, curries and noodle dishes.

Hjørten (☎ 86 82 93 20, Tværgade 4) Lunch specials 49kr, dinner mains 90-150kr. This is a decent steak restaurant that has also added Mexican fare such as chicken enchiladas to its menu.

Zorba (☎ 86 81 21 55, Vestergade 35) Lunch/dinner mains 55/125kr. This inviting candlelit restaurant serves Greek speciali-ties such as grilled lamb and moussaka.

Piaf (☎ 86 81 12 55, Nygade 31) 3-course meals 268kr. This upmarket French dinner restaurant has a changing menu that in-cludes such dishes as fish soup, beef medal-lions and sumptuous gateaux.

Føtex (☎ 86 82 50 88, Torvet 4) Salads & cakes 10-30kr. This supermarket has an in-formal cafe with tempting cakes and a good self-service salad bar.

You'll find *bakeries* on the corner of Søndergade and Møllegade and at the north-eastern corner of Torvet.

Getting There & Away

Silkeborg is 37km south of Viborg on route 52 and 43km west of Århus on route 15.

Hourly trains connect Silkeborg with Århus (52kr, 45 minutes) via Ry.

A paddle steamer sails from Silkeborg to Himmelbjerget daily during the summer; see Getting There & Away in the Himmel-bjerget section for details of departure times and costs.

Getting Around

You can park along the streets in the town centre and at car parks on the western side of rådhus and at Torvecentret on Fredensgade.

Bicycles can be hired at the camping grounds and hostel; they cost around 60kr per day.

RY

postcode 8680 • pop 4800

A smaller town in a more rural setting than Silkeborg, Ry could make a good place from which to base your exploration of the Lake District. Although there aren't really any notable sights in the town centre, there are lots of options for activities and excur-sions into the surrounding countryside.

Information

The Ry Turistbureau (☎ 86 89 34 22, fax 86 89 35 52, e ryturist@post6.tele.dk), in the train station at Klostervej 3, is open 9am to 5pm Monday to Friday and 8.30am to 1.30pm on Saturday between mid-June and August; it's open 9am to 4pm on weekdays and 9am to noon on Saturday during the rest of the year.

The post office (☎ 76 26 86 00) is north of the train station and there's a branch of Danske Bank (☎ 87 88 00 44) nearby at Klostervej 2.

Hiking

The tourist office sells an English-language brochure called *On Foot in Ry and Environs* (20kr) that maps out and briefly describes 10 hikes in the Ry area. One of the nicest hikes from Ry is the two-hour, 7km walk to Himmelbjerget. The starting point for the hike is the dirt road that begins off Rodelundvej about 400m south of the Ry bridge. The path, which is signposted, leads to the Himmelbjerget boat dock before climbing the hill to the tower.

Cycling Tour

A good half-day outing is the cycle ride from Ry to **Boes**, a tiny hamlet that boasts an array of picturesque thatched houses and bounteous flower gardens. From there, continue through the countryside to **Øm Kloster** (☎ 86 89 81 94, Munkevej 8; adult/child 30/10kr; open 10am-5pm daily May-Sept, 10am-6pm July-Aug, 10am-4pm Apr & Oct), the ruins of a medieval monastery. There are just enough bricks and rocks left to show what the monastery was once like. In the underground tombs, where the high altar once stood, you can peer through glass-topped enclosures at the 750-year-old skeleton of Bishop Elafsen of Århus and the bones of many of his abbots. There's also a small museum with more skulls and monastery artefacts.

The whole trip from Ry and back is about 18km.

Canoeing

If you want to explore the surrounding lakes and rivers on your own, Ry Kanofart (☎ 86 89 11 67), Kyhnsvej 20, has canoes for hire (50/250kr per hour/day). In addition, Danhostel Ry has a few canoes that it hires out for the same price.

Places to Stay

Sønder Ege Camping (☎ 86 89 13 75, fax 86 89 02 07, e info@sdregecamping.dk, Søkildevej 65) Camping per person 57kr.

Open Apr-Sept. This three-star lakeside ground 1km north of Ry is the closest camping ground to town.

Danhostel Ry (☎ 86 89 14 07, fax 86 89 28 70, e mail@danhostel-ry.dk, Randersvej 88) Dorm beds 100kr, doubles 250/400kr in summer/winter. Open Jan-Nov. This hostel, opposite the same bathing lake as the camping ground, is just 100m from the beach. To get to the hostel from the train station, cross over the tracks, turn left and continue on for 2.5km.

Staff at the tourist office can book **rooms** in private homes around Ry for around 200/275kr for singles/doubles. They also book cottages in the Ry area, most of which can sleep four people and cost from 2400kr a week.

Ry Park Hotel (☎ 86 89 19 11, fax 86 89 12 57, e ryparkhotel@mail.dk, Kyhnsvej 2) Singles/doubles with breakfast 695/895kr. This 80-room hotel is in the centre of town. Rooms have modern amenities including TV and minibar and there's an indoor swimming pool and sauna.

Places to Eat

Peking Grill (☎ 86 89 24 84, Klostervej 26) Meals 40-55kr. This simple place just west of the train station has good-value Chinese dishes served with rice.

Pizzeria Italia (☎ 86 89 31 33, Skanderborgvej 3) Pizza & pasta dishes 60kr. This pizzeria also serves pasta and is 300m from the train station on the eastern side of the tracks.

Restaurant Sønder Ege (☎ 86 89 18 66, Søkildevej 69) 2-course meal 98kr. This quintessentially Danish place near Sønder Ege Camping has a lovely lake view and good food, including trout with salad and traditional beef dishes.

Bagergaarden (☎ 86 89 10 48, Klostervej 12) Sandwiches 25kr. This bakery is opposite the train station and has good sandwiches and pastries.

Getting There & Around

If you have your own transport, Ry is on route 445, 24km south-east of Silkeborg and 35km west of Århus.

Hourly trains connect Ry with Silkeborg (24kr, 20 minutes) and Århus (37kr, 30 minutes).

Ry Cykel (☎ 86 89 14 91), which is at Skanderborgvej 19, rents bikes for 50/250kr per day/week.

HIMMELBJERGET

The Lake District's most visited spot is the whimsically named Himmelbjerget (Sky Mountain) which, at just 147m, is one of Denmark's highest hills. The hill top is crowned with a 25m tower (admission 5kr) erected in 1875. From here you'll have a fine 360° view of the lakes and surrounding countryside, which is part woodland, part farmland. On a clear day it's a lovely vista.

There are marked hiking trails in the woodland area, including one that leads 1km down to the lake.

The parking area for Himmelbjerget is next to a hotel, restaurant and souvenir kiosks. It's a five-minute walk from the car park to the hill-top tower.

Places to Stay & Eat

Hotel Himmelbjerget (☎ 86 89 80 45, fax 86 89 87 93, Ny Himmelbjergvej 20) Singles/doubles with breakfast 490/645kr. This pleasantly rustic lodge has 18 rooms with shared bathrooms. The restaurant at the hotel has a nice view of the woods as well as reasonable prices. There's also a kiosk selling fast food.

Getting There & Away

Bus No 311 runs from Ry train station to Himmelbjerget four to seven times a day; check the schedule with the Ry tourist office as it varies with the day of the week. Himmelbjerget is a 10-minute drive west of Ry on route 445.

It can also be reached by a pleasant 7km hike from Ry or by a scenic boat ride from either Ry or Silkeborg.

Boat The paddle steamer *Hjejlen* (☎ 86 82 07 66), sails from Silkeborg to Himmelbjerget daily during the summer, leaving Silkeborg at 10am and 1.45pm. The trip takes 1¼ hours and costs 100kr return or 63kr one way; children's tickets are half-price. The same company also operates an ordinary boat on this route up to six times a day, so be sure to request the *Hjejlen* when you book.

Ry Turistbåde (☎ 86 82 88 21) operates boats from Ry to Himmelbjerget daily in summer, leaving Ry at 10am, noon and 2pm, and leaving Himmelbjerget one hour later. The fare is 40kr one way, 60kr return, 25/35kr for children.

A Paddle Steamer Cruise

The *Hjejlen*, one of the world's oldest operating paddle steamers, has been faithfully plying the waters of the Lake District since it was first launched in 1861. King Frederik VII was among the passengers on that inaugural cruise.

Built by the Burmeister & Wain shipyard in Copenhagen, the boat is such an antique that, when the engine needed rebuilding a few years ago, an engineer had to be called out of retirement to do the work. These days the boat makes a couple of daily runs shuttling tourists from Silkeborg to Himmelbjerget during the summer season. The 15km route takes in a wealth of river and lake scenery along the way and is one of the most popular outings in the Lake District.

NC

Djursland & Mols

Djursland and Mols are the names, respectively, of the northern and southern halves of the large peninsula north-east of Århus. It's a pleasant area of gently rolling hills and farmland interspersed with patches of woodland. There are small villages and a scattering of old manor houses throughout. The main destinations are the towns of Ebeltoft and Grenaa, both of which have fine, white-sand beaches that attract the summer tourists.

There are a handful of other sites around the peninsula that could also be toured. The southern town of Rønde contains the ruins of **Kalø Slot**, a coastal brick fortress erected in the early 14th century. The Swedish king Gustav Vasa was a prisoner here in 1519. Although those who like to soak up history should enjoy this site, all that's left is the outline of the fortress foundation and the partial remains of one of the towers.

For a different sort of experience, there's **Djurs Sommerland**, an amusement park featuring water chutes and slides and other recreational activities geared towards children. It's about 20km west of Grenaa on Randersvej 17 in Nimtofte.

There's some particularly pretty countryside along the eastern side of the peninsula. If you're travelling by bicycle or car between Ebeltoft and Grenaa, consider taking the unfrequented rural route that leads through Dråby and continues as the easternmost through-road north.

EBELTOFT
postcode 8400 • pop 5300
Ebeltoft has an enjoyable tourist centre with cobbled pedestrian streets lined with souvenir shops, cafes and ice-cream stands.

In medieval times Ebeltoft was a successful market town trading with Zealand, Germany and Sweden. The town's prosperity came to an abrupt end in 1659 when the Swedish navy sacked Ebeltoft and torched its merchant fleet. It wasn't until the 1960s, when the Swedes 'reinvaded' (this time as tourists), that the economy shook off three

centuries of stagnation. The central town quarters are more historic than modern, the streets around the old rådhus thick with period, timber-framed buildings topped with red-tiled roofs.

The town sits on a calm, protected bay fringed with white-sand beaches; you'll find a nice stretch right along Strandvejen, the coastal road that leads north from the town centre. Another bathing area begins on the southern side of Ebeltoft, just below the harbour.

Orientation
The tourist office, the *Fregatten Jylland* and the harbour are along Strandvejen. From the harbour walk east on Jernbanegade to reach Adelgade, the main shopping street. Torvet, the town square, is at the southern end of Adelgade. All of these places are within a five-minute walk of each other.

Information
The Ebeltoft/Mols Turistbureau (☎ 86 34 14 00, fax 86 34 05 28, [e] ebeltoft@post6 .tele.dk) is at Strandvejen 2 on the harbour. It's open 9.30am to 6pm Monday to Friday, 9.30am to 5pm on Saturday and 9.30am to 4pm on Sunday between mid-June and August. The opening hours are 9.30am to 4pm or 5pm on weekdays and 10am to 1pm or 2pm on Saturday from September to mid-June.

There are several banks on Jernbanegade, including a Unibank (☎ 86 34 17 11) at No 7, about 100m east of the tourist office.

The post office (☎ 87 12 89 00), on the waterfront north of the tourist office, is open 9.30am to 5pm Monday to Friday and to noon on Saturday.

Things to See
Ebeltoft's old rådhus, which claims to be Denmark's smallest town hall, is a quaint half-timbered building erected in 1789. It now houses the **Ebeltoft Museum** (*☎ 86 34 55 99, Torvet; adult/child 25/5kr; open 11am-4pm daily June-Aug, 11am-3pm Tues-Sun in spring & autumn)*, a worthwhile little collection that exudes a sense of the town's history.

Down at the harbour is **Fregatten Jylland** (☎ 86 34 10 99; adult/child 50/20kr; open 10am-7pm daily mid-June-Aug, 10am-5pm Sept–mid-June), a 19th-century wooden frigate that has undergone an extensive restoration.

Ebeltoft Kirke dates back to at least 1301, at the time when the town received its charter from Erik VI. The church has a 13th-century sandstone font and a few simple early-16th-century frescoes, including a drawing of the *Maria*, a Danish warship that was used to attack Sweden in 1517. Ebeltoft Kirke is about a 10-minute walk south from Torvet via Overgade; the door to the church is usually open during the day and admission is free.

Another attraction is the **Glasmuseum** (☎ 86 34 17 99, Strandvejen 8; adult/child 40/5kr; open 10am-5pm daily, until 9pm in July), which displays both decorative and functional works in glass.

Places to Stay

There are several camping grounds in the Ebeltoft area. **Vibæk Camping** (☎ 86 34 12 14, fax 86 34 55 33, [e] lejerfar@hotmail .com, Strandvej 23) Camping per person 58kr. Open year-round. This three-star camping ground is on a white-sand beach 1km north of town.

Danhostel Ebeltoft (☎ 86 34 20 53, fax 86 34 20 77, [w] www.danhostel.dk/ebeltoft, Søndergade 43) Dorm beds 100kr, singles/doubles 200/250kr. Open Feb-Nov. This cosy 72-bed hostel is in a residential neighbourhood south of the centre, a 10-minute walk from Torvet.

Ebeltoft Parkhotel (☎ 86 34 32 22, fax 86 34 49 41, [e] post@ebeltoftparkhotel.dk, Adelgade 44) Singles/doubles with breakfast 595/735kr. This modern, mid-range hotel, 500m east of the town centre, has full amenities including an indoor pool.

Hotel Ebeltoft Strand (☎ 86 34 33 00, fax 86 34 46 36, [e] hotel@ebeltoftstrand.dk, Nedre Strandvej 3) Singles/doubles 905/1150kr, family room 795kr. This Best Western hotel, on the shoreline 500m north of the town centre, has a pool, sauna and 72 rooms with balconies. Rates include breakfast.

Places to Eat

You'll find several places to eat along Adelgade between Jernbanegade and Torvet.

Gryden (☎ 86 34 13 00, Adelgade 32) Fast food 25-40kr. This place serves pizza, burgers and pitta-bread sandwiches.

Café Bageriet (☎ 86 34 10 71, Adelgade 60) Lunch/dinner mains 45/70kr. This pleasant cafe has good chicken and steak lunch deals.

Mellem Fyder (☎ 86 34 11 23, Juulsbakke 3) Lunch/dinner mains 65/85kr. Try this half-timbered restaurant just south of Torvet for traditional Danish food and a cosy historic atmosphere.

Restaurant Vigen (☎ 86 34 14 33, Adelgade 5) Mains 160-180kr. This upmarket dinner restaurant merges French and Danish influences, and has a good reputation for its fish dishes.

Underground Ice Cream (☎ 86 34 10 70, Adelgade 2) Cones 18kr. Head here for some delicious all-natural ice cream after a day on the cobbled streets.

Getting There & Away

Ebeltoft is on route 21, 54km east of Århus and 35km south-west of Grenaa.

Bus No 123 runs between Århus and Ebeltoft about hourly on weekdays, less frequently at weekends; it takes 1½ hours and costs 48kr. There's also the No 351 regular bus service (32kr, 40 minutes) between Ebeltoft and Grenaa.

Mols-Linien (☎ 70 10 14 18) operates a large hydrofoil car ferry between Ebeltoft and Odden in north-western Zealand. The service runs 12 to 16 times a day and takes just 45 minutes. The cost is 130kr for adults, 65kr for children, 170kr for a motorcycle with two riders and 425kr for a car and up to five people.

Getting Around

Bicycles can be hired from LP Cykler (☎ 86 34 47 77), Nørreallé 5, for 50kr a day.

GRENAA

postcode 8500 • pop 14,400

Grenaa, at the eastern tip of Jutland, is a relatively young town, having largely taken its

CENTRAL JUTLAND

present form in the late 19th century when its commercial harbour was dug and a rail link was established with the rest of Jutland. It now serves as a port for ferries to Sweden.

Grenaa is divided into two sections. The centre of town, Torvet, is 3km inland from the harbour. Torvet is an engaging main square with a rådhus, town church and the usual mix of shops, restaurants and bakeries. The train station is two blocks east of Torvet. A second commercial area has built up along the inland side of the harbour and has similar services, including banks and eateries. The harbour itself is a sizable complex with a popular marina, ferry docks and fishing port.

A wide inviting beach, backed by gentle sand dunes, runs south from the harbour for nearly 7km. The inshore waters are shallow and popular with families who flock here on warm summer days.

Information

Djurslands Turistforening (☎ 87 58 12 00, fax 87 58 12 12, e dt@djurslands-turistforening .dk), Torvet 1, is open 9am to 5.30pm Monday to Friday and 9.30am to 5pm on Saturday from June to August; it's open 9am to 4pm on weekdays and 10am to 1pm on Saturday for the rest of the year.

There's a branch of Djurslands Bank (☎ 86 32 16 22) at Strandgade 2, opposite the fishing harbour and a couple of other banks on Torvet in the town centre.

The post office (☎ 87 12 89 00) is at Stationsplads 2, west of the train station; it's open 9am to 5pm on weekdays and 9am to noon on Saturday.

Things to See & Do

Although the main tourist draw is the beach, the town offers a couple of attractions to keep visitors occupied on rainy days.

Kattegatcentret (☎ 86 32 72 00, Færgevej 4; adult/child 90/55kr; open 10am-6pm daily June-Aug, 10am-4pm Sept-May) on the harbour and north of the marina, is a modern aquarium housing several tanks of cold-water and tropical fish, including several sharks. There's also an outdoor tank that houses a number of seals.

The regional-history museum, **Djurslands Museum & Dansk Fiskerimuseum** (☎ 86 32 48 00, Søndergade 1; adult/child 30kr/free; open 10am-4pm Mon-Fri, 1pm-4pm Sat & Sun in summer; 1pm-4pm Tues-Fri & Sun in winter) is in a timber-framed merchant's house on the south side of Torvet. It has antique toys, old coins, archaeological finds and displays on the Danish fishing industry.

Places to Stay

Polderrev Camping (☎ 86 32 17 18, fax 86 30 95 55, Fuglsangvej 58) Camping per person 57kr. Open Apr-Sept. This three-star camping ground is opposite the beach about 2km south of the harbour. It has a grocery shop and a restaurant.

Danhostel Grenaa (☎ 86 32 66 22, fax 86 32 12 48, W www.danhostel.dk/grenaa, Ydesvej 4) Dorm beds 100kr, doubles 300kr. Open early Jan–mid-Dec. This modern 108-bed hostel is at a sports centre about 1.5km south-east of the town centre.

The tourist office maintains a list of private **rooms** (around 150kr per person) in the Grenaa area and has information on beachside holiday cottages that are rented by the week.

Hotel Grenaa Strand (☎ 86 32 68 14, fax 86 32 07 92, e info@grenaastrand.dk, Havneplads 1) Singles/doubles with breakfast 420/595kr. Rooms in this atmospheric little hotel opposite the harbour have a private bath and TV.

Places to Eat

In the town centre you'll find a variety of places to eat on Lillegade, the street that runs north-west from Torvet.

Otto's Bageri (☎ 86 32 12 06, Lillegade 10) Light meals 20-40kr. This bakery-cafe combo has good sandwiches, pizza and salads.

Alberto's (☎ 86 32 48 11, Lillegade 22) Dishes 55kr. Here you can get moderately priced pizza, lasagne and spaghetti.

Den Gyldne Krus (☎ 86 32 47 22, Lillegade 18) Mains 60-90kr. This pub-style restaurant doubles as a summertime pavement cafe and has an extensive menu, including various grilled meat dishes.

Fiskerestauranten (☎ *86 30 03 07, Kystvej 14)* Mains 130-160kr. A pleasant option for a relaxing upmarket dinner is this popular fish restaurant by the harbour.

Getting There & Away

Grenaa is 63km north-east of Århus on route 15 and 57km east of Randers along route 16.

Both bus (No 121 or 122) and train services run throughout the day between Århus and Grenaa, cost 52kr and take about 1½ hours.

For information on boats between Grenaa and Varberg, Sweden, see the Getting There & Away chapter.

Getting Around

Both buses and trains leave from the DSB station at Stationsplads 4.

Bicycles can be hired from Viggo Jensen (☎ 86 32 06 83) near the harbour at Strandgade 14 for 50kr per day.

GAMMEL ESTRUP

Gammel Estrup (☎ *86 48 30 01, Randersvej 2; bus No 119 from Århus; adult/child 65kr/free, includes both museums; open 10am-5pm daily Apr-Oct, 10am-4pm Tues-Sun Nov-Mar)* in the village of Auning, 33km west of Grenaa, is an impressive estate dating back to the 14th century. It makes an interesting detour if you want a historical perspective on rural Danish life or if you haven't yet toured one of Zealand's impressive castles.

The moat-encircled manor house, along with its period furnishings, tapestries and paintings, has been turned into a museum called the **Jyllands Herregårdsmuseum**. Visitors can wander through numerous rooms, including the kitchen, chapel, reception halls and sleeping quarters.

The estate farm buildings, adjacent to the manor house, have been set aside as a farming museum, **Dansk Landbrugs-museum**, which depicts the more earthy lives of those who worked the land. Its halls are packed with farm tools, old tractors and carriages, milk jugs and the like; in summer there are often demonstrations of rural trades such as blacksmithing.

The Interior

This inland part of Jutland is a mixed landscape with some small industrial towns and cities, as well as wooded areas and farmland. The two most interesting places are the 1000-year-old Fyrkat Viking ring fortress in Hobro and the Rebild Bakker National Park, part of Rold Skov, Denmark's largest public woodland.

RANDERS
postcode 8900 • pop 60,000

Randers is the fourth largest city in Jutland. Situated at the spot where the river Gudenå and the Randers Fjord merge, Randers' central location has made it an important trading town since its founding in 1302. In the 19th century the railway linked Randers with the rest of Jutland and heavy industry developed. Lofty smokestacks are still a dominant feature of the skyline. Randers is not a major tourist destination, but because so many main roads and trains pass through Randers there's a good chance you'll pass through as well.

Orientation

The train station is west of the city centre. It's a 15-minute walk to the tourist office (go east on Jernbanegade and Tørvebryggen) or a 10-minute walk via Vestergade to Rådhustorvet, the central square.

Information

The Randers Turistbureau (☎ 86 42 44 77, fax 86 40 60 04, e randers@randersturist .dk), Tørvebryggen 12, is open 9am to 6pm Monday to Friday and 9am to 3pm on Saturday between mid-June and August; it's open 9.30am to 4.30 or 5pm Monday to Friday and 9am to noon on Saturday during the rest of the year.

The Danske Bank (☎ 87 10 33 00) on the southern side of Rådhustorvet has a 24-hour ATM.

The post office (☎ 87 12 89 00), north of Rådhustorvet at Nørregade 1, is open 9.30am to 5.30pm Monday to Friday and 9.30am to 1pm on Saturday.

CENTRAL JUTLAND

Things to See & Do

By far the most interesting part of the city is its central area, where there is a cluster of period brick and half-timbered buildings. Three buildings that date from the late 15th century are **Paaskesønnernes Gård**, a three-storey brick building on Rådhustorvet; **Helligåndshuset**, once part of a medieval monastery, at Eric Menveds Plads; and **Sankt Mortens Kirke** on Kirketorvet. All are within a few minutes' walk of each other.

The local-history and art museums are at **Kulturhuset** to the east of the city centre, a 10-minute walk from either Rådhustorvet or the tourist office. The history museum *(☎ 86 42 86 55, Stemannsgade 2; adult/child 20kr/free; open 11am-5pm Tues-Sun)* has a prehistory section and collections of church art, period interiors, weapons and glass. The art museum *(☎ 86 42 29 22, Stemannsgade 2; adult/child 20kr/free; open 11am-5pm Tues-Sun)* features Danish paintings from the late 19th century to the present.

The city's most visited attraction is **Randers Regnskov** *(☎ 87 10 99 99, Tørvebryggen 11; adult/child 65/40kr; open 10am-6pm daily June-mid-Aug; 10am-4pm Mon-Fri, 10am-5pm Sat & Sun rest of the year)*, a dome-enclosed tropical zoo about 300m west of the tourist office. Trails within the sultry domes pass through enclosures housing crocodiles, monkeys, pythons, iguanas, orchids, hibiscus and other rainforest flora and fauna.

Places to Stay

Danhostel Randers *(☎ 86 42 50 44, fax 86 41 98 54, e randers.danhostel@adr.dk, Gethersvej 1)* Dorm beds 80kr, doubles 240-300kr. Open 15 Feb-1 Dec. This hostel is just west of the city centre, a 10-minute walk north of the train station. It has 136 beds in 30 rooms.

The tourist office can provide a list of private homes with *rooms* for rent in the Randers area; prices vary, but expect a double to cost around 300kr.

Hotel Kronjylland *(☎ 86 41 43 33, fax 86 41 43 95, e hotelkronjylland@dk-online .dk, Vestergade 53)* Singles/doubles with breakfast 695/895kr. This hotel, a five-minute

walk east of the train station, has 33 modern rooms with bath, TV and phone.

Hotel Randers *(☎ 86 42 34 22, fax 86 40 15 86, e hr@hotel-randers.dk, Torvegade 11)* Singles/doubles 845/1050kr, weekend rate for all rooms 825kr. This pleasantly old-fashioned hotel is centrally located just 100m from Rådhustorvet. It has 79 comfortable rooms with bath, TV and minibar. There's a restaurant, a lounge and free parking. Rates include breakfast.

Places to Eat

All of the following places are in the town centre near Rådhustorvet.

Belvedera Pizza *(☎ 86 40 79 75, Rådhustorvet 6)* Pizza slices 20kr, kebab sandwiches 35kr. This pizzeria, opposite the post office, gives you good value in a pizza slice.

Café Borgen *(☎ 86 43 47 00, Houmeden 10)* Light meals 32-45kr. A block southwest of Rådhustorvet, this cosy candlelit cafe is a favourite place to linger over a drink or light meal including sandwiches, salads and lasagne.

Jensen's Bøfhus *(☎ 86 43 43 00, Rådhusstræde 3)* Lunch specials 45kr, dinner mains 100kr. This restaurant, specialising in grilled chicken and steaks, is in an attractive building just off the square.

China Wok House *(☎ 86 42 71 72, Eric Menveds Plads 4)* Takeaway 25kr, lunch/dinner buffet 49/108kr. This place has all-you-can-eat buffets that include a good salad bar and numerous Chinese dishes. There is also a three-item takeaway box special.

Niels Ebbesen's Spisehus *(☎ 86 43 32 26, Storegade 13)* Mains 100-150kr. This upmarket restaurant occupies a charming period building offering good steak and fish dishes.

Getting There & Around

All trains between Århus and Aalborg stop in Randers. The fare is 52kr to Århus and 76kr to Aalborg.

Randers is 76km south of Aalborg and 36km north of Århus on the E45 and 57km west of Grenaa and 41km east of Viborg on route 16.

Jørgen Schmidt Cykler (☎ 86 41 29 03), Vestergade 35, hires bicycles for 50kr a day.

HOBRO

postcode 9500 • pop 10,800

Hobro is best known as the site of Fyrkat, an intact 10th-century Viking ring fortress.

The town, which sits at the head of the Mariager Fjord, is otherwise a rather utilitarian place, being a mix of small industry and commercial facilities serving the farms and villages in the surrounding district.

The train station is on the western edge of town; from the station to the town centre, 1km away, walk east along Jernbanegade.

Information

Hobro Turistbureau (☎ 98 52 56 66, fax 98 52 28 70, e hobroturistkontor@hobro-erhverv .dk), Sondre Kajgade 16, is at the head of the Mariager Fjord. It's open 9am to 5pm on weekdays and 9am to 2pm on Saturday between mid-June and 31 August; hours are 9am to 4pm on weekdays and 9am to noon Saturday during the rest of the year.

There's a branch of Jyske Bank (☎ 98 52 41 11) at Adelgade 10. The post office (☎ 80 20 70 30) is at Adelgade 8.

Town Centre

Over the centuries, fires have robbed Hobro of its finer buildings. The oldest remaining structure is a merchant's house erected in 1821. It now houses the **Hobro Museum** (☎ 98 51 05 55, Vestergade 21; adult/child 25/5kr; open 11am-5pm daily May-Sept), which displays local-history exhibits, including excavated items from Fyrkat.

Fyrkat

Although it's somewhat smaller than the better-known Trelleborg in southern Zealand, the 1000-year-old Fyrkat fortress (☎ 98 51 19 27, Frykatvej 45; adult/child 50/15kr includes entry to Vikingegården Fyrkat; open 10am-4pm daily Easter weekend–mid-Oct, 10am-5pm June-Aug) outside Hobro so closely resembles Trelleborg that both are presumed to have been built by the Viking king Harald Bluetooth in around 980.

Fyrkat was part of a farmer's overgrown field until the 1950s, when archaeologists from the national museum excavated the site. Items found during the excavation indicate that Fyrkat not only quartered about 800 Viking soldiers but that women and children were also part of the camp life. Many of the finds were singed, suggesting that the wooden longhouses that sat within the rampart walls had been destroyed by fire, probably within a few years of the completion of the fortress, and that the site was then abandoned.

Today you can walk out onto the grass-covered circular ramparts for an impressive view of the fort's symmetrical design. The four cuts in the earthen walls, all formerly gates, face the four points of the compass. Within the rampart walls the fortress is divided into four equal quadrants, each once had a central courtyard surrounded by four symmetrical buildings. Stone blocks placed within the fortress show the foundation shape of these elongated buildings, which housed the inhabitants of Fyrkat. Sheep grazing in the fields add a timeless backdrop to it all.

No structures now stand within the ramparts but just outside is a replica Viking house built of oak timbers utilising a stave-style construction technique.

At the entrance to Fyrkat there are some period farm buildings, including a 200-year-old, working water mill and a half-timbered house with an old-fashioned restaurant.

Fyrkat is 3km south-west of Hobro town centre via Fyrkatvej and about a 90kr taxi ride from the train station. If the weather is good, stop at the Viking farmstead and then walk the last kilometre to the fortress site.

Vikingegården Fyrkat To augment the Fyrkat fortress site, a Viking-style farmstead has been constructed along Fyrkatvej, 1km north of the fortress. It is believed that farms such as this sat outside the fortress walls and served to provide food for the soldiers encamped within.

All nine Viking farm buildings were erected using period-authentic materials and hand tools – a process that took over a decade and was only recently completed. The most impressive, a 33m longhouse, has a frame made of oak hewn by hand using an adze, a roof constructed of reeds fastened by willow shoots, a ridge of local peat and

CENTRAL JUTLAND

Viking Play

Fyrkatspillet, a local amateur theatre troupe, presents a Viking play at Fyrkat annually during a two-week period from late May to early June. A new play is performed each season.

Plays are performed at the reconstructed Viking house. Although the performances are in Danish, the general theme is usually easy to follow and someone will gladly provide you with a little rundown on the plot before the action begins.

Themes commonly involve Viking kings; one play depicts the marriage of Sweyn Forkbeard and the strong-spirited Polish princess Swietoslawa, which was undertaken in a contrived effort to unite Denmark and Poland against the German kaiser. Whatever the storyline, you can expect beautiful damsels, sword-wielding Viking warriors, conflicts and resolutions, and lots of light-hearted laughter.

It's all quite a pleasant event with the inviting spirit of a neighbourhood party. On Friday and Saturday the performance is accompanied by a dinner featuring lamb roasted over an open spit. Admission to the play alone costs 70kr; with dinner it costs 150kr. Tickets can be reserved through the Hobro Turistbureau (for contact details, see under Information in this section), but book well in advance as tickets always sell out.

walls made from a mixture of cow dung, blue clay and straw.

Costumed interpreters provide demonstrations of silverwork, archery and other Viking activities. Many of these people are volunteers who come to Fyrkat every year for a week or so to live as the Vikings did: sleeping in the longhouse, eating grains and smoked fish that they prepare for themselves, and mastering Viking-era crafts. They'll be happy to answer any questions you might have and most of them also speak English.

The farmstead area has the same opening hours as the Fyrkat fortress site. Admission is also included in the cost of entry to the fortress.

Places to Stay

Hobro Camping Gattenborg (☎ 98 52 32 88, fax 98 52 56 61, Skivevej 35) Camping per person 60kr. Open Apr-Sept. This three-star camping ground has a swimming pool and is just 1km south of the train station.

Danhostel Hobro (☎ 98 52 18 47, fax 98 51 18 47, e danhostelhobro@adr.dk, Amerikavej 24) Dorm beds 100kr, singles/doubles 295/315kr. Open 15 Jan-15 Dec. This modern 116-bed hostel is at a sports centre, 1.5km east of the town centre.

Staff at the tourist office can provide a list of *rooms* in private homes; doubles cost around 300kr.

Places to Eat

Bæch's Conditori (☎ 98 52 48 00, Adelgade 38) Sandwiches 25kr. On the pedestrian street running through the town centre, this bakery with cafe tables sells hearty sandwiches.

Musikcaféen Hobro (☎ 25 51 52 07, Havnen) Daily meal special 48kr. This cafe at the harbour, west of the tourist office, has good, reasonably priced Danish food and occasional live jazz.

Fyrkat Møllegaard (☎ 98 52 10 65, Frykatvej 45) Lunch 70-100kr, dinner 200kr. This atmospheric restaurant in a period building at Fyrkat offers Danish country meals including omelettes, minced beef with pumpkin and dinner steaks.

Getting There & Away

Route 180 runs straight through Hobro, connecting it with Randers, 27km to the south-east and to Aalborg, 49km to the north. The speedier E45 runs along the outskirts of Hobro connecting with the same cities.

Hobro is on the main Frederikshavn to Århus railway line. There are trains about twice hourly between Hobro and Randers (29kr, 20 minutes), and between Hobro and Aalborg (52kr, 34 minutes).

MARIAGER

postcode 9550 • pop 2500

Although it's a bit out of the way, Mariager can be an interesting stop for those who want to unwind. This quiet little fjordside town has a solid grip on the past. Not only are its cobblestone streets lined with picturesque centuries-old buildings but it's home to two other relics, a vintage steam train and a paddle steamer.

The Mariager Turistbureau (☎ 98 54 13 77, e mariager@mariagerturist.dk), in the old rådhus on Torvet, is open 9am to 5pm Monday to Friday and 9am to 2pm on Saturday between mid-June and August, and 9am to 4pm on weekdays and 9am to noon on Saturday the rest of the year.

Things to See & Do
You'll find the best collection of old buildings around Torvet, the central square, a 10-minute walk south of the harbour. The **Mariager Museum** (☎ 96 68 25 25, Kirkegade 4; adult/child 15kr/free; open 1pm-5pm daily 15 May-15 Sept), just a minute's walk south of Torvet, occupies an 18th-century merchant's house and contains the usual collection of historical artefacts.

The 21m-long **paddle steamer** Svanen (☎ 98 54 14 70; one-way/return 45/75kr adults, children half price; Tues, Thurs & Sun June-Aug; Sun only late June-July) plies the Mariager Fjord in summer, making a return journey between Mariager and Hobro. The departure times may vary.

In summer, the smoke-belching **steam train** Veteranjernbane (☎ 98 54 18 64; return 50/25kr adult/child; 11.30am & 2.40pm Sun late June-Aug) is taken out of its winter mothballs to carry passengers on a 45-minute joyride to the village of Handest, where it stops for 30 minutes before making the return journey.

Places to Stay
Mariager Camping (☎ 98 54 13 42, fax 98 54 25 80, e mariager@dk-camp.dk, Ny Havnevej 5A) Camping per person 62kr. Open Apr-Sept. This fjordside, three-star camping ground is just a few hundred metres west of the boat dock and the steam train station.

Hotel Postgaarden (☎ 98 54 10 12, fax 98 54 24 64, Torvet 6) Singles/doubles with breakfast 475/650kr. This hotel, in a restored 300-year-old half-timbered building

right on Torvet, has 14 rooms with bath, TV and phone.

Places to Eat
Hotel Postgaarden (☎ 98 54 10 12, Torvet 6) Lunch 98kr, dinner 150kr. A fun place to soak up the village atmosphere, this restaurant has traditional Danish fare and tables right on the cobbled square.

Opposite the harbour there's a *grill* serving hot dogs and burgers. There's also a grocery shop in this area.

On Torvet you'll find a *bakery*, an *ice-cream shop* and a *pizzeria*.

Getting There & Away
Mariager is 15km east of Hobro on route 555. Other than the vintage tourist steam train, there's no train service to Mariager. Buses run every couple of hours from Hobro (20kr) and hourly from Randers (30kr); both routes take about 30 minutes.

REBILD BAKKER
postcode 9520
Rebild Bakker, with its rolling heathered hills, is Denmark's only national park. In 1912 a group of Danish-Americans purchased 200 hectares of property at this site and presented it to the Danish government with three provisions: that it would remain in a natural state, be open to all visitors and be accessible to Danish-Americans for the celebration of US holidays.

To augment the park area the Danish forest service acquired adjacent woodland tracts that are now set aside as nature reserves. Collectively the area, referred to as **Rold Skov**, is the largest forest in Denmark. Still, don't expect a vast wilderness, as it does not take much to lay claim to being Denmark's largest forest – the entire area accounts for only 77 sq km and at its greatest width can be walked across in a matter of hours.

Rebild Bakker is a pleasant area in which to stroll, its hills covered with heather, juniper, crowberry, blueberry, cranberry, mountain tobacco and club moss, while its scrubby woods contain European aspen, beech and oak trees.

Things to See & Do

The **Lincoln Log Cabin** *(Cimbrervej 3; adult/child 20kr/free)*, just west of the car park at the start of the trails, contains bits of Americana as seen through Danish eyes, plus displays on Danish emigration to the USA. The building, modelled on the log cabin that US president Abraham Lincoln grew up in, is itself a replica, the original having been destroyed by arsonists in 1993.

At the car park is **Spillemandsmuseet** *(Fiddlers' Museum;* ☎ *98 39 16 04, Cimbrervej 2; adult/child 20/5kr)*, a simple regional museum featuring a varied collection of exhibits including fiddles, guns and traps, textiles and a 19th-century kitchen.

There are numerous walking **trails** crisscrossing the park. One pleasant 4km route begins in a sheep meadow west of the car park. It goes past Tophuset, a small century-old thatched house that was built by the first caretakers; the Lincoln log cabin; a large glacial boulder called Cimbrerstenen, sculpted in the form of a Cimbrian bull's head by Anders Bundgaard; the hollow where the 4 July celebrations are held; and Sønderland, the park's highest hill at 102m. It's a particularly lovely area in summer and autumn when the heather adds a purple tinge to the hillsides.

Places to Stay

Safari Camping *(*☎ *98 39 11 10, fax 98 39 17 94,* e *safari@dk-camp.dk, Rebildvej 17A)* Camping per person 60kr. Open year-round.

This three-star facility is just a few minutes' walk from the entrance to Rebild Bakker.

Danhostel Rebild *(*☎ *98 39 13 40, fax 98 39 27 40,* e *rebild@danhostel.dk, Rebildvej 23)* Dorm beds 100kr, 4-person rooms 350kr. Open Feb-Nov. This thatched, 100-bed hostel has a handy location right next to the park entrance.

Scanticon Comwell *(*☎ *98 39 12 22, fax 98 39 24 55,* e *hotel@scanticoncomwell-rebild .dk, Rebildvej 36)* Singles/doubles with breakfast 895/1095kr. This modern hotel, opposite the park entrance, has 151 rooms with bath, TV, minibar and balcony. The excellent facilities include a large indoor swimming pool, saunas and tennis courts.

Places to Eat

Bette Grill *(*☎ *98 39 12 00, Cimbrervej 1)* Light meals 15-40kr. This place, right at the car park, sells hot dogs, burgers, fried chicken and fish & chips.

Rebild Hus *(*☎ *98 39 12 00, Cimbrervej 1)* Meals 100kr. Adjacent to the grill, this is the park's sit-down restaurant, featuring moderately priced meat dishes.

Harvard *(*☎ *98 39 12 22, Rebildvej 36)* 3-course dinner 238kr. This dinner restaurant, at the Scanticon Comwell, is Rebild's fine dining option.

Getting There & Away

Route 180 runs through the Rold Skov forest, connecting Rebild Bakker with Hobro, 23km to the south.

Danish-American Festivities

Every 4 July thousands of Danes and Americans gather at Rebild Bakker to celebrate US Independence Day. The festivities, known as the Rebild Festival, have occurred annually since 1912 except during the two world wars, and are the largest US Independence Day celebrations held outside the USA. Many of the American participants are descendants of Danish immigrants, some 300,000 of whom went to the USA in the Danish emigration boom of the late 19th and early 20th centuries.

The festivities include singing, square-dancing and country music as well as speeches by prominent Danes and Americans. Among the keynote speakers in recent times have been members of the Danish royal family and US presidents Bush and Clinton.

Although the main celebration occurs at Rebild, in the days preceding the event there are also receptions and various activities in Aalborg, where most of the participants stay overnight. More information about the Rebild Festival can be obtained from the Aalborg Turistbureau.

From Aalborg, Århus-bound trains stop in Skørping (39kr, 16 minutes), from where it's 3km west to Rebild Bakker. Bus No 104 runs between Aalborg and Rebild Bakker (36kr, 45 minutes) via Skørping hourly on weekdays, less frequently on weekends. There are also frequent trains from Hobro to Skørping (29kr, 15 minutes).

VIBORG
postcode 8800 • pop 12,700
Viborg's history can be traced back to the 8th century. In 1060 it became one of Denmark's eight bishoprics and a century later, in 1150, it was granted its municipal charter. Viborg grew into a major religious centre and, prior to the Reformation, had 25 churches and abbeys though ecclesiastical remnants from that period are few.

The old part of town consists of the streets around Viborg Domkirke. Sankt Mogens Gade, which is between the cathedral and the tourist office, has some handsome old homes, including Hauchs Gård at No 7 and the Willesens House at No 9, both dating back to around 1520.

Viborg has a pleasant setting, bordering two lakes and surrounded by woods and moors. If you have your own transport, the Hald-Viborg reserve 6km south-west of Viborg has trails through woodlands and the ruins of a castle.

The train station is about 1km south-west of the tourist office.

Information
The Viborg Turistbureau (☎ 86 61 16 66, fax 86 60 02 38), Nytorv 9, is in the centre of town. It's open 9am to 5pm Monday to Friday and 9am to 3pm on Saturday in summer; it closes at 4pm on weekdays and at 12.30pm on Saturday in winter.

Things to See & Do
The twin-towered cathedral, **Viborg Domkirke** (☎ 87 25 52 50, Sankt Mogens Gade 4; admission free; open 10am-5pm Mon-Sat June-Aug, 11am-3pm in low season, from noon Sun year-round), just a two-minute walk down the hill from the tourist office, is one of Denmark's largest granite churches.

Archaeological excavations in 1974 indicate that the first church on this site was a wooden structure dating back to Viking times. A series of stone churches followed and, although there are traces of the first stone crypt dating from 1130, the current cathedral was virtually rebuilt in its entirety in 1876.

The interior of the cathedral is splashed with grand frescoes painted over five years (1901–06) by artist Joakim Skovgaard. The frescoes in the nave depict scenes from the Old Testament, those in the transept depict the life of Christ, while the choir frescoes feature scenes from the Resurrection and Ascension.

Skovgaard Museet (☎ 86 62 39 75, Domkirkestræde 4; adult/child 10kr/free; open 10am-12.30pm & 1.30pm-5pm daily May-Sept, 1.30pm-5pm Oct-Apr), to the south of Viborg Domkirke, also features works by Joakim Skovgaard, but here the scenes are more varied including nudes, portraits and landscapes. Works by friends and family members, including his father, PC Skovgaard and his brother, Niels Skovgaard, are also on display.

There's a local-history museum, **Viborg Stiftsmuseum** (☎ 87 25 26 20, Hjultorvet 9; adult/child 20kr/free; open 11am-5pm daily June-Aug; low-season hours shorter), a minute's walk south-west of the tourist office. The museum features relics from the Viking Age, church sculpture of the Middle Ages and regularly changing theme exhibits that more deeply explore Viborg's long history.

Places to Stay
Viborg Sø Camping (☎ 86 67 13 11, fax 86 67 35 29, e viborg@dcu.dk, Vinkelvej 36) Camping per person 58kr. Open late Mar-late Sept. This three-star camping ground is on the eastern side of lake Søndersø.

Danhostel Viborg (☎ 86 67 17 81, fax 86 67 17 88, e vibhoste@post8.tele.dk, Vinkelvej 36) Dorm beds 100kr, doubles 270-330kr. Open Mar-Nov. This pleasant, modern 112-bed hostel is adjacent to Viborg Sø Camping, just a kilometre's walk from town. Bicycles are available for hire.

CENTRAL JUTLAND

Staff at the tourist office can book *rooms* in private homes for around 200/275kr for singles/doubles, plus a 25kr booking fee.

Palads Hotel (☎ 86 62 37 00, fax 86 62 40 46, e info@hotelplads.dk, Sankt Mathias Gade 5) Singles/doubles 895/995kr, weekend & summer rate 795kr per room. A Best Western affiliate, this pleasant historic hotel, a short walk north of the train station, has 75 rooms with baths. Prices include breakfast.

Places to Eat

Take Away Spisested (☎ 86 61 10 90, Kompangnistræde 45) Pizza 35kr. Just 200m south of the tourist office, this unpretentious place has good inexpensive pizza.

Bone's (☎ 86 60 36 66, Preislers Plads 3) Meals 100kr. About 300m west of the tourist office, this steak and spareribs restaurant, well known for its large servings, is always bustling.

Kafé Arthur (☎ 86 62 21 26, Vestergade 4) Lunch 50kr, 2-course dinner 218kr. This cosy candlelit restaurant in the same area as Bone's, offers quiche and salads at lunch and fresh fish dishes at dinner.

Getting There & Away

Viborg is 66km north-west of Århus on route 26 and 41km west of Randers on route 16. Trains from Århus (92kr, 70 minutes) run hourly on weekdays, less frequently at weekends.

HJERL HEDE

Seven kilometres east of the small village of Vinderup is Hjerl Hede *(☎ 97 44 80 60, Hjerl Hedevej 14; adult/child 70/25kr; open 9am-5pm daily Apr-Oct)*, an open-air museum that traces the development of a Danish village from 1500 to 1900. Scenically set against a lake and moors, it has a collection of about 40 period buildings, many of them timber-framed with thatched roofs, which were brought here from around Jutland. You can wander around visiting a forge, a dairy, a grocery shop or village school.

From mid-June to late-August about 100 traditionally costumed men, women and children act as villagers doing such tasks as baking bread, dipping candles and tilling

the fields. There's also a small settlement where 'Stone Age people' in costume make flint instruments and pottery and practise spear fishing from dugout canoes.

Because of the activities, the summer high season is by far the most interesting time to go. The nearest train station is at Vinderup. There's no bus service from Vinderup; a taxi costs around 100kr. Trains run hourly between Viborg and Vinderup (37kr, 55 minutes).

SPØTTRUP SLOT

In the countryside 20km west of Skive, on route 573, is Spøttrup Slot *(☎ 97 56 16 06, Slotsvej 1; adult/child 30/10kr; open 10am-6pm daily May-Aug, 10am-5pm Sept, 10am-4pm Oct)*. Spøttrup castle was built in the 1500s by Jørgen Friis, the region's last Catholic bishop, at a time when the Church was under siege by the impending Lutheran Reformation. Not surprisingly, the heavy brick structure, encircled by a high rampart and double moats, more closely resembles an austere fortress than a castle. Although it may lack the grand scale and splendour of other Danish castles, Spøttrup is unique in that it has survived the centuries without any significant alteration and is thus one of the best-preserved medieval castles in Denmark.

The national government, which took over Spøttrup Slot and restored it 50 years ago, still maintains it today. You can walk around the entire castle, which is purposely kept in its original state with minimal furnishings and decor.

The nearest train station is in Skive; from there you can take bus No 43 or 44, which cost 22kr and leave about hourly on weekdays, less frequently at weekends. Trains run hourly between Skive and Viborg (29kr, 26 minutes).

HERNING

postcode 7400 • pop 29,200

Herning is an industrial town that developed in the late 19th century when the railway came chugging through. Textile mills followed but have been largely replaced by wood-processing and computer-technology

Traditional half-timbered houses with thatched roofs are part of many Jutland streetscapes.

industries. The community has a keen interest in the arts, which is visible in the many sculptures around town.

The Herning Turistbureau (☎ 96 27 22 22, fax 96 27 22 23), Torvet 1, right on the central square, is two blocks north-west of the train station.

Things to See & Do

Herning Museum (☎ 97 12 75 18, Museumsgade 32; adult/child 30kr/free; 10am-4.30pm Tues-Fri, 11am-4.30pm Sat & Sun), 300m south-west of the train station, features period furnishings and a collection of prehistoric items.

Herning Kunstmuseum (☎ 97 12 10 33, Birk Centerpark 3; adult/child 40kr/free; noon-5pm Tues-Sun), 2km east of town, has a respectable collection of modern Danish art, including works by Asger Jorn, Richard Mortensen and Carl-Henning Pedersen.

Places to Stay & Eat

Danhostel Herning (☎ 97 12 31 44, fax 97 21 61 69, Holingknuden 2) Bus No 1. Dorm beds 100kr. Open Feb-Nov. Herning's hostel is 3km north of town.

Hotel Eyde (☎ 97 22 18 00, fax 97 21 01 65, ⓔ info@eyde.dk, Torvet 1) Singles/doubles 695/895kr. This cheery old-fashioned hotel, on the central square, has comfortable rooms with full amenities.

There are lots of cafes and restaurants on the central square and in the nearby streets.

Bryggeriet Herning (☎ 96 26 02 70, Torvet 3) Meals 120kr, beer 20-40kr. This fun place brews its own organic beer and serves herring plates, chicken and lamb.

Getting There & Away

Herning is 50km west of Silkeborg on route 15. Trains from Silkeborg run hourly to Herning (45kr, 45 minutes).

Central West Coast

The central west coast, north of Esbjerg, is lined with sandy beaches, making it a popular summer holiday destination. One area particularly thick with summer cottages is Holmsland Klit, the thin neck of sand and dunes stretching nearly 35km from north to south, separating the North Sea from the Ringkøbing Fjord. This sandy neck, only about 1km wide, has its appeal but don't expect the drive to be overwhelmingly scenic as the dunes block the ocean view almost the entire way.

Ringkøbing Fjord attracts scores of windsurfers with conditions that are suitable for all levels, including beginners, while the North Sea side of Holmsland Klit offers more challenging action for advanced windsurfers.

HENNE STRAND
postcode 6854

Henne Strand is a small seaside resort that is especially popular with German visitors. The road into the village, Strandvejen, ends at the beach and is lined with a touristy collection of souvenir shops, boutiques and eateries, all in a row one after the other. The grassy dunes that separate the village from the beach are dotted with summer holiday homes, including some attractive thatched cottages.

The beach itself is long and lovely. On warm summer days when the wind is calm, swimmers take to the waters, although caution should be used as strong North Sea undertows can be experienced anywhere along the west coast. The northern end of the beach is a popular spot for nude sunbathing.

Places to Stay & Eat
Henne Strand Camping (☎ 75 25 50 79, *Henne Strandvej 418*) Camping per person 60kr. Open Apr-Oct. This three-star facility, 300m east of the village centre, is about a 10-minute walk from the beach and has a swimming pool.

Danhostel Henne Strand (☎ 75 25 50 75, e hennestrand@danhostel.dk, *Strandvejen 458*) Dorm beds 85kr, doubles 325kr. Open May-Oct. The little 44-bed hostel is right in the village, just minutes from the beach. Private rooms are often not available.

Henne Strand Feriehusudlejning (☎ 75 25 56 00, fax 75 25 51 20), Strandvejen 436, can book *summer houses* from 2200kr to 6500kr a week.

Along Strandvejen you'll find a *grocery shop*, *hot dog stands*, a couple of *bakeries* and a few *pizzerias* where you can get a meal for between 40kr and 80kr.

Getting There & Away
Henne Strand is at the end of route 465. Almost all visitors arrive by car but public transport is available. The easiest way is to take a train to Henne Strandby from Varde (37kr, 30 minutes) and from there catch a taxi, which will cost about 125kr. Alternately you could take the train to the more northerly Nørre Nebel (37kr, 45 minutes)

and catch one of the infrequent buses that run from there to Henne Strand.

HVIDE SANDE
postcode 6960 • pop 3200

The town of Hvide Sande came into existence in 1931 with the opening of a sluice channel and lock between the Ringkøbing Fjord and the North Sea. The sluice regulates both the water level and salinity of the Ringkøbing Fjord and protects the fields on the inland side of the fjord from being flooded. The lock, which is 16.5m wide, allows ships to enter the fjord, which is otherwise sealed off from the sea. The channel cuts across the centre of town and you can get a view of it all from the bridge.

Hvide Sande has a busy deep-sea fishing harbour, with trawlers, fish-processing factories and an early morning fish auction. There's also a little fishing museum adjacent to the tourist office. Most visitors, however, aren't here for the fish but to take advantage of the wind.

Information
The Holmsland Klit Turistforening (☎ 97 31 18 66, fax 97 31 28 80), Nørregade 2, is on the northern side of the channel. It's open 10am to 5pm Monday to Friday and 9am to noon on Saturday.

Windsurfing
Ringkøbing Fjord has ideal wind and water conditions, and Hvide Sande attracts scores of windsurfers. Surfcenter Hvide Sande Nord (☎ 97 31 25 99, Gytjevej 15), a Westwind operation on the northern side of Hvide Sande, offers a three-hour introductory course for 400kr as well as more comprehensive classes. It also rents boards with rigs starting at 200kr per half-day.

A Web site about windsurfing in the area is at w www.ringkobingfjord.dk/windsurfing.

Places to Stay
Beltana Camping (☎ 97 31 12 18, fax 97 31 33 11, e beltana@dk-camp.dk, *Karen Brandsvej 70*) Camping per person 55kr. Open early Apr–mid-Oct. This two-star camping ground is south of town opposite a

popular windsurfing beach. There are other camping grounds both north and south of Hvide Sande.

Danhostel Hvide Sande (☎ 97 31 21 05, fax 97 31 21 96, e danhostel@hvidesande .dk, Numitvej 5) Dorm beds 100kr, doubles 400kr. This modern 88-bed hostel has a central location at a sports centre on the northern side of the harbour. It has comfortable rooms, many with their own shower and toilet. The sports centre itself has a large indoor swimming pool, plus handball and badminton courts.

The tourist office can provide information on private *rooms* and summer cottages to rent.

Hvide Sande Sømandshjem (☎ 97 31 10 33, Bredgade 5) Singles/doubles 325/495kr which includes breakfast. This hotel is on the southern side of the harbour. There are 15 straightforward rooms with baths.

Places to Eat

There are *bakeries* on the southern side of town on the corner of Metheasvej and Stormgade and on the northern side of town at Nørregade 50.

Edgar Madsen (☎ 97 31 14 33, Metheasvej 11) Snacks 10-20kr. This place near the waterfront street Auktionsvej on the southern side of town sells smoked fish by the piece, deli salads and a few other takeaway items.

Bella Italia (☎ 97 31 30 00, Parallelvej 3) Lunch specials 39kr, dinner pizza 60kr, meat dishes 100kr. This Italian restaurant on the northern side of the harbour has a good steak-and-chips lunch deal, but also offers pizza and meat dishes.

Getting There & Away

Hvide Sande is on route 181. Bus No 58 runs to Hvide Sande from Ringkøbing train station (18kr, 20 minutes) and Nørre Nebel train station (26kr, 35 minutes) about hourly on weekdays, half as frequently on weekends.

RINGKØBING

postcode 6950 • pop 9100

Ringkøbing, on the northern side of the Ringkøbing Fjord, is an old market town that was granted its municipal charter in 1443. The town originated as a North Sea port but from the 17th century shifting sands caused the mouth of the fjord to slowly migrate south and threatened to cut off Ringkøbing's access to the sea. It was not until the lock at Hvide Sande was built in 1931 that the town was once again assured a reliable North Sea passage.

Today Ringkøbing has a shipyard, some industry and county administrative offices.

Information

Ringkøbing Turistbureau (☎ 97 32 00 31, fax 97 32 49 00, e rt@ringkobing-tourist .dk) is on Torvet, the central square. It's open 9.30am to 5pm Monday to Friday and 10am to 1pm on Saturday.

There are a couple of banks on Torvet. The post office (☎ 96 26 74 00), Nørredige 1, is to the west of the train station.

Things to See

There are a few **period buildings** in the centre of town around Torvet, the oldest of which is Hotel Ringkøbing, whose timber-framed wing dates from about 1600. The church north-west of the hotel dates from medieval times and has a sundial from 1728 on its western buttress.

Ringkøbing Museum (☎ 97 32 16 15, Østerport; adult/child 20kr/free; open 11am-5pm daily in July & Aug, shorter hours rest of year), east of Torvet, features displays on the Greenland expedition (1906–08) of Mylius Erichsen and such intriguing local items as a chastity belt from 1600.

Places to Stay

Ringkøbing Camping (☎ 97 32 08 38, fax 97 32 52 08, e info@ringk-camp.dk, Vellingvej 56) Camping per person 55kr. Open Apr-Oct. This three-star camping ground is on the eastern side of town.

Danhostel Ringkøbing (☎ 97 32 24 55, fax 97 32 49 59, e rofi@rofi.dk, Kirkevej 28) Dorm beds 100kr, 4-person rooms 400kr. Open year-round. This modern hostel is at a sports centre 1.5km north of the train station via Holstebrovej. It has 118 beds in 24 rooms, most with bath.

Hotel Ringkøbing (☎ 97 32 00 11, fax 97 32 18 72, Torvet 18) Singles/doubles 525/625kr. This historic hotel in the town centre has 15 rooms with bath.

Hotel Fjordgården (☎ 97 32 14 00, fax 97 32 47 60, ℮ rec@fjordgaarden.dk, Vesterkær 28) Singles/doubles 895/1095kr; weekend & summer rate 795kr per room. This modern hotel, on the western side of town, has 98 commodious rooms with bath and minibar. There's a sauna and indoor swimming pool.

Places to Eat

Café Victoria (☎ 97 32 42 01, Torvet 12) Light meals 45-60kr. This pleasant cafe has courtyard dining on sunny days with a menu offering sandwiches, omelettes and salads.

Ristorante Pizzeria Italia (☎ 97 32 01 23, Algade 11) Dishes from 60kr. This pizzeria has pizza, pasta and Italian meat dishes at moderate prices.

Hotel Ringkøbing (☎ 97 32 00 11, Torvet 18) 3-course dinner 178kr. This atmospheric fine-dining restaurant overlooks the central square and features Danish beef and fish meals.

Hvidbergs Bageri (☎ 97 32 44 22, Østergade 17) Sandwiches 25kr. This bakery east of Torvet makes good sandwiches.

Getting There & Away

Ringkøbing is on route 15, 46km west of Herning and 9km east of the North Sea.

It is on the railway line between Esbjerg (76kr, 1¼ hours) and Struer (68kr, one hour).

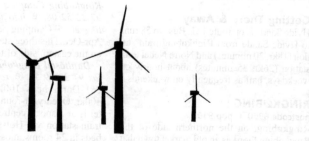

Northern Jutland

Northern Jutland, which is separated from the rest of Jutland by the Limfjord, has a coastal landscape dominated by heathlands, dunes and sandy beaches.

The region has only one large city, Aalborg, and a handful of mid-sized towns. Although road maps are peppered with the names of numerous smaller villages, these are often little more than a string of roadside houses broken by farmland and fields of grazing sheep.

Among the most interesting places in northern Jutland is the Lindholm Høje Viking burial ground on the northern outskirts of Aalborg, the vast, shifting sand dunes of Råbjerg Mile and the arty resort town of Skagen. The sandy tip of Skagen marks Denmark's northernmost point, called Grenen.

AALBORG
postcode 9000 • pop 154,000

Strategically situated at the narrowest point of the Limfjord, the long body of water that slices Jutland in two, Aalborg has been a bustling port since Viking times. Today it is the second-largest city in Jutland.

An industrial and trading centre, the economy of Aalborg relies on shipbuilding, cement and steel. It's also well known to bar hoppers as the leading producer of Danish schnapps, *akvavit*.

Although it's skipped over by most foreign travellers Aalborg does have a few worthwhile sights, the paramount attraction is Lindholm Høje, Denmark's largest Viking burial ground.

Orientation

Aalborg spreads along both sides of the Limfjord, with its two halves linked by bridge and tunnel. The heart of the city, and most of the services that a traveller would need are on the southern side. These include the tourist office and the cathedral, which are about 1km north of the train and bus stations along Boulevarden.

Highlights

- Reflect on the past at the Viking burial ground at Lindholm Høje (Aalborg)
- Get lost in vast stretches of deserted beaches
- Explore the extensive sand dunes of Råbjerg Mile
- Wander about seaside Skagen with its distinctive houses, museums and artists community
- Cycle out to the 'buried church' in the dunes south of Skagen
- Taste the windsurfing action at Klitmøller

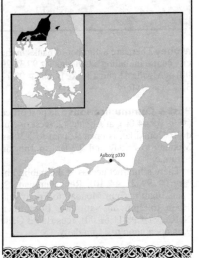

Aalborg p330

Information

Tourist Offices The Aalborg Turistbureau (☎ 98 12 60 22, fax 98 16 69 22, e info@ visitaalborg.com) is at Østerågade 8. It's open 9am to 5.30pm Monday to Friday and 10am to 1pm on Saturday between mid-June and August; 9am to 4.30pm Monday to Friday and 10am to 1pm on Saturday during the rest of the year.

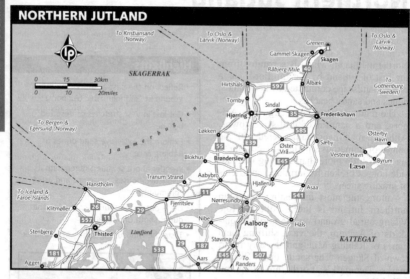

NORTHERN JUTLAND

Money There are a number of banks in the city centre including a Unibank (☎ 99 33 20 00) at Algade 41 and a Jyske Bank (☎ 98 12 31 22) at Nytorv 1.

Post & Communications The post office (☎ 99 35 44 00), at Algade 42, west of Budolfi Domkirke, is open 9.30am to 5.30pm Monday to Friday and 9.30am to 1pm on Saturday.

There's Internet access at the public library (☎ 99 31 44 10), Rendsburggade 2, open 10am to 7pm Monday to Friday and 10am to 2pm on Saturday. Boomtown NetCafe (☎ 98 11 61 00), Jens Bangs Gade 9, is open noon to 11pm daily.

Gay & Lesbian Travellers There is a branch of Landsforeningen for Bøsser og Lesbiske (LBL; ☎ 98 16 45 07), the national organisation for gays and lesbians in Aalborg. This branch provides a phone service rather than a drop-in centre.

Bookshops Vigeo Madsens Boghandel (☎ 98 13 21 44), Bispengade 10, is an international bookshop with a wide selection of maps and guides.

Laundry You'll find a coin laundry (☎ 98 16 40 11) on the corner of Vesterbro and Borgergade.

Medical Services Budolfi Apotek (☎ 98 12 06 77), on the corner of Vesterbro and Algade, is open 24 hours.

Danish Emigration Archives Det Danske Udvandrerarkiv (☎ 99 31 42 20, W www .emiarch.dk), Arkivstræde 1, behind the Vor Frue Kirke, keeps records of Danish emigration history and is set up to help foreigners of Danish descent trace their roots. It's open 9am to 4pm Monday to Thursday and 9am to 2pm on Friday and Saturday.

Budolfi Domkirke

This whitewashed cathedral *(Algade 40; admission free; 9am-4pm Mon-Fri, 9am-2pm Sat May-Sept; 9am-3pm Mon-Fri, 9am-noon Sat Oct-Apr)*, which dates from the 12th century, marks the centre of the old town.

As you enter the cathedral interior from Algade, look up at the foyer ceiling to see colourful frescoes. The interior boasts some beautifully carved items, including a gilded

Baroque altar and a richly detailed pulpit. Interestingly, despite their different appearances, both were created by Danish sculptor Lauridtz Jensen; apparently the altar, carved in 1689, was too flashy for the parish so in 1692 Jensen used an older Renaissance style for the pulpit.

Aalborg Historiske Museum

On the block west of Budolfi Domkirke is the Aalborg Historiske Museum (☎ 98 12 45 22, Algade 48; adult/child 20/10kr; open 10am-5pm Tues-Sun). This local-history museum features excavated artefacts, the requisite Renaissance furnishings and fine collections of silver and ancient Danish coins. It also displays some interesting oddities, such as a mid-18th-century hearse embellished with motifs of a skull and crossbones.

Other Central Sights

The alley between the Aalborg Historiske Museum and the post office leads to the rambling **Helligåndsklostret**, or Monastery of the Holy Ghost, which dates from 1431. The interior can only be visited on a guided tour arranged through the tourist office (see Organised Tours later in this section).

East of Budolfi Domkirke on Østerågade are three noteworthy historic buildings: the Baroque-style **old rådhus** (circa 1762), the five-storey **Jens Bangs Stenhus** (circa 1624), and **Jørgen Olufsens House** (circa 1616) at Østerågade 25. The latter two are lovely Renaissance buildings, one built by a wealthy merchant, Jens Bang, and the other by a wealthy mayor, Jørgen Olufsen.

In addition, the neighbourhoods of half-timbered houses around **Vor Frue Kirke** on Peder Barkes Gade are worth strolling through, particularly the cobbled street Hjelmerstald. **Aalborghus Slot**, near the waterfront, is more an administrative office than a castle but there's a small dungeon you can visit (admission free).

Ask at the tourist office for the English-language *Good Old Aalborg* booklet, which maps out two suggested walking tours and provides details of buildings and sights along the way.

Nordjyllands Kunstmuseum

This regional museum of contemporary and modern art (☎ 98 13 80 88, Kong Christian Allé 50; adult/child 30kr/free; open 10am-5pm daily July & Aug, 10am-5pm Tues-Sun Sept-June) is in a striking marble building designed by Finnish architect Alvar Aalto. It has a fine collection of Danish art dating from the late 19th century to the present day, including works by JF Willumsen, Asger Jorn, Richard Mortensen and Edvard Weie.

To get there take the tunnel beneath the train station, which emerges into Kildeparken, a green space with statues and water fountains. Go directly through the park, cross Vesterbro and continue through a wooded area to the museum, a 10-minute walk in all.

Aalborgtårnet

The hill behind Nordjyllands Kunstmuseum is topped with Aalborgtårnet (☎ 98 77 05 11, Søndre Skovvej; open 11am-5pm Apr-Sept, 10am-7pm in July, weather permitting), an ungainly tower offering a panoramic view of the city's steeples and smokestacks. The ride to the top of the tower costs 20kr (children 10kr).

Aalborgtårnet sits at the edge of an expansive wooded area, **Mølleparken**, which has walking trails, views and also the Aalborg Zoo.

Aalborg Zoo

This zoo (☎ 96 31 29 29, Mølleparkvej 63; bus No 1; adult/child 70/35kr; open 9am-6pm daily May-Aug, 10am-4pm Apr, Sept & Oct, 10am-2pm Nov-Mar) in Mølleparken, to the south-west of the city centre, has some pleasant aspects including a wooded setting and a children's zoo with goats and other tame creatures.

In all, Aalborg Zoo is home to more than 800 animals including elephants, zebras, tigers, giraffes, orang-utans, crocodiles and polar bears. The zoo also boasts golden-lion tamarins, which are almost extinct in the wild but have been successfully bred here. There's a cafeteria that serves moderately priced food.

Tivoliland

This amusement park (☎ 98 11 12 55, Karolinelundsvej; bus No 5; adult/child 40/20kr; open Apr-Sept; hours vary, but 10am-10pm at height of season), to the east of the city centre, has a roller coaster, a carousel, bumper cars and about 70 other rides and attractions as well as the usual carnival-style food.

Aalborg Marinemuseum

This waterfront museum (☎ 98 11 78 03, Vestre Fjordvej 81; bus No 2; adult/child 60/30kr; open 10am-6pm daily May-Aug, 10am-4pm Sep-Apr), 3km west of the city centre, features a 54m submarine, a torpedo boat, model ships and other maritime exhibits.

Lindholm Høje

On a hill-top pasture overlooking the city, Lindholm Høje (admission free; open dawn-dusk) is the site of 682 graves from the Iron Age and Viking Age. Many of the Viking graves are marked by stones placed in an oval ship shape, with two larger end stones as stem and stern. Interpretive plaques on the grounds provide historical insights in both English and Danish. It's an intriguing place to walk around; there's something almost spiritual about the site.

Lindholm Høje Museet (☎ 96 31 04 28, Vendilavej 11; adult/child 30/15kr; open 10am-5pm daily Apr-Oct, 10am-4pm Tues & Sun Nov-Mar), by the site's car park, features archaeological displays that attempt to re-create a sense of life during Viking times. The museum has a cafe serving simple sandwiches and salads at reasonable prices.

Lindholm Høje is 15 minutes from Aalborg via bus route No 6; cross the fence 50m beyond the bus stop and you'll be in the burial field. If you have your own transport, head north from the city centre over Limfjordsbroen to Nørresundby, and following Lindholmsvej north to Hvorupvej. After Hvorupvej intersects with Vikingevej take the first left, which will bring you up the driveway to the museum.

Organised Tours

In summer there's a convenient two-hour city bus tour, with a guide who is fluent in both Danish and English, at 1pm on Monday, Wednesday and Friday. It cruises past the city's main sights and stops for visits at Lindholm Høje and its Viking museum. Tickets, which include admission to the museums, can be bought in advance from the tourist office; the cost is 60kr (children 25kr).

The tourist office also organises a tour of the 15th-century Helligåndsklostret at 1.30pm on Monday, Wednesday and Friday. The tours cost 40kr (children 10kr).

Places to Stay

Camping & Hostels The following facilities are in the marina area about 4km west of the centre of Aalborg.

Strandparken Camping (☎ 98 12 76 29, fax 98 12 76 73, e info@strandparken.dk, Skydebanevej 20) Bus No 8. Camping per person 50kr. Open mid-Apr–mid-Sept. This three-star camping ground is on the eastern side of the marina, 300m from Fjordparken.

Danhostel Aalborg (☎ 98 11 60 44, fax 98 12 47 11, e aalborg@danhostel.dk, Skydebanevej 50) Bus No 8 (twice hourly, 6am-midnight). Dorm beds 100kr, 1-4–bed private rooms 398kr. Open year-round except mid-Dec–mid-Jan. This hostel has 35 rooms, each with four beds and a bath. The hostel also runs an adjacent two-star camping ground, **Fjordparken** where camping is 60kr per person. It's open 15 May to October.

Private Rooms & Hotels Staff at the tourist office can book *rooms* in private homes; singles/doubles 200/300kr plus a booking fee of 25kr.

Aalborg Sømandshjem (☎ 98 12 19 00, fax 98 11 76 97, e hansen@hotel-aalborg.com, Østerbro 27) Singles/doubles 475/625kr. This hotel, about 1km east of the city centre, is part of a small hotel chain originally geared to seamen but now open to all. It has 54 rooms with bath, TV and phone. The hotel has a fitness room and free parking.

Park Hotel (☎ 98 12 31 33, fax 98 13 31 66, e parkhotel@email.dk, JF Kennedys Plads 41) Singles/doubles 675/790kr. This traditional hotel has a convenient location opposite the train station. Ask for one of the courtyard rooms, which are the quietest.

Prinsens Hotel (☎ *98 13 37 33, fax 98 16 52 82, Prinsensgade 14)* Singles/doubles 695/895kr. This central hotel has 37 rooms with private bath, TV, phone and minibar. The rooms are comfortable enough but some are on the small side.

The following top-end hotels are in the city centre. In addition to the regular rates listed here, all of these hotels sometimes offer discounted rates at weekends, in summer or anytime business is slow, so always inquire about specials.

Hotel Chagall (☎ *98 12 69 33, fax 98 13 13 44,* e *chagall@isa.dknet.dk, Vesterbro 36)* Singles/doubles 790/995kr. The Chagall has 72 rooms with TV, phone and minibar. There is also a sauna, a jacuzzi and an exercise room.

Hotel Hvide Hus (☎ *98 13 84 00, fax 98 13 51 22,* e *aalborg@hotelhvidehus.dk, Vesterbro 2)* Singles/doubles 895/1095kr. This modern 200-room hotel has all the usual amenities. There's a fitness room, a sauna, an outdoor pool and a restaurant.

Radisson SAS Limfjord Hotel (☎ *98 16 43 33, fax 98 16 17 47,* e *limfjord@ aalzh.rdsas.com, Ved Stranden 14)* Singles/doubles 1035/1235kr. Best known as the site of the local casino, this hotel has 180 rooms; some are set aside for nonsmokers.

Helnan Phønix Hotel (☎ *98 12 00 11, fax 98 10 10 20,* e *hotel@helnan.dk, Vesterbro 77)* Singles/doubles 1050/1250kr. This old-fashioned hotel has 180 pleasantly furnished rooms. There's a bar, a restaurant, a sauna and a fitness room.

Places to Eat
Jomfru Ane Gade The best place to head at meal times is Jomfru Ane Gade, a boisterous pedestrian street lined with cafes and restaurants, some with alfresco dining. With so much competition you can always find tempting deals, simply stroll the street and see what takes your fancy. A few of our favourites are detailed here.

Fellini (☎ *98 11 34 55, Jomfru Ane Gade 23)* Lunch buffet 39kr, pizza or pasta 50-90kr. Open noon-4pm Mon-Fri. This Italian restaurant is best known for its good-value lunch buffet of pizza, pasta and salad.

Fyrtøjet (☎ *98 13 73 77, Jomfru Ane Gade 17)* Lunch specials 49kr, dinner 70-100kr. Open 11.30am-late Mon-Sat, from noon Sun. If it looks like might be going to rain, consider this place, which has a glass-roofed courtyard, competitive prices and good food.

Gaucho (☎ *98 13 70 30, Jomfru Ane Gade 21)* Mains 50-125kr. Open 11.30am-11pm Mon-Sat, 11.30am-10pm Sun. If you're up for a hearty Argentinian steak this is where you'll find it.

Elsewhere The usual fast-food chain eateries can be found around the city centre on Østerågade.

Café Luna (☎ *98 13 22 75, Boulevarden 38)* Dishes 20-60kr. Open noon-midnight Mon-Wed, noon-2am Tues-Sat, 2pm-midnight Sun. A short walk north of the train station, this pleasant cafe has reasonably priced lasagne, sandwiches and salads.

Water of Life

Akvavit (or aquavit), which means water of life, is the most popular spirit produced in Denmark. There are some 30 types of Danish akvavit on the market, most made from fermented potato mash. During the distilling process this dry spirit is flavoured with herbs, berries or spices, the most common being caraway seeds.

Akvavit is served in special long-stemmed glasses and is not sipped but swallowed straight in one gulp. The bottle is commonly kept in the freezer and the liquor served so ice-cold that it frosts the glass when it is poured. In Denmark, akvavit is often followed by a beer chaser and is usually not drunk as an aperitif but as a complement to traditional Danish meals such as smørrebrød or herring.

Most akvavit is 40% alcohol and all varieties produce a strong fiery sensation on the way down the throat. The city of Aalborg has been producing akvavit since the 17th century and its namesake Aalborg brand is the world's most famous.

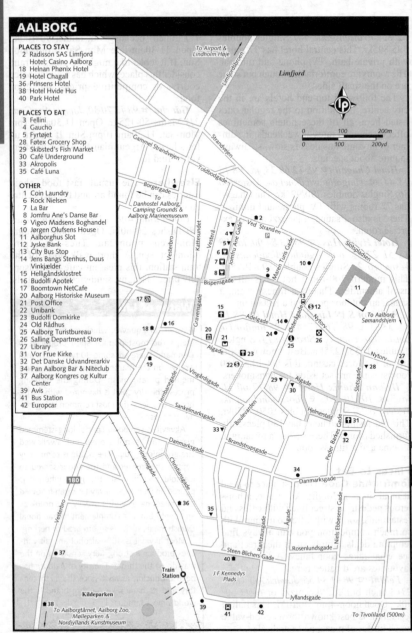

AALBORG

PLACES TO STAY
2 Radisson SAS Limfjord Hotel; Casino Aalborg
18 Helnan Phønix Hotel
19 Hotel Chagall
36 Prinsens Hotel
38 Hotel Hvide Hus
40 Park Hotel

PLACES TO EAT
3 Fellini
4 Gaucho
5 Fyrtøjet
28 Føtex Grocery Shop
29 Skibsted's Fish Market
30 Café Underground
33 Akropolis
35 Café Luna

OTHER
1 Coin Laundry
6 Rock Nielsen
7 La Bar
8 Jomfru Ane's Danse Bar
9 Vigeo Madsens Boghandel
10 Jørgen Olufsens House
11 Aalborghus Slot
12 Jyske Bank
13 City Bus Stop
14 Jens Bangs Stenhus, Duus Vinkjælder
15 Helligåndsklostret
16 Budolfi Apotek
17 Boomtown NetCafe
20 Aalborg Historiske Museum
21 Post Office
22 Unibank
23 Budolfi Domkirke
24 Old Rådhus
25 Aalborg Turistbureau
26 Salling Department Store
27 Library
31 Vor Frue Kirke
32 Det Danske Udvandrerarkiv
34 Pan Aalborg Bar & Niteclub
37 Aalborg Kongres og Kultur Center
39 Avis
41 Bus Station
42 Europcar

Akropolis (☎ *98 11 44 08, Sankelmarksgade 1A)* Mains 50-90kr, children's menu 29kr. Open noon-midnight Mon-Sat, 5pm-midnight Sun. This restaurant features authentic Greek food and drinks at moderate prices.

Skibsted's Fish Market (☎ *98 12 35 92, Algade 23)* Dishes 15-25kr. Open 8am-5pm Mon-Fri, 8am-1pm Sat. Here you can get fresh takeaway salmon burgers and fish and chips.

Café Underground (☎ *98 11 33 20, Algade 21)* Snacks 12-50kr. Open 11am-6pm daily. This little cafe serves delicious natural ice cream as well as crepes and sandwiches.

Duus Vinkjælder (☎ *98 12 50 56, Østerågade 9)* Light meals 15-40kr. Open until at least midnight Mon-Sat. A superb way to cap off the evening is with a glass of wine at this smoulderingly romantic 300-year-old candlelit wine cellar in Jens Bangs Stenhus. Drink prices are surprisingly reasonable and it offers a few cheap light meals such as burgers, chips and sandwiches.

Salling (☎ *98 16 00 00, Nytorv)* The basement supermarket at this department store, 100m to the east of Østerågade, has a quality deli selling smoked fish, salads and cheeses to take away.

Føtex (☎ *98 13 70 00, Slotsgade 8)* This grocery store, a few minutes east of Salling, has a bakery, a fast-food kiosk and a cafeteria where a filling meal of the day is 35kr.

Entertainment

Jomfru Ane Gade is a popular spot for nightlife. You'll find drinks, music and dancing along this street.

Rock Nielsen (☎ *98 13 99 29, Jomfru Ane Gade 11)* This lively club has live rock bands Thursday to Saturday nights.

Jomfru Ane's Danse Bar (☎ *98 16 37 08, Jomfru Ane Gade 3)* This place attracts an older crowd with '70s music on Friday and Saturday nights.

La Bar (☎ *98 11 37 37, Jomfru Ane Gade 7)* For cheap drinks, this is the place to go.

Aalborg Kongres og Kultur Center (☎ *99 35 55 55, Europa Plads)* This centre, north of Kildeparken, is the venue for classical music, opera, ballet and theatre performances.

Pan Aalborg Bar & Niteclub (☎ *98 12 22 45, Danmarksgade 27A)* Open nights Thurs-Sat. This is Aalborg's main gay venue, with a bar and dance club.

Casino Aalborg (☎ *98 10 15 50, Ved Stranden 14)* Open 8pm-4am daily. This casino has roulette, blackjack and poker.

Getting There & Away

Air Aalborg airport is 6km north-west of the city centre. Those coming from outside Denmark usually have to change planes in Copenhagen; Scandinavian Airlines operates several flights daily between Aalborg and Copenhagen.

An airport bus (27kr) coincides with flight times and runs between the airport and the bus station on Jyllandsgade. A taxi between the airport and the city centre costs about 120kr.

Bus Express buses (☎ 70 10 00 10) run to Copenhagen (220kr, five hours) two to four times daily.

Train Trains run about hourly to Frederikshavn (68kr, one hour) and a little more frequently to Århus (132kr, 1½ hours).

Car & Motorcycle Aalborg is 112km north of Århus and 65km south-west of Frederikshavn. The E45 bypasses the city centre, tunnelling under the Limfjord, while route 180 (which links up with the E45 both north and south of the city) leads into the centre.

To get to Lindholm Høje, or points north of the centre of Aalborg, take route 180 (Vesterbro), parallel to the E45, which crosses Limfjordsbroen.

Rental Hertz, Avis and Europcar have booths at the airport. Avis (☎ 98 13 30 99) has an office at the train station and Europcar (☎ 98 13 23 55) is at Jyllandsgade 4.

Getting Around

Bus Almost all city buses leave from Østerågade and Nytorv, near Burger King. The standard bus fare is 12kr, or you can buy a 24-hour tourist bus pass (70kr). The detailed city maps in the tourist office's free

Aalborg Guide show bus routes in blue; there's a bus information line (☎ 98 11 11 11) if you need further assistance.

Car & Motorcycle Apart from a few one-way streets that may have you driving in circles a bit, Aalborg is easy to travel around by car. There's free parking along many side streets, and metered parking in the city centre. If you're unable to find a parking space, there are several large commercial car parks, including one at Ved Stranden 11.

Taxi Taxis line up at the train station and are usually plentiful at the airport around flight times. You can also order one (☎ 98 10 10 10 or ☎ 98 12 12 12).

FREDERIKSHAVN
postcode 9900 • pop 25,700

Frederikshavn, the largest town north of Aalborg, is Jutland's busiest international ferry port.

Frederikshavn is a young town that is quite modern in appearance with not many historical attractions. It has an industrial waterfront of boat terminals and shipyards, while the town centre is chock-a-block with supermarkets selling liquor, canned hams and frozen meats to Swedes and Norwegians on shopping excursions.

Although overtaxed Scandinavians may be drawn here for bargains, Frederikshavn is not terribly appealing to most other foreign travellers who generally pass right through without pause. If you have time to spare, there are a couple of local sights, the most interesting being Bangsbomuseet.

Orientation
An overhead walkway leads from the ferry terminals to the tourist office, which sits at the edge of the central commercial district. The train station and adjacent bus terminal are a 10-minute walk north from the ferry terminals.

Information
The Frederikshavn Turistbureau (☎ 98 42 32 66, fax 98 42 12 99, e turistbureau@ frederikshavn-tourist.dk), at Brotorvet 1, is

opposite the harbour. It's open 8.30am to 7pm Monday to Saturday and 11am to 7pm on Sunday between mid-June and August; opening hours are 9am to 4pm Monday to Friday from September to mid-June.

There are several banks in the town centre, including a Danske Bank (☎ 96 20 61 60) at Danmarksgade 70.

The post office (☎ 80 20 70 30), beside the train station, is open 9.30am to 5pm on weekdays and 9.30am to noon on Saturday.

Things to See
If you're waiting for a train it's an ideal time to climb the nearby whitewashed **Krudt-tårnet** *(Gunpowder Tower;* ☎ *98 42 31 11, Kragholmen 1; adult/child 15/5kr; 10.30am-5pm daily June–mid-Sept)*, a remnant of the 17th-century citadel that once protected the port. Until 1974 this squat round tower stood 270m to the east of its present position but an expansion of the shipyards necessitated its move farther inland. Within the tower's 2m-thick walls are a few displays of antique swords, helmets and guns, and a steep stairway leading to a top galley mounted with cannons.

On Parallelvej 14, 500m west of the train station, there's a **cultural complex** with a modest art museum, swimming pools and the public library.

Bangsbomuseet
The Bangsbo Museum *(*☎ *98 41 09 37, Margrethesvej 1; adult/child 30/5kr; open 10.30am-5pm daily, except Mon in winter)*, 3km south of Frederikshavn town centre, is an old country estate with an eclectic mix of items. The manor house holds local-history exhibits, Victorian furniture, antique dolls and a peculiar collection of ornaments woven from human hair.

The farm buildings contain old ship figureheads, military paraphernalia and exhibits relating to the Danish Resistance to the German occupation of WWII. The most intriguing exhibit is the Ellingåskib (Ellingå Ship), the reconstructed remains of a 12th-century, Viking-style merchant ship that was dug up from a stream bed 5km north of Frederikshavn.

If you're up to a walk, a gate just outside the museum leads into Dyrehaven, a wooded area that's home to red, fallow and sika deer. Bus No 3 stops near the entrance to the estate; from there it's an enjoyable 500m walk through the wood to the museum.

Places to Stay

Nordstrand Camping (☎ 98 42 93 50, fax 98 43 47 85, e *nordstrand-camping.dk, Apholmenvej 40)* Camping per person 56kr. Open Apr-Oct. This four-star camping ground near the coast, 4km north of Frederikshavn centre, is the closest to town. Skagen-bound buses and trains (13kr) stop nearby.

Danhostel Frederikshavn (☎ 98 42 14 75, fax 98 42 65 22, W *www.danhostel.dk/ frederikshavn, Buhlsvej 6)* Dorm beds 70-90kr, singles/doubles 200/270kr. Open Feb–mid-Dec. This hostel, 1.5km north-west of the train station, has 130 beds. From the ferry harbour it's a 30-minute walk or a 50kr taxi ride.

The tourist office can book private *rooms* for singles/doubles 175/275kr, plus a 25kr booking fee.

Frederikshavn Sømandshjem (☎ 98 42 09 77, fax 98 43 18 99, e *info@fshotel.dk, Tordenskjoldsgade 15B)* Singles/doubles with breakfast 495/675kr. This hotel, 200m south of the train station, has 40 rooms with bath and TV.

Hotel Herman Bang (☎ 98 42 21 66, fax 98 42 21 07, W *www.hermanbang.dk, Tordenskjoldsgade 3)* Singles/doubles 295/395kr, with bath 395/495kr. This hotel, just off the pedestrian street Danmarksgade, has a fresh coat of paint and the cheapest rooms in the town centre. The room rates include breakfast.

Radisson SAS Hotel (☎ 98 42 42 00, fax 98 42 38 72, W *www.radisson.com, Havnepladsen 1)* Singles/doubles 915/1115kr, weekend & summer rate 850kr. This multistorey hotel opposite the harbour has comfortable rooms with modern amenities. Breakfast is included in the room rates.

Places to Eat

Both the train station and the ferry terminals have simple eateries. There are plenty of restaurants on Lodsgade, just west of the harbour, and the nearby streets of Danmarksgade and Tordenskjoldsgade.

Bacchus (☎ 98 43 29 00, Lodsgade 8A) Lunch specials 48kr, dinner mains 100-150kr. This restaurant has good lunch deals of steak, pizza and taco and pricier Mexican and Italian dinners.

Empire (☎ 98 42 60 02, Tordenskjoldsgade 3) Burgers 55kr, mains around 100kr. This place specialises in designer burgers (such as pineapple, basil, chilli etc) and also has steaks and spareribs.

Restaurant Venezia (☎ 98 42 37 50, Danmarksgade 73) Pizza & pasta 50-80kr. Head here for excellent Italian food in a pleasant atmosphere.

Hos Thanh (☎ 98 42 09 36, Danmarksgade 60) 3-course lunch/dinner 59/188kr. This candlelit Asian restaurant serves upmarket Chinese and Vietnamese food.

Getting There & Away

Bus & Train An express bus runs a couple of times daily from Frederikshavn and Esbjerg (215kr, five hours).

Frederikshavn is the northern terminus of the DSB railway line. Trains depart about hourly south to Aalborg (68kr, one hour), Århus (172kr, 2½ hours) and Copenhagen (300kr, five hours).

Nordjyllands Trafikselskab (NT) runs both a train (40 minutes) and a bus service (one hour) north to Skagen (39kr). NT sells a *klippekort* (clip card) costing 82kr and valid for 120kr-worth of travel; several people can clip the same card.

NT also sells a 24-hour ticket for 70kr (children 35kr) valid for unlimited travel along its bus and train routes, which take in most of northern Jutland as far afield as Skagen, Råbjerg Mile, Hirtshals, Hjørring and Løkken.

Car & Motorcycle Frederikshavn is 65km north-east of Aalborg on the E45 and 41km south of Skagen on route 40.

As Frederikshavn is a port of entry, there are several car-rental offices, including Avis (☎ 98 43 19 77) at Paradiskajen 1 and Hertz (☎ 98 42 86 77) at Danmarksgade 15.

Boat For information on ferries from Frederikshavn to Sweden and Norway see the Getting There & Away chapter.

LÆSØ
postcode 9940 • pop 2400

Læsø, 28km south-east of Frederikshavn, is a quiet island with a landscape of small farms, heathlands, dunes and sandy beaches. Although it measures only 25km at its greatest width, this 114-square-km island is the largest in the Kattegat.

According to legend, Queen Margrethe I was saved from a shipwreck off Læsø in the 14th century and rewarded her rescuers with a stunning dress, giving them the right to adapt it as an island costume. Although such regional customs had largely disappeared elsewhere in Denmark by the 19th century, Læsø women wore their traditional island dress up until the post-WWII period and continue to wear the costume today on special occasions.

Another island tradition continues in the making of Læsø salt, at one time an island export; it's now sold in small bags as a tourist souvenir.

Læsø is free of large resort hotels and attracts visitors looking for a low-key summer holiday. The island has a few small towns, two medieval churches, a seaweed-roofed farm museum and a straw-roofed fishing museum.

Information
The Læsø Turistbureau (☎ 98 49 92 42, fax 98 49 92 83, e turistbureau@laeso-tourist .dk), Vesterø Havnegade 17, is 200m east of the ferry terminal in Vesterø Havn.

Places to Stay & Eat
There are two three-star camping grounds on Læsø. *Østerby Camping (☎ 98 49 80 74, fax 98 49 80 73, e oesterby-camping@ image.dk, Campingpladsvej 8, Østerby Havn)* Camping per person 52kr. Open mid-April–Sept. This camping ground is on the north-eastern side of the island right in the village of Østerby Havn.

Læsø Camping (☎ 98 49 94 95, fax 98 49 94 55, e laesoe@dk-camp.dk, Agersigen 18, Vesterø Havn) Camping per person 52kr. Open May-Sept. This camping ground is on the north-western side of the island, 1.5km from the ferry terminal.

Danhostel Læsø (☎ 98 49 91 95, fax 98 49 91 60, e ts@laesoe-vandrerhjem.dk, Lærkevej 6, Vesterø Havn) Dorm beds 100kr, singles or doubles 350kr. Open Apr-Sept. This 90-bed hostel is 500m south-east of the ferry harbour.

Læsø Turistbureau can provide information on *holiday cottages* and *flats* available around the island.

Danhostel Læsø (☎ 98 49 91 95, Lærkevej 6, Vesterø Havn) Dinner 85kr. In the evening you can get a standard two-course dinner or a pizza at the hostel.

There are *bakeries*, food *markets* and small *restaurants* in the main villages.

Getting There & Away
Færgeselskabet Læsø (☎ 98 49 90 22) ferries sail two to six times a day between Læsø and Frederikshavn year-round. The crossing takes 1½ hours. The regular return fare is 160kr for adults, 80kr for children, 570kr for a car and up to two passengers. In summer there are also same-day return tickets that include the boat and a 3½-hour bus tour for adult/child 160/80kr.

Getting Around
A public bus runs about hourly on weekdays and every couple of hours at weekends between the villages of Vesterø Havn, Byrum and Østerby Havn.

Bicycles can be rented from Jarvis Cykelservice (☎ 98 49 94 44) at Vesterø Havnegade 29 in Vesterø Havn and from the camping grounds.

SKAGEN
postcode 9990 • pop 10,500

A fishing port for centuries, Skagen's luminous heath-and-dune landscape was discovered in the mid-19th century by artists and, in more recent times, by holidaying urbanites.

The town's older neighbourhoods are filled with distinctive yellow-washed houses, each roofed with red tiles edged with white. Skagen is half arty and half touristy, with a mix of galleries, souvenir shops and ice-cream parlours. The peninsula is lined with fine beaches, including a sandy stretch at the eastern end of Østre Strandvej, a 15-minute walk south-east from the town centre.

Sankt Laurentii Vej, Skagen's main street, runs almost the entire length of this long thin town and is never more than five minutes' walk from the waterfront.

Information

The Skagen Turistbureau (☎ 98 44 13 77, fax 98 45 02 94, e turistbureau@skagen-tourist .dk, w www.skagen-tourist.dk) is in the train station at Sankt Laurentii Vej 22. It's open at least 9am to 5pm Monday to Saturday and 10am to 2pm on Sunday from June to August; at least 9am to 4pm on weekdays and 10am to 1pm on Saturday during the rest of the year.

There are several banks in town, including an Egnsbank Nord (☎ 98 48 86 66) at Sankt Laurentii Vej 39 and a Danske Bank (☎ 96 79 10 50) at Havnevej 1. The post office (☎ 98 44 23 44) is at Christian X Vej 8, 400m west of the station.

Museums

Skagens Museum This fine museum (☎ 96 44 64 44, Brøndumsvej 4; adult/child 50kr/free; open 10am-6pm daily June-Aug, 10am-5pm May & Sept; shorter low-season hours) displays the paintings of PS Krøyer, Michael and Anna Ancher and other artists who flocked to Skagen between 1830 and 1930 to 'paint the light'. Take a close look at *Johannisfeuer*, Krøyer's early-20th-century work that shows a bonfire on the Skagen beach; among the notable Skagen residents depicted on the left side of the painting are Anna Ancher, in a blue cape, and Holger Drachmann, in a brown cloak with a white beard and cane. Skagens Museum is just a few minutes' walk east from the train station.

A Mariner's Nightmare

The waters off northern Jutland have always been extremely treacherous for mariners and have claimed many hundreds of ships over the centuries. Not only are the waters tempestuous and the currents strong, but the land is flat and devoid of landmarks, offering few reference points by which ships can be guided.

Historically, when ships did wash up on shore, local residents would go straight to work pillaging the contents and dismantling the ships for their timber. Some unscrupulous souls are even said to have hung lanterns in such a manner as to imitate waterways and in so doing would lure captains into venturing too close to the shoreline, where they would strand on shallow shoals.

The situation got so out of hand that in 1521 a decree was passed to control salvaging. Gallows were erected along the coast to remind would-be pillagers of the new penalty for the looting of shipwrecks. At the same time, simple wooden seesaw-style 'lighthouses' called *vippefyret* were erected along the coastline. Each had a basket that could be pulled down and filled with coal, and a counterweight that raised the basket high where it burned throughout the night. These forerunners of present-day lighthouses helped to guide ships safely around the point.

Although none of the original coal lights still exists, there's a reconstructed one at Skagen above the beach at the north-eastern end of Østre Strandvej.

NC

Michael & Anna Anchers Hus The house that Michael and Anna Ancher purchased in 1884 was turned into a museum (☎ 98 44 30 09, Markvej 2; adult/child 40/10kr; open 10am-5pm daily May-Sept, 10am-6pm in summer high season; shorter low-season hours) after the death of their daughter Helga in the 1960s. Preserved to look much as it would have during the artists' lifetimes, it is of note mainly to those with a particular interest in the Anchers. It's 300m north-east of the station.

Drachmanns Hus The house where poet/ artist Holger Drachmann lived from 1902 until his death six years later is now a museum (☎ 98 44 51 88, Hans Baghs Vej 21; adult/child 20kr/free; open 11am-3pm daily June–mid-Sept; shorter low-season hours) dedicated to his life. It is near Sankt Laurentii Vej, to the west of the town centre.

Skagen By og Egnsmuseum Evocatively presented, this open-air museum (☎ 98 44 47 60, PK Nielsen Vej 8; adult/child 30/5kr; open 10am-4pm daily May-Sept; 11am-4pm Mon-Fri Mar, Apr & Oct), 200m south-west of the harbour, depicts Skagen's maritime history. It features interesting displays on Skagen's lifeboat rescue service, including dramatic photos of ships in distress, as well as the preserved homes of fisherfolk with their original furnishings, and a picturesque Dutch windmill.

Grenen

Denmark's northernmost point is the long, curving sweep of sand at Grenen, 3km north-east of Skagen town centre. From the car park at the end of route 40, the path to the beach crosses rose-covered dunes and at its highest point passes the grave of poet Holger Drachmann (1846–1908).

It's a 30-minute walk out along the vast beach to its narrow tip where the waters of the Kattegat and Skagerrak clash and you can put one foot in each sea. Swimming is not permitted near the point, however, as the strong currents have been responsible for sweeping unsuspecting bathers out to sea in the past.

If you're short on time you might want to walk one way and take the Sandormen in the other direction. This tractor-drawn 'bus' drives out to the point from the Grenen car park every half-hour in summer and spends 15 minutes at the site before it returns. The cost is 15kr return.

Tilsandede Kirke

The Tilsandede Kirke (Buried Church) is a whitewashed, medieval church tower that still rises above the sand dunes that buried the surrounding village and farms in the late 18th century. The church itself, once the largest in the county, was closed in 1795 because of drifting sand that obscured the doorways, and in 1810 the main part of the church was finally torn down. The lofty tower (adult/child 8/4kr; interior open 11am-5pm daily June-Aug), however, was left standing to serve as a navigational landmark.

The picturesque church tower and the surrounding area comprise part of Skagen Klitplantage, a nature reserve. It's 5km south of Skagen and well signposted from route 40. The nicest way to get there is by bike; take Gammel Landevej from Skagen. You could also take the train (13kr) to Højen, a rural stop near the church; in Skagen let the conductor know you want to get off in Højen, and on the return you'll need to push the button on the platform that signals the train to stop.

Gammel Skagen

Gammel Skagen, 4km west of Skagen, is an upmarket summer cottage community on the Skagerrak coast, known for its lovely evening sunsets. It was a fishing hamlet in centuries past, before sandstorms ravished this windswept area, forcing many of its inhabitants to move to Skagen on the more protected east coast. If you have your own transportation, it makes a nice spot to head to in the late afternoon. Højensvej, the road to Gammel Skagen, leads right to the main beach and sunset spot.

Bus No 79 runs between Skagen and Gammel Skagen (13kr), but service is not frequent, so an outing is best suited for people with a bicycle or a car.

Places to Stay

Camping There are two three-star camping grounds about 1.5km north of Skagen's centre.

Grenen Camping (☎ 98 44 25 46, fax 98 44 65 46, e grencamp@post6.tele.dk, Fyrvej 16) Camping per person 62kr. Open early May–early Sept. This camping ground has a fine seaside location.

Poul Eeg Camping (☎ 98 44 14 70, fax 98 45 14 60, Batterivej 31) Camping per person 62kr. Open mid-May–early Sept. This camping ground is inland from the beach but is otherwise an agreeable place.

Rooms & Hostels Staff at the tourist office will book *rooms* in private houses for singles/doubles 200/350kr, plus a 50kr booking fee.

Danhostel Skagen Ny (☎ 98 44 22 00, fax 98 44 22 55, e danhostel.skagen@adr.dk, Rolighedsvej 2) Dorm beds 100kr, doubles 300-500kr. Open mid-Feb–Nov. This modern 112-bed hostel is 1km west of the town centre, on the road to Frederikshavn.

Hotels & Pensions The room rates for each of the following places to stay include breakfast.

Marienlund Badepension (☎ 98 44 13 20, fax 98 45 14 66, e badepension@marielund .dk, Fabriciusvej 8) Singles/doubles with shared bathroom 295/560kr. This 12-room pension is on the western side of town near Skagen By og Egnsmuseum.

Clausens Hotel (☎ 98 45 01 66, fax 98 44 14 64, e bestilling@clausenshotel.dk, Sankt Laurentii Vej 35) Singles/doubles 450/595kr, with bath 550/695kr. This hotel is opposite the train station.

Skagen Sømandshjem (☎ 98 44 25 88, fax 98 44 30 28, Østre Strandvej 2) Singles/doubles 340/585kr, with bath 510/690kr. This 29-room place with straightforward rooms is near the harbour.

Finns Hotel Pension (☎ 98 45 01 55, e info@finnshotelpension.dk, Østre Strandvej 63) Singles/doubles 375/650kr, doubles with bath 875kr. This gay-friendly pension, in town opposite the ocean, has six delightful rooms furnished with antiques.

Places to Eat

Havnevej, the main road connecting the harbour and the town centre, has the main cluster of inexpensive eateries.

Blue Burger (☎ 98 45 07 11, Havnevej 4) Cheeseburger 35kr. This place offers burgers and other fast food.

China House (☎ 98 44 65 62, Havnevej 7) Dishes served with rice 65kr. This restaurant has numerous, standard Chinese meals.

Alfredo (☎ 98 44 17 46, Havnevej 13) Lunch pizzas 49kr, dinner mains 65-100kr. This place specialises in pizza and pasta but has fish and meat dishes as well.

Clausens Hotel (☎ 98 45 01 66, Sankt Laurentii Vej 35) Cafe lunch 78kr. This old-fashioned hotel restaurant, opposite the train station, offers a cafe lunch of either a smørrebrød plate or a half-lobster with salad, plus a glass of beer.

Pakhuset (☎ 98 44 17 46, Rødspættevej 6) Cafe mains 90-120kr, restaurant mains 150-200kr. This popular fish establishment, which is right at the harbour, has an upstairs restaurant serving Skagen's best seafood. There's also a cheaper ground-floor cafe serving good food, but for gourmet fare head upstairs.

Havnegrillen (☎ 98 44 63 85, Rødspættevej 10) Fast food 15-40kr. For a cheap harbourside eat, try this grill, opposite Pakhuset, which has hot dogs, burgers, beer and outdoor picnic tables.

Stendys Is-Café (☎ 98 44 38 78, Sankt Laurentii Vej 37) Cones 17kr. This place opposite the train station has delicious Italian ice cream.

Getting There & Away

Skagen is 41km north of Frederikshavn on route 40 and 49km north-east of Hirtshals via routes 597 and 40.

Either a bus or a train leaves Skagen station for Frederikshavn (39kr) about once an hour.

NT's seasonal Skagerakkeren bus (No 99) operates about half a dozen times each day from Skagen to Hirtshals (32.50kr, 1½ hours) between mid-June and mid-August. The same bus also continues on to Hjørring and Løkken.

Getting Around

In summer, buses run between Skagen station and Grenen (13kr) hourly until 5pm.

Taxis (☎ 98 43 34 34) are available at the station or charge about 60kr from Skagen town centre to Grenen.

Skagen Cykel (☎ 98 44 10 70), a stand on the western side of the station, rents bicycles for 75kr a day.

RÅBJERG MILE

Denmark's largest expanse of shifting sand dunes are these undulating, 40m hills that are almost large enough to disappear in and good fun to explore. The dunes, which are carried eastward about 10m each year by prevailing west winds, are a legacy of the 17th-century deforestation and overgrazing that left northern Jutland susceptible to the ravages of sandstorms. While other dunes in northern Jutland have been stabilised by the planting of beach grasses, the dunes at Råbjerg Mile have purposely been left in a migratory state.

Råbjerg Mile is 16km south-west of Skagen, off route 40 on the road to Kandestederne. Between mid-June and mid-August, the Skagerakkeren bus (No 99) runs six times daily from Skagen station to Råbjerg Mile (19.50kr, 25 minutes) and on to Hirtshals. The dunes themselves are a 750m walk from the Råbjerg Mile bus stop.

HIRTSHALS

postcode 9850 • pop 6900

Hirtshals takes its character from its commercial fishing harbour and ferry terminal. The main street is lined with supermarkets catering to Norwegian shoppers who pile off the ferries to load up with relatively cheap Danish meats and groceries.

The town boasts an impressive aquarium with the largest tank in Europe. There are coastal cliffs and a lighthouse on the more scenic western side of Hirtshals but if you want beaches and dunes head south to Tornby Strand.

Information

The Hirtshals Turistbureau (☎ 98 94 22 20, fax 98 94 58 20) is 1km south of the ferry harbour at Nørregade 40. It's open 9am to 5pm Monday to Saturday and 10am to 1pm on Sunday mid-June to August; 9am to 4pm Monday to Friday and 9am to noon on Saturday the rest of the year.

You'll find banks one block south of the train station, including a Danske Bank (☎ 96 56 10 00) at Jørgens Fiblers Gade 23. The post office (☎ 98 94 17 33) is adjacent to the train station.

Nordsømuseet

The main sight in town is Nordsømuseet (☎ 98 94 44 44, Willemoesvej 2; adult/child 90/45kr; open daily 10am-10pm mid-June–mid-Aug, 9am-5pm mid-Aug–mid-June), 1km east of the town centre, where visitors can view North Sea marine life in a four-storey, state-of-the-art oceanarium that holds 4.5 million litres of sea water. The main viewing area is an amphitheatre that looks into the circular tank through an 8m-high window as feeding sharks and schools of herring, mackerel and other pelagic fish swirl by. A diver enters the tank at 1pm daily to feed the fish and entertain visitors. There are also educational displays about fishing and marine biology as well as a children's section and an outdoor seal pool with feedings at 11am and 3pm.

Places to Stay

Hirtshals Camping (☎ 98 94 25 35, fax 98 94 33 43, e hirstshals@dk-camp.dk, Kystvejen 6) Camping per person 57kr. Open mid-April–mid-Sept. This three-star camping ground is in an open field on the coast, 150m south of the hostel.

Danhostel Hirtshals (☎ 98 94 12 48, fax 98 94 56 55, e danhostel.hirtshals@adr.dk, Kystvejen 53) Dorm beds 95kr, doubles 300kr. Open Mar-Oct. This 72-bed hostel is 1km south-west of the train station.

Staff at the tourist office can book *rooms* in private homes for around 150kr per person plus a 25kr booking fee.

Sømandshjemmet (☎ 98 94 53 33, fax 98 94 53 36, Havnegade 24) Singles/doubles 230/380kr, with bath 280/480kr. This local hotel, which has comfortable rooms and a convenient location opposite the ferry terminal, is Hirtshals' cheapest.

Skaga Hotel (☎ 98 94 55 00, fax 98 94 55 55, e info@skagahotel.dk, Willemoesvej 1) Singles/doubles 595/795kr. This modern hotel, opposite Nordsømuseet, has 108 rooms with full amenities and there's an indoor pool, fitness room and restaurant.

Places to Eat

You'll find the following eateries close together in the town centre.

Jasmine (☎ 98 94 35 55, Hjørringgade 4) Fish & chips 40kr, Chinese meals 50kr. This good-value place has both Danish fast food and Chinese fare.

Restaurant Rosa (☎ 98 94 19 44, Nørregade 4) Pizza 39kr until 4pm, 60kr after 4pm. This place specialises in pizza but also has Mexican dishes.

Sundbæk Bageri (☎ 98 94 44 80, Hjørringgade 15) Sandwiches 20kr. This bakery has tempting pastries and sandwiches; another *bakery* is opposite the tourist office.

Getting There & Away

Hirtshals is 49km south-west of Skagen via routes 40 and 597 and 41km north-west of Frederikshavn via the E39 and route 35.

Bus The summer Skagerakken bus runs between Hirtshals station and Skagen (32.50kr) six times daily.

Train Hirtshals' train station is 500m south of the ferry terminal, but trains connecting with ferry services continue down to the harbour. A private railway, operated by Hjørring Privatbaner, connects Hirtshals with Hjørring (19.50kr), 20 minutes to the south. Trains run at least hourly, with the last departure from Hjørring to Hirtshals at 10.25pm. At Hjørring you can connect with a DSB train to Aalborg or Frederikshavn.

Boat Color Line runs ferries year-round to the Norwegian ports of Oslo, Kristiansand and Larvik. See the Sea section of the Getting There & Away chapter for information.

TORNBY STRAND

Tornby Strand, 5km south of Hirtshals, is a lovely undeveloped stretch of beach and dunes. It generally has good swimming conditions in summer, which is the only time you can expect to find much company.

The beach sand is packed hard enough to drive on and indeed many visitors park their cars right on the sand at the spot where they sunbathe. It's possible to drive south on the beach for about 4km, at which point a river slices across the beach en route to the sea. Use caution however, as it's easy to misjudge the tides or hit a soft spot.

There are plenty of possibilities for hiking on the beach, along the high mounded dunes and in the coastal woodlands that back the southern side of the beach. Other than a bit of sea-bird watching there's nothing more to see or do here – which is what makes Tornby Strand an attractive little getaway.

Places to Stay & Eat

Munch's Badehotel (☎/fax 98 97 71 15, Tornby Strand, 9850 Hirtshals) Doubles 290kr, with bath 390kr; cottages low/high season 1400/2600kr per week. This family-run place, right on the beach at the end of Tornby Strandvej, has nine rustic rooms. The management also books cottages in the dunes and operates a small grocery store and a reasonably priced restaurant with an ocean view.

Getting There & Away

Tornby Strand can be reached from Hirtshals via route 55 and Tornby Strandvej. In summer the bus from Hirtshals to Hjørring stops en route at Tornby Strand six times daily; the fare from Hirtshals is 13kr.

HJØRRING

postcode 9800 • pop 24,800

Hjørring, an old market town, is the capital of Vendsyssel county and a regional centre, with the district hospital and central rail connections.

It's a tidy town with streets and walkways enlivened by some 150 statues and bronze sculptures. The oldest part of Hjørring is built around the central squares: Springvandspladsen, where the municipal offices are located, and the nearby Sankt Olai Plads, which is bordered by three medieval churches. Springvandspladsen is a short five-minute walk north from the train station along Jernbanegade; continue 200m farther north on the pedestrian walkway Strømgade to reach Sankt Olai Plads.

Although Hjørring is not a very exciting destination in itself, it has an engaging small-town character and can be an enjoyable place to spend a few hours (or break for the night) if you are leisurely touring the region.

Information

The Hjørring Turistbureau (☎ 98 92 02 32, fax 98 92 04 52) is on Markedsgade 9, 750m east of the train station. It's open 9am to 4pm weekdays and 9am to noon on Saturday, except mid-June to August when it closes at 5pm on weekdays and 2pm on Saturday. You can also pick up a tourist map of the town at the ticket window in the train station.

There's a Danske Bank (☎ 96 23 63 60) at Springvandspladsen 2. The post office (☎ 80 20 70 30) is on the western side of the train station.

Churches

Hjørring is unique in that it managed to retain three medieval churches despite the consolidations that occurred throughout Denmark following the Reformation. All three churches are within 200m of each other, on the northern side of Sankt Olai Plads.

The oldest, **Sankt Olai Kirke**, dates from the 11th century and has a Romanesque chancel and a 16th-century altarpiece. **Sankt Catharinæ Kirke**, the current parish church, retains traces of its medieval beginnings in the transept and has a 13th-century Gothic crucifix, although the church has been altered over the centuries and was largely rebuilt in the 1920s. The Romanesque **Sankt Hans Kirke** has a nave built from medieval brick, a fresco painted in 1350 and an altarpiece and pulpit dating from the early 17th century.

Museums

Vendsyssel Historiske Museum (☎ 96 24 10 50, Museumsgade 3; adult/child 30kr/free; open 10am-5pm daily Apr-Oct, 11am-4pm Mon-Fri Nov-Mar) occupies an old deanery and a couple of 19th-century school buildings on Museumsgade, about 250m south of

Sankt Catharinæ Kirke. It features some local-history exhibits from prehistoric times, as well as an ecclesiastical art collection, period furnishings and displays on farming.

There's also an art museum, **Hjørring Kunstmuseum** (☎ 98 92 41 33, Brinck Seidelinsgade 10; adult/child 25kr/free; open 10am-4pm Tues-Sun), a five-minute walk north-east of the train station, that's devoted to regional art and crafts.

Places to Stay

Both the camping ground and hostel are about 2.5km north-east of the train station and can be reached by local bus.

Hjørring Campingplads (☎ 98 92 22 82, fax 98 91 06 99, Idræts Allé 45) Camping per person 50kr. Open May–mid-Sept. This small three-star camping ground has an outdoor swimming pool.

Danhostel Hjørring (☎ 98 92 67 00, fax 98 90 15 50, e danhostel.hjoerring@adr.dk, Thomas Morildsvej 11) Dorm beds 100kr, singles/doubles 350/380kr. Open Mar-Sept. This large, modern hostel has 140 beds.

Hotel Phønix (☎ 98 92 54 55, fax 98 90 10 37, e hotel@phoenix-hjoerring.dk, Jernbanegade 6) Singles/doubles 595/795kr, with breakfast. This hotel, 300m north of the train station, has 70 comfortable rooms with bath and TV.

Places to Eat

Pizza King (☎ 98 92 23 00, Jernbanegade 24) Pizza 29kr. This pizzeria just opposite the train station also has hot dogs and other fast food.

Peking Grill (☎ 98 91 10 33, Jernbanegade 13) Dishes with rice 42kr. This restaurant serves various curries, chop suey and other Chinese favourites.

Hotel Phønix (☎ 98 92 54 55, Jernbanegade 6) Lunch 65kr, dinner mains 100kr. This hotel has a pleasant solarium dining room with a menu that ranges from smørrebrød to steaks.

Getting There & Away

Hjørring is 35km west of Frederikshavn on route 35 and 17km south of Hirtshals on route 55 or the E39.

Hjørring is served by NT, which operates bus services to Skagen, Løkken, Frederikshavn and Hirtshals. The bus station is 150m north-east of the train station, near the intersection of Jernbanegade and Asylgade.

Hjørring is on the Århus-Frederikshavn DSB railway line and is also the terminus of a private railway line to Hirtshals. The fare is 19.50kr to Hirtshals, 37kr to Frederikshavn, 52kr to Aalborg and 172kr to Århus.

LØKKEN
postcode 9480 • pop 1300

Fronted by a broad sandy beach, Løkken is a small town that is packed each summer with an invasion of beachgoers. Not surprisingly, its character is that of a popular resort area, more commercial than quaint, with a bustling centre of shops, ice-cream stands and cafes. Although the beach is the major attraction there's also a summertime museum (Nørregade 12) in a former sea captain's house that features exhibits on the town's history as a trading and fishing port.

Information
The Løkken Turistbureau (☎ 98 99 10 09, fax 98 99 11 59), Møstingsvej 3, is on Torvet, the central square. It's open 9am to 5pm Monday to Saturday June to August; 9am to 4pm on weekdays and 10am to 1pm on Saturday, September to May.

Places to Stay
There is a string of camping grounds along Søndergade, the street that runs south from Torvet.

Josefines Camping (☎ 98 99 13 26, fax 98 99 03 26, Søndergade 57) Camping per person 60kr. This three-star facility is 500m from both the town centre and the beach.

Hotel Klitbakken (☎ 98 99 11 66, fax 98 99 17 76, e klitbakken@loekken.dk, Nørregade 3) Singles/doubles 500/600kr including breakfast. The hotel, near Torvet, has 24 inviting rooms with bath and balconies.

Most of the other hotels and apartment complexes in Løkken are geared to holidaymakers planning longer stays and offer their best prices for weekly bookings. The tourist office can provide a booklet with a brief description of each place and a detailed price list.

Places to Eat
There are several places to eat on Torvet and along Nørregade and Strandgade, which radiate out from Torvet.

Løkken Snack Bar (☎ 98 99 20 31, Nørregade 18) Light meals 30-50kr. More a cafe than a snack bar, this place makes good sandwiches and pizza.

China Grill (☎ 98 99 22 66, Strandgade 3) Three-item meals 35kr. Head here for inexpensive Chinese fare.

Løkken Badehotel (☎ 98 99 27 12, Torvet) Lunch/dinner meals 79/150kr. This popular hotel restaurant, on the central square, specialises in traditional Danish fish and beef dishes.

Getting There & Away
Løkken is on route 55, 18km south-west of Hjørring. Buses run every couple of hours between Løkken and Hjørring (26kr, 30 minutes) and between Løkken and Aalborg (48kr, one hour).

HANSTHOLM
postcode 7730 • pop 3200

Hanstholm is a new town built around a large commercial harbour that was completed in 1967; it's now one of Denmark's largest fishing ports. It was originally thought that the population would quickly grow to 20,000, but Hanstholm has only reached a fraction of that size.

There's no other reason to come to Hanstholm unless you're planning to take a ferry to Norway or Iceland. Those who do find themselves here might want to visit the lighthouse, which claimed to beam the world's most powerful beacon when it was first erected in 1843. It now contains local-history exhibits.

Early risers scratching for something to do might want to watch the harbourside fish auction, held at 7am on weekdays.

Information
Hanstholm Turistbureau (☎ 97 96 12 19, fax 97 96 21 54), Centervej 31, is in Hanstholm

Treasure of the Sea

Amber is fossilised tree resin, translucent and brittle. It's usually a golden-yellow colour but can appear in other hues, most notably reddish-brown. Some pieces of amber contain fossilised ferns or insects that were trapped inside the resin aeons ago, when it was still sticky.

In Denmark, amber is most commonly found on the western coast of Jutland. The best time to hunt for amber is in the wake of a storm or strong gale, when the amber gets stirred up from the seabed, bobs to the surface and is washed ashore. Look for it up on the beach mixed with other lightweight items such as driftwood and seaweed.

Amber is not easily found by novices, however, and most first-time collectors end up with a pocketful of small yellow stones instead. There are two key identification points: amber is significantly lighter than rock and it floats in salt water; it also collects a small negative charge when rubbed and will warm to the touch after being held.

Professional amber collectors have their own tools of the trade, primarily a meshed net on a long frame with which they can snatch the amber as it's tossed around in breaking waves.

Amber is often polished and made into jewellery, particularly pendants, beaded necklaces, earrings and rings. If you're unable to find your own pieces, they can be readily purchased at jewellery shops all over Denmark.

Centret, about 1km inland of the harbour. It's open 8.30am to 4pm on weekdays and 9am to noon on Saturday, with slightly later closing times in summer.

Hanstholm Centret, a shopping complex, also contains two banks, the post office, a library, a pharmacy and eateries.

Places to Stay & Eat

Havnehotellet Sømandshjem (☎ 97 96 11 45, fax 97 96 27 80, Kai Lindbergsgade 71) Singles/doubles 395/600kr. This seamen's hotel at the harbour is a utilitarian place with adequate rooms, each with bath and TV.

Hotel Hanstholm (☎ 97 96 10 44, fax 97 96 25 84, e hotel-hansholm@hotel -hansholm.dk, Christian Hansens Vej 2) Singles/doubles 575/750kr, with breakfast. This modern 70-room hotel is inland from the harbour and close to Hanstholm Centret. It has full amenities, including a swimming pool.

Harbour Grill (☎ 97 96 11 45, Kai Lindbergsgade 71) Sandwiches & light meals 25-50kr. This inexpensive eatery at Havnehotellet Sømandshjem is a good place to rub shoulders with local fishers.

Hanstholm Centret (☎ 97 96 18 05, Centervej 31) has a bakery, steak restaurant, cafeteria and a Super Brugsen supermarket.

Getting There & Away

Hanstholm is at the terminus of routes 181, 26 and 29.

Thisted, 21km to the south via route 26, has the nearest train station. Bus No 40 runs to Thisted train station from Hanstholm harbour about hourly on weekdays, less often on weekends (18kr, 45 minutes).

There are car ferries from Hanstholm to the Norwegian cities of Bergen and Egersund, as well as to Iceland and the Faroe Islands. See the Sea section of the Getting There & Away chapter for details.

KLITMØLLER

postcode 7700

Klitmøller is a small fishing village that attracts lots of windsurfers, both German and Danish, with some of North Jutland's best wind conditions. The main windsurfing spot is right in town; follow the central road, Ørhagevej, to the waterfront. When the winds are down there's good swimming at the beaches north and south of the village.

The landscape around Klitmøller, dunes backed by stark heathlands, continues for more than 10km to the north and south. The section between Hanstholm and Klitmøller looks particularly barren as you zip along the road, but there are bogs and ponds inland

and the entire area is a bird reserve known as Hanstholm Vildtreservat; human access is restricted.

Windsurfing

In addition to the challenging North Sea waters, Vandet Sø, a lake to the east of Klitmøller, is a popular windsurfing spot, with conditions suitable for all levels.

Windsurfing Klitmøller (☎ 97 97 56 56), near the beach at Ørhagevej 151, rents gear (300kr a day) and offers four-hour lessons for beginners (450kr, gear included).

Places to Stay & Eat

Most visitors to Klitmøller stay in one of the three camping grounds right in town; the first two listed are just a few minutes' walk from Ørhagevej.

Klitmøller Camping (☎ 97 97 50 20, fax 97 97 50 85, e klitcamp@post12.tele.dk, Vangvej 16) Camping per person 50kr. Open year-round. This is a two-star facility.

Nordsø Camping (☎ 97 97 50 71, fax 97 97 59 71, e klitmoller@dk-camp.dk, Vangsåvej 25) Camping per person 57kr. Open year-round. This is a three-star facility.

Nystrup Camping (☎ 97 97 52 49, fax 97 97 57 52, Trøjborgvej 22) Camping per person 62kr. Open Apr-Sept. This camping ground is a three-star facility.

All three camping grounds have *mini-markets* and *grill-style eateries*. There's an *ice-cream shop*, *bakery*, *food market* and a few cafes and restaurants along Ørhagevej within 1km of the waterfront.

Getting There & Away

Klitmøller is 10km south-west of Hanstholm on route 181 and 15km north-west of Thisted on route 557. From Klitmøller, bus No 22 goes to Thisted, which has the nearest rail connections. Bus No 24 connects Klitmøller and Hanstholm. Both bus services run about hourly on weekdays, less often on weekends.

Language

Together with Swedish, Norwegian, Icelandic and Faroese, Danish belongs to the northern branch of the Germanic language group. Consequently, written Danish bears a strong resemblance to all these languages. Spoken Danish, however, has evolved in a different direction, developing sounds and quirks of pronunciation not found elsewhere.

Grammatically, Danish has the same general rules and syntax as the other Germanic languages of Scandinavia. There are two genders: common (or 'non-neuter'), and neuter. Articles ('a/an' and 'the' in English) are suffixed to the noun: -en for common singular nouns and -et for neuter singular nouns.

Danish has both a polite and an informal mode of address (where English uses the universal 'you'); the polite form uses the personal pronouns De and Dem, the informal, du and dig. The translations in this chapter are mostly in the informal, except where it's appropriate to use the polite form. In general, use the polite form when speaking to senior citizens and officials, and the informal in all other instances.

Most Danes speak English, and many also speak German. However, any effort to learn even the basics, such as the Danish words for 'Thank you', 'Good-bye', 'Hello' and 'I'm sorry', will be greatly appreciated. With an increased command of the language, you'll be rewarded by gaining a greater insight into the people and their country.

Note that Danish has all of the letters of the English alphabet plus three others, æ, ø and å. These come at the end of the alphabet and we have used this order thoughout the book.

Pronunciation

You may find Danish pronunciation difficult. Consonants can be drawled, swallowed and even omitted completely, creating, in conjunction with vowels, the peculiarity of the glottal stop or stød. Its sound is rather as a Cockney would say the 'tt' in 'bottle'.

Stress usually falls on the first syllable. As a general rule, the best advice is to listen and learn. Good luck!

Vowels

a	as in 'father'; as in 'act'
e	a short, flat 'e' as in 'met'
e(g)	as the 'i' in 'high'
i	a short, flat 'e' as in 'met'; as the 'i' in 'marine'
o	a short 'o' as in 'pot'; as the 'a' in 'walk'; as the 'oo' in 'zoo'
o(r)	as in 'or' but with little emphasis on the 'r'
o(v)	as the 'ow' in 'vow', but shorter
u	as in 'pull'; as the 'oo' in 'zoo'
u(n)	as the 'a' in 'walk'
y	a long, sharp 'u' – purse your lips and say 'ee'
æ	as the 'e' in 'bet'; as the 'a' in 'act'
ø	as the 'er' in 'fern', but shorter
å	as the 'a' in 'walk'

Consonants

Consonants are pronounced as in English with the exception of the following:

b	as in 'box'
c	as in 'cell'
ch	as in 'cheque', but sharper
(o)d	as the 'th' in 'these'
g	before vowels, a hard 'g' as in 'get'
h	as in 'horse'
j	as the 'y' in 'yet'
k	as in 'kit'
ng	as in 'sing'
r	a rolling 'r' abruptly cut short
sj	as the 'sh' in 'ship'
w	as the 'v' in 'Volkswagon'

Greetings & Civilities

Hello.	Goddag/Hej. (polite/informal)
Goodbye.	Farvel.
Yes.	Ja.
No.	Nej.

Could I please have ...?	Jeg vil gerne bede om ...
Please ... (when making a request)	Vær så venlig at ...
Please (sit down).	Værsgo (at sidde ned).
Thank you.	Tak.
That's fine/ You're welcome.	Det er i orden/Selv tak.
Excuse me (Sorry).	Undskyld.
May I/Do you mind?	Må jeg/Tillader De?

Language Difficulties

Do you speak English?	Taler De engelsk?
Does anyone speak English?	Er der nogen, der kan tale engelsk?
I understand.	Jeg forstår.
I don't understand.	Jeg forstår ikke.
Could you speak more slowly please?	Kunne De taler langsommere?

Small Talk

What's your name?	Hvad hedder du?
My name is ...	Jeg hedder ...
Where are you from?	Hvorfra kommer du?
I'm from ...	Jeg kommer fra ...
How old are you?	Hvor gammel er du?
I'm ... years old.	Jeg er ... år gammel.

Getting Around

What time does the ... leave/arrive?	Hvornår går/ ankommer ...?
boat	båden
bus (city)	bussen
bus (intercity)	rutebilen
train	toget
I'd like (a) ...	Jeg vil gerne have ...
one-way ticket	en enkeltbillet
return ticket	en tur-retur billet
1st class	første klasse
2nd class	anden klasse

Directions

Where is ...?	Hvor er ...?
I want to go to ...	Jeg vil gerne til ...
Can you show me (on the map)?	Kan De vise mig det (på kortet)?
Go straight ahead.	Gå ligeud.

Signs

Indgang	Entrance
Udgang	Exit
Åben	Open
Lukket	Closed
Forbudt	Prohibited
Information	Information
Politistation	Police Station
Toiletter	Toilets
Herrer	Men
Damer	Women

Turn left.	Drej til venstre.
Turn right.	Drej til højre.
near	tæt på
far	langt væk

Around Town

I'm looking for ...	Jeg leder efter ...
a bank	en bank
the city centre	centrum
the ... embassy	den ... ambassade
my hotel	mit hotel
the market	markedet
the museum	museet
the police	politiet
the post office	postkontoret
a public toilet	et offentligt toilet
the telephone centre	telefoncentralen
the tourist office	turist-informationen

beach	strand
castle	slot
cathedral	katedral/domkirke
church	kirke
main square	hovedtorv/torvet
monastery	kloster
old city	den gamle bydel
palace	palads

Accommodation

Where's a cheap hotel?	Hvor ligger det et billigt hotel?
What's the address?	Hvad er adressen?
Could you write down the address, please?	Kunne De skrive adressen ned?
Do you have any rooms available?	Har I ledige værelser?

I'd like ...	*Jeg vil gerne have ...*
a single room	*et enkeltværelse*
a double room	*et dobbeltværelse*
a room with a bathroom	*et værelse med bad*
to share a dorm	*plads i en sovesal*
a bed	*en seng*

How much is it per night/ per person?	*Hvor meget koster det per nat/per person?*
May I see it?	*Må jeg se værelset?*
Where is the bathroom?	*Hvor er badeværelset?*

Shopping

How much is it?	*Hvor meget koster den/* (common) *det?* (neuter)
bookshop	*boghandel*
camera shop	*fotohandel*
clothing store	*tøjforretning*
delicatessen	*delikatesse*
laundry	*vaskeri*
market	*marked*
newsagency	*aviskiosk*
souvenir shop	*souvenirbutik*
stationers	*papirhandel*

Health

Where is the ...?	*Hvor er ...?*
hospital	*hospitalet*
chemist	*apotkeket*

I'm ill.	*Jeg er syg.*
My friend is ill.	*Min ven er syg.*

I'm ...	*Jeg er ...*
asthmatic	*astmatiker*
diabetic	*diabetiker*
epileptic	*epileptiker*

I'm allergic to antibiotics/ penicillin.	*Jeg er allergisk over for antibiotika/ penicillin.*

I need medication for ...	*Jeg skal bruge noget medicin imod ...*
I have a prescription.	*Jeg har en recept.*
I have a toothache.	*Jeg har tandpine.*
I'm pregnant.	*Jeg er gravid.*

antiseptic	*antiseptisk*
aspirin	*aspirin*
condoms	*kondomer*
contraceptive	*præventiv*
dentist	*tandlæge*
diarrhoea	*diarré*
doctor	*læge*
medicine	*medicin*
nausea	*kvalme*
stomachache	*ondt i maven*
soap	*sæbe*
sunblock cream	*solcreme*
tampons	*tamponer*

Time & Dates

What time is it?	*Hvad er klokken?*
It's ... o'clock.	*Klokken er ...*

today	*i dag*
tonight	*i aften/i nat*
tomorrow	*i morgen*
day after tomorrow	*i overmorgen*
next week	*næste uge*
yesterday	*i går*
in the morning	*om morgenen*
in the afternoon	*om eftermiddagen*
in the evening	*om aftenen*
early	*tidlig*

Monday	*mandag*
Tuesday	*tirsdag*
Wednesday	*onsdag*
Thursday	*torsdag*
Friday	*fredag*
Saturday	*lørdag*
Sunday	*søndag*

January	*januar*
February	*februar*
March	*marts*
April	*april*
May	*maj*
June	*juni*
July	*juli*
August	*august*
September	*september*
October	*oktober*
November	*november*
December	*december*

Emergencies

Help!	*Hjælp!*
Go away!	*Forsvind!*
It's an emergency!	*Det er en nød-situation!*
Call a doctor!	*Ring efter en læge!*
Call the police!	*Ring efter politiet!*
Call an ambulance!	*Ring efter en ambulance!*
I want to contact my embassy/ consulate.	*Jeg vil kontakte min ambassade/ mit konsulat.*
I'm lost.	*Jeg har gået vild.*
Where are the toilets?	*Hvor er toiletterne?*

Numbers

0	*nul*
1	*en*
2	*to*
3	*tre*
4	*fire*
5	*fem*
6	*seks*
7	*syv*
8	*otte*
9	*ni*
10	*ti*
11	*elleve*
12	*tolv*
13	*tretten*
14	*fjorten*
15	*femten*
16	*seksten*
17	*sytten*
18	*atten*
19	*nitten*
20	*tyve*
21	*enogtyve*
30	*tredive*
40	*fyrre*
50	*halvtreds*
60	*tres*
70	*halvfjerds*
80	*firs*
90	*halvfems*
100	*hundrede*
1000	*tusind*

one million   *en million*

FOOD & DRINK

I'd like today's special, please.	*Jeg tager dagens ret, tak.*
I'm a vegetarian.	*Jeg er vegetar.*
breakfast	*morgenmad*
lunch	*frokost*
dinner	*middag*
menu	*spisekort*
set menu	*dagens middag*
children's menu	*børnemenu*
daily special	*dagens ret*
dishes, courses	*retter*
starters, appetisers	*forretter*
main dishes	*hovedretter*
self-serve buffet	*tagselvbord*

Food Glossary

Note that æ, ø and å come after z in the Danish alphabet.

Dishes

engelsk bøf	steak, commonly served with onions
forårsrulle	spring roll, egg roll
gryderet	casserole or stew
karry	curry
oksehaleragout	oxtail stew
parisertoast	toasted ham and cheese sandwich
pommes frites	French fries, chips
smørrebrød	open sandwich
æggekage	scrambled eggs with onions, potatoes and bacon

Soups

gule ærter	split pea soup served with pork
hønsekødsuppe	chicken soup
klar suppe	clear soup
suppe	soup
øllebrød	beer and bread soup

Salads

agurkesalat	sliced cucumber with vinegar dressing
grøn salat	green salad
kartoffelsalat	potato salad

Desserts

chokolade	chocolate, also hot chocolate
fromage	a pudding
ingefærbrød	gingerbread
is	ice cream, ice
kage	cake
kringle	type of Danish pastry
lagkage	layer cake
pandekage	pancake or crepe
ris à l'amande	rice pudding with almonds
tærte	tart
vaffel	waffle
vandmelon	watermelon
vanilleis	vanilla ice cream
wienerbrød	Danish pastry

Meat

dyresteg	roast venison
flæskesteg	roast pork, often served with crackling
frikadelle	fried meatball
fårekød	mutton
hakkebøf	ground-beef burger
haresteg	roast hare
kalvekød	veal
kotelet	cutlet
kød	meat
kødbolle	boiled meatball
kødretter	meat dishes
lamme, lammekød	lamb
lammesteg	roast lamb
lever	liver
leverpostej	liver pâté
oksefilet	tenderloin
oksekød	beef
oksemørbrad,	fillet of beef,
oksesteg	roast beef
pølse	sausage, hot dog
skinke	ham
svinekød	pork
tunge	tongue

Poultry

and, andesteg	duck, roast duck
gås	goose
høns/hønsekød	chicken
hønsebryst	chicken breast
kalkun	turkey
kylling	chicken

Seafood

ansjoser	anchovies
blæksprutte	octopus
fisk	fish
fiskefilet	fish fillet
fiskefrikadelle	fried fishball
fiskeretter	fish dishes
fiskesuppe	fish soup, usually creamy
flynder	flounder
forel	trout
helleflynder	halibut
hummer	lobster
klipfisk	dried, salted cod
krabbe	crab
kryddersild	herring pickled in various marinades
kuller	haddock
laks	salmon
makrel	mackerel
marineret sild	marinated herring
musling	mussel
rejer	shrimp
rødspætte	plaice
røget laks	smoked salmon
røget sild	smoked herring
sild	herring
skaldyr	shellfish
søtunge	sole
torsk	cod
torskerogn	cod roe
tun, tunfisk	tuna
ørred	trout
østers	oyster
ål	eel

Vegetables

agurk	cucumber
asparges	asparagus
bagt kartoffel	baked potato
blomkål	cauliflower
bønner	beans
champignon	mushroom
grøn bønne	green bean
grøntsager	vegetables
gulerødder	carrots
hvidløg	garlic
kartoffel	potato
kartoffelmos	mashed potatoes
kål	cabbage
løg	onion
majs	corn

oliven	olive
porre	leek
rødbeder	beets, commonly served pickled
rødkål	red cabbage
salat	salad, lettuce
selleri	celery
snittebønner	string beans
spinat	spinach
syltede agurker	pickled cucumbers
ærter	peas

Nuts

hasselnød	hazelnut
jordnød	peanut
mandel, mandler	almonds
nødder	nuts
valnød	walnut

Fruit

abrikos	apricot
ananas	pineapple
appelsin	orange
banan	banana
blomme	plum
blåbær	blueberry
brombær	blackberry
citron	lemon
fersken	peach
frugt	fruit
grapefrugt	grapefruit
hindbær	raspberry
jordbær	strawberry
kirsebær	cherry
pære	pear
æble	apple

Eggs

blødkogt æg	soft-boiled egg
flæskeæggekage	scrambled eggs with bacon
hårdkogt æg	hard-boiled egg
røræg	scrambled eggs
spejlæg	fried egg, sunny side up
æg	egg
æggeblomme	egg yolk

Dairy

crème fraîche	sour cream
fløde	cream
flødeost	cream cheese
flødeskum	whipped cream
hytteost	cottage cheese
kærnemælk	buttermilk
letmælk	low-fat milk
mælk	milk
ost	cheese
skummetmælk	skimmed (nonfat) milk
smør	butter
sødmælk	whole milk
tykmælk	a pourable yoghurt

Bread

bolle	soft bread roll, also a meatball or fishball
brød	bread
flute	type of French bread
kryddere	crispy bread rolls
rugbrød	rye bread
rundstykke	crispy poppy-seed roll

Condiments, Herbs & Spices

dild	dill
eddike	vinegar
honning	honey
ingefær	ginger
jordnødsmør	peanut butter
krydderi	spice
peber	pepper
pebermynte	peppermint
peberrod	horseradish
persille	parsley
purløg	chives
remoulade	mayonnaise-based tartar sauce
sennep	mustard
sukker	sugar
syltetøj	jam

Cooking Methods

bagt	baked
dampet	steamed
friturestegt	deep fried
gennemstegt	well-done
grilleret, grillstegt	grilled
kogt	boiled
marineret	marinated
mellemstegt	medium cooked
ovnstegt	roasted
pocheret	poached
ristet	toasted
røget	smoked
stegt	fried

Useful Words

benfri	boneless
frisk	fresh
fyld	stuffing
fyldt	stuffed
glasur	glaze, frosting
hakket	chopped, minced
hjemmebagt	home-baked
hjemmelavet	home-made
hvide	white (as in white potatoes, rice etc)
iskold	ice cold
kold	cold
nudler	noodles
olie	oil
ris	rice
rå	raw
saltet	salted, cured
skive	slice
sky	meat juice (for gravy)
sovs	gravy, sauce
stegeretter	fried dishes
sød	sweet
tilberedt	cooked
varm	warm, hot
vegetar/ vegetarianer	vegetarian
vildt	game

Drinks

alkoholfri	nonalcoholic
appelsinjuice	orange juice
citronvand	lemonade
fadøl	draught (draft) beer
kaffe	coffee
koffeinfri	caffeine-free
mineralvand	mineral water
sodavand	soft drink, carbonated water
te	tea
vand	water
øl	beer

Glossary

Note that the Danish letters æ, ø and å fall at the end of the alphabet.

akvavit – schnapps
amt – county
apotek – pharmacy, chemist

bageri – bakery
bakke – hill
banegård – train station
bibliotek – library
billetautomat – automated parking-ticket dispenser
bro – bridge
bugt – bay
by – town
børnemenu – children's menu

campingplads – camping ground
cykel – bicycle

dag – day
dagens ret – special meal of the day
Danmark – Denmark
Dansk – Danish
domkirke – cathedral
DSB – abbreviation and common name for Danske Statsbaner (Danish State Railway), Denmark's national railway

EU – European Union

folkehøjskole – folk high school
Fyn – Funen, both a county and an island
færge – ferry
færegehavn – ferry harbour

gade – street
gammel – old
gård – yard, farm

have – garden
havn – harbour
HI – Hostelling International, the main international hostel organisation (formerly IYHF)
hygge – cosy

IC – intercity train
IR – inter-regional train

jernbane – railway
Jylland – Jutland

keramik – ceramic, pottery
kirke – church
kirkegård – churchyard, cemetery
klint – cliff
klippekort – a type of multiple-use transport ticket
kloster – monastery
koldt bord – buffet-style meal, mostly cold food
konditori – bakery with café tables
kro – inn
København – Copenhagen
køreplan – timetable

lur – Bronze Age horn

morgenmad – breakfast
museet – museum
møntvask – coin laundry

nord – north

plantage – plantation, tree farm, woods
prefect – chief administrative officer of the county government
pølsemandens – wheeled food carts

rådhus – town hall, city hall
rundkirke – fortified round church, found on Bornholm
røgeri – fish smokehouse

samling – collection, usually of art
Sjælland – the island of Zealand
skov – forest, woods
slagter – butcher
slot – castle
smørrebrød – open sandwich
strand – beach, shoreline
stykke – piece (fruit)
sund – sound

svømmehal – swimming pool
syd – south
sø – lake

tog – train
torv, torvet – square, marketplace
tårn – tower

uge – week

vandrerhjem – youth and family hostel
vej – street, road

vest – west
værelse – room (to rent)

wienerbrød – Danish pastry, literally 'Vienna bread'

ø – island, usually attached as a suffix to the proper name
øl – beer
øst – east

å – river

LONELY PLANET

You already know that Lonely Planet produces more than this one guidebook, but you might not be aware of the other products we have on this region. Here is a selection of titles that you may want to check out as well:

Norway
ISBN 1 74059 200 X
US$19.99 • UK£11.99

Germany
ISBN 1 74059 078 3
US$24.99 • UK£14.99

Sweden
ISBN 0 86442 721 2
US$17.99 • UK£11.99

Scandinavian & Baltic Europe
ISBN 1 86450 156 1
US$21.99 • UK£13.99

Scandinavian phrasebook
ISBN 1 86450 225 8
US$7.99 • UK£4.50

Europe on a shoestring
ISBN 1 86450 150 2
US$24.99 • UK£14.99

Read This First: Europe
ISBN 1 86450 136 7
US$14.99 • UK£8.99

Copenhagen
ISBN 1 86450 203 7
US$14.99 • UK£8.99

Available wherever books are sold

Lonely Planet Guides by Region

Lonely Planet is known worldwide for publishing practical, reliable and no-nonsense travel information in our guides and on our Web site. The Lonely Planet list covers just about every accessible part of the world. Currently there are 16 series: Travel guides, Shoestring guides, Condensed guides, Phrasebooks, Read This First, Healthy Travel, Walking guides, Cycling guides, Watching Wildlife guides, Pisces Diving & Snorkeling guides, City Maps, Road Atlases, Out to Eat, World Food, Journeys travel literature and Pictorials.

AFRICA Africa on a shoestring • Botswana • Cairo • Cairo City Map • Cape Town • Cape Town City Map • East Africa • Egypt • Egyptian Arabic phrasebook • Ethiopia, Eritrea & Djibouti • Ethiopian Amharic phrasebook • The Gambia & Senegal • Healthy Travel Africa • Kenya • Malawi • Morocco • Moroccan Arabic phrasebook • Mozambique • Namibia • Read This First: Africa • South Africa, Lesotho & Swaziland • Southern Africa • Southern Africa Road Atlas • Swahili phrasebook • Tanzania, Zanzibar & Pemba • Trekking in East Africa • Tunisia • Watching Wildlife East Africa • Watching Wildlife Southern Africa • West Africa • World Food Morocco • Zambia • Zimbabwe, Botswana & Namibia
Travel Literature: Mali Blues: Traveling to an African Beat • The Rainbird: A Central African Journey • Songs to an African Sunset: A Zimbabwean Story

AUSTRALIA & THE PACIFIC Aboriginal Australia & the Torres Strait Islands •Auckland • Australia • Australian phrasebook • Australia Road Atlas • Cycling Australia • Cycling New Zealand • Fiji • Fijian phrasebook • Healthy Travel Australia, NZ & the Pacific • Islands of Australia's Great Barrier Reef • Melbourne • Melbourne City Map • Micronesia • New Caledonia • New South Wales • New Zealand • Northern Territory • Outback Australia • Out to Eat – Melbourne • Out to Eat – Sydney • Papua New Guinea • Pidgin phrasebook • Queensland • Rarotonga & the Cook Islands • Samoa • Solomon Islands • South Australia • South Pacific • South Pacific phrasebook • Sydney • Sydney City Map • Sydney Condensed • Tahiti & French Polynesia • Tasmania • Tonga • Tramping in New Zealand • Vanuatu • Victoria • Walking in Australia • Watching Wildlife Australia • Western Australia
Travel Literature: Islands in the Clouds: Travels in the Highlands of New Guinea • Kiwi Tracks: A New Zealand Journey • Sean & David's Long Drive

CENTRAL AMERICA & THE CARIBBEAN Bahamas, Turks & Caicos • Baja California • Belize, Guatemala & Yucatán • Bermuda • Central America on a shoestring • Costa Rica • Costa Rica Spanish phrasebook • Cuba • Cycling Cuba • Dominican Republic & Haiti • Eastern Caribbean • Guatemala • Havana • Healthy Travel Central & South America • Jamaica • Mexico • Mexico City • Panama • Puerto Rico • Read This First: Central & South America • Virgin Islands • World Food Caribbean • World Food Mexico • Yucatán
Travel Literature: Green Dreams: Travels in Central America

EUROPE Amsterdam • Amsterdam City Map • Amsterdam Condensed • Andalucía • Athens • Austria • Baltic States phrasebook • Barcelona • Barcelona City Map • Belgium & Luxembourg • Berlin • Berlin City Map • Britain • British phrasebook • Brussels, Bruges & Antwerp • Brussels City Map • Budapest • Budapest City Map • Canary Islands • Catalunya & the Costa Brava • Central Europe • Central Europe phrasebook • Copenhagen • Corfu & the Ionians • Corsica • Crete • Crete Condensed • Croatia • Cycling Britain • Cycling France • Cyprus • Czech & Slovak Republics • Czech phrasebook • Denmark • Dublin • Dublin City Map • Dublin Condensed • Eastern Europe • Eastern Europe phrasebook • Edinburgh • Edinburgh City Map • England • Estonia, Latvia & Lithuania • Europe on a shoestring • Europe phrasebook • Finland • Florence • Florence City Map • France • Frankfurt City Map • Frankfurt Condensed • French phrasebook • Georgia, Armenia & Azerbaijan • Germany • German phrasebook • Greece • Greek Islands • Greek phrasebook • Hungary • Iceland, Greenland & the Faroe Islands • Ireland • Italian phrasebook • Italy • Kraków • Lisbon • The Loire • London • London City Map • London Condensed • Madrid • Madrid City Map • Malta • Mediterranean Europe • Milan, Turin & Genoa • Moscow • Munich • Netherlands • Normandy • Norway • Out to Eat – London • Out to Eat – Paris • Paris • Paris City Map • Paris Condensed • Poland • Polish phrasebook • Portugal • Portuguese phrasebook • Prague • Prague City Map • Provence & the Côte d'Azur • Read This First: Europe • Rhodes & the Dodecanese • Romania & Moldova • Rome • Rome City Map • Rome Condensed • Russia, Ukraine & Belarus • Russian phrasebook • Scandinavian & Baltic Europe • Scandinavian phrasebook • Scotland • Sicily • Slovenia • South-West France • Spain • Spanish phrasebook • Stockholm • St Petersburg • St Petersburg City Map • Sweden • Switzerland • Tuscany • Ukrainian phrasebook • Venice • Vienna • Wales • Walking in Britain • Walking in France • Walking in Ireland • Walking in Italy • Walking in Scotland • Walking in Spain • Walking in Switzerland • Western Europe • World Food France • World Food Greece • World Food Ireland • World Food Italy • World Food Spain **Travel Literature:** After Yugoslavia • Love and War in the Apennines • The Olive Grove: Travels in Greece • On the Shores of the Mediterranean • Round Ireland in Low Gear • A Small Place in Italy

Lonely Planet Mail Order

L onely Planet products are distributed worldwide. They are also available by mail order from Lonely Planet, so if you have difficulty finding a title please write to us. North and South American residents should write to 150 Linden St, Oakland, CA 94607, USA; European and African residents should write to 10a Spring Place, London NW5 3BH, UK; and residents of other countries to Locked Bag 1, Footscray, Victoria 3011, Australia.

INDIAN SUBCONTINENT & THE INDIAN OCEAN Bangladesh • Bengali phrasebook • Bhutan • Delhi • Goa • Healthy Travel Asia & India • Hindi & Urdu phrasebook • India • India & Bangladesh City Map • Indian Himalaya • Karakoram Highway • Kathmandu City Map • Kerala • Madagascar • Maldives • Mauritius, Réunion & Seychelles • Mumbai (Bombay) • Nepal • Nepali phrasebook • North India • Pakistan • Rajasthan • Read This First: Asia & India • South India • Sri Lanka • Sri Lanka phrasebook • Tibet • Tibetan phrasebook • Trekking in the Indian Himalaya • Trekking in the Karakoram & Hindukush • Trekking in the Nepal Himalaya • World Food India **Travel Literature:** The Age of Kali: Indian Travels and Encounters • Hello Goodnight: A Life of Goa • In Rajasthan • Maverick in Madagascar • A Season in Heaven: True Tales from the Road to Kathmandu • Shopping for Buddhas • A Short Walk in the Hindu Kush • Slowly Down the Ganges

MIDDLE EAST & CENTRAL ASIA Bahrain, Kuwait & Qatar • Central Asia • Central Asia phrasebook • Dubai • Farsi (Persian) phrasebook • Hebrew phrasebook • Iran • Israel & the Palestinian Territories • Istanbul • Istanbul City Map • Istanbul to Cairo • Istanbul to Kathmandu • Jerusalem • Jerusalem City Map • Jordan • Lebanon • Middle East • Oman & the United Arab Emirates • Syria • Turkey • Turkish phrasebook • World Food Turkey • Yemen **Travel Literature:** Black on Black: Iran Revisited • Breaking Ranks: Turbulent Travels in the Promised Land • The Gates of Damascus • Kingdom of the Film Stars: Journey into Jordan

NORTH AMERICA Alaska • Boston • Boston City Map • Boston Condensed • British Columbia • California & Nevada • California Condensed • Canada • Chicago • Chicago City Map • Chicago Condensed • Florida • Georgia & the Carolinas • Great Lakes • Hawaii • Hiking in Alaska • Hiking in the USA • Honolulu & Oahu City Map • Las Vegas • Los Angeles • Los Angeles City Map • Louisiana & the Deep South • Miami • Miami City Map • Montreal • New England • New Orleans • New Orleans City Map • New York City • New York City Map • New York City Condensed • New York, New Jersey & Pennsylvania • Oahu • Out to Eat – San Francisco • Pacific Northwest • Rocky Mountains • San Diego & Tijuana • San Francisco • San Francisco City Map • Seattle • Seattle City Map • Southwest • Texas • Toronto • USA • USA phrasebook • Vancouver • Vancouver City Map • Virginia & the Capital Region • Washington, DC • Washington, DC City Map • World Food New Orleans **Travel Literature:** Caught Inside: A Surfer's Year on the California Coast • Drive Thru America

NORTH-EAST ASIA Beijing • Beijing City Map • Cantonese phrasebook • China • Hiking in Japan • Hong Kong & Macau • Hong Kong City Map • Hong Kong Condensed • Japan • Japanese phrasebook • Korea • Korean phrasebook • Kyoto • Mandarin phrasebook • Mongolia • Mongolian phrasebook • Seoul • Shanghai • South-West China • Taiwan • Tokyo • Tokyo Condensed • World Food Hong Kong • World Food Japan **Travel Literature:** In Xanadu: A Quest • Lost Japan

SOUTH AMERICA Argentina, Uruguay & Paraguay • Bolivia • Brazil • Brazilian phrasebook • Buenos Aires • Buenos Aires City Map • Chile & Easter Island • Colombia • Ecuador & the Galapagos Islands • Healthy Travel Central & South America • Latin American Spanish phrasebook • Peru • Quechua phrasebook • Read This First: Central & South America • Rio de Janeiro • Rio de Janeiro City Map • Santiago de Chile • South America on a shoestring • Trekking in the Patagonian Andes • Venezuela **Travel Literature:** Full Circle: A South American Journey

SOUTH-EAST ASIA Bali & Lombok • Bangkok • Bangkok City Map • Burmese phrasebook • Cambodia • Cycling Vietnam, Laos & Cambodia • East Timor phrasebook • Hanoi • Healthy Travel Asia & India • Hill Tribes phrasebook • Ho Chi Minh City (Saigon) • Indonesia • Indonesian phrasebook • Indonesia's Eastern Islands • Java • Lao phrasebook • Laos • Malay phrasebook • Malaysia, Singapore & Brunei • Myanmar (Burma) • Philippines • Pilipino (Tagalog) phrasebook • Read This First: Asia & India • Singapore • Singapore City Map • South-East Asia on a shoestring • South-East Asia phrasebook • Thailand • Thailand's Islands & Beaches • Thailand, Vietnam, Laos & Cambodia Road Atlas • Thai phrasebook • Vietnam • Vietnamese phrasebook • World Food Indonesia • World Food Thailand • World Food Vietnam

ALSO AVAILABLE: Antarctica • The Arctic • The Blue Man: Tales of Travel, Love and Coffee • Brief Encounters: Stories of Love, Sex & Travel • Buddhist Stupas in Asia: The Shape of Perfection • Chasing Rickshaws • The Last Grain Race • Lonely Planet ... On the Edge: Adventurous Escapades from Around the World • Lonely Planet Unpacked • Lonely Planet Unpacked Again • Not the Only Planet: Science Fiction Travel Stories • Ports of Call: A Journey by Sea • Sacred India • Travel Photography: A Guide to Taking Better Pictures • Travel with Children • Tuvalu: Portrait of an Island Nation

Index

Text

Note that the Danish letters æ, ø and å fall at the end of the alphabet.

Bold indicates maps.

Bold indicates maps.

Boxed Text

MAP LEGEND

CITY ROUTES

Freeway	Freeway
Highway	Primary Road
Road	Secondary Road
Street	Street
Lane	Lane
	On/Off Ramp
= = = =	Unsealed Road
	One Way Street
	Pedestrian Street
	Stepped Street
⟩ = =	Tunnel
	Footbridge

HYDROGRAPHY

	River, Creek
	Canal
	Lake
	Dry Lake; Salt Lake
⊙	Spring; Rapids
⊛ ⊣⊢	Waterfalls

REGIONAL ROUTES

	Tollway, Freeway
	Primary Road
	Secondary Road
	Minor Road

BOUNDARIES

—·—··—	International
—··—··—	State
— — —	Disputed
▬▬▬	Fortified Wall

TRANSPORT ROUTES & STATIONS

⊢—Ra—⊣ Train	-----◻ Ferry
⊢—S—⊣ S-Train	----- Walking Trail
⊢—O—⊣ Private Train	·········· Walking Tour
⊢ + + + ⊣ Underground Train	Path
▬▬▬ Tramway	Pier or Jetty

AREA FEATURES

Building	Market
⊛ Park, Gardens	Sports Ground
Beach	Campus
+ + Cemetery	Plaza

POPULATION SYMBOLS

◎ CAPITAL National Capital	● CITY City	● Village Village
◉ CAPITAL State Capital	● Town Town	Urban Area

MAP SYMBOLS

● Place to Stay	▼ Place to Eat	● Point of Interest

✈ Airport	⊞ Cinema	※ Lookout	▣ Pub or Bar
⊖ Bank	☗ Cycling	▲ Monument	⊗ Shopping Centre
⊟ Bus Stop	▣ Embassy, Consulate	⊞ Museum	▥ Stately Home
▣ Bus Terminal	☂ Fountain	▣ Parking	▣ Swimming Pool
⚠ Camping	⊕ Hospital	◉ Petrol or Gas Station	▣ Theatre
▥ Castle, Chateau	▣ Internet Cafe	▣ Police Station	❶ Tourist Information
▣ Cathedral, Church	✕ Lighthouse	▣ Post Office	▣ Zoo

Note: not all symbols displayed above appear in this book

LONELY PLANET OFFICES

Australia
Locked Bag 1, Footscray, Victoria 3011
☎ 03 8379 8000 fax 03 8379 8111
email: talk2us@lonelyplanet.com.au

USA
150 Linden St, Oakland, CA 94607
☎ 510 893 8555 TOLL FREE: 800 275 8555
fax 510 893 8572
email: info@lonelyplanet.com

UK
10a Spring Place, London NW5 3BH
☎ 020 7428 4800 fax 020 7428 4828
email: go@lonelyplanet.co.uk

France
1 rue du Dahomey, 75011 Paris
☎ 01 55 25 33 00 fax 01 55 25 33 01
email: bip@lonelyplanet.fr
www.lonelyplanet.fr

World Wide Web: www.lonelyplanet.com *or* AOL keyword: lp
Lonely Planet Images: lpi@lonelyplanet.com.au